Florida Real Estate

Law and Practice

Explained

2nd Edition

Volume 1 in Series:

All Florida School of Real Estate – Real Estate Mastery

PAMELA S. KEMPER

AND HEATHER L. RANEY

With Content and Editorial Contribution by Jeffrey V. Kemper

All Florida School of Real Estate

Real Estate Mastery Series

Volume 1:   Florida Real Estate Law and Practice Explained

Volume 2:   Florida Real Estate Law and Practice Simplified

Volume 3:   Florida Real Estate Law Primer

Volume 4:   Florida Real Estate Math Primer

Volume 5:   Florida Real Estate Math Formula Reference Guide

Volume 6:   Florida Real Estate Vocabulary Primer

Volume 7:   Florida Real Estate Sales Exam Practice

DEDICATION

To my husband, Jeff Kemper
"Jeff, you are the reason for my every day!"
Pamela S. Kemper

To my mother, Diana Raney
"Mom, thank-you for always being there for me!"
Heather L. Raney

CONTENTS

ACKNOWLEDGMENTS

The content of this book is original and was written to comply with
The Florida Real Estate Curriculum Syllabus for the Real Estate Sales Associate Pre-Licensing Course I.
See Sources and Resources at the end of the book for clarification of content credit and for further resource materials.
Utilize the Topic Index to navigate the 122 state required study topics.

For advice regarding real estate, legal, and accounting issues; always consult a professional.

1 The Real Estate Business

Learning Objectives:
- Describe the various activities of real estate brokerage
- Distinguish among the five major sales specialties
- Identify the role of property managers
- Explain the appraisal process and the role of the appraiser
- Understand the mortgage process and the role of mortgage loan originator
- Explain the three phases of development and construction
- Distinguish among the three categories of residential construction

Key Terms:

absentee owner	comparative market analysis	real estate brokerage
appraisal	(CMA)	special-purpose property
appraiser	dedication	subdivision plat map
broker price opinion (BPO)	farm area (target market)	USPAP
business opportunity	follow-up	MLS
	property management	

Overview of the real estate industry

Many Industries Are Dependent on Real Estate Activity

The real estate industry has a huge impact on our economy. Understanding the impact on job creation and overall financial health of our economy is addressed here including issues of:

- The real estate industry's role in the nation's economy including providing jobs, providing housing and providing investment opportunities.

- Many industries are dependent on real estate activity including construction, banking, appraising, title companies, insurance agents, attorneys, surveyors, etc.

The Real Estate Industry's Role in the Nation's Economy

Real estate is an important part of the economy in the United States. Millions of jobs are created from real estate in many industries. Residential real estate meets families' most basic needs as it provides housing. For many people, purchasing a home is the largest and most important investment. Investors utilize real estate as an income source stemming from construction, sales, and rentals. The real estate market peaked at $1.195 trillion in 2006 - providing 8.9% of the Gross Domestic Product.

Following the peak in 2006, the real estate market experienced a decline in both construction activities and sales. This meant that individuals experienced a loss of jobs in mass numbers, both within and outside the real estate profession.

Nearly all homeowners experienced a loss in their home's value, regardless of whether they were actively selling or not. Many people had been using lines of credit from home equity loans to make purchases in the general economy. Thus, spending across industries slowed dramatically.

Contributing to the housing crisis was the fact that excessive amounts of loans issued between 2005 and 2007 were subprime loans which increased the risk of buyer default. Even loans issued through the prime market began to default as the loss of home prices took effect. These loans had been packaged and sold as mortgage-backed securities and thus, the value of these securities plummeted. Many had been sold to pension funds, corporations and individual investors.

There is no doubt, as the lessons from the housing crisis demonstrates, the real estate industry affects most aspects of our national economy - from the individual home owner to the stock market – and to individuals working in fields even outside of real estate.

http://useconomy.about.com/od/grossdomesticproduct/f/Real_estate_faq.htm

How Does Real Estate Affect the U.S. Economy?

The real estate industry is also key to funding a city or county's finances. Most cities and counties rely on the funds generated from taxes paid from the real estate market. Funds come from ad valorem property tax plus documentary and intangible taxes collected on every property bought and sold in the city and county.

http://useconomy.about.com/od/grossdomesticproduct/f/Real_estate_faq.htm

Real Estate is a Business of Many Specializations

Expert information is the product that a broker or a sales associate must market and contribute to a real estate transaction including: knowledge of property transfer, knowledge of market conditions, and knowledge of how to market real estate.

So how does all of this affect you as a real estate professional? As a real estate professional, you are marketing yourself and your skill set. People seek out real estate agents expecting them to have extensive knowledge of market conditions and how to successfully market real estate.

"Is it a good time to buy," is a common question casually put to a real estate licensee. The public looks to the licensee to guide them in their real estate investment. Most importantly, consumers expect licensees to have expert knowledge regarding property transfers ensuring their interests are protected.

Special Emphasis: Expert Knowledge

Real estate licensees must develop expert knowledge which includes the areas of property transfer, market conditions, and how to market real estate.

Special Emphasis: Overview of the Real Estate Industry

The real estate industry plays a vital role in the nation's overall economy and many industries are directly and indirectly dependent upon real estate activity.

Sales and Leasing

Real estate licensees work in Sales and Leasing.

1) **A brokerage is a business in which real estate license-related activities are performed under the authority of a real estate broker**

2) **The broker acts as an agent or intermediary between two or more people in the negotiation of the sale, purchase or rental of real estate**

3) **A sales associate works for the broker, providing services to prospective buyers and sellers or landlords and tenants**

4) **It requires expert information that the average layperson does not possess**

5) **It is more efficient to acquire this information through a real estate professional**

6) **Real estate brokers and sales associates often specialize in a particular geographic area or property type. This method of target marketing is often called "farming"**

A Real Estate brokerage is a business where a "managing" broker oversees the Broker Associate/Sales Associates that work for the brokerage and provide real estate services to clients for compensation. All clients and commission technically belong to the brokerage and are the responsibility of the broker. More specifically, brokerage activities involved assisting clients in the buying and selling or leasing of real estate for a fee. A real estate broker acts as an intermediary between buyers and sellers, landlords and tenants. Real estate brokers can also be called real estate salespersons or real estate agents. (Don't confuse this with a distinction in license level status from the state as a broker, broker associate or sales associate.)

http://www.investorwords.com/4059/real_estate_broker.html#ixzz3ybvEcwZf

Buying and selling real estate is a complex process and generally involves large sums of money. Therefore, many people chose to seek the services of a real estate professional instead of trying to acquire the knowledge to protect their interests themselves. A real estate professional has extensive knowledge in everything required to successfully negotiate the terms of the sale, purchase or leasing of real property. Rules regarding home sales are always changing, and it is a licensee's job to stay on top of those market dynamics and provide the best service for the client.

The National Association of REALTOR®'s 2015 Profile of Home Buyers and Sellers noted that about 88% of home buyers purchased their home through a real estate agent.

http://www.realtor.com/advice/why-you-should-use-realtor

Expert Service

Real estate professionals require an advanced understanding of the real estate industry. Clients expect licensees to provide expert service and advice in the areas of property transfer, market conditions, and ow to market real estate or businesses.

Farm Area or Target Market

Real estate brokers and sales associates often specialize in a geographic area or property type. This method of target marketing is often called "farming."

A farm area is an area/neighborhood picked by a licensee to market to on a very regular basis; thus, cultivating buyers and sellers. This requires extensive and continued follow-up by "touching" these individuals monthly or on a regular basis with mailings, emails, door hangers, etc. *"Farm Area or Target Market" does NOT refer to a type of Real Estate rather it is an industry jargon used to describe a business-building activity.*

Most seasoned agents will have one or two farm areas. These are neighborhoods or specific areas of town that an agent will continually market. By continuing to feed marketing material or making face to face or phone contacts with the individuals in these areas, top of mind awareness is created. The goal is for the individuals within the households in these locations to think of you first when they have a need for a real estate agent. This top of mind awareness is what generates business.

Target marketing can also mean picking certain demographics and marketing regularly to a specific group of individuals based on demographic information rather than geographic area. *Note: Target marketing is not the same as working a group of people that you have met over the years.*

5 Major Types of Real Estate

Real estate licensees can handle the transfer of five different types of real estate. Some agents choose to handle any type of property that they have an opportunity to work with, while most choose to specialize in one or several property types. The five types of real estate include:

- Residential
- Commercial
- Industrial
- Agricultural
- Businesses

Residential

Residential real estate is the sale of property which includes single family homes (also called detached homes), condominiums (condos), and property which houses up to a **maximum of 4 individual units or ten or fewer acres of land.** Property that has more than four units is considered commercial property. Don't confuse condominiums as having more than four units as the ownership of each unit is separate and is therefore considered residential real estate. A duplex is an example of a residential multi-unit property. Property with more than 10 acres is considered agricultural.

Most real estate licensees that work in the sale of residential real estate work with individuals who purchase the property for their own use- as their home. As such, many real estate agents enjoy specializing in working with first time home buyers, or home buyers that are moving up into their next home, or downsizing to their final homes.

The sale of residential real estate also opens the opportunity to work with investors. In addition to understanding what attracts an individual to an area such as community amenities, investors require the knowledge of how to calculate return on investment and risk assessment among other things.

Each type of buyer and seller creates opportunities and challenges for real estate agents as the licensee develops his or her business and serves clients.

Commercial

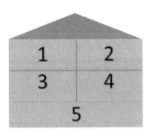

Commercial property consists of residential properties that contain more than four individual units and includes property that houses retail, restaurant, professional offices and other businesses that are not manufacturing or industrial related. Commercial property is an area that can be very lucrative for real estate agents as they tend to sell at large price points. However, commercial property also tends to have a much longer period involved to get the property sold.

Most real estate licensees that sell commercial property sell only this type of property as it takes knowledge and community contacts that is quite different from residential real estate. One of the differences is in how commercial property is marketed. There are commercial services that specialize in listing only commercial property which maximizes exposure to potential clients, also community groups that licensees are involved with to find potential contacts.

Clients also expect commercial real estate agents to be able to guide them to the best income producing opportunities with the least risk.

Industrial

Industrial real estate generally consists of properties used for manufacturing, recycling, distribution, and other "industrial" type uses. Industrial real estate is in a category separate from commercial real estate as it involves issues that can be quite different from office and retail spaces.

Real estate licensees who work in industrial real estate should understand zoning and building codes. They also must understand the process of assessing whether an existing property has adequately handled its emissions and effluents. Whenever there is a production of a product there is most often also the production of a by-product, which is a potential pollution if not handled correctly. This can create costly clean-up situations for an unsuspecting purchaser if appropriate inspections are not conducted.

There is a lot of risk involved with this type of real estate. However, a real estate licensee that specializes in industrial real estate is well rewarded.

Agricultural

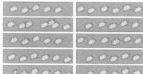 Agricultural real estate includes farming and uses of land for animals such as horses or cows which are of more than 10 acres. It can be anything from a tree farm to a dog breeder or an orange grove to simply a mass of acreage.

Specializing in agricultural real estate involves knowledge about what attributes to land making it usable for different types of ventures. In Florida, there are rules about land use which involves the protection and preservation of wildlife and wetlands.

It is imperative that a licensee be versed on land use restrictions when working with buyers and sellers of these types of properties.

Business Opportunity

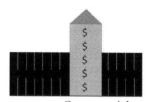 Real estate licensees, per Florida Statutes, are licensed to sell business opportunities as well as the sale of the business real estate or lease of the real estate. So - **a restaurant, clothing store, gas station, and any business that is sold with the assistance of another for compensation, requires that the individual handling the sale or lease be a real estate licensee.** People mistakenly put these types of sales in the commercial category. Commercial only involves the sale of an empty building without a viable business still in place.

Business opportunity brokerages is another specialty that real estate agents tend to either handle, or refer out to other agents. A **business opportunity** (or bizopp) involves a sale or lease of any product, service, equipment, etc. that will enable the purchaser-licensee to begin a business. It involves not only the sale of the property but of the business itself. And it may be for the sale of a business without the real estate, as many businesses operate in locations utilizing a lease.

The licensor or seller of a **business opportunity** usually declares that it will secure or assist the buyer in finding a suitable location, or provide the product to the purchaser-licensee. Handling this type of transaction involves being able to inventory and value personal property as business assets, as well as the good will of the business. Businesses are larger than its physical collection of assets as in business, the clientele and reputation is often the most valuable component.

https.en.wikipedia.org/wiki/Business_opportunity

Florida Statutes 475.278

Special Emphasis: Real Estate Brokerages

A Real Estate brokerage is a business where a "managing" broker oversees the Broker Associate/Sales Associates that work for the brokerage, and provide real estate services to clients for compensation.

Special Emphasis: Farm Area or Target Market

A farm area is an area/neighborhood picked by a licensee to market to on a very regular basis; thus cultivating buyers and sellers.

Special Emphasis: Business Brokers

Real estate professionals specializing in selling businesses are called **Business Brokers**.

The law in Florida assumes that businesses come with real property and although that is not always true the law requires business brokers and anyone that assists in selling or buying businesses for a commission to have a real estate license.

Special Emphasis: Licensees Work Under Brokers

Real estate licensees are the employee of the broker. It is the broker who is employed by the client and works as an intermediary on the client's behalf. It is the broker that receives compensation for real estate services (not the licensee).

Special Emphasis: Five Areas of Specialty

Real estate licensees that have an opportunity to work within one of the five major types of real estate, without having experience to do so, can look to their broker for guidance about how to proceed.

- Specialty areas include residential, commercial, industrial, agricultural, and business.

Many licensees pair up with experienced agents to learn the craft of the different real estate specialties. Real estate licensees can refer business to another agent and be paid a referral fee, so there is always an opportunity for compensation whenever the licensee comes across an opportunity to represent a client – without risking providing poor or inferior service through inexperience.

In addition to assisting buyers and sellers in the transfer of property, real estate licensees may also work in **property management**.

The study of this area includes:

1)Need for property managers

   (a) Absentee owner: A person or entity who owns a piece of real estate but does not live in it. Often the person may reside in another state. An absentee owner entity may be a corporation or real estate investment trust (REIT).

2) Services typically provided by a property manger

   (a) Distinguish between Community Association Manager (CAM).

3) Scope of work detailed in a management agreement

4) Property manager's charge is to protect the owner's investment and maximize owner's returns

Property Management

Property management is the process of "managing" property that is available for lease. Duties of the property manager include maintaining and handling all the activities that are centered around the leasing and care of the piece of real estate.

Property management may involve seeking out tenants, collecting rent, holding advance rents and deposits in escrow, and maintaining the property.

The property manager is considered the local representative of an absentee property owner. **The property manager's job is to protect and maintain the property while maximizing the owners return on their investment.**

Absentee Owners

The need for qualified property managers has grown due to an increase in absentee owners.

Absentee owner: A person or entity who owns a piece of real estate but does not live in it. Often the owner of the property may reside in another state. An absentee owner entity may be a corporation or real estate investment trust (REIT).

The nature of real estate in Florida involves a large amount of people who have invested in real estate without the intention of living in the property themselves. They do sometimes make use of the property on an occasional basis allowing the property to be rented on a "seasonal" basis.

http://www.businessdictionary.com/definition/property-management.html

Property Management

Types of Property Needing Services

Property managers handle all different type of residential property. Types of properties range from single family homes to apartment buildings. Single family homes require more time dedicated to the single unit as it is generally positioned away from other properties being managed. Therefore, on a unit to unit comparison, owners of single family properties generally are charged a higher fee than owners who have invested in multi-unit properties.

Also with Florida being a vacation destination, many properties are rented out on a seasonal or even weekly basis as opposed to a yearly rental. These properties are rented "turnkey furnished" meaning that everything is in place that someone could need, right down to towels and pots and pans. Seasonal property management and weekly property management is more time intensive and therefore also tends to bring a higher rate for the management fee charged to the owner.

http://www.businessdictionary.com/definition/property-manag

Property Management

Rental Agent vs. Property Manager

Many people use the terms "rental agent" and "property manager" interchangeably.

However, some owners hire a professional to handle just the leasing of the rental property without ongoing management activities.

In the real estate industry, the person who handles the "leasing only" by finding a tenant and collecting the initial fees is referred to as a "rental agent" rather than as a "property manager."

- Rental agents find a tenant and collect a fee.

- Property managers continue to manage the property once a tenant is secured.

http://www.rentalagentguide.com/is-there-a-difference-between-a-rental-agent-and-a-property-manager-2

Property Management

Management Agreement

When a property owner wishes to engage in the services of a property manager, a contract will be utilized that will spell out the terms of the agreement.

This contract identifies the duties that the licensee is expected to perform. It also identifies the amount of compensation and when it will be paid.

This contract is between the broker and the property owner. In essence, it is a type of employment contract with the broker agreeing to work for the property owner. Although a real estate licensee, rather than the broker, may handle the follow-up of the agreement. The licensee is employed by the broker not the property owner. **All compensation for the property management work done must be paid to the broker and not directly to the licensee.**

http://www.businessdictionary.com/definition/property-management.html

Community Association Manager (CAM)

Note that a **Community Association Manager** (called a CAM) is NOT the same thing as a property manager. CAMs manage the workings of associations such as Home Owner Associations. In fact, the licensing requirements with the state of Florida are different for CAMs.

Anyone responsible for community association management of more than 10 units or a budget of $100,000 or greater must be licensed with the Department of Business and Professional Regulation (does not include apartment complexes) as a Community Association Manager.

- Generally, includes condominium associations, manufactured housing parks, etc.

- Apartment complexes, commercial, and single-family properties are exempt from CAM licensure.

Homeowners that also have legal use of community property will utilize a community association manager to assist with the property.

The tasks of the community association manager can seem like that of a property manager including the collection of fees, preparation of financial statements, and overall dealing with complaints within the community.

The community association manager works directly for the association board members while interacting with all the homeowners. Community association managers ensure that homeowners are complying with the rules of the association. These rules may involve use of common areas. Yet, they also may involve details such as approving paint colors for homes within the neighborhood, fencing, etc. Disputes that escalate may result in legal action.

http://www.allpropertymanagement.com/faq/community-association-manager_p16.html

Florida Statutes 468.432

Special Emphasis: Property Manager

Property management involves finding tenants to occupy the space, collecting monthly rental payment, maintaining the property, and upkeep of the grounds.

Special Emphasis: Absentee Owner

An absentee owner is a person or entity who owns a piece of real estate but does not live in it.

Special Emphasis: Community Association Manager

Community Association Managers (called a CAM) manage the workings of community associations.

Special Emphasis: Property Manager

Anyone who is paid a commission or paid on a transactional basis for conducting property management services must be licensed.

To conduct these services without a real estate license is "practicing real estate without a license and is punishable as a third-degree felony." Exemptions apply. See Section 2.

Florida Statutes 475

APPRAISING

Assisting clients in real estate also involves the area of appraisals. The topic of appraisals covers the following facts:

1) The process of estimating the value of real estate

2) Types of real estate activities that require appraisal services

3) State-certified, licensed and registered appraisers are regulated by the Florida Real Estate Appraisal Board

4) Real estate licensees may appraise real property provided they do not represent themselves as state-certified, registered or licensed appraisers

5) Real estate licensees must comport to USPAP when conducting appraisals of real property--define USPAP

6) Comparative market analysis versus appraisal--define CMA

(a) CMAs exempt from USPAP

1) Broker Price Opinion (BPO)

2) USPAP's Ethics Rule regarding compensation

Appraising

Conducting appraisals is the process of estimating the value of real estate. (There are other types of appraisals that do not involve real estate which are not covered.) Appraisals are used for many reasons, including to verify the value of the property as collateral when a buyer is utilizing a loan to fund a purchase, to verify the value of property for the satisfaction of a buyer's peace of mind, such as when the buyer is an investor who is considering buying property for investment purposes, and for legal proceedings such as dividing property for a divorce and estate settling.

The Florida Department of Business and Professional Regulation licenses and registers appraisers under the Florida Real Estate Appraisal Board. To be a state certified appraiser, you must meet training and education requirements established by the Appraisal Qualifications Boards, and the appraisals must follow the guidelines established by the Appraisal Standards Board.

USPAP are the standards that must be followed for an appraisal. USPAP is short for the Uniform Standards of Professional Appraisal Practice. USPAP rules regulate how an appraisal is performed and written.

According to Florida Statutes 475, real estate licensees may perform an appraisal for compensation if the appraisal follows USPAP standards, are not being performed for a federally-related transaction, and the licensee is not referring to him or herself as an actual certified appraiser.

Although appraisers and real estate licensees who are conducting appraisals may collect a fee for an appraisal, it may only be a flat fee and not a commission based on purchase price. If a fee was charged for an appraisal based on purchase price, then it would create a conflict of interest—appraisals might be falsely inflated to earn the appraiser more money.

http://theappraisaliq.com/for-consumers/appraisal-steps-determining-market-value-of-property/

Special Emphasis: Appraising

Appraising is the process of estimating the value of property.

Appraisals are used when a buyer is getting a bank loan, an investor is considering buying for investment purposes, or for a legal proceeding; divorce, estates, dividing assets.

Special Emphasis: Appraisal / Appraiser

An appraisal is a professional opinion of the market value of a property including homes and businesses.

An appraiser is a professional who has the knowledge and expertise necessary to estimate the value of property.

http://www.investopedia.com/terms/a/appraiser.asp#ixzz3wrxEU21u
http://www.investorwords.com/237/appraisal.html#ixzz3wrwIjElb

Special Emphasis: Appraisals

USPAP is the Uniform Standards of Professional Appraisal Practice.

USPAP is promulgated by the Appraisal Standards Board of the Appraisal Foundation.

USPAP is revised on a regular basis.

http://www.realpropertyappraisalsllc.com/WhatisUSPAP

Special Emphasis: Who can perform appraisals

Real estate licensees may appraise real property for compensation provided:

- The appraisal is NOT for federally regulated transactions

- The licensee CANNOT claim to be a certified appraiser.

- BOTH appraisers and real estate licensees must abide by USPAP

- A set of guidelines (standards of practice) to follow when providing appraisal services

Appraisers (and licensees) may ONLY charge a fee - not a commission.

Special Emphasis: USPAP Ethics rule regarding compensation

The payment of undisclosed fees, commissions, or things of value regarding procurement of an assignment is unethical.

- *Comment: Disclosure of fees, commissions, or things of value connected to the procurement of an assignment must appear in the certification and in any transmittal letter in which conclusions are stated. In groups or organizations engaged in appraisal practice, intracompany payments to employees for business development are not considered unethical. Competency, rather than financial incentives, should be the primary basis for awarding an assignment.* Excerpt from USPAP The Appraisal Foundation – Ethics.

http://alappraisal.com/uspap/Ethics%20Rule.pdf

CMAs and BPOs

Although a real estate licensee may conduct appraisals, there are two other methods for obtaining value that licensees more commonly use rather than an actual appraisal: the Comparative Market Analysis (CMA) and the Broker's Price Opinion (BPO).

Both the CMA and BPO determine value with a process like a certified appraisal, yet they are not quite as restrictive in methodology as USPAP standards do not have to adhere to either of these valuation methods.

Generally, real estate agents perform a **comparative market analysis** (CMA) for a client to help them determine a price to list when selling a home, or a price to offer when buying a home.

Since no two properties are identical, agents make adjustments for the differences between the sold properties and the one that is about to be purchased or listed to determine a fair offer or sale price. Essentially, a comparative market analysis is a less-sophisticated version of a formal, professional appraisal.

A **broker price opinion** (BPO) is the estimated value of a property as determined by a real estate broker, or other real estate licensee working under the direction of a broker. A broker price opinion is based on the characteristics of the property being considered as compared to other properties in the area currently listed and having recently sold.

BPOs are often requested by relocation companies which work as an advocate to move employees from one part of a country to another, and either need a property sold or bought to facilitate the move. BPOs are also ordered by banks in the early stages of a foreclosure to gauge the value of the property.

Both CMAs and BPOs may be conducted by real estate licensees and payment for these services may be charged.

However, as this is a type of real estate service, the licensee must work under a broker and be paid by the broker, not the client. The client may only pay the broker per Florida Statutes 475.

Also note, that although payment for comparative market analysis is allowed, many licensees offer these for free to try to compete for a listing of a property for sale.

http://www.investopedia.com/terms/c/comparative-market-analysis.asp#ixzz3wsBA0saI

http://www.investopedia.com/terms/b/broker_price_opinion.asp#ixzz3wsC6hu

Special Emphasis: Comparative Market Analysis - CMA

CMA is short for Comparative Market Analysis. A CMA is an opinion of value based on an examination of the prices at which similar properties in the same area are currently listed, recently sold, and failed to close. CMAs are often conducted to determine value to list a property or offer to purchase a property.

- Cannot be referred to or be represented as an **appraisal**

- Can charge a fee for the completed CMA

- Does not have to comply with USPAP

Special Emphasis: Broker's Price Opinion - BPO

BPO is short for Broker's Price Opinion. A BPO is the estimated value of a property as determined by a real estate broker or other real estate licensee working under the direction of a broker. A broker price opinion is based on the characteristics of the property being considered. BPO's are often requested by relocation companies and banks holding pre-foreclosure properties.

- Sales associates may complete a BPO for compensation when supervised by the broker

- Compensation must be **paid to broker;** Broker pays the sale associate

- Does not have to comply with USPAP

FINANCING

Assisting clients in real estate also involves having basic knowledge in financing. The topic of financing covers the following facts:

1) Financing is the business of providing funds for real estate transactions

2) Sources of funds to finance real estate transactions

3) Importance of expertise in financing matters and knowledge of how to solve financing problems

4) Mortgage loan originator and mortgage bankers must be licensed as such

Financing

Financing is the business of providing funds for real estate transactions.

The purpose of acquiring the property may be for personal, business or investment reasons. Financial institutions, banks, mortgage lenders and private lenders are in the business of financing by providing capital for the purchase.

Years ago, if someone wanted a loan, they obtained it from someone they knew personally simplifying the application and approval process. Today, it is a much more complicated process. There are many factors that go into the completion of funding a loan and allowing the transfer of property based on the loan being accomplished. Therefore, it is imperative that a real estate licensee have a strong working knowledge of how to assist clients in navigating the lending process.

This is true regardless of whether the licensee is representing the seller or when the licensee is representing the buyer.

Real estate licensees develop relationships with mortgage brokers and mortgage bankers (or loan officer) to refer clients to for financing. Both a mortgage broker and a loan officer are individuals who work in the mortgage industry. The main difference between them is basically how they're paid.

Mortgage brokers work independently of a lending institution to match buyers and lenders together for a loan. They are paid a percentage of the final negotiated loan value and loan terms. Whereas loan officers work directly for an institution like a bank, a mortgage lender or a credit union. Loan officers are paid as employees to write loans for their company—although it may also be on a percentage basis.

http://www.investopedia.com/terms/f/financing.asp#ixzz3ykfkS8

Mortgage Loan Origination (MLO)

Mortgage loan origination is the actual process of working with a buyer to process loan applications and negotiate the terms and conditions of a loan between the borrower and the lender. Both mortgage brokers and mortgage bankers engage in mortgage loan origination activities.

Following the difficulties of the housing and the mortgage crisis, in 2008 the Secure and Fair Enforcement for Mortgage Licensing Act (SAFE Act) was passed. The act created minimum standards for the licensing and registering of Mortgage Loan Originators.

The act requires that MLO's must register with the Nationwide Mortgage Licensing System (NMLS). In addition, mortgage Loan Originators not employed by Federally chartered and regulated institutions must also be state licensed to conduct loans and work under state regulations. This included MLOs working for mortgage brokers and depositories chartered at the state level rather than the federal level.

http://www.investopedia.com/terms/f/financing.asp#ixz

Mortgage Brokers

Many buyers prefer to work with mortgage brokers rather than a mortgage banker, as mortgage brokers don't work for a specific institution. Instead, they develop relationships with many lending institutions and then try to find the best loan for the buyer.

A broker doesn't lend money, they find someone who will.

A broker starts the mortgage loan origination process by having a buyer fill out an application to get an idea of a buyer's financial situation. They also pull credit as part of the application process. The broker then takes the credit score and accompanying financial information to match to loan options offered by different lenders. Mortgage brokers often have better results for people with low credit scores than mortgage bankers, as they have so many more loan options to turn to in challenging buyer situations.

A broker's job is to negotiate the best mortgage rate, terms and cost for the buyer.

Because of the flexibility in the loans offered through mortgage brokers, real estate licensees usually have several mortgage brokers to refer their clients to for a loan.

http://www.quickenloans.com/blog/differences-between-mortgage-brokers-and-loan-officers#Dj7pBbAysBiCpukM.99

Mortgage Banker/Loan Officer

A mortgage banker is someone who works for a bank or lender to write loans for that company. They're also called loan officers, home loan consultants, mortgage planners, mortgage consultants and mortgage loan originators.

Like a mortgage broker, a loan officer conducts mortgage loan origination duties which starts with the application process. They also pull credit and gather financial information to get an understanding of the buyer's financial situation. The loan officer will then recommend the best loan out of his or her company's loan options.

Keep in mind, a mortgage broker must specialize in a broad range of lenders and individual loan programs, while a loan officer must only specialize in the individual programs from their own company's offering. This may be an advantage as the loan officer may better know how to apply a specific loan package to a buyer.

http://www.quickenloans.com/blog/differences-between-mortgage-brokers-and-loan-officers#Dj7pBbAysBiCpukM.99

Mortgage Banker/Loan Officer

Real estate licensees also have a variety of mortgage bankers that they refer their clients to for loans.

In fact, best practices are to refer clients to a variety of reputable mortgage brokers and bankers and to let the client make his or her own choice.

This limits liability for the licensee.

http://www.quickenloans.com/blog/differences-between-mortgage-brokers-

Special Emphasis: Financing

Financing is the business of providing funds for real estate transactions.

Financial institutions, banks, and private lenders are in the business of financing as they provide capital to achieve goals toward property ownership.

Special Emphasis: Mortgage Loan Originator (MLO)

Mortgage loan origination is the actual process of working with a buyer to process loan applications and negotiate the terms and conditions of a loan between the borrower and the lender.

The Secure and Fair Enforcement for Mortgage Licensing Act (SAFE Act) of 2008:

- Requires MLO's to register with the Nationwide Mortgage Licensing System (NMLS)
- Mortgage Loan Originators not employed by Federally chartered and regulated institutions must also be state licensed to conduct loans and work under state regulations.

http://www.investopedia.com/terms/m/mortgage_originator.asp

Special Emphasis:

Funds to finance real estate can come from many sources.

Commercial Banks, Mortgage Brokerages, Credit Unions, Savings Associations, Corporations, and Private Individuals.

Special Emphasis:

A working knowledge of financing is important to a licensee to help them work smarter and save time by:

a) Being able to pre-qualify buyers; can they most likely buy?

b) Having an idea how much a buyer will qualify to buy

c) Know what loans will work for which buyers and/or properties

d) Assist with solving issues that come up during the process

Special Emphasis: Mortgage loan originators and mortgage bankers must be licensed as such

- Mortgage Loan Officers and Mortgage Bankers are required to register with the Nationwide Mortgage Licensing System (NMLS)

- Mortgage Loan Originators not employed by Federally chartered and regulated institutions must also be state licensed to conduct loans and work under state regulations.

COUNSELING

Assisting clients in real estate as a real estate counselor is another form of real estate activity. The topic of counseling covers the following facts:

1) Real estate counseling is the service of analyzing existing or potential projects and providing advice

   a) Generally used by entities making large scale purchases for investment purposes.

1) Requires extensive knowledge and expertise

Counseling

Counseling is a unique real estate activity involving assisting clients in making strategic investment decisions.

The goal of real estate counseling is to provide clients with the best results in achieving their investment goals. The ability to analyze information is at the core of a successful counseling process.

Mergers and acquisitions can only happen successfully after a careful review of existing problems within existing real estate opportunities, and the potential to overcome the problems with a well-crafted plan.

Due to the size of the investments involved, most real estate licensees interested in operating as a real estate counselor for investors earn a "Counselor of Real Estate" designation – also referred to as a CRE.

http://www.cre.org/aboutcre/what_is_counseling.cfm

Special Emphasis: Counseling

Real estate counseling is the service of analyzing existing or potential projects, and providing advice to clients who are generally making large scale purchases for investment purposes. Real Estate Counselors require extensive knowledge and expertise.

DEVELOPMENT AND CONSTRUCTION

Assisting clients in real estate also involves having basic knowledge in development and construction. The topic of development and construction covers the following facts:

1) Land acquisition

2) Subdividing and development

3) Subdivision plat map is recorded

4) Developer often dedicates land to a governmental body for public use

5) Types of construction

- Residential: Spec Homes, Tract Homes and Custom Homes

Development and Construction

There are three phases of development and construction that each project goes through. It includes land acquisition, subdividing, and development.

Land Acquisition is the process of acquiring the land that will be developed.

Although this isn't a difficult concept, there are factors that should be considered. The developer must have an idea of how many lots to be developed, how big the lots will be, and how much area is needed for green space, roads, sidewalks and other items that will require land. The developer will also have in mind an estimate of the price range of homes intended to be built.

Once the developer acquires land, the property is then "subdivided" into individual lots while reserving some land for other purposes such as roads and sidewalks.

Development, then, is the actual building up of the land. Developers often start with building the roads, sidewalks, and other common areas. Some will then build houses on some or all the lots depending on the developer's choice of residential construction methods.

Before the developer can proceed with the project, a subdivision plat map must be submitted and approved. The plat map shows the subdivision of land into lots and/or tracts. Typical annotation includes a boundary description, lot dimensions, directional bearings, street names, lot numbers, tracts, easements, and right-of-way's.

There are three approaches developers take when developing residential property; Spec or Speculative homes, Tract homes, or Custom homes.

- **Spec homes** are when the developer buys lots and constructs homes without having a buyer in mind.

- **Tract homes** are when the developer buys lots and builds a few "model" homes, and buyers then pick from among the specific floor plans offered by the developer.

- **Custom homes** are built by a developer to the specific requirements of the buyer.

Subdividing Property

Real estate licensees may specialize in working in new construction. This specialization may focus on working with developers during the acquisition phase of development to the transfer of property to buyers.

A brief explanation of the subdividing process follows with more information to be obtained from the section on planning, zoning, and environmental hazards.

The first step when subdividing land is to call the planning, zoning and/or development office. Specific rules on development per area is available from the appropriate office including building codes.

Surveyors and engineers are required to professionally draw up the plat map.

The plat map and application will be submitted for approval. This may require it then being reviewed by the planning board or similar council in a regular or public meeting.

http://www.kompareit.com/homeandgarden/developers-engineers-subdividing-property.html

Special Emphasis: Special Purpose Property

Keep in mind, all construction is not for residential and not all construction fits into predesigned architectural formats.

A **special purpose property is a** property that is designed specifically for one type of use.

This generally involves a unique design and layout which makes it difficult to use the property for another purpose without a major redesign.

Examples of special purpose properties are churches, theaters, and schools.

http://definitions.uslegal.com/s/special-purpose-property/

Special Emphasis: Land Acquisition

Land Acquisition is the process of acquiring the land that will be developed.

Special Emphasis: Subdividing

Subdividing is when a developer acquires a large piece of land and then "subdivides" it into individual lots reserving some land for other purposes such as roads and sidewalks.

Special Emphasis: Development

Real estate development is a group of similarly constructed buildings placed in an area by a developer.

http://dictionary.cambridge.org/us/dictionary/english/real-estate-development

Special Emphasis: Plat Maps

Subdivision plat maps show how a land will be developed with details including lot lines, lot dimensions, directional bearings, street names, lot numbers, tracts, easements, and right-of-way's.

https://www.bcpao.us/mainhtml/subdivisionplats.asp

Special Emphasis: Spec Homes

Speculative homes, also called spec homes, are built by developers before a buyer is found for the property.

Special Emphasis: Tract Homes

Tract homes are built by developers who buys lots and builds a few "model" homes and then the buyers pick from one of the specific floor plans offered.

The buyer often can choose details such as cabinets, light fixtures, countertops, etc.

Special Emphasis: Custom Homes

A **custom home** is built by a contractor exactly to the specifications of a buyer.

Special Emphasis: Dedication

Dedication is the voluntary transfer of private property by its owner to the public for some public use, such as for streets or schools.

http://www.propertywords.com/dedication.html

Special Emphasis: There are three phases of development and construction that each project goes through.

Land Acquisition, Subdividing, and Development.

Special Emphasis: Dedication

Developers often dedicate land to a governmental body for public use when developing land.

http://www.propertywords.com/dedication.html

Special Emphasis: Plat Maps

Per Florida Statutes 177.091, plats maps must be recorded into the public records.

THE ROLE OF GOVERNMENT

Assisting clients in real estate also involves having a basic understanding of how government affects real estate at each level of government. The role of government in real estate involves the following levels:

1) Local government

2) State government

3) Federal government

Local Government

The local government, such as the city and county, heavily rely on revenue from the real estate industry via property taxes. Local government also regulates parts of the real estate industry through zoning and building codes and through the issuance of building permits and occupancy certificates. Real estate licensees need to be familiar with issues of property taxation, zoning, building codes, building permits, and occupancy certificates.

The State government also receives revenue from the real estate industry through Documentary "Doc" stamps and taxes. The state is also involved in the regulation of protected land areas and license law regulations.

The Federal government affects real estate in all states. The federal government has several agencies that create laws and regulations with oversight of the real estate industry.

Special Emphasis: Local Government affects real estate through

Property Taxation, Zoning, Building Codes, Building Permits, and Occupancy Certificates.

Special Emphasis: State Government

Document Stamps, Taxes, Protected areas, and License Law.

Special Emphasis: Federal Government

Department of Housing and Urban Development, Federals Housing Administration, Department of Veteran Affairs, Environmental Protection Agency, and Internal Revenue Service.

PROFESSIONAL ORGANIZATIONS

Real estate licensees have multiple options available to join professional organizations for networking and ongoing training, support, and resources.

These include:

1) National Association of REALTORS®

2) Florida REALTORS®

3) Local Board (Association) of REALTORS®

4) Multiple Listing Service (MLS)

Licensees must understand the difference between holding a Real Estate license vs. being a Realtor.

National Association of REALTORS

The National Association of Realtors, referred to as NAR, has a voluntary membership of brokers who can then refer to themselves as "Realtors®" and sales associates and broker associates who can then refer to themselves as "Realtor® associates." NAR is the largest trade association in North America.

NAR has over 1.1 million members. NAR functions as a self-regulatory organization creating industry standards that are even higher than required by law. Due to its size and activities, NAR is a powerful lobbying group in politics that specifically affect real estate.

https://en.wikipedia.org/wiki/National_Association_

There is a difference in being a real estate licensee and a Realtor®. The only people that can use the designation as Realtor® with their names are licensees that belong to the National Association of Realtors®.

And belonging to NAR requires adherence to a strict code of ethics.

NAR adopted its Code of Ethics and Standards of Practice in 1913. Unlike the appraiser's USPAP standards, the NAR standards are not imposed by law. Rather, it has been adopted voluntarily to self-elevate the profession to high standards. Members must complete two hours and thirty minutes of ethics training every four years to keep membership in compliance. Once a real estate licensee and a member of NAR, the Code of Ethics training can be found at: http://www.realtor.org/code-of-ethics/training

While the Code of Ethics establishes obligations that may be higher than those mandated by law, in any instance where the Code of Ethics and the law conflict, the obligations of the law takes precedence.

The preamble sets the tone for cooperation among licensees: "Realizing that cooperation with other real estate professionals promotes the best interests of those who utilize their services, Realtors® urge exclusive representation of clients; do not attempt to gain any unfair advantage over their competitors; and they refrain from making unsolicited comments about other practitioners."

And Article 1 sets the tone for putting clients first: "When representing a buyer, seller, landlord, tenant, or other client as an agent, Realtors® pledge themselves to protect and promote the interests of their client. This obligation to the client is primary, but it does not relieve Realtors® of their obligation to treat all parties honestly. When serving a buyer, seller, landlord, tenant or other party in a non-agency capacity, Realtors® remain obligated to treat all parties honestly."

And Article 2 sets the tone for honesty in transactions: "Realtors® shall avoid exaggeration, misrepresentation, or concealment of pertinent facts relating to the property or the transaction. Realtors® shall not, however, be obligated to discover latent defects in the property, to advise on matters outside the scope of their real estate license, or to disclose facts which are confidential under the scope of agency or non-agency relationships as defined by state law."

The full Code of Ethics and Standards of Practice can be found in class resources and at:

http://www.realtor.org/sites/default/files/policies/2016/2016-NAR-Code-of-Ethics.pdf

Florida REALTORS®

Another association that licensees can join is the Florida Realtors® Association (FAR). FAR is a professional trade association for licensed real estate practitioners in the state of Florida serving 58 local and regional Realtor® associations.

The organization serves residential and commercial agents as well as appraisers, property managers, and real estate counselors. To legally sell real estate in Florida, it is NOT a requirement for the licensee to be a member of FAR.

According to the FAR website, Florida Realtors' membership totals more than 155,000 real estate licensees. "It's the largest professional trade association in the Sunshine State." It is largely responsible for providing ongoing education and resources to licensees such as state approved contracts and a legal hotline.

http://media.floridarealtors.org/about-florida-realtors/

Local Board(Association) of Realtors®

At the local level, real estate licensees can join their local board association of Realtors®. The local realtor association is the "go to" as an immediate source for training, support, and networking with other real estate licensees.

Local boards also sponsor events which allows licensees to meet and develop relationships with vendors to the real estate community such as property inspectors, insurance companies, lenders, etc.

Multiple Listing Service (MLS)

The Multiple Listing Service is where information about houses for sale listed by real estate agents are compiled into a computer. The information is shared with other agents through the system.

Real estate agents use the MLS to search for homes for prospective buyers.

While buyers don't have direct access to the MLS, buyers can now indirectly access the MLS through their agents or by accessing websites like Realtor.com and Trulia. These websites post MLS listings to share with the public.

- Local MLSs have made agreements with third party vendors allowing listing information to be shared on websites such as Zillow.com, Trulia.com, etc.

https://www.lendingtree.com/glossary/what-is-multiple-listing-servic/

Multiple Listing Service (MLS)

One of the key elements of the MLS, is that members who list their properties in the MLS agree to compensate an agent representing a buyer in a sale. This is called co-brokering. The amount of compensation to be "shared" with the buyer's agent is not dictated by the MLS. However, the amount of compensation is included within the listing information of the MLS.

The rules for listing properties on a MLS varies from MLS organization to organization. Licensees are advised to study the rules well as most organizations impose fines for failure to comply. The fines can become costly.

Upon joining, training will be available and mandated to take advantage of the system.

Special Emphasis: REALTOR®

Only real estate licensees that have joined the National Association of Realtors and have agreed to follow the Code of Ethics and Standard of Practice may use the words REALTOR® with their name.

2 REAL ESTATE LICENSE LAW AND QUALIFICATIONS FOR LICENSURE

Learning Objectives:
- Identify the qualifications for a sales associate's license
- Describe the application requirements for licensure including nonresident application requirements
- Explain the importance of responding accurately and completely to the background information questions on the licensure application
- Illustrate the background check procedure conducted by the DBPR
- Describe the education requirement for pre- and post-license education and continuing education
- Distinguish among the various license categories
- Identify services of real estate where licensure is required
- Recognize actions that constitute unlicensed activity
- Recognize exemptions from real estate licensure
- Distinguish between registration and licensure
- Explain mutual recognition agreements

Key Terms:

adjudication withheld	compensation	prima facie evidence
broker	Florida resident	real estate services
broker associate	license/registration	sales associate
caveat emptor	nolo contendere / no contest	expungement vs. sealing

It is important that licensees understand how license laws were put into place and the purpose of the laws that affects the profession of real estate. Issues in this topic include:

A) History of Florida's real estate license law
      a) Department of Business and Professional Regulation

        b)   Division of Real Estate

        c)   Florida Real Estate Commission

B) Need for regulation
C) Caveat emptor
        a)   Purpose of regulation
D) Consumer protection
E) Important real estate statutes and rules

Prior to licensing laws, all risk and responsibility was on the buyer, known as **caveat emptor** meaning "Let the buyer beware!"

When Florida was young, the Florida constitution was passed establishing three branches of government **Legislative, Executive and Judicial**. The Florida Legislature passed **Florida Statute 20** to create the organizational structure of the Executive Branch of the Florida government. The purpose of the **Executive Branch** is to carry out the executive duties of the government that were established in the state constitution.

The Florida Legislature had come to understand that some professions should be regulated when the unregulated practice can harm the public, the public is not adequately protected by other laws, and less restrictive means of regulation are not available.

So, under Statute Chapter 20, **The Department of Business and Professional Regulation (DBPR)** was established to implement policies and oversee professions to be regulated.

Florida Statute 455 was then passed as **The Regulation of Professions and Occupations** to define the general legal practice and procedures for the DBPR. Statute 455 set a standard from profession to profession.

- For Example, under 455 it was established that you do NOT have to be a US Citizen to obtain any license to practice a profession!

Florida Statute 120 was then passed as the **Procedural Process** for ALL governmental professions authorized under the Florida Constitution. *If you are going to regulate something, then you need rules to regulate the regulator!*

- For example, under Statute 120, the DBPR must process and respond to deficiencies in applications for licensure within 30 days!

Statute 120 also established **discipline procedures** for licensees.

Every state now requires that individuals who practice real estate for another for compensation be licensed. So, the Florida Legislature passed the Real Estate License Law via Chapter 475 of the Florida Statutes to **regulate** real estate. The intent of real estate regulation is to protect the health, safety, and welfare of the public. It follows the standards of professional regulation set forth under Chapter 455 and is called the **Real Estate Professions Act.**

Statute 475 is divided into 4 Areas:

- Part I pertains to Real Estate **Brokerages**

- Part II pertains to Real Estate **Appraisers**

- Part III, **Commercial** Real Estate **Sales** Commission Lien Act

- Part IV, **Commercial** Real Estate **Leasing** Commission Lien Act.

Having developed laws to oversee real estate as a licensed profession, the Florida government needed a body of people to implement, interpret, and enforce the provisions of Chapter 475. Thus, the Florida Legislature created The Florida Real Estate Commission- also known as FREC or "the Commission."

FREC was **granted the authority** to keep records, conduct investigations, and the power to grant, deny, suspend, and revoke licenses.

And to hold FREC and licensees to specific standards, the Florida Real Estate Commission Rules were established in the Florida Statute Chapter 61J2.

- For Example, Florida Statute 120 states that a fee can be charged to a licensee while Chapter 61J2 states how much will be charged for a Real Estate License.

Statute 475 is divided into 4 Areas:

Part I REAL ESTATE BROKERS, SALES ASSOCIATES, AND SCHOOLS

Real estate licensees are regulated under Part I of Statute 475. It includes licensees, brokers, and schools. Licensees are responsible for knowing the rules and laws that pertain to the practice of real estate.

The best way to become familiar with the rules and regulations is to read the Statutes. This course is based on Part I of Statute 475.

Chapter 475 of the Florida Statutes can be found at:
http://www.leg.state.fl.us/STATUTES/index.cfm?App_mode=Display_Statute&URL=0400-0499/0475/0475PartIContentsIndex.html&StatuteYear=2013&Title=%2D%3E2013%2D%3EChapter%20475%2D%3EPart%20I

Part II APPRAISERS

Establishes similar rules, regulations, and procedures for real estate appraisers that Part I establishes for real estate agents. Where Part I established FREC, Part II Established FREAB -the Florida Real Estate Appraisal Board (FREAB). FREAB regulates the training and licensing of appraisers.

Part III COMMERCIAL REAL ESTATE SALES COMMISSION LIEN ACT

Part III regulates the lien rights of brokers who earned a commission but haven't been paid.

Pursuant to Florida's Commercial Real Estate Sales Commission Lien Act, a commercial broker has a lien upon the owner's net proceeds from the sale of commercial real estate for any commission earned by the broker under a written broker's agreement.

According to the Act, the lien upon the owner's net proceeds for a broker's commission is a lien upon personal property. It attaches to the owner's net proceeds only, and **it does NOT create a lien right against the real estate that is being sol**d.

Part IV COMMERCIAL REAL ESTATE LEASING COMMISSION LIEN ACT

Provides similar broker commission protections and rights as Part III, however, Part IV applies to commercial leases. A broker has a lien upon the owner's interest in commercial real estate for any commission earned by the broker pursuant to a brokerage agreement with respect to a lease of the commercial real estate.

- F.S. 475.803 If the owner obligated to pay the commission is the landlord, the broker's lien attaches to the landlord's interest in the commercial real estate identified in the brokerage agreement, but not to the tenant's leasehold estate. If the individuals obligated to pay the commission is the tenant, the broker's lien attaches to the tenant's leasehold estate, but not to the landlord's interest in the commercial real estate.

Important Real Estate Statutes and Rules

CHAPTER 475; PART I; REAL ESTATE BROKERS, SALES ASSOCIATES, AND SCHOOLS (ss. 475.001-475.5018)

CHAPTER 455; BUSINESS AND PROFESSIONAL REGULATION: GENERAL PROVISIONS

Chapter 20; ORGANIZATIONAL STRUCTURE

CHAPTER 120; ADMINISTRATIVE PROCEDURE ACT

61J2; Florida Real Estate Commission

Important Dates Regarding the History of Florida Real Estate

1923----Florida Legislature created real estate license laws; Chapter 475 REAL ESTATE BROKERS, SALES ASSOCIATES, SCHOOLS, AND APPRAISERS

1925---- Florida Legislature set forth the Florida Real Estate Commission to enforce the laws under Chapter 475 and gave FREC the power to do so.

- Since then, the Florida Legislature created the Division of Real Estate to assist FREC with the administrative tasks and support services.

Special Emphasis: Licensing Laws

Every state now **requires** that individuals who provide real estate services for another, for compensation, be licensed.

Special Emphasis: Statute 20

Established the Department of Business and Professional Regulation (DBPR) to: **implement policies and oversee**

professions to be regulated.

Special Emphasis: Chapter 20 ORGANIZATIONAL STRUCTURE

Chapter 20 established the Organizational Structure of the DBPR. It is part of the Executive Branch of the Florida government and carries out the **"executive"** duties of the government established in the state constitution.

Special Emphasis: Chapter 455; BUSINESS AND PROFESSIONAL REGULATION: GENERAL PROVISIONS

Chapter 455 applies to Regulation of Professions by the department. It defines the procedures and general legal practices for the DBPR. And it sets the standards for all professions regulated under the statute.

- For Example, under 455 it was established that you do NOT have to be a US Citizen to obtain any license to practice a profession!

Special Emphasis: Chapter 475; REAL ESTATE BROKERS, SALES ASSOCIATES, SCHOOLS, AND APPRAISERS

Chapter 475 established Real Estate License Law to **regulate** Real Estate.

Special Emphasis: FREC

Having developed laws to oversee real estate as a licensed profession, the Florida government needed a body of people to implement, interpret, and enforce the provisions of Chapter 475, so the Florida Legislature created

- The Florida Real Estate Commission (FREC).
- FREC was **granted the authority** to keep records, conduct investigations, and the power to grant, deny, suspend, and revoke licenses.

Special Emphasis: CHAPTER 120; ADMINISTRATIVE PROCEDURE ACT

Chapter 120 is the **Procedural Process** for ALL governmental entities authorized under the Florida Constitution including the DBPR. If you are going to regulate something, then you need rules to regulate the regulator!

For example, under Statute 120, the DBPR must process and respond to deficiencies in your application for licensure within 30 days!

- It also established discipline procedures for licensees

Special Emphasis: Florida Administrative Code 61J2

The Florida Administrative Code 61J2 established the Florida Real Estate Commission Rules holding both FREC and licensees to specific standards.

For Example:

- Florida Statute 120 states that a fee can be charged to a licensee

- Chapter 61J2 states how much will be charged for a Real Estate License

Special Emphasis: Need for Regulation

Prior to licensing laws, all risk and responsibility was on the buyer known as

- Caveat emptor – "Let the buyer beware."

The Florida Legislature had come to understand that some professions should be regulated when:

- The unregulated practice can harm the public.

- The public is not adequately protected by other laws.

- Less restrictive means of regulation are not available.

Special Emphasis: Purpose of Regulation

The intent of real estate regulation is to protect health, safety, and welfare of the public.

Special Emphasis: Statute 475 is divided into 4 Areas

- Part I REAL ESTATE BROKERS, SALES ASSOCIATES, AND SCHOOLS

- Part II APPRAISERS

- Part III COMMERCIAL REAL ESTATE SALES COMMISSION LIEN ACT

- Part IV COMMERCIAL REAL ESTATE LEASING COMMISSION LIEN ACT

LICENSE CATEGORIES

There are three types of Real Estate licenses available in Florida that allow licensees to help other people buy and sell or lease real property and be paid a commission for that work:

II) License Categories

A) Broker

B) Sales associate

C) Broker associate

Another distinction that many people ask about is the REALTOR® designation. The REALTOR® designation is a personal choice and not required by any state.

Real Estate Agent, Sales Associate, Broker, or REALTOR®?

Many people unfamiliar with the real estate industry use the terms real estate agent, broker and *REALTOR®* interchangeably.

However, there are important differences between the titles.

A real estate agent is a real estate professional who has taken and passed all required real estate classes and passed the real estate licensing exam. It is the most encompassing of the titles, yet it is not a legally recognized term by the DBPR.

New licensees are licensed as Sales Associates. If the licensee chooses to join the National Association of Realtors, the licensee may refer to him or herself as a Realtor® Associate.

> http://www.investopedia.com/ask/answers/101314/what-are-differences-among-real-estate-agent-broker-and-realtor.asp

Real Estate Agent, Sales Associate, Broker, or Realtor®?

A real estate broker has continued his or her education past the real estate agent level and passed the real estate broker licensing requirements per the rules of Statute 475. Real estate brokers can work as independent real estate agents and may have other agents working for them.

The most notable distinction with the license level of a broker is that the broker can work on his or her own and receive compensation for real estate activities.

Broker associates are licensees that have qualified as a broker including required time as a licensee, education requirements, and testing requirements. However, the broker associate chooses to continue working under the direction of a broker.

> http://www.investopedia.com/ask/answers/101314/what-are-differences-among-real-estate-agent-broker-and-

Special Emphasis: Broker

Brokers act as an intermediary between buyers and sellers and tenants and landlords. They oversee the activities of sales agents in a brokerage or real estate office. They are licensed by the DBPR to carry out real estate services and may receive compensation for their services.

Special Emphasis: Sales Associate

Real estate sales associates are licensed and registered by the DBPR to work under the direction of a broker. They are employed by the broker and receive compensation from the broker.

http://homeguides.sfgate.com/real-estate-salesperson-vs-broker-39659.html

Special Emphasis: Broker Associate

A broker associate qualifies for licensure as a broker, however, chooses to work under the direction of a broker.

http://www.businessdictionary.com/definition/associate-broker.html#ixzz3wgvoFQWC

GENERAL LICENSURE PROVISIONS

To become a real estate licensee in Florida, there are certain provisions that must be met. Provisions to become a licensee covered here include:

III) General Licensure Provisions

    A) Age

    B) High school diploma or its equivalent

    C) Honest, trustworthy, of good moral character

    D) Disclose if under investigation, convicted of a crime or ever entered a plea of nolo contendere / no contest or guilty

    E) Aliases—A/K/A

    F) Disclose if denied, or had a license disciplined or pending discipline in another jurisdiction

    G) Disclose if Denied, surrendered, or revoked license or registration to practice a regulated profession in any jurisdiction

   H) Guilty of any conduct or practice that would have been grounds for suspension or revocation under Chapter 475, F.S.

   I) U.S. citizenship (Chapter 455.10)

   J) Qualification of immigrants for examination (Chapter 455.11, F.S.)

   K) Requirement for United States social security number (Chapter 559, F.S.)

Basics for Getting a License

The process to become and remain a real estate licensee is not hard to learn but takes time to *memorize the details!*

In order to become a real estate licensee in Florida, the applicant must be at **least 18 years of age**. The applicant must have **a High school diploma or an equivalen**t level of education such as a GED. And the applicant must have a **Social Security Number**.

Per Chapter 455.10, realize that it is possible for a "non" U.S. Citizen to obtain a Social Security Number. The qualification requirement is not for the applicant to be a U.S. Citizen – only that the applicant have a Social Security Number.

It is also a requirement that a licensee be of **Honest and of Good Character** and the applicant be **Competent and Qualified**.

Honest and of Good Character

What does it mean to have honest and good character? To be of honest, trustworthy, and good moral character is the mental and moral qualities distinctive to an individual. It may be measured through the testimony of others along with any existing criminal records that would indicate the contrary.

The opposite of honest and good character includes individuals who lie, cheat, or steal. It is imperative that as real estate licensees handling transactions that often represent the largest investment that individuals make to act in a manner that is ethical and conscientious.

John H. Sklare, Ed.D, and Lifescript Personal Coach stated in **A Person of Moral Character Daily Inspiration**, Published March 24, 2010: "In my opinion, there are few things that contribute more to your sense of self and overall image than your moral character. By definition, moral character is *the existence or lack of virtues such as integrity, courage, fortitude, honesty and loyalty.* In other words, it means that you're a good person and a good citizen with a sound moral compass."

http://www.lifescript.com/well-being/articles/a/

Disclose Crimes

Applicants and licensees are expected to disclose when under investigation, convicted of a crime or ever having entered a plea of nolo contendere/no contest, or a guilty plea.

Therefore, when submitting an application, the applicant should attach **full details** of all cases if the applicant has been found guilty of or pleaded nolo contendere or no contest.

If you have any charges that were supposed to be sealed, expunged, or had adjudication withheld, verify that they are not on your record.

Sometimes there are additional steps required to get those situations finalized. Make sure you submit the full details and a personal statement pertaining to any crimes that are on your record for any and all states not just Florida.

The failure to disclose is considered falsifying an application.

Nolo Contendere (no contest)

Nolo contendere, also called a plea of no contest, is a Latin term meaning "I will not contest" the charges as a defendant in a criminal charge.

The result is the same as having plead guilty.

http://definitions.uslegal.com/n/nolo-contendere/

Adjudication Withheld

Withheld adjudication means that instead of having been found guilty by a judge, a person is put on probation.

If the person fails to meet the conditions of the probation, a guilty verdict would be found and further punishment placed upon the person.

http://definitions.uslegal.com/w/withheld-adjudication/

Aliases A/K/A

When filling out an application, applicants must include all versions of their name that they have ever used. These name variations are called aliases or A/K/A.

This means that applicants must include maiden names and name changes, if applicable. It is also a good idea if there is a common misspelling of the applicant's name that is associated with the applicant's history, to include it as well.

Disclose if Ever Denied

Applicants must disclose if the applicant has ever been denied a license, or had a license disciplined or pending discipline in another jurisdiction.

This means that the applicant must disclose if there was ever any action taken against the applicant regarding any field that requires licensure.

This includes, at any time throughout the individual's entire lifetime, having had a professional license for application denied, suspended, or revoked.

And it includes disclosing if there was ever any type of discipline or pending discipline regarding a professional license in Florida or any other state.

Conduct of Practice

Once an applicant has obtained a license, the licensee must disclose if the licensee is ever found guilty of any conduct or practice that would have been grounds for suspension or revocation under Chapter 475, F.S. Also, the licensee must disclose if they enter a plea of nolo contendere regardless of adjudication.

This is very important for licensees to note. Except for minor traffic violations that do not need to be reported, if a licensee gets in trouble after having obtained a license – even if in another state besides Florida– the licensee must report the infraction to the DBPR. Failure to do so is a violation of licensure.

This disclosure must be made within 30 days.

U.S. citizenship is not required (Chapter 455.10)

As already noted, it is not a requirement for any professional license in Florida for the applicant to be a United States Citizen.

- F.S. 455.10☐ Restriction on requirement of citizenship.—No person shall be disqualified from practicing an occupation or profession regulated by the state solely because he or she is not a United States citizen.

However, the individual will need to apply for a social security number.

- F.S. 559.79 Applications for license or renewal.—(1)☐ Each application for a license issued by the Department of Business and Professional Regulation shall include a statement showing the name, address, and social security number of each person.

Qualification of Immigrants for Examination

Florida Statute 455.11 specifically addresses an immigrant's right to sit for the state examination for licensure.

Simply put, immigrants that have taken the required educational requirements and are otherwise qualified may take the examination.

- 455.11☐ Qualification of immigrants for examination to practice a licensed profession or occupation.—
    (2)☐ Any person who has successfully completed, or is currently enrolled in, an approved course of study created pursuant to chapters 74-105 and 75-177, Laws of Florida, shall be deemed qualified for examination and reexaminations for a professional or occupational license......

Special Emphasis: Nolo contendere

Nolo contendere is a Latin term meaning "I will not contest" the charges, which is a plea made by a defendant to a criminal charge, allowing the judge to then find him/her guilty. It has the same effect as a plea of guilty.

Special Emphasis: Adjudication Withheld

Withheld adjudication refers to a decision by a judge to put a person on probation without a guilty verdict. In effect, then, the person has not been found guilty legally by the court.

http://definitions.uslegal.com/w/withheld-adjudication/

Special Emphasis: Basic Requirements for Licensure

- Being 18 years of age or older

- Have a high school diploma or equivalent

- Possessing a social security number

- Being of honest and of good character

- Being competent and qualified

Special Emphasis: Applicants Must Disclose

Applicants and Licensees must report if the person has ever:

- Been convicted of a crime

- Been found guilty

- Entered a plea of guilty or *nolo contendere* (no contest)

- And be sure to disclose this information even if court action (*adjudication*) was withheld.

- If the applicant has ever had an application for any other type of professional license or registration denied, suspended, or revoked. Or if you received any type of discipline or pending discipline regarding any professional license in Florida or any other state.

- All aliases must be disclosed.

Special Emphasis: Licensees Must Disclose

Once an applicant has obtained a license, the licensee must disclose if the licensee is ever found guilty of any conduct or practice that would have been grounds for suspension or revocation under Chapter 475, F.S.

Failure to disclose required information on an application is viewed as falsifying an application.

APPLICATION REQUIREMENTS

Basics for applying for licensure will be reviewed here and involve:

IV) Application Requirements

A) Fees

B) Application form

1) Responding accurately and completely to background information on the application

C) Background check procedure

D) Period to check for errors and omissions

E) Period to inform applicant of approval or denial of application

F) Rights of an applicant

G) The length of time a licensure application is valid

1) Initial application

2) Exam eligible

H) Nonresident application requirements

I) Regulations pertaining to pre-license courses

J) Identify what is public record

Application and Fees

Individuals that want to apply for licensure do so by filling out a DBPR application and paying an application and license fee. The application for sales associates, referred to as form **# DBPR RE 1, is** available on the DBPR website (Form DBPR RE2 for Broker application). The form can be submitted in print or online. If submitting for the Real Estate Sales Associate License- in print, attach a check for the current license and application fee of $83.75 made payable to the Florida Department of Business and Professional Regulation ($91.75 for Real Estate Broker level application). If submitting online, payment can also be made online with a debit/credit card or an electronic check. The application form must be filled in completely and honestly.

- The Printable Form is available at:
  http://www.myfloridalicense.com/dbpr/re/documents/DBPR_RE_1_Sales_Associate_Application.pdf

- The Online Form is available at:
  https://www.myfloridalicense.com/datamart/introduction.do?applicationId=4

APPLICATION CHECKLIST – IMPORTANT

For an application to be approved all required information must be provided. The DBPR has prepared a checklist to help the applicant. Submitting everything on the checklist will ensure faster processing.

ALL License Applicants must submit:

- A fee of $83.75 for Sales Associate Real Estate License ($91.75 for Real Estate Broker level).

- Electronic fingerprints.

- Supporting legal documentation, if necessary (such as for convictions).

Sales Associate License Applicants must:

Present their pre-licensure course certificate to the exam vendor at the time of examination.

http://www.myfloridalicense.com/dbpr/re/documents/DBPR_RE_1_Sales_Associate_Application.pdf

Fee

The fee that is paid covers the initial license period and the initial application fee. Licensees are charged a license fee at every renewal period. The first renewal period will be between 18 to 24 months from initial licensure with subsequent renewals every 24 months thereafter.

The licensee may be slightly higher if the Real Estate Recovery Fund fee is active.

There are also fees required for fingerprinting and for the state exam. However, these fees are not controlled by the state and not paid to the state.

http://www.myfloridalicense.com/dbpr/re/documents/DBPR_RE_1_Sales_Associate_Application.pdf

Fee Waiver Program

In 2017, the Florida Senate passed the Occupational Opportunity Act. This offers some advantages to individuals with good standing with the military or who has low income. Anyone who has served in the military and their spouse (or surviving spouse) is exempt from initial licensing fees (with documentation).

Also, low income individuals may have the initial fee waived. Low income is defined as a household income that is at or below 130 percent of the federal poverty guideline based on household size.

file:///C:/Users/artve/AppData/Local/Microsoft/Windows/INetCache/Content.Outlook/HQP4OPCB/h0615c.GOT.PDF

Background Check Procedure

Applicant must submit electronic fingerprints.

To assist in the background checks of applicants, Florida Statutes 475 mandates that electronic fingerprinting be provided for all real estate sales associate, real estate broker, and real estate appraiser applicants.

Electronic fingerprinting allows applicants to have their fingerprints scanned and electronically submitted to the Florida Department of Law Enforcement (FDLE) and Federal Bureau of Investigation (FBI).

Applicants can use any Livescan vendor that has been approved by the Florida Department of Law Enforcement to submit their fingerprints to the department.

The applicant must include the appropriate Originating Agency Identification (ORI) number to the vendor submitting the electronic fingerprints. Failure to provide the correct ORI will result in the Department of Business and Professional Regulation not receiving fingerprint results.

- The Real Estate Sales and Brokers ORI# to provide is FL920010Z.

  The total fee charged by each fingerprinting vendor varies.

Applicants must provide two forms of identification to the electronic fingerprinting site one bearing a picture and signature such as a driver's license, state identification card or passport. A list of Livescan vendors can be found at: http://www.fdle.state.fl.us/cms/Criminal-History-Records/Documents/ApplicantLivescanService-ProvidersVendors.aspx

> http://www.myfloridalicense.com/dbpr/re/documents/DBPR_RE_1_Sales_Associate_Application.pdf

What is the difference between a record sealing and record expungement?

When the goal is to remove an arrest record from public view, either sealing the record or expungement of the record will work. There is a difference, though, in what each means and how the record itself is affected.

A sealed record is simply hidden from the public by designating it as non-public.

An expunged record is physically removed so that the record no longer exists.

If the case was dismissed by the judge, dropped by the state attorney, or never filed by the state attorney, then the case can be expunged.

Cases involving adjudication withheld MAY BE ELIGIBLE to seal the case. Dangerous crimes cannot be sealed.

Never assume that a record has been expunged even if told that it was. The licensee applicant should do a background check before submitting the application to make sure that it doesn't show on the record.

An applicant that fails to disclose something that shows up is deemed as having *__falsified the application!__*

> http://sealmyrecord.com/sealing-expungement/difference-between-seal-expunge

Period to Check for Errors and Omissions

The state has 30 days from the receipt of an application to notify the applicant of any errors or omissions.

F.S. 120.60

Period to Approve or Deny Application

The Department of Business and Professional Regulation has 90 days from the time of complete application to approve or deny the application.

Florida Statutes 120.60

The Length of Time a Licensure Application is Valid

Once an application has been received by the applicant, it is valid for two years. This means that if the application is approved to take the license exam, the applicant has up to two years to complete licensing requirements and become a licensee.

Florida Statutes 475.181

Exam Eligible

Once an applicant has been approved to take the pre-license real estate exam, the licensee has up to two years to successfully pass the exam.

Upon approval, the state will provide a "PIN" to the applicant. The state also notifies the testing center that the applicant is eligible to take the exam. For the applicant to schedule the exam, the PIN will have to be supplied. The PIN replaces the applicant's social security number in the interest of protecting applicant private information.

To take the exam, the licensee will need to provide proof that the applicant passed the 63-hour pre-license course. Proof is supplied at the time of testing to the testing vendor – it is not provided to the state. The applicant will also have to have two forms of identification to take the test.

Nonresident Application Requirements

There is no requirement for an applicant to be a resident of Florida to apply for a Florida real estate license.

Therefore, application requirements for a non-resident applicant (that does not have a current real estate license in a state with Mutual Recognition) are the same as a resident applicant.

However, if the nonresident applicant has a real estate license in a state that Florida recognizes as mutual recognition; the applicant should follow the application process for mutual recognition.

Sales associate's license requirements include the following topics for a licensee to know:

V) Sales Associate License Requirements

    A) Education exemptions

    B) Sales associate pre-license course

    C) State licensure examination

Education Exemptions

Individuals applying for the Sales Associate license who also have a 4-year college degree in real estate are entitled to some education exemptions.

These individuals are exempt from the 63-hour associate sales pre-license course also called Course I. They are also exempt from the broker course also called Course II and are exempt from the subsequent post sales and post broker courses.

However, they must take and pass the state sales associate exam and the broker exam.

And they must complete all other continuing education to stay current with their knowledge.

Individuals applying for the Sales Associate license who also are an attorney in good standing with the Florida bar are exempt from the 63-hour sales associate pre-license course - Course I.

They must take the state sales associate exam and must take the post license sales associate course.

They are NOT exempt from the broker course – Course II or the broker post licensing courses.

However, they will not be required to do any other continuing education to maintain their license. (This makes sense considering they do take continuing education to maintain their attorney license.)

Exemptions from Licensing Education Requirements	
4-year College Degree in RE	**Florida Attorney**
• Exempt from Courses I & II	• Exempt from Courses I
• State exam required	• State exam required
• Exempt from Post-license education	• Post-license education required
• Must complete continuing education	• Exempt from continuing education

Sales Associate pre-license course

Applicants for a sales associate license in real estate must pass a <u>63-hour Sales Associate Pre-license</u> course before taking the State Sales Associate exam.

The course is designed to teach an applicant the fundamentals of real estate and specific licensing laws in the state of Florida.

Out of the 63 hours, 60 hours involve class room instruction (can be computer delivered) based on 50-minute periods. The remaining three hours are allotted for the end-of-course exam. A maximum of 8 hours may be missed of class time.

The end-of-course exam is a total of 100 multiple choice questions which allows for 1.7 minutes per question. The exam tests principles and practices of real estate with 45 questions, Florida real estate law with 45 questions, and math skills with 10 questions.

70% correct is required to pass. Should the licensee not pass, a second and different test may be taken after 30 days. If that test is not passed, the applicant would have to retake a pre-license course per statute.

State Licensure Examination

Once you have completed the 63-hour Sales Associate class and passed, you can take the State Brokers exam. This exam is administered by Pearson Vue.

Schedule the exam at

> https://www1.pearsonvue.com/testtaker/signin/SignInPage.htm?clientCode=FLREAPP

> Applicants can request that the exam be given in English or Spanish.

The state exam also consists of 100 questions with the same 45/45/10 question format followed by the end-of-course exam. However, the state requires a passing grade of 75%. Applicants will be immediately told whether the individual has passed the exam.

It takes about 24 hours for the DBPR website to update reflecting that license requirements have been met. Keep in mind that a licensee cannot practice real estate until their license has been made active by an employing broker.

Special Emphasis: State licensure examination

The 63-hour Sales Associate course – Course I requires a passing grade of 70% on the end-of course exam.

The Florida state Sales Associate exam requires a passing grade of 75%.

The **Candidate Information Booklet** is a useful source to help guide you through the application process.

Use this link or find it in the course resources to review this booklet.

> http://www.myfloridalicense.com/dbpr/servop/testing/documents/RE_sales_cib.pdf

To qualify for a broker's license, the individual must meet some additional criteria. This topic includes:

VI) Broker License Requirements

    A) Education exemptions

    B) Experience requirement

    C) Broker pre-license course

    D) State licensure examination

Broker Education Exemptions

As with the Sales Associate licensing, persons with a 4-year college degree in real estate are entitled to some exemptions. They are exempt from the 72-hour Broker course or Course II. However, they must take the broker exam. They are also exempt from the post license broker course.

They will be required to do the continuing education component to maintain their license.

Persons that are attorneys in good standing with the Florida bar ARE required to take the 72-hour broker pre-license course or Course II. They must take the state exam and must take the post license broker's course.

However, they will not be required to do any other continuing education to maintain their license.

Experience Requirement

One big part of qualifying for a broker's license is the experience component. To qualify to sit for the broker state exam, a licensee must have had a sales associate license with active experience for 2 years of the last 5 years.

Working for a contractor/developer is not considered active experience (if the developer is not registered as a broker). Any time that the license has been considered inactive would not count towards the 2-year active experience criteria either. However, the required experience/ time does not have to be as a sales associate licensed in Florida. Time spent as an active agent in other states qualifies.

- <u>Requires Active Experience of 24 months in the previous 5 years</u>

- Working for a contractor does not count as "active" experience

Broker Pre-License Course

A licensee must complete a 72-hour Broker Pre-license course, also called Course II, before taking the broker level state exam.

The course is like the sales associate course; however, content is geared toward brokerage level handling of issues and the operation and management of brokerages.

This course must be passed with a score of 70%. Should the end-of-course exam not be passed, the licensee may take one more different exam after 30 days. If that test is not passed, the licensee would be required to take another Broker Pre-license course.

Broker State Licensure Examination

Once a broker applicant has completed the Brokers class, has 2 years of experience, and has gone through the application process with the DBPR, the individual will be eligible to take the State Brokers exam.

This exam is also administered by Pearson Vue:

https://www1.pearsonvue.com/testtaker/signin/SignInPage.htm?clientCode=FLREAPP

A passing score of 75% is required.

Special Emphasis

Experience Requirement

To qualify to sit for the broker state exam, a licensee must have had a sales associate license with active experience for 2 years of the previous 5 years.

MUTUAL RECOGNITION

The state of Florida currently has Mutual Recognition agreements with seven states. The topics addressed with this issue are:

VII) Mutual Recognition Agreements with Other States

    A) Florida resident defined

    B) Distinguish between mutual recognition and reciprocity

Mutual Recognition Agreements with Other States

If someone is already a licensed real estate agent in a state that Florida has "Mutual Recognition" agreement, that individual may be exempt from some of the education and testing requirements.

The purpose of mutual recognition is that the state of Florida recognizes the education and experience of these individuals and, therefore, provides special licensing provisions.

The definition of a Florida Resident is applied to see if someone can get their license through Mutual Recognition! Even if the individual is licensed by one of the states recognized for mutual recognition, if the individual is a "resident" of Florida, the rules of mutual recognition do NOT apply.

Florida currently has mutual recognition agreements with:

- Alabama, Arkansas, Connecticut, Georgia, Illinois, Mississippi, and Nebraska.

Anyone applying for a Florida license under mutual recognition will not have to take the pre-license courses. If applying as a sales associate – exempt from Course I. If applying as a broker – exempt from Course II.

Instead of regular 100 question exam, the applicant will instead be required to take the Florida law portion of the Florida Real Estate exam. This is a 40-question exam pertaining to Florida specific real estate practice and laws. This verifies that the person's knowledge transfers to specific Florida licensing provisions. This exam must be passed at 75% or higher.

http://www.myfloridalicense.com/dbpr/re/MutualRecognition.html

Florida Residents

Anyone who has resided in Florida continuously for a period of four calendar months or more within the preceding year is considered to be a Florida Resident.

Florida residents are NOT allowed to be licensed under the mutual recognition provision.

Florida residents who hold an active license in one of the states recognized under mutual recognition will still need to pass the pre-licensing courses and the regular 100 question state exam.

Distinguish Between Mutual Recognition and Reciprocity

Mutual Recognition is not the same thing as **Reciprocity** – which is not allowed in Florida!

Reciprocity is the exchange of licensing privileges between states, nations, businesses or individuals.

Regarding real estate, reciprocity refers to recognizing the license of a real estate agent from another state without the necessity of taking the local state's examination, whereas mutual recognition credits the experience and education yet still requires proof of competency through passing the Florida law exam.

Florida does NOT have reciprocity with any state.

http://legal-dictionary.thefreedictionary.com/Reciprocity

Special Emphasis: To Qualify for Mutual Recognition

- Proof of U.S. citizenship **is not** required

- Applicants **must possess** a Social Security number

- Florida residency **is not** allowed at time of licensing

- Nonresident licensees must complete post-license and continuing education as required of all Florida licensees

- Resident licensees who become nonresidents must notify the Commission within **60 days** of change in residency

Special Emphasis: Mutual Recognition

An agreement between states to recognize the education and experience of real estate licensees and to provide special licensing provisions.

Special Emphasis: Florida Resident Defined

A person who has resided in Florida continuously for a period of four calendar months or more within the preceding year is considered to be a Florida Resident.

Licensees must understand rules regarding the actual real estate license. This topic covers:

VIII) Information included on the real estate license

A) Prima facie evidence that holder of a real estate license possesses current and valid licensure

Prima Facie Evidence

What is PRIMA FACIE?

Prima Facie is Latin meaning at first sight; on the first appearance; on the face of it; so far as can be judged from the first disclosure; presumably.

Licensees are required to have their wallet license in their possession anytime they are conducting real estate activities with the public.

A real estate license is considered prima facie evidence that the individual holding the license has a valid license and may conduct real estate services. The license contains all identifying license information including name, license number, type of license and expiration date. The code at the start of the license number indicates the type of license granted.

http://thelawdictionary.org/prima-facie/

IX)   Registration vs. Licensure

What is the difference between registration and licensure?

Licensure is generally issued at the state level and is a mandatory credentialing process that allows an individual to legally perform certain skills. As dictated by law, there is usually a requirement to pass certain tests and exhibit the ability to perform certain skills.

Registration indicates that a person whose name is listed on an official record or register has met certain requirements in their profession. The registry list of names can then be accessed to determine if a potential employee has met certain requirements.

http://www.answers.com/Q/What_is_the_difference_between_certification_registration_licensure

The Department of Business and Professional Regulation maintains a database of all professionals who are licensed within the state of Florida. This database is a "registration" of licensee information. This is different from the actual license, which is also issued by the DBPR.

It includes information such as the licensee's address, dates of licensing, the status of the license and the licensee's employer.

There are also situations that do not require a license, however, require registration. For example, Real Estate Brokerages that are corporations must register corporate officers that are not also real estate licensees.

It is extremely important that licensees understand ongoing education renewal of license requirements.

X) License Renewal Education

    A) Post licensure requirement

    B) Continuing education

    C) Reactivation education

Post Licensure Requirement

Sales Associate

Being a real estate licensee involves a great deal of knowledge that is difficult to learn completely in the pre-license course. Therefore, Florida requires that every real estate licensee that has passed the 63-hour pre-license course and has successfully obtained a license as a sales associate take a post licensing 45-hour course.

This course must be completed prior to the first renewal period which will be between 18 and 24 months depending upon the license date.

It's to the licensee's advantage to take this course right away as it covers skills that new licensees need to have to prospect, build business and work successfully with buyers and seller.

If the licensee fails to take this course before the renewal period, his or her license will be NULL AND VOID, meaning the person lost the license and would have to start all over to practice real estate!

Broker and Broker Associate

Being a real estate broker and broker associate also involves a great deal of knowledge that is difficult to learn completely in the pre-license course. Therefore, Florida requires that every real estate licensee that has passed the 72-hour pre-license broker course and has successfully obtained a license as a broker or broker associate take a post licensing 60-hour course (2, 30-hour courses).

These courses must be completed prior to the first renewal period which will be between 18 and 24 months depending upon the license date.

If the licensee fails to take this course before the renewal period, his or her BROKER license will be NULL AND VOID, meaning the person lost the license and would have to start all over to practice real estate! The licensee could request to be reinstated at the sales associate level.

Post Licensure Passing Requirement

Licensees must pass the end-of-course exam of a post licensure course at 70% or higher. Failure to do so means the licensee can retake a different version of the exam after 30 days. If the licensee fails that exam the licensee would have to retake the course. Keep this in mind when scheduling your course. Best practice is to take the course as soon as possible after becoming initially licensed.

Licensees who also have a four-year degree in real estate are exempt from both the sales associate and the broker post licensing courses.

Continuing Education

Regardless of whether a sales associate, broker associate, or broker, licensees must take 14 hours of continuing education before every renewal period ends after the initial renewal period. It doesn't apply during the first renewal period as post license courses are taken instead.

Three of the 14 hours must be in the area of core law. Another three must be in Ethics & Business Practices. The other eight hours can be a specialty course offered by approved schools. Often the 14 hours are offered as one course to easily fulfil the requirement. (The three hours of ethics applies for licensees with expiration date of 9/30/18 and thereafter.)

Due to the desire of keeping licensees abreast of the most current legal issues, a licensee may take a second three hours of core law during the second year if the first three hours were taken during the first year for a total of six hours of core law.

Three of the eight specialty course credit hours may be gained by attending a legal agenda session of the Florida Real Estate Commission- FREC. This can be done one time during a renewal cycle.

A point of fact is that if a licensee is REQUIRED to attend a legal session due to a disciplinary action against the licensee – this would not be allowed to count to replace the core law continuing education requirement!

Also, to get credit for attendance, the licensee must notify the Division of Real Estate (DRE) at least seven days in advance of the session.

Note that licensees who also have a four-year degree in real estate are NOT exempt from continuing education. However, licensed Florida lawyers in good standing are exempt.

Reactivation Education

Occasionally a licensee fails to renew his or her license before the end of a license renewal period. To renew a license, the licensee must have completed the continuing education or post education requirements AND have paid the renewal fee.

If the licensee fails to renew the license by the first renewal term, the license is lost with no chance to recover it. The license is null and void.

After the first renewal period, if the licensee fails to take the required 14 hours of continuing education the license will be considered involuntarily inactive and the licensee cannot practice real estate until the license is once again active.

If the license has expired for no more than 12 months, the licensee simply needs to make up the 14 hours of continuing education to activate the license.

If more than 12 months have passed but less than 24 months, then the licensee is required to take a special Reactivation Course which equals 28 hours of education.

If the licensee fails to renew the license and allows 24 months to pass, then the license cannot be renewed.

More information related to license status will be covered in Session 3 Real Estate License Law and Commission Rules.

Special Emphasis: Post Licensure Requirement

Sales Associate: Sometime between getting your initial license and your first license renewal you must take the 45-hour sales associate post-license course.

Broker: Sometime between getting your initial broker's license and your first license renewal you must take the 60-hour broker post-license course.

Special Emphasis: Continuing education

All real estate licensees must take 14 hours of continuing education between each renewal period, or every two years.

Special Emphasis: Reactivation Education

Any licensee that let's their license expire for more than 12 months , but less than 24 months can reactivate their license by taking the required 28-hour course.

Florida Statutes 475 defines what activities require a real estate license and what activities are exempt from licensure:

XI) Real Estate Services

A) Individuals who are required to be licensed

B) Individuals who are exempt from licensure

As already stated, performing the services of real estate on behalf of another person, for compensation, requires a real estate license.

The term "real estate" is defined in statute to include both interest in land or real property and business opportunities. The term "compensation" includes monetary compensation as well as valuable consideration, which includes benefits other than cash or tangible goods.

This means that if someone receives anything of value in exchange for "helping" someone sell or lease property, the person may be breaking license law which is a third-degree felony.

To further clarify the licensing requirements, the statutes have very carefully laid out who must have a license as compared to who is exempt from licensure.

Individuals Required to be Licensed

So, Who Must Have a Real Estate License?

Per Florida Statutes, ANYONE receiving a "commission" or transaction-based compensation for the buying, selling, or leasing of real estate MUST have a real estate license.

First, the statutes have clarified that just being paid for conducting real estate activities for a fee does not automatically mean that a license is required. The reason that this clarification exists is that there are exemptions for individuals that are paid a regular salary or hourly wage who are paid regardless of whether a property sells. These specific exemptions will be reviewed shortly.

Know, though, that anytime a fee, commission, or even a "bonus," is tied directly to a property being sold or rented, then a license would ALWAYS be required.

Individuals Required to be Licensed

What are Real Estate Activities?

Unless an individual is exempt from licensure, performing real estate services for any type of compensation requires a real estate license. Real Estate Activities cover a broad range of activities designed to result in the transfer of property or the lease of property.

It starts with ADVERTISING a property for sale. Advertising is a real estate activity if instead of being paid a flat fee for the advertising service, such as running an ad in a newspaper, the person is paid upon a successful sale or lease.

Assisting a buyer to purchase or BUY a property is a type of real estate activity. As well as assisting a seller to SELL a property. (This includes Time Shares.)

http://www.myfloridalicense.com/dbpr/pro/division/Servicesthatrequirealicense_re.htm

Individuals Required to be Licensed

What are Real Estate Activities?

When assisting sellers to sell a property by AUCTIONING the property, this is considered a real estate activity and a license is required – unless exempt by already being licensed as an auctioneer.

Facilitating the EXCHANGE of property- even if no money changes hands between the buyer and seller—and being paid to do so is a form of real estate activity.

Assisting a tenant to RENT a property, or assisting a landlord in LEASING out a property, are both real estate activities.

And finally, APPRAISING a property is a type of real estate activity.

Note that although mortgages are involved, financing is not a real estate activity as it is not regulated under Chapter 475 of the Florida Statutes.

Individuals Exempt from Licensure

Not everyone needs a license to sell real estate.

- **Owners** may buy, sell, exchange or lease their own property without a license. Know that a corporation, partnership, trust, joint venture, or other entity which sells, exchanges, or leases its own real property count as owners and are exempt. (Therefore, **owner developers** can employ salaried employees to sell property if there is NOT compensation based on the actual sales.)

- Any person acting as an **Attorney in Fact having Power of Attorney** or a **Court Appointed Individual** for the execution of contracts or conveyances only

- An **attorney at law or certified public accountant** acting within the scope of her or his duties

- Any **employee of a public utility**, a rural electric cooperative, a railroad, or a state or **local governmental agency** who acts within the scope of her or his employment, for which no compensation in addition to the employee's salary is paid.

- Any salaried employee of an owner, or of a registered broker for an owner, of an **apartment community** who works in an onsite rental office of the apartment community in a leasing capacity.

- **Any salaried manager of a condominium or cooperative apartment complex** for the renting of individual units within such condominium or cooperative apartment complex if rentals arranged by the person are for periods no greater than 1 year.

- Employees purchasing, selling, or leasing a business that are **radio, television, or cable enterprises** licensed and regulated by the Federal Communications Commission- if real estate property is not included in the sale (the business only!)

- Any property management firm or any owner of an apartment complex for the act of paying a **finder's fee** or referral fee to an unlicensed person who is a tenant in such apartment complex provided the value of the fee does not exceed $50 per transaction.

- Any person, partnership, corporation, or other legal entity which, for another and for compensation or other valuable consideration, rents or advertises for rent, for **transient occupanc**y, any public lodging establishment licensed under Chapter 509—this includes **hotels and motel**s.

- An **owner of one or part of one or more timeshare** periods for the owner's own use and occupancy who later offers one or more of such periods for resale.

Special Emphasis: Compensation

Compensation means payment for work done and includes anything of monetary value, not just money.

http://www.yourdictionary.com/compensation#ZGiETsAHlIDZ5UIE.99

Special Emphasis: What are Real Estate Activities?

Real estate activities include:

BUYING, SELLING, AUCTIONING, EXCHANGING, RENTING, LEASING, AND APPRAISING PROPERTY OR BUSINESSES.

Special Emphasis: Individuals Required to be licensed

Unless an individual is exempt from licensure, performing real estate services for any type of compensation requires a real estate license.

- ANYONE receiving a "commission" or transaction-based compensation always requires a license.

Special Emphasis: Individuals Exempt

Owners are exempt and can sell their own property. This includes corporations, LLCs, etc.

Unauthorized Practice of Law

Just as individuals must be careful not to engage in practicing real estate without a license, it is extremely important that licensees be careful not to practice "law" without a license. Only lawyers are authorized to practice law and as such are licensed by the state to do so. This includes activity that a real estate licensee may unknowingly begin to engage in while trying to be "extra helpful" in the interaction with clients.

Know that only lawyers can give "legal" advice to clients. This includes matters of real estate law such as advice on the title and transfer of property.

Just as licensees are taught information about mortgages for the purpose to better interface between clients and their lenders – real estate licensees are also taught about legal issues that can impact your clients. However, it is not the licensees place to advise clients on legal matters. It is the licensee's place to stay within the law for the licensee's own behavior and pass on requirements such as legal disclosures that must be made by sellers, etc. This is different from giving legal advice.

A licensee must remember to always refer clients to other professionals including lawyers as appropriate.

This means that real estate agents cannot:

- Explain potential legal outcomes of a dispute

- Evaluate legal issues and offer advice on the best way to proceed

- File a lawsuit for a client

- Make arguments in court on a client's behalf

Finally, licensees MUST follow real estate contract law rules as defined in Section 11.

http://www.legalmatch.com/law-library/article/real-estate-agent-liability-unauthorized-practice-of-law.html#sthash.Jiz0DpKq.dpuf

3 REAL ESTATE LICENSE LAW AND COMMISSION RULES

Learning Objectives:
• Describe the composition, appointment and member qualifications of the Florida Real Estate Commission
• Define the powers and duties of the Commission
• Explain the different licensure statuses
• Distinguish between active and inactive license status
• Describe the regulations regarding involuntarily inactive status
• Distinguish between multiple and group licenses

Key Terms:

active/inactive	group license	null and void
canceled	involuntarily inactive	voluntarily inactive
cease to be in force	license authority voided	
current	multiple licenses	

At the core of real estate licensing are the regulations by the Department of Business and Professional Regulation.

The topics reviewed here include:

1) Organizational structure

2) Definitions; F.S. 455.01

3) Legislative intent; requirements; F.S. 455.02

4) Department powers and duties; F.S. 455.203

5) Licensing examinations

6) Licenses, fees, statuses, and renewal

  a) Active status

  b) Inactive status

     (i) Voluntarily inactive status

     (ii) Involuntarily inactive status

  c) License ceases to be in force (F.S. 475.23)

  d) Members of armed forces (F.S. 455.02)

7) Types of real estate license

  a) Multiple and group licenses

Legislative Intent

As explained in Section 2 of this course, the **Department of Business and Professional Regulation**, or the DBPR, was established under Florida **Statute 20** as part of the executive branch of government to implement policies and oversee professions.

The Florida Legislature had come to understand that some professions should be regulated when the unregulated practice can harm the health, safety, and welfare of the public; the public is not effectively protected by other means, including, but not limited to, other state statutes, local ordinances, or federal legislation; and less restrictive means of regulation are not available.

Therefore, the intent of the Legislature, through the creation of the DBPR, is that persons desiring to engage in any lawful profession regulated by the department shall be entitled to do so as a matter of right-if otherwise qualified.

And the intent of the DBPR is to protect the public.

Legislative Intent

Yet, in the efforts to "protect the public," the statutes also safeguard against the department becoming unreasonably restrictive by creating extraordinary standards that work only to deter qualified persons from entering a profession.

- Per **Florida Statute 455.201**, "neither the department nor any board may take any action that tends to create or maintain an economic condition that unreasonably restricts competition."

Think about this. What if a bunch of established real estate agents got together and convinced the DBPR to raise the initial application fees for real estate? These agents would be happy since they wouldn't have to pay the fee as they are already licensed. Individuals trying to enter the field would suddenly find themselves unreasonably burdened by the "economic condition" of the fee that was being placed upon them. The result would be less competition and more income for currently licensed agents!

Department Powers and Duties

Fortunately, Florida Statutes have regulations in place governed by **Chapter 120, F.S.** which keeps a situation such as the one just described from happening.

So, although **Chapter 455 of the Florida Statutes** gives the DBPR the power to investigate consumer complaints, issue subpoenas upon conducting investigation, issue cease and desist orders, and issue citations--these powers are muted by **Chapter 120** which holds the DBPR to standards of conduct within the department.

Today, the DBPR summarizes their mission on their website as

- "To license efficiently, regulate fairly, and …strive to meet this goal in our day-to-day operation."

Organizational Structure

The DBPR's role of licensing and regulating professions has turned into a large task with many professions falling under licensing restrictions:

- Architecture and Interior Design, Auctioneers, Barbers' Board, Building Code Administrators and Inspectors, Construction Industry, Cosmetology, Electrical Contractors, Employee Leasing Companies, Landscape Architecture, Pilot Commissioners, Engineers, Geologists, Veterinary Medicine, Home inspections, Mold-related services . . . This list goes on and on.

As such, the Department of Business and Professional Regulation follows a well-developed organizational structure which licensees are expected to understand.

Organizational Structure

The organizational structure, as mandated by Chapter 20, starts with the Governor of Florida who appoints the **Secretary of the DBPR**. This appointment is subject to confirmation by the state senate. This is a very important position as the Secretary of the DBPR is the chief executive officer of the DBPR.

- F. S. 20.165 (1) The head of the Department of Business and Professional Regulation is the Secretary of Business and Professional Regulation. The secretary shall be appointed by the Governor, subject to confirmation by the Senate. The secretary shall serve at the pleasure of the Governor.

The Secretary is responsible for planning, directing, coordinating and executing the powers, duties and functions vested in the Department, its divisions, bureaus and other subunits.

Because there are so many professions for the DBPR to regulate, separate divisions under the DBPR were created.

- The Secretary of the DBPR appoints a director for each division established within this section- including the **Director of the Division of Real Estate** (DRE). The Director of the DRE is confirmed by the Florida Real Estate Commission.

- The **Division of Service Operations** handles license applications, processes license fees, issues licenses (upon approval) and handles renewals. They also have a Customer Contact Center to handle questions from licensees: 1-850-487-1395.

- The **Division of Professions** regulates education courses and license examinations.

- The **Division of Real Estate** protects the public by regulating real estate and appraisal licensees through education and compliance and provides administrative support to the Florida Real Estate Commission (FREC).

- The **Division of Florida Condominiums, Timeshares, and Mobile Homes** provides consumer protection for Florida residents living in the regulated communities through education, complaint resolution, mediation and arbitration and developer disclosure.

http://www.myfloridalicense.com/dbpr/os/os-info.html

F.S 20.165

Licensing Examinations

As stated, the Division of Service Operations handles licensing and processes fees.

- Per Florida Statutes 475.175, a person shall be entitled to take the license examination to practice real estate in Florida if the person has submitted to the DBPR an application, digital fingerprint data, and the fee for licensing. To take the actual exam, the person would be asked to supply proof of identification and certification of having passed the Pre-license course.

Licensure

- The Department shall license any applicant whom the commission certifies to be qualified to practice as a broker or sales associate.

Fees

The commission by rule may establish fees to be paid for application, examination, reexamination, licensing and renewal.

License Statuses

Once a licensee has obtained a license, there is more than one type of status that the license can be attributed as.

Active status indicates that the licensee has fulfilled all requirements (including if a sales or broker associate having an employer on record with the DBPR) and may practice real estate.

Inactive means that there is a license in place, but the licensee may not practice real estate.

An inactive status can be voluntary specifically by choice and request of the licensee. This would be appropriate for a licensee who would like to retain the license but is not currently working in real estate. When a licensee's license is inactive, the licensee is still required to pay all renewal fees and complete post license education and/or continuing education and renewal requirements.

Florida Statute 475.183

License Statuses

Involuntary inactive is when the licensee fails to fulfill the renewal requirements. However, the state allows a licensee to reactivate a license if the licensee fulfills the renewal requirements within two years of expiration. Reactivation is not possible if the licensee fails to meet requirements of the first renewal period.

After 2 years, the license becomes null and void and the licensee would have to repeat the entire application process by retaking the pre-license course to obtain a new license.

A license with a "Current" status indicates that all requirements have been completed and the license has not expired.

Florida Statute 475.183

Renewal

It is important for a licensee to track his or her license renewal dates to avoid having a license lapse.

Remember that failure to renew within the first renewal period would result in an immediate loss of license. The license would be null and void.

Licenses are only renewed during one of two dates in a year- Either March 31st or September 30th.

Once a license is approved, the license is in effect (not the same as active) and the first renewal date will be between 18 to 24 months from the license date. To calculate the first renewal period date, add 2 years to the calendar year of the new license. Because a license must be renewed within 24 months, go backwards to the either March 31st or September 30.th This will be the renewal date.

Florida Statute 475.183

Calculate License Renewal Date

If a licensee received his or her license on September 10th, 2016, when is the end of his or her first renewal period?

Add 2 years to 2016: 2018 is the renewal year.

Move backwards from the September 10th date to March 31st.

The renewal date is March 31st, 2018.

Although closer to September 30th, technically September 30th would take the licensee past a 24-month renewal time frame which is not allowed.

Involuntary Inactive License

To Reactivate:

If a license has been involuntarily inactive for 12 months or less

- Complete 14 hour continuing education course

More than 12 months but less than 24 months

- Complete 28 hours of a Commission-prescribed education course

More than 24 months

- The license would be null and void

Involuntary Inactive

There are other ways for a license to become involuntarily inactive other than failure to renew.

When an employing broker has his or her license suspended or revoked for discipline reasons (or retires, quits or is fired from the brokerage), the licenses of all sales associates and broker associates employed by the broker are automatically placed in involuntary inactive status.

A licensee may activate the license by having the license registered under a new employing broker.

License Ceases to be in force (F.S. 475.23)

A license shall cease to be in force whenever a broker changes her or his business address and fails to notify the department of the change. Per Florida Statutes 475.23, the licensee must notify the department of address changes within 10 days after the change.

The distinction here is that upon verifying a license within the DBPR system, it would appear to be active and valid even though they are unaware of the infraction. Yet technically, the license would fail to be in force until notification was made and the licensee could not practice real estate.

Statuses

A license is considered canceled when the commission mistakenly approved a license.

Know that falsifying an application is a Third-Degree Felony.

Members of the Armed Forces (F.S. 455.02)

Recall from Section 2 that military members and their spouses are exempt from license fees.

In addition, in an attempt to honor their situations, members of the armed forces and their spouses get additional special treatments:

The DBPR may issue a **real estate license** to practice real estate in Florida to a spouse of an active duty member of the Armed Forces assigned to duty in Florida. The spouse must hold a valid real estate license in another state.

Plus, a licensee in good standing, who is a member of the U.S. Armed Forces, is exempt from renewal requirements during active duty and for two years after discharge from active duty. If military duty is out of state, the exemption also applies to a licensed spouse.

Special Emphasis: Multiple Licenses

Multiple licenses are issued to a broker who qualifies as the broker for more than one business entity or brokerage.

For each business/brokerage that a person is a broker, a separate broker license must be obtained.

According to the Florida DBPR, "A multiple broker license is not transferrable. Once you have canceled the license, it will be set to License Authority Voided and you will have to apply for new multiple licenses in the future should you decide to operate for multiple entities at the same time."

http://myfloridalicense.custhelp.com/app/answers/detail/a_id/1774/~/how-do-real-estate-brokers-cancel-a-multiple-license-when-it-is-no-longer

Special Emphasis: Group License

According to the Florida DBPR, a group license is for an owner/developer who owns properties through various entities, but all such entities are connected so that such ownership or control is by the same individual or individuals. A sales associate or broker associate may have a "group license" to sell for all the entities owned by the owner/developer.

Owner-developer sends the DBPR a list of legal company names and the sales associate or broker associate receives ONE license under ONE employer.

http://myfloridalicense.custhelp.com/app/answers/detail/a_id/481/~/what-is-a-real-estate-group-license%3F

Special Emphasis: Null and Void License

A license is null and void when it no longer exists

- License has been involuntarily inactive for more than two years

- Revoked following disciplinary proceedings

- Voluntarily relinquish (does not involve disciplinary action)

Special Emphasis: The Intent of Regulation

The Legislature regulates the real estate professions only for the health, safety, and welfare of the public.

(a) Their unregulated practice can harm or endanger the health, safety, and welfare of the public.

(b) The public is not effectively protected by other means.

(c) Less restrictive means of regulation are not available.

Special Emphasis: Florida Statute 455 granted the DBPR the legal powers to:

- Investigate complaints

- Issue subpoenas

- Issue cease and desist orders

- Issue citations

Special Emphasis: Organizational Structure F.S 20.165

The head of the Department of Business and Professional Regulation is the Secretary of Business and Professional Regulation.

The secretary shall be <u>appointed by the Governor</u>, subject to <u>confirmation by the Senate</u>.

The secretary shall serve at the pleasure of the Governor.

The chief administrator of the DBPR is Secretary of the DBPR who is **appointed by the governor and confirmed by the Florida Senate.**

Special Emphasis: DRE

The following board and commission are established within the Division of Real Estate:

- Florida Real Estate Appraisal Board, created under part II of Chapter 475.

- **Florida Real Estate Commission**, created under part I of Chapter 475.

Special Emphasis: License Statuses

1) Active Status (Current/Active)

2) Inactive Status

    a) Voluntary Inactive Status (Current/Inactive)

        i. Licensee requests inactive status

        ii. Voluntary inactive licensees must complete education and renewal requirements

    b) Involuntary Inactive Status (not Current)

        i. Failed to renew license before the expiration date

        ii. After 2 years, involuntary inactive license is null and void

Special Emphasis: Involuntary Inactive

When a broker:

1) Has their license suspended or revoked for discipline

2) Retires, quits or is fired from the brokerage

- The licenses of sales associates and broker associates employed by the broker are automatically placed in involuntary inactive status

- Associates may become active again under a new employer or new broker

Special Emphasis: License Ceases to be in force (F.S. 475.23)

Licensee cannot conduct business when it ceases to be in force due to:

- Broker or school (or licensee) changes business address without notification to the DBPR

- Sales associate or instructor changes employer without notification to the DBPR

DBPR must be notified within 10 days of either change.

*This is not the same thing as null and void which means the license cannot be reactivated.

Special Emphasis: Renewal

Renewal period is two years. Licenses expire on March 31 or September 30. Must renew prior to expiration date.

Post-license or continuing education requirement must be completed. Late fee charged if renewed after expiration date.

Special Emphasis: Members of the Armed Forces (F.S. 455.02)

Military members and their spouses are exempt from <u>license fees.</u>

Special Emphasis: Armed Forces

The DBPR may issue a real estate license to a spouse of an active duty member of the Armed Forces assigned to duty in Florida:

- Spouse must hold valid real estate license in another state or jurisdiction.

- Must make application, provide proof of license, and pass background. Florida course and test is not taken.

Special Emphasis: Armed Forces Renewal Exemption

Licensee in good standing, who is a member of the U.S. Armed Forces, is exempt from renewal requirements during active duty and for 2 years after discharge from active duty.

- If military duty is out of state, the exemption also applies to a licensed spouse.

DIVISION OF REAL ESTATE

The Division of Real Estate protects the public by regulating real estate and appraisal licensees through education and compliance.

The Division is responsible for the examination, licensing and regulation of more than a quarter of a million individuals, corporations, real estate schools and instructors.

Located in Orlando, the Division also provides administrative support to the Florida Real Estate Commission (FREC) and the Florida Real Estate Appraisal Board (FREAB).

The Director of the Division of Real Estate is appointed by the Secretary of the DBPR and is confirmed by FREC.

Each division director shall directly administer the division and shall be responsible to the Secretary of the DBPR.

The secretary may appoint deputy and assistant secretaries as necessary to aid the secretary in fulfilling the secretary's statutory obligations.

- The Director of The DRE coordinates the duties of FREC with the DBPR.

Special Emphasis: Organizational Structure F.S 20.165

Division of Real Estate (DRE) - The director of the division shall be appointed by the secretary of the department, subject to approval by a majority of the Florida Real Estate Commission (FREC).

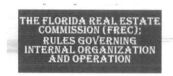

THE FLORIDA REAL ESTATE COMMISSION (FREC); RULES GOVERNING INTERNAL ORGANIZATION AND OPERATION

Purpose of Regulation

The purpose of real estate regulation is to protect health, safety, and welfare of the public. The Florida Real Estate Commission was established under Florida Statute 475 for the purpose of specifically regulating Real Estate. Also called FREC or the Commission.

The Florida Real Estate Commission, created by Chapter 475, Part I, F.S., is a regulatory agency and performs its functions pursuant to Chapter 475, Part I, F.S.

FREC is also charged with promoting and regulating educational and competency standards.

The principal office of the Commission is located at 400 West Robinson Street, Orlando, Florida 32801-1757. The Commission may also be contacted through the Department of Business and Professional Regulation, 1940 North Monroe Street, Tallahassee, Florida 32399-0750.

General Structure

Composition and Qualification of FREC Members

There are seven members total:

- Five members who are real estate **professional** (licensed) members

  - Four must have held active broker licenses for five years

  - One must be a licensed broker or sales associate who has been active two years

  - Two **consumer** members who have never been licensed

  - One must be 60 years of age or older

The seven members of FREC are appointed by the Governor and confirmed by the senate. The members serve 4 year terms but no more than two members' terms can expire during the same year. FREC members are volunteers and not employees.

The board must have at least two consumer members that have never been in the real estate industry.

FREC members cannot be held for civil liability for any official action taken.

Meeting and Minutes

The Florida Real Estate Commission (FREC) meets monthly.

The commission meeting is usually the third Wednesday of the month and the immediately preceding Tuesday. The schedule can be found at:

http://www.myfloridalicense.com/dbpr/re/frec.html

Minutes of the FREC meetings can be found at:

http://www.myfloridalicense.com/dbpr/re/FRECMeetings.html

The FREC meeting is a two-day meeting. The start time for the meeting is 8:30 for both days. The Legal Docket is the first day of the meeting (Tuesday). Sign in will begin at 8:15 a.m. If you plan to attend to obtain continuing education credit, you will need to attend the full day when the Legal Docket is heard.

Please contact the Division of Real Estate Education Section, either by phone at (850) 921-8547 or by fax to (407) 317-7245, seven (7) days prior to the meeting to be placed on the registration form.

You will receive three (3) hours of specialty education. You will be required to sign out at the end of the meeting.

http://www.myfloridalicense.com/dbpr/re/EDUCEFRECMeeting.html

FREC Powers and Duties

FREC powers and duties include these specific responsibilities:

-Adopt a seal
-Foster education
-Make determinations of violations
-Regulate professional practices
-Create and pass rules and regulations
-Establish fees
-Grant and deny applications for licensure
-Suspend or revoke license and impose fines

http://activerain.com/blogsview/2291212/frec-powers-and-duties

FREC Powers and Duties

The powers of FREC are limited to administrative matters and do not extend to criminal actions. The FREC may NOT impose imprisonment as a penalty. However, FREC can refer the criminal activity to a criminal court where imprisonment can be imposed.

The primary purpose of FREC is to enforce duties and obligations as they apply to individuals and firms actively engaged in the real estate business.

Decisions and policies are carried out by the (DRE) Division of Real Estate.

http://activerain.com/blogsview/2291212/frec-powers-and-duties

Duties and powers of the Commission

FREC has three types of powers:

- Executive Power

- Quasi-legislative

- Quasi-judicial

Duties and Powers of the Commission

Executive Power:

- Regulate and enforce license law

- Foster education

- Adopt a seal

- Establish fees

Quasi-legislative

- Create and pass rules and regulations

- Regulate professional practices

Quasi-judicial

- Grant or deny applications

- Suspend or revoke licenses and issue administrative fines

- Make determinations of violations

Special Emphasis: General Structure

- FREC members are appointed for a 4-year term

- FREC members can serve up to 2 consecutive terms

- FREC members are volunteers and not employees

Special Emphasis: FREC Members

FREC members are appointed by the governor and confirmed by the Florida Senate.

Special Emphasis: Note the Comparison

The Secretary of the DBPR is appointed by the <u>governor and confirmed by the Florida Senate.</u>

FREC Members are appointed by the <u>governor and confirmed by the Florida Senate.</u>

The Director of the DRE is appointed by the <u>Secretary of the DBPR and is confirmed by FREC Members.</u>

Special Emphasis: Purpose of Regulation

The Florida Real Estate Commission was established under Florida Statute 475 for the purpose of specifically regulating Real Estate.

Consult Florida Administrative Code for 61J1-8.002 for Disciplinary Guidelines and the Florida DBPR's Printable Law book found at:

http://www.myfloridalicense.com/dbpr/servop/testing/documents/Printable_LawBook.pdf

4 AUTHORIZED RELATIONSHIPS

Learning Objectives:

• Describe which provisions of the Brokerage Relationship Disclosure Act apply only to residential real estate sales and list types of real estate activities that are exempt from the disclosure requirements
• Define residential transaction
• Distinguish among nonrepresentation, single agent and transaction broker
• List and describe the duties owed in the various authorized relationships
• Compare and contrast the fiduciary duties owed in a single agent relationship and the duties owed in a transaction broker relationship
• Describe the disclosure procedures for the various authorized relationships
• Describe the required content and format of the various disclosure forms
• Explain the procedure for transition from a single agent to a transaction broker
• Describe the disclosure requirements for non-residential transactions where the buyer and seller have assets of $1 million or more
• List the events that will cause an agency relationship to be terminated
• Distinguish between and explain the disclosure requirements and forms pursuant to Florida Statute
• Identify Information that is Subject to Public Record

Key Terms:

agent	fiduciary	single agent
caveat emptor	general agent	special agent
consent to transition	limited representation	sub agency
customer	nonrepresentation	transaction broker
designated sales associate	principal	
dual agent	residential sale	

CONCEPT
OF
AGENCY

Throughout the course of any given day working in real estate, a licensee interacts with other agents, brokers, buyers, sellers, renters, landlords, business proprietors, investors and a multitude of professionals. It is crucial that licensees understand what type of legal relationships are allowed and in what situations. Issues with this topic to be reviewed here include:

Concept of agency

    A. Historical perspective of agency relationships

        1) Statutory law

        2) Common law

    B. Types of agents

        1) General agent

        2) Special agent

    C. Fiduciary relationships

        1) Dealing at arm's length

        2) Caveat emptor

        3) Dual agency

        4) Sub agency

        5) Customer vs. client

    D. Agency relationships determined by broker

Imagine a young boy riding his bike to the store on an important mission: he had been sent by his mother to purchase several items that she needed to prepare their evening dinner.

The boy zoomed along; the money that his mother entrusted him was tucked deep into the left pocket of his blue jeans. In his right pocket was the grocery list and written in his mother's careful handwriting were the words lettuce, flour, corn beef and eggs.

A block from the store, the boy saw two friends from school throwing stones into a creek. So the boy stopped and discovered that they were targeting a log on the other side of the bank. And they had a bet going- whichever boy successfully struck the log the most would win ten dollars! All the boy needed to get into the game was his own five dollars.

So, the boy reached into his left pocket and he pulled out the folded money. And then the boy guiltily thought about the grocery list, so he pulled it out from the other pocket.

As much as the boy wanted to join his friends, he hurried on to the store.

Once there, he again dug into his right pocket to retrieve the list. He shoved his hand as deep as it would go, his fingers trolling for the list to no avail. Somehow it hadn't made it back into his pocket. Thankfully, the boy did find the money still safe in his left pocket.

Relying on his memory, the boy collected the items on the list, paid for them and hurried back out of the store. When he passed the spot where his friends had been, he noticed they were gone. Unable to resist, he stopped just long enough to throw a few stones at the log – convinced he would have won if only he had stayed!

When the boy returned to his bike, he realized that it had fallen over and had crashed down onto the groceries. Grumbling, he retrieved the groceries, righted his bike and hurried home where the boy's mother greeted him warmly.

"You're home!" she cried. "Now I can get busy making a salad." But instead of pulling out a head of lettuce from the bag, she pulled out a head of cabbage. "Oh, well," she said, "At least cooked cabbage will be good with the corn beef." But instead of corn beef, the boy had gotten roast beef. "I can make that work," his mother said cheerfully. "And while it's cooking, it will give me time to make you your favorite cake." But when she pulled out the flour she found sugar in its place. Luckily the boy had gotten the eggs she had requested – but not so luckily; all the eggs were broken from the fall with the bike!

So, what does this story have to do with the issue of how real estate licensees can legally work with others? The answer is: EVERYTHING – when the boy agreed to go to the store for his mother; he had in effect become an agent for his mother acting on her behalf.

Historical Perspective of Agency Relationships

An agency relationship is formed when a person delegates authority to another to act in a **fiduciary relationship.**

The boy was in a fiduciary relationship with his mother having been entrusted with money for the task of making a purchase on her behalf - and he was to do his best to see to her request.

Licensees can become agents for others without even realizing it. And just as the boy had a responsibility to his mother, when an agency relationship is formed, licensees have duties that are legally required of them- even when the agency relationship has not been formally recognized!

The concept of agency is deeply entrenched in our society and in our laws dating back to the feudal system of the middle ages. At the core of the feudal system is the idea that both parties have obligations and corresponding rights with the agent owing strict loyalty to the other (known as the principal).

https://en.wikipedia.org/wiki/Feudalism

Statutory Law

Failure to adequately tend to the duties and obligations in the relationship can result in legal consequences.

Today, agency is supported legally through two legal components: Statutory law and Common Law.

Statutory law or statute law is written law set down by a body of legislature. The rules specifically outlined in Section 3 and 4 (Florida Statutes Chapter 20, 455 and 475 are Statute Laws whereas 61J2 is Administrative Code) of this course are rules that were put into place because of statutory laws. Statutes may be put into place by national or state legislatures or by local governments.

Common Law

It is important to note that statutory laws can never be written to override a higher constitutional law.

The advantage of statutory law over **Common law** is that the rules of Statutory law are easy to follow as they are clear and easy to look up.

Common law, on the other hand, is case law that takes shape from the decisions judges make in the courts as each judicial case is decided upon. Each decision in the court room is then held up as case law to mold decisions of future court cases.

This means that an individual can find themselves unknowingly in a situation that is at odds with case law.

Keep in mind that the rules and regulations of agency relationships are clearly outlined in statutory law and licensees not upholding these are held accountable with significant consequences. Many licensees, unfortunately, find themselves involved in court cases involving issues of agency.

Special Emphasis: Statutory Law

Statutory law or statute law is written law specifically created by the legislative body.

https://en.wikipedia.org/wiki/Statutory_law

Special Emphasis: Common Law

Common law is case law created when a judge rules in a case setting precedent. Future cases will look to the ruling as law now in place.

https://en.wikipedia.org/wiki/Common_law

Law of Agency

When a principal delegates authority to an agent to act on their behalf, an agency relationship is created. A **Principal** is the person who delegates authority to another acting in a fiduciary relationship. An **Agent** is the person who is authorized to represent and act for principal. A **Fiduciary** is the relationship of trust and confidence between the agent and the principal (Does not have to be a "paid" relationship).

Special Emphasis: Fiduciary Relationship

As defined by Florida Statutes 475.01 (1)(f)☐

- "Fiduciary" means a broker in a relationship of trust and confidence between that broker as agent and the seller or buyer as principal. The duties of the broker as a fiduciary are loyalty, confidentiality, obedience, full disclosure, and accounting and the duty to use skill, care, and diligence.

Types of Agents

There are three potential types of agency relationships recognized by law. However, only two of three apply to relationships real estate licensees will engage in through the practice of real estate.

The three types of agency relationships are: Universal agent, General agent, and Special agent.

The two types of agency relationships relevant to real estate are: **General agent and Special agent.**

Universal Agent

A **universal agent** is the broadest and most comprehensive form of agency.

It's considered a broad form of agency in that the agent can do a broad range of things for the principal. For example, anyone who is a superhero movie fan might recall when Tony Stark (Iron Man) wanted to check out of his business; basically, check out of his entire life. To "walk away" he had to "turn over" all decision making powers to his associate. In his absence, she could make all decisions. These decisions would have ranged from hiring and firing staff for his company, donating money to the needy from his personal funds, and even buying and selling property. Because Tony Stark's holdings were massive, his beautiful associate found herself acting in broad categories of his life. She was, in effect, his universal agent.

As such, she had a duty to make decisions that would better his life – not hurt him. She certainly could NOT make decisions that would advantage herself over him.

To have such broad powers, universal agents are commonly created via a power of attorney – with the agent becoming an attorney in fact. In real life, a power of attorney is sometimes used when the principal is travelling or living overseas or hospitalized with limited mobility. Appointing an attorney in fact can give peace of mind for spouses or family members as they give each other power of attorney in case of accident or absence.

A power of attorney does not automatically define the agency as universal. It would only create a universal agency if broad powers are given for the agent to act on the principal's behalf. More often, though, a power of attorney is limited to a particular act - such as signing the deed to transfer property from the principal to another.

The power of attorney can be stopped like any other agency appointment.

Know that real estate licensees do NOT act as universal agents.

http://EzineArticles.com/5943706

Special Emphasis: Universal Agent

- is given power to do everything for the principal. Generally, given through a power of attorney, often because the principal is unable to take care of their own business for some reason.

General Agent

A second type of agency relationship recognized by law is that of a **general agent**.

A general agent's power may seem broad, which makes it easy to confuse with a universal agent, but in fact it is **much**

more limited. General agents are empowered to perform a multitude of acts associated with one area of the principal's life, such as for operation of a business.

The general agent can make contracts and do things for the principal that is necessary in the normal course of ordinary business of the principal. The difference between the general agent and the universal agent is that the power of the general agent stops there. It doesn't reach into the rest of the principal's life.

For example, someone may hire an individual to manage all the principal's florist shops, or maybe act as a travelling representative, or a broker may hire a real estate sales associate to work as a licensee under the broker-- making the licensee a general agent of the broker-engaging in activities to further the broker's real estate business.

Keep in mind then, that by the very definition of a **general agent**, **real estate licensees are general agents of the employing broker.** The licensee works to further the broker's real estate business. The agent prospects for new business and works directly with clients. The agent even creates contracts on behalf of the principal – the employing broker. These contracts bind the broker to the buyers and sellers as the client's agent.

Sometimes, it is the broker who acts as a general agent—but not to the licensee. **When a broker is hired to be a property manager the broker is a general agent of the property owner.** Property management is an ongoing activity that encompasses many tasks. It is the broker's duty, as a general agent to the property owner, the principal, to work in the best interest of the principal.

http://EzineArticles.com/5943706

Special Emphasis: General Agent

A general agent is given a general power to do basic tasks within the ordinary course of duties. Often an employer-employee situation.

Special Agent

The third type of agent is a **special agent** which is extremely limited and has narrowly defined powers. The boy who went to the store for his mother was acting as a special agent.

The special agent is appointed for a specific purpose or to do something such as to handle a single business transaction. Often the activity is outside of the individual's usual course of business. Many occupations including accountants and travel agents fit in this type of agency.

Where a real estate broker is a general agent when services are engaged for property management; the **broker acts as that of a special agent when working to sell a property for a seller or assist a buyer in purchasing a property.**

This qualifies as a special agent rather than a general agent in that the agent's duties are to create and/or assist in the transfer of property. Once that single transaction is accomplished, the agency relationship ends.

http://EzineArticles.com/5943706

Special Emphasis: Special Agent

A special agent is given authority to do certain specific tasks or specific duties.

Fiduciary Relationships

As already defined, a **Fiduciary Relationship** is a relationship of trust and confidence between an agent and the principal.

Fiduciary relationships

      1)   Dealing at arm's length

      2)   Caveat emptor

      3)   Dual agency

      4)   Sub agency

      5)   Customer vs. client

A **fiduciary** is someone who acts in a special position of trust and confidence- the **Fiduciary relationship.**

The boy was entrusted with money to carry out an act on his mother's behalf.

The exact opposite of a fiduciary relationship is when someone deals with another in what is said to be an "arm's length transaction." In an arm's length transaction, each party is acting only to the benefit of themselves. It assumes that each person will strive to create the best deal for him or herself and that they are not responsible for whether the deal is equitable and fair to the other party.

In a real estate transaction, the buyers and sellers negotiating a deal are said to be operating as if in an arm's length transaction, and the rule of caveat emptor (buyer beware) applies. (With disclosure exceptions.)

The agent, on the other hand, is to work to the advantage of the party they are representing – although there are specific rules about the extent this can go.

http://www.businessdictionary.com/definition/fiduciary-relationship.html

Special Emphasis: Dealing at arm's length

When dealing with another party at arm's length, the parties are said to be acting freely and independently of the other.

http://dictionary.law.com/Default.aspx?selected=2433#ixzz3wVibv8b1

Special Emphasis: Caveat Emptor

Latin for "let the buyer beware." A doctrine that places on buyers the burden to reasonably examine property before purchase and take responsibility for its condition after the purchase.

https://www.law.cornell.edu/wex/caveat_emptor

Special Emphasis: Fiduciary Relationship

The duties of the broker as a fiduciary are loyalty, confidentiality, obedience, full disclosure, and accounting and the duty to use skill, care, and diligence.

Dual Agency

Because the very definition of a fiduciary relationship involves acting in a position of trust and confidence, the question becomes in real estate as to how a broker can act as a fiduciary for both a buyer and a seller at the same time.

The term for this is acting as a **Dual Agent.** Because Florida legislature believes that it is impossible to fulfill fiduciary duties to two parties of the same transaction; dual agency is not allowed.

Following this rule can be a bit tricky for a licensee working for a large brokerage as it is, in fact, the broker that is held accountable to the dual relationship. Remember that it is the broker that is the actual agent to the principal – the buyer or seller. Therefore, if one licensee has contracted on behalf of the employing broker to list a house for sale and the buyer who buys the house is working with another licensee who is employed by the same broker; then both the buyer and the seller are being represented by the same broker! This could potentially create a dual agency.

Know that when a licensee works on behalf of a broker for either a buyer or a seller, the licensee does also owe fiduciary duties to the principal just as the broker does.

This is because **the licensee, who is a general agent of the broker, is now a subagent of the broker's principal when dealing with the broker's principal.**

Special Emphasis: Dual Agency

Dual Agency in a real estate transaction means that the listing broker represents both the seller and the buyer equally in a fiduciary manner.

 DUAL AGENCY **is illegal** in Florida as the very nature of the relationship makes it impossible to be totally loyal to opposing parties at the same time!

http://homebuying.about.com/od/glossaryd/g/DualAgency.htm

Florida Statutes 475.278

Sub-agent

So, if it is the broker that is in the actual agency relationship with the buyer or the seller, then what is the sales associate or the broker associate to the buyer or the seller? The real estate licensee is a sub-agent to the buyer or the seller, meaning that the licensee must honor the same duties that the broker has with the principal.

https://en.wikipedia.org/wiki/Sub-agent

Special Emphasis: Sub-agent

A Sub-agent is an agent of a principal who is authorized to act on the principal's behalf.

A real estate licensee is a subagent to the buyer or seller with the broker acting as the actual "agent."

Special Emphasis: Types of Agents

- The broker acts as that of a special agent when working to sell a property for a seller or assist a buyer in purchasing a property.

- When a broker is hired to be a property manager the broker is a general agent of the property owner.

- Real estate licensees are general agents of the employing broker.

- The licensee, who is a general agent of the broker, is now a subagent of the broker's principal when dealing with the broker's principal.

The Difference Between a Client and Customer in Real Estate

The difference between a **Client** and a **Customer** is a significant issue for real estate licensees to understand as not all work done for buyers and sellers constitute the creation of an agency relationship and the distinction between the two roles blur together legally.

Client

A client in common language often refers to a **principal** who is in a binding contractual relationship with a broker obligating the broker, to act in an agency capacity.

This relationship is often created through a formal Buyer Representation Agreement or a Listing Agreement. Be aware, however, that even without a formal agency agreement; a broker (and the licensee) can be held accountable for an agency relationship that was created through the implication of the actions taken by the licensee or broker.

Customer

A customer, in common language, is when the broker provides a limited task for the buyer or seller. Customers must be treated honestly and fairly.

> http://www.lakelbj.com/real-estate-info--The-Difference-Between-a-Client-and-Customer-in-Real-Estate/1034

Per Florida Statutes

There is no definition of client in the Florida real estate statutes. Refer instead to the definition of "principal" and "Customer."

- F.S. 475.01 (1)(h)☐ "Principal" means the party with whom a real estate licensee has entered into a single agent relationship.

- Per Florida Statutes 475.01 (1) (d) "Customer" means a member of the public who is or may be a buyer or seller of real property, and may or may not be represented by a real estate licensee in an authorized brokerage relationship.

Agency relationships are determined by the broker

Real estate involves the transfer of property which is a vitally important transaction. Yet, the general public rarely has the knowledge to understand what the differences are between a client and a customer, or what is being given up when not being represented in an agency relationship.

Therefore, the Florida legislature found it necessary to protect the public by imposing specific agency rules for the licensee to follow.

Part of the clarification of the statutes is because it is the licensee who has the advantage of knowledge of agency- **it is the broker who is ultimately responsible for determining what type of agency relationship applies.** If the agency relationship that the broker knows to be appropriate is somehow not acceptable to the buyer or the seller, then the broker should not proceed with working with that person as it is the broker who is held responsible by law.

http://www.lakelbj.com/real-estate-info--The-Difference-Between-a-Client-and-Customer-in-Real-Estate/1034

When determining what type of relationship is most fitting for the situation, a broker in Florida has four types of legal relationships that are allowed when conducting a real estate transaction:

- **Transaction Broker** for buyer and/or seller

- **Single Agent** for EITHER a buyer or seller (not both in same transaction)

- **No Brokerage Relationship** (nonrepresentation so can represent the other party either as a transaction broker, single agent, or no brokerage relationship).

- **Designated Sales Associate** (allowed for only certain **nonresidential** sales transactions).

Florida Statutes 475.255

Events That Terminate an Agency Relationship

All agency relationships eventually end. There are many ways to terminate an agency relationship.

Ways to terminate an agency relationship include:

- Lapse of time: The agency relationship terminates when the time period passes that was agreed upon at the formation of the relationship.

- Purpose achieved: Once the purpose is achieved that the relationship was formed to accomplish, the agency relationship is terminated.

- Mutual agreement: An agency relationship can be terminated early if both parties agree to do so.

- Certain events: An agency relationship will not continue if certain events happen such as one of the parties dying, or being declared mentally incompetent, or declaring bankruptcy.

- Court action: If all parties will not agree to terminate the relationship, a court action to do so may be sought.

DISCLOSURE REQUIREMENTS

To avoid confusion about what type of agency relationship exists, if any; licensees are subject to certain disclosure requirements. The types of disclosures addressed here are residential sales disclosures:

A) Applies to residential sales only

B) Disclosure requirements do not apply to:

1) Non-residential transactions

2) The rental or leasing of real property, unless an option to purchase all or a portion of the property improved with four or fewer residential units is given

3) Auctions

4) Appraisals

5) Dispositions of any interest in business enterprises or business opportunities, except for property with four or fewer residential units

Brokerage Disclosure Act

When a licensee is working with a buyer or a seller of property for transferring ownership of the property, agency disclosure requirements must be met as outlined in the **Brokerage Disclosure Act.**

Florida has three types of legal relationships that are allowed when conducting a residential real estate sales transaction.

The broker can work as a **transaction broker** for either a buyer or a seller. The broker may work as a transaction broker for both the buyer and seller in the same transaction. This type of relationship provides duties and obligations from the broker to the buyer; however, since it is not a true fiduciary relationship- dual agency is avoided.

The broker may work as a **single agent**, which creates fiduciary obligations, but only with either a buyer or a seller and never both in the same transaction.

Furthermore, the broker may work in a **no brokerage relationship** capacity, meaning the buyer or the seller is agreeing to not be represented by the broker.

Applies to Residential Sales *Only*

With some exceptions, in Florida, **a broker is presumed to be working in the capacity of a transaction broker** <u>unless a disclosure is made in writing</u> to the buyer or seller of residential property that either a single agency, or a no brokerage relationship has been formed.

Notice that the rule requires that the disclosure be made in writing. It does not require that it be signed to create the relationship.

This rule that the disclosure must be made applies to residential sales only. This means that if a broker is working in the capacity of a property manager, the disclosure does NOT need to be made.

Disclosures do have to be made for **residential sale** as defined as being an improved residential property of four units or fewer, or the sale of unimproved residential property intended for use of four units or fewer, or the sale of agricultural property of 10 acres or fewer.

Exceptions to Residential Sales Disclosure Requirements

There are times that a broker is not required to make the disclosure even in a residential sales transaction. These situations include:

- When the licensee knows that a single agent or transaction broker already represents the buyer or seller.
- At a bona fide open house or model showing.
- In unanticipated casual encounters.
- When responding to general questions of advertised property.
- While communicating about real estate services being offered.
- When selling new residential units and working for the owner/developer.

Disclosure Requirements Do Not Apply To:

Agency Disclosure requirements apply to residential sales only. They do not apply, then, to the following transactions.

- If the property being sold qualifies as a nonresidential property, no disclosure is required.
- If the licensee is working in the capacity to rent a property, then the licensee does not have to provide agency disclosures to either the landlord or the tenant.
- Nor do disclosures have to be made when selling property via an auction.
- Appraisal services do not require agency disclosures.
- Business opportunity sales do not require disclosures.

Note however, that licensees are still bound to the duties of agency; it is the disclosure of the duty that is exempt in these situations.

Special Emphasis: Brokerage Relationship Disclosure Act

The Florida Statutes that outline requirements regarding agency relationship disclosures starts with F.S. 475.2701 and continue through F.S. 475.2801.

These statutes combined are officially known as the **Brokerage Relationship Disclosure Act.**

Topics here further detail the No Brokerage Relationship.

A) Nonrepresentation

    1) Customer means a member of the public who is or may be a buyer or seller of real property and may or may not be represented by a real estate licensee in an authorized brokerage relationship

    2) Duties

        (a) Dealing honestly and fairly

        (b) Disclose all known facts that materially affect the value of residential property which are not readily observable to the buyer

        (c) Accounting for all funds entrusted to the licensee

    3) Disclose the no brokerage relationship (nonrepresentation) notice in writing before the showing of property (Section 475.278(4)(b), F.S.)

No Brokerage Relationship (Nonrepresentation)

Florida Statutes 475.01 defines a **customer** as a member of the public who is or may be a buyer or seller of real property and may or may not be represented by a real estate licensee in an authorized brokerage relationship.

To reword this, a seller or a buyer can choose not to be represented.

A broker's assistance may be requested to facilitate a sale/purchase through such tasks as filling out a contract. However, the customer may feel confident in their own negotiation skills and not desire the assistance or representation of the broker through an agency relationship.

This is perfectly acceptable. In the **No Brokerage Relationship**, the broker still has duties to the customer. These duties include:

- **Deal honestly and fairly.**

- **Disclose all known facts that materially affect the value of residential property that are not readily observable to the buyer.**

- **Account for all funds entrusted to the licensee.**

These duties must be fully described and disclosed in writing to the buyer or seller.

The disclosure must be made before the showing of property to a buyer.

When working with a seller, the required disclosure notice <u>may be</u> included within the listing agreement. If it is within the listing agreement, then the disclosure must be of the same size type, or larger, as the other provisions of the document and the disclosure must be obvious in where it is placed within the listing agreement with the first sentence of the information identified in paragraph printed in uppercase bold type.

F.S. Statute 475.278 (4) (a) & (b)

Deal Honestly and Fairly

So, what does it mean to **deal honestly and fairly**?

Remember that part of the requirement to qualify as a licensee, the individual must be of honest, trustworthy, and of good moral character. It is imperative that as real estate licensees handling transactions that often represent the largest investment that an individual makes to act in a manner that is ethical and conscientious.

So, even though the broker is working in the no brokerage relationship, the broker is held to a standard of only making statements to the customer that is in fact true and accurate.

F.S. Statute 475.278 (4) (a) & (b)

Disclose All Known Material Facts

So, what does it mean to d**isclose all known facts that materially affect the value of the residential real property which are not readily observable to the buyer?**

A material defect is any fact about what is wrong with a property that may have a significant and reasonable impact on the market value. The issue of whether a disclosure was made is a major source of litigation not just against property owners but against the broker handling the transaction. This can result in the broker and licensee being charged with misrepresentation or fraud.

Although buyers have an opportunity to have the property inspected, this duty to disclose is NEVER relieved. So, if there are hidden cracks to the structure or damage to walls or floors that are covered from sight – the broker must disclose this information. Note that "ignorance is not always bliss" as a broker may be held accountable for having "should have known!"

F.S. Statute 475.278 (4) (a) & (b)

Account for All Funds

So, what does it mean to **account for all funds entrusted to the licensee**?

Recall the boy who went to the store for his mother. What if he would have used the money his mother had entrusted him with to join in the stone throwing bet? Had he done that, it would have been an example of conversion – using someone else's money that he had been entrusted with and converting it to his own use. He would have been guilty of this even if he had won the contest and replaced the money shortly after.

Brokers are entrusted with earnest money deposits as buyers enter into purchase and sale agreements with sellers. Or with rental deposits and monthly rental charges. Care must be taken when handling these funds to follow specific procedures outlined in the statutes. Ultimately, the broker must do more than report where the money is – they must produce it!

F.S. Statute 475.278 (4) (a) & (b)

FLORIDA REAL ESTATE LAW AND PRACTICE EXPLAINED

Topics here further detail the Single Agent Relationship.

B) Single agent relationship

    3) Duties

        (a) Dealing honestly and fairly

        (b) Loyalty

        (c) Confidentiality

        (d) Obedience

        (e) Full disclosure

        (f) Accounting for all funds

        (g) Skill, care and diligence in the transaction

        (h) Presenting all offers and counteroffers in a timely manner

        (i) Disclosing all known facts that materially affect the value of residential real property that are not readily observable.

Single Agent Relationship

A single agent is a broker who represents, as a fiduciary, **either** the buyer or seller but **not both** in the same transaction.

The party with whom a real estate licensee has entered a single agent relationship with is called the principal.

There are **nine duties** that Florida Statutes dictate must be upheld within the single agent relationship.

The first three are the same as required with a no agency relationship:

- Deal honestly and fairly.

- Disclose all known facts that materially affect the value of residential property that are not readily observable to the buyer.

- Account for all funds entrusted to the licensee.

Single Agent Relationship

The other six of the nine duties include:

- Loyalty

- Confidentiality

- Obedience

- Full disclosure

- Skill, care, and diligence in the transaction

- Presenting all offers and counteroffers in a timely manner.

Give the single agent disclosure, before or at the time of, entering into a listing agreement or an agreement for representation or before showing the property, whichever occurs first.

475.278 (b) (1)

Single Agent Relationship

So, what does the duty of **loyalty** mean?

Again, recall the boy who went to the store for his mother. Can you imagine how badly he must have wanted to join into the bet with his friends? When he resisted his impulses and instead went on to the store where he did his best to follow her instructions – although with admittedly poor results- the boy was acting with loyalty to his mother.

Recall the Iron Man Tony Stark and his beautiful assistant. It would have been easy for her to take advantage of the situation and profit from it while diminishing his interests.

Real estate brokers have similar opportunities to do wrong.

Refer to the case law referenced at the end of the discussion of the "Concept of Agency."

475.278 (c) (1)

Single Agent Relationship

In that case, a licensee was found guilty in the courts for having breached her fiduciary duty when she purchased a property several years after her client's original offer was rejected on that property.

Seemed innocent enough, right? But the judge ruled that even though several years had passed since the offer had been made; the licensee still had a duty to notify the client about the new opportunity to purchase the property. In essence, the licensee was still obligated to put the principal before her own desires to own the property!

475.278 (c) (1)

Single Agent Relationship

So, what does the duty of **confidentiality** mean?

Throughout the course of a real estate transaction, the licensee will discover very personal information about the principal. Much of it that could directly hurt the principal's bargaining power if it was inadvertently revealed.

The licensee is not allowed to share this information with anyone (except the broker or the other subagents within the same brokerage).

For example, if a broker in a single agency relationship with a seller discovers that the sellers are listing the property because the sellers are getting a divorce– the broker and the agents within the brokerage must keep this information private.

Sometimes, licensees will advertise a property as "Seller is highly motivated – bring all offers!" This would be unlawful as a single agent unless the seller had given permission for the wording. And the permission must be in writing!

475.278 (c) (1)

Single Agent Relationship

So, what does the duty of **obedience** mean?

Simply put, the licensee is to follow the instructions of the principal.

Sometimes this can create a conflict if the licensee doesn't believe that the instructions are in the best interest of the licensee. If this is the case, the licensee should share his or her opinion with the principal. However, if the principal isn't persuaded to change the instructions; then the licensee must either follow the instructions or formally end the relationship.

If the request of the principal is for the licensee to do something that is unlawful, then the licensee cannot follow the principal's instructions!

For example, if a licensee discovers that the air conditioner system is faulty but the seller keeps filling it with Freon before showings – the licensee must disclose this defect despite the seller demanding that it be kept a secret.

475.278 (c) (1)

Single Agent Relationship

So, what does the **full disclosure** mean?

The broker is required to share all information that may work to the benefit of the principal to know.

Consider the example of the sellers that were selling because they were getting a divorce. Now imagine that a buyer is being represented by a single agent. Upon calling the listing agent to inquire about showing the home, the listing broker happens to let it slip that the sellers are divorcing. Because the buyer's agent is acting as a single agent for the principal (the buyer), not only is it a good idea for the agent to mention the divorce situation – the agent would be obligated by law to do so under the rule of full disclosure!

Having this knowledge would likely benefit the buyer by knowing that the stress of a divorce may make the couple more eager to sell resulting in a lower offer being made and accepted.

475.278 (c) (1)

Single Agent Relationship

So, what does **presenting all offers** mean?

A single agent is obligated to present all offers and counteroffers in a timely manner, unless the principal has previously directed the licensee otherwise in writing.

Sometimes an offer may seem ridiculous to a licensee and the licensee dreads the time that it takes to present an offer to a seller (or a buyer) only to have it turned down. Temptation is for the licensee in these common situations to simply ignore the offer and not even tell the seller (or buyer) about it.

By law, the licensee is required to present all offers. This includes all verbal offers.

Only if a seller directs in writing not to present offers is the licensee relieved of this obligation – this includes once a property is under contract!

475.278 (c) (1)

Topics here detail the Transaction Broker Relationship

    C) Transaction broker relationship

        1) Presumption of transaction brokerage relationship

        2) Transaction broker means a broker who provides limited representation to a buyer, a seller, or both, in a real estate transaction, but does not represent either in a fiduciary capacity or as a single agent

        3) Transaction brokers provide a limited form of no fiduciary representation to a buyer, a seller, or both in a real estate transaction

        4) Duties include:

            a) Dealing honestly and fairly

            b) Accounting for all funds

            c) Skill, care and diligence in the transaction

            d) Disclosing all known facts that materially affect the value of residential real property that are not readily observable.

            e) Presenting all offers and counteroffers in a timely manner

            f) Limited confidentiality

            g) Any additional duties that are mutually agreed to with a party

Presumption of Transaction Broker Relationship

Per Florida Statute 475.278 (b), there is a **"Presumption of transaction brokerage"** meaning that it shall be assumed that all licensees are operating as transaction brokers unless a single agent or no brokerage relationship is established, in writing, with a customer.

Because of the presumption, a transaction broker disclosure is not required to be made in writing or otherwise.

A transaction broker means a broker who provides limited representation to a buyer, a seller, or both, in a real estate transaction; but does not represent either in a fiduciary capacity or as a single agent. Transaction brokers provide a limited form of non-fiduciary representation to a buyer, a seller, or both in a real estate transaction.

- *In a transaction broker relationship, a buyer or seller is not responsible for the acts of a licensee.*

Presumption of Transaction Broker Relationship

The parties to a real estate transaction must understand that they are giving up their rights to the undivided loyalty of a licensee. This aspect of limited representation allows a licensee to facilitate a real estate transaction by assisting both the buyer and the seller, but a licensee will not work to represent one party to the detriment of the other party when acting as a transaction broker to both parties.

There are seven **duties** that must be upheld.

The first three are the same as required with a no agency relationship and single agency relationship:

- Deal honestly and fairly.

- Disclose all known facts that materially affect the value of residential property that are not readily observable to the buyer.

- Account for all funds entrusted to the licensee.

Transaction Broker Relationship

Two of the other four duties are the same as with a single agent relationship:

- Skill, care, and diligence in the transaction

- Presenting all offers and counteroffers in a timely manner.

The remaining two duties are:

- Exercise limited confidentiality, unless waived in writing by a party

- Perform additional duties mutually agreed to with a party.

Notice that this type of relationship does not obligate the licensee to either disclosure or full confidentiality. Limited Confidentiality will prevent disclosure that the seller will accept a price less than the asking or listed price, that the buyer will pay a price greater than the price submitted in a written offer, of the motivation of any party for selling or buying property, that a seller or buyer will agree to financing terms other than those offered, or any other information expected by a party to remain confidential.   F.S. 475.278 (1)(b)

Transaction Broker Relationship

Let's apply this idea to the couple that is divorcing and needing to sell their home. And let's assume that the broker requires all agents to only work as transaction brokers.

The licensee being eager to get the home sold for the divorcing couple goes around the office telling everyone about how wonderful the home is in hopes of finding an agent with a buyer that would like to buy the home. One agent begins asking a lot of questions and learns that the couple is under pressure to sell in a hurry due to their divorce.

However, because both licensees are working with their prospective customers as a transaction broker under the same broker; the licensee working with the buyer CANNOT disclose the issue of the divorce to the buyer! To do so would be breaking the rule of limited confidentiality.

F.S. 475.01 (1)(l)

Special Emphasis: Brokerage Relationship Limitations

If a brokerage firm is a

- Transaction broker for the seller, then the broker can be a
    - Transaction broker for buyer or in a
    - No brokerage relationship with buyer
- Single agent for a seller, then
    - No brokerage relationship with buyer is the only option to work with both the buyer and the seller.

Special Emphasis: Single agent relationship

- Single agent is a broker who represents, as a fiduciary, **either** the buyer or seller but **not both** in the same transaction
- The party with whom a real estate licensee has entered into a single agent relationship is the principal

Special Emphasis: No Brokerage Relationship and Single Agency Disclosures (Nonrepresentation)

Both the no brokerage and the single agency disclosure must be disclosed in writing;

- To a buyer before showing of property or upon agreement of the representation, whichever comes first.
- To a seller before/at the time of listing.
- (Signatures are not required!)

F.S. Statute 475.278 (4) (a) & (b)

Special Emphasis: Transaction Broker Relationship

Under Florida law, it is presumed that licensees are operating as transaction brokers unless a single agent or no brokerage relationship is established.

A transaction broker disclosure is not required.

- Provides limited representation to customer (buyer, seller or both)
- Does not represent either buyer or seller as a fiduciary or as a single agent
- Customer is not responsible for actions of transaction broker

Authorized Brokerage Relationships

Special Emphasis

Also with Single & Transaction!

Duties in No Brokerage Relationship

- Account for all funds
- Dealing honestly and fairly
- Disclosure of all known facts that materially affect the value of residential real property that are not readily observable to the buyer

Authorized Brokerage Relationships

Special Emphasis

Also with No Disclosure & Transaction!

Duties of a Single Agent

- Account for all funds
- Dealing honestly and fairly
- Disclosure of all known facts that materially affect the value of residential real property that are not readily observable to the buyer
- Use skill, care, and diligence in the transaction
- Presenting all offers and counteroffers in a timely manner

Also with Transaction!

- Loyalty
- Obedience
- Confidentiality
- Full disclosure

Authorized Brokerage Relationships

Special Emphasis

Also with No Disclosure & Single!

Duties of a Transaction Broker

- Account for all funds
- Dealing honestly and fairly
- Disclosure of all known facts that materially affect the value of residential real property that are not readily observable to the buyer
- Use skill, care, and diligence in the transaction
- Presenting all offers and counteroffers in a timely manner
- Exercise limited confidentiality, unless waived in writing by a party
- Perform additional duties as mutually agreed to

Also with Single Agent!

Consent to Transition from Single Agent to Transaction Broker

Topics here detail the Consent to Transition from Single Agent to a Transaction Broker Relationship.

A) A single agent relationship may be changed to a transaction broker relationship at any time during the relationship between an agent and principal, provided the agent gives the transition disclosure and the principal consents to the transition before a change in relationship.

B) Procedure

    1) Give the single agent disclosure before, or at the time of, entering into a listing agreement or an agreement for representation, or before showing of property, whichever occurs first

    2) Give transition disclosure and secure consent (signature) from party

C) Required information on the disclosure per Statute

D) Required format of the disclosure per Statute

Consent to Transition from Single Agent to Transaction Broker

Sometimes, despite having entered into a relationship as single agent with a principal, it makes sense to transition back to a transaction broker.

For example, let's take the couple selling their home because of a divorce. When the agent listed the home, the agent may have wanted to provide the best service possible, so a single agency relationship was formed with the sellers.

However, if she also had them sign a consent to transition from single agent to transaction broker form– then, when she drummed up interest in her own office for a buyer; the brokerage could represent both the sellers and the buyer. Furthermore, the licensee who had discovered that the sellers were getting a divorce wouldn't be able to use it to a negotiating advantage.

Consent to Transition from Single Agent to Transaction Broker

Recall that, had a single agency relationship not been entered into, the licensee automatically would have been in a transaction broker relationship with the customer.

Once the single agent relationship has been formed, it may be changed to a transaction broker relationship at any time during the relationship between an agent and the principal, provided the agent gives the transition disclosure and the principal consents to the transition in writing before a change in the relationship.

Limited representation means that a buyer or seller is not responsible for the acts of the licensee. Additionally, parties are giving up their rights to the undivided loyalty of the licensee. This aspect of limited representation allows a licensee to facilitate a real estate transaction by assisting both the buyer and the seller, but a licensee will not work to represent one party to the detriment of the other party, when acting as a transaction broker to both parties.

Procedure

The procedure to do this requires that the single agent disclosure be given before, or at the time of entering into a listing agreement, or an agreement for representation, or before showing of property, whichever occurs first.

Then a transition disclosure is given and a secure consent (signature) from the party is obtained.

- This means that the Consent to Transition to Transaction Agent form MUST be signed!

Special Emphasis: Transition to Transaction Broker

F.S. 475 permits a licensee to change the relationship from a single agent to a transaction broker, the principal *must* sign.

Presented here is a disclosure that involves Non-Residential Transactions

V) Designated sales associate

    A) Non-residential transaction limitations

    B) Disclosure requirements

    C) Single agent duties

Designated Sales Associate

In residential real estate, a broker is not allowed to act as a single agent for both a buyer and a seller. To do so would create a dual agency which is illegal in Florida.

However, in non-residential real estate there is a twist on this concept known as the Designated Sales Associate which is allowed per Florida Statutes.

In a non-residential transaction, where the buyer and seller each have assets of $1 million or more, the broker, at the request of the customers, may **designate sales** associates to act as single agents for different customers in the same transaction.

Such designated sales associates shall have the duties of a single agent including the requirement to disclose in writing the duties of the relationship. In addition to disclosure requirements presented about residential real estate, the buyer and seller as customers shall both sign disclosures stating that their assets meet the threshold of **$1 million or more,** and requesting that the broker use the designated sales associate form of representation.

Florida Statutes 475.2755

The duties of a **Designated Sales Associate** are the same as a regular single agent, and must be fully described and disclosed in writing to a buyer or seller in agreements for representation including the following:

- Account for all funds

- Dealing honestly and fairly

- Disclosure of these duties must be made before or during entrance into a listing/representation agreement, or before the showing of property.

- Use skill, care, and diligence in the transaction

- Presenting all offers and counteroffers in a timely manner

- Loyalty

- Obedience

- Confidentiality

- Full disclosure

Confidentiality

Regarding the duty of confidentiality, what this rule does is that it removes the broker from having direct contact with the buyer and seller and to instead act as an advisor of the sales associates who interface with the principals.

THE PURPOSE OF this provision is to allow each agent to seek advice from the broker for the benefit of the customer regarding the transaction. And any information obtained by the broker during these discussions must be held confidential from the other sales associate, and the other principal.

This allows each party to be equally benefited by the relationship with the sales associate and the broker, without detriment to their dealings.

Special Emphasis: Nonresidential Transactions Only

At the request of the buyer and seller, the broker may designate sales associates to act as single agents for different customers in the same transaction.

Buyer and seller each must have assets of at least $1 million

Requires written and signed disclosures

- Single agent disclosure

- Designated sales associate disclosure

VI) Discipline

A) Violations and penalties

As Seen in Florida Statutes

475.42 Violations and penalties

(2) PENALTIES.—

Any person who violates any of the provisions of subsection (1) is guilty of a misdemeanor of the second degree, punishable as provided in s. 775.082 or s. 775.083, or, if a corporation, it is guilty of a misdemeanor of the second degree, punishable as provided in s. 775.083, except when a different punishment is prescribed by this chapter. Nothing in this chapter shall prohibit the prosecution under any other criminal statute of this state of any person for an act or conduct prohibited by this section; however, in such cases, the state may prosecute under this section or under such other statute, or may charge both offenses in one prosecution, but the sentence imposed shall not be a greater fine, or longer sentence than that prescribed for the offense which carries the more severe penalties. A civil case, criminal case, or a denial, revocation, or suspension proceeding may arise out of the same alleged state of facts, and the pendency or result of one such case or proceeding, shall not stay or control the result of either of the others.

There are a lot of things that are potential violations, but if you do the right thing and follow the rules and laws you will be fine. However, if you are ever unsure of a rule or law - look it up or ask your broker.

If your broker doesn't know or you still are unsure or just want another opinion you can always call the Florida Association of Realtors legal hotline at 407-438-1409.

Maintaining copies of your disclosure documents is imperative.

VII) Record keeping and retention

A) Documenting agency disclosure

Florida Statutes 475.5015 requires that brokerages maintain business records for five years.

These records must also be made available to the DBPR in the event of an audit. Records include books, accounts, and records that pertain to the real estate business.

This includes records of receipt of any money, funds, deposits, checks, or drafts entrusted to the broker or, in the event no funds are entrusted to the broker. And it includes executed listing agreements, buyer broker agreements, offer to purchase, rental property management agreement, rental or lease agreement, or "any other written or verbal agreement which engages the services of the broker."

This also includes disclosure documents which must be kept for 5 years by the real estate licensee in all transactions that result in a written contract to purchase to sell real property.

Special Emphasis: Record Keeping

Agency disclosure documents need to be retained by the real estate licensee in all transactions that there is a written contract to purchase or sell property, or retain the services of a real estate brokerage for at least 5 years.

Disclosure documents required under ss. 475.2755 and 475.278 shall be retained by the real estate licensee in all transactions that result in a written contract to purchase and sell real property.

Special Emphasis – Disclosure Document Retention

Brokers must retain agreements that engage their services for 5 years.

Brokers must retain brokerage relationship disclosure documents for 5 years.

- All residential transactions that result in a written contract
- Includes files of properties that fail to close
- Commercial transactions that involve a designated sales agent

Public Record

In reality, there is more information that is subject to public record. In addition to the above mentioned information, the public can access your employer's information and any disciplinary action that has been taken against you; not to mention any additional information that is public.

As Seen in Florida Statutes

F.S. 455.229 **Public inspection of information required from applicants**; exceptions; examination hearing.—

(1) All information required by the department of any applicant shall be a public record and shall be open to public inspection pursuant to s. 119.07, except financial information, medical information, school transcripts, examination questions, answers, papers, grades, and grading keys, which are confidential and exempt from s. 119.07(1) and shall not be discussed with or made accessible to anyone except members of the board, the department, and staff thereof, who have a bona fide need to know such information. Any information supplied to the department by any other agency which is exempt from the provisions of chapter 119 or is confidential shall remain exempt or confidential pursuant to applicable law while in the custody of the department.

5 REAL ESTATE BROKERAGE ACTIVITIES AND PROCEDURES

Learning Objectives:
- Identify the requirements for real estate brokerage office(s) and the types of business entities that may register
- Explain what determines whether a temporary shelter must be registered as a branch office
- List the requirements related to sign regulation
- List the requirements related to the regulation of advertising by real estate brokers
- Explain the term *immediately* as it applies to earnest money deposits
- Describe the four settlement procedures available to a broker who has received conflicting demands, or who has a good-faith doubt as to who is entitled to disputed funds
- Explain the rule regarding the advertisement of rental property information, or lists, or negotiation of rentals
- Describe the obligations placed on a sales associate who changes employers and/or address

Key Terms:

arbitration	escrow account	limited partnership
blind advertisement	escrow disbursement order	litigation
commingle	general partnership	mediation
conflicting demands	good-faith doubt	ostensible partnership
conversion	interpleader	professional association (PA)
corporation (INC)	kickback	point of contact information
deposit	limited liability company (LLC)	sole proprietorship
earnest money	limited liability partnership (LLP)	trade name

BROKERAGE OFFICES

The hub of all real estate activities starts with a brokerage office. Understanding how brokerages are formed and may legally operate is an important component of preparing to enter the real estate field.

Issues with this topic to be reviewed here include:

I)   Brokerage offices

A) Sales associates must be registered and work under direction and control of broker's office or branch office

B) Entrance Sign Requirements

C) Temporary shelters

Office

When someone takes the plunge to run his or her own real estate brokerage—it all starts with the opening of an "office."

Florida Legislature has specific rules about what is and isn't allowed in regard to offices and general real estate brokerage operations. And although real estate licensees, new to real estate, start at the licensee level; these rules and regulations impact the licensee as well as the broker.

- According to Florida Statutes 475.22 each real estate brokerage must open and register a brokerage office with the Florida Department of Business and Professional Regulation.

To physically qualify as an office, the location need only have at least one enclosed room in a building of stationary construction.

Home Office

It's perfectly fine for the office to be a "home office."

- A brokerage office may be in a residential location if that is not contrary to local zoning ordinances. It is the responsibility of the broker to learn the applicable zoning regulations (Rule 61J2-10.022).

Branch Office

Brokers tend to operate real estate business as they move out and about in the community. And at times, this opens up the opportunity to spend extra time in a location to generate leads. Upon doing this, the broker is giving the appearance that the location is a real estate office; the FREC has a right to require the broker to register that location as a branch office and pay associated fees.

Branch Office

- If, in the judgment of the FREC, the business conducted at a place other than the principal office is of such a nature that public interest requires registration of the branch office, the office must be registered as a branch office. If the name or advertising of a broker is displayed in a location other than the principal office in such a manner as to lead the public to reasonably believe that the other location is owned or operated by the broker, that location must be declared a branch office (Section 475.24, F.S., and Rule 61J2-10.023).

If a broker closes a branch office and opens a new branch office at a different location, the registration may not be transferred (to avoid paying another fee). The new location must be registered and a fee is required. However, a broker may reopen the first branch office at the same location during the same license renewal period without paying an additional fee (Rule 61J2-10.023(3)).

Out of State Office

As a result of federal case decisions affecting other state real estate commissions, the FREC now allows a Florida brokerage office to be located outside the State of Florida.

Prior to registering such an office or branch office, the broker must agree in writing to cooperate with any investigation by the DBPR, DRE, or FREC, including promptly supplying any requested documents and personally meeting with an investigator either in Florida or elsewhere as reasonably requested.

If the DBPR or the DRE sends by certified mail to the broker's last known business address a notice or request to produce documents or to appear for an interview, and the broker fails to comply with that notice or request, then the broker is in violation of the license law and is subject to the penalties of Section 475.25, F.S. (Section 475.22(2), F.S.).

https://ims.orlrealtor.org/PDF/Brokerage%20Office%20and%20Sign%20Requirements.pdf

Sales associates must be registered and work under direction and control of broker's office or branch office

Although a sales associate or broker associate may never step foot into the actual physical location that has been registered by the broker as a brokerage office or branch office, this is still the licensee's official office that is registered with the DBPR.

When registering as a new licensee, there are also rules about how the licensee's name can be registered. F.S. 475.161 prescribes that a broker associate or sales associate can register as an individual or as a professional corporation (P.A.), limited liability company, or professional limited liability company- if the status as such has been approved by the Department of State. (Many choose to do this for tax and liability purposes.)

If the licensee is registering with one of the above options, then the license shall be issued in the licensee's legal name including the entity designation.

Sales associates must be registered and work under direction and control of broker's office or branch office

Know that a broker associate or sales associate is not permitted to register or be licensed as a general partner, member, manager, officer, or director of a brokerage firm per Florida Statute. 475.15.

475.161☐ Licensing of broker associates and sales associates.—The commission shall license a broker associate or sales associate as an individual or, upon the licensee providing the commission with authorization from the Department of State, as a professional corporation, limited liability company, or professional limited liability company. A license shall be issued in the licensee's legal name only and, when appropriate, shall include the entity designation. This section shall not operate to permit a broker associate or sales associate to register or be licensed as a general partner, member, manager, officer, or director of a brokerage firm under s. 475.15.History.—s. 26, ch. 2003-164; s. 1, ch. 2006-210.

Entrance Sign Requirements

When a broker opens a brokerage office or branch office there are rules to follow regarding signage.

The broker must maintain a sign at the entrance of the principal office and each branch office. The sign must be noticeable and easy to read by any person about to enter the office.

Each sign must contain the name of the broker, together with the trade name (DBA/Doing Business as Name) if any.

And either the words "licensed real estate broker" or "lic. real estate broker" must also appear on the office entrance signs." (No other abbreviations are allowed.)

If the brokerage is registered as a partnership or a corporation (instead of as a sole proprietor), the sign must contain the name of the firm or corporation or trade name of the firm or corporation, together with the name of *at least* one of the brokers. And the words "licensed real estate broker" or "lic. real estate broker."

F.S. 475.22

Brokerage Offices

Entrance Sign Requirements

If brokerage is owned by an "individual" (sole proprietor), signs must contain:

- Trade name (if used) ———————→ Davis Realty
- Broker's name ———————————→ Bryan Davis
- Words "Licensed Real Estate Broker" —→ Lic. Real Estate Broker
- or "Lic. Real Estate Broker"

Brokerage Offices

Entrance Sign Requirements

If the brokerage entity is a partnership, corporation, or limited liability partnership/company sign must contain

- Name of firm or corporation ————→ Davis Realty LLC
- Name of at least one active broker ——→ Heather Davis
- Words, "Licensed Real Estate Broker" —→ Licensed Real Estate Broker
- or "Lic. Real Estate Broker"

Temporary Shelters

As subdivisions are being built and homes sold, it is common for a temporary shelter to be utilized for the convenience of sales associates.

These offices do not have to be registered if:

- A mere temporary shelter, on a subdivision being sold by the broker, for the protection of salespersons and customers and at which transactions are not closed and salespersons are not permanently assigned, *is not deemed to be a branch office.*

- The permanence, use, and character of activities customarily conducted at the office or shelter shall determine whether it must be registered.

61J2-10.023

Trade Name

Names or designations used by companies to identify themselves and distinguish their businesses from others in the same field.

Trade names are used by profit and non-profit entities, political and religious organizations, industry and agriculture, manufacturers and producers, wholesalers and retailers, sole proprietorships and joint ventures, partnerships and corporations, and a host of other business associations.

A trade name may be the actual name of a given business or an assumed name under which a business operates and holds itself out to the public.

http://legal-dictionary.thefreedictionary.com/Trade+Name

Special Emphasis: Sales Associates Work Under Direction and Control of Broker

Sales associates must be registered and work under direction and control of broker's office or branch office.

Signage must be in place at the front entrance with designating clearly who the broker is of the brokerage.

GUIDELINES FOR ADVERTISING

Licensees must take care to follow advertising guidelines as presented here:

II) Guidelines for advertising

    A) False or misleading advertising

        1) Penalties for false advertising

B) Any advertising must be worded so that a reasonable person knows that the advertiser is a real estate licensee.

C) "Blind" advertising is prohibited; it must always reveal the licensed name of the brokerage firm.

D) Any person advertising real estate services is interpreted as acting as a broker.

E) Sales associates cannot advertise or conduct business in his or her own name.

F) All types of Internet advertising

    1) Point of contact information

Advertising

First and foremost, when advertising – whether it is to offer a real estate service or a property for sale – any advertising must be worded so that a reasonable person knows that the advertiser is a real estate licensee or it can be deemed as false or misleading advertising.

Recall from Section 4 of this course that licensees are general agents of the broker. This means that anytime a licensee advertises some type of real estate service or property for sale, the brokerage name must also be clearly identified.

- All advertising must be in a way which reasonable persons would know they are dealing with a real estate licensee. All real estate advertisements must include the licensed name of the brokerage firm. No real estate advertisement placed or caused to be placed by a licensee shall be fraudulent, false, deceptive or misleading. 61J2-10.025

If advertising is not clear that a real estate brokerage is involved and the real estate broker is not clearly identified, the advertising is called **blind advertising**.

61J2-10.02

Blind Advertising

Blind advertising is prohibited. Advertising must always reveal the licensed name of the brokerage firm.

It is okay to also include your own personal name in the advertisement- although it is not required. The broker's name (brokerage name) IS required.   Keep in mind, though, that if you include your own name, that your *last* name must appear *exactly* as it is registered with the DBPR.

The licensee may use a nickname or initials for the first name, and is not required to display the first and/or middle name as registered with the FREC (Rule 61J2-10.025(2)).

Otherwise, any person advertising real estate services is interpreted (by the unknowing public) as acting as a broker. Know that it is unlawful for sales associates to advertise or conduct business in her or her own name.

- Know that false, deceptive, or misleading information in advertisements for real estate is illegal and is a second-degree misdemeanor.

61J2-10.025

False or Misleading Advertising

The standards of advertising apply to advertising with yard signs, newspaper and magazine ads, mail outs, business cards, billboards, benches, internet ads, or any other medium or vehicle by which services or property are displayed.

No real estate advertisement placed or caused to be placed by a licensee shall be fraudulent, false, deceptive, or misleading

Section 475.25(1)(c), F.S., and Rule 61J2-10

Internet Advertising

Today, much of a licensee's advertising is conducted on the internet.

When advertising on a site on the Internet, the brokerage firm name must be placed **adjacent to or immediately** above or below the point of contact information.

"Point of contact information" refers to any means by which to contact the brokerage firm or individual licensee including mailing address(es), physical street address(es), e-mail address(es), telephone number(s) or facsimile telephone number(s).

61J2-10.025

Advertising Licensee Information

When a licensee is registered with the DBPR, an identifying license number will be assigned. There is NO requirement for a licensee to display his or her license number or the registration number of the brokerage firm.

In addition, there is no requirement that the licensee display the license status. However, Article 12 of the National Association of REALTORS ® Code of Ethics requires licensees to include their professional status (e.g., broker, appraiser, property manager, etc.) or status as Realtors®. There is also a FREC rule that states that a licensee is not permitted to use an identification or designation of any association or organization unless the licensee is entitled to use such identification or designation. (Don't call yourself a Realtor® if you do not belong to NAR!)

FREC does not regulate the use of telephone numbers in ads. Therefore, a licensee may use either office or personal telephone numbers without qualifying the number as such. However, if using a personal number then the licensee should identify it as such or risk the advertising as being deemed "misleading".

61J2-10.027

https://ims.orlrealtor.org/PDF/Brokerage%20Office%20and%20Sign%20Requirements.pdf

Faxing Advertisements

Fax advertisements are also regulated.

Section 365.1657, F.S., makes it unlawful for any person to send unsolicited advertising material via a facsimile machine for the sale of any real property, goods, or services.

The Attorney General may bring an action to impose a civil penalty and to seek injunctive relief. The civil penalty cannot exceed $500 per violation. Each transmission is considered a separate violation.

Requirements to send fax advertisements includes having an established business relationship with the recipient; having voluntarily received the fax number, having clearly state opt-out procedures (with every fax), and opt-outs MUST be honored within 30 days.

https://ims.orlrealtor.org/PDF/Brokerage%20Office%20and%20Sign%20Requirements.

Telephone Solicitation Regulations

Both Florida and the Federal government maintain a Do Not Call Registry. It is important that licensees are checking both lists before making unsolicited calls.

Florida's Do Not Call Registry is maintained by Dept. of Agriculture & Consumer Services. The fine for contacting someone on the Florida Do Not Call Registry is $10,000 per infraction. Florida DOES allow licensees to call For-sale-by-owners that are on the Do Not Call Registry for soliciting a listing.

However, if that same person is on the Federal Do Not Call Registry, then the licensee cannot call them as it is prohibited by Federal law. Those who violate the National Do Not Call Registry or place an illegal robocall can be fined up to $16,000 per call.

It is important that brokerages have a procedure in place, best when incorporated into an employee manual that outlines procedures for making calls.

Per the **Telephone Consumer Protection Act of 1991 (TCPA),** a company-specific "do-not-call" (DNC) list of consumers who asked not to be called must be maintained for five years.

The TCPA also prohibits solicitors from calling residences before 8 a.m. or after 9 p.m., local time.

https://www.donotcall.gov/

https://www.fldnc.com/

https://en.wikipedia.org/wiki/Telephone_Consumer_Protection_Act_of_1991

Exceptions

A company with which a consumer has an established business relationship may call for up to 18 months after the consumer's last purchase or last delivery, or last payment, unless the consumer asks the company not to call again. In that case, the company must honor the request not to call. If the company calls again, it may be subject to a fine of up to $16,000.

If a consumer makes an inquiry or submits an application to a company, the company can call for 3 months. Once again, if the consumer makes a specific request to that company not to call, the company may not call, even if it has an established business relationship with the consumer.

http://www.donotcallcompliance.com/do_not_call_laws.html#established_business_relationship

Special Emphasis: Exceptions to National Do-Not-Call List

- When representing a potential buyer, you may call a FSBO seller, provided the buyer is interested in the property.

- May contact individuals with whom associate had an established business relationship for up to 18 months

- May contact a customer for 3 months after a business inquiry

- You may call FSBOs unless they are on the National DNC List!

Special Emphasis: Penalties for False Advertising

False, deceptive, or misleading information in advertisements for real estate is illegal and is a second-degree misdemeanor.

Special Emphasis: Advertising Rules

- All advertising must always reveal the licensed name of the brokerage firm.

- Any advertising must be worded so that a reasonable person knows that the advertiser is a real estate licensee.

- Any person advertising real estate services is interpreted as acting as a broker.

- Sales associates cannot advertise or conduct business in his or her own name.

Special Emphasis: Blind Advertising

Advertising must inform people they are dealing with a licensee or a brokerage firm.

All ads must include name of brokerage firm or it is blind advertising which is illegal.

Special Emphasis: Internet Advertising

In internet advertising, the brokerage name must appear adjacent to or immediately above/below point of contact information. Point of contact information is mailing and/or physical addresses, email addresses, and telephone or fax numbers.

Special Emphasis: Unsolicited Fax Ads are Prohibited

Requirements to send fax advertisements

- Established business relationship

- Voluntarily received fax number

- Clearly state opt-out procedures

- Honor opt-out requests within 30 days

Special Emphasis: Telephone Solicitation Regulations

Florida maintains a Do Not Call Registry

- Maintained by Dept. of Agriculture & Consumer Services

- $10,000 fine for calling someone illegally that is on the list

- For-sale-by-owner exception (Federal law supersedes state law)

Licensees must take care to follow guidelines for handling client funds as presented here:

III) Handling of deposits

A) Requirement to deposit in an escrow account monies received from a client or customer

  1) Definition of escrow account

  2) Sales associate must deliver funds by end of next business day

  3) Meaning of "immediately" for a broker

  4) Deposit notification if deposited with title company or attorney within 15 days

Definition of Escrow

Handling funds for a client in relation to a real estate transaction is an extremely important part of a licensee's tasks. Failure to comply with the proper legal requirements and procedures regarding the handling of client funds has significant legal ramifications.

Take time to clearly understand the rules presented here including the timelines involved.

With this topic, the best way to start is with basic definitions involving escrow and escrow accounts.

An **earnest money deposit**, also called a binder deposit, escrow, or a good-faith deposit is a sum of money given to bind the sale of real estate, or a sum of money given to ensure payment, or an advance of funds in the processing of a loan.

Definition of Escrow Account

In real estate, the earnest money cannot be placed into a broker's general operating account. Instead, it must be placed in special account for "escrowing" or placing the money in "trust."

This is called an **escrow account**.

An escrow account must be held in a bank or trust company, or a title company having trust powers, a credit union, or a savings and loan association within the State of Florida.

- No personal funds of any licensee shall be deposited or intermingled with any funds being held in escrow, trust or on condition except as provided in subsection 61J2-14.010(2), F.A.C.

Sales Associate Must Deliver Funds by End of Next Business Day

When a buyer and seller enter a purchase sale agreement, it is common for the buyer to put down an earnest money deposit to show good-faith intention to close on the sale. Often this money is given directly to the sales associate to handle.

Once the sales associate receives the deposit, the sales associate must deliver the funds to the broker by the end of the next business day.

Every sales associate who receives any deposit, as defined in Rule 61J2-14.008, F.A.C., shall deliver the same to the broker or employer no later than the end of the next business day following receipt of the item to be deposited. Saturday, Sundays and legal holidays shall not be construed as business days. Receipt by a sales associate or any other representative of the brokerage firm constitutes receipt by the broker for purposes of paragraph 61J2-14.008(3), F.A.C

Meaning of "Immediately" for a Broker

Regardless of when the licensee gives the check to the broker, the broker must deposit the check in the escrow account no later than end of the third business day following the date the LICENSEE received the check.

Note: the broker's timeline starts after the day after the sales associate receives the deposit

Administrative Code 61J2-14.008

- **"Immediately"** means the placement of a deposit in an escrow account no later than the end of the third business day following receipt of the item to be deposited. Saturdays, Sundays and legal holidays shall not be considered as business days.

Examples: So, What if???

Sales Associate gets the check on <u>Monday</u>

- Sales Associate must give it to broker by end of business day <u>Tuesday</u>

- Broker must deposit the check in the escrow account no later than end of the business day <u>Thursday</u> (By the end of the third business day from Monday).

Sales associate gets the check on <u>Friday</u>

- Sales Associate must give check to broker by end of business day <u>Monday</u>

- Broker must deposit the check in the escrow account no later than end of business day <u>Wednesday</u> (By the end of the third business day from Friday).

Title Company/Attorney Escrow Accounts

Deposit notification if deposited with title company or attorney

Many brokers avoid handling earnest money by having title companies handle them instead.

When this is the case, these are the rules that must be followed:

- Indicate on the purchase sale contract the name, address, and telephone number of the title company or attorney

- Within 10 business days after deposit is due, the buyer's broker shall make written request to the title company (attorney) for verification of receipt of deposit (Unless, held by a title company or by an attorney nominated in writing by a seller or seller's agent).

- Within 10 business days after broker made written request, provide seller's broker with a copy of written verification.

Definition of Deposit

A sum of money given to bind the sale of real estate, or a sum of money given to ensure payment or an advance of funds in the processing of a loan. Also see earnest money deposit.

http://www.propertywords.com/deposit.html

Definition of Earnest Money

Money deposited by a buyer under the terms of a contract. Also referred to as a binder deposit or good-faith deposit.

http://www.propertywords.com/Earnest_Money.html

Special Emphasis: Deposit of Earnest Money

Sales Associates - Deliver the deposit to the broker no later than end of the <u>next business day</u>

Brokers - Deposit the check in the escrow account no later than end of the <u>third business day</u> after sales associate receives the deposit.

III) Handling of deposits

B) Management of escrow accounts

1) If the account is interest bearing, requirement for written authorization for distribution of interest

2) Requirement to inform broker immediately of any conflicting demands concerning disbursement of escrowed funds

3) Good-faith doubt procedure when it is not clear which party should receive the escrowed property

(a) Situations that are considered good-faith doubt

Management of Escrow Accounts

Written Authorization for Distribution of Interest

A broker can place escrow funds in either an interest-bearing or a non-interest-bearing escrow account. If the broker places the funds in an interest-bearing account, there is a requirement for written authorization of distribution of interest.

This authorization is a written agreement as to who will receive the interest earned on the funds and when the interest will be disbursed. All parties involved in the transaction must sign the authorization.

Know too, that an escrow account must be in an insured account in a depository located and doing business in Florida.

Before the broker can disburse the interest to either the buyer or the seller, the broker first transfers the earnest money deposit and earned interest into a non-interest-bearing escrow.

However, if the broker has been designated by all parties to receive the interest, only the amount of the earnest money is transferred to the non-interest-bearing escrow account while the interest is transferred directly to the broker's operating account.

An alternative method is for the broker to deposit the escrow into an interest-bearing escrow account that was opened for the specific transaction. On the date agreed upon for disbursement, the broker closes the account by issuing checks to the appropriate person(s) for the earnest money and interest.

61J2-14.014

Broker as Signatory

The broker must be a signatory on all escrow accounts. If there is more than one broker for the brokerage, then one broker licensee may be designated as the signatory.

A broker may ONLY place and maintain up to $1,000 of personal or brokerage funds into a **sales escrow account**. A broker may place and maintain up to $5,000 of personal or brokerage funds into each **property management escrow account**.

If the escrow account is being used for both sales and property management escrow funds, then the $5,000 maximum is allowed.

A broker shall have 30 days from the date the last reconciliation statement was performed or should have been performed to correct escrow errors if there is no shortage of funds and such errors pose no significant threat to economically harm the public.

61J2-14.010

Misappropriation of Escrow Funds

Know that to misappropriate funds is a serious infraction.

- Trust funds (client funds/binder deposit/earnest money) must be kept in an account separate from the company's or broker accounts.

In regard to earnest deposit, misappropriation can take two forms: Commingling or Conversion.

Commingling is the illegal act of mixing deposits or monies belonging to a client with one's personal money.

http://www.propertywords.com/Commingling.html

Conversion is the appropriation of property belonging to another. It is illegal for a broker to convert trust funds to his own use – even if it is just temporary. (Remember the boy who went to store for his mother in Section 4 of this course? Had he used her money to participate in the bet; he would have been guilty of misappropriation of funds.)

http://www.propertywords.com/Conversion.html

Conflicting Demands

Requirement to inform broker immediately

Whenever there are conflicting demands regarding the distribution of the earnest money deposit, the licensee is required to IMMEDIATELY inform the broker.

Conflicting demands, by definition, is when the parties each make claims that are inconsistent with each other.

Not every real estate deal goes smoothly. Occasionally, they will even fall apart. When that happens, the broker will attempt to deliver the funds per the terms of the purchase and sale agreement. However, both the buyer and seller are requested to sign a form authorizing that they approve how the money is to be distributed.

Sometimes in these situations, both the buyer and seller believe that the money should be distributed to them and they refuse to authorize the distribution of the funds. When that happens, the broker may decide as to who should receive the funds and distribute the money without their authorization. (This doesn't mean that the broker can't be sued in civil court by the aggrieved party!)

Good Faith Doubt Procedure

Yet, sometimes, the broker will have an honest doubt as to which party has the legal rights to the funds. This is called a good-faith doubt.

When there is a good-faith doubt, the broker must provide written notification to the Commission within 15 business days of the last party's demand, and the broker must institute one of the settlement procedures as set forth in Section 475.25(1)(d)1., Florida Statutes, within 30 business days after the last demand.

Also within that same 30-day period, the broker must notify the Commission of which settlement procedure was instituted – unless the settlement procedure utilized was to request that the Commission issue an Escrow Disbursement Order, which would make the notification redundant.

61J2-10.0

Good Faith Doubt Procedure

If the broker has requested an Escrow Disbursement Order (EDO), and as a result, the broker is notified in writing by FREC that no Escrow Disbursement Order will be issued by FREC-- then the broker has another 30 days to institute a different settlement procedure and notify the Commission of the procedure chosen. (Remember the FREC and the Commission are two different ways to refer to the Florida Real Estate Commission!)

Or, if the broker has requested an Escrow Disbursement Order from the FREC and the dispute is subsequently settled between the buyer and seller or goes to court because one of them decided to sue before the order is issued, the broker must notify the Commission within 10 business days of such event.

Good Faith Doubt Procedure

For purposes of these rules, where a broker is required to provide written notification within a certain period, the effective date of that notification is the date of the postmark or other dispatch of notification. Therefore, a request for an Escrow Disbursement Order as a settlement procedure is deemed instituted when the completed request form is mailed or otherwise dispatched to the Commission.

Here's an exception to the above Good-faith Doubt Procedure:

Brokers who are holding earnest money as part of a residential sales contract utilized by the **Department of Housing and Urban Development** (HUD) in the sale of property owned by HUD, are NOT required to notify the FREC of settlement procedures. Instead, the broker is to follow HUD's rules and procedures outlined in HUD's Broker Participation Requirements.

61J2-10

Good Faith Doubt Procedure

Escrow Held by Title Companies

When escrow is being held by a title company rather than the brokerage office, the broker is not subject to notify the FREC as described in the administrative code 61J2-10.032(1)(a). This code does not apply to title companies. And since the broker isn't holding the funds, the broker does not institute a settlement procedure either.

In most cases, a title company will require clear written instructions from both parties before releasing the deposit. If the parties can't provide matching instructions within a reasonable period, the title company will likely deposit the funds with the local clerk of courts, and either party may then file a court case to argue why they believe they're entitled to the deposit.

Situations that are considered good-faith doubt:

- The transaction has closed and the broker has not received any claim or request for the funds to be disbursed.

- The transaction has not closed and one of the parties has expressed a desire to back out of the transaction and the broker has not received any claim or request for the funds to be disbursed.

- The broker has received a conflicting request for disbursement of the funds.

Special Emphasis: Commingling

Mixing funds belonging to a client with one's personal funds.

Special Emphasis: Conversion

The appropriation of property belonging to another – even if just temporarily.

Special Emphasis: Conflicting demands

When the parties each make a claim toward the deposit that is inconsistent with each other.

Special Emphasis: Good-faith doubt

An honest doubt as to whom the earnest money should go to.

http://definitions.uslegal.com/g/good-faith/

Special Emphasis: Escrow Account

If the broker is maintaining an escrow account:

- Brokers may place $1,000 personal or brokerage funds in a sales escrow account.

- Brokers may place $5,000 personal or brokerage funds in property management escrow account.

Special Emphasis: Good-Faith Doubt

If you have a "good faith" doubt as to whom the earnest money should be given to you must:

a) Inform your broker immediately

b) Request that the commission issue an escrow disbursement order determining who is entitled to the escrowed property

Special Emphasis

Conflicting Demands

- Must notify the FREC in writing within 15 business days of receiving conflicting demands

- Begin settlement procedure within 30 business days of receiving conflicting demands and notify the FREC of the procedure implemented.

III) Handling of deposits

    4) Settlement procedures

        (a) Mediation

        (b) Arbitration

        (c) Litigation

(1) Interpleader

(2) Declaratory judgment

(d) Escrow disbursement order

Settlement Procedures

Recall that once a broker has a good-faith doubt as to how to distribute the escrow funds, the broker notifies the FREC of the conflicting demands on the deposit within 15 days, and within 30 days of having received conflicting demands; the broker will institute one of the following Settle Procedures:

- Mediation

- Arbitration

- Litigation

- Escrow disbursement order.

Following is a review of each procedure.

Mediation

The least conflictual option of the settlement procedures is the option to take the matter to **mediation**.

Mediation is the attempt to settle a legal dispute through active and neutral participation of a third party (mediator), who works to find points of agreement and encourage those in conflict to agree on a fair result.

Because mediation is inherently an informal process, it is not binding to the parties. This means that they can change their minds after a mediation session has been conducted and still not agree to the disbursement of funds.

Many times, though, this is the least conflictual, yet most productive way to resolve the issue.

The broker has only 90 days for the mediation process to produce results or per the Florida Statutes, the broker would have to implement one of the three remaining settlement procedures.

The purpose of this rule, is that the statute attempts to prevent a broker from having funds remaining in the broker's account for excessive periods of time. (Think of the interest that a broker could earn when in an interest-bearing account if the broker was not held to a timeline!)

475.25 Discipline.—

- (1)(d)1. (a) With the written consent of all parties, submit the matter to mediation. The department may conduct mediation or may contract with public or private entities for mediation services. However, the mediation process must be successfully completed within 90 days following the last demand or the licensee shall promptly employ one of the other escape procedures contained in this section. Payment for mediation will be as agreed to in writing by the parties.

http://dictionary.law.com/Default.aspx?selected=1233#ixzz3yOBlxJj4

Arbitration

Another one of the four settlement procedures is to submit the dispute for **arbitration**. An arbitrator is an unbiased third person designated by the parties who agree in advance to comply with the decision—a decision to be issued after a hearing at which both parties have an opportunity to be heard.

Unlike mediation, the decision made by the arbitrator is binding to all the parties. Because it is binding, all parties must agree to the arbitration procedure in advance and in writing.

Arbitration is a well-established and widely used means to end disputes. It provides the parties an option that is less extreme than litigating the matter in court.

http://legal-dictionary.thefreedictionary.com/arbitration

Unlike litigation, which is discussed next, arbitration takes place out of court: the two sides select an impartial third party, known as an arbitrator; agree in advance to comply with the arbitrator's award; and then participate in a hearing at which both sides can present evidence and testimony.

As the arbitrator's decision is considered final, and courts rarely reexamine it.

- 475.25☐ Discipline.—

(1)(d)1. b.☐ With the <u>consent of all parties</u>, submit the matter to <u>arbitration</u>;

Litigation

Another one of the four settlement procedures is to submit the dispute to the courts for **litigation**.

If the parties have not come to some type of resolution, or if the broker wishes to be relieved of the responsibility, the broker may submit the matter to the court.

Know that what is being described here are the procedures that the broker must take per the Florida Statutes. There is nothing that prevents the buyer or seller from taking the matter to court themselves.

Litigation as a settlement procedure takes one of two forms: either as an Interpleader or as a Declaratory Judgment. The form that applies depends upon whether the broker is making a demand on the deposit.

http://law.freeadvice.com/litigation/litigation/litigation.htm#ixzz3yOOLGi

Interpleader

Listing agreements with sellers and purchase agreements between buyers and sellers sometimes include a provision that if a deal fails to close, that the broker can retain part or even all the earnest money deposit.

Keep in mind, that a licensee and broker may put hours of time into creating a deal and into attempting to keep the deal together. The retaining of all or more commonly a portion of the earnest money helps to offset this.

Florida law provides for a broker who has chosen NOT to have a right to any of the deposit to submit the matter to the courts and request an **interpleader**. By using an interpleader, the broker deposits the funds with the clerk of the court and is relieved of further duties in overseeing the matter.

- An interpleader action is defined in the Florida Rules of Civil Procedure under Rule 1.240. The rule states "persons having claims against the plaintiff may be joined as defendants and required to interplead when their claims are such that the plaintiff is or may be exposed to double or multiple liability." The State of Florida bases this rule on the theory that conflicting parties should litigate their claims among themselves without involving the plaintiff or middleman in their dispute.

The broker is then dismissed as a party to the interpleader action and the buyer and seller must litigate and argue for their rights to the money among themselves.

http://www.pompanolaw.com/2012/01/07/business-law/escrow_disputes

Declaratory Judgment

When the broker IS making a claim on the deposit, the broker must request a **declaratory judgment**.

A declaratory judgment is a judgment of a court which determines the rights of parties.

By seeking a declaratory judgment, the broker is seeking an official declaration of the status of a matter in controversy—how the funds will be distributed. A petition for a declaratory judgment asks the court to define the legal relationship between the parties and their rights with respect to the matter before the court.

http://definitions.uslegal.com/d/declaratory-judgment/

Escrow Disbursement Order

The final of the four settlement procedures is for the broker to make a request with the Commission to issue an **escrow disbursement order** (EDO).

An escrow disbursement order is a determination by the FREC as to who is entitled to disputed funds.

However, the FREC isn't obligated to decide. Sometimes based on the facts of the case, the FREC will notify the broker that the broker needs to institute a different settlement procedure and must do so within 30 days of having received the notification.

If the parties resolve the issue while the broker waits for a decision from the FREC, the broker must notify the FREC within 10 business days that the EDO is no longer necessary. This same rule applies if one of the parties takes the matter to the courts for litigation.

Know that just because it is the FREC that issues the EDO, the broker can still be sued by the aggrieved party for how the funds are distributed!

http://francesjarvis.com/2015/03/22/what-is-an-escrow-disbursement-order/

475.25 (1)(d)

Postdated Checks

Circumstances may prevent a buyer from making a deposit upon an accepted offer. Instead, the buyer may write a postdated check and give it to the licensee to hold as escrow deposit, which will be given to their agent who then must to turn it over to his/her broker.

Licensees should avoid taking a postdated check, however, Florida law does allow it. It must be approved by the sellers and noted in the contract.

The licensee must implement deposit procedures with the same timeline as a regular check once the check is current.

Florida statute (F.S. 673

http://activerain.com/blogsview/4341349/fl-buyers-can-give-post-dated-escrow-deposit---but

Special Emphasis: Mediation

The attempt to settle a legal dispute through active participation of a third party (mediator) who works to find points of agreement and make those in conflict agree on a fair result.

Mediation differs from arbitration, in which the third party (arbitrator) acts much like a judge in an out-of-court, less formal setting but does not actively participate in the discussion.

Special Emphasis: Arbitration

With the consent of all parties, submit the matter to arbitration. Binding decision from a neutral third party.

The submission of a dispute to an unbiased third person, known as an arbitrator, who agree in advance to comply with the decision to be issued by the arbitrator after a hearing at which both parties have had an opportunity to be heard.

Unlike litigation, arbitration takes place out of court.

Special Emphasis: Litigation

Litigation is the term used to describe proceedings initiated between two opposing parties to enforce or defend a legal right.

Litigation as a settlement procedure takes one of two forms: either as an Interpleader or as a Declaratory Judgment.

Special Emphasis: Escrow Disbursement Order

A settlement procedure when there is a good faith doubt by the broker. The FREC decides how the funds should be distributed.

Special Emphasis: Misappropriation of Escrow Funds

Trust funds (client funds/binder deposit/earnest money) must be kept in an account separate from the company's or broker accounts.

Special Emphasis: Settlement Procedures

Within 30 days of having received conflicting demands; the broker will institute one of the following Settlement Procedures:

- Mediation

- Arbitration

- Litigation

- Escrow disbursement order.

Special Emphasis: Litigation - Interpleader

Florida law provides for a broker who has chosen NOT to have a right to any of the deposit to submit the matter to the courts and request an interpleader.

By using an interpleader, the broker is relieved of further duties in overseeing the matter.

Special Emphasis: Settlement Procedures - Litigation

Declaratory judgment

When the broker IS making a claim on the deposit, the broker must request a declaratory judgment.

A declaratory judgment is a judgment of a court which determines the rights of parties.

Special Emphasis: Escrow Disbursement Order (EDO)

Request that the commission issue an escrow disbursement order determining who is entitled to the escrowed property.

- The Commission (FREC) issues a determination of who is entitled to disputed funds.

- You must inform FREC within 10 business days if dispute is settled or it goes to court.

IV) Rental Lists and Rental Companies

    A) Requirement

        1) Provide a receipt when offering rental information for a fee

            (a) Required language under Rule 61J2-10.030, F.A.C.

        2) Refund procedures

            (a) Fail to attain rental

            (b) Material misrepresentation

            (c) Request must be made within 30 days

Requirements Regarding the Sale of Rental Information

Although not common practice in all areas of the country, a broker may charge a prospective tenant a fee to receive a list of available rentals. This is common in areas where rentals are in high demand such as New York City.

- Per Florida Statutes **475.453,** each broker or sales associate who furnishes a rental information list to a prospective tenant, for a fee paid by the prospective tenant, shall provide such prospective tenant with a contract or receipt.

The receipt must describe the conditions for which a refund can be received by the prospective tenant.

If the prospective tenant fails to obtain a rental, the person is entitled to a 75% refund if a request for the refund is made within 30 days of having received the list.

If the rental information list provided by the broker or sales associate to a prospective tenant is not current or accurate in any material respect, the full fee (100%) shall be repaid to the prospective tenant upon demand.

The contract or receipt shall also conform to the guidelines adopted by the commission to provide full disclosure regarding the prospective tenant's rights.

Special Emphasis: Refund Procedures

- Fail to attain rental; can get 75% of the fee paid back---person does not find a rental from the list provided.

- Material misrepresentation of rental information; you can get 100% of the fee paid back--The information is old and outdated or has inaccurate information such as price or availability.

- Request must be made within 30 days of the contract date—must give the person a refund if requested within 30 days of purchasing the list.

IV) Rental Lists and Rental Companies

    B) Penalties for advertising obsolete or otherwise inaccurate rental lists

        1) License suspension or revocation

        2) First degree misdemeanor

            (a) Punishable by up to one year of imprisonment and/or fine of up to $1,000

The Selling of Rental Information and Lists is Regulated

The selling of rental lists that are not current or accurate is illegal, and per Florida Statutes is a first-degree misdemeanor.

This is punishable by up to one year of imprisonment and/or fine of to $1,000.

See Florida Statutes 475.453 and Administrative Code 61J2-24.001.

Licensees must take care to follow guidelines as presented here or risk legal consequences:

V) Broker/Sales associate licensee as an expert in specific aspects of property transfer

    A) Requirement to avoid offering an opinion of title since it can be relied on as expert opinion.

    B) Ability to offer a representation of value, avoiding misrepresentation through exaggeration, etc.

    C) Misrepresentation of value by a licensee as fraud, breach of contract, or breach of trust

    D) Unauthorized practice of law

Requirement to avoid offering an opinion of title since it can be relied on as expert opinion

The process of working with buyers and sellers or landlords and tenants involves aspects from fields of various expertise. In fact, much of the information included in the course involves how these different areas intertwine with real estate. Yet a licensee must be careful not to cross the line and engage in behavior that will be legally viewed as practicing a profession (other than real estate) that requires a license.

For example, all too often, real estate agents and brokers go over the line and practice law without a license.

If a buyer or seller asks a broker or agent to check out the title to a piece of property and give an opinion of the condition of title, this is breaking the law.

Although title is a real estate issue, figuring out if a property has a "clouded title" is legally complex.

http://aboutfloridalaw.com/2015/03/24/when-is-a-florida-real-estate-agent-or-broker-guilty-of-the-unauthorized-practice-of-law/#sthash.6wNP3gB4.dpuf

Requirement to avoid offering an opinion of title since it can be relied on as expert opinion

Real estate licensees offer knowledge of title transfer to their clients. Do not confuse this with offering opinion of title marketability. Giving an opinion of title is practicing law. The opinion of title must come, instead, from a Florida real estate lawyer. Once that opinion has been shared with the licensee, the licensee may pass opinion on to the client.

If a real estate licensee were to give an opinion of title, per Florida Statutes the licensee is subject to losing his or her real estate license:

- [h]as rendered an opinion that the title to any property sold is good or merchantable, except when correctly based upon a current opinion of a licensed attorney at law, or has failed to advise a prospective purchaser to consult her or his attorney on the merchantability of the title or to obtain title insurance. Florida Statute 475.25(j)

http://aboutfloridalaw.com/2015/03/24/when-is-a-florida-real-estate-agent-or-broker-guilty-of-the-unauthorized-

Ability to Offer a Representation of Value

Real estate licensees assist clients with the buying and selling of homes which often represents clients' largest investments.

Licensees are expected to utilize industry experience and knowledge to assist clients in obtaining the best deal. This starts with the knowledge to assist clients in the assessment of property value.

Appraisals, comparative market analyses and broker price opinions are within the scope of the real estate license. However, care must be taken not to misrepresent value through exaggeration.

http://realtyabsolute.com/articles/the-real-estate-agents-value-proposition/

Avoiding Misrepresentation Through Exaggeration, etc.

When marketing a property for sale or presenting it to a prospective buyer, licensees must take care not to misrepresent the value of the property.

Misrepresentation includes embellishing, obfuscation, omissions, and lying. These types of behaviors can result in the loss of a real estate license.

According to the National Association of Realtors®, failure to disclose is one of the most common reasons that results in lawsuits against licensees

Exaggeration is a statement that represents something as better or worse than it really is, which is unlawful. However, puffing is when a person talks about something in an overly flattering way without distorting facts by merely expressing an opinion. Generally, puffing is lawful. Licensees must be careful not to cross over the line into misrepresentation.

"This property has the best view in town," would be considered puffing and is lawful if the client was with the licensee looking at the house. The buyer can form their own opinion about the view. On the other hand, if the buyer was buying the property sight unseen, this could cross over into misrepresentation.

http://realtormag.realtor.org/law-and-ethics/law/article/2002/09/ten-ways-lose-or-least-endanger-your-license

Puffing

Talking up the good points without misstating facts.

http://legal-dictionary.thefreedictionary.com/puffing

Exaggeration

Representing something as being better or worse than fact.

Powered by Oxford Dictionaries · © Oxford University Press

Misrepresentation

Fraudulent, or negligent, or innocent misstatement, or failure to supply complete information regarding material facts.

http://www.businessdictionary.com/definition/misrepresentation.html#ixzz3yTmkB7mu

Misrepresentation of value by a licensee as fraud, breach of contract, or breach of trust

When a sales associate misrepresents value of a property, the licensee and the broker may be found guilty of fraud, breach of contract, or breach of trust.

- To be fraudulent means that the licensee intentionally misrepresented material facts or deceived the party.

- Part of the agreement or contract that a broker has with a party to a contract is to represent all information accurately. Failure to do so is a breach of contract.

- The licensee and broker is in a position of trust with a client and as such misrepresenting value is a breach of that trust.

Therefore, one instance of misrepresentation of value may result in all three of these separate charges. Know that even if the broker is not aware of the misrepresentation, the broker may be held liable as it is the broker who is responsible.

Unauthorized Practice of Law

Article 13 of the NAR Code of Ethics states that "REALTORS® shall not engage in activities that constitute the unauthorized practice of law."

In addition to not giving an opinion of value, a licensee and/or broker may be charged with the unauthorized practice of law by drawing up contracts that is not allowed per Florida Statutes.

The intent of the law is to prevent the public from being damaged by unskilled practitioners.

To limit legal advice liability: Know the parameters of what you may and may not do. See Section 11 of this course for specific information about how to legally deal with real estate contracts. For additional assistance, licensees should look to their brokers for instruction or contact the Florida Association of Realtors® hotline.

http://realtormag.realtor.org/law-and-ethics/law/article/2000/03/top-10-legal-issues-facin

COMMISSIONS

VI) Commissions

    A) "Fixing" commissions or fees is illegal

    B) A Sales associate cannot contract directly with a principal

        1) The sales associate's commission is by agreement with the broker

        2) A sales associate cannot sue a principal over a commission

"Fixing" commissions or fees is illegal

Activities That Violate Antitrust Laws

Competing brokers are supposed to compete for business. The following is illegal, as it applies to real estate, per Antitrust laws:

- Price Fixing - Fixing commissions or fees for services between brokerages

- Market Allocation - Splitting up market areas between brokerages to avoid competition

It is unlawful for brokerages who are supposed to be "competing" to get together and decide what commission to charge or to divide up the market to lower competition. This practice drives up profits which drives up the costs to consumers and is therefore illegal per the U.S. Supreme Court antitrust

                  lawhttps://www.grec.state.ga.us/infobase/tableofcontents/chapter12.html

To participate in price fixing or market allocation is to violate antitrust laws which were put into place at the Federal level back in 1890.

The law attempts to prevent the artificial raising of prices by restriction of trade or supply. The law directs itself not against conduct which is competitive, even severely so, but against conduct which unfairly tends to destroy competition itself.

                  https://en.wikipedia.org/wiki/Sherman_Antitrust_Ac

A Sales Associate Cannot Contract Directly with a Principal

Recall that a sales associate or a broker associate is a general agent of the broker. It is the licensee who is engaged in a relationship to deliver services to a buyer, seller, landlord or tenant. And as such, only the broker may collect direct compensation from any of these parties for a real estate related transaction.

Violation of this is covered under Florida Statutes 475.42 Violations and penalties.—

- (1)(d) A sales associate may not collect any money in connection with any real estate brokerage transaction, whether as a commission, deposit, payment, rental, or otherwise, except in the name of the employer and with the express consent of the employer; and no real estate sales associate, whether the holder of a valid and current license or not, shall commence or maintain any action for a commission or compensation in connection with a real estate brokerage transaction against any person, except a person registered as her or his employer at the time the sales associate performed the act, or rendered the service for which the commission or compensation is due.

The sales associate's commission is by agreement with the broker

Each brokerage will have their own compensation plans and programs. Licensees should carefully read the employment contract or the Independent Contractor Agreement carefully and thoroughly. Brokerages vary widely in the type of commission structure offered.

In most cases, licensees are employed as an independent contractor. Less common, though, is the possibility of working as a regular employee. Both contracts will detail your working relationship with the broker. And both types of contracts will detail how much you will be paid as a real estate agent.

In all cases, only the broker can be paid by a party for real estate services. The licensee may be paid on a transaction basis (which is one of the requirements to be considered an independent contractor). However, the pay comes directly from the broker not the principal.

A sales associate cannot sue a principal over a commission

As it is the broker who is contracted with the principal to assist in the real estate transaction, it is ONLY the broker that may sue in the event that the principal refuses to pay the commission.

475.42 Violations and penalties.—

(1)(d) ...no real estate sales associate, whether the holder of a valid and current license or not, shall commence or maintain any action for a commission or compensation regarding a real estate brokerage transaction against any person, except a person registered as her or his employer at the time the sales associate performed the act, or rendered the service for which the commission or compensation is due.

Commission Liens

So, what happens if a principal refuses to pay a commission on a real estate transaction? If the transaction involved residential real estate, the broker would have to take the buyer or seller to court.

If it involves a commercial property, there are other options under **The Florida Commercial Real Estate Sales Commission Lien Act and the Florida Commercial Real Estate Lease Commission Lien Act.**

Both provide that when a broker has earned a commission by performing licensed services under a brokerage agreement, the broker may:

- Upon a sale, claim a lien against the net sales proceeds for the broker's commission.

- Upon a lease, the broker may claim a lien against interest in the property for the broker's commission or an interest in the leasehold, depending upon whether it is the landlord or the tenant that owes the commission.

- Only allowed if broker is given that authority in a contract, otherwise seek civil judgment

475.703, 475.803

F.S. 475, Part III

Commercial Real Estate Sales Commission Lien Act

Gives broker lien rights on seller's net proceeds from sale of commercial property

Not lien rights on the real property

Brokerage agreement (listing contract) must clearly state broker's lien rights

F.S. 475, Part IV

Commercial Real Estate Leasing Commission Lien Act

Gives broker lien rights for commission earned for leasing commercial real estate

- If landlord agreed to pay commission, lien is against landlord's interest in the real property
- If tenant agreed to pay commission, lien is on tenant's leasehold estate

Special Emphasis: Price Fixing

PRICE FIXING - Agreements among competing brokers to set commissions at fixed levels. This is a violation of antitrust laws.

Special Emphasis: Antitrust Laws Apply to Real Estate Agents

Competing brokers are supposed to compete.

Therefore, it is illegal to:

- Fix commissions or fees for services (price-fixing)
- Conspire to split up market areas to avoid competition (market allocation)

VI) Commissions

C) "Kickbacks" are legal only under limited conditions

1) All parties to the transaction must be fully informed of the kickback

2) It must not be prohibited by other law

3) It is unlawful to share a commission with an unlicensed person, except for the seller or buyer of the

property.

4) It is unlawful for a licensee to pay any unlicensed person for performing real estate service

"Kickbacks" are Legal Only Under Limited Conditions

A **KICKBACK** is a payment for doing a task related to a real estate transaction. However, the task itself cannot be something that requires a real estate license to perform.

To be legal, the kickback must meet the following conditions:

- All parties to the transaction must be fully informed about the kickback

- It must not violate any other law

- It cannot involve the sharing of a commission unless the person receiving the kickback is the buyer or the seller in the transaction.

- It is unlawful for a licensee to pay any unlicensed person for performing real estate service

Title or casualty insurance companies cannot provide a kickback to other types of professionals in the field. For example, a title company cannot throw a party for a brokerage company as a thank-you for sending them title business.

So, when is a kickback lawful?

It is lawful to share a commission in the form of a rebate to a buyer or seller involved in the property transaction.

It is also lawful to pay a $50 referral fee to a current tenant of an apartment complex for finding a tenant.

It is legal to share a sales commission with the buyer or seller involved with a transaction with full disclosure to all parties to the transaction.

http://activerain.com/blogsview/4472842/real-estate-kickbacks

Kickbacks or Rebates

All parties to the transaction must be fully informed of the kickback.

Provide all clients with a disclosure stating any "kickbacks", rebates, or referral fees before the transaction closes. Create a form and have clients sign it upon initial contracting.

How is this information disclosed? The licensee is required to disclose in the agency agreement all details about any kickbacks.

If the licensee is not receiving or giving any kickbacks, a statement should also be provided to this effect.

http://www.reaa.govt.nz/ForBuyersAndSellers/Documents/Information%20Sheets/Disclosure%20Information%2 0Sheet%20July%201%202011%20reformated.pdf

It Must Not Be Prohibited by Other Law

Any "kickback", rebate or referral fee must not be prohibited by any federal or state law such as RESPA.

RESPA: The Real Estate Settlement Procedures Act

Section 8: Kickbacks, Fee-Splitting, Unearned Fees

Section 8 of RESPA makes it unlawful for a person to give or accept a fee, kickback or anything of value in exchange for referrals of settlement services in a federally related transaction. Fee splitting and receiving unearned fees for services not actually performed is also unlawful.

A person violating RESPA by giving unlawful kickbacks may face a fine up to $10,000 and imprisonment for up to one year.

http://library.hsh.com/articles/government-programs/respa-the-real-estate-settlement-procedures-act/

Special Emphasis: Kickbacks or Rebates

It is unlawful to share a commission with an unlicensed person, except for the seller or buyer of the property.

Licensees may share their commission with the buyer or seller in that transaction (with full disclosure).

May not share commission with any other unlicensed person.

May not pay an unlicensed person for referral of real estate business (finder's fee of up to $50 to a tenant exception).

Personal Assistants

It is unlawful for a licensee to pay any unlicensed person for performing real estate services. This means that brokers as well as licensees must be careful when they hire an assistant to aid them in their real estate services.

Per FREC website: "Unlicensed assistant is defined as support staff for a real estate corporation or other licensed individuals."

Unlicensed Personal Assistant

- Administrative tasks
- May not perform duties requiring a license
- May not be paid a commission
- Licensee who employs unlicensed assistants
    - Must comply with state and federal employment laws

Licensed Personal Assistant

- Can perform services of real estate

- Must be registered with employing broker

- Broker must pay licensed assistant for brokerage activities

Commissions

FREC has issued the following specific guidelines as to the tasks which Unlicensed Assistants may perform under their broker's supervision:

- Answer the phone and forward calls

- Fill out and submit listings and changes to any multiple listing service

- Follow-up on loan commitments after a contract has been negotiated and generally secure the status reports on the loan progress

- Assemble documents for closing

- Secure documents (public information) from courthouse, utility district, etc.

- Have keys made for company listings, order surveys, termite inspections, home inspections and home warranties with the licensed employer's approval

- Write ads for approval of the licensee and the supervising broker, and place advertising (newspaper ads, update web sites, etc); prepare flyers and promotional information for approval by licensee and the supervising broker

- Receive, record and deposit earnest money, security deposits and advance rents

- Only type the contract forms for approval by licensee and supervising broker

- Monitor licenses and personnel files

- Compute commission checks

- Place signs on property

- Order items of repair as directed by licensee

- Prepare flyers and promotional information for approval by licensee and supervising broker

- Act as a courier service to deliver documents, pick-up keys

- Place routine telephone calls on late rent payments

- Schedule appointments for licensee to show a listed property

http://www.myfloridalicense.com/dbpr/re/documents/Permissibleactivitiesrev092009.pdf

The details of commission agreements with sales associates should be part of a broker's policy manual

Policy Manual

The standards and procedures of an office should be stated specifically and clearly in a Policy Manual.

> http://www.flashcardmachine.com/florida-realestatesalesassociate.html

VI) Commissions

  D) The details of commission agreements with sales associates should be part of a broker's policy manual

The details of commission agreements with sales associates should be part of a broker's policy manual

A smooth-running brokerage office requires written documentation about office policies and procedures. A broker's policy manual is an easy-to-understand guidebook for salespeople to refer to in their daily business.

> **The details of commission agreements with sales associates should be part of a broker's policy manual**

A smooth-running brokerage office requires written documentation about office policies and procedures. These policies and procedures should be compiled into a policy manual. According to the National Association's "Field Guide to Real Estate Office Policy Manuals", policy manuals should:

- "Provide a clear understanding of the relationship between broker and sales associates, management and employees, and administrative functions and sales functions.

- Permit the anticipation of and resolution of controversies before they arise.

- Stabilize both management and sales by building confidence that both management and sales associates know the rules by which the game is to be played.

- Forbid favoritism, since all must operate within the framework of the manual's predetermined rules and guidelines.

- Provide stability of organization and permit the staff to function effectively in the absence of **management."**

http://www.realtor.org/field-guides/field-guide-to-real-estate-office-policy-manuals

VII) Change of Employer

    A) A sales associate must inform the FREC about a change of employer.

        1) Within ten days

        2) On a prescribed form

    B) A Sales associate's obligation of confidentiality with respect to principals or the broker does not end with termination of employment.

    C) Duplication of records from a previous employer constitutes breach of trust, even if the one copying the records originated them, if done for taking listings to the new employer.

    D) Removal of records from a previous employer's office constitutes theft.

Notice of Change of Employer

A sales associate must inform the FREC whenever a change in employer is made. This notification may be done on a prescribed form by mail or online at the DBPR website www.myfloridalicense.com. This notice must be given within 10 days. Until the change is noted on the DBPR website, the licensee may not practice real estate as the license would cease to be in force.

F.S. 475.23

A Sales associate's obligation of confidentiality with respect to principals or the broker does not end with termination of employment

Even once a change of employment is made, sales associates must honor the confidentiality of their previous employer and the principals served.

REALTORS® Code of Ethics Article

http://www.realestateabc.com/codeofethics/dutiestoclients.htm

Duplication of Records

Duplication of records from a previous employer constitutes breach of trust, even if the one copying the records originated them, if done for taking listings to the new employer.

Removal of records from a previous employer's office constitutes theft. Because of the just stated facts, a licensee should carefully examine the employment contract. A provision of the contract may be added that the clients that a licensee procures during the relationship may be released under this provision.

Use of Association Names

Only members of the NAR may refer to themselves as a "Realtor®." There are also many other designations that can be obtained to further a licensee's education and status. Only include them if they have been earned.

- 61J2-10.027 **Use of Association Names.**

  - No licensee shall use an identification or designation of any association or organization having to do with real estate unless entitled to use such identification or designation.

IX) Change of address procedure and penalty for failure to notify the FREC

As Seen in the Florida Statutes

61J2-10.038 Mailing Address

(1) Pursuant to Section 455.275(1), Florida Statutes, the Commission defines "current mailing address" as the current residential address which is used by a licensee or permit holder to receive mail through the United States Postal Service.

(2) Each licensee and permit holder is required to notify the DBPR in writing of the current mailing address and any change in the current mailing address within 10 days after the change.

This is not the same thing as notifying change of Florida residency which allows for 60 days in notification.

Special Emphasis: Change of Address

Licensees must notify DBPR within 10 days of change to current mailing address. Failure to notify DBPR:

- Citation

- Fine of $500.

X) Types of Business Entities

    A) Entities that may register as a brokerage

        1) Sole proprietorship

        2) General partnership

        3) Limited partnership

            (a) Ostensible partnerships are prohibited

        4) Corporation

            (a) For profit

            (b) Not for profit

        5) Limited liability company

        6) Limited liability partnership

The following business entities may register as real estate brokers:

- Sole Proprietorship
- General Partnership
- Limited Partnership
- Limited Liability Partnership (LLP)
- Corporation
- Limited Liability Company (LLC)
- Professional Association (PA)

Sole Proprietorship

A person doing business as him or herself and under his or her own name is a sole proprietorship.

Anyone who does business without formally creating a business organization is a sole proprietor. Many small businesses including real estate licensees operate as sole proprietorships.

Creating this type of business often requires the least startup costs as compared to other business entities.

A sole proprietorship is not a separate legal entity, like a partnership or a corporation. Therefore, it is the business owner that assumes all legal and tax liability.

http://legal-dictionary.thefreedictionary.com/Sole+Proprietorship

General Partnership (General Partner)

When more than one person joins together to operate a business, they share in the profits and responsibilities including the legal and tax liabilities. Each general partner is liable for <u>all the debts</u> of the partnership.

http://legal-dictionary.thefreedictionary.com/general+partnership

Limited Partnership

Limited partnerships are when there are two or more persons involved in the business, however, some are designated as general partners and others are designated as limited partners.

There must be a written agreement defining the roles.

Limited partners make an investment of funds into the partnership and receive a share of the profit. They are not held liable for the business. To qualify as a limited partner, the person cannot participate in the management of the business

- Limited partnerships are commonly used for investments in a real estate development.

Limited partnerships must file the partnership name and the names and addresses of general partners with the state so the public has notice as to who the responsible parties are.

http://legal-dictionary.thefreedictionary.com/limited+partnership

Ostensible Partnership

Be very careful to not take on the liability of a partnership appearing to give the impression to others that you are in a partnership with someone else.

An ostensible partnership is not a real partnership. Rather it is the appearance of a partnership due to how multiple individuals are presenting themselves to the public by giving the appearance that they are a partnership.

When this happens, each party can be held liable for the actions of the other.

It is common for brokers to share office space with other professionals. It is important to make sure that signage and physical space division exists in such a way as to give notice to the public that the businesses are separate.

Also, make sure all advertising clearly distinguishes the different business entities even when co-advertising takes place.

Operating as an ostensible partnership is unlawful. Real estate licensees who operate as ostensible partners may lose their license.

http://activerain.com/blogsview/4471403/ostensible-partnership

Limited Liability Partnership

To avoid personal liability that a general or limited partnership creates for general partners, a limited liability partnership may be formed.

The Limited Liability Partnership (LLP) provides each of its individual partners protection against personal liability – not just limited partners.

When this form of partnership is created and registered, the words "Registered Limited Liability Partnership" or the abbreviation "LLP" is included in the name.

http://legal-dictionary.thefreedictionary.com/Limited+liability+partnership

Corporations

Corporations are not an actual person. Yet, corporations are treated as such by having legal rights and taking on the tax and legal liabilities of the company.

Types of Corporations

Corporations can be private, nonprofit, or owned by the government.

- Private corporations are in business to make a profit.

- Nonprofit corporations are designed to use profits to benefit the public rather than the company or company owners.

Private corporations can be publicly traded or closely held by the original company owners.

Most corporations are closely held.

http://legal-dictionary.thefreedictionary.com/Corporation

For Profit Corporation

A business or other organization whose primary goal is making a profit. *Can be registered as a real estate brokerage.*

Not for Profit Corporation

A not for profit organization is a type of organization that does not earn profits for its owners. Instead money is used for the public good. *A not for profit corporation can be registered as a real estate brokerage.*

Limited Liability Company

The limited liability company (LLC) has both the characteristics of a corporation and a partnership. It's like a corporation in that it protects the owners against personal liability. It's like a non-corporate business in the way profit or loss is passed straight to the owners for tax purposes rather than taxed at the company level.

http://legal-dictionary.thefreedictionary.com/Limited+Liability+Company

Professional Association

Florida allows for professionals to provide services under a special type of corporation known as a Professional Association.

It provides the same insulation that a corporation does from tax and legal liabilities.

Real estate licensees can register themselves as a professional association.

When conducting business as a professional association, the licensee must use P.A. at the end of their name.

- Professional Associations cannot be registered as a real estate brokerage. However, the licensee can register as a P.A. with the DBPR.

http://www.businessandtaxlawyerblog.com/business-formation/what-is-a-florida-professional

Special Emphasis: Real Estate Brokerage General Partnership

- Must Register Partnerships with the DBPR
- At least one partner must be an active broker
- Partners who deal with public and perform real estate services must be active brokers
- Sales associates may not be *general partners*

Special Emphasis: Real Estate Brokerage Limited Partnership

- Register Limited Partnerships with the DBPR
- General partners who perform real estate services must be active brokers
- At least one general partner must be active broker
- All other general partners must register with DBPR
- Sales associates may not be general partners
- Limited partners do not register with DBPR

X) Types of Business Entities

    B) Entities that may not register as a brokerage

        1) Corporation sole

        2) Joint venture

        3) Business trust

        4) Cooperative association

5) Unincorporated associations

Entities That May Not Register as a Brokerage

Corporation sole – A type of ecclesiastical corporation

http://www.merriam-webster.com/dictionary/corporation%20sole

Joint venture – Not an actual business entity. Rather two or more businesses coming together to accomplish a business opportunity.

*http://www.businessdictionary.com/definition/joint-venture-JV.html#ixzz3yT88cb*wo

Business trust – A trust held by a business and managed by appointed trustees for the benefit of one or more beneficiaries.

http://www.businessdictionary.com/definition/business-trust.html#ixzz3yT8fKzXY

Cooperative association – A group of people brought together to achieve a common goal such as maintaining jointly held property.

http://thelawdictionary.org/cooperative-association/

Unincorporated association – A group of people brought together to achieve a common goal, however, the entity is not legally incorporated.

http://definitions.uslegal.com/u/unincorporated-association/

X) Types of Business Entities

C) A sales associate is prohibited from being an officer or director in a real estate brokerage corporation, or a general partner in a brokerage limited partnership XI

Sales associates are prohibited from being an officer or director in a real estate brokerage corporation, or a general partner in a brokerage limited partnership

As Seen in the Florida Statutes

475.161 Licensing of broker associates and sales associates

….. This section shall <u>not</u> operate to <u>permit</u> a <u>broker associate or sales associate to register or be licensed</u> as a <u>general partner, member, manager, officer, or director of a brokerage firm</u> under s. 475.15.

Business Entities That May Register as Real Estate Brokers

May register as real estate brokers:

- Sole Proprietorship
- General Partnership
- Limited Partnership
- Limited Liability Partnership (LLP)
- Corporation
- Limited Liability Company (LLC)
- Professional Association (PA)

May NOT register as a brokerage

- Corporation sole
- Joint venture
- Business trust
- Cooperative association
- Unincorporated associations

TRADE NAMES

XI) Trade names

A) No trade name (fictitious name or DBA) may be used by a sales associate; sales associates must register under their true name only.

No Trade Name (Fictitious Name) May Be Used

As Seen in the Florida Statutes

Per Florida Statutes 75.161, a <u>license shall be issued in the licensee's legal name only and, when appropriate, shall include the entity designation.</u>

- An *individual broker, partnership or corporation* may use a trade name and, if so, it must be disclosed upon the request for license, and be placed upon the registration or license. 61J2-10.034

6 VIOLATIONS OF LICENSE LAW, PENALTIES, AND PROCEDURES

Learning Objectives:
• Explain the procedures involved in the reporting of violations, the investigation of complaints and the conduct of hearings
• Define the elements of a valid complaint
• Discuss the composition of the probable-cause panel
• Recognize events that would cause a license application to be denied
• Distinguish actions that would cause a license to be subject to suspension or revocation
• Identify individuals who would be eligible and the procedure to seek reimbursement from the Real Estate Recovery Fund
• Identify individuals who are not qualified to make a claim from the Real Estate Recovery Fund
• Describe the monetary limits imposed by law on the Real Estate Recovery Fund
• Explain the penalty for a first and second -degree misdemeanor and what real estate activities are first-degree misdemeanors
• Provide Examples of Unlicensed Practice of Law
• Illustrate Presumptions for a Party Performing Real Estate Services

Key Terms:
breach of trust
citation
complaint
commingle
concealment
conversion
culpable negligence failure to account for and deliver
formal or administrative complaint
fraud

legally sufficient
mediation
misrepresentation
moral turpitude
notice of noncompliance
probable cause
recommended order
stipulation
subpoena

summary/emergency suspension order
voluntary relinquishment for permanent revocation

DEFINITIONS

Culpable Negligence

Failing to use the same care a reasonable person would exercise in each situation.

http://www.flashcardmachine.com/florida-real-estate6.html

Moral Turpitude

Conduct that goes against standards of behavior involving honesty or good morals.

http://legal-dictionary.thefreedictionary.com/Moral+Turpitude

Misrepresentation

Fraudulent, negligent, or innocent misstatement, or an incomplete statement, of a material fact.

http://www.businessdictionary.com/definition/misrepresentation.html#ixzz3yfQACqX8

Subpoena

Being ordered to appear in court in a legal case.

http://www.thefreedictionary.com/subpoena

Stipulation

A formal legal agreement made between opposing parties to avoid the case being formally heard.

https://en.wikipedia.org/wiki/Stipulation

Failure to Account for and Deliver

Failing to produce the money that a person was entrusted.

Legally Sufficient

Appearing to have enough evidence to be admissible in court and support a decision or verdict.

http://dictionary.thelaw.com/legally-sufficient-evidence/

Breach of Trust

When an agent, someone that has been placed in a position of trust, acts against the terms of the agreement to the detriment of the principal.

http://thelawdictionary.org/breach-oftrust/

Concealment

Intentionally failing to share information known that could change the other's decision if communicated.

http://legal-dictionary.thefreedictionary.com/Concealment

Conversion

Using someone else's trust funds for your own use.

http://legal-dictionary.thefreedictionary.com/conversion

Complaint

Claim made by a plaintiff against another stating someone has done something wrong.

https://en.wikipedia.org/wiki/Complaint

Commingle

Mixing trust funds from another with the agent's personal or business funds.

http://dictionary.cambridge.org/us/dictionary/english/commingle

Fraud

Intentionally deceiving another by concealing, misleading, or lying through words or actions.

http://legal-dictionary.thefreedictionary.com/Fraud

Probable Cause

Based on facts gained through an investigation, it appears that a crime may have been committed and should be prosecuted. It is NOT a proclamation of guilt.

http://www.lawyerlocator.com/criminal-defense/what-is-probable-cause/

Mediation

A meeting led by a neutral third party to resolve a conflict between two opposing parties. The agreement is nonbinding.

http://www.thefreedictionary.com/mediation

DISCIPLINARY PROCEDURE

I) Disciplinary Procedure (Chapters 120, F.S.; 455, F.S.; 475, F.S.; 60Q and 61J2 of the Florida Administrative Code)

    A) The complaint
        1) Filed with DBPR
        2) The complaint must be legally sufficient
        3) Notice of noncompliance for first-time offense of a minor violation

    B) DBPR conducts investigation
        1) Anonymous complaints
        2) Withdrawal of complaints
        3) When an investigation of a subject is undertaken the DBPR forwards a copy of the complaint to the subject (notice exception for criminal violation)
        4) Investigative report is submitted by legal means to the probable-cause panel

    C) Probable-cause Panel
        1) Composition of probable-cause panel
        2) Purpose is to determine whether probable cause exists
        3) Letter of guidance

    D) If Probable cause is found, a formal/administrative complaint is filed

    E) Licensee is entitled to an informal or a formal hearing

      1) Election of rights form

      2) If no dispute of material fact, the case can be presented in an informal hearing before the FREC

Disciplinary Proceedings

When the public is unhappy with the behavior of a licensee or when the board becomes suspicious of a licensee's behavior, there are disciplinary procedures that are implemented. The basis for these procedures are the same across professions and are detailed in Florida Statute Chapter 455.

- (1)(a)☐ ...shall cause to be investigated any complaint that is filed before it if the complaint is in writing, signed by the complainant, and legally sufficient.

A **complaint is legally sufficient** if it provides facts that demonstrate a violation of Florida Statutes Chapters 120, 455, 475, and 61J2 of the Florida Administrative Code. The department may require supporting information or documentation from the complainant to investigate.

Know that the department may continue the investigation even though the original complainant withdraws the complaint. The department may also investigate an **anonymous complaint** if the complaint is in writing and is legally sufficient.

The department may initiate an investigation without a complaint having been made if it has reasonable cause to believe that a licensee or a group of licensees has violated a Florida statute, a rule of the department, or a rule of a board.

455.225☐ Disciplinary Proceedings

Normally, the person who is under investigation will receive a copy of the complaint and be given 20 days to respond. However, if revealing the existence of the complaint is detrimental to the investigation, then the notice does not have to be given.

Once the investigation is complete, the department always submits an investigative report to a probable cause panel. However, despite submitting it to the probable cause panel, the investigator could immediately dismiss the case if there does not seem to be enough evidence. Any case dismissed prior to review by the probable cause panel would be kept confidential – not available as a public record.

If the offense is a first offence that is considered a minor violation, the department may issue the licensee a notice of noncompliance. The FREC has a list of violations that are considered "minor." If a licensee receives a notice of noncompliance, the licensee has 15 days to provide the department with proof that the behavior has been corrected. Failure to take the corrective action could result in further action being taken against the licensee.

The probable cause panel examines the investigative report and decides as to whether probable cause exists. This is not a determination of guilt. The panel is made up of two FREC members. One member must be a current member and one member must be a current real estate licensee.

Decisions of the probable cause panel become public 10 days after probable cause has been found.

If the probable cause panel requires additional investigative information, they must make a request to the department within 15 days of having received the case. A decision by the panel must be made within 30 days of receipt of all investigation reports unless an extension is granted by the DBPR Secretary.

The panel will either issue a letter of guidance or file a formal complaint against the licensee.

If a formal complaint has been filed against the licensee, the case will be heard before an administrative law judge *if the facts are being disputed by the licensee.*

If the facts are not being disputed by the licensee, then the case is heard by remaining FREC members who did not serve on the probable cause panel.

The complainant will be kept informed of the process.

Once the investigation is complete, a licensee can request to see the file regarding their case.

The person filing the complaint and anyone called as a witness will not be held civilly liable unless it can be proved that they made the complaint in bad faith and with malice.

Special Emphasis

If someone believes that they have been wronged by a licensee, there is a complaint process that can be initiated.

Keep in mind that a person can violate license law and be subject to this process even if they do not have a real estate license.

There are 7 Steps in the process.

Step 1: Filing the Complaint

A complaint is LEGALLY SUFFICIENT if it appears to have violated:

- Florida statute

- DBPR rule

- FREC rule

(This is not yet called a formal complaint)

Notice of Noncompliance

When a complaint is received, the department may provide a licensee with a notice of noncompliance for an initial offense of a minor violation.

- if it does not demonstrate a serious inability to practice the profession

- result in economic or physical harm to a person,

- or adversely affect the public health, safety, or welfare or create a significant threat of such harm.

- Failure of a licensee to take action in correcting the violation within 15 days after notice may result in the institution of regular disciplinary proceedings.

Notification

- When an investigation is undertaken, the DBPR forwards a copy of the complaint to the subject (notice exception for criminal violation).

- However, if there is concern that sending a notice would cause further harm, jeopardize the case, or is a criminal violation they are not required to send the notice

- A written response may be sent within 20 days that will be presented at the probable cause hearing.

Step 2: Investigation

DBPR conducts investigation

If the investigation reveals that the public is endangered, the DBPR or FREC may decide not to allow a licensee to continue to work **during** the disciplinary process.

- DBPR Secretary can issue a **summary suspension** (also called emergency suspension).

The Department of Business and Professional Regulation conducts investigations by taking depositions and gathering witness statements along with complaint facts. The person having had the complaint made against him or her may also be interviewed.

- Once completed, the Department submits an investigative report to the probable cause panel.

Step 3: Probable Cause

The determination of probable cause is the third step.

The DBPR issues an investigative report to the Probable-cause panel. The probable cause panel convenes to review the report.

Determination is made, by majority vote, as to whether probable cause exists:

- May dismiss the case or
- Dismiss with a letter of guidance
- Issue a Formal Complaint

Purpose is to determine whether probable cause exists

The purpose of the probable cause panel is to determine whether probable cause exists which is different than determining actual guilt. By not including all FREC members on the probable cause panel, they are able to operate like a "grand jury." The FREC members who do not sit on the probable cause panel are later in the position to be objective when hearing the case.

The panel reviews the facts of the case and then decides as to whether probable cause exists.

If probable cause is found, the DBPR (or the FREC) gives written notice to the licensee's broker.

If the panel finds that probable cause does not exist, the Department of Business and Professional Regulation is allowed to still file charges.

Or if the Department believes that the panel was unwise in deciding that probable cause existed, it may choose not to prosecute a complaint.

Composition of probable-cause panel

The probable cause panel is made up of (two) current FREC members or one current and one former FREC member.

The panel must include at least one professional member. If a former professional board member serves on the panel, the former commissioner must currently hold an active real estate license.

A consumer member, if available, may also serve on the probable cause panel.

61J1-1.009

Special Emphasis: Letter of guidance

A letter of guidance is a written reprimand. It is like a "slap on the hand" to let the licensee know that the behavior should not continue. A letter of guidance is only used for minor violations.

http://samaan-law.com/practice-areas/professional-license-defense/real-estate-license-defense/

www.floridarealtors.org/.../DBPR-Complaint-Processlegal-library-question

If probable cause is found, a formal/administrative complaint is filed

If the probable cause panel determines that probable cause does exist, the process continues with the issuance of a Formal Complaint which the DBPR files against the licensee.

http://samaan-law.com/practice-areas/professional-license-defense/real-estate-license-defense/

Special Emphasis: The probable cause panel has three options.

1. Dismiss the complaint - complaint remains confidential.

2. Issue a letter of guidance - which is a written reprimand and is also kept confidential.

3. Find probable cause and go forward with the case - becomes public 10 days after probable cause is found.

http://www.floridarealtors.org/LegalCenter/HotTopics/upload/DBPR-Complaint-Processlegal-library-question.docx

Step 4: Formal Complaint

The DBPR Files the Formal Complaint.

The DBPR outlines facts and charges against the licensee and sends a copy to the to the licensee's broker.

The respondent is entitled to an Election of Rights to choose how to have the case heard.

- Not dispute the allegations and waive the right to be heard

- Not dispute the allegations and request an informal hearing

- Dispute the allegations and request a formal hearing

http://samaan-law.com/practice-areas/professional-license-defense/real-estate-license-defense/

Stipulation

To avoid the hearing process completely, the licensee may agree to a stipulation.

Licensee-respondent can meet with a DRE attorney prior to a hearing to discuss a settlement called a Stipulation. A Stipulation is an agreement as to the facts of the case and the penalty reached. The Stipulation must be approved by FREC.

COMMISSION MEETING

II) Commission meeting (probable cause panel members are excused)

    A) Formal hearings are conducted by administrative law judges

        1) hears evidence

        2) makes findings of fact

        3) submits a recommended order to FREC

    B) FREC (probable cause members excused) consider the administrative law judge's report and recommended order and then issues a final order

        1) Summary/Emergency suspension order

    C) Judicial Review (appeal process)

        1) Stay of enforcement

        2) Writ of supersedeas

Step 5: Informal or Formal Hearing

Informal Hearing

An informal hearing is held if there are no disputed facts. The licensee presents information regarding the case to the FREC at a Commission meeting where the case is considered and possible penalty decided upon.

A formal hearing is required if the licensee is disputing the facts of the case. Instead of being heard by FREC, the case is heard by an administrative law judge who issues a Recommended Order to the FREC.

http://samaan-law.com/practice-areas/professional-license-defense/real-estate-license-defense/

Formal Hearing

When a licensee elects to dispute the material facts, the Department of Business and Professional Regulations arranges for the case to be heard by an Administrative Law Judge.

The Administrative Law Judge is assigned to hear the case by the Division of Administrative Hearings - Department of Management Services. The law judge assigned must be a member of the Florida Bar in good standing for the preceding five years.

Notice must be given to the parties charged. The notice must include: the date, time and place of the hearing; the jurisdiction and legal authority under which the hearing is to be held; and a list of the rules purported to be broken; a short summary of the case.

The licensee has the right to be represented by an attorney and to present evidence to support the licensee. Witnesses may also be called.

Step 6: Final Order

Once the Administrative Law Judge issues the Recommended Order, it is reviewed by FREC.

The FREC then issues the **Final Order,** which is a final decision as to innocence or guilt and penalty imposed. Don't confuse the Recommended Order given by the Administrative Law Judge with the Final Order decided by FREC. It is FREC that makes the final determination of penalty and action taken against the licensee not the Judge.

The FREC will issue a Final within 90 days of having received the Recommended Order.

The FREC may accept, modify or reject the Administrative Law Judge's Recommended Order and impose penalties at the FREC's discretion.

Penalties can include:

- Fines – Up to $5,000 for each offense

- License Suspension – Up to 10 years.

- License Revocation – Permanent loss of the ability to practice real estate in the state of Florida.

A licensee has 30 days to appeal a Final Order by filing a petition for judicial review or the Final Order becomes effective.

http://samaan-law.com/practice-areas/professional-license-defense/real-estate-license-defense/

Summary/Emergency Suspension Order

If during the early investigative process, the alleged facts, if true, puts the public's health, safety or welfare in jeopardy, the DBPR may impose a summary suspension ordering the licensee not to practice real estate until the case is resolved.

http://www.cram.com/flashcards/florida-real-estate-principles-chapter-6-review-questions-295580

Step 7: Judicial Review (Appeal)

A licensee may APPEAL the Final Order within 30 days. An appeal is filed with the DBPR and the district court. If the Final Order had included license suspension or revocation, the licensee may request a **stay of enforcement** to stop the enforcement of the suspension or revocation. To put a stay of enforcement in place, the court issues a **writ of supersedeas.**

This appeal must be made within 30 days to the District Court of Appeals.

Voluntary Relinquishment for Permanent Revocation

A licensee that has had a complaint filed against him or her can voluntarily surrender his or her real estate license. This is a permanent loss of the license meaning the licensee may never hold a real estate license in the state of Florida again. (Not the same thing as "Voluntary Relinquishment.)

Judicial Review

Step seven of the complaint process is that the licensee may appeal the FREC's decision.

If it was FREC's decision that the license be suspended or revoked, then the licensee can request a stay of enforcement from the courts to issue a writ of supersedeas which will allow the licensee to practice real estate while under appeal.

https://quizlet.com/44956540/unit-6-flash-cards/

III) Violations and Penalties

    A) The Florida Real Estate Commission is authorized to:

        1) Deny a license application

           a) Grounds for denial

        2) Refuse to renew a license

        3) Suspend a license up to 10 years

        4) Revoke a license

           a) Exceptions to permanent revocation

               (1) Filed for renewal without complying with the continuing or post licensing education requirement

               (2) Filed an application for licensure which contained false or fraudulent information

           b) Revoke without prejudice

        5) Issue citations

6) Impose a fine

    (a) Maximum $5,000 per violation of Chapter 455, F.S.

    (b) Maximum $5,000 per violation of Chapter 475, F.S.

7) Impose probation

8) Issue notice of noncompliance

9) Mediation

B) Violations and recommended penalties (see Disciplinary Guidelines, 61J2-24.001, F.A.C.)

C) Penalties that may be issued by a court of law

    1) Second degree misdemeanor

    2) First degree misdemeanor

        (a) Failing to provide accurate and current rental information for a fee

    3) Civil penalties

        (a) Denial and recovery of compensation

    4) Third degree felony

        (a) Unlicensed activity

            (1) Fine of not more than $5,000 and/or up to 5 years in jail

        (b) Falsifying an application

Types of Penalties

There are 3 types of penalties that can be imposed for violation of license law

<u>Administrative penalties</u>

- Issued by FREC
  - suspending a license
  - Imposing fines
  - Revoking licenses

<u>Civil penalties</u>

- Handled in court
  - Sue licensee for monetary damages

<u>Criminal penalties</u>

- Handled in court; the FREC notifies the state of criminal violations
  - The FREC does not have to power to imprison individuals!

Administrative Penalties

Per Florida Statutes 475, The Florida Real Estate Commission is authorized to:

- deny an application for licensure, registration, or permit, or renewal thereof;
- place a licensee, registrant, or permittee on probation;
- suspend a license, registration, or permit for a period not exceeding 10 years;
- revoke a license, registration, or permit;
- impose an administrative fine not to exceed $5,000 for each count or separate offense;
- issue a reprimand,
- all of the foregoing.

Denial of License:

If a license is denied, the DBPR mails a copy of the order to the applicant by registered or certified mail. The applicant has 21 days from date of receipt to request a hearing with the FREC to dispute the denial.

- The following reasons may be the basis for denial of a license:
  "Did not correct an error or omission on an application,
  Did not take the examination within two years from date of application,
  Did not pass the state exam or cheated on the exam,
  Did not prove qualifications for licensure,
  Has a reputation for bad business dealings or incompetence,
  Is being investigated by another state for an act that would be a violation of Florida law,
  Has committed an act in the previous year that could have resulted in discipline had the applicant been licensed at the time.
- Refusal to renew a license may be the following:
  Did not file the proper paperwork in a timely fashion,
  Did not pay the appropriate fee,
  Did not take the continuing education or post-license courses,
  Has a reputation for incompetent or bad business dealings,
  Is being investigated in another state for an act that would be a violation of Florida law,
  Has committed an act while licensed which resulted in discipline."

https://quizlet.com/44956540/unit-6-flash-cards/

Criminal History

Failure to disclose criminal history may be cause for denial or disciplinary action against your license.

An applicant may still be accepted for licensing even with a criminal history. Details of the criminal history must be included with the application. Include an explanation of the facts and how the applicant's life has changed since the infraction. Letters of recommendation are also helpful.

https://realtypronetwork.com/wp-content/uploads/2010/12/FREC-Licensing-FAQs.pdf

What do I need to submit with my application if I answer yes to one of the background questions?

Applicants must provide a written explanation supported by the following documents:

Copy of the arrest report, copies of the disposition or final order(s), and documentation proving all sanctions have been served and satisfied.

Applicants who are unable to supply the above state documents may supply a certified statement from the clerk of court stating the status of the records required.

If on probation, the applicant must supply a letter from the probation officer.

> https://realtypronetwork.com/wp-content/uploads/2010/12/FREC-Licensing-FAQs.pdf

Can I request that Florida Real Estate Commission reconsider the denial of my application?

If the applicant receives a "Notice of Intent to Deny", the applicant can:

1. Request an informal hearing to appear before the Florida Real Estate Commission, or

2. Request a formal hearing in front of an Administrative Law Judge

This is explained within the Election of Rights section of the Notice of Intent to Deny. The request for the hearing must be made within 21 days from the receipt of the notice.

The petition is mailed to: Division of Real Estate 400 West Robinson Street, Orlando Florida 32801

> https://realtypronetwork.com/wp-content/uploads/2010/12/FREC-Licensing-FAQs.pdf

I have been denied by the Florida Real Estate Commission twice what can I do? I still want to be licensed.

You still have the right to apply again.

> https://realtypronetwork.com/wp-content/uploads/2010/12/FREC-Licensing-FAQs.pdf

Special Emphasis: FREC has Authority to:

- Deny a license application
- Refuse to renew a license
- Suspend a license up to 10 years
- Revoke a license
- Impose an administrative fine
- Issue a reprimand

Revoke Without Prejudice

Per Florida Statutes 475.25, "a license may be revoked or canceled if it was issued through the mistake or inadvertence of the commission." The individual may reapply for a license.

Issuance of Citations

The DBPR/DRE has the authority to issue citations for minor violations. The licensee has 30 days to accept or reject the penalty. The penalty involved with a citation are fines from $100 to $500 per infraction. Additional education could also be placed on the licensee. See Administrative Code 61J2-24.02 for a complete list under Citation Authority.

Issuance of Fines

Per Florida Statutes 475.25, the FREC may impose an administrative fine not to exceed $5,000 for each count or separate offense.

Impose Probation

Per Administrative Code 61J2-24.006, the FREC may place the licensee on probation. Generally, probation will last 90 days with the probation period to begin 30 days after the filing of the final order.

Mediation

Per Administrative Code 61J2-24.004, Mediation may be appropriate to resolve an issue with a licensee when the matter is administrative in nature. Examples include the "Failure to maintain office or sign at entrance of office pursuant to Section 475.22, F.S." or the "Failure to register a branch office pursuant to Section 475.24, F.S." or having "Failed to deliver to a licensee a share of a real estate commission if the licensee has obtained a civil judgment and the judgment has not been satisfied pursuant to Section 475.25(1)(d), F.S."

Civil Penalties

If someone feels that they have been harmed by a licensee, they may sue the licensee in court and seek a civil remedy such as compensatory and punitive damages. This action may be taken in addition to or in place of reporting the licensee for administrative action.

Criminal Penalties for certain license law violations

A licensee may also face criminal penalties depending upon the nature of infraction. Criminal penalties range as follows:

Third degree felony	= $5000 fine and up to 5 years in prison
First degree misdemeanor	= $1000 fine and up to 1 year in prison
Second degree misdemeanor	= $500 fine and up to 60 days in jail

Criminal Violations Compared

The unlicensed practice of real estate (practicing real estate with a license resulting from a falsified application)

- Third Degree Felony

Selling a rental list that is inaccurate

- First Degree Misdemeanor

Just about every other violation you may be asked about

- Second Degree Misdemeanor

Violations and Penalties

Top 5 FREC Charging Statutes

VIOLATION	FLORIDA STATUTE
Emergency Suspension Order If the agency finds that immediate serious danger to the public health, safety or welfare...	Sections 455.225(8) and 120.60(6)
Making misleading, deceptive or fraudulent representations in or related to the practice of licensee's profession or employing a trick or scheme related to the practice of a profession	Sections 455.227(1)(a) and (m)
Guilty of Fraud, misrepresentation, concealment, false promises, false pretenses, dishonest dealings by trick scheme or device, culpable negligence, or breach of trust in any business transaction in this State	Section 475.25(1)(b)
Failed to keep and make available to the department such books, accounts, and records...	Section 475.5015
Obstruction or Hindering A person may not obstruct or hinder in any manner the enforcement of this chapter or the performance of any lawful duty by any person acting under the authority of this chapter	Section 475.42(1)(h)

http://www.myfloridalicense.com/dbpr/re/documents/DBPR_OGCPresentation.ppt

IV) Real Estate Recovery Fund

A) Applies to real estate brokerage transactions:

1) Involving Florida real estate

2) Involving a licensee under Chapter 475, F.S

3) Violating any part of Chapter 475, F.S.

B) Persons not qualified to make a claim

C) Payment for claims from the fund

D) Authorized fund limit and fees

Florida Real Estate Recovery Fund Explained

The Florida Real Estate Recovery Fund was designed specially to protect members of the public – also called consumer members. It was not designed to protect the licensee!

When someone in the public has been defrauded or suffered financial harm as the result of the actions of the licensee that is in violation of Florida Statute 475, the consumer member can be compensated from the real estate recovery fund. A judgment can be made against the licensee in court and the compensation is made from the fund only if the consumer member was unable to successfully collect the judgment from the licensee.

The consumer member can collect up to $50,000.00 for a single case of misconduct. However, only $150,000.00 will be paid out in total from the fund for the actions of one licensee.

The wrongdoing by the licensee results in immediate suspension of the licensee until the licensee has paid back the amount paid by the fund, plus interest.

The Recovery Fund can also be used to reimburse a consumer who won a court case against a broker who followed an Escrow Disbursement Order (EDO). In this case, the fund would pay the broker's costs and legal fees. Punitive damages will not be paid. In this case, the broker's license would not be suspended.

http://www.themiamilaw.com/blog/2014/11/florida-real-estate-recovery-fund/

F.S. 475.482

Special Emphasis

Only applies to real estate brokerage transactions. To collect from the real estate recovery fund, there must be a judgment for monetary damages against someone who is a Florida real estate licensee. The license must have been current and valid at the time of the incident.

How is the Real Estate Recovery Fund Funded?

The Real Estate Recovery Fund is funded by a fee of $3.50 added to the license fee of new and renewal broker's licenses, as well as a fee of $1.50 added to the license fee of new and renewal sales associate licenses.

In addition, all moneys collected from fines imposed and collected by the FREC are transferred to the RF.

https://view.officeapps.live.com/op/view.aspx?src=http%3A%2F%2Fwww.floridarealtors.org%2FLegalCenter%2FHotTopics%2Fupload%2FFREC-Real-Estate-Recovery-Fund-legal-library-question.docx

Collecting from the Fund

If a customer believes that they have been damaged by the actions of another licensee in Florida, the licensee should speak with an attorney concerning their claim.

https://view.officeapps.live.com/op/view.aspx?src=http%3A%2F%2Fwww.floridarealtors.org%2FLegalCenter%2FHotTopics%2Fupload%2FFREC-Real-Estate-Recovery-Fund-legal-library-question.docx

What Circumstances Allow Someone to Claim on the Recovery Fund?

If a legal person or entity has suffered monetary damages because of any act committed as part of a real estate brokerage transaction involving real property in Florida, a claim can be made against the fund – if also:

- The person the claim was made against was the holder of a current, valid, active real estate license; and

- The person the claim was made against was neither the seller, buyer, landlord, or tenant in the transaction; and

- There must have been some violation of Florida Statute 475.

The Real Estate Recovery Fund may be used to reimburse a broker or sales associate who lost a court case involving an Escrow Disbursement Order.

- However, no payment shall be made unless the broker or sales associate makes all the required statutory notifications under 475, and has defended the case against him or her in court.

https://view.officeapps.live.com/op/view.aspx?src=http%3A%2F%2Fwww.floridarealtors.org%2FLegalCenter%2FHotTopics%2Fupload%2FFREC-Real-Estate-Recovery-Fund-legal-library-question.docx

Limitations to Claims on the Fund:

If the person making the claim holds a valid real estate license, then a claim cannot be made against the fund.

If the person making the claim is also the spouse of the person that the judgment was against, then a claim cannot be made against the fund.

If the real estate licensee involved in the transaction was also the owner of the property involved, then a claim cannot be made against the fund.

If the person who the claim is against did not hold a valid real estate license at the time of the infraction, then a claim cannot be made against the fund.

If the judgment is against a real estate brokerage corporation, partnership, limited liability company, or limited liability partnership, then a claim cannot be made against the fund.

https://view.officeapps.live.com/op/view.aspx?src=http%3A%2F%2Fwww.floridarealtors.org%2FLegalCenter%2FHotTopics%2Fupload%2FFREC-Real-Estate-Recovery-Fund-legal-library-question.docx

Special Emphasis

The following individuals cannot make a claim to the Real Estate Recovery Fund:

1.   A licensee that participated in the subject transaction as an agent is not entitled to make a claim for an unpaid commission.

2.   A licensee that participated in the subject transaction as an agent and the licensee owned or controlled the subject property.

3.   Anyone that bases their claim against a licensee that did not hold a valid and current license at the time of the transaction.

4.   A spouse of the judgment debtor or the spouse's personal representative.

5.   If the judgment is against a business entity such as corporation, partnership, limited liability company or limited liability partnership.

http://activerain.com/blogsview/4473637/the-florida-real-estate-recovery-fund

Special Emphasis

The Real Estate Recovery Fund was created to compensate for compensatory damages when:

- A person won a civil lawsuit against a licensee.

- They attempted to collect a judgment against the licensee, but the licensee failed to pay.

The licensee's license will be **Mandatorily Suspended** upon payment from the fund unless payment was made because of an EDO, or escrow disbursement order.

The license of the licensee will not be reinstated until the fund has been repaid with interest.

Special Emphasis: Monetary Limits of Claims

Maximum amount paid from fund

- $50,000 per transaction

- $150,000 against one licensee total.

Court costs and attorney fees can be reimbursed as well as actual money lost.

Punitive damages, treble damages, and interest cannot be paid from the fund.

Special Emphasis: Claim Resulting from an EDO

When a broker is sued for complying with an EDO;

- No disciplinary action will be taken against the broker.

- The broker must notify the FREC of the court case and defend the EDO in court.

- FREC may reimburse broker reasonable attorney fees and court costs along with compensatory damages awarded to the claimant.

7 FEDERAL AND STATE LAWS PERTAINING TO REAL ESTATE

Learning Objectives:
- Explain the significance of the Jones vs. Mayer court case
- List the real estate included under the different fair housing acts
- Recognize the groups protected under the 1968 Fair Housing Act
- List the property exempt from the 1968 Fair Housing Act
- Understand the provisions of the 1988 Fair Housing Amendment
- Describe the types of discriminatory acts that are prohibited under the 1968 Fair Housing Act
- Describe the HUD process for handling a complaint under the 1968 Fair Housing Act
- Describe the objectives and major provisions of the Americans with Disabilities Act
- Describe the major provisions of the Florida Residential Landlord and Tenant Act
- Describe the major provisions of the Interstate Land Sales Disclosure Act

Key Terms:

blockbusting	property report	subdivided land
familial status	public accommodation	steering
handicap status	redlining	

FEDERAL LAWS

A)   Civil Rights Act of 1866
      1) Jones v. Mayer case
B)   Civil Rights Act of 1964
C)   Civil Rights Act of 1968
    1) Fair Housing Act of 1968 and amendments
        (a) Prohibits discrimination in sales, leasing, advertising sales or rentals, financing or brokerage services
        (b) Protection from discrimination based on race, color, religion, sex, national origin, handicap or familial status
            (1) Familial status defined
            (2) Handicap defined
        (c) Groups not covered
            (1) Marital status
            (2) Age
            (3) Occupation

        (d) Two categories of housing covered by the 1968 Fair Housing Act:

            (1) Single-family

            (2) Multifamily

        (e) Real estate transactions exempted under the Act

        (f) Acts prohibited:

            (1) Refusing to rent

            (2) Quoting different terms

            (3) Discriminatory advertising

            (4) Steering

            (5) Blockbusting

            (6) Redlining

            (7) Denying membership

            (8) False statements regarding availability

      (g) Housing for older persons

      (h) Equal housing opportunity poster

      (i) Enforcement of the Fair Housing laws

          (1) Complaints filed with HUD under the 1968 Fair Housing Act (as amended)

          (2) Civil suits filed in Federal district court

(3) Action taken by the Department of Justice

(j) Responsibility and liability of real estate licensees

D) Americans with Disabilities Act of 1990

    (1) Access to public transportation, public accommodation and commercial facilities

    (2) New construction and renovation of public accommodations and commercial facilities

E)   Interstate Land Sales Full Disclosure Act II

There are federal and state laws in place designed to protect the public regarding real estate and housing activities.

Civil Rights Act of 1866

Civil rights laws that affect real estate date back to 1866 when the Civil Rights Act of 1866 was passed. The act makes it illegal to discriminate in the sale or leasing of real estate (housing) based on race – without exception.

Fast forward to mid twentieth century when despite the existence of the 1866 law, discriminatory practices were still common place.

The Supreme Court upheld in the case *Jones v. Mayer* that the Civil Rights Act of 1866 made discrimination based on race unlawful. This is true whether within the public or private housing domain.

Jones v. Alfred H. Mayer Co.

- The Supreme Court case held that the **Civil Rights Act of 1866** prohibited both private and state-backed discrimination and that the 13th Amendment authorized Congress to prohibit private acts of discrimination against race.

                    https://en.wikipedia.org/wiki/Jones_v._Alfred_H._Mayer_Co.

Civil Rights Act of 1964

To further quell discrimination, the Civil Rights Act of 1964 was passed. (This act was not specific to housing.) The legislation was enacted July 2, 1964 outlawing discrimination based on race, color, religion, or national origin.

It ended unequal application of voter registration requirements and racial segregation in schools, at the workplace and by facilities that served the public.

                    https://en.wikipedia.org/wiki/Civil_Rights_Act_of_1964

Special Emphasis: Civil Rights Act of 1866

Ended housing discrimination based on race without exception.

Special Emphasis: Civil Rights Act of 1964

Ended racial segregation in schools, workplaces and public accommodations

Prohibits discrimination based on race, color, religion, or national origin in:

- Public accommodations such as hotels, restaurants, gas stations, places of entertainment
- Public facilities: government-run facilities

Civil Rights Act of 1968 – Fair Housing Act

Just four years after passing the Civil Rights act of 1964, The Civil Rights Act of 1968 was passed to follow-up the Civil Rights Act of 1964.

Considered a landmark part of U.S. legislation, Title VIII of the Civil Rights Act of 1968 provided for equal housing opportunities "regardless of race, creed, or national origin" and made it a federal crime to "by force or by threat of force, injure, intimidate, or interfere with anyone … due to their race, color, religion, or national origin."

Title VIII of the Civil Rights Act of 1968 is referred to as the Fair Housing Act, as it expanded the 1964 legislation to prohibit discrimination in the sale, rental, and financing of housing based on race, religion, national origin, and since the 1974 Amendment, gender; since the 1988 Amendments, the act protects people with disabilities and families with children.

The United States Department of Housing and Urban Development enforces the fair housing act.

https://en.wikipedia.org/wiki/Fair_Housing_Act

Special Emphasis: Title VIII of Civil Rights Act of 1968

Discrimination is illegal in sales, leasing, advertising sales or rentals, financing, or brokerage services if based on:

- Race
- Color
- Religion
- National origin

- Sex (as amended in 1974)
- Familial Status (as amended in 1988)
- Handicap Status (as amended in 1988)

Definition of Familial Status Protection

Protection from discrimination based on familial status means that under United States law **24 CFR 100.20**, one or more individuals (who have not attained the age of 18 years) living together cannot be discriminated against.

This includes:

(a) A parent or another person having legal custody of such individual or individuals; or

(b) The designee of such parent or other person having such custody, with the written permission of such parent or other person.

This protection extends to someone who is pregnant or in the process of getting custody.

http://www.fairhousing.com/index.cfm?method=page.display&pagename=regs_fhr_100-201

Definition of Handicap Status Protection

Protection from discrimination based on handicap status means that under the United States law 24 CFR 100.201, anyone with a physical or mental impairment, which substantially limits one or more major life activities, cannot be discriminated against.

Under CFR 100.21

a) Physical or mental impairment includes:

(1) Any physiological disorder or condition, cosmetic disfigurement, or anatomical loss affecting one or more of the following body systems: Neurological; musculoskeletal; special sense organs; respiratory, including speech organs; cardiovascular; reproductive; digestive; genitourinary; hemic and lymphatic; skin; and endocrine; or

(2) Any mental or psychological disorder, such as mental retardation, organic brain syndrome, emotional or mental illness, and specific learning disabilities. The term physical or mental impairment includes, but is not limited to, such diseases and conditions as orthopedic, visual, speech and hearing impairments, cerebral palsy, autism, epilepsy, muscular dystrophy, multiple sclerosis, cancer, heart disease, diabetes, Human Immunodeficiency Virus infection, mental retardation, emotional illness, drug addiction (other than addiction caused by current, illegal use of a controlled substance) and alcoholism.

(b) Major life activities mean functions such as caring for one's self, performing manual tasks, walking, seeing, hearing, speaking, breathing, learning and working.

(c) Has a record of such an impairment means has a history of, or has been misclassified as having, a mental or physical impairment that substantially limits one or more major life activities.

(d) Is regarded as having an impairment means:

(1) Has a physical or mental impairment that does not substantially limit one or more major life activity but that is treated by another person as constituting such a limitation;

(2) Has a physical or mental impairment that substantially limits one or more major life activity only because of the attitudes of other toward such impairment; or

(3) Has none of the impairments defined in paragraph (a) of this definition but is treated by another person as having such an impairment.

http://www.fairhousing.com/index.cfm?method=page.display&pagena

Special Emphasis: Fair Housing Act Amendment in 1988 Added Protection

Familial status

- Families with children under 18 and pregnant women

Handicap status

- Any physical or mental impairment that interferes with normal life functioning

- Includes persons recovering from alcoholism and drug addiction

Special Emphasis: Fair Housing Act

Remember all the protected classes are:

- Race
- Color
- Sex
- Religion
- National origin
- Familial Status
- Disability

Fair Housing Act: Groups NOT Covered

Under the Fair Housing Act, there is no protection for age, occupation, marital status, sexual orientation. *However, many State and local laws add additional protected classes such as these.*

(1) Marital status

(2) Age

(3) Occupation; source of income

(4) Sexual Orientation

There are two categories of housing covered by the 1968 Fair Housing Act:

(1) Single-family

(2) Multifamily

Complying with Fair Housing

If it is a **Single-family house** and

- Government owned housing or

- Privately owned if real estate agent is employed to sell or rent it or

- Property owned by person who owns four or more residential properties total or

- If someone has sold two or more houses (not owner-occupied) in the past 2 years

... *then requires compliance with the act.*

If it is **Multifamily/unit housing** and

- Has Five (5) or more units or

- Has Four (4) or fewer units (when the owner doesn't live in one of the units)

... *then requires compliance with the act.*

Fair Housing Act

Real estate transactions exempt under the Act

Who does NOT have to comply with Fair Housing Act?

- If the seller owns three or fewer single-family dwellings or

- If the seller was not living in the house and was not the most recent resident when the property was sold or rented, still allowed one exempt sale within a 24-month period or

- For rentals in multifamily dwellings with four or fewer family units when the owner lives in one of the units or

- In 55 and up housing communities officially registered as such (age exemption only)

... then exempt from Fair Housing ACT if ALSO a real estate agent was not involved in the sale or lease and there was no discriminatory advertising involved.

Fair Housing Act

Real estate transactions exempt under the Act

Housing operated by religious organizations and private clubs

Sometimes clubs and churches will offer housing exclusively to their members. This is legal under limited circumstances.

- Religious organizations may restrict units to members of their religion **provided** they do not discriminate in accepting membership.

- Private clubs may restrict units to its members **provided** they do not discriminate in accepting membership.

Special Emphasis: Fair Housing Act - Real estate transactions exempted under the Act

Know that Exemptions apply only under two additional conditions

- A real estate licensee is not involved

- There is no discriminatory advertising!

Fair Housing Act - Acts Prohibited

(1) Refusing to rent

(2) Quoting different terms

(3) Discriminatory advertising

(4) Steering

(5) Blockbusting

(6) Redlining

(7) Denying membership

(8) False statements regarding availability

Fair Housing Act

Under the Fair Housing Act, it is unlawful to refuse to rent, sell, negotiate with, or deal with a member of a protected class. It is also unlawful to quote different terms, conditions or privileges for buying or renting. For example, it is unlawful to tell a Caucasian man that a home rents for $1,800 a month while telling a woman with children that the same home rents for $2,400 a month.

It is absolutely unlawful to advertise that housing is available only to people of a certain race, color, sex, religion, national origin, handicap status, or familial status. For example, it would be unlawful to advertise "only adults with no children may apply."

It is unlawful to steer a group of people away or toward housing based on being a member in a protected class. In addition, it is unlawful to "bust up a block" by scaring owners into selling by telling them that members of a protected class would move into the area and drive down prices. It is also unlawful to deny loans and insurance services based on being a member of a protected class.

It is unlawful to deny membership or use of any real estate service based on a protected class. It is also unlawful to make false statements concerning availability of housing for inspection, rent, or sale. For example, it is unlawful to tell someone that the home is no longer for rent to deny housing to the person.

Discriminatory Advertising

As clarified by the U.S. Department of Housing and Urban Development, "it is unlawful to make, print, or publish any statement, about the sale or rental of a dwelling, that indicates a preference, limitation, or discrimination based on race, color, religion, gender, disability, familial status, or national origin."

http://portal.hud.gov/hudportal/HUD?src=/program_offices/fair_housing_equal_opp/HousingProviders#E

Steering

It is unlawful to steer a group of people away or toward housing based on being a member in a protected class.

http://legal-dictionary.thefreedictionary.com/Steering

Blockbusting

Convincing owners to sell property cheaply by scaring them that the property will lose value due to members of a protected group moving into the neighborhood, and thus profiting by reselling at a higher price.

https://en.wikipedia.org/wiki/Blockbusting

Redlining

When lenders and insurance companies refuse services based on an area being made up of a high concentration of a protected group.

http://homebuying.about.com/od/glossaryqr/g/053107Redlining.htm

Denying Membership

Deny anyone access to or membership in a facility or service due to being a member of a protected class when the membership is related to the sale or rental of housing – such as being able to join a multiple listing service or real estate association.

False Statements Regarding Availability

Falsely claim that housing is no longer available for inspection, sale, or rental in order to avoid selling or renting to a member of a protected class.

Housing for Older Persons Act of 1995

The question becomes, then, that if the Fair Housing Act prohibits discrimination based on familial status, how are certain communities able to insist that residents must be 55 years of age or older to live there?

The answer is that a specific amendment to the Fair Housing Act was passed to address this issue.

The act was amended by defining "housing for older persons" as being exempt from the law for housing intended and operated for occupancy by persons 55 years of age or older, and--

- (i) at least 80 percent of the occupied units are occupied by at least one person who is 55 years of age or older

- (ii) the housing facility or community publishes and adheres to policies and procedures that demonstrate the intent required under this subparagraph; and

- (iii) the housing facility or community complies with rules issued by the Secretary for verification of occupancy, which shall--

- (iv) provide for verification by reliable surveys and affidavits; and

- (v) include examples of the types of policies and procedures relevant to a determination of compliance with the requirement of clause (ii). Such surveys and

Because of the amendment, it is legal for communities to market themselves as "55+" or "age-restricted." For the exemption to apply, they must maintain that 80 percent of the occupied units are occupied by at least one person who is 55 years of age or older. By letting the number fall below 80 percent, they could lose the status as an age-restricted community.

Public Law 104–76 104th Congress

Special Emphasis: Fair Housing Act Housing for Older Persons - Exempt from The Familial Status Protection Provided

- All units are occupied by persons 62 or older; or

- At least 80% of the units are occupied by one or more persons 55 or older

Fair Housing Posters

The Fair Housing Act combined with regulation through The U.S. Department of Housing and Urban Development (HUD) requires that a Fair Housing Poster be displayed per 24 CFR, part 110. As such:

- Owners and managers are required to display a fair housing poster with its logo at rental offices. This applies to rentals covered by the federal Fair Housing Act, and to dwellings rented through a real estate broker/agent. See 24 C.F.R. §§ 110.1 – 110.30.

- If a single-family dwelling is offered for sale or rental through a real estate broker, agent, salesman, or person in the business of selling or renting dwellings, such person must post and maintain a fair housing poster at any place of business where the dwelling is offered for sale or rental. 24 C.F.R. § 110.10(a)(1).

- Any place of business where the dwelling is offered for sale or rental, and

- The dwelling itself (may be in a model home rather than at each of the individual dwellings). 24 C.F.R. § 110.10(a)(2).

- With respect to new construction, the fair housing poster must be posted at the beginning of construction and maintained throughout the period of construction and sale or rental. 24 C.F.R. § 110.10(a)(3).

- HUD does not require the posting and maintaining of a fair housing poster on vacant land. 24 C.F.R. § 110.10(b)(1).

- All real estate brokers and agents must post and maintain a fair housing poster at all their places of business. 24 C.F.R. § 110.10(c).

Location of Posters

All fair housing posters must be prominently displayed "to be readily apparent to all persons seeking housing accommodations or seeking to engage in residential real estate-related transactions or brokerage services." C.F.R. § 110.15.

Availability of Posters

Fair housing posters can be obtained from HUD's regional and area offices or through the following HUD website:

http://portal.hud.gov/hudportal/HUD?src=/program_offices/fair_housing_equal_opp/marketing

Failure to Display Poster

Failure to display the fair housing poster as required by this part shall be deemed prima facie evidence of a discriminatory housing practice. 24 C.F.R. § 110.30

Enforcement of the Fair Housing laws

(1) **Complaints filed with HUD under the 1968 Fair Housing Act** (as amended)

(2) **Civil suits filed in Federal district court**

(3) **Action taken by the Department of Justice**

Fair Housing Complaint Process

When Fair Housing Rights have been violated, the aggrieved person can file a complaint with HUD. The following eight step process has been outlined by the U.S. Department of Housing and Urban Development and is out lined on their website at:

http://portal.hud.gov/hudportal/HUD?src=/program_offices/fair_housing_equal_opp/complaint-process

Step 1 - Intake

Anyone can file a complaint with the HUD at no cost. Fair housing complaints can be filed by any entity, including individuals and community groups. Those that file fair housing complaints are known as complainants. Those against whom fair housing complaints are filed are called respondents. The agency must begin to work with the complainant within 30 days, or the HUD can take the complaint back.

Step 2 - Filing

Within 10 days after receipt of a signed complaint, the HUD will send the respondent notice that a fair housing complaint has been filed against him or her along with a copy of the complaint. At the same time, the HUD will send the complainant an acknowledgement letter and a copy of the complaint. Within 10 days of receiving the notice, the Respondent must submit an answer to the complaint to the HUD.

Step 3 – Investigation

As part of the investigation, the HUD will interview the complainant, the respondent, and pertinent witnesses.

Step 4 - Conciliation

The Fair Housing Act requires the HUD to bring the parties together to attempt conciliation in every fair housing complaint. The choice to conciliate the complaint is completely voluntary on the part of both parties.

Step 5 - No Cause Determination

If, after a thorough investigation, the HUD finds no reasonable cause to believe that housing discrimination has occurred or is about to occur, the HUD will issue a determination of "no reasonable cause" and close the case.

Step 6 - Cause Determination and Charge

If the investigation produces reasonable cause to believe that discrimination has occurred or is about to occur, HUD will issue a determination of "reasonable cause" and charge the respondent with violating the law. HUD will send a copy of the charge to the parties in the case. After HUD issues a charge, an HUD Administrative Law Judge (ALJ) will hear the case unless either party elects to have the case heard in federal civil court. Parties must elect within 20 days of receipt of the charge.

Step 7 - Hearing in a U.S. District Court

Within 30 days after either party elects to go to federal court, DOJ will commence a civil action on behalf of the aggrieved person in U.S. district court. If the court finds that a discriminatory housing practice has or is about to occur, the court can award actual and punitive damages as well as attorney's fees.

Step 8 - Hearing before an HUD ALJ

If neither party elects, an HUD ALJ will hear the case. An attorney from the HUD will represent the aggrieved party before the ALJ. Within 15 days of the issuance of the ALJ's initial decision, any party adversely affected by the ALJ's initial decision can petition the Secretary of the HUD for review. The Secretary of the HUD has 30 days after the initial decision to affirm, modify, or set aside the ALJ's initial decision, or remand the initial decision for further proceedings. Any party aggrieved by the Department's final decision can appeal to the appropriate court of appeals.

Civil Suits Filed in Federal District Court

In addition to filing a complaint with the U.S. Housing and Urban Development, a person could file a civil lawsuit in federal court. The lawsuit must be filed within two years after the discriminatory act occurred or ended, or after a conciliation agreement was breached, whichever occurs last. This lawsuit can be filed even if a complaint had been filed with the HUD, provided that an Administrative Law Judge has not yet begun a hearing.

The judge will decide as to relief and damages including actual and punitive damages, attorney fees and temporary or permanent injunctions. When the facts of the lawsuit seem significant, the U.S. Attorney General may step in and declare that involvement is warranted due to public importance.

http://www.peoples-law.org/laws-against-housing-discrimination#sthash.FkXHwMhM.dpuf

Action Taken by the Department of Justice

Under the Fair Housing Act, the Department of Justice may bring lawsuits, where there is reason to believe that a person or entity is engaged in a "pattern or practice" of discrimination. This means that there doesn't have to be a complaint made by an individual for an investigation to begin. If there is evidence of "force or threat" then the Department of Justice may also pursue criminal proceedings.

http://civilrights.uslegal.com/the-fair-housing-act/#sthash.En2zL5Ux.dpuf

Responsibility and Liability of Real Estate Licensee

Any real estate licensee assisting in a real estate transaction IS prohibited by law from discriminating based on race, color, religion, sex, handicap, familial status, or national origin.

Know that if a home seller or landlord requests that a licensee act in a discriminatory manner in the sale, lease or rental – THE LICENSEE MUST NOT DO SO!

http://www.realtor.org/programs/fair-housing-program/what-everyone-should-know-about-equal-opportunity-housing

D) Americans with Disabilities Act of 1990

(1) Access to public transportation, public accommodation and commercial facilities

(2) New construction and renovation of public accommodations and commercial facilities

The American with Disabilities Act of 1990 applies to real estate dealings as well as the Fair Housing Act which prohibits discrimination against individuals with disabilities.

The Americans with Disabilities Act - An Overview

The Americans with Disabilities Act (ADA) became U.S. law on July 26, 1990.

The purpose of the act is to make society more accessible to people with disabilities.

Amendments were passed to the Act in 2008 (ADAAA) to broaden the definition of disability.

Title 1 of the ADA applies specifically to employment (including real estate brokerages). It requires covered employers to provide "reasonable accommodations for applicants and employees with disabilities and prohibits discrimination based on disability in all aspects of employment."

Reasonable accommodation includes things like making adjustments to work-sites to accommodate the individual.

Federal laws define a person with a disability as "any person who has a physical or mental impairment that substantially limits one or more major life activities; has a record of such impairment; or is regarded as having such an impairment."

- In general, a physical or mental impairment includes hearing, mobility and visual impairments, chronic alcoholism, chronic mental illness, AIDS, AIDS Related Complex, and mental retardation that substantially limits one or more major life activities. Major life activities include walking, talking, hearing, seeing, breathing, learning, performing manual tasks, and caring for oneself.

http://askjan.org/links/adasummary.htm

Special Emphasis: Americans with Disabilities Act Continued

The ADA is a wide-ranging civil rights law that is intended to protect against discrimination based on disability.

The law provides similar protections as does the Civil Rights Act of 1964 which made discrimination based handicap status illegal.

Unlike the Civil Rights Act, though, the ADA also requires covered employers to provide reasonable accommodations to employees with disabilities, and imposes accessibility requirements on public accommodations.

Private and Public – Reasonable Accommodations

The ADA requires reasonable accommodations as necessary to suit the needs of the person with the disability. This includes changes in rules, policies, practices, or services to accommodate the person. Reasonable accommodations may be necessary in the housing itself or in the process of providing housing such as in how an application is taken.

http://portal.hud.gov/hudportal/HUD?src=/program_offices/fair_housing_equal_opp/disabilities/inhousing

Private and Public - Reasonable Modifications

Federal law requires that reasonable modifications must be allowed to alter housing to suit a person with a disability. This applies to private as well as public housing. However, these modifications are to be made at the resident's expense.

Examples:

- Installing an entrance ramp

- lowering the entry threshold

- or installing grab bars in a bathroom.

Multi-family Housing

The law further requires that "covered" housing built and ready for occupancy after March 13, 1991 must follow design requirements to ensure that housing is accessible to persons with disabilities. Per the HUD website, "these requirements apply to most public and private housing. However, there are limited exemptions for owner-occupied buildings with no more than four units, single-family housing sold or rented without the use of a broker, and housing operated by organizations and private clubs that limit occupancy to members."

These requirements apply to multi-family housing consisting of 4 or more units *with an elevator.*

1. Accessible Entrance on an Accessible Route

2. Accessible Public and Common-Use Areas

3. Usable Doors

4. Accessible Route into and Through the Dwelling Unit

5. Accessible Light Switches, Electrical Outlets, Thermostats, and Environmental Controls

6. Reinforced Walls in Bathrooms

7. Usable Kitchens and Bathrooms

For multi-family housing consisting of 4 or more units *without an elevator*, all ground floor units must comply with the seven design requirements noted above.

Special Emphasis: Americans With Disabilities Act (ADA)

Protects employment and **accessibility** rights of individuals with mental and physical disabilities.

Disabled cannot be denied access to public transportations, public accommodations, and commercial facilities.

Includes real estate brokerage offices even if located in a private residence.

- Modifications may be required if readily achievable.

Florida Americans With Disabilities Implementation Act

- Mirrors the ADA standards and places design guideline on new construction per F.S. 553.

Special Emphasis: New Construction

The **new construction** requirements of the **Fair Housing Act** apply if a building with four or more units was ready to live in after March 13, 1991:

- Public and common areas must be accessible to individuals with disabilities.
- Doors and hallways must be wide enough for wheelchairs.

Each unit must have:

- An accessible route into and through the unit,
- Accessible light switches, electrical outlets, thermostats and other environmental controls,
- Reinforced bathroom walls to allow later installation of grab bars, and
- Kitchens and bathrooms that can be used by people who use wheelchairs.
- If there is an **elevator**, the requirements apply to every floor and every unit.
- If there is not an elevator, the requirements only apply to ground floor units.

http://disabilityrightsflorida.org/resources/disability_topic_info/fair_housing_act

Special Emphasis: Reasonable Accommodations

A **reasonable accommodation** is a change, exception, adaptation or modification to a **policy, program or service** that allows a person with a disability to use and enjoy a dwelling. The term also applies to public and common use spaces.

The **Fair Housing Act** requires owners and landlords to make reasonable accommodations if the accommodation is necessary to ensure that a person with a disability has equal opportunity to use and enjoy the dwelling or space.

What are some examples of reasonable accommodations?

- Allowing a person with a disability to mail the rent instead of delivering it to the office;
- Assigning a parking space closest to the exit or unit to tenants with mobility disabilities;
- Allowing persons with disabilities to keep service or quality of life animals, despite a general "no pets" policy;
- Not counting a home health aide, therapist, nurse, etc. as an additional tenant or guest;
- Allowing a tenant to move to a more suitable unit when one becomes available;
- Releasing a tenant with disabilities, who must move because of his/her disability, from lease requirements.

http://disabilityrightsflorida.org/resources/disability_topic_info/fair_housing_act

Special Emphasis: Reasonable Modifications

A **reasonable modification** is a physical change made to a tenant or owner's living space or to a common area that is necessary to ensure that the tenant or owner who has a disability has full enjoyment of the dwelling or space. Modifications are usually made **at the tenant's or owner's expense**, except in the case of federally funded housing.

The **Fair Housing Act** requires owners and landlords to allow the reasonable modification of a living space of a person with a disability, if the modification is necessary to ensure full enjoyment.

What are some examples of reasonable modifications?

- Building ramps over steps to allow wheelchair access;
- Installing lever door openers instead of knob openers;
- Widening door openings by installing swing-away hinges or wider pocket doors;
- Installing grab bars and hand rails;
- Installing wheelchair accessible shower stalls;
- Changing tub faucets to an off-set location;
- Removing under-the-sink cupboards in bathrooms;
- Lowering light switches.

Funds are often available to assist individuals to pay for modifications. Check with both your area Center for Independent Living and your city and county government to request financial assistance paying for a modification.

http://disabilityrightsflorida.org/resources/disability_topic_info/fair_housing_act

Interstate Land Sales Full Disclosure Act (ILSA)

The Interstate Land Sales Full Disclosure Act was passed by Congress in 1968 to protect consumers from risk of fraud when purchasing or leasing land.

Land developers must register developments of 100 or more lots with the Consumer Financial Protection Bureau (CFPB). For developments of 25 or more lots, the developer must give purchasers Property Report prior to the buyer signing the purchase agreement.

The Property Report is a disclosure that details information about the subdivision.

Developers who fail to comply with the disclosure requirements risk the buyers rescinding the contract.

https://en.wikipedia.org/wiki/Interstate_Land_Sales_Full_Disclosure_Act_of_1968

Special Emphasis: Property Report

A summary of facts about undeveloped land that must be given to purchasers when 25 or more lots are being developed per the Interstate Land Sales Full Disclosure Act.

The Complete Real Estate Encyclopedia by Denise L. Evans, JD & O. William Evans, JD. Copyright © 2007 by The McGraw-Hill Companies, Inc. http://financial-dictionary.thefreedictionary.com/property+report

Special Emphasis: Subdivided land

The Interstate Sales Full Disclosure Act was designed to protect buyers of land that have been subdivided.

http://www.propertywords.com/Subdivided_Land_Law.html

Special Emphasis: The Interstate Land Sales Full Disclosure Act (ILSA)

- Created to protect consumers from fraud.

- Federal law that regulates sale or lease of land.

- Administered by Consumer Financial Protection Bureau (CFPB).

- Developers must register developments (100 and more lots) and disclose to prospects facts regarding the real estate, and provide prospective purchasers a property report (25 and more lots) prior to the buyer signing a purchase agreement.

- Pertains to any development being advertised across state lines.

State Laws

A) Florida Fair Housing Law

B) Florida Americans with Disabilities Accessibility Implementation Act

C) Florida Residential Landlord and Tenant Act

    (1) Overview of the law

    (2) Deposits and advance rents

    (3) Landlord's obligation to maintain premises

    (4) Tenant's obligations

    (5) Landlord's access to premises

    (6) Vacating premises

    (7) Termination of rental agreements by the tenant

(8) Termination of rental agreements by the landlord

(9) Eviction procedure

Florida Fair Housing Law

Florida's Fair Housing Law protects the same 7 classes as the federal fair housing law.

Prohibits:

- Refuse to rent or sell housing.

- Falsely deny that housing is available for inspection, rental, or sale.

- Refuse to make a mortgage loan.

- Impose different conditions or terms on a loan.

- Threaten, coerce, or intimidate any individual exercising a fair housing right.

- Refuse reasonable changes to a dwelling to accommodate a disability.

Florida Fair Housing Law

The Florida Fair Housing Act makes it illegal to discriminate in the sale, rental, advertising, financing, or providing of brokerage services for housing.

- The Fair Housing Act parallels the Federal Fair Housing Act.

- The Florida laws do not add any additional covered groups or classes of people.

http://fchr.state.fl.us/resources/the_laws/florida_fair_housing_laws

Chapter 760 of the Florida Statutes

Real estate licensees violate law if the licensee coerces a homeowner to sell or rent with discriminatory intent.

Florida Americans with Disabilities Accessibility Implementation Act Housing

http://fchr.state.fl.us/fchr/complaints__1/housing

Florida Americans with Disabilities Accessibility Implementation Act

Passed in 1993 by Florida Statutes to adopt accessibility requirements of the Americans with Disabilities Act of 1990, Public Law No. 101-336, 42 U.S.C. Section 12101 et. seq. ADA. Florida laws.

http://publiccodes.cyberregs.com/st/fl/st/b200v07/st_fl_st_b200v07_11_sec001.htm

Florida Residential Landlord and Tenant Act - Overview of the law

Regardless of whether a rental property is being managed by a real estate brokerage property manager or the owner handling the property him or herself, there are landlord and tenant laws that must be followed per Florida Statutes Chapter 83, Part II.

Florida's Landlord/Tenant Law Summary of Chapter 83, Part II - Florida Statutes

http://www.freshfromflorida.com/Divisions-Offices/Consumer-Services/Consumer-Resources/Consumer-Protection/Publications/Landlord-Tenant-Law-in-Florida

Overview of the Law

The purpose of Florida's landlord and tenant laws is to try to place landlords and tenants in an equitable legal basis.

Landlord tenant laws apply to rental of residential dwelling units.

- Not renting of mobile home lots.

- Not commercial properties.

F.S. 83.40-49

Landlord must account for deposits and advance rents

When the landlord is holding the deposit without the use of a property manager, the landlord must choose one of the following methods to hold security deposits;

- Hold money in a separate noninterest-bearing Florida bank account for the benefit of tenant.

- Hold money in a separate interest-bearing Florida bank account, and pay the tenant at least 75% interest or 5% per year simple interest.

- Post a bond for amount of security deposits and advance rents or $50,000 (whichever is less) and pay tenant 5% per year simple interest.

How the money is being kept must be disclosed to the tenant.

The landlord must provide written notice to tenant within 30 days of collecting deposit as to which method was chosen.

Landlord's Obligation to Maintain Premises

Landlords must comply with the requirements of building, housing, and health codes in the maintenance of property including:

- Maintenance of the roof, windows, screens, floors, steps, porches, exterior walls, foundations and structural components and keep the plumbing in reasonably good working condition.

http://www.flarent.com/Landlord_tenant_law.pdf

According to the state statute as detailed in the brochure **Florida's Landlord/Tenant Law Information** developed by the Florida Department of Agriculture & Consumer Service, landlords are obligated to:

- Provide for extermination;
- Provide locks and keys;
- Provide heat during winter;
- Provide running water and hot water;

- Provide clean and safe conditions of common areas;
- Provide a smoke detection device; and
- Provide garbage removal and outside receptacles.

http://www.flarent.com/Landlord_tenant_law.pdf

Tenant's Obligation to Maintain Premises

According to the brochure **Florida's Landlord/Tenant Law Information** developed by the Florida Department of Agriculture & Consumer Service, tenants are obligated to:

A tenant, at all times during the tenancy shall:

- Comply with all building, housing and health codes;
- Keep the dwelling clean and sanitary;
- Remove garbage from the dwelling in a clean and sanitary manner;
- Keep plumbing fixtures clean, sanitary and in repair;
- Not destroy, deface, damage, impair or remove any part of the premises or property belonging to the landlord, nor permit any person to do so;
- Conduct him/herself, and require other persons on the premises with his/her consent to conduct themselves, in a manner that does not unreasonably disturb the tenant's neighbors or constitute a breach of the peace;
- Use and operate in a reasonable manner all electrical, plumbing, sanitary, heating, ventilating, air-conditioning and other facilities and appliances, including elevators.

http://www.flarent.com/Landlord_tenant_law.pdf

Special Emphasis: Obligations to Maintain Premises

Landlord

- Meets health and building codes

- Working heat and running hot water

- Insect extermination, garbage receptacles and pickup

- Working smoke detectors

Tenant

- Meets health and building codes

- Use reasonable care in operation of equipment

- Not disturb peace of others

Landlord's Access to Premises

Tenants cannot withhold permission for a landlord to enter the premises without cause.

Special Emphasis: Landlord's Access to Premises

Tenant must allow landlord to enter property to make inspections, provide services, make repairs, and to show property.

- Landlord may enter property at any time in case of emergency
- Otherwise, obligated to give tenant reasonable notice (at least 12 hours).

Vacating Premises

Ending a lease can be frustrating for either the landlord or tenants. It is common for there to be disputes as to who has rights to security deposits. By law, each has rights and responsibilities to help guide and settle the disputes.

Leases are written with lease provisions which specifically address the ending lease process.

In addition to statutes regarding tenant and landlord laws, the lease itself, may have requirements that go above and beyond the law.

For example, the lease can increase the time required to give notice of lease termination.

> When Vacating a Lease. SFGate. January 2016. http://homeguides.sfgate.com/tenant-landlord-responsibilities-vacating-lease-64370.html

Appropriate Notice

- Yearly Lease Termination – Either party must give notice no less than 60 days prior to the end of any annual period. This is per Florida Statute 83.57(1).

- Quarterly Lease Termination – Either party must give notice of no less than 30 days prior to the end of any quarterly period. This is per Florida Statute 83.57(2).

- Monthly Lease Termination – Either party must give notice of no less than 15 days prior to the end of any monthly period. This is per Florida Statute 83.57(3).

- Weekly Lease Termination - Either party must give notice of no less than 7 days prior to the end of any weekly period. This is per Florida Statute 83.57(4).

- A Landlord may terminate a lease for nonpayment of rent with only 3 days' notice (business days excluding Saturday, Sunday, and legal holidays). This is per Florida Statute 83.56(3).

- Either party may terminate a lease if the other party is not living up to the terms of the lease, (such as maintaining sanitary conditions) by giving the other Notice of the Violation and a 7-day opportunity to correct the situation. This is per Florida Statutes 83.56(2).

- Landlord must give notice before entering the property; 12 hours- unless an emergency. This is per Florida Statutes 83.53(2).

Hall, Lucas. Landlordology. January 2016 https://www.landlordology.com/florida-landlord-tenant-laws/

Vacating Premises

When landlord is holding a security deposit, the landlord must:

- Return the deposit to tenant within 15 days if no claim is to be made, or

- Send written notice by certified mail within 30 days if claim is made on the deposit.

- Tenant allowed 15 days to respond to landlord's written claim.

- Disputes are handled in civil court.

Breaking a Lease in Florida - Tenants

Marcia Stewart, a Nolo editor and author of tenant rights since 1989, has noted that at times it is justifiable for a tenant to break a lease in Florida.

Regarding:

Military Duty

- Anyone who enters the military after having signed a lease may break the lease due to military duty taking the person out of the area.

Unsafe Housing Conditions

- To legally vacate based on condition, the tenant must have given the tenant notice to make corrections. The problem must be "truly serious, such as the lack of heat or other essential service."

Violation of Your Privacy Rights

- Landlords who fail to follow notice requirements about entry into the property are violating the law, and the tenant may pursue canceling the contract per Florida Statute.

Steward, Marcia. Tenant's Right to Break a Rental Lease in Florida. NOLO. January 2016. http://www.nolo.com/legal-encyclopedia/tenants-right-break-rental-lease-florida.html

Special Emphasis: Termination of Rental Agreement by Tenant

If the landlord fails to maintain the property, the tenant may give a 7-day written notice of intent to cancel the lease.

- Gives landlord this time to make corrections

- Notice must be given in writing and delivered

  - Personally or

  - Mailed.

Termination of Rental Agreement by Landlord

If the tenant fails to comply with agreement, a 7-day written notice must be given to the tenant.

However, if it is for reason of non-payment of rent, then only a 3-business-day written notice need be given.

The notice must be delivered:

- Personally or

- Mailed or

- Posted on door.

Eviction in Florida:

There are 4 steps that must be taken to complete an eviction process.

1. Serving the Eviction Notice (3-Day or 7-Day)

2. Filing a Complaint and Summons

3. Going to Court

4. Writ of Possession

3-Day Notice or 7-Day Notice

To evict a tenant for non-payment of rent, the landlord uses the 3-Day Notice. Otherwise, the landlord should use the 7-Day Notice.

The notice must be "delivered" in writing – either through the mail, in person, or by posting on the door.

If after the notice period, the tenant is still there, then the landlord would file a "complaint" with the County Clerk.

Complaint and Summons

Once the landlord files the complaint, the Clerk of the Court issues a summons to the tenant. The summons gives the tenant notice that he or she is being sued for eviction. The summons must be served to the tenant.

Going to Court

Following the summons having been served, the tenant will have 5 days to file an objection to the summons. If an objection is filed, then the matter will be heard in court.

Writ of Possession

Once the judge has ruled in the landlord's favor, the clerk of the court will issue a Writ of Possession to be served by the sheriff to the tenant.

The Tenant will then have 24 hours to vacate the premises.

Evictionresources.com January 2016.

http://www.evictionresources.com/eviction_process_articles/florida_eviction_process.html

Special Emphasis: Eviction Requirements

- Notify tenant in writing (3-business-day or 7-day)

- After time period is up, file complaint for eviction

- Tenant has 5 business days to respond to complaint

- If tenant continues to occupy without responding, obtain final judgment from court

- Post 24-hour notice

- Sheriff signs writ of possession.

Broker Property Management

Recall, that there are specific laws that a landlord must follow regarding how the landlord can hold the tenants' advance rents and security deposits.

These rules regarding escrow accounts changes when the money is being held by a broker who is functioning as the property manager.

If a broker holds the funds on behalf of the landlord, then the broker follows license law regarding escrow funds.

All deposits and advance rents are treated as trust funds, and must be deposited into the broker's escrow.

Although, it is best to open a separate escrow for property management, it is not required. Therefore, the broker could put the money in the sales escrow account.

Escrow accounts held for property management may have up to $5,000 of the broker's personal or business funds to maintain the account.

All licensees must deliver rent and rental deposits to broker by end of next business day with the broker making the deposit by the end of the third business day, following the day the licensee received the funds.

Special Emphasis: Broker Property Management

- If a broker holds the funds on behalf of the landlord, broker must abide by license law regarding escrow funds
- Deposits and advance rents are trust funds that must be deposited into the broker's escrow
- Best to open a separate escrow for property management but not required
- $5,000 broker's funds to maintain the account
- Sales associates must deliver rent and rental deposits to broker by end of next business day.

8 PROPERTY RIGHTS: ESTATES AND TENANCIES, CONDOMINIUMS, COOPERATIVES, AND TIME-SHARING

Learning Objectives:

- Define *real property* based on the definition in Chapter 475, F.S.
- List and explain the physical components of real property
- Explain the four tests courts use to determine if an item is a fixture
- Distinguish between real and personal property
- Describe the bundle of rights associated with real property ownership
- List the principal types of estates (tenancies) and describe their characteristics
- Describe the features associated with the Florida homestead law
- Distinguish between cooperatives, condominiums and time-shares and describe the four main documents associated with condominiums

Key Terms:

community development districts	homestead	remainderman
condominium	joint tenancy	right of survivorship
cooperative	land	separate property
declaration	leasehold estate	tenancy at sufferance
estate for years	life estate	tenancy at will
exempt property	personal property	tenancy by entireties
fee simple estate	proprietary lease	tenancy by entireties
fixture	Prospectus	time-share
freehold estate	real estate	
homeowner associations	real property	

REAL PROPERTY

Understanding the difference between land, real estate and real property is an important part of understanding the transfer of property and property rights.

Issues with this topic to be reviewed here include:

I)   Land, Real Estate and Real Property

  A) Definition of real property (Section 475.01, F.S.)
  B) Physical components of real property

      1) Surface Rights

      2) Subsurface Rights

      3) Air Rights

Land

As a real estate sales licensee, you will be in business to sell real property which includes land, real estate, and the bundle of rights included in ownership.

Land is defined as the surface and everything attached to the land by nature. This includes things like the lakes, streams, ponds, trees, shrubs, plants, grass and even weeds. Land includes all the elements beneath the surface such as minerals, petroleum, and natural gas. Land also includes all that is above it – the air and the space containing the air. Land is said to go from the center of the earth into the sky and into infinity.

Land = Sky Above + Trees (etc.) + Ground + Below the Ground

Real Estate

Real estate is defined as land plus man-made improvements that are permanently attached to the land. This includes the buildings, factories, houses, fences, streets, sidewalks, fencing, wells, sewers, and any other structure that has been attached.

Land + Man-made Improvements = Real Estate

Definition of Real Property (Florida Statutes 475.01)

So, we have land which includes all that is naturally attached to the land and that which is naturally above and below the land. Then we have real estate which includes the land plus the man-made improvements to the land. Now we have real property which includes the real estate plus the legal bundle of rights that goes with owning real estate. When you own real estate, you own the right to use, possess, enjoy, dispose, exclude others from using, or the right not to exercise any of these rights regarding real estate.

- Per Florida Statutes 475.01, "Real property" or "real estate" means any interest or estate in land and any interest in business enterprises or business opportunities, including any assignment, leasehold, sub-leasehold, or mineral right; however, the term does not include any cemetery lot or right of burial in any cemetery; nor does the term include the renting of a mobile home lot or recreational vehicle lot in a mobile home park or travel park.

http://definitions.uslegal.com/b/bundle-of-rights-property-law

Real Property = Real Estate + Bundle of Rights

Physical Components of Real Property

As already stated, land is defined to include the physical components of the land such as the surface, everything that nature has attached to the surface; everything beneath the surface. Land extends from the middle of the earth into the infinity of the sky.

The rights of land use, then, can be divided up by separating these different physical components. As such, there are surface rights, subsurface rights and air rights. Each right can actually be separated from the other and transferred from one person to another.

Land rights are divided into three areas. Surface rights include both land and water rights. Subsurface rights include mineral rights and the rights to petroleum and natural gas. Air rights include right to use the space above the land.

- Subsurface rights (mineral rights)

    - Minerals

    - Petroleum

    - Natural gas

- Air rights involve space above

- Surface rights
    - Include land rights

- Water rights

Subsurface Rights

In Florida, mineral property beneath land can be severed and sold to a separate owner other than the land owner. Mineral owners retain the right of access to their minerals. Florida mineral rights are wide and varied. Control of mineral rights is required for drilling oil and gas wells, but is not required for conducting geophysical surveys.

Florida statutes define the lawful right to drill, develop or explore for oil and gas as having majority control (through ownership or lease) of the mineral acreage within a drilling unit. Mineral owners who lease their mineral rights to an oil company are paid for the lease regardless of whether the oil company drills, discovers oil and gas, or sets up production.

http://www.dep.state.fl.us/water/mines/oil_gas/docs/OilGasMineralRightsFactSheet.pdf

Subsurface Rights

Florida's first producing oil well, the Sunniland No. 1, was drilled in September 1943 by the Humble Oil Co. This well site is next to the Big Cypress Preserve and is located half an hour from Naples. Most of the producing mineral rights in Florida are located north of Pensacola near the Alabama border.

The other primary areas in Florida with mineral rights that are under production are toward the southern end of the state.

- Mineral and oil rights are a form of subsurface rights.

http://www.mineralweb.com/mineral-rights-by-state/florida-mineral-rights/

Air Rights

The incentive to develop structures on air rights is a result of two aspects of urban growth — rising land values and expanding transportation facilities. With the desire that so many people have to live near the Gulf of Mexico, air rights in Florida are especially driven to build high rise buildings and condominiums to enjoy and maximize water views.

With condominiums, for example, individuals end up owning space that literally occupies the sky without owning the space that touches the ground. Air rights involve the space above the land. Even though you may occupy only 20 feet of the air for a long time, under the common law principle, you can later decide to build a 200-foot building unless it would be a nuisance.

Conflict emerges when the development of the air interferes with the views from others. This interference has included the development of railway systems that are suspended in the air. Think of the New York and Chicago systems as an example.

https://www.planning.org/pas/at60/report186.htm

Although the upper limit of an owner's airspace isn't clearly defined, it certainly doesn't extend into navigable airspace.

The upper airspace belongs to the public and is open to air travel.

Zoning and other statutes often restrict the height of buildings. Such statutes don't declare the unused airspace to belong to the public. However, they merely restrain the owner's use of that space. So, landowners may own more airspace than the law allows them to use.

Not only can the landowner use and enjoy the airspace, but he or she can also convey it to others. For example, a condominium may divide up airspace among individual unit owners. An owner can also give another party, such as a utility company, an easement to use some of the airspace.

- High rise buildings

- Condominiums

    - Individual/Conveyed Ownership or Interest of real estate in the air

http://www.dummies.com/how-to/content/the-property-rights-of-airspace.html

Issues reviewed here include:

I)   Land, Real Estate and Real Property

    C) Water rights

        1) Riparian rights

        2) Littoral rights

        3) Accretion and erosion

        4) Alluvion and Reliction

Surface Rights include Land & Water Rights

The owner of the surface title has control of the land's surface and the right to work it.

As such, you can sell or lease the land (or use of it).

Water rights can be divided into different types; riparian rights and littoral rights. Riparian rights are associated with land bordering moving water. This includes the land along the banks of a river or stream. Littoral rights are associated with land bordering tidal bodies of water: oceans and seas, ponds and lakes, and water is not flowing.

Water Rights

Ownership of waterfront property is highly sought after in Florida and involves unique real property considerations. When it comes to private waterfront property ownership, it can be difficult to distinguish where the private land rights cease and the public land begins.

As a result, a subset of real property law is in place to address what is called "riparian rights" and "littoral rights."

- Riparian vs. Littoral Rights

    - Riparian rights are associated with land bordering, moving or "flowing" water such as the land along the banks of a river or a stream.

    - Littoral rights are associated with land bordering tidal bodies of water such as oceans and seas and ponds and lakes. The water is not "flowing."

http://www.jdsupra.com/legalnews/riparian-rights-in-florida-22935/

Riparian Rights

Someone who owns property along a flowing body of water, such as a river or a stream, has riparian water rights.

Riparian rights include the rights of ingress, egress, boating, bathing, fishing and even the right to an unobstructed view of the water.

The Florida Constitution mandates that navigable waters shall be held in trust for the people of Florida. This means that the person doesn't own the actual water or the land under the water. Their actual ownership ends where the bank ends. The boundary between publicly owned navigable waters and adjacent privately-owned uplands is the ordinary high-water boundary.

Yet, riparian rights give the owner the right to use the water adjacent to property including navigating the waterway.

http://www.jdsupra.com/legalnews/riparian-rights-in-florida-22935/

- Per Florida Statutes 253.141 (1) **Riparian Rights** are those incident to land bordering upon navigable waters. They are rights of ingress, egress, boating, bathing, and fishing and such others as may be or have been defined by law. Such rights are not of a proprietary nature. They are rights inuring to the owner of the riparian land but are not owned by him or her.

- They are appurtenant to and are inseparable from the riparian land. The land to which the owner holds title must extend to the ordinary high watermark of the navigable water for riparian rights to attach.

- Conveyance of title to or lease of the riparian land entitles the grantee to the riparian rights running therewith whether or not mentioned in the deed or lease of the upland.

Water Rights

Littoral Rights

The person who owns land along a tidal body of water such as an ocean, lake, or even a pond; has **littoral rights**.

The water itself is not owned. Instead, littoral rights relate to the ownership of the property that abuts an ocean, sea, or lake and is concerned with the use and enjoyment of the shore.

The question becomes, though, with the constant flux of tides as to where the ownership begins and ends. The federal rule for calculating ownership is the average height of the water over a period of 18.6 years. Florida's constitution asserts, then, that state ownership of beaches as being the area below the average high-water mark.

Florida is known for its snowy-white beaches that draw tourists from around the world. Yet, over the last two decades, access to the state's 1,200 miles of coastline has become a point of contention.

http://www.obxbeachliving.com/waterfront-homes-information/littoral-rights--whats-a-high-mean-water-mark-mean.shtml

Beachgoers often find "No Trespassing" signs on beaches previously open to the public. These incidents have emphasized the growing conflict between landowners desiring privacy and those who seek the beaches for public use. Florida's Department of Environmental Protection reports that 60% (plus) of Florida beaches are private without public access. These beachfront homeowners have claimed the beaches as their own.

Florida law requires the state to ensure "the public's right to reasonable access to beaches." Yet, local governments have allowed waterfront communities to exclude others from the beach in exchange for property tax revenues these communities provide.

While this move can increase property values and benefit private landowners, other Florida residents and visitors to the state find it contrary to the Florida experience of walking along the shore - finding their passage barred.

http://www.floridabar.org/DIVCOM/JN/JNJournal01.nsf/8c9f13012b96736985256aa900624829/83d21148206bf5ef852575bb00532

Accretion and Erosion

The location of the edge of a body of water may change (and the edge of owned land may change) through such processes that add or take away from the land mass.

Accretion is the process of land being buildup from the water depositing rock, sand and soil. The land has increased.

Erosion is the loss of land due to natural forces including tides and currents. The land has been "swept away" slowly or quickly.

These naturally-occurring physical changes can result in changes to legal title describing land boundaries.

http://link.springer.com/chapter/10.1007%2F978-1-4684-4376-9_23

Water Rights

Alluvion and Reliction

Alluvion is the actual deposit of land material from the process of accretion.

Whereas accretion adds land through deposits (alluvion), land can also be gained through a "loss" of water:

Reliction is the gradual receding of water which leaves land to be claimed through new ownership descriptions.

http://link.springer.com/chapter/10.1007%2F978-1-4684-4376-

Special Emphasis: Land

Land includes the surface, everything that nature has attached to the surface, and everything beneath the surface. Land extends from the middle of the earth into the infinity of the sky.

Special Emphasis: Real estate

Real estate is defined as land + man-made improvements such as permanently attached buildings, factories, houses, fences, streets, sidewalks, fencing ,wells and sewers, etc.

Special Emphasis: Definition of Real Property (Florida Statutes 475.01)

Any interest or estate in land, and any interest in business enterprises or business opportunities, including any assignment, leasehold, sub-leasehold, or mineral right. Real estate + the legal bundle of rights.

Special Emphasis: Physical Components of Real Property

Land rights are divided into three areas: subsurface rights, air rights, and surface rights.

Special Emphasis: Riparian vs. Littoral Rights

Riparian rights are associated with land bordering moving or "flowing" water, such as the land along the banks of a river or a stream.

Littoral rights are associated with land bordering tidal bodies of water, such as oceans and seas and ponds and lakes. The water is not "flowing."

http://www.jdsupra.com/legalnews/riparian-rights-in-florida-22935/

Issues reviewed here include:

II) Real versus Personal Property

    A) Real property is basically land and improvements on the land.

    B) Personal property usually consists of items having a limited life, which are easily movable from one place to another.

        1) Personal property (or *chattel*, or *personalty*) includes any property that is not real property.

It is necessary to be able to identify what is real property and what is personal property when facilitating the sale of real estate. Real property rights are different from personal property rights.

- **Real property is basically land and improvements on the land.**

- **Personal property usually consists of items having a limited life, which are easily movable from place to another.** Personal property **(chattel or personalty)** includes any property that is not real property.

Personal property is a type of property which, in its most general definition, can include any asset other than real estate. The distinguishing factor between personal property and real estate is that personal property is movable. That is, the asset is not fixed permanently to one location as with real property such as land or buildings.

A notable distinction between real property and personal property is that personal property has a limited life and is easily moveable. An example of personal property is tables and chairs. However, a bench built into a kitchen nook may have started as personal property but has become part of the real property upon installation.

http://www.investopedia.com/terms/p/personalproperty.asp#ixzz3wuNzcBpi

The bench became real property through the act of **attachmen**t. The opposite can also happen in that real property can become personal property by the act of **severance**.

The dividing line between personal rights and property rights is not always easy to draw.

As a real estate licensee, it is important to use detailed purchase agreements that clearly defines what stays and what does not stay in a real estate transaction. Otherwise, the buyer and seller may not just find fault with each other but fault with the licensee – even filing suit in court.

Dealings between tenants and landlords can also result in questions about ownership.

Severance

- Real property becomes personal property by act of **severance.**

Attachment

- Personal property becomes real property by **attachment.**

https://en.wikipedia.org/wiki/Property

Issues reviewed here include:

II) Real Versus Personal Property

    C) Fixtures

        1) A fixture is an item that was once personal property, but is now legally considered to be real property

        2) Legal tests of determination:

(a) Intent of the parties

(b) Method or degree of attachment

(c) Agreement and/or relationship of the parties

(d) Adaptation of the item

Fixtures

Understanding the concept of personal versus real property expands to definition of what a fixture is.

A fixture is an item that was once personal property, but is now legally considered to be real property.

Fixtures are items that are attached to a house or building and that are not removed when the house or building is sold. Examples of fixtures are a light, toilet, sink, etc. Contracts are generally written to include fixtures as part of real property transferring ownership. Fixtures become real property through attachment and return to personal property through severance.

- Items attached to a house or building and that are not removed when the house or building is sold

  - A light, toilet, sink, etc.

- Fixtures become real property through attachment and return to personal property through severance.

http://www.merriam-webster.com/dictionary/fixture

Legal Tests of Determination:

Sometimes parties dispute whether something was supposed to be part of the real estate sale as a fixture.

If the matter ends up in court, the judge uses four legal tests to determine whether the item in question is personal property or has become part of the real estate.

- Intent of the parties

- Method or degree of attachment

- Agreement and/or relationship of the parties

- Adaptation of the item

Intent of the Parties

Considering the intent of the parties means examining whether the item was installed with the intent that it would permanently become part of the real estate.

An example of this type of test would be a tenant who brings in a washer and dryer. Upon the termination of the lease, the tenant begins to remove the washer and the dryer, but the landlord interrupts the process and tells the tenant that since the washer and dryer were attached to the properties, gas and water lines are now part of the real estate and belong to the landlord. If taken to court, the washer and dryer, even though partially installed, may likely be viewed as personal property by a judge if the tenant can show that the intent of the tenant was to install the washer and dryer temporarily only for the convenience of the tenant.

https://en.wikipedia.org/wiki/Fixture_(property_law)

Method or Degree of Attachment

Another legal test of determining whether an item is personal property or a fixture is the method or degree of attachment. This test examines whether the object can be detached without substantial damage being caused. The process also examines the process utilized to attach the item (screws, glue, etc.) and to what extent the installation altered the property.

If, for example, when a tenant installed a washer and dryer, the real estate property had to be altered to allow for the vents and the gas and water lines (there was never a washer and dryer installed on the property). It now becomes less clear that it belongs to the tenant.

http://prepagent.com/fixtures

Agreement and/or Relationship of the Parties

When determining whether an item is a fixture, a judge will take into consideration who's who in the relationship – landlord vs. tenant, buyer vs. seller and who is making what claim. The judge will compare the claims to the details of the agreement between the parties.

Buyers and tenants tend to prevail in these cases when there is doubt about ownership of items.

In the example of the tenant removing the washer and dryer, the judge would examine the lease agreement closely to see if the tenant had permission to alter the property to install the washer and dryer.

https://en.wikipedia.org/wiki/Fixture_(property_law)

Adaptation of the Item

The final test for determining whether something is a fixture is to look at the adaptation of the items. This means that if the item has become an integral part of the home or building then it now is part of the real estate. When an item is specially built or installed permanently for use with a property, then it has become a fixture and, hence, part of the real property.

Examples include a built-in stereo system, hot water solar heating pipes, wall-to-wall carpet and attic insulation.

In the example of the tenant removing the washer and dryer, because the washer and dryer is of standard size – easily replaced with any brand of washer and dryer, the tenant likely can show that the value of the property was increased by the ease of another tenant installing their own washer and dryer.

http://prepagent.com/fixtures

Issues reviewed here include:

II) Real Versus Personal Property

C) Fixtures

    1) Listing and sale contracts should clearly specify which items are considered real property in the transaction and any personal property that is to be included.

D) Definition of a trade fixture

    1) Fixture versus trade fixture

Fixtures

Listing and sales contracts should clearly specify which items are considered real property in the transaction and any personal property that is to be included.

Although an item may be personal property, it can be designated as staying per the terms of the contract.

Property in vacation areas are often sold furnished or "turnkey furnished." "Turnkey furnished" means that all the items remain such as pots, pans, towels…

In the agreement, fixtures can be "excluded" from the sale. However, if a seller wants to exclude an item, it is better to advise the seller to have the item removed before marketing the property. Buyers tend to want what they are not supposed to have!

Also, don't be confused by what is listed as staying in a listing contract. The final rule is what is included in the purchase contract. It will overrule the listing description.

Definition of a Trade Fixture

A trade fixture is a piece of equipment placed on or attached to commercial real estate, which is used in the tenant's trade or business. When a commercial property is rented, it is expected that the tenant will have to alter the property to suit the business. The items that the tenant attaches to the property is called a trade fixture.

Fixture Versus Trade Fixture

Trade fixtures differ from other fixtures in that they may be removed from the real estate (even if attached) at the end of the tenancy, while ordinary fixtures attached to the real estate become part of it.

Trade fixtures, unless otherwise designated within the lease agreement, will remain owned by the tenant and can be removed upon the end of the lease.

- Property attached by a commercial tenant as a part of tenant's business

- Considered personal property

- Can be removed by tenant upon the end of the lease

http://definitions.uslegal.com/t/trade-fixture/

Special Emphasis: Fixtures - Legal Tests of Determination:

- Intent of the parties

- Method or degree of attachment

- Agreement and/or relationship of the parties

- Adaptation of the item

Special Emphasis

- Real property is basically land and improvements on the land.

- Personal property usually consists of items having a limited life, which are easily movable from place to another. Personal property (chattel or personalty) includes any property that is not real.

http://www.investopedia.com/terms/p/personalproperty.asp#ixzz3wu

Special Emphasis: Fixtures

A fixture is an item that was once personal property, but is now legally considered to be real property.

Special Emphasis: Trade Fixture

Trade fixtures, unless otherwise designated within the lease agreement, will remain owned by the tenant and can be removed upon the end of the lease.

- Property attached by a commercial tenant as a part of tenant's business

- Considered personal property

- Can be remove by tenant upon the end of the lease.

PROPERTY RIGHTS

Issues reviewed here include:

III) Basic Property Rights A "Bundle of Rights" include the rights of:

　1) Possession

　2) Enjoyment

　3) Disposition

　4) Control

　5) Exclusion

Bundle of Rights Include the Rights of:

Basic property rights include what is known as the Bundle of Rights. The bundle of rights include the right of possession, the right of enjoyment, the rights of disposition, the right of control, and the right of exclusion.

- Possession

- Enjoyment

- Disposition

- Exclusion

- Control

http://www.investopedia.com/terms/p/property_rights

Possession

An owner also has the right to possess his or her own property. This means the right to occupy it. The right to possess a property can be given up on a temporary basis through a lease.

"Harold owned the property on the corner of 5th Street and Sampson Avenue and decided to move into it to live."

Possession

- Right to occupy

Enjoyment

The right of enjoyment means that the owner has the right to enjoy his or her own property. The legal phrase is the right of quiet enjoyment free of interference. Basically, because the owner owns the property, he or she has the right to use it any way the person pleases.

"Harold owned the property on the corner of 5th Street and Sampson Avenue and spent time there happily on the weekends to rest and relax."

- Quiet enjoyment

- Free of interference

Disposition

The right of disposition is the right to convey or transfer the ownership or other ownership interest in any real estate. Basically, it means that because a person owns it, the person has the right to sell or lease it.

"Harold owned the property on the corner of 5th Street and Sampson Avenue but decided to dispose of the property through a real estate auction."

- To convey or transfer the title to or other ownership interest in any real estate

- Sell it

- Lease it

Exclusion

Because the owner owns the property, the owner also has the right to exclude others from using it. It is the owner's right to prevent others from trespassing onto your property. It's the owner's property, which means the owner determines who can be there.

"Harold owned the property on the corner of 5th Street and Sampson Avenue and he put up a 6' fence to keep others from entering."

- Right to limit trespass

- Right to bar others from entering property

Control

The right granted to an owner enabling him or her to control property is the right to use the property in an uninterrupted manner.

"Harold owned the property on the corner of 5th Street and Sampson Avenue but decided to tear down interior walls to give it an open floor plan."

- Rights of use of property

- Uninterrupted

- Use must be for lawful activities

Special Emphasis : Bundle of Rights Include the Rights of:

- Possession

- Enjoyment

- Disposition

- Exclusion

- Control

http://www.investopedia.com/terms/p/property_rights.asp

Issues reviewed here include:

IV) Freehold Estates

    A) An estate refers to the degree, quantity, nature and extent of interest (ownership rights) a person can have in real property

    B) Estates are divided into two general groups:

        1) Freehold estates which are for an indefinite length

        2) Leasehold estates (or nonfreehold) which are for a fixed term

Ownership of property can be for different degrees, quantity, nature, and extent of interest.

The word estate refers to the degree, quantity, nature, and extent of the interest (ownership rights) a person can have in real property.

Estates are divided into two groups: freehold and leasehold estates. A freehold estate is ownership for an indefinite length (unknown) duration. **A leasehold or a (nonfreehold) estate is for fixed (known) duration.**

Note that a leasehold estate is NOT a type of freehold estate and is in fact the opposite of a freehold estate.

- The degree, quantity, nature, and extent of the interest (ownership rights)
- Two general groups freehold and leasehold
  - **Freehold** – indefinite length (unknown) duration
  - **Leasehold** – (nonfreehold) fixed (known) duration or term

Issues reviewed here include:

IV) Freehold Estates

 C) Freehold estates include:

    1) Fee simple estate

        (a) Fee, fee simple, fee simple absolute. . .defined as the largest bundle of rights we have. All three terms mean the same thing. Most titles are held in fee.

Freehold Estates Include:

The first form of estate that we are going to focus on are the types of freehold estates. They break down into either being a fee simple estate or a life estate.

Fee simple estates can be sold or willed or inherited. Whereas a life estate is given for the span of a person's life meaning they have use of it for their entire life but cannot themselves dispose of the property.

- Fee Simple

    - Can be sold or willed (inherited)

- Life Estate

    - Measured by a person's life span giving the person use of the estate during their life

Fee simple

A fee simple estate includes all of the bundle of rights. Remember, these rights include the rights of disposition, the right of enjoyment, the right of exclusion, the right of possession, and the right of control.

Fee Simple = Fee = fee simple absolute…is defined as the largest bundle of rights we have. All three terms mean the same thing. Most titles are held in fee.

A **fee simple estate** is the highest form of real estate ownership that is recognized by law. The owner can enjoy the property to its fullest extent, only limited by zoning laws or other similar restrictions. It has an unlimited duration and can be passed on to heirs. The fact that it can be passed onto their heirs, or sell the property, is the right to dispose or right of disposition. Know that the highest form of real estate ownership that is recognized by law or "the largest bundle of rights we have."

- The owner can enjoy the property to its fullest extent

- Unlimited duration and can be passed on to heirs

- Most titles are held in fee simple

When the fee simple ownership is in regard to a condominium, the owner of a unit is the owner only of his or her portion of the building, and jointly owns the land and the common areas of the property with the other owners.

- Condominium fee simple ownership

- The owner of a unit is the owner only of his or her portion of the building, and jointly owns the land and the common areas of the property with the other owners.

    http://www.businessdictionary.com/definition/fee-simple-estate.html#ixzz3wxZ1GcF9

Issues reviewed here include:

IV) Freehold Estates

   C) Freehold estates include:

      2) Life estate

         (a) Conventional life estates are created by action of the grantor

            (1) Use during life of holder or whoever's life the interest is based on. Often used by husband for wife with children as the *remaindermen.*

(2) Remainder estate

(3) Reversion estate

Freehold Estates Include:

Life Estate

"Conventional life estates are created by action of the grantor."

Another form of freehold estate is the life estate.

"Conventional life estates are created by action of the grantor."

Use of the property is granted during life of the holder or whoever's life the interest is based on. It is often used by a husband (spouse) for a wife (spouse) with children as a remaindermen.

- Use during life of holder or whoever's life the interest is based on

- Often used by husband for wife with children as a remaindermen

- Own for the length of designated lifetime

- Created by the action of the grantor(owner).

A life estate is a freehold form of ownership. However, the holder of the life estate does not have the right of disposition– one of the rights included in the full bundle of rights.

Instead, the person who created the life estate has control over who the property is to go to upon the death of the person with the life estate. If the person who created the life estate wanted use of the property to return directly back to that person it is called a reversion estate. If they pick an heir to inherit the property upon the death of the person with the life estate, then it is said to be a remainder estate with the person inheriting the property called the remainderman.

http://trusts-estates.lawyers.com/estate-planning/life-estates.html

Remainder Estate

A life estate is one way to avoid probate, because the children's interest in the property transfers when the life estate is created, not at the parent's death. Ownership is typically conveyed by deed. The deed includes language giving the tenant life estate rights. While the parent is alive, the children cannot dispose of the property.

- Is a life estate that wills the property to another heir upon the death of the person with the life estate

  - This person is called the remainderman.

http://trusts-estates.lawyer

Reversion Estate

If the details of the life estate dictate that upon the person whom the life estate is based on dies is to return to the original owner, then this is called a reversion estate.

If the grantor dies before the life estate ends, then the right of the reversion is extended to the estate of the grantor.

- After life estate expires, it reverts to original owner who had granted the life estate.

http://www.davephillipsproductions.com/the-life-estate-the-reversion-an-excerpt

Issues reviewed here include:

IV) Freehold Estates

    C) Freehold estates include:

        2) Life estate

            (b) Legal life estates are created automatically by law

                (1) Homestead is a legal life estate

                    (i) Homeowner's principal residence is protected from certain creditors

                    (ii) Not protected from real estate property

Legal Life Estates Are Created Automatically by Law

Homestead is a Legal Life Estate

A legal life estate can be created automatically by law rather than by action (will) of the person who died. Per Florida statutes, if the person died without providing for his or her spouse to have ownership of the **homesteaded property**, then a legal life **estate can be granted to the surviving spouse.**

Per Florida Statutes

- Descent of homestead. —(1) If not devised as authorized by law and the constitution, the homestead shall descend in the same manner as other intestate property; but if the decedent is survived by a spouse and one or more descendants, the surviving spouse shall take a life estate in the homestead, with a vested remainder to the descendants in being at the time of the decedent's death per stirpes. Florida Statutes 732.

…the surviving spouse may elect to take an undivided one-half interest in the homestead as a tenant in common, with the remaining undivided one-half interest vesting in the decedent's descendants in being at the time of the decedent's death

(a) The right of election may be exercised:

1. By the surviving spouse; or

2. With the approval of a court having jurisdiction of the real property, by an attorney in fact or guardian of the property of the surviving spouse. Before approving the election, the court shall determine that the election is in the best interests of the surviving spouse during the spouse's probable lifetime.

(b)☐ The election must be made within 6 months after the decedent's death and during the surviving spouse's lifetime.

F.S. 732

So, what does it mean to have a legal life estate created for a surviving spouse? The surviving spouse has a right to remain in the home!

Take for example a couple who had gotten married later in life after each had already been married and divorced with kids. Let's say a man (or woman) owned a home before marrying the new spouse and so the property was in his name only. Let's also say prior to the marriage the man had willed his home to his children. Now let's say, they hadn't put the wife on the deed or changed the will prior to his death, then the wife could request a life estate by law. Meaning the children couldn't take the home from her.

- Surviving spouse has a right to remain in the home!
- Purpose is to protect the family.

Homeowner's Principal Residence Is Protected from Certain Creditors

The legal life estate of homesteaded property is also demonstrated by the inability of a creditor to force the sale of a homesteaded property. If the debt is unrelated to the home such as with a mortgage or a mechanics lien, the home is protected.

This means you can NOT lose a homesteaded property to pay a medical bill or a car loan that was defaulted.

However, the home is **not protected from real estate property taxes, or from a mortgage for purchase, or cost of improvements.** The point of this type of legal life estate is to protect the family and keep them in their primary residence.

- Homeowner's principal residence is protected from certain creditors
- Not protected from real estate property taxes, or from a mortgage for purchase, or cost of improvements.

Special Emphasis: Freehold Estates Include

- Fee Simple - Can be sold or willed (inherited)
- Life Estate - Measured by a person's life span giving the person use of the estate during their life.

Special Emphasis: Life Estate

- Remainder Estate is a life estate that wills the property to another heir upon the death of the person with the life estate. This person is called the remainderman.

  - Reversion Estate is when after the life estate expires, ownership reverts to the original owner who had granted the life estate.

http://trusts-estates.lawyers.com/estate-planning/life-estates.html

Issues reviewed here include:

V) How Ownership Can Be Held

    A) Severalty—sole ownership. Only one party is needed to sign deed. (Spouse must sign if homesteaded.)

    B) Co-ownership

        1) Tenancy in common

        2) Joint tenancy with right of survivorship

            (a) Creating a joint tenancy

        3) Tenancy by the entireties

In looking at freehold estates in more detail, it is important to understand how ownership can be held.

Basically, you either own property all by yourself or along with other people. When you own it alone, you are said to have ownership **in severalty**. In severalty is sole ownership. Because it is owned by only one person, only one person needs to sign the deed when transferring the property to another owner.

However, this rule changes if it is homesteaded property. In that case, even though only one person is officially on the deed, if the owner has a spouse and has claimed the property as their homesteaded property then the spouse would also have to sign the deed upon the sale. This is because the spouse has a legal interest as the holder of the life estate on the property.

If more than one person is on the deed, meaning more than one person owns the property, then the property is held either as tenancy in common, joint tenancy, or as tenancy by the entireties.

To reiterate then, you can own property in severalty, as a tenancy in common, as joint tenancy, and as tenancy by the entireties. In severalty is sole ownership. The other three are forms of co-ownership also called concurrent ownership.

In **Severalty**

- Sole ownership, only one party needed to sign deed unless homesteaded – then spouse must sign (even though not on the deed).

Co-ownership

- Tenancy in common

- Joint Tenancy

- Tenancy by the entirety

In Severalty

Sole ownership, only one party needed to sign deed unless homesteaded – then spouse must sign (even though not on the deed).

This is absolute ownership and the owner can do anything with the property that he cares to do within legal bounds -- build on it, sell it, subdivide it, pass it on as an inheritance or lease it without consulting with or obtaining permission from other owners.

As the name implies, the owner's interests are severed from any others.

http://www.ehow.com/about_6134689_tenants-common-severalty.html

Co-ownership

Tenancy in Common

Let's take a close look at each type of co-ownership starting with tenancy in common.

A co-ownership does involve two or more people. Title is acquired at same or different times meaning that you can add someone to the deed later with your name and each hold tenancy in common.

Interest is in the whole property. It is an **UNDIVIDED** interest. What this means is that even though you own the property with someone else you have control and use of 100% of the property. You have a share in the WHOLE property, not a fraction of the property.

However, you can have an **unequal or an equal interest** and possession of the property. Meaning if there is just one other owner, then you could own 50% of the interest or perhaps you only own 20% of it or maybe 65% of it. As a tenancy in common, you have control over what happens to your interest meaning that you can will it or sell your share.

This right to will it to your heirs is referred to as "no right of survivorship." As the name would suggest, this is a common type of ownership and is the default form of ownership unless another type of ownership is expressed.

http://www.ehow.com/about_6134689_tenants-common-severalty.html

Tenancy in Common

- Two or more people
- Acquire title at same or different times
- Acquire title on same or different deeds
- Undivided Possession
- Interest in whole property (Undivided interest)
- Shares of ownership can be equal or unequal
- No right of survivorship

Joint Tenancy with Right of Survivorship

Let's compare how a joint tenancy with **right of survivorship** is different from a tenancy in common. First, joint tenancy always has right of survivorship. If you hold property that has a tenancy in common, when you die the property can be passed on to your heirs. This is not true for a joint tenancy. A joint tenancy has the right of survivorship meaning that it survives past your death. So, if you die holding a joint tenancy, the people you held the joint tenancy with would now equally own your interest in the property.

For this type of ownership, interest had to be created at the same time, meaning that you acquired title at the same time and on the exact same deed. This is a huge distinction from tenancy in common.

Another difference is that although tenancies in common may own different percentage of ownership, a joint tenancy is always an equal amount of ownership between the owners, though, again, it is an undivided possession or interest in the whole.

Joint Tenancy with Right of Survivorship

- Two or more people

- Acquire title at the SAME time – required

- Acquire title on the SAME deed - required

- Must have specific wording in Deed

- Undivided Possession

- Shares of ownership MUST be EQUAL

- Right of survivorship - Surviving joint tenants immediately become the owner of the whole property upon the death of the other joint tenant.

Creating a Joint Tenancy

Joint tenancy is described as having four unities. Unity of possession, interest, title, and time. They have equal possession of the property, with equal interest, and ownership is conveyed on the same deed and at the same time. The four unities of joint tenancy: possession, interest, title, and time.

http://www.investopedia.com/articles/pf/08/joint-tenancy.asp

Let's take a closer look at the right of survivorship. It's important to have a clear understanding of what it means. The "Right" belongs to the owners that you are owners with as joint tenants.

It is a right to have the ownership of one of the parties, to spring back to the other parties, in the event of your death. "Think of the owners as joined at the hips." So, when one dies, the property interest of the one who died springs back to the living or surviving owners. Hence the phrase survivorship. **Ownership survives the death**.

- Right of survivorship - Surviving joint tenants immediately become the owner of the whole property upon the death of the other joint tenant.

http://www.investopedia.com/terms/j/joint-tenancy.asp

So, if you choose to take ownership as joint tenancy with the right of survivorship, what are you giving up? You are giving up your right to pass your share on to your heirs.

- Right of survivorship

    - Surviving joint tenants immediately become the owner of the whole property upon the death of the other joint tenant.

    - What do owners give up in joint tenancy?

Here's an example:

Bob, Mark and Sarah all are owners by joint tenancy with right of survivorship. Bob dies and has willed all his possessions to his wife except he CAN'T pass this property on to his wife. So, Mark and Sarah are now equal owners of the property.

- Bob, Mark and Sarah all are owners by joint tenancy with right of survivorship.

- Bob dies and has willed all his possessions to his wife except he CAN'T pass this property on to his wife.

- Mark and Sarah are now equal owners of the property.

Here's another example:

Bob, Mark and Sarah all are owners by joint tenancy with right of survivorship. Bob dies. Thus, Mark and Sarah are now equal owners of the property. What happens if Mark then dies? Sarah is now the sole owner and her ownership is an estate in severalty.

- Mark and Sarah are now equal owners of the property.

- Mark died.

- Sarah is now the sole owner and her ownership is an estate in severalty.

But here's the rub. Although property owned by joint tenancy cannot be passed to an heir upon death, Bob could have sold the property while he was still alive!

Let's say that while Bob, Mark, and Sarah owned the property as joint tenants, Bob sold his interest to Connie. Now what happens to the ownership? Mark and Sarah would remain joint tenants. They would also share ownership with Connie who bought Bob's share. But Connie holds ownership as a tenancy in common with Mark and Sarah.

Remember that to have joint tenancy, you must take title at the same time. Because Connie took ownership later, she is automatically a tenancy in common. As a tenancy in common, not only does she have the right to sell her property, she also has the right to will it to her heirs! Even though there was a change in ownership by Connie replacing Bob, Mark and Sarah still hold joint tenancy. Thus. they cannot will their properties as they have right of survivorship with each other.

http://www.investopedia.com

Tenancy by the Entireties

This is the form of ownership that a husband and wife take when they buy property together. This type of ownership is automatically formed when they are both signing on the deed. The wording of the deed does not have to identify it as a tenancy by the entirety for the rules of this ownership to exist. The fact that they were married when they bought the property together automatically creates this type of ownership.

They have the same four unities that joint tenancy has: possession, interest, title, and time. This means they possess the whole property together with an undivided interest and they take title at the same time on the same deed.

With tenancy by the entireties, one cannot do anything such as mortgage or sell the property without the consent of the other. When one spouse dies, ownership interest transfers to surviving spouse by right of survivorship.

http://www.investopedia.com/terms/j/joint-tenancy.asp

Tenancy by the Entireties

- Husband and wife only

    - Must be married to each other when they take title

- Automatically formed if both sign the deed

- Four unities of a joint tenancy must exist

- Actions require consent of both spouses

- When one spouse dies, ownership interest transfers to surviving spouse by right of survivorship (becomes Estate in Severalty).

To recap, a husband and wife can own property together as a tenancy by the entirety. This is automatically created when they take title together. However, one of the spouses can own property without the other spouse. This property could be purchased before they were married or during the marriage. However, if only one spouse owns the property that is homesteaded, then a life estate is formed for the other spouse.

- A husband and wife can own property together as a tenancy by the entirety

- One spouse can own property without the other

    - Life Estate for Homesteaded property.

Special Emphasis: In Severalty

- Sole ownership, only one party needed to sign deed unless homesteaded – then spouse must sign (even though not on the deed).

Special Emphasis: Co-ownership

- Tenancy in common

- Joint Tenancy

- Tenancy by the entireties

Special Emphasis: Right of survivorship

- Surviving joint tenants immediately becomes the owner of the whole property upon the death of the other joint tenant.

http://www.investopedia.com/terms/j/joint-tenancy.asp

How Ownership Can Be Held

Tenancy in Common	Joint tenancy	Tenancy by the Entireties
• Two or more people	• Two or more people	• Must be Husband and Wife
• Acquire title at same or different times	• Acquire title at the SAME time – required	• Acquire Title at SAME time
• Acquire title on same or different deeds	• Acquire title on the SAME deed – required (Must have specific wording in Deed)	• Acquired Title on SAME deed (Specific wording not required)
• Undivided Possession	• Undivided Possession	• Undivided Possession
• Shares of ownership can be equal or unequal Interest	• Shares of ownership MUST be EQUAL Interest	• Shares of ownership MUST be EQUAL Interest
• No right of survivorship	• Right of survivorship	• Right of survivorship

The 4 "Unities" & Right of Survivorship

Special Emphasis : Exempt Property

- Exempt property, under the law of property, is property that can neither be passed by will nor claimed by creditors of the deceased if a decedent leaves a surviving spouse or surviving descendants.

(Used differently than exempt from licensing or exempt from taxation.)

https://en.wikipedia.org/wiki/Exempt_property

LEASEHOLD ESTATES

Issues reviewed here include:

VI) Leasehold (Non-freehold) Estates

A) An interest in real property for a definite period (measured in calendar time)

B) Types of leasehold estates

    1) Estate for years

    2) Tenancy at will

    3) Tenancy at sufferance

Opposite of the freehold estate where property ownership is held, is the **leasehold estate** which is **an interest in real property for a definite period (measured in calendar time).**

It is a transfer of use and possession rights for a known duration. More simply put, it is a lease.

A leasehold does not exist for an indefinite period of time. Meaning there is an end date.

This is not a freehold estate. The rights and interest are less than a freehold estate. Ownership rights are not transferred. Only a right to use and possess the property.

http://www.ehow.com/about_7366883_leasehold-property_.html

Types of Leasehold Estates

Parties may create a leasehold either in writing, or by any type of oral agreement in which the lessor gives the lessee either explicit or implicit permission to use the property. Leases lasting longer than a year, however, must generally be written.

There are three types of leasehold estates: estate for years, tenancy at will, and a tenancy at sufferance.

http://www.ehow.com/about_7366883_leasehold-property_.html

Estate(Tenancy) for Years

An estate for years, also called a tenancy for years has a specific start and end date of the lease.

To create an estate for years, this type of lease must be in writing.

It establishes tenant interest in property, although actual ownership of the property does not change hands.

Tenancy at Will

Tenancy at will is another type of leasehold estate that has a beginning date but does not have an ending date. It's basically a week to week or a month to month lease with the determination date to be determined at will in the future. However, a notice must still be provided.

If it is a week to week lease, then a seven-day notice must be provided to terminate the lease. If it is a month to month lease, then a 15-day notice must be provided.

Tenancy at Sufferance

Tenancy at sufferance is a leasehold estate where the lease has ended but the tenant has retained possession of the property without the permission of the landlord.

This is called a holdover or holding over. If the landlord then gives written consent, then it becomes a tenancy at will.

Special Emphasis: Non-Freehold Estate is a Lease Estate

- An interest in real property for a definite period
- Measured in calendar time
- Transfer of use and possession rights
- Known duration- a lease
- Does **not** exist for an indefinite period
- Less interest than freehold
- Not an ownership interest – A use interest.

Special Emphasis: Types of Leasehold Estates

- Estate for years – specific start and end date
- Tenancy at will – beginning date but no ending date
- Tenancy at sufferance – lease has ended but tenant has retained possession without permission.

VARIOUS OWNERSHIPS

Issues reviewed here include:

VII) Cooperatives, Condominiums, Community Development Districts (CDD), Homeowner Associations (HOA) and Time-Sharing

    A) Cooperatives

        1) Own stock in a corporation

        2) Stock ownership carries right of occupancy through a proprietary lease

        3) Corporation pays property tax; each shareholder pays prorated tax

        4) Transfer is accomplished by sale of stock

        5) Disclosures required by The Cooperative Act (F.S. 719)

Cooperatives

Freehold and leasehold are not the only types of interest in property.

Cooperative ownership is an alternative form of ownership. Cooperatives, also called a co-op, is when you own stock instead of the actual property.

Because the stock is connected to a specific unit, a propriety lease is also given. Meaning that the right to possess is yours through the lease. With a co-op, the Corporation pays the property tax bill, however, each shareholder pays a prorated share of the tax, meaning the shareholders are carrying the cost of the tax.

When someone wants to sell their ownership rights to the co-op, they do so by transferring the sale of stock and by assigning the lease over to the new owner.

There are disclosure requirements that must be followed with the sale of a new or resale coop. These disclosures are governed by The Cooperative Act (Florida Statutes 719).

The disclosure requirements for cooperatives are governed by The Cooperative Act (Florida Statutes 719).

The requirements change when the unit is sold as a resale versus when it was new and being sold by a developer.

A developer is required to disclose to the buyer that they have a right to cancel the sale **within 15 calendar days** of signing the purchase contract and having received all cooperative documents.

Whereas, when the property is being sold privately as a **resale**, then the purchase agreement must either include a clause that the buyer acknowledges that they were in possession of the cooperative documents for at least **3 days prior** to signing the purchase agreement or that because they didn't have the documents, they now have 3 business days upon receipt of the cooperative documents to cancel the sale.

Notice that with the developer it was a calendar day timeline, but with the resale it is a business day timeline.

Florida Statutes 719

Issues reviewed here include:

VII) Cooperatives, Condominiums, Community Development Districts (CDD), Homeowner Associations (HOA) and Time-Sharing

    B) Condominiums

        1) Own individual unit in fee simple

        2) Undivided interest in common areas

        3) Property tax levied on individual unit

        4) Transfer by deed

        5) Declaration and bylaws (a) Rights and obligations of condominium owners

6) Disclosures required by The Condominium Act (F.S. 718)

Condominiums

Condominium ownership is also an alternative form of ownership. Also referred to as condos.

This type of ownership creates ownership of the individual unit through fee simple ownership. Ownership is transferred by a deed, and use of common elements are legally attached and transferred as well.

Property taxes are levied on individual units and paid by each individual unit owner.

With every condominium development, comes the Declaration and bylaws which details the rights and obligations of owners.

Disclosure requirements for the sale of condominiums are governed by the condominium act, per Florida statute 718.

Upon the creation of a condominium development, the developer must file the condominium documents with the Division of Florida Condominiums, Timeshares, and Mobile Homes. Plus, if there are 20 or more residential units, then the developer must also prepare a prospectus which is a summary of the major points contained in the condominium documents and file it with the division as well.

Creation

- Condo Documents filed with

    - Division of Florida Condominiums, Timeshares, and Mobile Homes

- 20+ units also file a prospectus

    - Summarizes major points contained in the condominium documents.

When a condominium is sold, documents must be provided to the buyer. As a real estate agent, you could be found liable if you did not make sure that this happens.

Let's look at the documents involved with condominiums. A Declaration of condominium is a legal document filed in the county in which the condominium will be located.

Once filed, it establishes existence of the project and divides airspace into layers of ownership.

It describes property boundaries, the common elements, membership and voting rights in regard to the association, and the covenants and restrictions on the use of each individually owned unit plus the common areas.

Florida Statutes 718.504

Condominium Documents

Declaration of Condominium

- A legal document filed in the county in which the condominium will be located. Once filed, it establishes existence of the project and divides airspace into layers of ownership

- Describes property boundaries, the common elements, membership and voting rights in regard to the association, and the covenants and restrictions on the use of each individually owned unit plus the common areas.

http://www.businessdictionary.com/definition/condominium-declaration.html#ixzz3wyoNjOHT

Bylaws of the Association

Bylaws of the association are the official rules and regulation which govern a corporation's management. Bylaws are drawn up at the time of incorporation, along with the charter.

http://www.investorwords.com/660/bylaws.html#ixz

Frequently Asked Questions

Frequently Asked Questions is a prepared document that informs prospective buyers about restrictions on things such as leasing and pets, and provides general information about assessments, etc.

Also referred to as **FAQ**.

http://www.investorwords.com/660/bylaws.html#ixzz3wypchhEe

Articles of Incorporation

Articles of incorporation is a document, filed with a U.S. state (Florida) by a corporation's founders, describing the purpose, place of business, and other details of a corporation.

http://www.investorwords.com/258/Articles_of_Incorporation.html#ixzz3w

Rules of the Association

Rules of the association are the rules and regulations adopted by the board of directors of the association.

- The association elects a board of directors, which handles the maintenance and repair of common areas, disputes among unit owners, and enforcement of rules and regulations, and condominium fees. The rules and regulations are normally adopted by the board of directors of the association.

http://www.uslegalforms.com/us/US-03330BG.htm

Estimated Operating Budget or Most Recent Year-End Financial Report

The estimated operating budget outlines expected expenses for the condominium development. Whereas the Most Recent Year-End Financial Report is a snapshot of the previous year's finances. This is an important document to review when considering purchasing a condominium as it gives a picture of the financial health of the development.

- Outlines the expenses and operating budget of the condominium development

Utilities, Salaries, Insurance, Reserves …

Governance Form

Governance Form must be provided by condo sellers (who are not the original developer) to prospective buyers a disclosure from the Florida Department of Business and Professional Regulation (DBPR) which details the rights and responsibilities of condominium boards and unit owners, voting rights, meeting notices and other governance matters.

- Condo sellers of resales must provide prospective buyers a detailing of the rights and responsibilities of condo boards and unit owners, voting rights, meeting notices and other governance matters.

http://www.floridarealtors.org/NewsAndEvents/n7-121808.cfm

Cooperatives, Condominiums, Community Development Districts (CDD), Homeowner Associations (HOA) and Time-Sharing

Condominiums
Upon Resale, The Seller Must Provide the Buyer with
- 7 Forms
- Buyer has 3 business days to cancel contract
  - After signing contract and receiving docs
- These documents include:

Declaration of Condominium,   Bylaws of the association,
Frequently Asked Questions,   Articles of Incorporation,
Rules of the association,   Most Recent Year-End Financial Report,
Governance Form

http://www.legalscoopswflre.com/condominium/required-disclosures-to-buyers-of-resale-condominium-units-in-florida/

Cooperatives, Condominiums, Community Development Districts (CDD), Homeowner Associations (HOA) and Time-Sharing

Condominiums
Upon New Sale, The Developer Must Provide the Buyer with
- 6 Forms
- Buyer has 15 Calendar days to cancel contract
  - After signing contract and receiving docs
- These documents include:

Declaration of Condominium,   Bylaws of the association,
Frequently Asked Questions,   Articles of Incorporation,
Estimated Operating Budget,   Prospectus

Notice that the Rules of the Association and the Governance form that must be provided in resales are not provided by developers. Instead they provide the Prospectus. And the Most Recent Year-end Financial report is replaced with the Estimated Operating Budget.

Issues reviewed here include:

VII) Cooperatives, Condominiums, Community Development Districts (CDD), Homeowner Associations (HOA) and Time-Sharing

    C) Time-Share

        1) Share ownership or right of occupancy for a time interval in a unit

        2) Legal formats

            (a) Interval ownership

            (b) Right-to-use

        3) Disclosures required under Florida Vacation Plan and Time-Sharing Act (F.S. 721) and Rule 61J2, F.A.C.

Time-Share

Time-Shares are another form of ownership.

Time-Share ownership is right of occupancy for a time interval in a unit. Usually divided into weeks of ownership.

There are two legal formats that time-shares can take.

- **Interval Ownership** which is a right to occupy (with deeded interest) for a specific time period.
- Or the **Right to Use** the property for a specified number of years.

Disclosure requirements are mandated by The Florida Vacation Florida Vacation Plan and Time-Sharing Act (F.S. 721) and Rules 61J2, F.A.C.

Legal Formats:

- Interval Ownership
    - Right to occupy (deeded interest) for a specific time period
- Right to Use
    - For specified number of years

Disclosure required under Florida Vacation Plan and Time-Sharing Act (F.S. 721) and Rules 61J2, F.A.C

Interval Ownership

One of the two legal formats for time-shares is Interval Ownership. Interval ownership is fee simple ownership. It is the right to occupy and possess the property for a specific time period. It is a fractional ownership. The owner has right to dispose of property through selling it or willing it to an heir. The owner also has the right to rent out the fractional interest owned.

- Fee Simple Ownership

- Right to occupy for a specific time period

- Fractional Ownership

- Owner has right to Dispose of property through sale or will

- Owner has right to rent out the fractional interest

Right to Use

The other of the two legal formats for time-shares is the right to use. This is a Leasehold Estate with the right to occupy for a specific time period that can be as long as 20 to 40 years. At the end of the contract term, the usage rights revert to owner/developer. Keep in mind that the actual property ownership can be sold to an investor by the developer.

- Leasehold Estate

- Right to occupy for a specific time period

- Owner has right to use property—20 -40 years

- End of time period, usage reverts to owner/developer

- Property ownership can be sold to an investor by the developer.

Disclosure Required Under Florida Vacation Plan and Time-Sharing Act (F.S. 721) and Rules 61J2, F.A.C.

Disclosures required under Florida Vacation Plan and Time-Sharing Act (F.S. 721) and Rules 61J2, F.A.C include that a disclosure must be made to buyers that they have 10 calendar days to cancel purchase agreements after signing the contract. Licensees who sell time-shares must be versed with the disclosure requirements

- Disclosure must be made to buyer that the buyer has 10 calendar days to cancel purchase agreements after signing the contract

- Licensees who sell time-shares must be versed with the disclosure requirements.

Required Disclosure Wording per Florida Statute

You may cancel this contract without any penalty or obligation within 10 calendar days after the date you sign this contract, or the date on which you receive the last of all documents required to be given to you pursuant to section 721.07(6), Florida Statutes, whichever is later. If you decide to cancel this contract, you must notify the seller in writing of your intent to cancel. Your notice of cancellation shall be effective upon the date sent and shall be sent to (Name of Seller) at (Address of Seller). Any attempt to obtain a waiver of your cancellation right is void and of no effect. While you may execute all closing documents in advance, the closing, as evidenced by delivery of the deed or other document, before expiration of your 10-day cancellation period, is prohibited. Florida Statute 721.06.

Additional Resale Disclosures

Know that it is illegal to collect an advance fee for the listing of a time-share unit. Plus, FREC requires specific written disclosures in listings, advertisements, and sale contracts for resales of time-shares.

No Guarantees to Sell- Specific Wording

The "No Guarantees" to:

- "There is no guarantee that your time-share period can be sold at any particular price or within any particular period of time."

- This statement must be included in any agreement written about the resale of time-share periods and located immediately above the time-share owner's signature.

- The statement must be included with any advertising to solicit for listings.

Plus, a time-share listing must include:

Fees, or other compensation to broker, ability to extend term of agreement, management and each party obligations, broker rights and termination of agreement costs and timeline, allowing use of time period and profit use for period, and any judgments or pending litigation for fraud against the listing broker.

Issues reviewed here include:

VII) Cooperatives, Condominiums, Community Development Districts (CDD), Homeowner Associations (HOA) and Time-Sharing

    D) HOA (Chapter 720, F.S.)

        1) Define

        2) Disclose

HOA "Homeowners' Association"

Keep in mind that many homes in Florida that are owned as fee simple with the full bundle of rights may still have their usage rights restricted by Homeowner Association requirements.

A homeowner association is a Florida corporation responsible for the operation of a residential community or a mobile home subdivision. Voting membership is made up of parcel owners or their agents. Membership is a mandatory condition of parcel ownership, and is authorized to impose assessments that, if unpaid, may become a lien on the parcel.

F.S.720.30

HOA "Homeowners' Association"

A Florida corporation responsible for the operation of a community or a mobile home subdivision.

- Voting membership is made up of parcel owners or their agents

- Membership is a mandatory condition of parcel ownership

- Authorized to impose assessments that, if unpaid, may become a lien on the parcel

F.S.720.301

Disclose

The Florida Statute 720 requires that a disclosure summary be included with a purchase and sale agreement for property that is subject to mandatory Homeowner Association membership, fees and assessments, and restrictions.

The rule provides that the buyer be given a 3 day right of rescission upon receipt of the disclosure summary if the disclosure summary was not provided at the time the contract was signed.

The right to void (rescission) cannot be voided by the buyer.

This rescission right ends at closing. This means that if a buyer purchases a home without having ever read the disclosure summary, the buyer cannot back out of the deal after the deal is closed.

Keep in mind, though, that the licensee is responsible for the disclosure being made and could be sued by the buyer if the sale closed without the information being provided.

The Disclosure Summary specifically identifies the homeowner association by name, the fees to be paid and the fee schedule.

It advises the buyer that the failure to pay these fees could result in a lien being placed on the property. Because of the lien, the homeowner could ultimately lose the property. It advised the buyer that the homeowner associations can restrict usage of the property through the restrictive covenants, and that these covenants be amended.

It advises the buyer that they should refer to the actual homeowner association documents, not the disclosure summary, before purchasing the property.

http://www.leg.state.fl.us/Statutes/index.cfm?App_mode=Display_Statute&URL=0700-0799/0720/0720.html

Issues reviewed here include:

VII) Cooperatives, Condominiums, Community Development Districts (CDD), Homeowner Associations (HOA) and Time-Sharing

    E) CDD (Chapter 190, F.S.)

        1) Define

        2) Disclose

CDD "Community Development District"

A Community Development District (**CDD**) is a local, special purpose government authorized by Chapter 190 of the Florida Statutes as amended, and is an alternative method for managing and financing infrastructure required to support community development.

Be aware too that home ownership could also be restricted if the property is part of a community development district. This could be instead of, but more likely in addition to a home owner association.

A CDD is a local, special purpose government authorized by Chapter 190 of the Florida Statutes as amended and is an alternative method for managing and financing infrastructure required to support community development.

When a developer plans a community, he may take out a bond to finance the infrastructure. Infrastructure means the roads, utilities, water, and sewer systems that support a community. If the infrastructure isn't already in place, then the CDD becomes a way to provide the financing to make it happen without costing the local government. This aids in the approval of the development.

The cost of the bond is paid back over a number of years – 20 for example. Each property owner in a community development district has their share of the payment assessed, which is levied and collected through the property taxes.

A CDD in summary, then, is a Special Tax District created to take care of long-term needs of a community.

A CDD may impose taxes and/or assessments on property for public facilities, construction operations and maintenance of such.

These taxes and/or assessments are in addition to city and county taxes, usually financed by bonds and paid until bonds are paid back.

CDD disclosure must appear conspicuously, and boldfaced before the purchaser's signature space.

http://activerain.com/blogsview/24019/what-is-a-cdd-- community-development-district

Disclosure

The Florida Association of Realtors provides this statement in a Community Development District Addendum to be attached to the purchase and sale agreement. As a real estate licensee, you could be held accountable if the disclosure regarding the special taxes and assessments was not made.

- 190.048 …"THE (Name of District) COMMUNITY DEVELOPMENT DISTRICT MAY IMPOSE AND LEVY TAXES OR ASSESSMENTS, OR BOTH TAXES AND ASSESSMENTS, ON THIS PROPERTY. THESE TAXES AND ASSESSMENTS PAY THE CONSTRUCTION, OPERATION, AND MAINTENANCE COSTS OF CERTAIN PUBLIC FACILITIES AND SERVICES OF THE DISTRICT AND ARE SET ANNUALLY BY THE GOVERNING BOARD OF THE DISTRICT. THESE TAXES AND ASSESSMENTS ARE IN ADDITION TO COUNTY AND OTHER LOCAL GOVERNMENTAL TAXES AND ASSESSMENTS AND ALL OTHER TAXES AND ASSESSMENTS PROVIDED FOR BY LAW."

Special Emphasis: Cooperatives

- Co-op

- Own stock in the co-op (corporation)

- Stock ownership carries right of occupancy through a proprietary lease

- Corporation pays property tax

- Each shareholder pays a prorated share of the property tax

- Transfer is accomplished by sale of stock

- Disclosures required by The Cooperative Act (Florida Statutes 719)

Special Emphasis: Cooperatives

Disclosures required by The Cooperative Act (Florida Statutes 719)

- Disclosure in contract with developer

    - Buyer has right to cancel **within 15 calendar days** of signing contract and receipt of cooperative documents.

- Disclosure in resale contract

    - Buyer has received documents at least **3 business days** before signing, or

    - Buyer has right to cancel within **3 business days** of signing contract and receipt of cooperative documents.

Special Emphasis: Condominiums

Condo units and common elements

- Own individual unit in fee simple

- Plus, an undivided interest in common elements

- Property taxes levied on individual units

- Transfer by deed

- Declaration and bylaws

    - Rights and obligations of condominium owners

- Disclosures required by the Condominium Act (Florida Statutes 718)

Cooperatives, Condominiums, Community Development Districts (CDD), Homeowner Associations (HOA) and Time-Sharing

Condominium Required Documents Compared

New Sale	Resale
Declaration of Condominium ⟷	Declaration of Condominium
Bylaws of the association ⟷	Bylaws of the association
Frequently Asked Questions ⟷	Frequently Asked Questions
Articles of Incorporation ⟷	Articles of Incorporation
Estimated Operating Budget ⟹	Most Recent Year-End Financial Report
Prospectus	Rules of the association
	Governance Form

Special Emphasis: Additional Time-Share Resale Disclosures

Listings Include:

- Fees, or other compensation to broker

- Ability to extend term of agreement

- Management and each party obligations

- Broker rights and termination of agreement costs and timeline

- Allowing use of time period and profit use for period

- Any judgments or pending litigation for fraud against the agent

Florida **Statutes721 and Administrative Rule 61J2**

Special Emphasis: HOA "Homeowners' Association"

Disclose

- The Florida Statute 720

- Property that is subject to mandatory Homeowner Association

- Gives 3 day right of rescission upon receipt of documents

- Right to void (rescission) cannot be waived by the buyer

- Rescission right ends at closing

- Identifies the Association and fees to be paid

- Failure to pay fees could result in lien and loss of the property

- Restrictive covenants can be amended

- Advises buyer to refer to the actual homeowner association documents before purchasing the property

    http://www.leg.state.fl.us/Statutes/index.cfm?App_mode=Display_Statute&URL=0700-0799/0720/0720.html

Special Emphasis: CDD - Community Development District

- A Special Tax District

- Created to take care of long-term needs of a community

- A CDD may impose taxes and/or assessments on property for public facilities, construction operations and maintenance of such.

- These taxes and/or assessments are in addition to city and county taxes, usually financed by bonds and paid until bonds are paid back.

CDD disclosure must appear conspicuously, boldfaced before the purchaser's signature space.

9 TITLE, DEEDS, AND OWNERSHIP RESTRICTIONS

Learning Objectives:
- Differentiate between voluntary and involuntary alienation
- Explain the various methods of acquiring title to real property and describe the conditions necessary to acquire real property by adverse possession
- Distinguish between actual notice and constructive notice
- Distinguish between an abstract of title and a chain of title
- Explain the different types of title insurance
- Describe the parts of a deed and the requirements of a valid deed
- List and describe the four types of statutory deeds and the legal requirements for deeds
- List and describe the various types of governmental and private restrictions on ownership of real property
- Distinguish among the various types of leases

Key Terms:

abstract of title
acknowledgment
actual notice
adverse possession
alienation
assignment
chain of title
condemnation
construction lien
constructive notice
deed
deed restriction
easement

eminent domain
encroachment
escheat
further assistance
general warranty deed
grantee
granting clause
grantor
gross lease
ground lease
habendum clause
intestate
lien

net leases
percentage lease
police power
quiet enjoyment
quitclaim deed
seisin
sublease
testate
title
variable lease
warranty forever

CONCEPT OF TITLE

Understanding the methods of transferring title is reviewed here including the topics of:

    I)   Concept of Title
        A) Ownership in a bundle of rights
        B) Equitable title
        C) Transferred voluntarily or involuntarily by operation of law

Ownership in a Bundle of Rights

In property law, title refers to all rights that can be secured and enjoyed under the law. It is frequently referred to as absolute ownership– also known as fee simple ownership. However, the term title itself should not be confused with full and absolute ownership. Rights to property can be separated and transferred to others either as a whole unit or in individual rights and pieces.

Remember the **Bundle of Rights**. Basic property rights include what is known as "the bundle of rights." The bundle of rights include the right of possession, the right of enjoyment, the rights of disposition, the right of control, and the right of exclusion.

When transferring title, these are the rights that are designated as being transferred – either in as a whole or in pieces.

Equitable Title

The person who holds the ownership rights to property is said to have title. Ownership in bundle of rights. **Equitable title**, on the other hand, is the person that holds a beneficial interest in real property while waiting to receive legal title.

When a purchase and sales contract has been entered into between buyer and seller, the buyer has equitable title while the seller still has (legal) title.

Per rules of law, this is a trust beneficiary as the person who holds legal title (the seller) is the trustee.

http://definitions.uslegal.com/e/equitable-title/

Transferred Voluntarily or Involuntarily by Operation of Law

Title can be transferred from one person to another (equitable title and legal title) and can be done so either voluntarily or by operation of law which is said to be involuntarily.

The word **alienation** is the actual act of transferring title or an interest in real property from one person to another. The word alienation in common uses evokes negative imagery. In title law, the word alienation itself is not negative, but in fact is an emotionally neutral word.

When title is transferred through involuntary alienation, however, it is done so without the original owner's control and consent which can hold negative consequences.

Alienation may be:

- **Voluntary Alienation—with the owner's control and consent**
- **Involuntary Alienation—without owner's control and consent**

http://thismatter.com/money/real-estate/title-transfer.htm

Special Emphasis: Transferred Voluntarily or Involuntarily by Operation of Law

The word **alienation** is the actual act of transferring title or an interest in real property from one person to another.

Alienation may be:

- **Voluntary Alienation—with the owner's control and consent**
- **Involuntary Alienation—without owner's control and consent**

Understanding the methods of transferring title is reviewed here including the topics of:

II) Transfer by Voluntary Alienation

    A) Deed

        1) When real property is sold or conveyed by gift

    B) Will

        1) Parties to a will

            a) Deceased person who made the will is called a testator (if a male) or a testatrix (if female)

            b) Devisee is the person receiving real property, or beneficiary if it is personal property

        2) Property conveyed by will

            a) Devise if its real property

            b) Bequest if its personal property

Transfer by Voluntary Alienation

Title that is conveyed through voluntary alienation is done so with the control and consent of the original owner. It is accomplished in one of only two ways; Either through a deed or a will.

Both are legal instruments used to convey title.

- **Deed**
- **Will**

http://thismatter.com/money/real-estate/title-transfer.htm

Deed

When Real Property is Sold or Conveyed by Gift

The deed is a written document that voluntarily conveys the transfer of title. Working as a real estate licensee, a deed is the main form of title transfer that the licensee will interface with upon the closing of a sale and purchase agreement.

However, a deed may also be used when a property owner transfers property to another as a gift (instead of upon a sale).

The person transferring title is the grantor of the deed. The person receiving title is the grantee.

http://thismatter.com/money/real-estate/title-transfer.htm

Will

Parties to a Will

Property can also be conveyed in the form of voluntary alienation through a **will**. Even after passing, an owner can have control over the transfer of property by instructing the administrator of the estate to transfer the property to the stated person designated in the will.

Testate is the term meaning that a person died with a legal will in place. To die **intestate** is to die without a will.

So, although it may seem as if the transfer is out of the deceased person's control which would hint at involuntary alienation. It is, in fact, voluntary alienation as control is maintained through the implementation of the legal document "last will and testament."

The deceased person who made the will is called a testator if that deceased person is a male. The deceased person is called a testatrix if that deceased person is a female.

http://info.legalzoom.com/transfer-property-through-wills-3893.html

It is common to hear someone receiving property through a deceased relative being referred to as the beneficiary. And that person is, in fact, **a beneficiary if the property received is personal property.**

The devisee is the person receiving real property (real estate). So, when someone receives a transferred title to a home from a deceased relative, that person is a devisee rather than a beneficiary.

Property Conveyed by Will

Devise is the gift of real property, whereas it is a bequest if it is personal property.

http://whatis.thedifferencebetween.com/compare/bequeath-and-devise/

Use the following words to fill in the blanks: beneficiary, bequest, devise, devisee, grantee, grantor, testate, testator

George died. Prior to his death, George had prepared a will. In his will he left his home to his son Michael. He left his antique car collection to his son Timothy.   Because Michael already had a home, Michael deeded the house over to Timothy.

- George died _____. As the _____, George left a _____ to Michael. Michael was the _____ as the recipient of the home. George left a _____ to Timothy. Timothy was the _____. When Michael transferred the deed of the home to Timothy, Michael was the _____ and Timothy was the _____.

Answer

- George died testate.   As the testator, George left a devise to Michael. Michael was the devisee as the recipient of the home. George left a bequest to Timothy. Timothy was the beneficiary. When Michael transferred the deed of the home to Timothy, Michael was the grantor and Timothy was the grantee.

Special Emphasis: Transfer by Voluntary Alienation

Either through a **Deed or Will.**

INVOLUNTARY ALIENATION

Understanding the methods of transferring title is reviewed here including the topics of:

III) Transfer by Involuntary Alienation

    A) Transfer by descent

        1) Person who dies without a will died intestate

        2) A form of involuntary alienation because the state (not the deceased) determines the disposition of property

        3) Passes to legal descendants known as heirs

    B) Escheat

        1) Provides for the property of a person who dies intestate and who has no known heirs to pass to the state

    C) Eminent domain

        1) Governmental power to *take* land from an owner through the legal process called condemnation

    D) Adverse possession

        1) Conditions for alienation by adverse possession

Transfer by Involuntary Alienation

The opposite of voluntary alienation is **involuntary alienation**. This is when a person's property is transferred without the original owner's consent or control.

Involuntary Alienation includes:

- Transfer by Descent
- Transfer by Escheat
- Transfer by Eminent Domain
- Transfer by Adverse Possession

Transfer by Descent

When a person dies without a will, the person dies intestate. This is a **form of involuntary alienation because the state (not the deceased) determines the disposition of the property**. In the absence of a will, the deceased property **passes to any legal descendants known as heirs.**

When this happens, the courts will look to Florida's statutes regarding the disposition of property.

Florida Statutes 732

Transfer by Escheat

Florida Statutes **provide that the property of a person who dies intestate and who has no known heirs, to pass to the state.** The property is transferred to the state by escheat. This is a form of involuntary alienation.

Without this legal provision, property would remain in limbo and would languish eventually deteriorating from neglect.

Florida Statutes 732

Transfer by Eminent Domain

Eminent domain is the **governmental power to take land from an owner through the legal process called condemnation.** This is a form of involuntary alienation.

The taking of the land must always be for a public purpose and cannot be to benefit a private entity.

Governments (the Condemning Authorities) can delegate authority to take property to private entities such as utility companies, railroads, etc., for right of way, easements and necessary facilities – when doing so is believed to benefit the public. Under Florida law, the power of eminent domain is held by counties, municipalities, utility companies, railroads, transportation authorities, community development districts, water management districts, airports and the mosquito control districts, etc.

Condemnation refers to the process by which the power of eminent domain is exercised. The safeguards contained in the U.S. and Florida Constitutions and the Florida Statutes are designed to protect the rights of the property owner.

http://eminentdomainlawflorida.com/the-eminent-domain-process/frequently-asked-questions.html

Transfer by Adverse Possession

Adverse possession is when someone other than the owner takes control of a property. This is a form of involuntary alienation as it is a method of acquiring title to real property by possession for a statutory period under certain conditions.

By adverse possession, title to another's real property is acquired without paying for the property. The property is taken and is held in conflict with the original owner's rights and desires.

There are specific conditions for alienation by adverse possession that must be met:

The person making the claim must have taken the property by hostile means (without permission of the original owner) and have done so by possessing the property through physical occupation which is said to be open and notorious, because the taking is evident and not hidden. The person must have possessed the property for at least seven years and have paid taxes on the property for the seven years. Finally, the person must make an actual claim on the property with the property appraiser through a "return" (form).

Florida Statutes 95.18

Special Emphasis: Involuntary Alienation includes:

- Transfer by Descent

- Transfer by Escheat

- Transfer by Eminent Domain

- Transfer by Adverse Possession

Special Emphasis: Conditions for Adverse Possession

- Hostile Taking of (meaning without permission)

- Actual Possession which is (meaning physical occupation)

- Open and Notorious for (meaning the possession is obvious to onlookers and not hidden)

- Continuous Period of 7 Years

- Paid Taxes for the entire period

- Makes Claim of Title (without color of title through written instrument or court action)

Florida Statutes 95.18

Understanding the methods of transferring title is reviewed here including the topics of:

IV) Notice to Legal Title

   A) Actual notice

   B) Constructive notice

      1) Acknowledgment

      2) Lis Pendens

Notice to Legal Title

Whether you are the buyer or seller, it is a good idea to give notice to others that the exchange of property has taken place.

For the seller, it is in the interest of being relieved from any liability that the ownership could potentially bring. Let's say someone was hurt on the property after title had transferred from one person to another. Then, the seller would want the public to clearly understand that he or she is no longer responsible for anything that happens on the property.

For the buyer, let's say that the person wants to engage the services of a contractor. The buyer would want the contractor to know that the buyer is now the true owner and has the right to make changes and hire the contractor.

There are two ways to give notice to the public that something has taken place (property has been transferred). This can be through actual notice or through constructive notice.

Both methods are considered legally sufficient in the eyes of the law that notice was given.

- Actual Notice

- Constructive Notice

http://legal-dictionary.thefreedictionary.com/Notice

Actual Notice

Actual notice is when a party has awareness or direct notification of a fact or proceeding through reading, hearing, or seeing.

- So, actual notice has occurred when an individual was directly told about something -- for example, when a tenant notifies the landlord that a furnace isn't working, the landlord has actual notice of the faulty furnace even though the landlord hasn't personally met with the furnace.

- "Personal service" of court documents is another common method of delivering actual notice when the person accepts the documents.

ttp://www.nolo.com/dictionary/actual-notice-term.html

Constructive Notice

Constructive notice is knowledge which, according to law, a person can acquire by making normal and reasonable enquiries.

Recording something in public records is to give constructive notice.

- For example, the purchaser of a property is presumed to know the legal status of a property from documents recorded with the clerk of the court. These documents are available for public inspection.

- And a notice of a court action in a newspaper is a constructive notice.

Regarding real estate, all documents recorded with the clerk of the court are binding as legal notice having been sufficiently given. However, it is not required that a deed be recorded to be valid.

http://www.businessdictionary.com/definition/constructive-notice.html

Acknowledgment

Although it is not required to record a deed, recording documents pertaining to real estate puts the public on notice about ownerships, liens, etc.

To record a deed, the deed must first be acknowledged by the grantor and this acknowledgment must be notarized. To acknowledge the deed means the grantor asserts that the deed was signed voluntarily.

The signer must personally appear before the notary public and declare that he or she has signed the document voluntarily. The notary will ensure that the signer understands the document and has not been coerced into signing it.

- Acknowledgment is the formal declaration before a notary public declaring that the signing was voluntary.

- **Constructive Notice**

- **Lis Pendens**

- When a lawsuit for foreclosure is proceeding, the lender will give constructive notice of the suit by filing the **lis pendens** notice in the county where the property is located.

- The lis pendens is a recorded legal document.

- The purpose of this notice is to flag the lawsuit in case the mortgagor attempts to sell the property. An action that wouldn't be uncommon from an individual on the verge of losing property.

http://www.investorwords.com/14476/lis_pendens.html#ixzz3wbSwfw35

Special Emphasis: Notice to Legal Title

There are two ways to give notice to the public that something has taken place (property has been transferred).

- Actual notice is when a party has awareness or direct notification of a fact or proceeding through reading, hearing, or seeing

- Constructive notice is knowledge which, according to law, a person can acquire by making normal and reasonable enquiries.

Special Emphasis: Constructive Notice (legal notice)

- Recording in the public records

- Acknowledgment

  - Formal declaration before a notary public that the signing is a free act

* Lis Pendens is notice pending legal action in public records

PROTECTION OF TITLE

Understanding the methods of transferring title is reviewed here including the topics of:

V) Protection of Title

A) Title companies

B) Chain of title vs. Abstract of title

C) Title opinion

D) Title insurance

    1) Owner's policy

    2) Lender's policy

Title Companies

A title company makes sure that the title to a piece of real estate is legitimate and then issues optional title insurance for that property.

The title company will review previous ownership records of a property through chain of title and an abstract of title and execute a title opinion in regard to the marketability of the title – the ability of the owner to transfer the property to the buyer.

- Title companies also often maintain escrow accounts — these contain the funds needed to close on the home — to ensure that this money is used only for settlement and closing costs, and may conduct the formal closing on the home.

- At the closing, a settlement agent from the title company will bring all the necessary documentation, explain it to the parties, collect closing costs and distribute monies. Finally, the title company will ensure that the new titles, deeds and other documents are filed with the appropriate entities.

Chain of Title Vs. Abstract of Title

A **Chain of Title** is the "linking" of one owner to another as the property has been conveyed from one person to the next. Each person is connected through the ownership history and is said to form a "chain" of ownership.

An **Abstract of Title** is the search through recorded documents to find evidence of title transfer history and mortgages or other liens against the property, including judgments and unpaid taxes.

An abstract of title, or title abstract, briefly summarizes the various activities affecting ownership of a parcel of land. When an individual agrees to purchase real estate, an examination of the history of seller's property is examined. This examination is known as a title search. A title search is conducted to determine that the seller of the property in fact owns the property and has a *free-and-clear* title. A free-and-clear title has no *clouds* on it, which means that no person or business other than the seller has an interest in, or claim to, the property.

- http://legal-dictionary.thefreedictionary.com/Abstract+of+title

Title Opinion

Once the Chain of Title has been established and an Abstract of Title has been reviewed by an attorney, the attorney provides an opinion of title.

A **Title Opinion** is the written opinion of an attorney, based on the attorney's title search into a property, describing the current ownership rights in the property, as well as the actions that must be taken, if any to make the stated ownership rights marketable.

The Title Opinion is as the name implies an "opinion" and is usually not given with a guarantee that it is correct meaning the attorney cannot be held responsible for errors.

- Executed by an attorney who has studied the abstract
- Title is or is not marketable

Title Opinion is NOT a guaranteed.

Caution:

A real estate licensee must take care NOT to provide an opinion of title. This is not within the scope of real estate licensing.

An opinion of title can only be provided by an attorney. The licensee can only share the opinion that the attorney has formed.

http://en.wikipedia.org/wiki/Title_opinion

Title Insurance

Searching the history of a property and providing an abstract of title may uncover most problems with title ownership. However, there could also be some issues that remain hidden called defects of title.

To protect the parties against these problems, title insurance companies offer title insurance.

With title insurance if any claim is brought against the property because of a pre-existing problem with the title, the title insurance will likely cover the expense.

Title insurance is not required by law, however, because of the risk involved with an unmarketable title, title insurance may be required as part of the closing when a mortgage is involved.

Once the title search has shown the title to be valid, the title company will likely be willing to issue a title insurance policy. The policy protects owners or lenders against claims made against them and covers legal fees that may arise from disputes over the ownership of the property.

There are two main types of title insurance: owner's title insurance, which protects the property owner from title issues, and lender's title insurance, which protects the mortgage company.

http://www.finweb.com/real-estate/how-much-do-title-search-companies-typically-cost.html#ixzz3wfJF6fkk
http://www.zillow.com/mortgage-learning/title-company/

Owner's Policy Vs. Lender's Policy

As a real estate licensee, be sure to understand the subtle differences between an owner's policy and a lender's policy.

An Owner's policy is issued for the price of the house where as the lender's policy is issued for the price of the mortgage the policy is protecting. How much the lender's policy will cover goes down as the mortgage is paid – it protects the unpaid balance!

An owner's policy is to protect the new owners whereas the lender's policy is put into place only to protect the lender.

With the owner's policy if the owner dies and the property is passed on to an heir, the protection is still in place. However, the owner's policy does not pass to a new owner upon the sale of the property. Whereas with the lender's policy, the policy does pass (is transferable) to the new owner of the mortgage (mortgages are collateral that can be sold from investor to investor protected by the lender's policy).

Both the owner's policy and the lender's policy are paid as a one-time fee at closing.

http://www.buyerschoicerealty.com/learn/html/title_insurance_lenders_vs_own.html

Owner's Policy

- Issued for price of house (sale price)

- Protects the new owner (buyer) and his heirs

- Not transferable to another party upon a sale

- One-time premium is charged (at closing)

Lender's Policy

- Issued for unpaid mortgage amount (not the sale price)

- Protects the lender against title defects (not the owner)

- Transferable (assignable to someone else buying the loan)

- Protects the lender up to outstanding loan balance (not original amount)

- One-time premium paid at closing

- Most lenders require it as a condition of making loan

Special Emphasis: Chain of Title Vs. Abstract of Title

A **Chain of Title** is the "linking" of one owner to another as the property has been conveyed from one person to the next.

An **Abstract of Title** is the search through recorded documents to find evidence of title transfer history and mortgages or other liens against the property including judgments and unpaid taxes.

Protection of Title

Comparing Types of Title Insurance

Owner's Policy
- Issued for price of house (sale price)
- Protects the new owner (buyer) and his heirs
- Not transferable to another party upon a sale
- One-time premium is charged (at closing)

Lender's Policy
- Issued for mortgage amount
- Protects the lender against title defects (not the owner)
- Transferable (assignable to someone else buying the loan)
- One-time premium paid at closing

DEEDS

Understanding the methods of transferring title is reviewed here including the topics of:

VI) Deeds

    A) Parties to the deed

        1) Grantor

        2) Grantee

Parties to the Deed

The deed is a written document or "instrument" that voluntarily conveys the transfer of title of real property from one party to another.

As already stated, there are two parties to a deed.

The person transferring title is the **grantor** of the deed. The person receiving title is the **grantee**.

- Grantor – owner giving title
- Grantee – new owner receiving title

Understanding the methods of transferring title is reviewed here including the topics of:

VI) Deeds

  B) Parts of a deed

      1) Grantor and grantee

      2) Consideration

      3) Words of conveyance (granting clause)

      4) Interest or estate being conveyed (habendum clause)

      5) Deed restrictions

      6) Exceptions and reservations

      7) Appurtenances

      8) Legal description of property

      9) Voluntary delivery and acceptance

10) Signature of the grantor and two witnesses

Parts of a Deed

It is important to be able to identify and understand the different parts of a deed. These elements are present to clearly transfer title and to specify the terms and conditions of the ownership transfer. Included in a deed are:

- Names of grantee and grantor

- Consideration—detail of what is given in exchange for title

- Words of conveyance—Granting clause

- Interest (estate) being conveyed—Habendum clause

- Deed restrictions

- Exceptions and reservations

- Deed restrictions

- Appurtenances

- Legal description

- Voluntary delivery and acceptance (Legal title passes to grantee at this point)

- Signature of grantor and 2 witnesses

A deed is broken down into three basic parts. The premises section, the operative part and the conclusion.

Premises Section

The Premises section starts with the date that the deed is being transferred and then identifies the names of the **grantor and the grantee**. To further identify the grantor and grantee, known addresses of the parties are included.

The amount of compensation being paid for the property is also included in the premises section. The amount of compensation is called the **Consideration**.

Words of conveyance, which is the "Granting Clause," is then included leading the **legal description** (address) of the property being convey. The granting clause is important because it specifically states the intent of the grantor to "grant" or "convey" the property to the grantee.

http://chestofbooks.com/business/law/American-Commercial-Law-Series/Chapter-22-The-Parts-And-Essentials-To-Deeds.html

Deeds

Parts of a Deed – Premises Section

This Deed is made on this day of _____, 20__, between the
Grantor _____ of
address _____
_____ and the Grantee _____ of
address _____
_____ For consideration of the sum of $ _____,
the Grantor hereby bargain, deed and convey the following described real
property to the Grantee forever, free and clear with WARRANTY
COVENANTS:

Property
Address: _____
Legal Description: _____

http://www.free-real-estate-forms.com/general-warranty-deed.html#sthash.YhY6OYtO.dpuf

Granting Clause

Operative Section

The operative section leads with words describing the exact "interest" or type of estate being conveyed. This is called the **Habendum clause.**

The habendum clause is associated with the words to "have and to hold" and if it is a fee simple estate (as opposed to a life estate, for example) it includes the words "forever" designating the transfer of ownership as permanent.

If **deed restrictions** already exist, or if the grantor is placing them upon the new owner, then they are included next followed by any exceptions or reservations. An example of a deed restriction could be the seller to refuse that any alcohol be served on the property or the retaining of mineral rights by the seller "restricting" the new owner from being able to gain from the minerals.

Exceptions and reservations are then described, meaning that if there are any encroachments or encumbrances or any known impediments on the property it would be described here. This would include easements.

http://chestofbooks.com/business/law/American-Commercial-Law-Series/Chapter-22-The-Parts-And-Essentials-To-Deeds.html

Deeds

Deed – Operative Section & Conclusion

Grantor, for itself and its heirs, hereby covenants with Grantee, its heirs and assigns, that Grantor is lawfully seized in fee simple of the above described property; that it has a good right to convey, that the property is free from all encumbrances; that the Grantors and its heirs, and all persons acquiring any interest in the property granted, through or for Grantor, will, on demand of Grantee, or its heirs or assigns, and at the expense of Grantee, its heirs or assigns, execute and instrument necessary for the further assurance of the title to the property that may be reasonably required; and that Grantor and _ heirs will forever warrant and defend all of the property so granted to __ __rs, against every person lawfully claiming the same or any part ti ___

EXECUTED this day of _____, 20__.

Grantor Name: _____ Gra_ __ignature: _____

Witness Name: _____ Witness Signature: _____

Witness Name: _____ Witness Signature: _____

Habendum Clause

Next, in the operative section would be a description of **Appurtenances**. Appurtenances are any uses of areas that transfer with the property. These normally involve deeded use of parking garages or space, water rights and other improvements such as club houses and pools in community centers.

Finally, the **Conclusion** section of the deed contains the **voluntary delivery and acceptance,** which is the actual legal transfer of property from one party to the other (the grantor to the grantee).

Included to make the transfer legal is the **signature of the grantor and two witnesses.**

This deed will normally be notarized to be able to record the deed with the clerk of the court. Note that the deed does not have to be signed by the grantee or notarized for property transfer to legally occur.

http://chestofbooks.com/business/law/American-Commercial-Law-Series/Chapter-22-The-Parts-And-Essentials-To-Deeds.html

Understanding the methods of transferring title is reviewed here including the topics of:

VI) Deeds

    C) Requirements for a valid deed

        1) The deed must be in writing (Statute of Frauds)

        2) The names of grantor and grantee

        3) Grantor must have legal capacity

        4) Consideration must be described

        5) A granting clause or words of conveyance

        6) A habendum clause must define the quality of the ownership interest being conveyed

        7) Legal description of the property being transferred

        8) Grantor must sign

For a deed to be valid it must have each element required by Florida law including:

- The deed must be in writing– Per Statute of Frauds

- Names of grantor and grantee included

- Grantor must be of legal capacity

- Consideration must be described

- A Granting clause or words of conveyance must be included

- A Habendum clause must define the quality of ownership interest being conveyed

- Legal description of the property being transferred must be included

- Grantor must sign and have 2 witnesses included to show voluntary delivery

- Delivery and acceptance must occur – Although the grantee doesn't have to sign the deed; the acceptance must be agreed upon.

Understanding the methods of transferring title is reviewed here including the topics of:

VI) Deeds

    D) Types of statutory deeds

        1) General warranty deed

        2) Special warranty deed

        3) Bargain and sale deed

        4) Quitclaim deed

        5) Special purpose deeds

            (a) Personal representative's deed

            (b) Guardian's deed

            (c) Committee's

Types of Statutory Deeds

A statutory deed is a deed whose format is defined by a state statute.

Recall that state laws mandate that some agreements must take on a formal written format (unlike informal contracts) to be valid.

The state of Florida allows for four types of statutory deeds. These deeds are considered "condensed" as they refer to the warranties contained within the deed rather than describing each warranty in detail.

The four statutory deeds are:

- General Warranty Deed

- Special Warranty Deed

- Bargain and Sale Deed

- Quitclaim Deed

http://www.ehow.com/facts_5045871_statutory-warranty-deed.html

General Warranty Deed

The general warranty deed is the most commonly used deed. It is the "default" deed that is used if a contract does not specifically state that another type of deed will be issued, meaning it is so common that it is assumed that the parties plan to use this deed.

What sets this deed apart from other types of deeds is that it is the most comprehensive. It provides the greatest guarantee of protections from the grantor to the grantee – the grantor agrees to stand behind the conveyance should any problems arise.

Covenants included in this type of deed are the Covenant of Seisin, the Covenant Against Encumbrances, the Covenant of Further Assurance, the Covenant of Quiet Enjoyment, and the Covenant of Warranty Forever.

> http://www.ehow.com/facts_5045871_statutory-warranty-deed.html

> Florida Statutes 689.02

General Warranty Deed

Includes Covenants of:

- Seisin—promises grantor is the true owner and has right to convey title

- Against encumbrances—free of liens, etc. (unless disclosed)

- Further assurance—grantor will deliver legal instrument if required to stand behind the transfer

- Quiet enjoyment—peaceful possession undisturbed by claims of title

- Warranty forever—to defend grantee's title against all lawful claims

> http://www.ehow.com/facts_5045871_statutory-warranty-deed.html

> Florida Statutes 689.02

Special Warranty Deed

Sometimes the grantor may be uncomfortable fully warranting a property, particularly if that grantor has limited knowledge about the history of the property.

In that case, someone such as an executor of an estate (who must sign to transfer property) would choose to issue a Special Warranty Deed instead of a General Warranty Deed. The Special Warranty Deed ONLY guarantees that the grantor personally has done nothing to encumber the property.

(The special warranty deed does NOT include the Covenant of Seisin.)

(No special statutory format.)

> http://www.ehow.com/facts_5045871_statutory-warranty-deed.html

> Florida Statutes 689.02

Bargain and Sale Deed

The Bargain and Sale Deed is signed by the person who owns the property, therefore, it includes the Covenant of

Seisin. This means that the person signing the deed is guaranteeing that they own the property and therefore has the right to sell it or transfer it to another party.

However, they do not include ANY other covenants including the covenant against encumbrances. (Not even any assurances that the grantor didn't cause any liens as does the Special Warranty Deed).

This is the type of deed that a property owned by a bank would be issued with using. Because although the bank owns the property and has the right to sell it, no other guarantees are made with the sale.

Florida Statutes 689.02

Quitclaim Deed

Sometimes there are issues that come up showing a **"cloud" on a title**.

And sometimes it is even unclear whether someone truly owns a property or could later cause problems by asserting ownership. The Quitclaim deed is used when such a person agrees to "remise, release, or quitclaim" any claims on the property in the future.

This type of deed holds no covenants and it does not contain the Covenant of Seisin as the person is not claiming to own the property now but is agreeing to assert no ownership in the future by signing off the deed officially transferring away all ownership rights.

(No special statutory format).

Florida Statutes 689.02

Special Purpose Deeds

Because of the wording of the standard deeds, it may be impossible to convey title using either the general warranty deed, the special warranty deed, the bargain and sale deed or the quitclaim deed.

Therefore, 4 Special Purpose Deeds are now used to handle these situations.

Special Purpose Deeds includes:

- Personal Representative Deed
- Guardian's Deed
- Committee's Deed
- Tax Deed

Special Purpose Deeds

Personal Representative's Deed

- Personal representative is appointed by will or by court to settle estate of deceased person

Guardian's Deed

- Guardian acts on behalf of a minor

Committee's Deed

- Used when owner is legally incompetent

Tax Deed

- Used when property is sold for back taxes

http://francesjarvis.com/2012/07/30/what-are-special-purpose-deeds/

Special Purpose Deeds

Personal Representative's Deed

Regardless of whether a person died testate or intestate, someone will be appointed to settle the estate. One of the required activities involved may be transferring real estate from the deceased person to the new owner.

This is a special circumstance where the representative cannot claim to own the property. There is no covenant of seisin, however there is a covenant of no encumbrances

http://francesjarvis.com/2012/07/30/what-are-special-purpose-deeds/

Guardian's Deed

If someone is acting on behalf of a minor then this type of deed would be used to transfer the property. First, the guardian would get permission from the court to authorize the sale. Then, a Guardian's Deed would be issued to transfer the property.

http://francesjarvis.com/2012/07/30/what-are-special-purpose-deeds/

Committee's Deed

A committee's deed is used to transfer property on behalf of someone who has been found to be incompetent and can no longer sign a regular deed him or herself. There are normally several people who are appointed to act on a committee for the individual and all persons on the committee would be required to sign the committee deed.

http://francesjarvis.com/2012/07/30/what-are-special-purpose-deeds/

Tax Deed

Once a property is sold for nonpayment of taxes, a Tax deed is issued. A tax deed contains no covenants and warranties and buyer beware applies.

http://francesjarvis.com/2012/07/30/what-are-special-purpose-deeds/

Understanding the methods of transferring title is reviewed here including the topics of:

VI) Deeds

    E) Deed Clauses

        1) Covenant of seisin

        2) Covenant against encumbrances

        3) Covenant of quiet enjoyment

        4) Covenant of further assurance

        5) Covenant of warranty forever

Deeds
Deed Clauses

Deed Clauses	General Warranty	Special Warranty	Bargain & Sale	Quitclaim	Personal Representative	Guardian's	Committee's	Tax
Covenant of Seisin	★		★	None				None
Covenant Against Encumbrances	★	★ (During Time They Owned It)			★	★	★	
Covenant of Quit Enjoyment	★							
Covenant of Further Assurance	★							
Covenant of Warranty Forever	★							

Understanding the methods of transferring title is reviewed here including the topics of:

VI) Deeds

    F) Legal requirements

Legal Requirements

Remember that a person who has been assigned by the court to dispose of property on behalf of another – either alive or deceased– is exempt from licensure for real estate.

- F.S. 475.011(1) as the personal representative, receiver, trustee, or general or special magistrate under, or by virtue of, an appointment by will or by order of a court of competent jurisdiction; or as trustee under a deed of trust, or under a trust agreement, the ultimate purpose and intent whereof is charitable, is philanthropic, or provides for those having a natural right to the bounty of the donor or trustor.

Remember too that a real estate licensee is not allowed to draw up a deed UNLESS the licensee happens to also own an interest in the property. Furthermore, the licensee CANNOT give an opinion of title.

To do would be considered practicing law without a license.

Special Emphasis: Elements of a Valid Deed

- The deed must be in writing– Per Statute of Frauds

- Names of grantor and grantee included

- Grantor must be of legal capacity

- Consideration must be described

- A **Granting clause** or words of conveyance must be included

- A **Habendum clause** must define the quality of ownership interest being conveyed

- Legal description of the property being transferred must be included

- Grantor must sign and have 2 witnesses included to show voluntary delivery

- Delivery and acceptance must occur

Special Emphasis: Types of Statutory Deeds

The four statutory deeds are:

- General Warranty Deed

- Special Warranty Deed

- Bargain and Sale Deed

- Quitclaim Deed

Special Emphasis: General Warranty Deed

The general warranty deed is the most commonly used deed.

It provides the greatest guarantee of protections from the grantor to the grantee – the grantor agrees to stand behind the conveyance should any problems arise.

Covenants included in this type of deed are the Covenant of Seisin, the Covenant Against Encumbrances, the Covenant of Further Assurance, the Covenant of Quiet Enjoyment, and the Covenant of Warranty

Forever.

Special Emphasis: Special Warranty Deed

The Special Warranty Deed ONLY guarantees that the grantor personally has done nothing to encumber the property.

(The special warranty deed does NOT include the Covenant of Seisin.)

Special Emphasis: Bargain and Sale Deed

It includes the Covenant of Seisin.

However, they do not include ANY other covenants including the covenant against encumbrances.

This is the type of deed that a property owned by a bank would be issued with using.

Special Emphasis: Quitclaim Deed

Used to clear a **"cloud" on a title**.

The Quitclaim deed is used when such a person agrees to "remise, release, or quitclaim" any claims on the property in the future.

This type of deed holds no covenants.

Understanding the methods of transferring title is reviewed here including the topics of:

VII) Ownership Limitations and Restrictions

    A) Government restrictions

        1) Police power

        2) Eminent domain

        3) Taxation

    B) Private restrictions

Ownership Limitations and Restrictions

Even though a person owns the complete bundle of rights to a property, the person may still be restricted in the use of the property.

There are two major categories for Ownership Limitations and Restrictions. These are:

- **Government Restrictions which includes Police Power, Eminent Domain, and Taxation.**

- **Private Restrictions which includes Deed Restrictions, Easements, Leases, and Liens.**

Government Restrictions

Includes:

Police Power

- Federal and State Constitutions apply restrictions to protect citizenry for health and safety reasons —Broadest Gov't. Power

Eminent Domain

- The right to take private property for just compensation

Taxation

- Property can be foreclosed upon for nonpayment of taxes

Police Power

Police powers are the broadest of all government powers. It stems from U.S. Constitutional law. Under the Tenth Amendment, it passes the police powers to the states to regulate and enforce order within their boundaries for the betterment of the health, safety, morals, and general welfare of the people.

The states can pass these powers to local government. These regulations must not infringe upon any of the rights of the people protected under the U.S. or States constitutions.

Police powers translates to ownership limitations and restrictions in that it allows zoning regulations, implementation of building codes, heath codes and city planning.

http://www.changelabsolutions.org/sites/default/files/chapter5.pdf

Eminent Domain

Recall that eminent domain is the governmental power to take land from an ownership limitation and restriction.

Governments (the Condemning Authorities) can delegate authority to take property to private entities such as utility companies, railroads, etc., for right of way, easements and necessary facilities.

The taking of the land must always be for a public purpose and cannot be to benefit a private entity.

Someone who has had their property taken from them have the right to "just compensation." This means they must be fairly compensated for the loss of the property.

Taxation

Property owners collectively pay for benefits and protection from the schools, police, fire department, emergency services, roads, water lines, sewer lines, etc.

The failure to pay the taxes and assessments imposed upon individual property owners can result in the ultimate ownership limitation and restriction through the loss of ownership of the property – as the property can be foreclosed upon for nonpayment of taxes.

http://www.alllaw.com/articles/nolo/foreclosure/unpaid-property-taxes-sale-house.html

VII) Ownership Limitations and Restrictions

B) Private restrictions

1) Deed restrictions

(a) Restrictive covenants

Private Restrictions

Includes:

Deed restrictions

- Deed restrictions are created within the deed which limits how an owner can use a property. Deed restrictions include Restrictive Covenants which are placed within deeds of an entire development.

Easements

- Easements do not transfer ownership. Rather, it forces the right for others to have use of the property.

Leases

- Leases place restrictions on the owner by passing the right of use to the lessee.

Liens

- A lien is the right to retain the lawful possession of the property of another until the owner fulfills a legal duty to the person holding the property, such as the payment of lawful charges for work done on the property.

Deed Restrictions

Deed restrictions are a form of private restrictions and includes restrictive covenants.

Deed restrictions are written directly into a property's deed. These restrictions are imposed by past or present owners of the property or by the developer or builder and neighborhood or homeowners' associations.

These restrictions can take the form of conditions, covenants, and restrictions (CC&Rs). When deed restrictions are placed on an entire community – rather than just one property owner – it is called a **restrictive covenant**.

Restrictive covenants are aimed at ensuring that there is an aesthetic uniformity between neighboring properties and that certain activities are limited. The main motivation for including these restrictions are to maintain the value of a property and promote good relations and peaceful cohabitation within the community.

http://www.realtor.com/advice/deed-restrictions-can-limit-home/

Deed Restrictions- Examples

- A property owner that wants to keep the family farm from being "developed" can bar the development activity within the deed.

- A building owner that doesn't believe in drinking alcohol could write into a deed that alcohol cannot be sold or served on the premises.

Restrictive Covenants- Examples

- The developer places restrictions requiring a "minimum" size of houses that can be built, the type of fencing that can be installed and even paint colors that are allowed.

- Property may be subject to the covenants of a home owners' association. The association covenants include rules that pets are not allowed and the property cannot be rented.

Understanding the methods of transferring title is reviewed here including the topics of:

VII) Ownership Limitations and Restrictions

    B) Private restrictions

        2) Easements

            (a) Appurtenant

            (b) In gross

            (c) By prescription

            (d) By necessity

            (e) Implied easement

                (1) encroachment

Private Restrictions

Easements

Easements are a right to use a portion of an owner's land for a specific purpose. Ownership of the property is not transferred, only the right of use—as limited by the language of the easement.

There are five different types of easements:

- Appurtenant
- In Gross
- By Prescription
- By Necessity
- Implied – Encroachments

https://en.wikipediahttp://www.realtor.com/advice/deed-restrictions-can-limit-home/.org/wiki/Easement

Appurtenant Easement

An appurtenant easement is a right to use adjoining property that transfers with the land.

The parcel of land that benefits from the easement is the dominant tenement. The servient tenement is the parcel of land that provides the easement.

The appurtenant easement always transfers with the land within the deed unless the owner of the dominant tenement releases it.

https://en.wikipediahttp://www.realtor.com/advice/deed-restrictions-can-limit-home/.org/wiki/Easement

Appurtenant -Examples

- Developer Max bought a large plot of land near the lake for $70,000.

- He divided it into two plots and built two houses on each plot.

- However, because of rules about how the land had to be divided, only one of the two plots now had natural access to the lake.

- Max calculated that the property with the lake access would sell for $350,000. However, the other property would only sell for $250,000 without any lake access.

- His research indicated, though, that if he forced an easement for the second property onto the first, giving both access to the lake, each would sell for $325,000—increasing his profit. Owning both properties, he could sell each for $300,000.

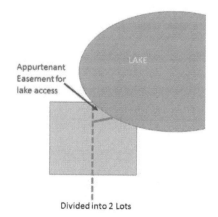

Appurtenant Easement for lake access

LAKE

Divided into 2 Lots

Easements in Gross

An easement in gross is an easement that benefits an individual or company instead of being tied to another parcel of land.

Commercial easements are freely transferable to a third party. They are divisible, but must be exclusive (original owner no longer uses it and exclusive to easement holder) and all holders of the easement must agree to divide. If subdivided, each subdivided parcel enjoys the easement.

The easement can be for a personal use or commercial use.

https://en.wikipedia.org/wiki/Easement

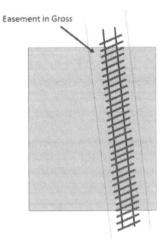

Easements in Gross - Example

An example of a personal easement in gross would be to use a boat ramp. An example of commercial use gross easement would be the rights obtained by a railroad to run tracks across property.

Easements by Prescription

Easement by prescription refers to an easement created by the open, notorious, uninterrupted, hostile, and adverse use of another's land for a period set by statute.

In Florida, the period required for an easement by prescription is 20 years.

As with all easements, the actual title of the property remains with the owner, however, use is granted based on the history of use.

http://www.realestatelawyers.com/legal-advice/real-estate/land-use-zoning/how-i-establish-easement-prescription-florida

Easements by Prescription - Example

In Florida access to beaches and the Gulf and bays are often a point of contention which requires the public to fall back on easements by prescription to keep access from the waterways and beaches from being blocked by their use. As such, the statutes have been written to ensure continued public use through an easement by prescription.

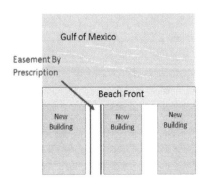

Florida Statutes 161.021

Easements by Necessity

An easement by necessity is an easement that is created by court order. Most commonly it is used when one property is land locked and has no access to the main access roads.

Judges will look to the original intention of the land; locked land was created to make a determination to impose an easement by necessity.

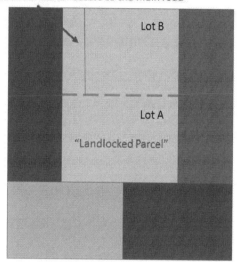

Easement in Gross for access to the main road

Easements by Necessity – Example

For example, a land developer divided a parcel into two lots and sold the property to two separate owners.

Lot A accessed the main road by crossing Lot B. The owners never questioned the arrangement and the owner of Lot B happily allowed Lot A to use the access to the main road.

However, the developer failed to officially write the easement into the deed of Lot B. So, when the owner of Lot B sold it just three years later, the new owner refused access of the property to the Lot A. (Notice that the use was not for 20 years per requirement of an easement by prescription.)

In this situation, the owner of Lot A would have to sue the new owner of Lot B. More than likely, the judge would grant Lot A an easement by necessity as the intention of the developer appeared to include it.

Florida Statutes 704.01

An Implied Easement

An implied easement can be created when a property owner has "encroached" onto another parcel, even if by mistake, for a period of seven years or more. After seven years, the right for the person who encroached upon the other's property to continue to have access would become permanent.

(This is for use other than being "landlocked," which constitutes an easement by necessity.)

- An Encroachment is defined as being an unauthorized use of another's property.

  - Examples of an implied easement would be a fence or garage located beyond boundary lines

  - Implied easement after seven years

http://www.bernsteinlegalgroup.com/home/articles/property-access-implied-easement-or-trespass-encroachment

Implied Easement - Example

When Property Owner A decided to add a garage onto his home, he mistakenly thought that the line of trees marked the edge of the property. He built his garage accordingly.

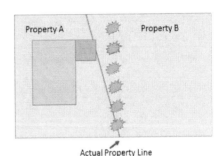

However, when Property Owner B noticed what Property Owner A had done, he notified him of the correct line which went right through the corner of the garage.

If Property Owner B allows the garage to remain in place, after 7 years it would be a permanent Implied Easement.

Understanding the methods of transferring title is reviewed here including the topics of:

VII) Ownership Limitations and Restrictions

    B) Private restrictions

        3) Leases

            (a)Types of leases

                i.   Gross
                ii. Net
                iii. Percentage
                iv. Variable/Index
                v.   Ground

Private Restrictions

Leases

A lease grants the right of possession and use to a lessee (tenant or renter). Leases do not transfer the actual ownership of the property. As leases grant rights of use, it is a private form of ownership limitation and restriction.

- Leases must be written and signed to be enforceable if for a period of over one year.

- Long-term leases also require signatures of two witnesses.

- Licensees are not able to draw up leases. Instead a real estate licensee can only use fill-in-the-blank lease forms approved by the Florida Supreme Court.

http://www.avvo.com/legal-guides/ugc/what-is-the-statute-of-frauds-in-florida

Lease Types to Know:

Gross

- Tenant pays fixed rent

Net

- Tenant pays fixed rent plus building expenses

Percentage

- Tenant pays percentage based on gross sales

Variable

- Tenant pays rent based on an index

Ground

- Lease on land

Gross Lease

With a gross lease, the tenant pays a fixed, predetermined amount for the lease as "rent" and the landlord pays all the expenses associated with ownership of the property.

It is common that utilities (electric, gas, water and sewer) be put in the tenant's name and be paid by the tenant.

The other expenses including property tax, insurance, and maintenance and repairs are paid by the landlord.

This is the most common lease that is used for residential property. It is also common for office building leases to use a gross lease.

http://www.investorwords.com/2244/gross_lease.html

Net Lease

With a net lease, the tenant pays a fixed rent amount. Plus, they are responsible for the other expenses associated with the property. This includes utilities, property taxes, property insurance, and maintenance and repairs.

This type of lease is common with commercial property.

The precise items that are to be paid by the tenant are specified in a written lease. When more than one tenant benefits from an expense, the cost is generally split fairly among the tenants based on the amount of square footage each carries with their occupancy.

https://en.wikipedia.org/wiki/Net_lease

Gross versus Net Lease

How to remember which is which?

The words gross and net are applied to leases the same as they are applied to other types of income.

With a paycheck, the gross is the amount of income before taxes and other expenses are subtracted from the check.

The net is the amount of "take home;" the amount "netted" or "captured."

Rent is income for the landlord. The gross lease is the gross income that the landlord earns BEFORE he pays for expenses associated with the property. On the other hand, the net lease already equals the amount that the landlord nets – captures.

https://en.wikipedia.org/wiki/Net_lease

Percentage Lease

A percentage lease is a lease that charges a base rent plus extra rent that is calculated as a percentage of gross sales.

This is a popular lease with retail and restaurants. It gives the property owner the opportunity to benefit from large sales revenues. It also gives the tenant the opportunity to keep their expenses under control in areas where business increases and decreases with the "season."

(Remember not to confuse the definition of a gross lease with a percentage lease. The confusion lies in the fact that this type of lease involves a percentage of "gross." Do not make that mistake.)

http://www.propertymetrics.com/blog/2014/01/16/percentage-rent/

Percentage Lease – Calculating Rent Due (1)

A percentage lease is a lease that charges a base rent, plus extra rent that is calculated as a percentage of gross sales.

- Pelican Pete wanted to open a food stand on the beach. Landlord Larry wanted $3,000 a month in rent. Pelican Pete couldn't afford to make the commitment of paying that much rent. So, Landlord Larry agreed to $1,000 a month plus 9% of gross sales. Things were slow the first three months with Pelican Pete only bringing in $15,000 in total gross sales for all three months together. But by the end of the first year, Pelican Pete's business had improved so much that he had earned total gross sales for the year of $200,000.

- How much total rent did Pelican Pete pay Landlord Larry for his first year?

Answer

- Calculate the amount of base rent due:

    - $1000 x 12 = $12,000

- Calculate the amount of percentage rent due:

    - $200,000 x .09 = $18,000

- Add the total yearly base rent with the total percentage rent due:

    - $12,000 + $18,000 = $30,000

Percentage Lease – Calculating Rent Due (2)

- Pelican Pete wanted to open a food stand on the beach. Landlord Larry wanted $3,000 a month in rent. Pelican Pete couldn't afford to make the commitment of paying that much rent. So, Landlord Larry agreed to $1,000 a month plus 9% of gross sales. Things were slow the first three months with Pelican Pete only bringing in $15,000 in total gross sales for all three months together. But by the end of the first year, Pelican Pete's business had improved so much that he had earned total gross sales for the year of $200,000.

- Was it a good idea for Pelican Pete to switch to a percentage lease?

Answer

- ...Landlord Larry agreed to $1,000 a month plus 9% of gross sales. ...But by the end of the first year, Pelican Pete's business had ... earned a total gross sales for the year of $200,000. How much total rent did Pelican Pete pay Landlord Larry for his first year?

- With the percentage lease, Pelican paid a total of $30,000 at the end of his first year. ($12,000 Base + $18,000 Percentage).

- Had Pelican Pete agreed to the $3,000 a month he would have paid $36,000 in total rent ($3,000 x 12 months).

- Pelican Pete paid $6,000 less by paying the Percentage Lease ($36,000 - $30,000). Plus, it allowed him to pay much less during the first few months he was building his business.

- If his business continues to grow, however, he could easily end up paying more than with the gross lease.

Variable Lease

A variable lease, also called an Index Lease, is a rent amount that changes at a set time based on the terms of the lease and based on an INDEX.

The specific timeline for allowed rent changes (increases) and the index that it is tied to is detailed in the lease.

It is common for the index to be tied to the Consumer Price Index (CPI). The Consumer Price Index (CPI) measures the average change in the prices paid for in the market for goods and services. Therefore, by tying to the CPI, it is viewed as a fair way to make systematic rent increases.

http://www.bls.gov/cpi/cpi1998d.htm

Variable Lease - Calculating Rent Due (1)

A variable lease, also called an Index Lease, is a rent amount that changes at a set time based on the terms of the lease and based on an INDEX.

- Gustav rented a 1,000-square foot unit with a rental rate of $15 per square foot with an CPI index of 1.3. The CPI increased to 1.9.

- How much will the new rental rate be?

Answer

- To figure the new rental rate, you need to know the **current rental rate, the current index, and the new index**. ($15, 1.3, 1.9)

- Begin by calculating what amount of % increase there was in the change of index:

- **CURRENT INDEX - NEW INDEX= INDEX DIFFERENCE**   1.9 - 1.3 = 0.6

- **INDEX DIFFERENCE ÷ CURRENT INDEX = % Increase**   0.6 ÷ **1.3** = .4615384615

- Add the **% increase** to 1.0 (100% of the Original Rent)   . 4615384615 + 1.0 =1.
  4615384615

- Then Multiply by the **ORIGINAL RENT:**   1. 4615384615 x **$15 = $21.92**

                                                                                            Rounded

EQUALS THE ADJUSTED RENTAL RATE

There's a much quicker way to calculate this same problem:

- Begin by calculating what amount of % increase there was in the change of index:

  - Divide the **NEW INDEX** by the **CURRENT INDEX.**

  - Multiply the answer by the **ORIGINAL RENT**

  - **1.9 ÷ 1.3 =** 1.4615384615

  - 1.4615384615 x **$15 = $21.92**

What if the question had asked how much total rent Gustav would now be paying?

- Same Process as before with 1 MORE STEP: Multiply by total square footage rented

  - **$21.92 x 1,000 = $21,920**

Ground Lease

With a ground lease, the lease is for the land only. The tenant erects buildings that will be used. These types of leases are usually for a very long period with 99 years not being uncommon.

An advantage of a land lease for a landlord is to avoid paying capital gain tax as the landlord would for a regular sale of property. Plus, the landlord retains fee ownership to the property. This is an important consideration to many family trusts and institutional owners who desire to maintain long-term ownership to put the property to economically productive use. Depending upon how the lease is written, the landlord may maintain control over usage.

An advantage of a land lease for the tenant is that it substantially reduces the tenant's front-end development costs because it eliminates land acquisition costs. Plus, all rent payments made under a ground lease are deductible by the tenant for federal and state income tax purposes.

http://www.wendel.com/knowledge-center/publications/2007/pros-and-cons-of-commercial-ground-leases

Understanding the methods of transferring title are reviewed here including the topics of:

VII) Ownership Limitations and Restrictions

    B) Private restrictions

        3) Leases

            b) Assignment

            c) Sublease

            d) Sale subject to lease

Assignment and Sublease

Just as a purchase, sales contract, and a mortgage may be assigned to a new buyer, a lease may be assigned to a new tenant or a sublease allowed. Whether either is permitted is dependent upon the terms of the original lease.

An **Assignment** is when the tenant assigns all leased property for the remainder of lease whereas a **Sublease** is when someone else can use the property for just a portion of the lease. This could be a sublease of part of the property (shared square footage) or it could be for the whole property but for a partial time period.

Sale Subject to Lease

A lease is binding even when a property is sold. This means that the new owner must honor the terms of a lease made with the previous owner of a property.

The fact that the renter is in place must be disclosed and handled in the terms of the Purchase and Sale Agreement.

The Florida Residential Landlord and Tenant Act requires that any security deposits and advance rents collected by the previous owner be transferred to the new owner upon the sale.

Any rent collected in advance by the new landlord would be prorated to the new owner and vice versa.

The new owner would then be required to handle rent deposits per the Florida Residential Landlord and Tenant Act, meaning the new owner would need to notify the tenant within 30 days as to how the landlord will be maintain the deposit.

Florida Statutes 83

Understanding the methods of transferring title is reviewed here including the topics of:

VII) Ownership Limitations and Restrictions

    B) Private restrictions

        4) Liens

(a) What is a lien?

(b) Types

    (1) Voluntary

    (2) Involuntary

Liens

A lien is the right to retain the lawful possession of the property of another unless the owner fulfills a legal duty to the person holding the lien against the property, such as the payment of lawful charges for work done on the property. A mortgage is a common lien.

Other common liens are property tax liens, mechanics liens and vendor liens.

The point of a lien is that, in some cases, it can force some properties to be sold to pay the lien.

The clerk of the court, where the property is located, will record the lien with appropriate documentation provided. The purpose of recording a lien is to give notice to others that the lien exists and to establish "lien order."

- Liens are encumbrances, recorded in public records

liens.uslegal.com

Voluntary Liens and Involuntary Liens

Although the word "lien" denotes a negative connotation, not all liens are forced on the property owner. Property owners may choose to have a lien placed against a property, such as when a mortgage is taken out with the property being used as collateral.

A **voluntary lien** is a lien created with the consent of the debtor. A mortgage, as just stated, or a vendor's lien are liens that have been voluntarily granted to a lender by a borrower.

An **involuntary lien** is a lien that is forced upon the property without permission from the property owner. Involuntary liens are created by law meaning that the lien will only attach to a property with the consent of the courts. A tax lien is an example of an involuntary lien.

Examples

- Voluntary

  - Mortgage

  - Vendor's lien

- Involuntary

  - Judgment liens

272

- Tax liens – property, income, and estate

- Mechanics/Construction liens

http://www.everify.com/resources/category/property-records/types-of-liens

Understanding the methods of transferring title is reviewed here including the topics of:

VII) Ownership Limitations and Restrictions

    B) Private restrictions

        4) Liens

           (c) Classifications

              (1) General

                  (i) Judgment

                  (ii) Income tax

                  (iii)Estate tax

Lien Classifications

As stated, liens can be viewed as either voluntary or involuntary. Liens can also be divided into the classification of either **general or specific**. General liens affect all properties that are held by an individual, such as from a judgment being placed against the person which is then filed against each property owned by that individual as a lien. A specific lien is filed against a property because it is a direct result of the property owner defaulting on a debt that was tied directly to the property itself.

General – May affect all properties of a debtor

- Judgment liens

- IRS liens

- Federal estate tax liens

Specific – Affect specific property only

- Property tax liens

- Special assessment liens

- Mortgages

- Vendor's lien

- Construction (mechanic's) lien

http://www.preservearticles.com/2012012621552/what-is-the-difference-between-particular-lien-and-general-lien-

Judgment Liens

General liens are never a voluntary lien. General liens are attached to property without the permission of the property owner with the intention of using the property to collect on an unpaid debt.

Judgment liens, an involuntary general lien, are attached to a property after a judgment has been made against an individual for a general unpaid debt, such as a medical bill. The unpaid bill has no relation on the property itself, but the lien is placed as an attempt to collect on the debt.

In Florida, a judgment lien can be attached to the debtor's real estate -- meaning a house, condo, land, or similar kind of property interest. Florida also allows judgment liens to be attached to the debtor's personal property -- things like jewelry, art, antiques, and other valuables.

Not all liens can force the sale of property. However, the lien will remain on the property until either the payment of the debt, forced sale of the property (if allowed), or it expires per the Florida Statutes.

http://www.preservearticles.com/2012012621552/what-is-the-difference-between-particular-lien-and-general-lien-lien.htm

Liens

Classifications

General

Income Tax Liens

Income tax liens, once filed, are another type of involuntary general lien. **It is the result of unpaid federal income taxes. As intimidating as any lien placed by the government may be, it cannot force the sale of property when the property is homesteaded.**

As stated on the IRS website, a "federal tax lien is the government's legal claim against your property when you neglect or fail to pay a tax debt. The lien protects the government's interest in all your property, including real estate, personal property and financial assets. A federal tax lien exists after the IRS: Puts your balance due on the books (assesses your liability); Sends you a bill that explains how much you owe (Notice and Demand for Payment); and You: Neglect or refuse to fully pay the debt in time. The IRS files a public document, the **Notice of Federal Tax Lien**, to alert creditors that the government has a legal right to your property."

It is possible to "discharge" the lien once the property tax debt has been paid.

- The income tax lien is not to be confused with a property tax lien or an estate tax lien

https://www.irs.gov/Businesses/Small-Businesses-&-Self-Employed/Understanding-a-Federal-Tax-Lien

Income Tax Liens

- 713.901☐ Florida Uniform Federal Lien Registration Act. —Notices of liens upon real property for obligations payable to the United States, and certificates and notices affecting the liens, shall be filed in the office of the clerk of the circuit court of the county in which the real property subject to the liens is situated…

- If a certificate of release, nonattachment, discharge, or subordination of any lien, or if a refiled notice of federal lien, is presented to the Secretary of State for filing, he or she shall: Cause a certificate of release or nonattachment to be marked, held, and indexed as if the certificate were a termination statement within the meaning of the Uniform Commercial Code, but the notice of lien to which the certificate relates may not be removed from the files.

Florida Statutes 713.913

Estate Tax Liens

An estate tax lien, or an involuntary general lien, is automatically created when any resident of the United States dies. No recorded notice is required for it to become effective.

It attaches to all of the assets that are part of the person's estate and is security for any estate taxes that may be determined to be due.

If a probate asset (assets in the name of the decedent at time of death) is transferred or liquidated without payment of the tax, generally the lien continues to attach to the asset.

If a non-probate asset is transferred or liquidated without payment of the tax, a liability equal to the value of the asset at the time of the decedent's death becomes due from the transferee.

The lien can be released against the property if the assessed value is paid in its place (or lien paid in full).

A lien can only be attached for ten years per IRS guidelines and must follow Florida Statutes 713.901 guidelines.

https://www.irs.gov/irm/part5/irm_05-005-008.html

Understanding the methods of transferring title is reviewed here including the topics of:

VII) Ownership Limitations and Restrictions

    B) Private restrictions

        4) Liens

            (c) Classifications

                (2) Specific

                    (i) Property tax & special assessment

                    (ii) Mortgage

                    (iii)Vendors

                    (iv)Construction (mechanics/materialman's)

Property Tax and Special Assessment

Property tax and special assessments are specific involuntary liens that are placed against the property immediately upon the property tax bill or assessment being levied. In fact, per Florida Statute, the lien is postdated to January 1st of the year the tax was levied and it becomes a superior lien over all other liens and is released only upon payment of the lien – forced sale for the tax debt.

The property tax is paid before the special assessment.

Although unpaid property taxes can also become a general lien against other property as well as a specific lien against the taxed property, a special assessment lien can only be applied to the property that benefited from the project for which the assessment was levied.

Florida Statutes 197.122

Mortgage Liens

A mortgage is a specific voluntary lien that is created when the borrower (mortgagor) signs a mortgage instrument pledging the property as collateral for a loan. The lien is created upon signing the mortgage. However, the mortgage lien is filed in the county where the property is located to establish lien order. If the borrower fails to pay the debt as agreed, the mortgagee can force the sale of the property.

On the other hand, within 60 days after the date of receipt of the full payment of the mortgage, a satisfaction of the mortgage should be issued and filed.

https://www.lawserver.com/law/state/florida/statutes/florida_statutes_701-04

Vendor's Lien

A vendor's lien is a specific voluntary lien that is created when the seller gives the buyer/borrower a purchase money mortgage.

A purchase money mortgage, also called seller financing or owner financing, is a home-financing technique in which the buyer borrows from the seller instead of, or in addition to, a bank. These are sometimes done when a buyer cannot qualify for a bank loan or for the full amount.

This becomes a lien against the property just as a regular bank mortgage does.

http://www.investorwords.com/3955/purchase_money_mortgage.html#ixzz3x4Q1csxI

Construction (Mechanics/Materialman's) Liens

A construction lien, also known as a mechanic's or materialman's lien, is an involuntary specific lien that results from nonpayment of a debt involving work specific to the property.

The contractor has only 90 days after the last date of work or delivery of supplies is made in order to file a lien against the property and establish lien priority over a mortgage that was taken out against the property after the work on the property began.

The contractor then has only one year to take the owner to court to force the payment of the debt or the lien against the property will be released.

Florida Statute 713

Understanding the methods of transferring title is reviewed here including the topics of:

VII) Ownership Limitations and Restrictions

    B) Private restrictions

        4) Liens

            (d) Lien priority

                (1) Satisfaction

                    (i) Superior

                    (ii) Junior

Liens

Lien Priority

Liens are designated as either a superior lien or a junior lien. Superior liens are paid before junior liens. Some superior liens include property tax, special assessments, and federal estate tax liens. Some junior liens include mortgages, vendor's, income tax, and judgments.

Superior liens

- Property tax
- Special assessments
- Federal estate tax

Junior liens

- Mortgages
- Vendors (Purchase Money Mortgage)
- Income Tax IRS Lien
- Judgment

Lien Priority

Who gets paid first when there is more than one lien against a property? Should a property be forced into foreclosure and there is more than one party holding a lien against the property, **the order of lien priority designates which party gets paid before the other.**

This can be especially important as the sale of the property does not always provide enough money to pay all the debts in full (if any).

With each lien that is paid a **satisfaction of the lien** must be issued by the creditor. This is also called a release of lien. The release must be sent to the debtor and filed in the same county that the lien was filed to give constructive notice that the lien has been released.

When a property is forced into foreclosure, not all unpaid liens are released and instead remain attached to the property.

Florida Statute 713

Senior Liens

While liens generally are prioritized (which is paid first) based on the date they're filed, government and municipal liens jump in line as a superior lien. If these superior liens are left unpaid even upon a foreclosure, they remain attached to the property —and the new owner is subject to the lien.

There is a lien priority even among superior liens as property tax liens are always paid first.

Although IRS liens are a type of government lien, it is not a superior lien and rarely attaches with property upon a foreclosure sale. Property tax liens, on the other hand, typically stay with the property regardless of a foreclosure.

People buying foreclosed properties should complete a title search to find out if they're buying a property in which they're responsible for back-property taxes.

http://homeguides.sfgate.com/happens-there-another-lien-foreclosure-property-34226.html

Junior Liens

Unpaid junior liens do not attach to a property upon foreclosure. This means that if there is not enough debt to pay these liens, the new owner of the property owns the property clear of the liens.

However, this does not free the original owner of the debt which can remain as a personal debt.

Junior liens are also an order of lien priority normally dictated by the date the lien was filed. A first mortgage taking priority over a second mortgage over a third, etc.

Recall that the construction lien, which is also a junior lien can override the date of a mortgage lien if the work was started before the mortgage was filed and the construction lien itself was filed with 90 days of the last work being done on the property.

http://homeguides.sfgate.com/happens-there-another-lien-foreclosure-property-34226.html

Special Emphasis: Government Restrictions Include:

Police Power

- Federal and State Constitutions apply restrictions to protect citizenry for health and safety reasons –Broadest Gov't. Power

Eminent Domain

- The right to take private property for just compensation

Taxation

- Property can be foreclosed upon for nonpayment of taxes

Special Emphasis: Private Restrictions Include:

Deed restrictions

- Deed restrictions are created within the deed which limits how an owner can use a property. Deed restrictions includes restrictive covenants which are placed within deeds of an entire development.

Easements

- Easements do not transfer ownership. Rather, it forces the right for others to have use of the property.

Leases

- Leases place restrictions on the owner by passing the right of use to the lessee.

Liens

- A lien is the right to retain the lawful possession of the property of another until the owner fulfills a legal duty to the person holding the property, such as the payment of lawful charges for work done on the property.

Special Emphasis: Private Restrictions - Easements

Appurtenant - a right to use adjoining property.

In Gross - benefits an individual or company instead of being tied to another parcel of land.

By Prescription - created by the open, notorious, uninterrupted, hostile, and adverse use of another's land for a period set by statute.

By Necessity - created by court order normally for land locked property.

Implied – when a property owner has "encroached" onto another parcel, even if by mistake, for a period of seven years or more.

Special Emphasis: Leases

- **Gross -**Tenant pays fixed rent

- **Net -**Tenant pays fixed rent, plus building expenses

- **Percentage -** Tenant pays percentage based on gross sales
- **Variable -** Tenant pays rent based on an index
- **Ground -** Lease on land

Special Emphasis: Lien Types

Voluntary

- Mortgage
- Vendor's lien

Involuntary

- Judgment liens
- Tax liens – property, income, and estate
- Mechanics/Construction liens

Special Emphasis: Lien Priority

Superior liens

- Property tax
- Special assessments
- Federal estate tax

Junior liens

- Mortgages
- Vendors (Purchase Money Mortgage)
- Income Tax IRS Lien
- Judgment

10 LEGAL DESCRIPTIONS

Learning Objectives:
- Describe the purpose for legal descriptions
- Understand the licensee's role and responsibilities as it pertains to legal descriptions
- Explain and distinguish among the three types of legal descriptions
- Describe the process of creating a legal description using the metes-and-bounds method
- Locate a township by township line and range
- Locate a particular section within a township
- Understand how to subdivide a section
- Calculate the number of acres in a parcel based on the legal description, and convert to square feet
- Explain the use of assessor's parcel numbers
- Apply the measurements associated with checks, townships and sections

Key Terms:

base line	lot and block	section
benchmark	metes and bounds	survey
check	monument	terminus
datum	point of beginning	township
government survey system	principal meridian	township line/tier
legal description	range	

PURPOSE OF
LEGAL
DESCRIPTIONS

Understanding the methods and purpose of creating legal descriptions are reviewed here including the topics of:

I)   Purpose of Legal Descriptions

    A) A legal description is a method of describing the location of real estate that will be accepted by a court

        1) Established boundary lines

Understanding the methods and purpose of creating legal descriptions are reviewed here including the topics of:

II) Types of Legal Descriptions

    A) Metes-and-Bounds

        1) Oldest method of land description

        2) Metes refers to *distance* (measured in feet) and bounds refers to *direction*

        3) Begin with reference point called a point of beginning (POB)

        4) Monuments are fixed objects used to establish boundaries

        5) Compass bearings are used to describe the direction of the boundary lines

            (a) Circle = 360°

            (b) Directions given in degrees (°), minutes (') and seconds (")

            (c) For example, N 45°25'20"E = North 45 degrees, twenty-five minutes, 20 seconds East

A real estate licensee, in the United States, may come into contact with three types of legal descriptions. The metes-and-bounds system is the oldest and was no longer being used by the time Florida was established as a state. Therefore, Florida property is either identified through the government survey system or the lot and block description

- **Metes-and-bounds**
- **Government survey system**
- **Lot and block description**

Metes-and-Bounds

The Metes-and-Bounds system is the oldest method of land description.

It was used for centuries in England and was the identifying system in place with the original thirteen colonies that became the original states of the United States.

The Metes-and-Bounds system was no longer being used by the time Florida became a state. However, licensees must know the basics of this system.

Know that **METES refer to distance (measured in feet) and BOUNDS refer to direction.** Every Metes-and-

Bounds description begins with a reference point called a **"POINT OF BEGINNING" (POB).** It ends there, as well, as it marks boundary points making its way back to the POB. An end point is referred to as a TERMINUS.

The Metes-and-Bounds system relies on **MONUMENTS which are fixed objects used to establish boundaries. Compass bearings are used to describe the direction of the boundary lines.**

Know that every **Circle = 360°** and directions are given in degrees (°) minutes ('), and seconds (").

So, How Do Compass Bearings Work?

It begins with an identified corner serving as benchmark marking the point of beginning. The description then gives distance, direction and various boundary descriptions as if one were walking the bounds pacing off the distance to the next corner where there is a change of direction.

The direction is described by a bearing which is the direction north or south followed by a degree measure out of **90 degrees** and another direction west or east. It stops at 90. From North to the right meets East or from South to the right meets the same East point, so 90 degrees is the largest measure used.

For example, such a bearing might be listed as N 45°25'20" E which equals North 45 degrees, twenty-five minutes, 20 seconds East.

https://familysearch.org/learn/wiki/en/Metes_and_Bounds

Plotting a Directional Point:

In addition to knowing the basic vocabulary and elements of a Metes-and-Bounds legal description, **licensees also need to know how to plot a Metes-and-Bounds descriptor on a circle (compass).**

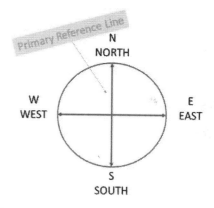

Circles can be divided into four quadrants with North at the top point, South at the bottom point, West at the far-left point and East at the far-right point.

The line running North and South is the primary reference line.

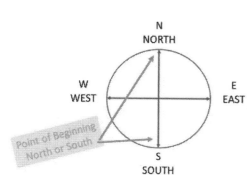

The Point of Beginning will either be at the North or South Point.

This means that a legal description using these points always start with either "N" or "S."

Here's an Example:

The Point of Beginning for N 45° E is the North point.

N 45° E then designates that the distance to travel from the North point is 45° to the East- away from the North Point toward the East point by 45°.

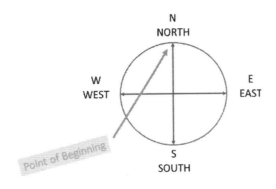
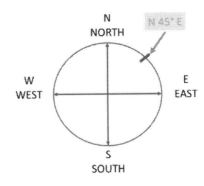

In addition to being able to plot a directional point, be able to find the exact opposite. The opposite of N 45° E is S 45° W. The points on the circle show that these two measurements are the exact opposite. However, a circle is not needed to answer this question. The opposite of North is always South and the Opposite of West is always East and vice versa. The number, which is the distance (bounds) never changes when finding the opposite.

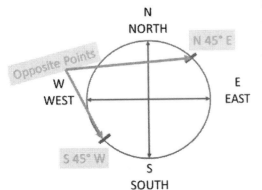

https://en.wikipedia.org/wiki/Metes_and_bounds

Write out a shortened version of each of the following legal descriptions:

1. North Sixty Degrees West =

2. South Seventy-five Degrees West =

3. **South Eighty-Nine Degrees East =**

Answer:

1. North Sixty Degrees West = N 60° W

2. South Seventy-five Degrees West = S 75° W

3. South Eighty-Nine Degrees East = S 89° E

What is the opposite of these following points?

1. **N 60° W**

2. **S 75° W**

3. S 89° E

Answers:

1. **N 60° W = S 60° E**

2. **S 75° W = N 75° E**

3. **S 89° E =N 89° W**

Understanding the methods and purpose of creating legal descriptions are reviewed here including the topics of:

II) Types of Legal Descriptions

    B) Government Survey System

        1) Based on the logic that you can identify any point on a plane by reference to two axes

        2) Primary reference lines running in a north-south direction are called principal meridians and lines running in an east-west direction are called base lines

        3) Range lines run north-south every 6 miles. The north-south strip of land formed by two range lines is called a range

        4) Township lines run east-west every 6 miles. The east-west strip of land formed by two township lines is called a tier or township

            (a) Numbering system of township lines and ranges

        5) Intersection of two range lines and two township lines form a 6-mile square called a township

            (a) There are 36 sections in a township

            (b) Numbering system of sections within townships

Government Survey System

An alternative method to the metes-and-bounds survey system is the government survey system which is also called the public land survey system or rectangular survey system. The government survey system was created by the Land Ordinance of 1785 to survey land brought into the United States because of the 1783 Treaty of Paris.

It is based on the logic that you can identify any point on a plane by reference to two axes. It relies on primary reference lines running in a north-south direction called the principal meridian and lines running in an east-west direction called base lines.

Originally proposed by Thomas Jefferson, the goal of the government survey system was to distribute land after the Revolutionary War – mostly to those who had served in the war and to raise money for the nation by selling land to settlers.

Before this could happen, the land needed to be surveyed. Through the government survey system, the land was then divided into sections for individual ownership.

Certain lands were excluded from the public domain and were not subject to survey and distribution. These lands include the beds of navigable bodies of water, military reservations, national parks, and areas such as land grants that had already passed to private ownership.

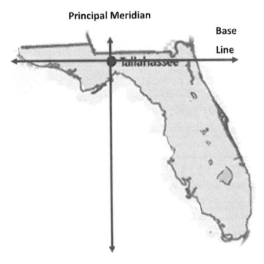

http://nationalmap.gov/small_scale/a_plss.html

https://en.wikipedia.org/wiki/Public_Land_Survey_System

To create the system intersecting principal meridian lines and base lines are positioned throughout the United States. There are 37 principal meridian lines.

In Florida, the principal meridian and base lines run through the center of Tallahassee.

Range lines are plotted that run north-south and the east of the principal meridian. Each It starts with an R to signify that it is a range tells you how many lines it is away from the ends with either a W or an E to signify that east from the principal meridian.

For example R3W is three range lines to the meridian.

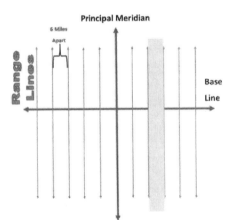

every **6 miles** to the west range line has an identifier. line. Then a number that principal meridian. And it it has moved to the west or

west of the principal

two range lines is called a

The north-south strip of and formed by range.

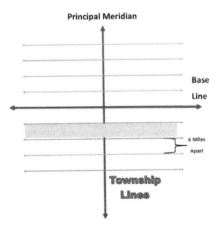

Township lines are plotted that run east-west every **6 miles** to the north and the south of the base line.

Each township line has an identifier. It starts with a T to signify that it is a township line. Then, a number that tells you how many lines it is away from the base line. It ends with either an N or an S to signify that it has moved to the north or the south away from base line.

For example, T3S is three township lines to the south of the base line.

The east-west strip of land formed by two township lines is called a tier or a township.

The range lines and the township lines intersect creating a grid system across the state that works from the original principal meridian and baseline through Tallahassee.

Understanding the methods and purpose of creating legal descriptions are reviewed here including the topics of:

II) Types of Legal Descriptions

    B) Government Survey System

        6) Correction lines

        7) Using the government survey system

            (a) Locating sections

            (b) Subdividing sections

            (c) Calculating size

            (d) "And" in legal description

        8) Fractional sections and government lots

Government Survey System

Correction Lines

The earth is not flat! The curvature of the earth combined with the crude instruments used in early days of the system means that few townships are exactly six-mile squares or contain exactly 36 square miles.

Therefore, correction lines and checks are used in the government survey system.

Every fourth township line is used as a correction line in which the placement of the range lines is measured and corrected to a full six miles. **A check contains 16 townships.**

http://www.propertywords.com/Correction_Lines.html

Townships

Intersection of two range lines and two township lines form a 6-mile square is called a township (note 6-mile square is NOT 6 square miles! Recognize the difference in how it is written.)

A **township** is identified by the range line and township line that borders the township farthest away from the principal meridian and the base lines. The township (not township line!) shown here is identified as T2S, R3W. The township line is always listed first reading from left to right.

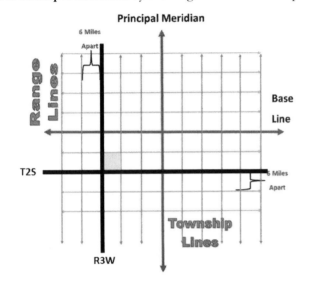

Remember that each range line is six miles from the principal meridian. Also remember that each township line is six miles from the base line. How many miles then is **T2S, R3W** located from the principal meridian? And how many miles is it located from the base line?

There are six miles between the principal meridian and R1W (the first range line). Plus, there is another six miles between R1W and R2W—the beginning point of the township. So there is a total of 12 miles (6+6) between the principal meridian and **T2S, R3W.**

There are six miles between the base line and **T1S** – which is the beginning point of the township. There is a total of 6 miles between the base line and **T2S, R3W.** Recall that the principal meridian and the base line intersect in Tallahassee. This means that **T2S, R3W** is just six miles south of the center point in Tallahassee and twelve miles west of the center point in Tallahassee. Considering that Tallahassee is 103.56 square miles total, that means that **T2S, R3W** is located in Tallahassee!

Recalling the shape of Florida and location of Tallahassee in Florida, the majority (not all) of legal descriptions using the government survey system in Florida will involve property that is to the south of the base line and the east of the principal meridian.

Townships, as stated, are 6 miles by 6 miles which equals **36 square miles**.

Remembering that the point of the system is to identify where a property is that someone owns and property owners rarely own as much as 36 square miles. Therefore, Townships are divided into 36 Sections which are each 1-smile square or 1 mile by 1 mile or 1 square mile.

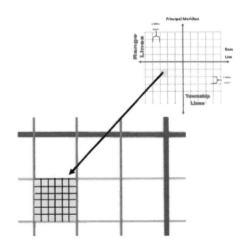

Each section then is identified as a number within the township.

There are 36 sections, so each section is numbered starting at the top far right as 1 then numbering to the left stopping at 6 at the far left, dropping down with 7 directly below 6 and stop with 12 and so forth working this pattern until it ends with the 36th section at the bottom right. To remember this pattern, realize that in the 1800's a surveyor actually walked these townships marking these sections. So, it makes sense that they would drop to the next section below the section they just walked or else they would waste time having to backtrack their steps.

A legal description that is located within section 1 of this township depicted is identified as: Section 1 of Township 2 South, Range 3 West of the Tallahassee Principal Meridian and Base Line. This is abbreviated as: **Sec 1, T2S, R3W.**

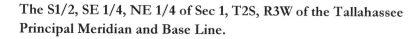

Subdividing Sections

Each section is one square mile which equals 640 acres.

Just as a property owner rarely owns a plot of land as large as a township (36 square miles), property owners rarely own an entire section (1 square mile) or 640 acres.

So, with legal descriptions using the government survey system, each section must be divided into smaller units. This is done by quartering a section into four quadrants. Then, each quadrant is quartered again and again until the remaining unit represents the property.

It is not uncommon for the last division to be a half unit instead of a quarter.

Legal descriptions are read from left to right (as is the tradition in the English language), but when working with them to identify the location of a property; **they are worked right to left.**

We have already identified the location of Sec 1, T2S, R3W of the Tallahassee Principal Meridian and Base Line. This would be 640 acres, so let's break it down even farther by identifying the location of:

The S1/2, SE 1/4, NE 1/4 of Sec 1, T2S, R3W of the Tallahassee Principal Meridian and Base Line.

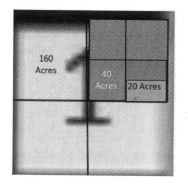

We start by recalling that we are starting at the Tallahassee principal meridian and base line intersection. We then find our township by plotting a line that is three range lines to the west of the principal meridian. Then we plot a line that is two township lines to the south of the baseline. This creates the intersecting outside lines of the township. Then, working our legal description further to the left, we see that we are working with section one of the township.

Working even farther to the left, we see that we now need to find the north east one quarter of the section 1. This means that section 1 is quartered and we are only working with the north-eastern quarter. The north east one quarter is then quartered again focusing in on the south-east quadrant which is then cut in half. Our property is the south half!

Properties rarely fit into the perfect world of quartered sections. So, it is common to have a legal description that adds together land from one section to land from another section. As townships physically butt up against each other, a property owner could own property that pulls from more than one township.

This requires identifying the property just as has been described. But it is done for each section that is part of the owner's land and added together in the description by using an "and."

Here's an example:

The S1/2, SE 1/4, NE 1/4 of Sec 1, T2S, R3W and the SW1/4, SW1/4, NW1/4 of Sec 6, T2S, R2W

Notice that Sec 6, T2S, R2W is immediately to the east of Sec 1, T2S, R3W. These two sections touch physically even though they are in different townships. The owner owns all the property as described in this legal description.

http://nationalmap.gov/small_scale/a_plss.html

Sec 1, T2S, R3W | Sec 6, T2S, R2W

Calculating Size

Not only does this legal description identify the location of the property, it also tells how the big it is. **So how big is the S1/2, SE 1/4 , NE 1/4 of Sec 1, T2S, R3W of the Tallahassee Principal Meridian and Base Line?**

With this legal description, we started with 640 acres in the entire section. First, we took one quarter of the 640 acres leaving 160 acres (640 ÷ 4=160). Then, 160 acres was quartered again leaving 40 acres 160 ÷ 4=40). Finally, the 40 acres were cut in half (40 ÷ 2=20) leaving a total of 20 acres in this property as described with the legal description.

- Calculator Tip: Enter 640 into your calculator. Starting at the right find the first denominator of the fraction of your section. In this case it is 4 so divide 640 by 4, look to the left and find the next denominator.   Keep entering the divide sign and the denominators until you run out and hit equal:

- 640 ÷ 4 ÷ 4 ÷ 2 = 20

The process is similar for calculating the size of The S1/2, SE 1/4 , NE 1/4 of Sec 1, T2S, R3W and the SW1/4, SW1/4, NW1/4 of Sec 6, T2S, R2W:

Each section of ownership is calculated separately and then added together.

The SW1/4, SW1/4, NW1/4 of Sec 6, T2S, R2W is worked as 640 ÷ 4 ÷ 4 ÷ 4 = 10.

The S1/2, SE 1/4 , NE 1/4 of Sec 1, T2S, R3W is worked as 640 ÷ 4 ÷ 4 ÷ 2 = 20.

Then add together: 10 + 20 = 30 acres.

Working with Conversion to Square Feet

1 Mile = 5,280 linear feet

1 Acre = 43,560 square feet

1 Section = 640 acres

The amount of linear feet in a mile, the total square feet in an acre, and the fact that one section has 640 acres are very important numbers to know when working with property size calculations.

If one section is one mile by one mile, then we also know that each section is 5,280 linear feet by 5,280 linear feet. And 5,280 multiplied by 5,280 equals 27,878,400 square feet. 27,878,400 divided by 43,560 square feet per miles means that there are 640 acres in each section.

5,280 feet x 5,280 feet = 27,878,400 square feet

27,878,400 square feet ÷ 43,560 square feet (in each acre) = 640 Acres

640 Acres = 1 Section

Convert Back to Acreage

1 Mile = 5,280 linear feet

1 Acre = 43,560 square feet

1 Section = 640 acres

Once a legal description has been used to calculate the amount of acreage it represents, it is a simple process to change to the total square feet. We have already determined that the following legal description has 30 acres in it. To convert to the total of square feet simply multiply the total acres, 30 by 43,560 (the number of square feet per acre). This provides you with the total square feet represented by the legal description.

The S1/2, SE 1/4, NE 1/4 of Sec 1, T2S, R3W and the SW1/4, SW1/4, NW1/4 of Sec 6, T2S, R2W

640 ÷ 4 ÷ 4 ÷ 2 = 20 plus 640 ÷ 4 ÷ 4 ÷ 4 = 10 becomes 20 + 10 to = 30 Acres

30 Acres x 43,560 = 1,306,800 Square Feet

So, an area that is ¼ mile by ½ mile is how many total square feet?

To work this problem, convert the ¼ and ½ miles to linear feet:

5,280 ÷ 4 (one quarter of a mile) = 1,320 linear feet

5,280 ÷ 2 (one half of a mile) = 2,640 linear feet

1,320 x 2,640 = 3,484,800 square feet

So, an area that is ¼ mile by ½ mile is how many **ACRES**?

Same as before, to work this problem convert the ¼ and ½ miles to linear feet:

5,280 ÷ 4 (one quarter of a mile) = 1,320 linear feet

5,280 ÷ 2 (one half of a mile) = 2,640 linear feet

1,320 x 2,640 = 3,484,800 square feet

3,484,800 ÷ 43,560 (square feet per acre) = 80

Which could also have been solved faster: 640 ÷ 4 ÷ 2 = 80 Acres

(Remember this is the shortcut calculator way to calculate the size of property when given government survey legal description.)

Fractional Sections and Government Lots

Dividing sections by a quarter is known within the government survey system as an **Aliquot part**—the standard subdivisions of a section, such as a half section, quarter section, or quarter-quarter section.

When the government began dividing land by this process, they ended up with areas of land which were less than an aliquot part (a fractional piece of a section) that frequently bordered water. This subpart of a section was designated by a number, for example, Lot 3 and is called a **Government Lot**.

http://nationalmap.gov/small_scale/a_plss.html

Understanding the methods and purpose of creating legal descriptions are reviewed here including the topics of:

II) Types of Legal Descriptions

    C) Lot and block survey method

        1) Also called recorded plat method

        2) Recorded survey called a plat map

        3) Platted subdivision divided into blocks and lots

Lot and Block Survey Method

A modern way to identify property is the lot and block survey method.

The lot and block survey method is also called the recorded plat method. It is used to locate and identify land, particularly for lots in densely populated metropolitan areas including suburban areas. This type of system came about as developers began to divide property into subdivisions. As such, it is an extremely widely used system.

With the lot and block system, specific parcels of land are identified by their lot number or letter within the "block", or subdivision plat, in which the lot is located. The block itself is located by using either the metes and bounds system or the rectangular survey system.

http://definitions.uslegal.com/l/lot-and-block-system/

The block or subdivision map is a recorded survey called plat maps.

To use this system, the plat map submitted by a developer must be reviewed and approved by a governing body such as the urban planning commission or zoning board. The plat map is then recorded and put into the official county records.

A Platted Subdivision Map shows the developed area divided into blocks and then lots – taking the property down to smaller parcels to be sold.

The plat map must show the survey data (datum) required to identify the location of the block. The plat map also shows proposed roads and rights of way and verifies that all parcels have access to main roads without being land locked. Easements are identified as well as any land being dedicated to the public for parks or other public uses.

As zoning often restricts placement of property on lots and minimum sizes of lots, the platting process allows government officials to ensure that all lots comply with regulations.

https://en.wikipedia.org/wiki/P

Understanding the methods and purpose of creating legal descriptions are reviewed here including the topics of:

III) Assessor's Parcel Number

    A) To aid in the assessment of property for tax collection

    B) Tax maps based on recorded plat maps

        1) Other land in county

    C) Assessment roll

        1) Every parcel in county listed by parcel number

        2) Shows owner's name and address of record

        3) Assessed value of land and structures

Tax Maps

Individual property, as explained, can be located through the designated legal description. Property can also be identified through an **assessor's parcel number,** referred to as PID, which is used **to aid in the assessment of property for tax collection.**

Tax maps assigning a parcel number are developed **based on recorded plat maps and other survey records of property** located throughout the county. The purpose of the tax map is simple – to make it easier to track property and impose assessments which are placed on properties annually and with special assessments.

Real estate licensees utilizing the multiple listing service identify property by the assessor's parcel number in addition to the legal description.

https://en.wikipedia.org/wiki/Assessor%27s_parcel_number

Assessment Roll

Every parcel in each county is listed by a parcel number within the assessment rolls.

Assessment rolls list information for every property in the assessing municipality or county including showing owner's name and address of record. Also included is the assessed value of land and structures. This information is used to levy ad valorem taxes and special assessments on each property. Every assessing municipality publishes tentative and final assessment rolls annually.

https://www.tax.ny.gov/pit/property/learn/asmtrolls.htm

Understanding the methods and purpose of creating legal descriptions are reviewed here including the topics of:

IV) Preparation and Use of Surveys

    A) Benchmarks

Preparation of Surveys

In summary, surveys include datum which are a set of reference points used to locate places on the Earth. Surveys rely on a point of beginning, monuments, and an ending point known as the terminus.

When a survey is conducted, a benchmark is put in place to make the property lines easier to identify by surveyors in the future. **The benchmark is a marked point of known or assumed elevation from which other elevations may be established.** These benchmarks may be placed on an iron post or brass marker.

The U.S. government maintains a register of these benchmarks so that the records are available for use. This registry is now maintained as a geographically searchable database with links to sketches, diagrams, photos of the marks, and any other technical details.

Use of Surveys

A property survey establishes and describes the legal description as a written word statement and as a sketch or map of a piece of land showing the property boundaries and physical features, like rivers, creeks, and roadways. Some surveys also note topographical information, like elevation and soil density; residential documents typically show the location of houses and other structures, too.

With a survey, not only can the property be identified as to exact location, but it also shows boundary lines between neighbors, it establishes exactly how much property is included, and it identifies encroachments.

Surveys are used to verify the information for the sale of property and for developers who divide the property or repurpose it for other uses other than how the property is currently being used. The methods to describe property may have changed over time, however, there are strict guidelines and standards that are in force per Florida Statutes for land surveyors, just as there are for real estate licensees.

The Florida Board of Professional Surveyors and Mappers has been charged by the Florida Legislature with protecting the public interest in regard to surveys.

Surveys Verify:

- Property Location
- Boundary Lines
- Amount of Land
- Identifies Encroachments

Surveys are Utilized to:

- Locate Property
- Resolved Boundary Disputes
- Resolve Encroachment Disputes
- Verify Information for a Sale and Purchase
- Divide into Smaller Parcels

Surveys Rely on:

- Datum
- Benchmarks
- Monuments
- Points of Beginning
- Terminus points

http://www.freshfromflorida.com/Divisions-Offices/Consumer-Services/Business-Services/Surveyors-and-Mappers

11 REAL ESTATE CONTRACTS

Learning Objectives:
- List and describe the essentials of a contract
- Distinguish among formal, parol, bilateral, unilateral, implied, expressed, executory and executed contracts
- Describe the various ways in which an offer is terminated
- Describe the various methods of terminating a contract
- Explain the remedies for breach of a contract
- Describe the effect of the Statute of Frauds and the Statute of Limitations
- Describe the elements of an option
- Differentiate among the various types of listings
- Explain and describe the various disclosures required in a real estate contract
- Recognize what constitutes fraud
- Recognize what constitutes culpable negligence

Key Terms:

assignment	fraud	Statute of Limitations
attorney-in-fact	liquidated damages	unenforceable
bilateral contract	meeting of the minds	unilateral contract
competent	net listing	valid contract
contract	novation	void contract
culpable negligence	open listing	voidable contract
exclusive-agency listing	option contract	
exclusive-right-of-sale listing	Statute of Frauds	

GENERAL CONTRACTS

Contracts utilized in real estate transactions are reviewed here including the topics of:

I)   Contracts in General

    A) Definition of a contract

B) Preparation of contracts

C) Statute of Frauds

D) Statute of Limitations

E) Void, voidable and unenforceable contracts

Definition of a Contract

Among the important skills real estate licensees offer clients is the expert ability to deal with contracts.

The definition of a contract is a legally binding agreement between two or more parties. It is an agreement to do a legal act for legal consideration.

Contracts, in one form or another, date back to the beginning of the formation of society. In fact, many standards for contract law that are in place today date back to Ancient Greek and Roman times that recognized the same basics for cancelling agreements.

Between the 17th and 18th centuries, English common law incorporated the principles of good faith, fair dealing, and the enforceability of seriously intended promises. The 1800s brought about the essential principles of an enforceable contract as an offer for certain terms, mirrored by an acceptance, supported by consideration, and free from duress, undue influence or misrepresentation.

A contract is:

- A legally binding agreement between two or more parties.

- An agreement to do a legal act for legal consideration

https://en.wikipedia.org/wiki/History_of_contract_law

Preparation of Contracts

A contract can be verbal, also called a parol or oral contract. Or a contract can be in writing. Another form of contract is an implied contract.

Despite the form of a contract, all contracts must follow a pattern that fits legal standards. Two of the standards that must be followed are the Statutes of Frauds and the Statutes of Limitations.

Modern American courts now require entirely clear information before onerous clauses can be enforced and the burden of proof shifted for businesses to show that misleading statements were not negligent.

- A contract can be verbal/Parol/Oral

- A contract can be in writing

- A contract can be implied

Statute of Frauds

Florida Statute of Frauds provides that certain types of contracts are not valid and cannot be enforced unless they are in writing and signed by the party against whom enforcement is sought. The purpose of the statute of frauds is to prevent injury from fraudulent conduct.

Someone who wishes to use the Statute of Frauds as a defense must raise it in a timely manner. The burden of proving that a written contract exists only comes into play when a Statute of Frauds defense is raised by the defendant. It is not imposed on individuals by the courts.

Once a defendant admits to the existence of the contract, then that individual cannot rely on the Statute of Frauds as his own defense.

- Certain types of contracts are not valid and cannot be enforced unless they are in writing and signed by the party against whom enforcement is sought.

- Purpose is to prevent injury from fraudulent conduct.

According to the Statute of Frauds, the following contracts must be in writing to be enforceable. Real estate purchase sales agreements, an option contract – because it contains an option to purchase real estate, deeds and mortgages, lease agreements that are for more than one year, listing agreements that are for longer than one year, and any contract (even if not real estate related) if it cannot be performed within one year of the date created.

Covered under the Statute of Frauds:

- Purchase and sale real estate contracts

- Option contracts

- Deeds and mortgages

- Lease agreements for more than one year

- Listing agreements for more than one year

- Any contract that cannot be performed for more than one year

Not all contracts have to be in writing to be legal. However, verbal contracts that may be legal and valid are only enforceable if it can be proven.

Imagine how difficult it would be to go to court based on a verbal contract. You would be relying on testimony of witnesses. Winning the case could come down to a he said, she said, scenario. A written contract reduces the chance of future litigation, and gives the parties the opportunity to take a second look at the terms and conditions of their agreement before finalizing it.

- Legality of Verbal contracts

  - Enforcing a verbal contract legally requires the ability to prove the facts of the contract when the facts were never put in writing.

- A written contract reduces the chance of future litigation, and give the parties the opportunity to take a second look at the terms and conditions of their agreement before finalizing it.

Some contracts that would otherwise be invalid under a "statute of frauds" will still be enforced, based on "partial performance."

- A party who has accepted partial performance by another party under the contract, will typically be barred from asserting the "Statute of Frauds" to avoid meeting its own contractual obligations.

- If an oral contract has been formed and the buyer has paid part of the purchase price and either taken possession or made improvements, then the contract would be upheld in court.

http://www.avvo.com/legal-guides/ugc/what-is-the-statute-of-frauds-in-florida

Statute of Limitations

- A statute of limitations is a law which places a time limit on pursuing a legal remedy in relation to wrongful conduct. After the expiration of the statutory period, unless a legal exception applies, the injured person loses the right to file a lawsuit seeking money damages or other relief.

When the period of time specified in a statute of limitations passes, a claim can no longer be filed. The intention of these laws is to facilitate resolution in a reasonable length of time.

A case cannot be pursued after the period specified, and courts have no jurisdiction over cases filed after the statute of limitations has expired. However, once filed, cases do not need to be resolved within the period specified in the statute of limitations.

Florida Statute of limitations states that a legal remedy for a written contract can be pursued for 5 years. Oral contracts are enforceable within 4 years.

- Time period for seeking legal remedy

    - 5 Years for a written contract

    - 4 Years for a verbal contract (Oral/Parol)

http://www.expertlaw.com/library/limitations_by_state/Florida.html

Void, Voidable, and Unenforceable Contracts

A contract that is **"void"** cannot be enforced by either party., The law treats a void contract as if it had never been formed. A contract will be considered void, for example, when it requires one party to perform an act that is impossible or illegal.

A contract that is void is a contract that doesn't meet the definition of a valid contract.

- Cannot be performed under the law

- Cannot be enforced by either party

- Does not meet the definition of a valid contract

- Treated as though it had never been formed

A **voidable** contract is different than a contract that is void. A voidable contract is one that CAN be enforced. Usually only one party is bound to the contract terms. The unbound party can cancel the contract, which would make the contract void. However, whomever they're in contract with cannot void the contract.

A contract with a minor is an example of a voidable contract. The minor can void the contract. The person in contract with the minor cannot cancel the contract.

- A valid contract that CAN be enforced

- Only binds one party

- The unbound party is allowed to cancel the contract

- The other party cannot void the contract

Contracts that can be upheld in court are said to be **enforceable**. An enforceable contract is a legally binding contract that the law will recognize.

The point of entering into a contract is to have the terms of the contract fulfilled. Upon a dispute between the parties, only an enforceable contract can be upheld by the courts.

- Can be upheld in court

- Legally binding contract that the law will recognize

An **unenforceable** contract can appear to be valid with all the elements of a contract. However, the contract cannot be fully enforced due to some technical defect. Often it cannot be upheld due to lack of proof, or it fails to meet the requirements under Statute of Frauds, or the time requirements of the Statute of Limitations

Unenforceable Contracts:

- Valid Contract

- Cannot be upheld in court due to a technical defect

- Cannot be upheld due to lack of proof

- Or fails to meet the requirements under Statute of Frauds or the time requirements of the Statute of Limitations

http://www.legalmatch.com/law-library/article/void-vs-voidable-contract-lawyers.html#sthash.XYW5jkrO.dpuf

Contracts utilized in real estate transactions are reviewed here including the topics of:

II) Essentials of a Contract

A) Contractual capacity of the parties

B) Offer and acceptance

C) Legality of object

D) Consideration

The term agreement is wider in scope than a contract. All agreements are not valid contracts. Only agreements that are enforceable by law are valid contracts.

Essential elements of every valid contract are: Competent Parties, Offer and Acceptance, Legal Purpose, and Consideration. If any one of these elements are missing, the agreement will not be legally binding.

Remember, that the terms of a non-legally binding agreement can be met, however, the parties have no legal stance to enforce the contract if things do not proceed well between the parties.

- Contractual Capacity of the Parties
- Offer and acceptance
- Legality of object
- Consideration

> http://www.smallbusiness.wa.gov.au/business-topics/money-tax-and-legal/legal-matters/business-contracts/four-essential-elements-of-a-contract/

Contractual Capacity of the Parties

Contractual Capacity of the Parties means that the participating parties must have the legal and mental capacity to contract (otherwise contract is voidable by the incompetent party).

By law, minors do not have the legal capacity to enter into an enforceable contract. Therefore, a minor may enter into contract, but the contract is voidable by the minor. Keep in mind, though, if the other party is of legal capacity (an adult) then that party may NOT void the contract as the party is bound by the contract. The effect is that the contract is voidable by only one of the parties – the minor.

- Participating parties must have the legal and mental capacity to contract
- Minors may enter into contract, but contract is voidable by minor (not voidable adult other party)

> https://www.rocketlawyer.com/article/contracts-101:-elements-of-a-contract.rl

Offer and Acceptance

To have a valid contract, there must have been an offer made that was accepted. This offer and acceptance should be of a natural meeting of minds. Meaning they came to a decision under mutual assent. Mutual assent is the offer made by an offeror and accepted by the offeree.

The two sides to a contract, whether for the construction of a high-rise building or for having your lawn cut, must agree on the fundamental terms of the contract. There must be an intention to enter into a legally binding contract. Whether the parties have reached an agreement is determined by an objective standard.

- Meeting of the minds – two parties reach an agreement through mutual assent

- Mutual assent – the making and acceptance of an offer

  - Offeror makes the offer

  - Offeree accepts (or rejects)

https://www.rocketlawyer.com/article/contracts-101:-elements-of-a-contract.rl

Legality of Object

A contract would not be valid if put together for an illegal purpose. Illegality makes the contract null and void.

The point of a legally binding contract is that an aggrieved party can take the other party to court for enforcement of the contract. So, if an agreement was made to do something illegally such as a "contract to kill someone" or to "sell street drugs"… then things would not end well by either party. The result of forming an agreement to do something illegal makes the contract itself "null and void."

- The contract must be of a legal nature

- Illegality makes the contract null and void

https://www.rocketlawyer.com/article/contracts-101:-elements-of-a-contract.rl

Consideration

Consideration is the final element of a valid contract. Consideration is the promise to perform and fulfill the contract. Valuable consideration can be measured in terms of money. Good consideration cannot be measured in terms of money such as love and affection.

This element becomes a point of confusion for many people. The erroneous belief regarding real estate purchase contracts is that the earnest money deposit given after the initial contract is signed is the consideration given. The phrase valuable consideration leads to the confusion in that the contract normally involves the end goal of a "promise" to pay another party money at the conclusion of the contract. An example of good consideration would be the "promise" to get married.

- The promise to perform and fulfill the contract

  - Valuable consideration can be measured in terms of money

  - Good consideration cannot be measured in terms of money such as love and affection

https://www.rocketlawyer.com/article/contracts-101:-elements-of-a-contract.rl

Contracts utilized in real estate transactions are reviewed here including the topics of:

III) Authority of Real Estate Licensees to Prepare Contracts

Authority of Licensees

As a licensee, it is important to understand what you can and cannot do in regard to contracts.

A distinction is made between how you are legally allowed to handle lease agreements versus other types of real estate contracts.

Lease Agreements

Licensees cannot draw up lease contracts from scratch. However, a licensee may use fill-in-the-blank contracts that have been approved by the Florida Supreme Court. Be aware, though, that these contracts are only allowed to be for a period that does not exceed one year.

Writing a lease agreement from scratch falls under the authority of an attorney. So, to do so would be practicing law without a license. A real estate licensee that is charged and found guilty of drawing up a lease agreement without a license would not only face legal consequences for doing so, but the licensee would lose their real estate license as well.

http://aboutfloridalaw.com/2015/03/24/when-is-a-florida-real-estate-agent-or-broker-guilty-of-the-unauthorized-practice-of-law/

Authority of Licensees

Real Estate licensees work with buyers and sellers. Under the authority of the real estate license granted by the Florida Department of Business and Professional Regulation, licensees can draw up four specific types of contracts:

Listing Contracts, Buyer Broker Contracts, Sale and Purchase Contracts, and Option Contracts

Real estate sales associates and broker associates can complete these types of contracts on behalf of the broker.

Listing Contracts

A listing contract is an agreement between a property seller and a listing broker for the broker to handle the details of marketing and handling the sale of the property.

Buyer Broker Contracts

A buyer broker contract is an agreement between a potential buyer and a broker; for the broker to represent the buyer in the purchase of the home starting with the home search and concluding upon the successful purchase of a home.

http://aboutfloridalaw.com/2015/03/24/when-is-a-florida-real-estate-agent-or-broker-guilty-of-the-unauthorized-practice-of-law/

Sale and Purchase Contracts

A sale and purchase contract is a contract for the purchase of property between a buyer and a seller. When the parties utilize the services of one or more brokers, the broker writes up the terms of the contract in an offer. Upon acceptance or a counter with final approval by both parties, it becomes a contract.

Option Contracts

Options are an agreement between a property owner and a buyer that gives the buyer the right to purchase a contract without the obligation to do so. Although associated with a lease, the actual option contract may be drawn up by a real estate licensee. There is some discrepancy about this rule and it is suggested that licensees be guided by their broker's on how to handle these types of contracts.

http://aboutfloridalaw.com/2015/03/24/when-is-a-florida-real-estate-agent-or-broker-guilty-of-the-unauthorized-practice-of-law

Liability

Be aware that it is best practice for real estate licensees to use fill-in-the-blank contracts for all their real estate activities. The Florida Realtors® have standardized contracts available developed by the Florida Bar as a benefit for members of the state association. Addendums are also provided for specific disclosures and common contract add-ons.

Even these standardized forms carry some risk of the Unauthorized Practice of Law by a non-lawyer. The more a licensee takes liberty to write their own verbiage into clauses, the more he or she increases liability in a deal should a clause misrepresent the best interests of the client.

These Addendum are legal documents and become part of the agreement. If the Addendum later results in that contract being unenforceable under Florida law, then the real estate agent and his or her real estate brokerage firm can be legally liable for the damages resulting from the deal gone bad — and the real estate professional could be accountable for practicing law without a license.

http://aboutfloridalaw.com/2015/03/24/when-is-a-florida-real-estate-agent-or-broker-guilty-of-the-unauthorized-practice-of-law/#sthash.HUH6N86n.dpuf

CLASSIFICATION OF CONTRACTS

Contracts utilized in real estate transactions are reviewed here including the topics of:

IV) Classification of Contracts

    A) Bilateral or unilateral contracts

    B) Expressed or implied contracts

    C) Executory or executed contracts

    D) Formal or informal contracts

Contracts can be divided into different classifications. There are eight classifications of contracts or 4 pairs of types of contracts.

They are Bilateral or Unilateral, Express or Implied, Executory or Executed, and Formal or Informal.

Bilateral or Unilateral

Looking first at bilateral and unilateral contracts:

A Bilateral Contract obligates both parties to perform per the terms of the contract, whereas a Unilateral Contract has only one party obligated to perform. A basic bilateral agreement is generally what comes to mind when someone is asked to describe a contract. In fact, most contracts fall into this category.

Examples of bilateral contracts are all around. When someone orders a meal at a restaurant or visits a physician, a bilateral agreement has been entered into between the participating parties. There's a promised action by one party (food or medical care) and a promised action by another (payment).

In real estate, a purchase and sale contract is an example of a bilateral contract. One party is obligated to sell and the other party is obligated to buy. An option contract, on the other hand, is an example of unilateral contract. Only the seller is obligated to sell in a unilateral contract. The buyer is not obligated to buy.

Expressed or Implied

The terms of an expressed contract is spelled out in detail in the contract. Implied Contracts, on the other hand are contracts where the parties never verbally or in writing formally agreed to enter into a contract but ended up in a contract based on the implication of their actions.

How can this happen? It is a misnomer to believe that you must formally agree to an agreement to be held liable for it. To establish the existence of an implied contract, it is necessary to show: an unambiguous offer, unambiguous acceptance, mutual intent to be bound, and consideration. However, these elements may be established by the conduct of the parties rather than through express written or oral agreements.

A contract which is implied is also called a quasi-contract and is a means for the courts to remedy situations in which one party would be unjustly enriched were he or she not required to compensate the other. Take, for example, an unconscious patient treated by a doctor in an emergency. This patient had not expressly agreed to pay the doctor for emergency services, but the patient would unjustly gain from the doctor's services should the doctor not be compensated.

If a real estate agent, for example, reasonably appears to be acting on behalf of a buyer by doing things that a buyer's agent would normally do such as saying, "I'll get you the best deal," the real estate agent may reasonably be held to agency obligations to the buyer such as confidentiality. This agent would be breaking an implied contract upon disclosing how much a buyer would be willing to pay for a property to a buyer.

https://en.wikipedia.org/wiki/Implied-in-fact_contract

Executory or Executed

Executory contracts are still to be finalized – they have actions that still must be completed by one or more parties; whereas executed contracts have been finalized, completed or "executed."

In real estate, while a buyer and seller are waiting to close a real estate contract, it is an executory contract. Once they sit down at the closing table and the contract is conveyed from one to the other, it has been executed.

Formal or Informal

A verbal (oral/parol) agreement is always considered to be an informal contract. However, a written agreement is only considered a formal contract if it is written in a format required by contract law. Most contracts are informal contracts despite being in a written fill-in-the-blank format. These formats are for convenience and legal protection of the users rather than actual requirement of contract law. Examples of these types of informal contracts in real estate are lease, purchase, and listing agreements. On the other hand, a promissory note -- an agreement between a lender and a borrower is a formal contract as contract law dictates how it is written.

http://www.businessdictionary.com/definition/implied-contract.html

Special Emphasis

Bilateral -Both parties must perform - Example – Real Estate Purchase Contract

Unilateral - One party must perform - Example – Option Contract

Expressed - Terms of the contract are expressed in the contract.

Implied - Terms of contract can be assumed by the actions of one or both parties

Executory - Contract still to be fully performed - A contract waiting to have the deed transferred from one owner to another

Executed - All conditions of the contract have been performed - All parties sat at the closing table and the deed was conveyed from one owner to another.

Formal - A written contract required in a specific format per contract law - A promissory note

Informal - An oral or verbal contract not required to be in specific format - A purchase and sale agreement

Contracts utilized in real estate transactions are reviewed here including the topics of:

V) Contract Negotiation

    A) Parties to the offer

        1) Offeror

2) Offeree

B) Ways an offer is terminated

Parties to the Offer

The ability of an agent to handle contract negotiations may very well be one of the most important services that a real estate licensee brings to clients. There are many details that must be considered when structuring a deal and analyzing a deal.

Every deal starts with an offer. With every offer that is made, there are multiple parties. Licensees must understand the verbiage involved with the parties.

The offeror is the person making an offer and the offeree has the offer made to him or her. The offeree may accept, reject, or counter the offer. If accepted, the parties are in contract. When making a counter offer, technically, the person that was the offeree becomes the offeror of the counter.

- **Offeror -** The buyer or person who makes the offer

- **Offeree -** The person who has the offer made to him/her

  https://www.biggerpockets.com/renewsblog/2010/03/24/7-tips-for-better-real-estate-negotiation/

Most people assume that negotiations are always about money, but often it is not. Experienced agents understand that often it's more important to solve a problem of one of the parties than to offer the most money.

For example, let's say two buyers (offerors) both want the same house. Each has a real estate licensee (a buyer's agent) that has made an offer for them. They are each then notified that there are multiple offers and that they should make their best offer.

The first buyer's agent assumes that the seller wanted the most money possible, and encourages the buyer to offer full asking price, but the second buyer's agent asked the listing agent if the seller (offeree) minded the agent disclosing why the seller was moving. When the second buyer's agent learned that the seller had a job offer and needed to move within two weeks, the second buyer's agent constructed a cash offer on behalf of the buyer that although it was not full asking price- it did allow the seller to close and move within two weeks.

Ways an Offer is Terminated

If the offer is terminated before acceptance, a contract cannot be formed. Once an offer has been made, it can be terminated by either the offeror or the offeree through one of these methods: counteroffer, acceptance, rejection, withdrawal, time, death/mental instability, and destruction of property.

  http://www.lawfiles.net/termina ting-an-offer-to-contract/

Withdrawal

Sometimes for many different reasons an offer is withdrawn by the buyer. If it has not been accepted before being formally withdrawn, it is then terminated. This is also called revoking the offer. **Example:** Latisha signed a written offer to purchase a home for $275,000. Her agent allowed the seller to take 48 hours to reply to the offer. While waiting for a response, a similar house came on the market for $30,000 less. Latisha withdrew her offer. Latisha's agent delivered the withdrawal to the seller's agent before the seller accepted Latisha's offer. The offer was effectively withdrawn freeing Latisha to purchase the second home.

Acceptance

If an offer is accepted, the offer is no longer an offer because it has become a contract. So, technically the offer is terminated and replaced by the contract. **Example:** Latisha signed a written offer to purchase a home for $275,000. Her agent allowed the seller to take 48 hours to reply to the offer. While waiting for a response, a similar house came on the market for $30,000 less. Before Latisha could request that her agent withdraw the offer, Latisha received an email with the seller's signatures accepting her offer. Latisha was legally in contract on the first house.

Counteroffer

When a seller (offeree) receives an offer with terms that the seller does not find acceptable, the seller can make a counteroffer proposing acceptable terms to the seller. Upon making the counteroffer, the seller has now become the offeror and the buyer has become the offeree. It is now up to the buyer to either accept, reject, or counter the new offer. It is important to note that once the counteroffer was made, the original offer has been terminated and cannot later be accepted should the seller's counter not be accepted. **Example**: Latisha signed a written offer to purchase a home for $275,000. The seller countered asking that Latisha agree to pay $300,000. However, while Latisha was waiting on the seller's reply, she spotted another new home on the market for $30,000 less. Latisha rejected the counter to purchase the second home. The seller of the first home attempted to accept her offer of $275,000 but that offer was terminated and their signature did not constitute legal acceptance.

Rejection

If an offer is rejected, it terminates the offer and it no longer holds any effect. If both parties wish to go forward, a new offer would have to be drawn up to restart the process. **Example:** Latisha signed a written offer to purchase a home for $275,000. Her agent informed Latisha that the offer was rejected. Latisha then made an offer on a second house. While she was considering whether she wanted to accept that seller's counter on the second home, she received word that the seller of the first house had reconsidered her offer and wanted to accept it. Latisha's agent wrote a new offer for the same amount for the first house. Upon both Latisha and the seller signing the new offer, Latisha was in contract to buy the first home. Latisha rejected the counteroffer on the second home.

Timed Out

Offers have a deadline that is open to be acted upon. If it is not acted upon in the time specified in the offer, it is terminated (expired). Some buyers think that a seller must respond to their offer. In fact, they do not. They can simply let the time run out without responding. **Example:** Latisha signed a written offer to purchase a home for $275,000. While waiting for the seller to respond to her offer, Latisha spotted a house for $30,000 less than the first house. However, Latisha liked the layout of the first house the best so she did not want to withdraw the offer. Yet, she also did not want to lose the second house. Latisha waited somewhat patiently for the first seller's response. She waited and waited until finally the offer time allowed in her offer passed. In the meantime, the second house sold. Latisha threatened to sue the first seller for not responding to her offer in order for her to make an offer on the second home but was told by a lawyer that her suit held no basis.

Death/Insanity

If mental capacity is challenged after an offer is made, any previous offers made would be terminated. Obviously death will terminate an offer as one party cannot fulfill their side of the contract should it become accepted. **Example:** Latisha signed a written offer to purchase a home for $275,000. Both Latisha and the seller were represented by the same broker. When the seller came to sign the offer, the seller saw Latisha leaving the brokerage and noticed she was pregnant. The seller was pleased to imagine his home filled with a happy family and decided to counter Latisha's offer at the low price of a $1! Before Latisha received word of the counter, the seller's son appeared at the brokerage with a court order to declaring the seller incompetent. The seller's offer was terminated and could not be accepted by Latisha based on mental capacity.

Destruction of the Property

If the property being offered is somehow destroyed, an offer is terminated. **Example:** Latisha signed a written offer to purchase a home for $275,000. She received word back that the seller was going to take the night to "think about it." At three o'clock a.m. a tornado blew through the area and ripped the roof off the house and destroyed more than half of the remaining structure. The seller hurriedly signed Latisha's offer and then called his agent to deliver to Latisha for a formal acceptance. The seller's agent informed the seller that Latisha's offer had been terminated along with the structure of the house!

Contracts utilized in real estate transactions are reviewed here including the topics of:

VI) Termination of Contracts

A) Methods of terminating contracts

B) Remedies for breach

C) Assignment of contracts

Methods of Terminating Contracts

Once an offer has become a contract, there are still ways that the contract can be terminated. Sometimes things just do not work out as hoped and one or all parties wish to terminate a contract.

Contracts are offers that have been accepted. Because there are specific legal obligations for both parties to perform per the contract, consequences can result upon attempting to cancel the contract.

Contracts can be terminated by: performance not accomplished, time specified not met, impossibility of performing (death), mutual agreement (both parties decide to cancel), or breach of contract.

http://www.dealmakerlibrary.com/a-lesson-on-the-basics-of-real-estate-contracts.aspx

Performance

Performance means that all parties have done everything agreed to in the contract. All contract terms and conditions have been executed. And all contract terms and conditions have been met.

In a real estate sales transaction, this means that property has been transferred from one party to another. When the contract has been performed as intended, the contract terminates. This is usually the best outcome for all involved.

- Execution of all contract terms and conditions
- The contract has been fulfilled.
    - Property transferred
    - Payment received.

http://thelawdictionary.org/performance-of-contract/

Time Runs Out (Expired)

All contracts are written with a time period for each party to perform and fulfill the contract. Often there are multiple timelines in a real estate contract that must be met as the contract is taken from acceptance to closing.

Time running out to perform on the contract terminates a contract. Time is of the essence, meaning all parties are to do their best to meet deadlines and the failure to do so terminates the deal unless the timeline is formally extended.

In real estate, for example, it isn't unusual for all involved in the buyer side of the deal racing to pull together a loan for the buyer to meet the deadlines of the contract.

- The time to perform should be specified by contract
- "Time is of the essence"
- If not performed by the date in the contract, the contract expires and is terminated

http://www.dealmakerlibrary.com/a-lesson-on-the-basics-of-real-estate-contracts.aspx

Performance Impossible

Performance of contractual duties can be excused under an impossibility theory. Types of impossibility theories observed by the court include acts of God, death, or legal impossibility.

If the contract cannot be performed, i.e. death of one party, the contract would be terminated as it takes at least two parties to have a contract. Destruction of the property would also terminate the contract.

- Performance is impossible for an unforeseen reason
- i.e. Death of one party or destruction of property.

http://www.dealmakerlibrary.com/a-lesson-on-the-basics-of-real-estate-contracts.aspx

Mutual Agreement (rescission)

If both parties agree to end the contract, the contact is terminated. This is called mutual rescission, or mutual agreement. This normally has the happiest end for all involved, as it means that buyers are free to buy other houses and sellers are free to sell the property to another buyer.

With a real estate sales purchase agreement, if the agreement to terminate the contract comes after the earnest money deposit has been made, both parties will be asked to sign an agreement about who will receive the earnest money. The contract may specify how the money will be handled upon cancellation but best practices of brokers requires the signed agreement for release of funds, to avoid a possible lawsuit claimed against the brokerage.

- Agreement between both parties

- Both parties agree to terminate the contract

http://www.dealmakerlibrary.com/a-lesson-on-the-basics-of-real-estate-contracts.aspx

Breach of Contract

A contract is a promise to perform. A breach of contract is a failure by one or both parties to perform.

If the party does not fulfill his or her contractual promise, or has given information to the other party that he or she will not perform the duty as mentioned in the contract, or if by action and conduct seems to be unable to perform the contract, the party is said to be in breach of the contract.

- One party failing to perform without a legally acceptable reason.

- Can lead to a lawsuit for failure to perform.

http://www.dealmakerlibrary.com/a-lesson-on-the-basics-of-real-estate-contracts.aspx

Remedies for Breach

A remedy is a way to correct a situation- a breach- and bring the situation to a satisfactory resolution.

There are several remedies for breach of contract with the most extreme requiring that the parties end up in court in a lawsuit over the breach. Remedies for breach of contract include specific performance, award of damages, rescission, and compensatory damages.

- Specific Performance

- Liquidated Damages

- Rescission

- Compensatory Damages

jec.unm.edu/education/online.../**contract**.../**remedies**-for-**breach-of-contrac**

Specific Performance

Specific performance is one of the remedies for breach of contract. It is when one party takes the other to court to force the parties to comply with the terms of the contract; an order of a court which requires a party to perform a specific act, usually what is stated in a contract.

Specific performance involving real estate is often sought through the remedy of a right of possession, giving the prevailing party the right to take or maintain possession of the property in dispute.

Keep in mind that if the specific performance (forcing a seller to transfer ownership of a property) would cause severe hardship to the defendant, the defendant normally prevails.

- Courts ordering performance of contract as stated per the terms of the contract

    http://www.floridabar.org/DIVCOM/JN/JNJournal01.nsf/Articles/DD80EFF3FC9685A685256ADB005D621

    7

Liquidated Damages

Most real estate purchase contracts specify how much of the earnest money could be retained by the seller as liquidated damages should the buyer fail to perform in the purchase of the property. Keep in mind that this may be better in theory than in practice.

Per the process and procedures of releasing earnest money, a seller who attempts to retain the earnest money from a buyer who agrees to sign a release of the money over to the seller may just end up tying up their house and keeping the home from being sold while the situation is in dispute. This is a better remedy reserved for substantial sums of earnest money that makes the struggle to retain a larger payoff for the seller.

- Money paid in case of default
- Usually loss of earnest money

    http://www.floridabar.org/DIVCOM/JN/JNJournal01.nsf/Articles/DD80EFF3FC9685A685256ADB005D62

Rescission

Rescission is when the court mandates that both parties are positioned back to where they were BEFORE the contract. Rescission is the unwinding of a transaction. This is done to bring the parties, as far as possible, back to the position in which they were before they entered into a contract. This position is forced through court action.

The court may decline to force rescission if substantial performance can be shown in implementing the contract – even if it was only partially implemented by one or both parties.

- To cancel or rescind the contract.
- Both parties to position BEFORE contract

    http://www.floridabar.org/DIVCOM/JN/JNJournal01.nsf/Articles/DD80EFF3FC9685A685256ADB005D621

Compensatory Damages

Sometimes when a party is injured (usually monetarily) by the breach of contract, the injured party may be awarded compensatory damages for this injury.

The amount of money awarded are for the sum of the loss. They may also be awarded expenses for lawyer and court fees. However, compensatory damages do not include punitive damages which also could be separately awarded.

The losses must have been unavoidable. If the non-breaching party could have prevented the losses but failed to do. Thus, it will disqualify them from receiving compensatory damages. This is known as "the doctrine of avoidable consequences."

- Injured party is awarded money equal to the loss

- Not punitive damages

http://www.legalmatch.com/law-library/article/compensatory-damages-in-breach-of-contract.html#sthash.YZEN0RYI.dpuf

Assignment of Contracts

Assignment of contract is a way for one party to be released from obligation to a contract without terminating the contract.

If permitted by the language in a contract agreement, a contact may be assigned replacing one of the original parties with another. The assignor legally transfers their rights to the assignee who is now in contract instead of the original party – the assignor.

Assignor-

Transfers legal rights of contract

Assignee-

Receives transfer of contract rights

Assignment of a Sale and Purchase Agreement

Once the buyer enters a purchase agreement with a seller, the buyer has equitable title. This means that the buyer has a legal interest in the seller. Investors will enter into a purchase agreement with a seller that includes the provision to allow the investor to assign the contract to another party. The intention of the investor is to receive a fee upon the successful closing for transferring his/her interest to the new party.

If the transaction is completed with full disclosure to all parties and that there is only one closing – meaning that the assignor does not orchestrate a "double closing" where the assignor closes on the deal immediately prior to the assignee closing and using the funds from the assignee as funds on the first deal—this is a legal transaction. (The double closing method described would not be a legal transaction.)

http://www.out-law.com/en/topics/projects--construction/construction-contracts/assignment

Novation

It is also possible for the mortgagor to assign a mortgage to a new party if the terms of the mortgage allow for an assignment of the mortgage. However, the original party will still be responsible for the debt should the new party default on the debt, unless the mortgage allows for novation to occur.

The difference comes in that the novation relieves the first party of legal responsibility. This is particularly important when the contract that is being assigned is a mortgage. Without the novation agreement, the original borrower is still responsible if the person who took over the mortgage defaults. With the novation agreement, the lender agrees to no longer hold the original borrower responsible.

- Substituting a new party on contract for original party

- Novation relieves the original party from the obligation.

Contracts utilized in real estate transactions are reviewed here including the topics of:

VII) Contracts Important to Real Estate

    A) Employment Agreements

        1) Conditions created by listing agreements

        2) Information included in listing agreements

        3) Types of listings:

            (a) Open listing

            (b) Exclusive-agency listing

            (c) Exclusive-right-of-sale listing

            (d) Net listing

        4) Buyer broker agreement

Employment Agreements

There are different types of contracts that real estate licensees interact with as a real estate agent.

The first contract that you are going to encounter as a new licensee is the employment contract that you sign with the broker that you work under.

In most cases, you will be employed as an independent contractor. Less common, though, is the possibility of working as a regular employee. Both contracts will detail your working relationship with the broker. Furthermore, both types of contracts will detail how much you will be paid as a real estate agent.

Independent Contractor Agreements must be paid on a per transaction basis to meet IRS independent contractor standards. Keep in mind that the commissions you pocket from each deal is something to be negotiated between you, as the agent, and the broker. You can negotiate various pay splits with your broker.

Some brokers take a flat fee for each day and pay the rest to the agent. Most brokerages offer a commission split. It is possible to find employment as a standard employee in real estate. Normally, this is when you are working as an assistant. Most assistants, though, are paid on a per transaction basis rather than an hourly or salary compensation.

The legality of paying real estate licensees as an independent contractor is held up by the IRS. According to the INTERNAL REVENUE CODE §3508. Treatment of real estate agents who performed services as a qualified real estate agent shall not be treated as an employee, and the person for whom such services are performed shall not be treated as an employer when compensated for the services performed by such individual as a real estate agent and not being paid directly based on the number of hours worked.

Independent Contractor Agreements-

- Paid by broker on per transaction basis

- Commissions paid negotiated between agent and the broker

- Flat Schedule of Fees or Commission Schedule

Employment Contract-

- Receives a salary or hourly compensation

- More popular when working as an assistant

Listing Agreements

Conditions (Terms) Created by a Listing Agreement

Listing agreements are another type of employment contract and is a primary contract that real estate licensees work with when marketing a home to sell.

The listing contract creates conditions that must be met between the parties. The parties are the seller of the property and the broker. The real estate agents work on behalf of the broker. The contract obligates the broker to attempt to find a buyer for the property. If a buyer is found, the property owner is obligated to compensate the broker per the terms of the listing contract.

Legally, per Florida Statutes Chapter 475, listing contracts can be in writing, verbal, or even implied. Remember that according to the Statute of Frauds, if a listing agreement is for longer than one year then it must be in writing to be enforceable. Also, remember that if something is not in writing that it is difficult to prove.

- Employment agreement between broker and property seller

  - Broker works to secure a buyer

  - Seller agrees to compensate broker

- Sales associate works on behalf of the broker

- Contracts can be-

  - Written

  - Verbal (unless longer than 1 year)

  - Implied

Florida Statutes Chapter 47

Information Included in Written Listing Agreements

According to Florida Statutes Chapter 475, written listing agreements must contain a definite expiration date, a description of the property, the listing price and acceptable sale terms, and the commission structure to be paid to the broker either at the time of listing or upon a sale. A written listing contract must be signed by all legal owners of the property. A copy of the signed listing agreement must be delivered to the owners either at the time of listing or within 24 hours. Finally, know that the listing agreement must not contain a provision for automatic renewal. A provision for automatic renewal would be an automatic extension of the expiration date if the property doesn't sell and this is not allowed by law.

Florida Statutes Chapter 475

Types of Listings

There are four basic types of listing agreements: Open Listing, Exclusive Agency Listing, Exclusive Right to Sell Listing, and a Net Listing.

Open Listing

An open listing means that the seller has listed with multiple brokerages. The first brokerage to bring an acceptable contract earns a commission. If the seller finds a buyer first, no commission is paid to any brokerage. An open listing is a unilateral contract. If a broker secures a buyer, the owner is obligated to pay the broker.

However, the broker is not being obligated to work to bring a buyer. They are instead being given the opportunity to bring a buyer. The key is the difference between obligation of a bilateral contract and the opportunity of the unilateral contract.

There was a time in history when this type of listing made more sense. Buyers used to go directly to sales offices to find out about listings in the area. With listings posted on multiple internet sites, brokers are less motivated to consider entering into this type of listing. The broker could find himself in the position of spending marketing dollars, creating buyer awareness of the property, then not being compensated for his efforts.

- An owner can sell a property himself or list with as many brokers as he wishes

- The first broker to bring an acceptable contract will earn the sale and commission

- If the owner sells the property him/herself, then no brokerage receives a commission

- Unilateral Contract

http://www.thetruthaboutrealty.com/open-listing/

Exclusive Agency Listing

The exclusive agency listing is a twist on the open listing. In this case the only brokerage who is going to get paid is the one broker who signs the agreement.

The agreement is written in such a way that it legally prevents the property owner from working with or paying any other brokers.

However, this agreement preserves the right of the property owner to find his or her own buyer. In that case, no broker would get paid.

This type of listing agreement is popular when agents work to list homes being sold "For Sale by Owner." This is a bilateral contract as the brokerage is obligated to try to find a buyer. As with the open listing, the broker may find himself putting out time and money for a home that he doesn't end up being compensated for upon a sale.

- The Broker earns a commission if the property owner has not found the buyer themselves

- They are the sole broker allowed to work with and be paid by the property owner per the agreement

- Bilateral contract

Exclusive Right of Sale Listing

The exclusive right of sale listing agreement, also known as the exclusive right-to-sell listing agreement, is the most popular form of listing agreement. This contract is preferred by brokers because it guarantees the broker payment if a buyer is secured within the listing timeline.

Brokers who are members of the Multiple Listing Service may advertise a commission split to other brokers who produce a buyer. Either way, the listing broker gets paid. If the owner brings a buyer himself, the broker still gets compensated per the terms of the listing agreement. Know that it is possible to exclude a buyer from an exclusive right of sale listing contract.

Often, when an agent meets with a potential seller to list a home, the agent may find the seller reluctant to commit due to one party who has been considering purchasing the home. By excluding that person from the agreement or altering the commission to be paid if that person does buy, the seller will be more likely to go forward with the contract. Rarely do the individuals excluded from a contract end up purchasing the property. Know that this type of listing contract is a bilateral contract.

- Broker is the only broker who can receive a commission. The broker receives a commission no matter who brings the buyer.

- May offer a co-brokerage to a buyer's agent in the MLS

- Bilateral Contract

Net Listing

A net listing is when the seller tells the broker how much he must net, or take away, from the closing. The broker calculates expected closing costs, adds in for his commission, and this sets a price to market the property for sale.

However, the bottom line is that anything above the acceptable net is how much the agent can pocket. A net listing creates an opportunity for an unethical agent to take advantage of a homeowner that isn't aware of the true value of their home. For this reason, a net listing is not legal in all states.

A net listing is legal in Florida, but taking advantage of sellers is not legal to misrepresent the true value of the property. Also know that a net listing is an example of a bilateral contract as both the seller and the broker are obligated to perform.

- The seller agrees to a net sale price.

- The broker keeps everything over this net price.

- Not legal in all states

- Legal in Florida

- Bilateral Contract

Calculating Net Listings

For a net listing, it is necessary to calculate the projected sale price based on how much the seller wants to net.

First, take the amount of net they want to walk away with from the sale. Add up their estimated costs to go to closing (not including commission) and add it to the amount they want to net.

(Estimated seller costs include things like title insurance, title closing fee, title search fees, recording fees, documentary stamp on the deed, property taxes, HOA estoppel fee, mortgage payoffs, and any expected repairs.)

Then, take 100% - % of Broker commission to equal a percentage that is then divided into the sum of the "net plus expenses." This gives the price needed to sell the house for in order for the seller to get the desired net.

• Seller NET	$200,000	
• Add Seller Fees and Expenses	+ 5,200	
• Net & Expenses (Not including commission)	$205,200	
• Deal % (100% - Broker Commission %)	÷ 94%	
• Net & Expenses ÷ Deal %	$218,298	Rounded Up

Buyer Broker Agreement

Best practice is when you work with a buyer to work under a formal buyer broker agreement. This agreement outlines the obligations of the broker to the buyer and the buyer to the broker, which means it details the buyer-broker relationship and the responsibilities between broker and buyer.

This type of contract is also considered to be an employment contract and it officially designates the broker as the agent working on behalf of the buyer. You can be either a single agent, a transaction agent or in no brokerage relationship and still have an official buyer broker agreement.

- The buyer broker agreement is an employment contract with a buyer.

- A common contract between home buyers and brokers.

- Bilateral contract

According to most buyer agency agreements, the buyer's agent must do these things:

- Protect their client's financial information

- Negotiate the best possible price for the buyer

- Must disclose to the buyer if they are working with another buyer interested in the same property

- Show all properties the buyer is interested in that fits their criteria and budget

- Connect you with the service providers—inspectors, lenders, home warranty companies—to best suit the buyer's needs.

Buyers also have obligations under the buyer broker agreement. The buyer must work with his or her buyer's agent exclusively, never give personal information to any other agent, not call other agents to see properties, even if they think they are saving their agent some time and effort, and clearly define their must haves and deal breakers to help their agent streamline the showing process.

The buyer must:

- Work with a buyer's agent exclusively

- Never give personal information to any other agent

- Not call other agents to see properties, even if they think they are saving their agent some time and effort

- Clearly define their must haves and deal breakers to help their agent streamline the showing process

http://www.realtor.com/advice/buyer-agents-work-free/

As a contract, Buyer Broker Agreements must identify the parties in the agreement – the buyers and the broker. The length of the agreement, the type of property desired, the broker and buyer obligations and the compensation. In some areas buyer brokers receive a retainer upfront which prepays them for their services. It is more common, however, for the agreement to state how much the broker will be paid upon the buyer closing on a home purchase.

Although the employment agreement with stated compensation is between the buyer and the buyer's broker – in most cases, the actual compensation comes through the listing broker paid by the seller. This fact will be detailed in the agreement. Most buyer broker agreements also include the fact that the buyer will owe the broker a commission even if the buyer goes around the broker to buy a house. The point being that if the agent commits time to work for the buyer, the buyer commits to making sure the broker gets paid.

These are the obligations under the contract.

- Parties and length of agreement

- Type and details of property desired

- Broker obligations

- Buyer obligations

- Compensation

- Brokerage relationship

Buyer Brokerage Agreements Compensation Example:

- A buyer entered into an agreement with a buyer broker, which ensures that the broker will earn 3% upon the successful purchase of a home by the buyer.

- The buyer purchased a home for $200,000

- The home that the buyer purchased was offered through the MLS with a co-broke amount of 2% to the buyer's agent.

- How much would the buyer be obligated to personally pay the buyer's broker at closing – to be included on the closing disclosure?

    Answer

    - $200,000 x .03 = $6,000 Total commission due

    - $200,000 x .02 = $4,000 Commission paid by seller

    - $6,000 - $4,000 = $2,000 Difference to be paid by buyer

Contracts utilized in real estate transactions are reviewed here including the topics of:

VII) Contracts Important to Real Estate

    B) Sales contracts

        1) Contract negotiation

            (a) Offers and counteroffers

            (b) Acceptance

        2) Earnest money deposits

        3) Equitable title

Sales Contracts

A purchase and sales agreement are another type of contract that you will be working with a as a real estate agent. It is a contract between a buyer (vendee) and seller (vendor) that outlines the provisions for the sale of real estate. A sales contract is a bilateral agreement where the seller is obligated to sell the house and the buyer is obligated to purchase the house. Other obligations, conditions, and contingencies of the deal are detailed in the agreement.

Purchase and Sale Agreement

- Contract between buyer (vendee) and seller (vendor)

- Outlines provisions for the sale of real estate

- Bilateral Contract

A purchase and sale agreement start as an offer. Normally, the offer is the buyer offering to buy the home. It can start with the seller offering to sell the home.

Once one of the parties makes an offer, the other party can accept, reject or counter the offer. The process of the buyer and seller going back and forth hammering out agreeable details is called negotiations. As agents representing the buyer and seller, the real estate licensees handle the negotiation details on behalf of their clients. Once both parties have agreed to all the details in the deal, they are in contract.

Contract Negotiation

- Offeror makes an offer
- Offeree can accept, reject or counter the offer

Earnest Money Deposit Definition

An earnest money deposit is a deposit paid by a buyer to a seller to demonstrate intention to complete the real estate purchase. It also called a good faith deposit or a binder deposit. Remember not to confuse the earnest money deposit as being the "consideration" in a deal! The consideration that the buyer is the promise to purchase.

http://www.investorwords.com/1616/earnest_money.html#ixzz3wZWRJKK5

Equitable Title Definition

Once a buyer and seller are in contract, the buyer has equitable title in the property. Equitable Title is defined by the interest retained by a person who has agreed to purchase a property but has not yet closed the transaction. Equitable title is like ownership in process. You have a contract, but it has not been finalized. There are certain rights that go with equitable title, even though the contract has not closed. It includes the right to acquire legal title once the deal has been completed.

http://www.investorwords.com/8581/equitable_title.html#ixzz3wZZ1GAwX

Contracts utilized in real estate transactions are reviewed here including the topics of:

VII) Contracts Important to Real Estate

B) Sales contracts

    4) Information included in sales contracts

        (a) Date, time and place of closing

        (b) Purchase price

        (c) Financing terms

        (d) Quality of title to be conveyed

        (e) Type of deed

        (f) Items of personal property included

        (g) Type of evidence of title to be provided

        (h) Items to be prorated

Information Included in the Contract

The sales contract must contain certain information to be a legal contract:

- Date, time and place of closing

- Price and Financing Terms of Purchase

- Quality of Title to Be Conveyed

- Type of Deed

- Items of Personal Property Included

- Type of Title

- Prorated Items

Contracts utilized in real estate transactions are reviewed here including the topics of:

VII) Contracts Important to Real Estate

    B) Sales contracts

        5) Required disclosures

           (a) Radon gas disclosure

           (b) Energy efficiency disclosure

           (c) Lead-based paint disclosure

           (d) Homeowner association disclosure

(e) Flood insurance disclosure

(f) Condominium and cooperative disclosures

(g) Property tax disclosure

(h) Building code violation disclosure

Sales Contracts Required Disclosures

As a licensee working with purchase and sale agreements, you must be aware that certain disclosures are required by law to be made. These include radon gas disclosure, energy efficiency disclosure, lead-based paint disclosure, H.O.A. disclosure, flood insurance disclosure, condo, coop disclosures, property tax disclosure, and building code violation disclosure.

Required Radon Disclosure

State law requires that buyers and renters who enter into a purchase or rental agreement must receive a written disclosure regarding radon gas before or at the time of executing the purchase or lease agreement. This disclosure must be contained in at least one document. The disclosure describes what radon gas is. Florida statutes do not require that testing be made, only the disclosure be provided.

- Radon gas-notification made on at least 1 document

- Describes what radon is

- Does not require testing

- Made before or at execution of purchase and sale contract

- Also required for lease agreements

The required wording per Florida statutes that must be included is:

"RADON GAS: Radon is a naturally occurring radioactive gas that, when it has accumulated in a building in sufficient quantities, may present health risks to persons who are exposed to it over time. Levels of radon that exceed federal and state guidelines have been found in buildings in Florida. Additional information regarding radon and radon testing may be obtained from your county health department."

http://www.leg.state.fl.us/statutes/index.cfm?App_mode=Display_Statute&URL=0400-0499/0404/Sections/0404.056.html

Energy Efficiency Brochure

Another disclosure that must be presented prior to signing a purchase and sale agreement, is the fact that a buyer may choose to get an energy-efficiency rating of the structure prior to closing. This disclosure is made through an information brochure. This requirement of disclosure is per the Florida Building Energy-Efficiency Rating Act, part of Florida statutes. This disclosure does not apply to leases.

Florida Building Energy-Efficiency Rating Act

- Buyers must receive an information brochure stating that they may choose to get an energy-efficiency rating of the structure prior to closing

- This disclosure must be made at the time of or prior to signing a purchase and sale agreement (does not apply to leasing)

http://www.leg.state.fl.us/statutes/index.cfm?App_mode=Display_Statute&URL=0100-0199/0163/Sections/0163.08.html

Lead-Based Paint Disclosure

A lead-based paint disclosure must be made to buyers and renters for homes built prior to 1978.

Congress passed the Residential Lead-Based Paint Hazard Reduction Act of 1992, also known as Title X, to protect families from exposure to lead from paint, dust, and soil.

Section 1018 of this law directed HUD and EPA to require the disclosure of known information on lead-based paint and lead-based paint hazards before the sale or lease of homes built before 1978.

- Built Prior to 1978

- Residential Lead-based Paint Hazard Reduction Act (federal law)

- Seller must disclose any known hazards and documents regarding lead hazards

- Buyers and renters must be given EPA booklet before the sale or lease

- Must allow a 10-day inspection period which buyer can waive

- It is the licensee representing the seller that must ensure that the disclosure is made

http://portal.hud.gov/hudportal/HUD?src=/program_offices/healthy_homes/enforcement/disclosure

HOA Disclosure Requirement

The Florida Statute 720 requires that a disclosure summary be included with a purchase and sale agreement for property that is subject to mandatory Homeowner Association membership, fees and assessments, and restrictions.

The rule provides that the buyer be given a 3 day right of rescission upon receipt of the disclosure summary if the disclosure summary was not provided at the time the contract was signed.

The right to void (rescission) cannot be voided by the buyer. This rescission right ends at closing, meaning that if a buyer purchases a home without having ever read the disclosure summary, the buyer cannot back out of the deal after the deal is closed.

Keep in mind, though, that the licensee is responsible for the disclosure being made and could be sued by the buyer if the sale closed without the information being provided.

- Gives 3 day right of rescission upon receipt of the disclosure summary

- Right to void (rescission) cannot be waived by the buyer

- Rescission right ends at closing.

http://www.leg.state.fl.us/Statutes/index.cfm?App_mode=Display_Statute&URL=0700-0799/

The Disclosure Summary specifically identifies the homeowner association by name, the fees to be paid and the fee schedule. It advises the buyer that the failure to pay these fees could result in a lien being placed on the property.

As a result of the lien, the homeowner could ultimately lose the property. It advised the buyer that the homeowner associations can restrict usage of the property through the restrictive covenants and that these covenants be amended.

It advises the buyer that they should refer to the actual homeowner association documents, not the disclosure summary, before purchasing the property.

http://www.leg.state.fl.us/Statutes/index.cfm?App_mode=Display_Statute&URL=0700-0799/0720/0720.html

Property Tax Disclosure

Florida Statutes also require that a Property Tax Disclosure be given to a buyer before or at the time of signing the purchase agreement. The Disclosure Summary may be included in the wording of the contract or Disclosure Summary may be separate from the purchase agreement.

If not included in the contract, it must be attached to purchase agreement. The Purchase agreement must also include a warning that the buyer should read the property tax disclosure prior to signing the purchase agreement.

The Property tax disclosure is designed to warn the buyer that the amount of ad valorem taxes for the existing owner may be different for the buyer. These differences can result from reassessment and the loss of prior Homestead exemption.

Must be given before or at the time of signing the purchase agreement. Disclosure Summary may be included in the wording of the contract. Or Disclosure Summary may be separate from the purchase agreement.

- Attached to purchase agreement

- Purchase agreement must include warning that buyer should read the property tax disclosure prior to signing the purchase agreement

Warns the buyer that the amount of ad valorem taxes for the existing owner may be different for buyer.

Wording for the disclosure must include:

- BUYER SHOULD NOT RELY ON THE SELLER'S CURRENT PROPERTY TAXES AS THE AMOUNT OF PROPERTY TAXES THAT THE BUYER MAY BE OBLIGATED TO PAY IN THE YEAR SUBSEQUENT TO PURCHASE. A CHANGE OF OWNERSHIP OR PROPERTY IMPROVEMENTS TRIGGERS REASSESSMENTS OF THE PROPERTY THAT COULD RESULT IN HIGHER PROPERTY TAXES. IF YOU HAVE ANY QUESTIONS CONCERNING VALUATION, CONTACT THE COUNTY PROPERTY APPRAISER'S OFFICE FOR INFORMATION.

http://www.leg.state.fl.us/Statutes/index.cfm?App_mode=Display_Statute&URL=0600-0699/0689/Sections/0689.261.html

Building Code Violation Disclosure

The building code violation disclosure is given prior to closing. Sellers are not required to rectify the situation, but must make available to the buyer notices and nature of the violation. Also, the new owner's name and address must be forwarded to code enforcement within 5 days.

Seller must disclose:

- If Seller has been notified of a violation and possible enforcement

- The nature of the violation

- Copy of notice(s)

- That buyer, upon closing, is responsible for bringing to code

- The seller, upon closing, must forward name and address of new owner to code enforcement within 5 days of the sale

Per the statute, if the sale closes prior to the date the seller was summoned to appear in court regarding the violation, the buyer/new owner must now appear and is responsible for the outcome. The new owner will be provided a reasonable period to correct the violation before the continuation of proceedings in county court.

If the property is transferred before the date the violator has been summoned to appear in county court, the proceeding shall not be dismissed, but the new owner will be substituted as the party of record and thereafter provided a reasonable period to correct the violation before the continuation of proceedings in county court.

Failure of the seller to disclose Building Code Violations may constitute Fraud and lead to civil charges.

"A failure to make the disclosure described in subparagraphs 1., 2., and 3. before the transfer creates a rebuttable presumption of fraud."

http://www.leg.state.fl.us/statutes/index.cfm?App_mode=Display_Statute&URL=0100-0199/0125/Sections/0125.69.html

Contracts utilized in real estate transactions are reviewed here including the topics of:

VII) Contracts Important to Real Estate

    B) Sales contracts

        6) FAR/BAR contract forms

Sale Contracts

Far/Bar Contract Forms

Approved Contracts and Addendums

There are different versions of purchase and sale contracts that as a Florida licensee can utilize. Remember that you are authorized only to fill in contracts not to write complete contracts.

To make it easier to comply with contract and disclosure requirements, approved contracts are available for licensees to use through the Florida Association of Realtors website: www.Floridarealtors.org These contracts are the work of the Far/Bar or Florida Realtors/Florida Bar.

As stated by the Florida Realtor Association in the CRSP Prep Manual: "The contract contains terms negotiated by the parties. It defines the party's rights and obligations. Therefore, the licensee who prepares the contract must be thoroughly familiar with its terms and with the expressed intent of the parties. The licensee (broker and sales associate or broker associate) is liable for mistakes."

- Florida Realtors/Florida Bar (FAR/BAR)
- Available from www.FloridaRealtors.org
- Licensee responsible for accuracy

Contracts utilized in real estate transactions are reviewed here including the topics of:

VII) Contracts Important to Real Estate

 B) Sales contracts

  7) Disclosure of defects that materially affect the value of residential property

   1) Johnson vs. Davis

   2) "As is" provision

   3) Duty for licensees to disclose

Sales Contracts

Disclosure of Material Defects

"That affect the value of residential property"

Any fact that may have a significant and reasonable impact on the market value of the property is material fact or a material defect and must be disclosed. The issue of whether a disclosure was made is a major source of litigation. These court cases involve suits against sellers and agent's real estate agents.

  http://www.legalmatch.com/law-library/article/disclosure-of-material-defects.html#sthash.UgCk0rT6.dpuf

Johnson Vs. Davis PL

Johnson vs. Davis is the landmark case that set the legal precedence that material defects must be disclosed by the seller. Per the Florida Supreme Court, it was found "We hold that where the seller of a home knows of facts materially affecting the value of the property which are not readily observable and are not known to the buyer, the seller is under a duty to disclose them to the buyer." Prior to this decision, the philosophy of caveat emptor, buyer beware ruled.

The case involved a seller that knew that a roof leaked, yet he concealed the facts to the buyer. The courts ruled that the buyer be returned the 10% deposit he had made on the home, plus interest and costs and fees.

> **Facts:** PL entered into a contract to purchase DF's home, and gave 10% down. DF knew the roof leaked, but represented to the PL there were no problems with the roof. PL entered the home after a heavy rain and found water gushing into the home. Under FL. Law, the seller of a home has a duty to disclose a latent material defect to the Pl. This was a fraudulent concealment, entitling PL to the return of his deposit plus interest, plus costs and fees.

http://www.4lawschool.com

http://www.casebriefs.com/blog/law/property/property-law-keyed-to-dukeminier/the-land-transaction/johnson-v-davis/

Sales Contracts "As is" Provision

Some contracts are written with an "As is" provision. This provision does not relieve the duty to disclose material defects. Buyers incorrectly fear that an "as is" sale would require that they give up their right to inspections.

The fact is that "as is" contracts include optional inspection periods that provide buyers with a number of days to inspect, which is negotiable. Buyer is protected during inspection period. Should the buyer, during the inspection period, determine that the property does not meet their buying criteria, the buyer can cancel the contract.

If the cancellation followed the guidelines of the contract, the buyer's earnest money deposit would be returned. Does not relieve the duty to disclose material defects. Buyers incorrectly assume that on an "as is" sale they're giving up their right to an inspection. The truth is you are covered by an inspection clause in an "as is" contract that's quite detailed.

The number of days to inspect is negotiable. The buyer is protected during inspection period.

Duties for Licensees to Disclose

Johnson vs. Davis clarified the seller's duty to disclose a material defect. However, licensees involved in a sale also have a duty to disclose material defects. **Rayner vs. Wise Realty** of Tallahassee set the precedence of the licensee's duties to disclose. In fact, failure to disclose can open a licensee up to misrepresentation or fraud charges.

- Extends duty to disclose material defects to licensees

- Misrepresentation

- Fraud

http://www.leagle.com/decision/19871865504So2d1361_11597/RAYNER%20v.%20WISE%20REALTY%20C O.

Contracts utilized in real estate transactions are reviewed here including the topics of:

VII) Contracts Important to Real Estate

    C) Option contracts

Option Contracts

Another type of sales contract for a licensee to be familiar with is the option contract. An **option contract** is an agreement between a buyer and seller that gives the purchaser of the **option** the right to buy or sell an asset, the real estate property, at a later date at an agreed upon price.

Options contracts are often used in securities, commodities, and real estate transactions. Option contracts can include the provision for the holder of the option to be able to assign the option for purchase. Options are unilateral contracts as only one party is obligated to perform. Under the option, the seller is obligated to sell per the terms of the contract. However, the buyer is not obligated to pursue the option and buy the property.

- Can be assigned per terms of the contract

- Unilateral Contract

www.investinganswers.com

The Optionee is the individual who takes an option. The optionor gives the option. In a purchase and sale option contract, the option specifies the terms and conditions that property can be purchased for should the option be pursued. This includes the price that would be paid for the property. If an option is not fulfilled by the optionee within the specified time, the optionor usually keeps the option fee, which paid for the option.

Option Contracts

The same provisions are included in the option contract as in a regular real estate purchase and sale valid contract. Option contracts must specify the time the option is in effect, the names parties involved, the price of the option and property, a legal description, terms of option, consideration, and type of deed to be delivered upon sale.

Contracts utilized in real estate transactions are reviewed here including the topics of:

VII) Contracts Important to Real Estate

    D) Installment sale contract

Installment Sale Contract

Another form of sales contract is the installment sales contract, often referred to as a land contract or contract for deed. With an installment contract, the sale of the real estate is completed over a period with installment payments made by the buyer to the seller per the terms of the contract. Some investors use this type of sale as a tax strategy as it can postpone capital gains tax.

- Land Contracts/Contracts for Deed

- Installment payments are made on a regular basis and taxes due during the period payment is received

- Installment payments are often used as a tax strategy.

http://homebuying.about.com/od/glossaryijk/g/Installment-Sales-Contract.htm

http://lockyeartitle.com/pdfs/October2008.pdf

R.E. Miscellaneous Considerations

CONTRACT CONSIDERATIONS

Contracts utilized in real estate transactions are reviewed here including the topics of:

VIII) Miscellaneous Real Estate Contract Considerations

   A) Procuring cause

   B) Telephone solicitation laws

   C) Multiple listing service

   D) Ethical practices

       1) When in doubt disclose

       2) Fraud

       3) Culpable negligence

Procuring Cause

There is no doubt that real estate contracts are a detailed issue for a student of real estate to tackle. Following are miscellaneous real estate contract consideration.

The Doctrine of Procuring Cause defines Procuring cause as referring to a broker's efforts to match a ready, willing and able purchaser with a seller and for a sale to take place because of the broker's continuous negotiation and/or involvement.

Basically, if a broker (or the agent acting on behalf of the broker) has introduced the buyer to the property and the buyer wishes to buy based on the efforts of the broker or licensee and the licensee has continuous involvement in the sale process; this is called procuring cause. The sale would not have taken place, but for the involvement of the broker/licensee. Procuring cause entitles the broke/licensee to commission for that sale.

The Doctrine of Procuring Cause

- Procuring cause refers to a broker's efforts to match a ready, willing and able purchaser with a seller and for a sale to take place because of the broker's continuous negotiation and/or involvement

- Entitles the broker the commission to the sale

http://moore-and-co.com/pdf/THE_DOCTRINE_OF_PROCURING_CAUSE-CLAY_NAUGHTON.pdf

Procuring Cause

Procuring cause disputes are disputes among brokers as to who should receive the commission for the sale. They are not disputes between the seller of the property and the broker who listed the property. Rather, they are claims for commission made to the listing broker who advertised a co-broker to the agent who produced the buyer.

If a seller refused to pay a broker per the terms of a listing contract, the listing broker would be forced to sue the seller in court to try to force the payment of the commission. Procuring cause disputes, on the other hand, are handled through dispute resolution arbitrated by the local REALTOR board.

All local REALTOR® associations must, as a benefit of membership, offer the ability to mediate otherwise-arbitral disputes. In some REALTOR® associations, mediation is required prior to an arbitration hearing. There are many reasons to have procuring cause dispute, yet all cases come down to interpretation of the rule and the specific facts in the case.

Disputes

- Procuring cause disputes between licensees are usually settled through an arbitration hearing.
- Disputes between a broker and buyer or seller may be settled in court

Many factors can influence a court or arbitration decision on procuring cause. A partial list from the NATIONAL ASSOCIATION OF REALTORS® Arbitration Manual highlights some of the most critical issues. These include the nature of the transaction (listing and buyer representation agreements), the offer of cooperative compensation, the conduct of the seller, the buyer, and the brokers and their affiliate licensees, the roles and relationships of the parties, the initial contact with the purchaser, and the continuity of contact.

Some licensees mistakenly believe that if they just introduced a buyer to a property that they have earned the commission. It is much more complicated than that. Abandonment and estrangement between the buyer and the agent can negate the right to receive payment. Real estate is littered with procuring cause cases.

Points of Consideration

- Nature of the transaction (listing and buyer representation agreements)
- Offer of cooperative compensation
- Conduct of the seller, the buyer, and the brokers and their affiliate licensees
- Roles and relationships of the parties
- Initial contact with the purchaser
- Continuity of contact (abandonment and estrangement)

Telephone Solicitation Laws

Remember that if you are working with a buyer or seller, you still must comply with Telephone Solicitation Laws. Important points include that calls must be limited to 8 a.m. – 9 p.m., that there are both State and National Registries, and that Federal Law Supersedes State Law.

Regarding individuals who have registered on the Do Not Call List – National or state: Individuals that inquire on properties that you have listed for sale, or people that have general real estate inquiries about your services open themselves up to receive calls from you but only for 3 months.

Once you have completed a sale for a buyer or seller, you can contact them by phone to solicit them for new business but only for 18 months after the sale was completed.

R.E. Miscellaneous Considerations

Telephone Solicitation Laws

Remember that if you are working with a buyer or seller, you still have to comply with Telephone Solicitation Laws. Important points include that calls must be limited to 8am - 9pm, that there are both State and National Registries, and that Federal Law Supersedes State Law.

Regarding individuals who have registered on the Do Not Call List – National or state: Individuals that inquire on properties that you have listed for sale, or people that have general real estate inquiries about your services open themselves up to receive calls from you but only for 3 months.

And once you have completed a sale for a buyer or seller, you are allowed to contact them by phone to solicit them for new business but only for 18 months after the sale was completed.

Do Not Call List	
Florida Law	**Federal Law**
No Solicitation Registry	National Do Not Call Registry
Calls only between 8am-9pm	Calls only between 8am-9
$10,000 fine/violation	$16,000 fine/violation
FSBO exception	No FSBO exception
Federal Law supersedes State Law	

https://www.donotcall.gov/

MLS – Multiple Listing Service

The **MLS** is used as a private offer of cooperation and compensation by listing brokers to other **real estate** brokers. The MLS is a tool to help listing brokers find cooperative brokers working with buyers to help sell their clients' homes. Access to information from MLS listings is provided to the public free-of-charge by participating brokers.

Data that is not publicly accessible includes information that would endanger sellers' privacy or safety, such as seller contact information and times the home is vacant for showings.

The point of the MLS is that real estate members can show and sell each other's listed property and receive compensation if the property sells. Listing contracts with sellers allow the seller to opt-in or opt-out of having their property included in the MLS.

- A service that allows Realtors© to share listing information with other members of the MLS

- Members can show and sell each other's listings and receive compensation if they sell

- Listing contracts allow sellers to opt-in or opt-out of having their property included in the MLS

http://www.realtor.org/topics/nar-doj-settlement/multiple-listing-service-mls-what-is-it

Ethical Practices

Real Estate Licensees are held to a high standard of ethics. Penalties are high for unethical behavior. Real Estate agents that join the National Association of Realtors and become REALTORS® are held to a standard of conduct established by the Code of Ethics.

The Code of Ethics establishes obligations that may be higher than those mandated by law. In any instance, where the Code of Ethics and the law conflict, the obligations of the law must take precedence. REALTORS® are required to complete ethics training of not less than 2 hours, 30 minutes of instructional time within four-year cycles. The training must meet specific learning objectives and criteria established by the National Association of REALTORS®.

- REALTORS® are members of National Association of REALTORS®

- REALTORS® are held to high stand of ethics

- Follows Code of Ethics and Standards of Practice

- Ethics Training Required

- 2 ½ hours every 4 years

- Learning objective of the National Association of REALTORS®

http://www.realtor.org/code-of-ethics/training

When in Doubt – Disclose

Behaving ethically includes disclosing material defects about the property. If you are in doubt about whether a disclosure needs to be made involving the condition of the property, disclose.

- Material defects must be disclosed

- Always in the best interest of the brokerage, to disclose about the material condition of the property if uncertain that you are supposed to disclose!

Fraud

Real estate licensees must not engage in fraud. Fraud consists of some deceitful practice or willful device, resorted to with intent to deprive another of his right, or in some manner to do him an injury. Whenever information is hidden from a buyer and damage is done, fraud can be an issue.

http://thelawdictionary.org/fraud/

4 Elements of Fraud

For a licensee to be found guilty of fraud, there are four elements or conditions that must be met.

1. Misstatement or failed to disclose material fact

2. The licensee knew or should have known the statement was inaccurate

3. The party relied on the misstatement

4. Damage resulted to the party who relied on the statement

http://shivamlawworld.blogspot.com/2012/07/elements-of-fraud.html

The level of criminal violation for fraud depends upon the amount of money involved in the value of the property:

Florida Statutes 775:

1. If the amount of property obtained has an aggregate value of $50,000 or more, the violator is guilty of a felony of the first degree, punishable as provided in s. 775.082, s. 775.083, or s. 775.084.

2. If the amount of property obtained has an aggregate value of $20,000 or more, but less than $50,000, the violator is guilty of a felony of the second degree, punishable as provided in s. 775.082, s. 775.083, or s. 775.084.

3. If the amount of property obtained has an aggregate value of less than $20,000, the violator is guilty of a felony of the third degree, punishable as provided in s. 775.082, s. 775.083, or s. 775.084.

Florida Statutes 775

Culpable Negligence

Real Estate Licensees must not engage in acts that can result in a charge of culpable negligence. You can be charged with Culpable Negligence, even if you did not know of a damaging issue, *but should have.*

Per Florida Statutes, whoever, through culpable negligence, exposes another person to personal injury commits a misdemeanor of the second degree, punishable as provided in s. 775.082 or s. 775.083.

Florida Statutes 775

Attorney-in-Fact

Acting in the role of a Real Estate Licensee on behalf of a buyer or seller does not give the licensee the power to bind a buyer or seller to a sale by signing in their place. Only someone who has a power of attorney can sign a contract for another person.

12 RESIDENTIAL MORTGAGES

Learning Objectives:
- Distinguish between title theory and lien theory
- Describe the essential elements of the mortgage instrument and the note
- Describe the various features of a mortgage including down payment, loan-to-value ratio, equity, interest, loan servicing, escrow account, PITI, discount points and loan origination fee
- Explain assignment of a mortgage and the purpose of an estoppel certificate
- Explain the foreclosure process and distinguish between judicial and non-judicial foreclosure
- Describe the mortgagor's and mortgagee's rights in a foreclosure
- Calculate loan-to-value ratio
- Explain the use of discount points and calculate approximate yield on a loan
- Distinguish among the various methods of purchasing mortgaged property

Key Terms:

acceleration clause	hypothecation	partial release clause
assumption	interest	PITI
blanket mortgage	lien theory	prepayment clause
buydown	lis pendens	prepayment penalty
contract for deed (land contract)	land development loans	receivership clause
defeasance clause	loan origination fee	right to reinstate
deed in lieu of foreclosure	loan servicing	satisfaction of mortgage
discount points	loan-to-value ratio	short sales
due on sale clause	mortgage	subject to
equity	mortgagee	subordination agreement
equity of redemption	mortgagor	take-out commitment
escrow	note	title theory
estoppel certificate	novation	

MORTGAGE CONCEPTS

Understanding the components of residential mortgages is essential to working in real estate. This topic is

reviewed here including:

I)   Mortgage concepts

    A) Mortgage law

        1) Title theory

        2) Lien theory

    B) Loan instruments

        1) Promissory note (essential elements)

        2) Mortgage instrument

            (a) Parties to a mortgage

            (b) Satisfaction of mortgage

        3) Hypothecation

    C) First mortgages versus junior mortgages

        1) Determining what priority a mortgage lien has

        2) Subordination agreements

Mortgage Law

Although you are being licensed as a real estate sales associate, part of your success in the business will stem from your understanding of how to interface between buyers and their need for mortgages.

There's more than one theory and standard about how to handle a mortgage. The question becomes, if a buyer has a mortgage on a property for almost the entire amount of the property's value, who owns the property? The borrower? Or the Lender?

- So, who owns the property?

  - The borrower?

    Or

  - The lien holder (lender)

Title Theory

Who owns the property depends upon which state you live in and which mortgage theory that state has adopted.

In a title theory state, the lender holds the title to the property until the mortgage is paid. Initially, upon closing of the home, the title is conveyed to the lender. Once the debt is paid in full, the lender conveys the title to the borrower.

- In a title theory state, the bank holds the title to the property until the mortgage is paid. At closing title conveyed to lender. Once the debt is paid in full, the lender conveys the title to the borrower

http://www.investorwords.com/18314/lien_theory_state.html#ixzz3wZF8KqdC

Lien Theory

In a lien theory state, **(Florida is a lien theory state)** the borrower owns the property. Title is conveyed to the borrower at the original closing. A lien is placed against the property by the lender. It makes it more difficult for a bank to foreclose on the property because the bank does not hold the title. Once the debt is paid in full, the lien is released.

In a lien theory state the borrower holds the title to the property.

- At closing, title conveyed to borrower and a lien is filed against the property. Once the debt is paid in full, the lien is released.

http://www.investorwords.com/18314/lien_theory_state.html#ixzz3wZF8KqdC

Loan Instruments

It is important to understand and be able to distinguish between the different loan instruments involved when a mortgage is placed against a property with a loan. The first is a promissory note. The second is a mortgage instrument. The third is hypothecation.

Promissory Note

Promissory note is the document signed by the borrower promising to repay a loan under agreed-upon terms. It is also called a note. Specific elements of the note include the specific terms of the loan such as rate, length of term, payment, etc. It also must be signed by the buyer to be valid.

- Accompanies the mortgage

- A document signed by the borrower promising to repay a loan under agreed-upon terms

- Also called note

Essential Elements

- Includes the specific terms of the loan such as rate, length of term, payment, penalties, etc.

http://www.investorwords.com/3896/promissory_note.html#ixzz3wZLHMoVt

Mortgage Instrument

The mortgage is the instrument that pledges the real estate property as collateral for a loan. A mortgage agreement must be in writing and recorded to be valid. The parties to the mortgage are the lender and the borrower. Once the debt has been paid a satisfaction of mortgage is given.

- Parties: Lender/mortgagee/creditor and borrower/mortgagor/debtor http://www.investorwords.com/3124/mortgage.html#ixzz3wZMwnyRc

Satisfaction of Mortgage / Release of Mortgage

Most home owners think that the most important document they can hold is the deed. In fact, if there has ever been a loan on the property, the importance of the satisfaction of mortgage trumps the importance of a deed. The satisfaction of mortgage is a release of mortgage that proves that a property is paid for free and clear of the original lien. The satisfaction of mortgage must be filed with the county office where the lien was officially registered to update the deed and create clear title to the property. The lender has 60 days to file the release of lien and this filing is considered constructive notice of the release.

Satisfaction of Mortgage Definition | Investopedia http://www.investopedia.com/terms/s/satisfaction-mortgage.asp#ixzz3wZfi2mSs

Hypothecation

Know that **Hypothecation** is the pledging of securities or other assets as collateral to secure a loan while not giving up possession of the property. This is what keeps the borrower in the home while the lien is in place.

A property owner can pledge the real estate as collateral for more than one mortgage. When a mortgage loan is recorded in the public records it becomes a lien on the real property. The mortgage lien is a voluntary lien created by the property owner (mortgagor). The question becomes then as to which lien or mortgage gets paid first upon the sale (or foreclosure) of the property.

The order or priority of which lien will be paid first is determined by the order in which they were recorded. The first mortgage recorded is called exactly that – the First Mortgage.

http://www.investorwords.com/2366/hypothecation.html#ixzz3wZVxHs8h

First Mortgages versus Junior Mortgages

All other subsequent mortgages are called Junior Mortgages, and they are paid in the order they were recorded. This means that there could be a second and third mortgage.

The second and third mortgages are both called junior mortgages. Assuming the second mortgage was recorded second it would be paid second in line behind the first mortgage. However, one lien holder can give up their place in line to another lien holder called a subordination agreement.
Determines what order liens will be paid.

- Becomes important when there is not enough money to cover all debts against the property.

http://www.nolo.com/legal-encyclopedia/understanding-mortgages-deeds-trust

Loan Instruments

It's important to keep the terminology straight. Generally speaking, when you have a word ending with –ee plus another word ending with –or, the –ee represents the person who is receiving something from the –or. For example, the lessee is the tenant who is receiving a lease from the lessor. The grantor is giving something to the grantee. The vendor is selling something to the vendee (the vendee is receiving what is being sold). The optionor is granting an option to the optionee. The offeror is making an offer to the offeree(seller). The assignor is assigning something (contract) to the assignee.

Who is whom?

Assignor/assignee	Lienor/lienee	Optionor/optionee
Grantor/grantee	Mortgagor/mortgagee	Vendor/vendee
Lessor/lessee	Offeror/offeree	

http://francesjarvis.com/2012/11/14/ees-and-ors/

Loan Instruments

This is also the same with the words mortgagor and mortgagee. Where people get confused though is that they think the lender is the mortgagor as they are giving the borrower a loan. This is not how it works. Remember that the mortgage is the instrument that pledges the home as collateral. Actually, it is the borrower who is giving or putting up the home to the mortgagee. The borrower, the home owner, is the mortgagor. The lender is the mortgagee. The lender receives the mortgage instrument. Another way that I've remembered this is that the mortgagor lives behind the door—tying the -ors together in my mind.

Who Owns What?

So, who owns what? In a Lien Theory State (Florida is a Lien Theory State), the Mortgagor is the Borrower who owns the property. The lender must foreclose on the property if the borrower defaults on the loan. The mortgagee is the lender and the lender owns the mortgage. The mortgage is personal property also called chattel or an investment. The mortgage can be sold to another investor in the secondary market.

In a Lien Theory State (Florida)

Mortgagor

- Mortgagor/Borrower owns the property
- Lender must foreclose to make the borrower leave
- Mortgagee
- Lender owns the mortgage
- The mortgage is personal property
- Chattel
- Investment
- Can be sold to another investor in the secondary market.

First Mortgages versus Junior Mortgages
Subordination Agreement

A Subordination Agreement is defined by a change in lien priority order. One lien holder gives up their place in line to another lien holder (Mortgagee).

So, why would a lien holder be willing to do this if it means the other lender would be paid first in the case of default? It is actually common when there is a mortgage on vacant land. Because the new mortgage to build the home will be so much larger (normally) than the original loan on the vacant land, the new lender will require that the original mortgagee sign a subordination agreement for the new lender to go forward with the building loan.

- Common when the First Mortgage is for vacant land
- Changes lien priority order
- Gives up place in line to another lien holder (Mortgagee)

ESSENTIAL ELEMENTS

Understanding the components of residential mortgages is essential to working in real estate. This topic is reviewed here including:

II) Essential elements of the mortgage
    A) Important mortgage provisions
        1) Promise to repay
        2) Taxes and insurance
        3) Covenant of good repair
    B) Other mortgage provisions
        1) Prepayment clause
            (a) Prepayment penalty clause
        2) Acceleration clause
        3) Right to reinstate
        4) Due on sale clause
        5) Defeasance clause

Important Mortgage Provisions

- Promise to Repay
- Taxes and Insurance (HOA)
- Covenant of Good Repair
- Covenant with Removal

Since the mortgage is used to pledge property as collateral, it is a very important instrument that requires oversight to make sure that essential elements are included and the borrower understands what is at stake in pledging the property. A mortgage includes a promise to repay the money that has been borrowed per the terms that are detailed in the promissory note. Along with the agreement to pay back the loan, they are agreeing to pay interest and any fees that apply.

A mortgage includes a promise for the borrower to maintain the payment of taxes and to keep the property insured, plus pay any home owner association fees. It is basically the borrowers pledge to prevent any liens being placed on the property which could jeopardize the collateral and the lien holder's position. Uninsured property puts the collateral at risk in case of fire or some other calamity. If a property owner fails to maintain insurance on the home, the lender will place insurance on the property and charge it to the homeowner. This is usually at a substantially higher fee than what the homeowner would otherwise have to pay for insurance.

A mortgage includes the covenant of good repair, which means the borrower will safeguard the condition of the property. This will usually be accompanied by a covenant not to remove the structure from the property. This may seem like a given, but I do know someone who had the fire department burn down his house to build a new home. Technically, he was required to get permission from the lien holder due to the covenant of removal—which he had failed to do.

Other Mortgage Provisions Include:

- Prepayment Clause
- Acceleration Clause
- Right to Reinstate
- Due on Sale Clause
- Defeasance Clause

Prepayment Clause
- Stipulates terms in which a mortgage loan can be prepaid; allows the borrower to pay off part or all the loan without penalty; automatically included in Florida unless specifically excluded

Acceleration Clause
- Calls the entire balance of the loan becomes due if the borrower defaults on the loan; Borrower has 30 days from date of notice of acceleration to pay all money due (the full loan).

Right to Reinstate
- Lender reserves the right to forgive the fact that the borrower defaulted and move forward with the loan either with late payments paid or renegotiated.

Due on Sale Clause
- Lender calls the mortgage due in full upon the sale of the property; Prevents assumption of mortgage or sale of property through land contract.

Defeasance Clause

- Finally, when the loan is paid in full, the defeasance clause defeats the prior action by the lender when the lien was placed upon the property. In a lien theory state where the borrower retained title and the lender placed a lien on the property (FLORIDA), the lien is defeated. In a title theory state where the lender was conveyed title, the defeasance clause defeats the conveyance of title to the lender and transfers title to the borrower.

www.freddimac.com/uniform/doc/3010-FloridaMortgage.doc

Understanding the components of residential mortgages is essential to working in real estate. This topic is reviewed here including:

III) Common mortgage features

    A) Down payment

    B) Loan-to-value-ratio

        1) Equity

    C) Interest

    D) Loan servicing

    E) Escrow (impound) account

        1) PITI

    F) Discount points

G) Loan origination fee

H) Take out commitment

Common mortgage features are important features that you often see with a mortgage but are not required to be part of a mortgage.

- Down payment

- Loan-to-Value ratio

- Interest

- Loan Servicing

- Escrow (impound) account

- Discount points

- Loan Origination Fee

- Takeout Commitment

- Buydown

- Partial Release Clause (Blanket Mortgage)

www.freddimac.com/uniform/doc/3010-FloridaMortgage.doc

Down Payment

A down payment is often required for a mortgage. A down payment is the part of the purchase price paid in cash up front, reducing the amount of the loan or mortgage. It becomes the amount the home owner personally has invested in the property. There are 100% loans requiring no down payments. This is less common in today's mortgage market except for VA and USDA loans. FHA requires a minimum of 3.5% down payment. Conventional mortgages require a range between 5-20%. If less than 20% is invested by the buyer with a conventional mortgage, Private Mortgage Insurance will be charged to help protect the lender in case of loss.

- The part of the purchase price paid in cash up front, reducing the amount of the loan or mortgage

- 100% Loan = No down payment (VA and USDA)

- 3.5% Required for FHA Loans

- 5-20% Standard for Conventional

    - Private Mortgage Insurance if less than 20% down

When a borrower puts money down on the purchase, the remaining cost of the home purchase is covered by the loan. The percentage amount covered by the loan compared to the entire value of the home is known as the loan-to-value ratio.

If an FHA buyer put down only the required 3.5%, then the loan to value ratio is 96.5%. If 20% has been put down, then the loan-to-value ratio would be 80%.

The remaining value of the home value minus the mortgage debt is the borrower's equity in the home. So if a home appraised at $270,000 and the borrower put down 10%, then he put down $27,000 which is the amount of his equity.

His loan-to-value ratio would be 90%. His equity ratio would be 10%.

Keep in mind equity increases both as the buyer pays off the mortgage debt and as the property increased in value due to a good market. But the opposite can happen as well. If the market is declining, the equity can decline.

http://www.investorwords.com/1568/down_payment.html#ixzz3waIPV48j

Loan-to-Value Ratio

The percent covered by the loan compared to the entire value of the property is called the loan-to-value ratio. Equity is the amount the owner has invested in the property.

- Current Market Value – Mortgage Debt = Equity

Home appraised at $270,000 & borrower puts 10% Down:

- Down Payment Required = $27,000

- Amount of Loan = $243,000

- Loan-to-Value = 90%

- Amount of Equity = $27,000

- Amount of Equity % = 10%

http://www.oxforddictionaries.com/us/definition/american_english/equity

2 Types of Loan-to-Value Math Formulas

Be prepared to calculate two different types of loan-to-value questions. The first formula utilized would be when you know the appraised value and the loan-to-value ratio. By multiplying these together, you can calculate the required loan amount.

- Appraised value $\times$ LTV ratio = Loan amount

  - What is the loan amount for a home that appraised at $100,000 with lender requiring an 80% loan-to-value?

  - $100,000 \times 80\% = \$80,000$ Loan Amount

This second formula would be when you know the loan amount and you divide it by the appraised value (price) to give you the loan-to-value-ratio.

- Loan Amount $\div$ Price (or value) = LTV ratio

- Buyer will get a loan of $80,000 with a $100,000 purchase price. What is her loan-to-value ratio?

- $80,000 ÷ $100,000 = .8 (80%)

Interest

Interest is the fee charged by the lender to the borrower for the use of borrowed money, usually expressed as an annual percentage of the principal.

- Interest for mortgages are usually paid in arrears, meaning that the June mortgage payment is paying the interest accrued in May.

> http://www.investorwords.com/2531/interest.html#ixzz3waOsCx50

Loan Servicing

If you are going to have a mortgage, someone must handle all the details of managing it.

- The process a lending institution goes through for all loans it manages

- Processing payments, sending statements, managing the escrow accounts, providing collection services on delinquent loans, ensuring that the insurance and property tax payments are made on the property, handling pay-offs and assumptions, etc.

- Can sell the loan on the secondary market passing on the loan servicing tasks or retaining loan servicing

    - Servicing Fees: 3/8 to 1% of the unpaid balance

> http://www.investorwords.com/13516/loan_servicing.html#ixzz3waQAraql.html#ixzz3waOsCx50

Escrow (Impound) Account

An escrow (Impound) account is an account held by the lender into which a homeowner pays money for taxes and insurance every month, so that the money is available when the bill is due. Money is collected from the borrower at closing to start the account to make sure that there will be enough there when the bill comes due.

- Generally, the amount charged monthly to the borrower is the total amount for the year for the taxes and interest divided into 12 payments. Federal Regulation limits the amount that can be held in escrow so occasionally when too much money has been accumulated (perhaps because taxes were lowered); then, the lender will issue the difference back to the borrower to keep the account balance in compliance.

- Money is collected from the borrower at closing to start the account

- Money is collected monthly for the property tax and property insurance

Federal Regulation limits the amount that can be held in escrow.

> http://www.investorwords.com/1747/escrow.html#ixzz3waSdGBSv
> http://www.investorwords.com/3707/PITI.html#ixzz3waRkbraW

Escrow (Impound) Account

- PITI is the acronym for principal, interest, taxes, and insurance.

These are the four components that make up a mortgage payment. If the borrower is taking on a fixed rate amortized mortgage, the total they pay on the combined interest and payment will not change. However, their total PITI payment can vary as the cost of taxes and insurance fluctuates.

http://www.investorwords.com/1747/escrow.html#ixzz3waSdGBSv
http://www.investorwords.com/3707/PITI.html#ixzz3waRkbraW

Discount Points

A discount point is an upfront fee that the lender charges the borrower that increases the lender's yield. The yield is the amount the lender is making on the loan, so by increasing the lender's yield, the lender's profit is increased.

Yield is expressed as an annual percentage rate (APR), so that one loan can be compared to another loan for fair competition. One discount point will increase the lender's yield by 1/8% of the new loan amount.

One discount point will cost the borrower 1%. The benefit to the borrower for buying a discount point is that it reduces the amount of interest that they pay. The amount it lowers the interest depends upon the deal offered by and negotiated with the lender. (It's not a consistent number.)

Keep in mind, as you memorize information about discount points that this is a different term and concept than discount rates. Also, keep in mind that interest rates are negotiated between borrower and lender and are NOT set or controlled by the government!

https://www.lendingtree.com/glossary/what-is-discount-points

Discount Points

For the Lender, a discount point is an added up-front fee that increases the lender's yield.

- Yield is the amount the lender is making on the loan

- Yield is expressed as an annual percentage rate (APR)

- 1-point equal to 1/8% increase in yield

For the Borrower, a discount point costs 1% of the purchase price per discount point.

- Benefit to borrower in that it lowers the interest rate they pay. Amount it lowers varies with the deal from the lender.

Calculate Lender's Yield

Work with discount points as a story problem:

- A lender charges 2 points on a loan of $450,000 for a quoted interest rate of 3.5% interest. What is the lender's yield?

- To calculate a lender's yield when 2 discount points are charged on a loan you must remember that each discount point is worth 1/8% to the lender.

- So, 2 discount points would be 1/8 plus 1/8, or 2/8 %. Taking the 2/8ths down to the lowest common denominator meaning that it is ¼%.

- Because the 3.5% is expressed as a decimal instead of a percentage, you then divide the numerator 1 by 4 to change the ¼ to .25.

- So then, 3.5 plus .25 equals a 3.75% yield to the lender.

- *3.5% + 2/8% becomes 3.5% + ¼% becomes 3.5% + .25% = 3.75% Yield*

Calculate Cost to the Borrower for Discount Points

Another type of story problem involving discount points:

A lender charges 2 points on a loan of $450,000 for a quoted interest rate of 3.5% interest. What is the cost to the borrower?

- Remember that each discount point is charged to the borrower as 1% of the loan. So, two points would be 2% times the loan amount of $450,000 equaling $9,000 charged to the borrower.

- 1 point = 1% of the loan; 2 points = 2% x $450,000 = $9,000 Cost

Loan Origination Fees

Loan Origination Fees are a one of the several add-on charges a lender may impose on a home loan. It is charged as a one-time flat fee at the time of the loan. The fee ranges 0.5 percent to 1 percent of the loan amount on FHA and VA loans. It ranges up to 2% of other types of loans. It is justified as covering administrative needs such as setting up the loan file, creating the mortgage, entering the loan into the lender's portfolio, preparing loan docs, loan underwriting, and as a general service charge; a one-time fee payable at the time of the loan.

- Ranges from 0.5 percent to 1 percent of the loan amount on FHA and VA loans

- Up to 2% of other types of loans.

http://www.investorwords.com/7384/loan_origination_fee.html#ixzz3wadaYQzR

Take Out Commitment

A take-out commitment, also called commitment fees, is a fee charged by a lender for holding credit available for a borrower. It is a written agreement obtained by developers or contractors certifying future financing on a project, so they can get a temporary construction loan. Without the commitment from the lender to finance the home once it is built, it would be more difficult for the developer or builder to acquire a building loan.

Commitment Fees

- A charge by a lender for holding credit available for a borrower.

- Written agreement obtained by developers or contractors certifying future financing on a project, so they can get a temporary construction loan http://www.investorwords.com/970/commitment_fee.html#ixzz3wafJykxp

Buydown

In addition to discount points, loan origination fees, and take out commitment fees, there are also buydown fees. A buydown can be charged by a lender to temporarily lower the interest rate charged to the buyer. Sometimes builders will use this as a negotiating tool to make a home purchase more attractive. By agreeing to pay for a buydown on the interest rate, the borrower will have a lower monthly payment for the term of the buydown. Often buyers find this appealing when they plan to later refinance the home.

- Upfront fee to temporarily lower the interest charged to the borrower for the term of the buydown

- Money saved by the interest charged on the loan offsets the fee

- Often paid by the seller when negotiated

https://www.lendingtree.com/glossary?searchTerm=buydown+fee

Partial Release Clause

A mortgage which creates a lien on two or more pieces of property is called a blanket mortgage. This type of mortgage is often used by individuals, builders, or developers that have more than one piece of real estate to finance and then sell. They take out a mortgage for the combined value of the properties. The mortgage will include a partial release clause which allows each property to be released as collateral from the mortgage as each property is sold.

A Blanket Mortgage:

- A mortgage which creates a lien on two or more pieces of property

- Used by builders/develops that have more than one piece of real estate to finance and then sell.

- They take out a mortgage for the combined value of the properties.

- The mortgage includes a partial release clause which allows each property to be released as collateral from the mortgage as each property is sold.

http://www.investorwords.com/7016/blanket_mortgage.html#ixzz3wanLifDf

Understanding the components of residential mortgages is essential to working in real estate. This topic is reviewed here including:

IV) Assignment of the mortgage

   A) Estoppel certificate

Assignment of Mortgage

With an assumption, the new owner takes title knowing that there is still a lien on the property. The legal instrument that transfers the mortgage and promissory note to the purchaser is called an **Assignment of Mortgage.** With the assignment, the buyer becomes responsible for that remaining debt. However, the seller is still responsible for the debt as well unless a novation agreement has been approved by the lender.

Assignment of Mortgage is the legal instrument that transfers the mortgage and promissory note to the purchaser.

- Buyer takes title also taking on lien to the property

- Assumption of the mortgage makes the new buyer responsible for the remaining debt

- Seller still responsible for the debt as well unless a novation agreement has been approved

http://www.investorwords.com/3360/novation.html

Estoppel Certificate

When a buyer assumes an existing mortgage, an estoppel certificate will be issued which verifies the amount of the unpaid balance, interest rate, and date to which interest has been paid prior to the assignment. The purpose is to stop a claim, because the amount could be different than what was claimed. Estoppel certificates or estoppel letters are also used to verify the amounts owed or not owed by a seller to a home owners association.

- Estoppel certificate verifies the amount of the unpaid balance, interest rate, and date to which interest has been paid prior to the assignment

- Purpose is to stop a claim, amount could be different than what was claimed

http://www.investorwords.com/14268/estoppel_certificate.html

Understanding the components of residential mortgages is essential to working in real estate. This topic is reviewed here including:

V) Methods of Purchasing Mortgaged Property

   A) Provisions under subject to the mortgage

   B) Provisions under assumed mortgage

      1) Effects of due on sale clause

      2) Novation

   C) Contract for deed (land contract)

1) Distinguish a contract from deed from a normal sales contract and a mortgage

2) Advantages and disadvantages of contract for deeds

3) How a contract for deed is typically used

Provisions Under Subject to the Mortgage

There are several ways that a buyer can purchase a property that has an existing mortgage lien against it.

One way is to purchase **subject to the mortgage**.

Subject to the mortgage means that the seller still holds the original mortgage on the property while the title to the property is transferred to the new buyer. Keep in mind that this does NOT make the buyer responsible for the original remaining debt. If the original creditor isn't paid, it is only the original owner (the seller) that is responsible for defaulting. However, because the debt is tied to the real estate property, it still can be foreclosed upon. This creates a risk for both the seller and the buyer.

It is risky for the seller if the buyer stops paying because the seller would still need to be able to clear the mortgage payments on his debt.

It is risky for the buyer because the buyer could be making his payments on time but if the payments are not also being made to the original creditor, then the property could be foreclosed upon.

- Transfer title to the new owner

- New buyer not responsible for the original debt

- Poses risk to the seller

- Poses risk to the buyer

http://www.investorwords.com/3360/novation.html

Effects of Due on Sale Clause

Be aware that you cannot always assign a mortgage or even sell a mortgage subject to a mortgage. When a mortgage includes a **Due on Sale Clause**, it calls the entire loan balance due upon a sale. Because both an assignment of mortgage and the selling of a home subject to a mortgage (such as through a land contract) are acts of selling the home, the entire loan balance would be called due in full.

- Calls the entire loan balance due upon a sale

- Prevents Assignment of Mortgage

- Prevents a Sale Subject to

  - Land Contract

http://www.investorwords.com/3360/novation.html

Novation Agreement

When an assignment of mortgage is allowed and the seller would like to be relieved of the debt, a **novation**

agreement would have to be granted from the lender. A novation agreement replaces one borrower with the other – relieving the first borrower from the debt and replacing him with the new buyer. Keep in mind that the new buyer must be approved by the lender.

So why would this ever occur? When a seller has trouble selling a home, the seller might be willing to risk someone else taking over the payments even if that seller is still responsible. Consider a market where interest rates are low when the seller originally obtained a loan. If the new buyer is facing higher interest rates, it makes the home purchase more appealing to be able to take over the original loan. In this situation, the seller particularly benefits when the seller is relieved from the debt with the novation agreement.

- Must be approved by the lender

- Replaces one borrower with the other

- New buyer must qualify as though for a new loan

http://www.investorwords.com/3360/novation.html

Definition of Contract for Deed - Also known as a Land Contract

A contract for deed, also known as a land contract, is a method to sell a property when the buyer doesn't have the means to pay the seller the full amount.

Here's the definition of contract for deed: it is a form of seller financing. The buyer makes payments over time, often with an initial down payment. The owner transfers title after all the payments are received but the buyer has possession of the property during the term of the land contract. IF there isn't a due on sale clause, the contract for deed can be used to purchase a property even if there is already an existing mortgage as "Subject to the Mortgage."

- Form of Seller Financing

- Buyer makes payments over time, often with an initial down payment

- The owner transfers title after all the payments are received

- Buyer has possession of the property during the term of the land contract

http://contractfordeed.uslegal.com/

Differences Between a Land Contract and a Normal Sale with a Regular Mortgage

Keep in mind the main difference between a land contract and a property sold with a regular mortgage is that the buyer takes equitable title instead of legal title with a land contract. Only after the property is completely paid for does title get transferred to a buyer of a land contract.

- Land Contract: Seller retains title/deed of the property

  - With a regular mortgage, the buyer has the deed conveyed to him and the lender holds a lien (in Florida)

- Land Contract: The buyer receives equitable title

  - Which means they have a legal interest in the property with the implication that they will receive title in the future

http://contractfordeed.uslegal.com/

Advantages of Contract for Deeds

- Provides a means for a buyer to purchase that may not have the cash or credit otherwise

- A recorded land contract qualifies the buyer to file for a homestead exemption, if other conditions are met

- Can provide the seller with a buyer for a property that may be difficult to sell or in a difficult market

- Seller can earn interest just as a regular lender

Disadvantages of Contract for Deeds

- If buyer defaults, seller must employ regular foreclosure proceedings to get the property back

- Buyers often find that the seller charges more interest than a regular lender does

http://contractfordeed.uslegal.com/

Why Use a Contract for Deed?

So, traditionally the main reason for using a contract for deed was to finance unimproved property, it is now a popular means for a seller to increase their return on the investment by earning interest on the contract for deed.

It also increases the selling opportunities for the seller and the buying opportunities for the buyer.

- Traditionally used to finance unimproved property

- Now used to increase revenue through interest for the seller

- Increase selling opportunities for the seller

- Increase buyer opportunities for the buyer

http://contractfordeed.uslegal.com/

DEFAULT

Understanding the components of residential mortgages is essential to working in real estate. This topic is reviewed here including:

VI) Default

    A) Consequence of default

    B) Judicial versus non-judicial foreclosure

1) Deed in lieu of foreclosure

2) Lis pendens

C) Rights of mortgagor in foreclosure

1) Equity of redemption

D) Rights of mortgagee

1) Surplus money action

Consequence of Default

When a borrower of a loan fails to keep up with the payments, he or she may be in default. The definition of default is the failure to meet the obligations promised through the promissory note.

The lender is left with two actions to take. The first is to file suit based on the promissory note. This type of suit can end up with a judgment against the mortgagor for other property they own – not just the property put up as collateral.

A foreclosure proceeding, the other action that the lender can take, targets just the property that was pledge as collateral. The mortgage is **accelerated** calling the entire amount due. The final judgment result of the lawsuit requires that the property be sold at a public auction and the lender paid out of funds from the sale.

htp://www.salcineslaw.com/statute-of-limitations-for-promissory-notes-and-deficiency-balances/

Judicial versus Non-Judicial Foreclosure

Deed in lieu of foreclosure

Court can be avoided, however when the buyer agrees to a non-judicial process of a **deed in lieu of foreclosure** - also known as a friendly foreclosure. With a deed in lieu of foreclosure the end result is the same. The lender regains possession of the property by the buyer signing over the deed to the lender. Yet, the expense for the lender, and the agony and repercussions for the mortgagor- can be muted when foreclosure proceedings are avoided.

- The act of giving a property back to the lender without undergoing foreclosure. While the end result is the same - the lender regains possession of the property - the expense and repercussions of the foreclosure proceedings is avoided.

- It is a non-judicial procedure

- Also called a friendly foreclosure

- The buyer signs the deed over to the lender

http:/www.investorwords.com/13159/deed_in_lieu_of_foreclosure.html#ixzz3wbR77Ipq

Lis Pendens

When a lawsuit for foreclosure is proceeding, the lender will give constructive notice of the suit by filing the **lis**

pendens notice in the county where the property is located. The purpose of this notice is to flag the lawsuit in case the mortgagor attempts to sell the property, which is an action that wouldn't be uncommon from an individual on the verge of losing property.

- Latin for "pending suit"

- Type of constructive notice of a pending legal action involving the real estate

- It's filed by the lender in the county where the property is located.

http://www.investorwords.com/14476/lis_pendens.html#ixzz3wbSwfw35

Rights of Mortgagor in Foreclosure

Right of Redemption

Keep in mind that property owners do have rights even once a foreclosure proceeding has been filed. According to Florida Statute 45.0315, property owners have the right to pay the balance in full, including court costs and attorney fees, and redeem ownership of the property. However, in Florida, this right ends once the property has been sold at auction to the highest bidder.

- The right of a property owner to redeem his or property from foreclosure (or tax sale) by paying off the full amount owed.

- This right ends upon the completion of foreclosure proceedings

http://www.investorwords.com/4285/right_of_redemption.html#ixzz3wbUjXvwM

Surplus Funds

Once a property is sold at foreclosure auction, the liens on the property are paid out of the proceeds. If there happens to be any money remaining, then the surplus is paid to the mortgagor – the person who lost the property to the forced sale.

- "Surplus funds" or "surplus" means the funds remaining after payment of all disbursements required by the final judgment of foreclosure and shown on the certificate of disbursements.

- Excess money is paid to the mortgagor

Florida Statute 45.032
http://www.investorwords.com/4285/right_of_redemption.html#ixzz3wbUjXvwM

Deficiency Judgments

However, if there isn't enough money to even pay off the debt to the mortgagee, then a deficiency judgment can be requested to be placed against the borrower. This is a personal judgment against other personal and real estate property owned by the mortgagor.

- There isn't enough money from the auction foreclosure sale to cover the debt

- Mortgagee requests a deficiency judgment against the mortgagor

  - Can extend to other personal and real estate property owned by the person who signed the note

http://www.investorwords.com/13164/deficiency_judgment.html#ixzz3wbj90M7Y

Receivership Clause

If a mortgagor stops making payments on the loan of an income-producing property, the mortgagee can be appointed to collect the income produced from the property to make the mortgage payments. This is only allowed if a Receivership Clause has been included in the mortgage.

Schecterlaw.com/tag/receivership=clause-in-mortgage

Understanding the components of residential mortgages is essential to working in real estate. This topic is reviewed here including:

VI) Default

    E) Results of foreclosure

        1) Effect on mortgagor/owner

           (a) Deficiency judgments

           (b) Effect on creditors or other claimants to title

           (c) Effect on mortgagee

           (d) Effect on title

    F) Short sales

Effects on Mortgagor and Creditors

Any junior liens on the property that are unpaid by the auction funds would be released.

However, release of lien on the property does not cancel the debt. Unsatisfied lienholders may sue the property owner for the unpaid debt. Deficiency judgments can result in other personal and real estate property being attached.

Keep in mind that homesteaded property cannot be forced into sale if it was not the foreclosed-on property. The mortgagor can also experience wage garnishments. Finally, know that it can make it difficult to get another mortgage.

- Any junior liens on the property unpaid by the funds would be released
- It cancels the lien on the property it does not cancel the debt
- Unsatisfied lienholders may sue the property owner for the unpaid debt
  - Deficiency judgment
  - Can result in other property being attached
  - Can result in a wage garnishment
  - Can make it difficult to get another mortgage

http://www.nolo.com/legal-encyclopedia/what-happens-liens-second-mortgages-foreclosure.html

Effect on Title

So, what happens to the property? Upon the property being sold at auction, the clerk of the court files a certificate of title and passes title to the purchaser at the foreclosure auction. All liens are released against the property. Title is given with no warranties meaning caveat emptor or buyer beware applies.

- The clerk files a certificate of title and title passes to the purchaser at the foreclosure auction

- No warranties

- Caveat emptor

- Florida Statute 45.031(5) CERTIFICATE OF TITLE.—If no objections to the sale are filed within 10 days after filing the certificate of sale, the clerk shall file a certificate of title and serve a copy of it to each party …

http://wwwg.state.l.us/statutes/index.cfm?App_mode=Display_Statute&URL=0000-
0099/0045/Sections/0045.031.html

Short Sales

The sale of property for less than the outstanding mortgage debt is called a **short sale**. The bank that holds the mortgage must approve the sale and agree to release the lien despite the shortage in funds. These sales are often approved as it may be preferable to a bank than foreclosing on the property.

- The sale of property for less than the outstanding mortgage debt is called a short sale.

http://www.investorwords.com/18484/real_estate_short_sale.html#ixzz3wbpwW0sV

13 TYPES OF MORTGAGES AND SOURCES OF FINANCING

Learning Objectives:
- Describe the mechanics of an adjustable rate mortgage and the components of an ARM
- Describe the features of an amortized mortgage and amortize a level-payment plan mortgage when given the principal amount, the interest rate and the monthly payment amount
- Distinguish among the various types of mortgages
- Describe the characteristics of FHA mortgages and common FHA loan programs
- Identify the guarantee feature of VA mortgage loans and the characteristics of VA loan programs
- Explain the process of qualifying for a loan and how to calculate qualifying ratios
- Distinguish among the primary sources of home financing
- Describe the role of the secondary mortgage market and know the features of the major agencies active in the secondary market
- Describe the major provisions of the federal laws regarding fair credit and lending procedures
- Recognize and avoid mortgage fraud

Key Terms:

adjustable rate mortgage (ARM)	level payment plan	package mortgage
amortized mortgage	lifetime cap	partially amortized/balloon
balloon payment	margin	mortgage
biweekly mortgage	MIP	payment cap
conforming loan	mortgage broker	periodic cap
disintermediation	mortgage fraud	purchase money mortgage
home equity loan	mortgage loan originator	reverse annuity mortgage
index	negative amortization	teaser rate
intermediation	nonconforming loans	UFMIP

CONVENTIONAL MORTGAGES

Years ago, if someone needed a loan, they walked into their small local bank.

They sat down with the banker and asked for the money. The banker knew the person's history; knew how hard the person worked; knew the person's character. The banker also knew about the person's job and how stable or how risky the person's income was.

The banker made the decision of whether to loan the money based on the likelihood of the bank getting paid their money back.

What the banker did, was to make or reject the loan based on risk.

Understanding the components of residential mortgages is essential to working in real estate. This topic is reviewed here including:

   I)   Conventional mortgages

      A) Neither government insured nor guaranteed

          1) Down payment and LTV ratio

      B) PMI

          1) Qualifying ratios

          2) Interest rate

          3) Assumption

          4) Prepayment

Neither Government Insured Nor Guaranteed

A conventional loan is a mortgage loan that is not guaranteed or insured by the government. The lender assumes all the risk. Non-conventional loans, on the other hand, are loans that are guaranteed by the government. They include loan programs offered by the Federal Housing Administration (FHA) and the Department of Veterans Affairs (VA).

A conventional loan is a mortgage loan that is not guaranteed or insured by the government

- Lender assumes all the risk of default

- A conventional loan is a mortgage loan that is not guaranteed or insured by the government.

                      http://www.ehow.com/info_8084842_nonconventional-loan.html

Down Payment and LTV Ratio

The buyer is required to make a down payment to help offset the risk to the lender. The loan-to-value (LTV) ratio is a financial term used by lenders to express the ratio of a loan to the value of an asset purchased. The term is commonly used by banks to represent the ratio of the first mortgage lien as a percentage of the total appraised value of real property. Ideally, lenders want 20% down leaving an 80% loan-to-value ratio (LTV).

- The buyer is required to make a down payment to help offset the risk to the lender.

- The loan-to-value (LTV) ratio is a financial term used by lenders to express the ratio of a loan to the value of an asset purchased.

https://en.wikipedia.org/wiki/Loan- to-value_ratio

PMI

PMI or private mortgage insurance is charged to a borrower when he has less than 20% equity in the residence. This insurance covers the lender if the borrower defaults on the debt.

Therefore, the only benefiting party in the transaction is the lender. To avoid this fee, a borrower must either make a down payment of 20% or more, or procure subordinate financing to cover the needed funds.

- Private Mortgage Insurance

- PMI is insurance that covers the lender if the borrower defaults on the debt.

- To avoid this fee, a borrower must either make a down payment of 20% or more, or procure subordinate financing to cover the needed funds.

http://homeguides.sfgate.com/conventional-mortgage-requirements-2035.html

$100,000 Purchase Price
$20,000 20% From Buyer
$80,000 80% From Lender

As this example shows, even with a $100,000 purchase, putting 20% down would equal $20,000. On a $250,000 purchase, the required 20% down payment would be $50,000.

Not everyone could afford 20% Down!

- 20% down payment

- 80% loan-to-value ratio

Depending upon other qualifying factors, a buyer may qualify for less down payment if they agree to add the cost of Private Mortgage Insurance to their monthly payment.

Private Mortgage Insurance (PMI)

- Used to insure the part of the loan above 80% LTV

- The Cost of the PMI is added to the Buyer's Payment!

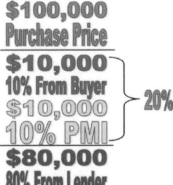

PMI Qualifying Ratios

- Loans are made in what is called the "Primary Market"

- Because most lenders "Sell" the loans they've made in the "Secondary Market," standards were created to determine whether a buyer qualified for the loan.

- Following these standards are said to be conforming loans.

- Down Payment/LTV, PMI, and Qualifying Ratios of the buyer's income to debt combine to mitigate the risk to the lender and subsequent investors that purchase the loan in the secondary market.

- Other loan approval requirements apply as well.

http://homeguides.sfgate.com/conventional-mortgage-requirements-2035.html

Total Obligation Ratio (TOR)

To qualify for a conforming conventional mortgage, a borrower cannot exceed maximum total monthly obligation ratio of 36%. TOR is designed to protect the borrower and lender by capping the amount of long term debt a borrower can take on as a monthly payment.

To calculate TOR, you must calculate the borrower's total monthly debt obligations. This is anything that is reported on the credit report including child support payments. Payments such as food, gas, and utilities are not included in the ratio.

The total monthly cost of the home that the buyer is trying to purchase must be added to the other long-term debt to equal the total monthly obligations. Dividing this total by the borrower's monthly gross income gives the TOR ratio. If it is 36% or less, then the buyer would qualify for the loan based on this one parameter.

- Cannot exceed 36% for a Conventional Conforming Mortgage

- Total Monthly Obligations ÷ Monthly Gross Income = TOR

- To Calculate Total Monthly Obligations

  - Total a buyer's Monthly INSTALLMENT debt already found on the Credit Report

    - Credit card payments, auto payments, student loans, child support payments

  - Add the proposed House Payment:

    - PITI (House Principal Payment, Interest, Taxes, & Insurance) + PMI

  - Divide Total Monthly Obligations by how much a buyer EARNS MONTHLY (not NET)

Apply the Total Obligation Ratio (TOR) to a story problem:

- Waldo wants to buy a home with a conventional mortgage. The total PITI on the home he wants to buy will total $1,000. He is already paying $800 in other long-term debt obligations (car payment of $525 and total credit cards of $275). Waldo's gross monthly income is $3,200. Will he qualify for this home?

  Answer:

  - Total Monthly Obligations ÷ Monthly Gross Income = TOR

  - Total Monthly Obligations = $800 + $1,000 = $1800

  - $1,800 ÷ $3,200 = .5625 or 56%   (Doesn't qualify!)

Interest Rate

Technically, interest rates are negotiable between the buyer and the lender. Going interest rates are set by the supply and demand for money in the capital markets. If more potential borrowers want more credit cards, mortgages and car loans, or want to issue more bonds, then the price of loanable money is bid up and interest rates rise.

Interest rates fall when people want to save more and borrow less. Supply and demand in the credit markets determines the "market rates of interest," meaning what interest rates would adjust to if left to the free market. However, the market rates of interest are manipulated by central banks and governments– the Federal Reserve. The corresponding surge in the money supply forces down interest rates.

- Interest rates are set by the supply and demand for money in the capital markets.

- Interest rates go up when there are more borrowers competing for loans.

- Interest rates go down when there are less borrowers competing for loans.

- However, the market rates of interest are manipulated by central banks and governments– the Federal Reserve. The corresponding surge in the money supply forces down interest rates.

  http://www.investopedia.com/articles/investing/122915/when-will-interest-rates-rise.asp#ixzz3x0YplH2I

Federal Reserve System

The Federal Reserve System, the Fed, is the central banking authority. The Fed was established to provide a safer and more stable monetary system and to influence the availability and cost of money and credit.

It conducts monetary policy through 3 ways: open-market operations, discount rate, and reserve requirements. The Fed also has regulatory and supervisory responsibilities over banks created by TILA and Equal Credit Opportunity Act.

Fed Monetary Policy

Open-Market Operations

The sale and purchase of U.S. securities is the principal method and most effective tool used to influence supply of available money.

The Federal Reserve's approach to the implementation of monetary policy has evolved considerably since the financial crisis, and particularly so since late 2008. From the end of 2008 through October 2014, the Federal Reserve greatly expanded its holding of longer-term securities through open market purchases with the goal of putting downward pressure on longer-term interest rates and thus, supporting economic activity and job creation by making financial conditions more accommodative.

www.federalreserve.gov

Discount Rate

The Discount Rate is the interest rate charged to commercial banks and depositories for loans received from the Federal Reserve Bank. Changing the discount rate is the 2nd most common method to control supply of money. It has the greatest impact on cost of short-term interest rate.

Increase in discount rate results in less lending and reduces money supply. Decrease in discount rate results in more lending and increases money supply. It is the least effective way to influence the interest rate charged with real estate loans.

http://www.investopedia.com/terms/d/discountrate.asp#ixzz3x0iZp5gk

Reserve Requirements

The Federal reserve requirement refers to the amount of funds that a bank must have on hand each night. The bank can hold it either as cash in its vault or as a deposit at its local Fed bank.

The Reserve Requirement has the most important impact on the money supply. Small increase in reserve requirement causes large reduction in money supply. Small decrease in reserve requirement causes large increase in money supply.

http://useconomy.about.com/od/glossary/g/Reserve_Require.htm

Mortgage Assumption

Conventional Mortgages do not allow for mortgage assumption: An assumable mortgage allows the purchaser of a property to assume the mortgage from the property's seller. The benefits of assuming a mortgage almost always stem from the buyer's ability to take on the assumed mortgage rate, which often is lower than prevailing market rates. Additionally, an assumable mortgage helps the purchaser avoid certain settlement costs.

Generally, loans made during the last 20 years of a mortgage are rarely assumable, with the notable exception of VA and FHA loans. Conventional Mortgages feature a due-on-sale clause: A provision which requires the mortgage to be repaid in full upon a sale or conveyance of partial or full interest in the property that secures the mortgage. Makes a conventional mortgage with a due-on-sale clause not assumable.

http://www.investopedia.com/terms/d/due_on_sale_clause

- An assumable mortgage allows the purchaser of a property to assume the mortgage from the property's seller.

Conventional Mortgages Feature a Due-on-sale Clause

- A provision which requires the mortgage to be repaid in full upon a sale or conveyance of partial or full interest in the property that secures the mortgage.

- Makes a conventional mortgage with a due-on-sale clause are not assumable.

http://www.investopedia.com/ask/answers/08/benefits-assumable-mortgage.asp#ixzz3x0X2eUrO

Prepayment Clause

Provisional clause in conventional mortgages under which a borrower may pay off or retire a loan ahead of the schedule without penalty.

- This is the clause that allows your 30-year mortgage to be paid in 2 years, 10 years, or whenever it suits the borrower if they wish to pay it off before the full term of the loan.

(This is different from a prepayment penalty clause which allows a fee to be charged with the loan is paid off early.)

http://www.businessdictionary.com/definition/prepayment-clause.html#ixzz3x0oyVHkx

Understanding the components of residential mortgages is essential to working in real estate. This topic is reviewed here including:

II) Common Types of Mortgages

    A) Amortized mortgage

        1) Monthly payment is constant for term of mortgage

        2) As loan is paid off, amount applied to principal increases as amount applied to interest decreases

        3) 30-year and 15-year terms

        4) Amortizing a level-payment plan mortgage

Amortized Mortgage

An amortized mortgage is one type of mortgage. It is a mortgage with a monthly payment that is constant, or the same amount paid every month on the combined principal and interest, for the term of mortgage. It is also called a level-payment plan. As loan is paid off, the amount applied to the principal increases and the amount applied to the interest decreases. The amortization schedule is based on either 15 or 30 years at the start of the mortgage, but can be paid off early.

Monthly Payment is Constant

The whole point of the amortized mortgage is for the buyer to have a predictable payment at the start of the loan that the buyer knows will be the payment all the way through the loan. This is an important feature that allows a buyer to budget for the cost of the home and ensures that the home will remain affordable for the buyer. Lenders and buyers like this type of schedule as it reduces the likelihood that a buyer will default on the mortgage.

Can you imagine how stressful it would be for most buyers to go forward with a home purchase if they didn't know what the payment would be in a year much less ten years? The reality is that the payment can still fluctuate as it is only the principal and interest that is held constant. The cost of the insurance and taxes that may be paid as part of the mortgage payment can vary from year to year. However, the amortized mortgage gives buyers a huge sense of control over their finances.

As the loan is paid off, the amount applied to the principal increases and the amount applied to the interest decreases. How does this work? At the outset of the mortgage, a payment is set that will cover both the principal and interest payment.

Of the total payment, interest is paid first-so the amount paid toward the interest versus the amount paid toward the payment is calculated based on the amount of interest due on the unpaid mortgage balance for that month.

So, the difference between the monthly payment and the monthly interest due is the amount that will be used to pay down the balance. As a result, each month the balance of the unpaid mortgage is decreasing. Therefore, the amount of monthly interest due is also decreasing which means more money is available each month from the payment to pay down the mortgage.

15 or 30-Year Mortgages

To calculate the payments, the lender presents the buyer with an amortization schedule which ensures that the interest will be covered and the balance paid off either on a 15 or 30-year mortgage schedule. The amount of payment required to cover both interest and principal is based on a mortgage term of either 15 or 30 years. A buyer will receive an amortization schedule which would show how much of each monthly payment would go toward the interest versus the payment. The balance is said to be "killed" by equal, regular, and consistent payments. However, remember the prepayment clause in a mortgage? This allows borrowers to be able pay extra money toward the mortgage to pay the balance off quicker. Or at any point, the borrower can pay the mortgage off completely with one large payment covering the balance and all fees due.

- Also called a level-payment plan

- Amortization Schedule

- Monthly payment is constant for term of mortgage

- As loan is paid off, amount applied to the principal increases and the amount applied to the interest decreases

- 30-year and 15-year terms

Amortizing a Level-Payment Plan Mortgage

The information needed to amortize a mortgage is your beginning principal balance, interest rate and the scheduled monthly payment.

Take the principal balance of the entire unpaid mortgage and multiply the interest rate. This gives you your annual interest rate. However, you need to take the annual amount into the amount due for just the one month, so the annual interest is divided by 12 (months). This is the amount of monthly interest due for that one month. That means that this is equal to how much of the monthly payment will go toward the interest payment.

To calculate how much is being paid toward the principal, you take this monthly interest total due and subtract it from the total payment. This is your amount paid on the principal or principal payment. Finally, you subtract the principal payment from the beginning principal balance and you have how much is now due on the entire mortgage which will be used to calculate the next month interest payment.

So, what do you know after doing this type of calculation? You know how much the balance owed at the start of the month. You know how much of the payment went toward principal and how much went toward interest. And now you know what your remaining balance is which is the balance you use to calculate the next month's payment breakdown information.

The information needed to amortize a mortgage is:

- Outstanding debt (principal), Interest rate, & Monthly payment

1. Beginning Principal Balance × Annual Interest= Annual Interest

2. Annual Interest ÷ 12 = Monthly Interest Due

3. Scheduled Monthly Payment – Monthly Interest Due = $ Paid on Principal

4. Beginning Principal Balance – $ Paid on Principal = New Balance

Let's try an amortization story problem:

Borrower Kate has a starting balance of $120,000 at the beginning of March. She is being charged at 6% interest. Her total monthly payment for combined principal and interest is $842.15

- How much of Kate's payment is interest?

- How much is paid toward the principal?

- And what will her new balance be?

Answer:

- How much of Kate's payment is interest?

    - $120,000 x .06 = $7,200.00 ÷ 12 = $600 paid toward interest

- How much is paid toward the principal?

    - $842.15 - $600 = $242.15 paid toward principal

- What will her new balance be?

    - $120,000 - $242.15 = $119,757.85 new balance of unpaid mortgage

What about Kate's second month?

(Borrower Kate has a starting balance of $120,000 at the beginning of March. She is being charged at 6% interest. Her total monthly payment for combined principal and interest is $842.15)

- How much of Kate's 2nd payment is interest?

- How much of the 2nd payment is paid toward the principal?

- And what will her new balance be at the end of month 2?

Answer

- How much of Kate's 2nd payment is interest?

    - $119,757.85 x .06 = $7,185.47 ÷ 12 = $598.79 paid toward interest

- How much is paid toward the principal in the 2nd payment?

    - $842.15 - $598.79 = $243.36 paid toward principal

- And what will her new balance be after the 2nd payment?

    - $119,757.85 - $243.36 = $119,514.49 new balance of unpaid mortgage

Understanding the components of residential mortgages is essential to working in real estate. This topic is reviewed here including:

II) Common Types of Mortgages

    B) Adjustable rate

        1) Mechanics of an adjustable rate mortgage

        2) Components of an ARM

            (a) Index

            (b) Margin

            (c) Adjustment interval

            (d) Interest rate caps

                (1) Periodic caps

                (2) Lifetime cap

            (e) Payment caps

                (1) Negative amortization

                (2) How negative amortization can result from payment caps

            (f) Teaser rates

Mechanics of an Adjustable Rate Mortgage

An amortized mortgage can be calculated using either a fixed rate mortgage or an adjustable rate mortgage.

A fixed rate mortgage charges the same interest rate throughout the entire term of the mortgage. As a result, the buyer knows the exact cost of the loan and total interest paid should payments be made exactly as the amortization schedule outlines.

However, a buyer could also obtain an adjustable rate mortgage. This type of loan allows for the interest charged to fluctuate depending upon the terms outlined in the loan. An adjustable rate mortgage is also referred to as an ARM.

- Fixed Rate - Same interest rate is charged throughout the entire term of the mortgage

- Adjustable Rate - Allows for the interest charged to fluctuate depending upon the terms outlined in the loan. Also referred to as an ARM

Components of an ARM

- Index
- Margin (spread)
- Adjustment interval
- Interest rate caps
- Payment cap
- Teaser rate

Index

- Interest rate can fluctuate during the term of the loan based on an agreed upon index
- Lenders base interest rates on a variety of indexes.
- Normally the index chosen is outside of the lender's control.
- The most common indexes are the one-year constant maturity treasury security, the cost of funds index, or the London interbank offered rate

http://files.consumerfinance.gov/f/201204_CFPB_ARMs-brochure.pdf

Margin

- The amount the lender adds to the index to make the loan profitable
- Index + Margin = Full Indexed Rate
- Margin may be based on credit
  - The better your credit, the lower the margin that is added.

http://files.consumerfinance.gov/f/201204_CFPB_ARMs-brochure.pdf

Adjustment Interval

Adjustment Interval for an adjustable rate mortgage is the period for which the payment rate can be changed is called the adjustment interval.

- The period for which the payment rate can be changed is called the adjustment interval
- The period between the change is called the adjustment period
- An adjustment period could be based on months, quarters or years
- A loan with an adjustment period of 1 year is called a 1-year ARM

- A loan with an adjustment period of 5 years is called a 5-year ARM

http://files.consumerfinance.gov/f/201204_CFPB_ARMs-brochure.pdf

Interest Rate Caps

An interest rate cap places a limit on how much the interest rate can increase.

- Periodic Caps

    - Limits the amount that the rate can increase from one interval period to another

- Lifetime Caps

    - Limits the amount that the rate can increase in total over the life of the loan

http://files.consumerfinance.gov/f/201204_CFPB_ARMs-brochure.pdf

Payment Caps

While interest rate caps control how much the interest rate can change, the payment caps set a limit of how much the payment can be increased in between terms. The purpose is to protect the borrower from payments being increased to a point that the borrower cannot afford to make the payment.

- Sets a limit of how much the payment can be increased in between terms.

- Protects the borrower from payments being increased to a point that the borrower cannot afford to pay

http://files.consumerfinance.gov/f/201204_CFPB_ARMs-brochure.pdf

Negative Amortization

Negative amortization is a possible unintended consequence of an amortized mortgage payment cap. Because payment caps keep the mortgage payment from rising past a certain level, the amount of interest being charged on the balance due could be higher than the total payment collected.

- Negative amortization arises when the payment made by the borrower is less than the **interest due** and the difference is added to the loan balance.

- The mortgage balance increases

http://www.mtgprofessor.com/a%20-%20amortization/how_does_negative_amortization_work.htm

Teaser Rates

Another feature you sometimes see with an adjustable rate mortgage are teaser rates. Teaser rates are also called discounted rates or start rate. It is an initial rate that is lower than the fully indexed rate. The lender charges a higher rate after the initial discounted rate period passes. These types of loans are often combined with larger initial loan fees. The initial low rate and subsequently lower payment, makes the loan appear to be more attractive.

- Initial rate is lower than the fully indexed rate

- Charges a higher rate after the initial discounted rate period passes

http://www.mtgprofessor.com/a%20-%20amortization/how_does_negative_amortization_work.htm

Learn More

A great resource for you and your clients to learn more about adjustable rate mortgages is the Federal Reserve Board Consumer Handbook on Adjustable-Rate Mortgages which can be found at The Consumer Financial Protection Bureau website.

www.consumerfinance.gov

http://files.consumerfinance.gov/f/201204_CFPB_ARMs-brochure.pdf

Understanding the components of residential mortgages is essential to working in real estate. This topic is reviewed here including:

III) Custom mortgages

    A) Partially amortized mortgage

        1) Balloon payment

    B) Biweekly mortgage

    C) Package mortgage

    D) Home equity loans

    E) Purchase money mortgage

    F) Reverse annuity mortgage

Partially Amortized Mortgage

With a fully amortized mortgage, the full balance of the mortgage is completely paid off by the end of the mortgage.

With a partially amortized mortgage, however, the payments are calculated using a longer term than what the mortgage requires to pay off the full balance. The loan balance that is unpaid at the end of the loan must be made in one large payment called a **Balloon Payment**. Borrowers can be attracted to a partially amortized mortgage because the payments are lower than with a fully amortized mortgage.

- http://www.mortgage101.com/article/fully-vs-partially-amortizing-loans

Balloon Payment

The loan balance that is unpaid at the end of the loan must be made in one large payment.

http://www.mortgage101.com/article/fully-vs-partially-amortizing-loans

Biweekly Mortgage

With a biweekly mortgage, the payments are based on a regular amortization schedule, but divided in half and set up to pay every 2 weeks instead of once a month.

It forces the borrower to make an extra monthly payment annually by having them pay a total of 26 payments. 52 weeks divided by 2 = 26 payments. This is not the same as taking your monthly mortgage and paying it twice a month. That would only have you making 24 payments. By using the biweekly payment strategy, the mortgage is paid off in 22.6 years instead of 30.

https://www.pamortgagepros.com/blog/biweekly-mortgages/

Package Mortgage

A Package Mortgage is a mortgage agreement that provides home financing including real property, property improvements and movable equipment. In other words, you get to finance a home along with the furniture, and other personal property such as tables and chairs. This is a popular type of mortgage for a business that is purchasing a turnkey business opportunity.

http://www.mortgagefit.com/package-mortgage.html

Home Equity Loans

A home equity loan is when you borrow money using the equity in your home as collateral. That is, you use the portion of your home that's paid for to back the loan.

- Because a home equity loan is secured by the value of your home, you could lose the property to foreclosure, the same as if you fail to make the payments on your regular mortgage.

- If there is already a mortgage on the home, a home equity loan is a type of second mortgage. That is, it's a secondary lien (junior lien) secured by the equity in your home.

A loan taken out using the equity on the home you already own as collateral.

Home equity loans come in two types:

- The standard home equity loan

  - You borrow a certain amount of money and repay it over a specified period of time.

- And the home equity line of credit, or HELOC

  - Allows you to borrow up to a certain limit as you see fit, in whatever amounts and at whatever times you wish. It's like a credit card, only one that allows you to borrow money instead of charging purchases to it.

Some people like the tax advantage that a home equity loan can offer:

- The interest paid on a mortgage can be deducted on your taxes which is why many prefer to take out home equity loan rather than use other non-tax-deductible loans.

- However, it puts a home at an increased risk that the other types of loans wouldn't pose on a homesteaded property.

https://www.mortgageloan.com/home-equity-loans

Purchase Money Mortgage

A purchase money mortgage, also called seller financing or owner financing, is a home-financing technique in which the buyer borrows from the seller instead of, or in addition to, a bank. Sometimes done when a buyer cannot qualify for a bank loan for the full amount.

- Title is transferred to the buyer as with a regular closing and the seller files a lien on the property

http://www.investorwords.com/3955/purchase_money_mortgage.html#ixzz3x4Q1csxI

Reverse Annuity Mortgage

A Reverse Annuity Mortgage, also called a Reverse Mortgage or a Home Equity Conversion Mortgage (HECM), is a mortgage for homeowners 62 and older who have a significant amount of equity built up in their house.

They can borrow against that equity — taking the cash in a lump sum, as a monthly income stream or a line of credit they can tap when needed.

The U.S. Department of Housing and Urban Development tightened lending criteria in 2015. The changes require that lenders determine whether would-be borrowers have enough income to keep up with property taxes and homeowner's insurance, so they don't default on the loan and, possibly, lose their home.

- Must be 62 years or older to qualify for this loan.

- They can borrow against the equity — taking the cash in a lump sum, as a monthly income stream or a line of credit they can tap when needed.

- The money doesn't have to be repaid until the owner moves, sells the house or dies.

- Upon the sale of the home, the loan must be repaid with any remaining proceeds going to the home owner, including heirs.

- HUD's Federal Housing Administration insures most reverse mortgages.

http://blog.aarp.org/2015/05/14/reverse-mortgages-now-harder-to-get/

FHA

Understanding the components of residential mortgages is essential to working in real estate. This topic is reviewed here including:

IV) Government Insured FHA Program

A) Purpose of FHA

B) Characteristics of FHA mortgage loans

1) Loan insurance

2) Lending source

3) Discount points

4) Amount of down payment

5) Loan limit

6) Insured commitment

7) Insurance premium

    (a) UFMIP

    (b) MIP

The government recognized that buyers didn't always have enough down payment available even with PMI making up some of the difference so they created an opportunity for nonconventional loans.

Nonconventional Loans

- by providing some risk protection to lender

  - FHA-insured

  - VA-guaranteed

  - Therefore, FHA/VA requires a smaller down payment than conventional loans

Purpose of FHA

The Federal Housing Administration, generally known as "FHA", provides mortgage insurance on loans made by FHA-approved lenders throughout the United States and its territories.

- FHA insures mortgages on single family and multifamily homes including manufactured homes and hospitals.

- It is the largest insurer of mortgages in the world, insuring over 34 million properties since its inception in 1934.

               http://portal.hud.gov/hudportal/HUD?src=/program_offices/housing/fhahistory

Purpose of FHA

When the FHA was created, the housing industry was flat on its back:

- Two million construction workers had lost their jobs. Terms were difficult to meet for homebuyers seeking mortgages. Mortgage loan terms were limited to 50% of the property's market value, with a repayment schedule spread over three to five years and ending with a balloon payment.

- America was primarily a nation of renters. Only 4 in 10 households owned homes.

In the 80 years since the FHA was created much has changed and Americans are now arguably the best housed people in the world. HUD has helped greatly with that success.

http://portal.hud.gov/hudportal/HUD?src=/program_offices/housing/fhahistory

Characteristic of FHA Mortgage Loans

Loan Insurance

- FHA mortgage insurance provides lenders with protection against losses as the result of homeowners defaulting on their mortgage loans.

- The lenders bear less risk because FHA will pay a claim to the lender in the event of a homeowner's default.

- Loans must meet certain requirements established by FHA to qualify for insurance.

http://portal.hud.gov/hudportal/HUD?src=/program_offices/housing/fhahistory

Lending Source

- FHA mortgage loans are made in the primary market from approved lenders.

- Nonconventional Mortgage providers

- FHA is not the actual lender. It's the insurer.

http://portal.hud.gov/hudportal/HUD?src=/program_offices/housing/fhahistory

Discount Points

- Buyers financing a home with a FHA loan may be charged discount points

- Discount Points may be paid by the buyer or the seller

- The purpose of the discount point is the lower the interest rate charged

http://portal.hud.gov/hudportal/HUD?src=/program_offices/housing/fhahistory

Amount of Down Payment

- Buyers financing a home with a FHA loan must put down 3 ½% of the purchase price or the appraised value (whichever is less)

- 96.5% Loan To Value (LTV)

- May be paid by a relative with an approved gift letter

- Cannot be paid by the seller

http://portal.hud.gov/hudportal/HUD?src=/program_offices/housing/fhahistory

Loan Limit

- FHA loan limits were established to define how much you can borrow for an HUD-backed mortgage

- Each state area has different limits based on the costs in the area

- In Florida, the range of loan limit varies dramatically depending upon where in the state the borrower is seeking an FHA loan. 2016 Florida Loan Limits, for example for a single-family home in Manatee County is $285,200 vs. $529,000 for a Single-Family Home in Key West, FL. Find loan limits at FHA.com

www.fha.com

http://www.fha.com/lending_limits_state?state=FLORIDA

Insured Commitment

Another characteristic of FHA mortgage loans is the Insured Commitment.

- Developer seeks an FHA commitment to insure the mortgage even though the project is in planning stage, rather than completed.

- It provides a conditional commitment to insure the mortgage loans on the finished homes if they are completed per FHA standards.

http://portal.hud.gov/hudportal/documents/huddoc?id=DOC_20698.pdf

Insurance Premium

Up-front Mortgage Insurance Premium (UFMIP)

Up-front Mortgage Insurance Premium (UFMIP) is charged to borrowers at closing as a closing fee.

- Goes into a fund in case the borrower defaults

- The fee charged can vary based on whether new or resale of a home and on the term of the loan.

www.fha.com

http://portal.hud.gov/hudportal/documents/huddoc?id=DOC_20698.pdf

Mortgage Insurance Premium (MIP)

An additional mortgage insurance fee that is charged to borrowers based on a yearly rate but divided between the monthly payments.

- Goes into a fund in case the borrower defaults

- Increases the total loan payment so must be used in calculating qualifying ratios

- (Both UFMIP and MIP are charged to borrowers of an FHA mortgage.)

http://portal.hud.gov/hudportal/documents/huddoc?id=DOC_20698.pdf

Understanding the components of residential mortgages is essential to working in real estate. This topic is reviewed here including:

IV) Government Insured FHA Program

    B) Characteristics of FHA mortgage loans

        8) Qualifying ratios

9) Interest rate

10) Appraisal

11) Closing costs

12) Assumption

13) Prepayment

Characteristic of FHA Mortgage Loans

Qualifying Ratios

To qualify for an FHA loan there are two measures that looks at a buyer's finances to gross income: The Total Obligation Ratio (TOR) and the Housing Expense Ratio (HER).

FHA loans allow for more long term debt than conventional loans. It allows up to 43% TOR for a FHA Mortgage, whereas a conventional mortgage cannot exceed 36%. However, even though the TOR standards are more relaxed, FHA adds a second requirement. It limits the amount of debt that a buyer can acquire for the housing expense. Called the Housing Expense Ratio (HER), FHA borrowers cannot exceed 31% for the PITI + MIP.

What FHA is doing is acknowledging that although may not have any other debt at the time of a loan, such as a car payment, they are better protected financially if they leave room in their budget for that possibility to happen. FHA tries to prevent what in laymen's term is "house poor" because so much of a person's earnings are going into housing expenses.

http://www.fhaloan.com/fha_debt.cfm

Total Obligation Ratio (TOR)

- FHA loans allow for more long-term debt than conventional loans

- Up to 43% TOR for a FHA Mortgage

- Compared to up to 31% TOR for a Conventional Conforming Mortgage

Housing Expense Ratio (HER)

- Also limits the amount of total housing debt a borrower can take on with the FHA loan

- Cannot exceed 31% HER

- No HER requirement for conventional mortgages.

http://www.fhaloan.com/fha_debt.cfm

Try a qualifying ratio story problem, remember Waldo?

- Now Waldo wants to buy a different home with an FHA loan. The total PITI + MIP on the home he wants to buy will total $625. He is already paying $800 in other long-term debt obligations (car payment of $525 and total credit cards of $275). Waldo's gross monthly income is $3,200. Will he qualify for this home?

Answer

- Monthly housing expenses (PITI and MIP) ÷ monthly gross income = HER

- $625 ÷ $3,200 = .20 or 20% HER

- Total Monthly Obligations ÷ Monthly Gross Income = TOR

- Total Monthly Obligations = $800 + $625 = $1,425

- $1,425 ÷ $3,200 = .45 or 45% TOR

- Would qualify by HER (below 31%) standards but does not qualify due to TOR ratio (must be below 43%).

Interest Rate

As with conventional loans, the interest rate for an FHA loan is not set by FHA or the government. Instead, it is negotiated between borrower and lender. Furthermore, it is said to be part of the free-flowing market and part of the open money market.

- Not set by FHA or the government

- Negotiated between borrower and lender

- Free flowing and Part of the open money market

Appraisal

An appraisal is required for an FHA loan.

- If you use an FHA loan to buy a house, the property will have to be appraised and inspected by an HUD-approved home appraiser. This individual will determine the current market value of the property, and will also inspect it to ensure it meets HUD's minimum property standards.

http://fhahandbook.com/appraisal-guidelines.php#ixzz3x585FXIn

Closing Costs

FHA defines allowable closing costs that may be charged to the borrower. These costs are determined as reasonable and customary by each local FHA office.

They may include:

- The appraisal fee and any inspection fees, actual cost of credit reports, lender's origination fee, deposit verification fees, home inspection service fees up to $200, cost of title examination and title insurance, document preparation (by a third party not controlled by the lender), property survey, attorney's fees, recording fees, transfer stamps and taxes, test and certification fees, water tests, etc.

Closing costs do not include the 3 ½% down payment required for an FHA loan. A helpful feature of an FHA loan is that sellers can pay up to 6% of the sales price towards the buyer's closings costs.

http://www.myfha.net/FHAassistance/closingcosts.html

Assumption

FHA loans allow for assumption because FHA loans do not have a Due-on-Sale Clause. A buyer of a home with an existing FHA loan can assume the existing mortgage if the new buyer qualifies and is approved by the existing lender. This provision is not open to investors as you must agree to be owner occupied.

http://portal.hud.gov/hudportal/documents/huddoc?id=DOC_20698.pdf

Prepayment Clause

FHA loans include a Prepayment Clause. This is the clause that allows the borrower to pay off the loan at any point. Although FHA loans do have a prepayment clause, FHA loans do NOT include a prepayment penalty clause. This means that when the loan is paid off early. The buyer is not penalized with a fee.

- FHA loans include a Prepayment Clause allowing the borrower to pay off the loan at any point.

- FHA loans do NOT include a prepayment penalty.

http://portal.hud.gov/hudportal/documents/huddoc?id=DOC_20698.pdf

Understanding the components of residential mortgages is essential to working in real estate. This topic is reviewed here including:

IV) Government Insured FHA Program

    C) Common FHA loan programs

        1) Section 203(b); homeownership; fixed rate

            (a) Loan assumption criteria

        2) Condominium units

        3) Homeownership; adjustable rate

Common FHA Loan Programs

Section 203(b)

An FHA Mortgage can be utilized in several variations of the loan programs. Section 203(b) is the FHA loan insurance program for people who want a single-family FHA insured mortgage loan. The FHA 203(b) "may be used to purchase or refinance a new or existing one-to-four family home in both urban and rural areas including manufactured homes on permanent foundations."

This loan is designed to promote homeownership for families. It is a Fixed Rate Amortized Mortgage that can be assumed by qualified buyer approved by lender.

- Homeownership for families

- Fixed Rate Amortized Mortgage

- Loan Assumption by qualified buyer approved by lender

http://portal.hud.gov/hudportal/documents/huddoc?id=DOC_20698.pdf

http://www.fha.com/fha_article?id=246

Section 203(k)

The Section 203(k) program is different in that it is FHA's primary program for the rehabilitation and repair of single family properties. As such, it is an important tool for community and neighborhood revitalization, as well as to expand homeownership opportunities. It includes money for rehab and repair of the home right in the loan.

- Rehab and Repair money combined with home loan

- Homeownership for families

- Includes money for rehab and repair of the home

- Loan Assumption by qualified buyer approved by lender

http://portal.hud.gov/hudportal/documents/huddoc?id=DOC_20698.pdf

http://www.fha.com/fha_article?id=246

Condominiums

Home buyers who wish to use an FHA loan for a purchase on a condominium can only do so if it is on an FHA-approved Condominium Projects list.

- What criteria must a condominium project meet to be included on the "approved" list? FHA guidelines state, "to be eligible for FHA mortgage insurance, the project must have been declared and exists in full compliance with applicable State law requirements of the jurisdiction in which the condominium project is located and with all other applicable laws and regulations."

Check with your lender for the approved list of Condominiums.

https://entp.hud.gov/idapp/html/condlook.cfm

http://www.fha.com/fha_article?id=244

Adjustable Rate Mortgages

There is also an Adjustable Rate Mortgages option with the FHA ARM.

- The FHA ARM is an HUD mortgage specifically designed for low and moderate-income families who are trying to make the transition into home ownership.

- This program, used in conjunction with other FHA programs, can help keep initial interest rates and mortgage payments to a minimum.

- Also referred to as Section 251, FHA's Adjustable Rate Mortgage Program insures home purchases or loan refinances on loans with interest rates that may increase or decrease over time.

http://www.fha.com/adjustable_rate

Points in Summary about FHA Mortgage

- Government Insured Mortgage

- Loans made by approved lenders

- Requires 3.5% Down

- Loan Maximums

- Can be Assumed

- Upfront Mortgage Insurance Charged

- Monthly Mortgage Insurance Charged

- Interests Rates are negotiable

- Up to 31% HER; Up to 43% TOR

Understanding the components of residential mortgages is essential to working in real estate. This topic is reviewed here including:

V) VA loan guarantee program

    A) The guarantee features

    B) Characteristics of VA mortgage loans

        1) Qualifications

        2) Eligibility

            (a) Licensees should rely on the VA lender to determine eligibility

        3) Lending source

        4) Eligible property

        5) Discount points

The Guarantee Feature

Another type of nonconventional loan is the Veteran's Administration Loan (VA).

On June 22, 1944, the Servicemen's Readjustment Act of 1944 was signed into law by President Roosevelt, commonly known as the G.I. Bill of Rights. The act included the benefit of low-cost NO down payment mortgages.

Whereas the G.I. Bills of 1944 and 1952 were given to compensate veterans for wartime service, the Veterans Readjustment Benefits Act of 1966 (P.L. 89-358) changed the nature of military service in America by extending benefits to veterans who served during times of war and peace.

The GI Bill helped increase the home ownership rate between 1940 and 1960 by over 18 %.

Home ownership rates by 2015 were up to 64%. "Before the war, college and homeownership were, for the most part, unreachable dreams for the average American."

Once the GI Bill passed, millions took advantage of its home loan guaranty. "From 1944 to 1952, VA backed nearly 2.4 million home loans for World War II veterans."

- Partial Guarantee - The Guarantee Feature of the VA loan is that it is a Partial Guarantee.

- It Guarantees a portion of the loan, enabling the lender to provide favorable terms. It helps Service members, Veterans, and eligible surviving spouses become homeowners.

- Service members, Veterans, and eligible surviving spouses become homeowners.

                                http://www.benefits.va.gov/homeloans/

Qualifications

Let's exam the Characteristic of VA Mortgage Loans. To qualify for a VA loan, you must be a veteran, un-remarried surviving spouses of veterans, or active military personnel.

Eligibility

- Based on eligibility periods of active duty service and or continuous service

- Real Estate Licensees should rely on the VA lender to determine eligibility

http://www.benefits.va.gov/HOMELOANS/purchaseco_loan_limits.asp

Lending Source

VA Home Loans are provided by VA approved private lenders, such as banks and mortgage companies.

- VA only makes direct loans to Native Americans on trust land or in other special circumstances per their guidelines. If the veteran does not want to live on trust land, he can use the VA loan anywhere else, for example.

Eligible Property

Homes that qualify are single Family Residences or up to 4 Units buildings with the borrower living in one of the units as an Owner-Occupied Residence.

- Home loans for new construction or existing construction

- Refinance of homes

- Single Family Residences or up to 4 Units of Owner Occupied Residence

http://www.benefits.va.gov/HOMELOANS/purchaseco_loan_limits.asp

Discount Points

Lenders may charge Discount Points

- Lenders set the costs of these points which can be negotiated between the borrower and the lender

- The purpose of the discount point for the buyer is to pay down the interest rate and lower the payment

http://www.benefits.va.gov/HOMELOANS/purchaseco_loan_limits.asp

Understanding the components of residential mortgages is essential to working in real estate. This topic is reviewed here including:

V) VA loan guarantee program

    B) Characteristics of VA mortgage loans

6) Qualifying ratios

7) Loan limits

8) Loan guarantee

9) Amount of down payment

10) Entitlement

11) Reusing the entitlement

Characteristic of VA Mortgage Loans

Qualifying Ratios

As with FHA loans, VA has a Total Debt Obligation ratio requirement for VA loans. VA does not have a requirement for the Housing Expense Ratio, which is a difference from the FHA qualifying requirement.

- Total Obligation Ratio (TOR) of up to 41%

Also, different from FHA loans is that the VA loan does not have a maximum loan amount or home price that can be purchased if the buyer meets the TOR requirement and that, the value of the property has been supported by the Certificate of Reasonable Value.

- No loan limit with VA loans

- Buyer must qualify for mortgage amount based on qualifying ratios

- Property must match purchase price with a

  - Certificate of Reasonable Value

  http://www.benefits.va.gov/HOMELOANS/purchaseco_loan_limits.asp

Loan guarantee

However, the VA does have established loan guarantee limits.

- Limits the purchase price that can be bought without a down payment

- VA does not set a cap on how much you can borrow to finance your home. However, there are limits on the amount of liability VA can assume, which usually affects the amount of money an institution will lend you.

- The loan limits are the amount a qualified Veteran with full entitlement may be able to borrow without making a down payment.

- These loan limits vary by county, since the value of a house depends in part on its location.

  http://www.benefits.va.gov/HOMELOANS/purchaseco_loan_limits.asp

Entitlement

The amount that the VA will guarantee is referred to as Entitlement.

- Test for Entitlement is based on 25% of the home's value

    - $417,000 is the Maximum Guarantee Loan Amount allowed in MOST of the country for VA loans

    - $417,000 x .25 = $104,250 Maximum Entitlement

- For loan amounts that pass the Maximum Entitlement, the buyer would need to make a down payment for the difference.

http://www.benefits.va.gov/HOMELOANS/purchaseco_loan_limits.asp

Down Payment

Whether a buyer utilizing a VA loan will need a down payment depends upon the price of the house they are purchasing combined with their eligible Entitlement.

Homes with a purchase price of up to $417,000 do not require a down payment.

A buyer's entitlement can be reduced by previous usage which could trigger a down payment to meet a purchase price. Buyer can choose a more expensive home and make up the difference with a down payment. A buyer can choose to make a down payment to lower the amount of debt and the monthly payment.

http://www.benefits.va.gov/HOMELOANS/documents/docs/guaranty_calculation_examples.pdf

Here's a sample of how the maximum entitlement can be applied to a home purchase:

- Maximum Entitlement

    - $417,000 x .25 = $104,250 Maximum Entitlement

- Buyer wants a $300,000 home purchase

- If he/she has 100% of their entitlement available

- $300,000 x .25% = $75,000 Covered by Guarantee and below available entitlement so no down payment is required because the VA is guaranteeing the top $75,000 of the loan.

http://www.benefits.va.gov/HOMELOANS/documents/docs/guaranty_calculation_examples.pdf

Reusing the Entitlement

It is possible to use up only part of an entitlement. The amount that is used up is equal to the amount that is being guaranteed by an existing VA loan. The unused entitlement is still available.

- When the VA loan is completely paid off, then the full entitlement is again available.

- Certificate of Eligibility

    - States the amount of entitlement available to the veteran or serviceman

http://www.benefits.va.gov/HOMELOANS/documents/docs/guaranty_calculation_examples.pdf

Understanding the components of residential mortgages essential to working in real estate. This topic is reviewed here including:

V) VA loan guarantee program

    B) Characteristics of VA mortgage loans

        12) Appraisal

        13) VA funding fee

        14) Loan origination fee

        15) Prepayment

        16) Assumption

        17) Interest rate

Appraisal

An appraisal for a purchase utilizing a VA loan must use a VA approved appraiser.

- Must retain current residential appraiser licensure or certification issued by the State in which VA appraisals will be completed.

- Approved appraisers must have submitted evidence showing at minimum, five years' experience in appraising residential properties.

- VA appraisers determine the value of a property for VA home loan guaranty purposes.

                                                http://www.benefits.va.gov/HOMELOANS/appraiser.asp

VA Funding Fee

A funding fee is charged for a VA loan. The fee is in place to reduce the loan's cost to taxpayers.

- The funding fee is a percentage of the loan amount

- The fee percentage varies based on the type of loan and military category

- The funding fee can be financed into the loan or paid at closing

                                    http://www.benefits.va.gov/HOMELOANS/purchaseco_loan_fee.asp

Loan Origination Fee

Loan origination fees can also be charged. This is a cost lenders charge to offset their administrative costs of the loan.

- May be charged to VA borrowers

- 1% of the loan amount, is the maximum origination fee allowed

Interest Rate

Interest rates are negotiated between the borrower and the lender.

Other Closing Costs

Other closing costs such as the VA appraisal, credit report, state and local taxes, and recording fees may be paid by the purchaser, the seller, or shared.

The seller can pay for some closing costs.

- Seller's "concessions" can't exceed 4% of the loan.

    - But only some types of costs fall under this 4% rule.

    - Examples are: payment of pre-paid closing costs, VA funding fee, payoff of credit balances or judgments for the Veteran, and funds for temporary "buy downs."

    - Payment of discount points is not subject to the 4% limit.

- Buyer is not allowed to pay for the termite report

    - Unless the loan is a refinance.

    - To be paid by the seller.

- No commissions, brokerage fees, or "buyer broker" fees may be charged to the buyer

Prepayment Clause

VA loans have a Prepayment Clause which allows the loan to be paid off early.

- VA does not have a Prepayment Penalty Clause, so there is no fee charged for paying the loan off early.

Assumption

VA loans do not have a Due-on-Sale Clause, so the loan can be assumed.

For VA loans taken out before March 1, 1988, they are assumable without a credit check. The original borrower remains liable in case the new borrower defaults. For VA loans taken out after March 1, 1988, there is a Novation Agreement. This means that the new borrower must be approved by VA, because the original borrower is no longer liable in case new borrower defaults.

- VA loans taken out before March 1, 1988

    - Assumable without a credit check, original borrower liable in case new borrower defaults

- VA loans taken out after March 1, 1988

- Novation Agreement:
- New borrower must be approved by VA, original borrower NOT liable in case new borrower defaults

Points in Summary about VA Mortgage

- Government Guaranteed Mortgage
- Loans made by approved lenders
- Requires NO Down (Maximum Entitlement Benefit)
- No Loan Maximum
- Can be Assumed
- No Upfront or Monthly Mortgage Insurance Charged
- Funding Fee is Charged
- Interests Rates are negotiable
- Loan Origination Fee Maximum of 1% of the Loan
- No HER requirement, TOR up to 41%

Understanding the components of residential mortgages is essential to working in real estate. This topic is reviewed here including:

VI) Qualifying for a loan

    A) Qualifying the Buyer

        1) The loan application process—Uniform Residential Loan Application

        2) Credit evaluation and credit scoring

        3) Qualifying ratios

            (a) Housing expense ratio

            (b) Total obligations ratio

        4) Qualifying the property

5) Information required by lender

The Loan Application Process

Regardless of what type of loan a borrower seeks, the borrower must quality.

The loan Application Process: As a real estate licensee you should qualify the buyer before house-hunting ever begins. It is good to know just how much house the borrower can afford. Doing this saves time and aggravation in the long run by not bidding on properties that cannot be obtained.

It also puts the buyer at a better negotiating advantage when they can produce the loan approval with an offer.

If bidding on a house owned by a lender, or a bank repo, this is a requirement to make the bid. Lenders use the Uniform Residential Loan Application to collect information they need to qualify the borrower such as employment, credit, assets, liabilities.

http://www.mortgagecalculator.org/helpful-advice/mortgage-qualifications.php

Credit Evaluation and Credit Scoring

Lenders review credit histories through a request to credit bureaus. Through the credit report, lenders acquire the borrower's credit score, also called the FICO score. There are three major credit bureaus: TransUnion, Experian, and Equifax.

- The FICO score represents the statistical summary of data contained within the credit report. It includes bill payment history and the number of outstanding debts which a lender can compare to the borrower's income.

- The higher the borrower's credit score, the easier it is to obtain a loan or to pre-qualify for a mortgage.

- A lower score may persuade the lender to reject the application, require a large down payment, or assess a high interest rate to reduce the risk they are taking on the borrower.

http://www.mortgagecalculator.org/helpful-advice/mortgage-qualifications.php

Qualifying for a Loan

Qualifying the Buyer - Qualifying Ratios

Remember that the buyer will have to meet qualifying requirements to obtain a loan.

- If the loan is for a conventional mortgage, the buyer's total obligation ratio cannot exceed 36%.

- For a VA loan it cannot exceed 41%.

- FHA allows for the highest total obligation ratio at 43%, however FHA also requires the buyer stay at or under 31% for the buyer's Housing Expense Ratio.

http://www.mortgagecalculator.org/helpful-advice/mortgage-qualifications.php

Qualifying Ratios		
Loan Comparison	HER	TOR
Conventional Loan		36%
FHA Loan	31%	43%
VA Loan		41%

Qualifying the Property

Whenever there is a loan involved, the lender orders an appraisal to make sure that the property supports the loan amount.

- If the loan would exceed the amount the property is worth, the lender will not loan the money.

    - If the appraisal shows the property is worth less than the offer, the terms can sometimes be renegotiated with the seller.

    - Or the borrower may pay the difference between the loan and the sales price.

http://www.mortgagecalculator.org/helpful-advice/mortgage-qualifications.php

Information Required by Lenders

- Income: A buyer should be prepared to provide information about employment history. Lenders will document the information from W2s, pay stubs and federal tax returns (1040's) and Year-to-Date Profit and Loss Statements if self-employed.

- Assets: A buyer should be prepared to provide bank statements on all accounts, stocks, mutual funds, bonds, and 401K statements. The buyer will need to explain any large deposits and sources of those funds. And the copy of the closing disclosure if the buyer recently sold a home.

- Credit Verification: A buyer should be prepared to provide the Landlord's name, address, and phone number (if renting), an explanation for any credit report late payments, inquiries, charge-offs, collections, judgments, and liens. And a copy of bankruptcy papers if filed bankruptcy within the last seven years.

- If the lender verifies the majority of this information at the outset, a Credit Pre-Approval will be provided to the buyer.

- If the lender takes verbal information from the buyer without enough documentation, then a pre-qualification is provided.

All this information will be used in combination with the property appraisal to determine whether the buyer qualifies for the mortgage.

http://www.mortgagecalculator.org/helpful-advice/mortgage-qualifications.php

Understanding the components of residential mortgages is essential to working in real estate. This topic is reviewed here including:

VII) Primary sources of home financing

    A) Mortgage Lenders

        1) Savings associations

(a) Types of loans offered

2) Commercial banks

(a) Types of loans offered

3) Credit unions

(a) Types of loans offered

So, where exactly does a buyer go to get a loan? There are multiple sources to go to for a loan.

- Buyers obtain a loan in what is referred to as the Primary Mortgage Market.

- Buyers can obtain a loan from Mortgage lenders, which are institutions specifically in business to loan money.

  - Mortgage lenders are not depositories for checking or savings

- Or Buyers can obtain a loan from Savings associations, Commercial banks, or Credit Unions who are also in business as depositories.

Mortgage Lenders

Mortgage lenders are specifically in business to loan money.

- The money the lender loans is either from the company's personal funds (investor's funds) or from borrowed capital.

- They do not hold the loans once the loan is made.

  - They bundle the loans together, package them, and sell them to the secondary market

    http://www.mortgageqna.com/mortgage-terms-glossary/mortgage-lender-definition.html

Savings Associations

Also called Savings Banks, Savings Associations are institutions that accept savings at interest and lends money to savers for home mortgage loans and may offer checking accounts.

- They are either chartered with the state or the federal government. If they are Federally charted SAs have either Federal or F.A. in their name

  - Charted means authorized and regulated by

- All Savings Associations are insured by the FDIC up to $250,000 per depositor per account.

- They mostly make loans for single family homes or for home equity loans or lines of credit

- Makes primarily conventional loans but will make FHA or VA loans

    http://www.oxforddictionaries.com/us/definition/american_english/savings-and-loan?q=savings+and+loan+association

Commercial Banks

Commercial banks are in the business to provide "on demand" accounts which are checking accounts. They also have savings accounts and make loans.

- They are either chartered with the state or the federal government. If they are Federally charted, they have either Federal or N.A. in their name

  - If federally charted, referred to as National Banks.

- All commercial banks are insured by the FDIC the same as Savings Associations.

- They mostly make commercial loans as well as single family home loans.

- They provide conventional, FHA and VA loans

http://banking.about.com/od/businessbanking/a/commercialbank.htm

Credit Unions

Credit unions are financial institutions that are owned by members. They are not-for-profits that operate to serve members rather than to maximize profits.

- Overall, credit unions typically offer higher savings rates, lower fees, and lower rates on loans.

- Provide savings and "on demand" accounts which are checking accounts.

- They are either chartered with the state or the federal government

- Credit Unions are insured by The National Credit Union Administration (NCUA) of up to $250,000 in deposit.

- They make single family home loans and home equity loans.

- They provide conventional, FHA and VA loans

http://www.mycreditunion.gov/about-credit-unions/Pages/default.aspx

Understanding the components of residential mortgages is essential to working in real estate. This topic is reviewed here including:

VII) Primary sources of home financing

   B) Mortgage broker

   1) Their role - how they operate

   C) Mortgage loan originator

   D) Seller financing

   1) Contract for deed (land contract)

2) Amortized mortgage

E) Government programs

1) Mortgage bond financing

Mortgage Broker

Mortgage brokers conduct Loan Origination Activities by acting as an intermediary who brokers mortgage loans on behalf of individuals or businesses.

- Mortgage brokers (mortgage brokerages) do not lend their own money or service loans.

- Their role is to find a bank or a direct lender for individuals seeking loans.

- Banks and other lending institutions offer mortgages directly without the involvement of a mortgage broker, however, as markets for mortgages have become more competitive, the role of the mortgage broker has become more popular.

- Many people prefer to work with mortgage brokers because they can connect the person to the right loan source that best meets their needs.

https://en.wikipedia.org/wiki/Mortgage_broker

Mortgage Loan Originator (MLO)

Mortgage loan origination is the actual process of working with a buyer to:

- Process loan applications

- Negotiate the terms and conditions of a loan between the borrower and the lender

- The Secure and Fair Enforcement for Mortgage Licensing Act (SAFE Act) of 2008

  - Created minimum standards for licensing and registering Mortgage Loan Originators.

  - Requires MLO's to register with the Nationwide Mortgage Licensing System (NMLS)

  - Mortgage Loan Originators not employed by Federally chartered and regulated institutions must also be state licensed to conduct loans and work under state regulations.

http://www.investopedia.com/terms/m/mortgage_originator.asp

Mortgage Loan Originator (MLO)

- "The objectives of the SAFE Act include aggregating and improving the flow of information to and between regulators; providing increased accountability and tracking of MLOs; enhancing consumer protections; supporting anti-fraud measures; and providing consumers with easily accessible information at no charge regarding the employment history of and publicly adjudicated disciplinary and enforcement actions against MLOs."

http://files.consumerfinance.gov/f/201203_cfpb_update_SAFE_Act_Exam_Procedures.pdf

Seller Financing

Seller's also provide a direct source of home financing for buyers.

- Recall that sellers can agree to sell their home as a contract for deed (land contract). With the contract for deed, the seller holds legal title to the property and the buyer holds equitable title.

- Or the seller could transfer the deed to the buyer and act as the lender filing a mortgage lien against the property.

- These are purchase money mortgages that are amortized to pay off the amount due through the loan term or may require a balloon payment at the end of the term.

Government Programs

Mortgage Bond Financing

State Bond loans or Mortgage Revenue Bond (MRB) loans are a local State Bond Loan program.

- Loan well suited for qualified first-time homebuyers.

- Provides eligible borrowers a below-market interest rate to purchase a home that they intend to own and occupy.

- Obtained through the Housing Finance Agency (HFA) which is most often a state-wide agency.

- Not every mortgage lender offers the State Bond Loan, so you need to carefully interview and select from the loan officers who do.

> http://www.firsthomeadvisor.com/index.php/first-time-home-buyer-loan-mortgage/

USDA Guaranteed Rural Housing Loans

The USDA Guaranteed Rural Housing Loan is another type of government loan program specifically for homes purchased in qualifying rural areas.

- 100% financing without monthly mortgage insurance premiums.

- Does require an upfront mortgage insurance premium, which can be financed into the loan.

> http://www.firsthomeadvisor.com/index.php/first-time-home-buyer-loan-mortgage/

SECONDARY MARKET

Understanding the components of residential mortgages is essential to working in real estate. This topic is reviewed here including:

VIII) Secondary Mortgage Market

    A) Effects of the mortgage market

1) Circulate the mortgage money supply

    (a) Intermediation and disintermediation

2) Standardize loan requirements

    (a) Conforming loans

    (b) Portfolio lenders

The Secondary Mortgage Market

Buyers obtain loans in the primary market. Lenders have the option to hold the loan or sell the loan in what is called the secondary mortgage market.

- When a lender makes a loan, the mortgage becomes personal property of the lender.

- As personal property, the loan can be bought and sold as chattel.

- The secondary mortgage market is where loans are bought and sold.

- Loans are pooled together and traded as mortgage-backed securities.

http://www.nasdaq.com/investing/glossary/s/secondary

Effects of the Mortgage Market - Circulates the Mortgage Money Supply

Selling loans provides the lender with proceeds which the banks access as new funds to offer more mortgages to more people.

- Before the secondary market was established, only larger banks had pockets deep enough to tie up bank funds for 15 – 30 years to cover the typical length of home loan.

  - As a result, potential homebuyers had a more difficult time finding mortgage lenders.

  - Since there was less competition between lenders, lenders could charge higher interest rates.

- This freeing up of mortgage money increases the supply of money for loans, which drives down rates through competition among lenders competing for the same buyers.

Useconomy.about.com/od/glossary/g/secondary_marke.htm

Intermediation and Disintermediation

Intermediation is the normal flow of money into financial institutions from the public in the form of deposits.

- These deposits are combined and accessed to loan out to earn income for the institution.

- Opposite of Disintermediation which occurs when depositors take their money out of financial institutions because they can earn more money in other investments.

http://financial-dictionary.thefreedictionary.com/intermediation

Standardized Loan Requirements

Lenders planning to resell mortgages in the secondary market follow a strict standard of loan guidelines established by the government-sponsored enterprises (GSEs) Fannie Mae and Freddie Mac.

- By meeting these guidelines, they can ensure the investors, those buying the loans, and that the loans are a good risk.

- Lenders use standardized loan documents to facilitate loan evaluation by potential investors.

http://financial-dictionary.thefreedictionary.com/intermediation

Conforming Loan

Loans that follow the standards expected to be sold in the secondary market are said to be conforming loans.

- A non-conforming loan is a loan that doesn't conform to guidelines established Fannie Mae or Freddie Mac.

- Because these loans cannot be sold in the secondary market, they can cost the borrower more money to obtain the loan - Higher closing costs and higher rates

- Because non-conforming mortgages do not have to conform to GSE guidelines, their underwriting standards and loan features can offer the borrower more flexibility.

https://www.lendingtree.com/glossary/what-is-non-conforming-loan

Portfolio Lenders

Remember the days when if someone walked into the bank and sat face to face with a lender, someone who lived in the small town with them and knew them well? A banker who could make a judgment based on the character and behavior of the person that he knew well?

Well in that story, if the banker actually chose to make the loan, the bank would have been acting as a portfolio lender. Portfolio lenders make loans to borrowers that are non-conforming mortgages. Instead of selling these loans in the secondary market, the loans are held in the bank's portfolio of assets.

- Non-conforming mortgages are held by portfolio lenders.

- Portfolio-lenders holds the loans that they make in a portfolio instead of selling them

http://financial-dictionary.thefreedictionary.com/Portfolio+Lender

Understanding the components of residential mortgages is essential to working in real estate. This topic is reviewed here including:

VIII) Secondary Mortgage Market

    B) Fannie Mae

        1) Private (not a government agency) corporation that trades on NYSE

        2) Secondary market for VA, FHA and conventional loans

3) Issues mortgage-back securities to investors

4) Largest single private mortgage purchaser

Fannie Mae

Fannie Mae is a private (not a government agency) corporation that trades on the NYSE. Fannie Mae was established by Congress in 1938 for the purpose of stimulating the economy after the great depression and to create more opportunities for home ownership through increased money supply. Because of the problems that resulted in the mortgage market around, in 2008, Fannie Mae came under "Conservatorship" of the federal government. This means that Fannie Mae is still a private corporation (not government owned) but is under strict government oversight.

- Fannie Mae is the Secondary Market for VA, FHA and conventional loans.

- All three of these loan types are bought and sold by Fannie Mae.

- Fannie Mae issues mortgage-back securities to investors

- Fannie Mae is the largest single private mortgage purchaser.

What does it mean: "Fannie Mae issues mortgage-back securities"?

1. Mortgage loans are purchased from banks and other lenders.

2. The purchaser (Fannie Mae) assembles these loans into collections or "pools".

3. Fannie Mae "securitizes" the pools by issuing mortgage-backed securities.

    - The securities are "secured" or backed by the real estate the mortgages are held against

4. The investors, by holding the security, now have a liquid asset that is easier to buy, sell, or trade through securities dealers.

https://en.wikipedia.org/wiki/Mortgage-backed_security

Understanding the components of residential mortgages is essential to working in real estate. This topic is reviewed here including:

VIII) Secondary Mortgage Market

    C) Government National Mortgage Association (GNMA)

        1) Wholly owned government corporation under HUD

        2) Provides a secondary market for VA and FHA loans

        3) Mortgage-backed securities program

Government National Mortgage Market Association (GNMA)

GNMA is a WHOLLY owned government corporation under HUD that provides a secondary market for VA and

FHA loans. **Ginnie Mae**, was established in the United States in 1968 to promote home ownership. Even in uncertain times, investors are guaranteed payment of interest and principal, in full and on time. The benefits of this process are passed on to the lenders who can then make more mortgage loans at more affordable rates.

- The mortgage-backed securities program provided by GNMA are pass-through securities as GNMA acting as a GUARANTOR of these securities rather than the actual purchaser or creator of the securities.

- GNMA mortgage-back securities carries the FULL FAITH and CREDIT GUARANTEE of the U.S. Government.

- GNMA charges a fee for this guarantee but the guarantee adds value to the securities which enables them to be sold at a higher profit for the investors.

http://portal.hud.gov/hudportal/HUD?src=/hudprograms/Ginnie_Mae_I

Understanding the components of residential mortgages is essential to working in real estate. This topic is reviewed here including:

VIII) Secondary Mortgage Market

   D) Freddie Mac

       1) Created by Congress in 1970

       2) Shares sold publicly

       3) Buy conventional loans

Freddie Mac

The Federal Home Loan Mortgage Corporation (Freddie Mac) was created by Congress in 1970 to expand the secondary market. Oversight is said to be needed primarily because of the inherent conflict and flawed business model embedded in the GSE structure, and to the ongoing housing correction. Critics in Washington claim the business model faces conflict due to its combination of government mission and private ownership.

- Freddie Mac buys conventional mortgages on the secondary market, pools them, and sells them as a mortgage-backed security to investors on the open market.

- Shares of Freddie Mac are sold publicly

- In 2008, it came under conservatorship of the Federal Government. The action has been described as "one of the most sweeping government interventions in private financial markets in decades."

"The government mission required them to keep mortgage interest rates low and to increase their support for affordable housing. Their shareholder ownership, however, required them to fight increases in their capital requirements and regulation that would raise their costs and reduce their risk-taking and profitability."

The Housing and Economic Recovery Act of 2008 passed by Congress in 2008 expanded regulatory authority over Fannie Mae and Freddie Mac by the newly established FHFA, and gave the U.S. Treasury the authority to advance funds to stabilizing Fannie Mae, or Freddie Mac. As a result, both Fannie Mae and Freddie Mac are now under a conservatorship.

https://en.wikipedia.org/wiki/Federal_takeover_of_Fannie_Mae_and_Freddie_Mac

Understanding the components of residential mortgages is essential to working in real estate. This topic is reviewed here including:

VIII) Secondary Mortgage Market

    E) Nonconforming loans

        1) Broker and correspondent loans

        2) Private investors through mortgage brokers and bankers

Nonconforming Loans

Broker and Correspondent Loans

Loans that do not fit the conforming standards can still be sold in the secondary market under special conditions. These are nonconforming loans. Broker and Correspondent Loans are nonconforming loans.

- Brokers who act as correspondent lenders are one example of this exception.

- Acting as a direct mortgage lender, correspondent lenders have the authority to underwrite their own loans funded by their investors. Their goal is to do loans in great quantities, package them together, and sell them in the secondary market before the first payment from the borrowers are due.

- Correspondent lenders have **secured trade lines from investors**– acting as direct lenders – in which loans are funded.

        https://qna.mortgagenewsdaily.com/questions/what-is-a-correspondent-lender

Private Investors Through Mortgage Brokers and Bankers

There are also several other sources for lending through private investors.

Private investors often pool their money and participate in investment opportunities with mortgage brokers and bankers either in the primary or secondary market. Private investors have an opportunity to invest in real estate and mortgages that they wouldn't otherwise have the resources to do.

However, with these investments are increased risks compared to the conforming market.

- This is also a nonconforming loan

        https://qna.mortgagenewsdaily.com/questions/what-is-a-correspondent-lender

Private Investors Through Mortgage Brokers and Bankers

Another type of nonconforming loan are loans through private investors called Hard Money Lending. The industry is not well publicized.

- Hard Money Lenders are predominantly small, highly specialized mortgage brokers familiar with commercial real estate lending.

- Mortgage pools are structured and operate like commercial banks.

- Private Money Bankers or Real Estate Bankers, are groups, individuals, companies or funds, that pool private money, and then lend those pooled funds for profit.

https://en.wikipedia.org/wiki/Private_money_investing

Private Investors Through Mortgage Brokers and Bankers

Why do private investors get involved in these type of investment opportunities?

The motivation for investing includes: the simplicity of the underlying investment and a desire for: 1) An investment secured by real estate 2) Regular income derived from monthly dividend distributions; 3) Higher yields than those available from investing in money market funds or bonds; 4) An Active involvement in real estate finance.

A borrower seeking funds approaches a mortgage broker or private money lender and describes his borrowing needs. The mortgage broker or lender then assesses the proposed loan. If the borrower defaults on the loan, investors holding the investment recoup their capital by assuming the borrower's equity in the property.

https://en.wikipedia.org/wiki/Private_money_investing

Understanding the components of residential mortgages is essential to working in real estate. This topic is reviewed here including:

IX) Mortgage Fraud

    A) Common types of mortgage fraud

        1) Straw borrowers

        2) No document loans

    B) Red flags

        1) Inflated appraisal

        2) Inflated contract prices

    C) Ethical practices

Common Types of Mortgage Fraud

Working as a real estate licensee, it is important to recognize mortgage fraud.

Mortgage fraud occurs when someone deliberately falsifies information to obtain mortgage financing that would not have been granted otherwise.

- Mortgage fraud continues to be one of the fastest growing crimes in the United States and is generally classified into one of three categories:

    - Fraud for housing or property, fraud for profit, and fraud for criminal enterprise

- Each fraud type is unique based upon the intent of the fraud scheme and the perpetrators involved.

http://www.freddiemac.com/singlefamily/preventfraud/types.html

Straw Borrowers

Common types of mortgage fraud include using straw borrowers to make the purchase.

- **Straw buyers** are people who consent to the use of their names and personal details by companies or people who will obtain mortgage loans but do not intend to live in the homes.

- Sometimes a straw buyer will be offered money for this "favor," or doesn't know that his or her name and information have been used on the loan application.

- **They may even be** involved in "mortgage fraud rings" where the initiator of these schemes can successfully obtain large loan amounts for over-valued properties, and the straw buyers can end up being sued by the lenders who have extended the loan monies.

http://disb.dc.gov/page/things-know-about-mortgage-fraud-and-straw-buying

No Document Loans

No document loans is a type of loan program that became illegal because of the mortgage fraud that took over these programs.

- A **no-doc mortgage** does not require mortgage lenders to document the borrower's income or assets. No-doc mortgages are illegal today because they violate the requirement that lenders must verify the borrower's ability to repay before approving a mortgage.

- No-doc loans were designed to make home purchases easier for individuals who often had plenty of cash flow but couldn't document their income.

- However, lenders increasingly pushed the envelope, and eventually sub-prime loans with very high rates and fees and no down payment requirement or income verification hit the market.

- They are blamed by many for starting the foreclosure crisis in 2008.

http://www.freddiemac.com/singlefamily/preventfraud/types.html

Red Flags

Learning how to avoid and identify mortgage fraud can prevent you from becoming a victim either as a consumer or a licensee. It is imperative that you work within the parameters of people that you already know and trust. The evolution of mortgage fraud dictates that this may not always be possible though. If confusion or doubt persists, good practice suggests that you should have your documents reviewed by your broker or a neutral professional.

If you are a member of the state association, you can also contact the Florida Realtors Association Legal Hot Line for guidance.

Two types of red flags to watch involve:

- An appraiser acting in collusion with a borrower and providing a misleading appraisal report to the lender. The report inaccurately states an inflated property value.

- Significant sales price adjustments that are not supported by comparable market data possibly accompanied by request that list price in MLS be altered to reflect appraised value.

http://www.realtor.org/sites/default/files/Mortgage-REV.pdf

Inflated Appraisals

- A red flag that mortgage fraud is occurring is an inflated appraisal that doesn't match your experience with the market.

- Inflated appraisals involve an appraiser who acts in collusion with a borrower and provides a misleading appraisal report to the lender. The report inaccurately states an inflated property value.

- A red flag within the appraisal is significant sales price adjustments that are not supported by comparable market data possibly accompanied by request that list price in MLS be altered to reflect appraised value.

http://www.fortunebuilders.com/protect-mortgage-fraud-2/

Inflated Contract Prices

- Flips are another common type of mortgage fraud. They occur when ownership of one property changes several times in a brief period.

- Flips are often used to artificially inflate the value of the property to obtain larger loans than what might otherwise be possible and to skim the equity off the property.

- Warning signs of possible flips include frequent ownership changes within a brief period of time, not having the property seller on the title, references to a double escrow or other closing disclosures, and large fluctuations of the sales price over a period of a few weeks or months.

https://www.mortgageloan.com/mortgage-fraud/red-flags

Ethical Practices

- Real estate licensees that become suspicious or aware of mortgage fraud are obligated to report it. Not to do so could result in the licensee being charged as being culpable in the mortgage scheme.

- Mortgage fraud is a second-degree felony when the loan documents exceed $100,000.

- Fraud charges would also result in the loss of licensure as a licensee.

http://www.leg.state.fl.us/statutes/index.cfm?App_mode=Display_Statute&URL=0800-0899/0817/Sections/0817.545.html

CREDIT AND LENDING LAWS

Understanding the components of residential mortgages is essential to working in real estate. This topic is

reviewed here including:

X) Laws regarding fair credit and lending procedures

    A) Equal Credit Opportunity Act (ECOA)

        1) Prohibits discrimination in loan underwriting based on sex, marital status, race, religion, age, or national origin. (A lender cannot require an applicant's spouse to join in (sign) a loan application).

        2) Prohibits discriminatory treatment of income from alimony, child support, public assistance, or part-time employment

        3) Prohibits inquiry about, or consideration of, child bearing plans or potential for child bearing

The Equal Credit Opportunity Act (ECOA)

Laws are in place to protect consumers who apply for mortgage loans.

The Equal Credit Opportunity Act (ECOA) prohibits discrimination in loan underwriting based on:

-     sex, marital status, race, religion, age, or national origin.
- Plus, it prohibits discriminatory treatment of income from alimony, child support, public assistance, or part-time employment.
- And it prohibits inquiry about, or consideration of, child bearing plans or potential for child bearing.

The Consumer Financial Protection Bureau has issued regulations under ECOA. These regulations, known as Regulation B, provide the substantive and procedural framework for fair lending.

www.justice.gov/crt/equal-credit-opportunity-act-3

Understanding the components of residential mortgages is essential to working in real estate. This topic is reviewed here including:

X) Laws regarding fair credit and lending procedures

    B) Consumer Credit Protection Act (Truth in Lending Act)

        1) Implemented by Federal Reserve Regulation Z

        2) Requires disclosure of full credit costs

        3) Requires disclosure of annual percentage rate (APR)

Consumer Credit Protection Act (Truth in Lending Act)

Another protection is provided by the Consumer Credit Protection Act also called the Truth in Lending Act, passed in 1968.

The Truth in Lending Act (TILA), Title I of the Consumer Credit Protection Act, promotes the informed use of consumer credit by requiring disclosures about its terms and costs.

"This regulation applies to each individual or business that offers or extends credit when the credit that is being offered is subject to a finance charge or is payable by a written agreement in more than four installments; the credit is primarily for personal, family or household purposes; and the loan balance equals or exceeds $25,000.00 or is secured by an interest in real property or a dwelling."

https://usffcu.org/TruthinLendingAct.asp

Implemented by the Federal Reserve Regulation Z

The Truth In Lending Act pairs with the Federal Reserve Regulation Z for actual implementation of the act's provisions.

- The overall goal is to inform borrowers of the true costs of a loan.

It does not regulate loan charges, but instead it requires a "uniform standard disclosure" of loan costs and charges so that the consumer can fairly shop loans by comparing one to the other.

http://www.anz.com/guam/en/auxiliary/general-disclosures/

TILA requires disclosure of full credit costs.

Specifically, TILA requires disclosure of loan terms in 4 formats:

- Finance charge

- Total amount financed

- Total amount of payments

- Annual percentage rate (APR)

  - Within 1/8 of 1%

And it requires lenders to disclose interest, discount points, servicing fees, & origination fees

- but not title, legal, survey, appraisal, credit report, or deed preparation

http://www.nrec.ne.gov/legal/truthinlending.html

TILA requires disclosure of annual percentage rate (APR)

Specifically, TILA requires that the full credit costs must be disclosed in the form of the Annual Percentage Rate.

- Included in the APR is the interest rate, origination fees, discount points, and other loan costs. The APR represents the Annual Cost of Credit

- By expressing all loans in terms of the APR, potential borrowers can compare loans and better shop the terms for a more competitive deal

http://www.anz.com/guam/en/auxiliary/general-disclosures/

Advertising

Affects advertising also for the protection of consumers. If an advertisement for credit for real estate (mortgages) contains any of the following trigger terms, three specific disclosures must also be included in the advertisement.

- The triggering terms are:

1. The amount of the down payment, expressed either as a percentage or as a dollar amount.

2. The amount of any payment expressed either as a percentage or as a dollar amount.

3. The period of repayment (the total time required to repay)

- Triggering Terms means all three of these disclosures must be included:

1. The amount or percentage of the down payment;

2. The terms of repayment; and

3. The "Annual Percentage Rate," using that term spelled out in full. If the annual percentage rate may be increased after consummation of credit transaction, that fact must be disclosed.

So, what does this mean for a real estate licensee? If along with the real estate property you are advertising for sale, you also mention any of the following types of phrases (Triggering Terms), you are also subject to this rule:

"25% down"   **"90% financing"**   **"Monthly payments less than $67"**

"36 small payments are all you make"   **"4 year loans available"**

"Less than $100 interest"

Not all terms are triggering term:

"No down payment" and phrases that are vague and simply talk up the loan terms such as **"Easy monthly payments"** **"Pay weekly"** **"Terms to fit your budget"** **"5% below are standard Rate"** are not triggering terms. *Know that making bait and switch advertising or misleading advertising is unlawful so be clear in any statements made.*

http://www.nrec.ne.gov/legal/truthinlending.html

Sample Advertising

"Only $850 a month for this beautiful home!"

- Because this statement is a triggering term, to include this statement, the amount of required down payment, how long the term is, and the APR must also be clearly disclosed in the advertisement.

"Easy payments available on this lovely home!"

- To include this statement, no other loan details would have to be provided. This is considered too vague to be a triggering term.

http://www.nrec.ne.gov/legal/truthinlending.html

Right of Rescission

TILA also requires that the disclosure be made to consumers of credit and that they have a 3 day right of rescission.

- In a credit transaction in which a security interest is or will be retained or acquired in a consumer's principal dwelling, each consumer whose ownership is or will be subject to the security interest has the right to rescind the transaction.

- Lenders are required to deliver two copies of the notice of the right to rescind and one copy of the disclosure statement to each consumer entitled to rescind. The notice must be on a separate document that identifies the rescission period on the transaction and must clearly and conspicuously disclose the retention or acquisition of a security interest in the consumer's principal dwelling, the consumer's right to rescind the transaction, and how the consumer may exercise the right to rescind with a form for that purpose, designating the address of the lender's place of business.

https://usffcu.org/TruthinLendingAct.asp

Right of Rescission

TILA also requires that the disclosure be made to consumers of credit and that they have a 3 day right of rescission.

- This 3 day right of rescission applies to home equity lines of credit, second mortgages and to refinance loans.

- This 3 day right of rescission does NOT apply to new loans on a home the borrower did not previously own before securing the mortgage.

- It also does NOT apply to construction loans.

https://usffcu.org/TruthinLendingAct.asp

Understanding the components of residential mortgages is essential to working in real estate. This topic is reviewed here including:

X) Laws regarding fair credit and lending procedures

    C) Real Estate Settlement Procedures Act (RESPA)

        1) Applies to virtually any closing involving a "standard" home mortgage loan from a financial institution or mortgage banker

        2) Requires that the borrower be provided a booklet of information regarding closing costs

        3) Requires advanced estimates of closing costs

        4) Requires that the borrower can examine the RESPA-specified closing statement in advance

        5) Prohibits kick-backs to a lender from vendors of closing related services

Real Estate Settlement Procedures Act (RESPA)

Another type of consumer protective act, is the Real Estate Settlement Procedures Act (RESPA). The Real Estate Settlement Procedures Act (RESPA) was passed by Congress in 1974.

It was created because various companies associated with the real estate transactions, such as lenders and real estate agents, were often engaging in providing undisclosed kickbacks to each other which causes the cost of the transaction to increase for the consumer.

https://en.wikipedia.org/wiki/Real_Estate_Settlement_Procedures_Act

In 2010, Congress passed the Dodd-Frank Act, which established the CFPB and are now authorized to issue regulations under the Truth-in-Savings Act, Funds Availability Act, Equal Credit Opportunity Act and Truth-in-Lending Act.

On July 21, 2011, administration and enforcement of the Real Estate Settlement Procedures Act (RESPA) was transferred from the Department of Housing and Urban Development to the Consumer Financial Protection Bureau (CFPB).

Called TILA-RESPA Integrated Disclosure Rule (TRID), it consolidated consumer protection agencies under CFPB to simplify oversight and compliance. It took the four existing required disclosures regarding credit and the costs of credit down to two disclosures.

http://www.anz.com/guam/en/auxiliary/general-disclosures/

Real Estate Settlement Procedures Act (RESPA) applies to most any closing involving a "standard" home mortgage loan from a financial institution or mortgage banker.

RESPA applies to all federally related mortgage loans for the purchase of:

- 1 to 4 family structure (including construction loans)

- Manufactured homes using proceeds of a loan

- With the loan made by a lender, creditor, or dealer

- Made by or insured by an agency of the federal government

- Made regarding a federal housing program

- Made by and intended to be sold by a lender to FNMA, GNMA, or FHLMC

- Subject of a home equity conversion mortgage

- Made by a lender, dealer, or creditor to be used to fund an installment sales contract, land contract or contract for deed

http://www.federalreserve.gov/boarddocs/supmanual/cch/200601/respa.pdf

Consumer Booklet

Requires that the borrower be provided a booklet of information regarding closing costs.

- Under RESPA, a financial institution or mortgage broker is required to provide a borrower with a copy of the "special information booklet" at the time a written application is submitted or no later than 3 business days after application is received.

- If the application is denied before the end of the 3-day period, the institution does not have to supply the booklet.

http://www.federalreserve.gov/boarddocs/supmanual/cch/200601/respa.pdf

Loan Estimate

Requires advanced estimates of closing costs.

- RESPA also requires that no later than the third business day after the submission of a loan application, the borrower is provided with a loan estimate which discloses key features, costs, and risks of the mortgage loan for which the person has applied.

  http://files.consumerfinance.gov/f/201403_cfpb_tila-respa-integrated-disclosure-rule_compliance-guide.pdf

Closing Disclosure

Requires that the borrower can examine the RESPA-specified closing statement in advance.

A Closing Disclosure form must be provided to the borrower within 3 business days BEFORE the loan closing. This form details all the costs associated with the closing including lender fees, real estate agent commissions, title closing fees, APR, and prorations between the buyer and the seller.

  http://files.consumerfinance.gov/f/201403_cfpb_tila-respa-integrated-disclosure-rule_compliance-guide.pdf

Kick-backs

RESPA prohibits kick-backs, also called Fee-Splitting or Unearned Fees, to a lender from vendors of closing related services.

- A kickback is illegal under RESPA. A kickback is something of value given in exchange for referring a settlement service business to another person. Kickbacks are said to harm consumers by driving up the cost of transaction.

- Mortgage brokers can only pay other mortgage brokers a referral fee.

- Real Estate Licensees can only pay other real estate licensees a referral fee.

- And title companies may not pay a referral fee or give something of value in return for referring the business.

14 REAL ESTATE RELATED COMPUTATIONS AND CLOSING OF TRANSACTIONS

Learning Objectives:
• Compute the sales commission
• Calculate the percent of profit or loss, given the original cost of the investment, the sale price and the dollar amount of profit or loss
• Define settlement and title closing
• List the preliminary steps to a closing
• Prorate the buyer's and seller's expenses
• Calculate the dollar amount of transfer taxes on deeds, mortgages and notes
• Allocate taxes and fees to the proper parties and compute individual costs
• Explain the rules of thumb for closing statement entries
• Explain the major sections of the Uniform Settlement Statement
• Demonstrate ability to read and check the Uniform Settlement Statement for errors

Key Terms:

arrears	level payment plan	profit
credit	pre-closing inspection	proration
debit	principal	

I) Basic Real Estate Computations

   A) Sales commissions

   B) Calculating selling price, cost and profit

Basic Real Estate Computations

Real Estate calculations are important to both the sales associate and clients.

Part of your job as a real estate professional is to calculate commission earned and closing statement amounts. Commissions are an integral part of the transaction and are often divided between broker(s) and associate(s).

It is imperative that amounts are calculated correctly. Closing statements need to be correct or the sale will have trouble closing.

Calculate:

Commissions earned

Closing Statement amounts

Prorations

Real Estate Sales Commissions:

Traditionally, when a real estate sales professional lists a house for sale, they negotiate with the seller for compensation that will be paid to the brokerage upon a successful closing.

Fees charged and how and when the fees are collected can range dramatically. Some brokerages take a flat fee and are paid at the time of listing regardless of whether the sale closes. Real estate services may be broken down into tasks and charged to the seller depending upon the services taken.

Most listings, however, are taken by the brokerage not charging any fees upfront and instead taking a percentage of the sales price at closing. The brokerage and/or agents take on all the cost of marketing the home. If the home fails to sell, the agent does not receive any payment.

- Listing Commissions
- Buyer Agent Commissions
- Flat Fee verses Percentage of Sale Price

Evaluating the Risk

So, why are real estate brokerages willing to work on a commission basis? If a brokerage is skilled in understanding the market, the broker can judge the odds of being able to sell a home under the terms of the listing contract – meaning the condition of the home, the motivation of the seller, and the sales price. Top producing real estate brokers and their sales associates do not take on just any listing. They list properties that they believe will sell in the current market.

- Commission
- Percentage Paid at Closing
- All or nothing to gain
- Condition of the home
- Motivation of the seller

- Appropriate sales price
- Current market conditions

Sales Commissions

Co-Brokerage Agreements

Real estate brokerages that participate with the multiple listing service will enter the listing into the MLS. In doing so, they advertise to other agents the amount of commission that will be paid to a buyer brokerage who produces the buyer for the sale.

- Multiple Listing Service
- Agreement to share the commission between the selling broker and the buyers broker should a broker from a cooperating agency produce the buyer.

Sales Commissions

Example of Commission Computation

Let's look at some commission calculations.

A home is listed by Sales associate, Pam Beater with Real Realty at $195,000 for 6% commission. It is subsequently sold at full price by sales agent Jay of Bold Realty. The listing broker and selling broker share the commission equally. The broker of Real Realty keeps 45% of what his company received.

Solution for commission computation

Take the $195,000 sale price $\times$ 6 percent (as a decimal) commission to equal $11,700 total commission. Divide $11,700 by 2 to equal $5,850 commission to selling office (Bold Realty). $5,850 commission to listing office (Real Realty). 100% minus 45% of the commission kept by Bold Realty = 55% to Pam Beater. So take the $5,850 commission paid to Bold Realty and multiply it by 55% to equal $3,217.50 which is the total paid to Pam Beater for listing the home.

- $195,000 sale price $\times$ .06 = $11,700 total commission
- $11,700 $\div$ 2 = $5,850 commission to selling office (Bold Realty)
    - $5,850 commission to listing office (Real Realty)
- 100% - 45% = 55% to Pam Beater
- $5,850 commission to listing office x .55 =$3,217.50 to Pam Beater.

Sales Commissions

Graduated Commission Defined

Graduated Commission is defined as compensation where the percentage of commission earned increases incrementally as sales volume increases. This is used to create an incentive to increase sales volume. Sometimes a seller will use it to try to get a higher sales price for their home – paying one commission up to a sales price and then another commission on the sale price above the base.

It is also common for brokerages to pay their sales associates on a graduated commission basis. In this case, the brokerage might pay their sales associates on a 50/50 split, for example, up to two million dollars in sales volume and then pay 60% of the commission to the agent on sales above the two-million-dollar point. With this type of commission structure, it is normal to see increases in commission to the agent moving up through several increments.

- Compensation where the percentage of commission earned increases incrementally as sales volume increases. This is used to create an incentive to increase sales volume.

  http://www.businessdictionary.com/definition/graduated-commission.html#ixzz3wVvI5pv5

Sales Commissions

Graduated Commission Example

Bold Realty broker lists a waterfront home for $1,000,000. the listing calls for 4% commission up to $700,000, and 5% above $700,000 to $950,000.

Also, there is a provision for 6% above $950,000.

If the property is sold for $980,000 by Bold Realty, what is the commission paid to Bold Realty?

Graduated Commission Solution

Calculate the first $700,000 @ 4%, the next $250,000 @ 5%, and the next $30,000 @ 6% . This gives you $28,000 + $12,500 + $1,800 = $42,300 in total commission paid to Bold Realty.

1. $700,000 x .04 = $28,000
2. $250,000 x .05 = $12,500
3. $30,000 x .06 = $1,800
4. $28,000 + $12,500 + $1,800 = $42,300

$42,300 is the total commission paid to Bold Realty

Calculating Selling Price, Cost, and Profit (Loss)

You'll also need to be able to calculate profit and loss based on selling price and cost. Selling price is the price at which a property sells or is expected to sell. To help a seller or buyer make decisions, you'll need to be able to calculate their selling or buying costs. Costs involved in buying or selling a property involve many items that are paid for before or at closing.

Selling Price-

- Price at which a property sells.
- Usually an amount that a buyer would pay for an equal property.
- Often compared to similar SOLD properties in near vicinity.

Cost-

- Selling a property acquires costs, such as commissions, doc stamps and taxes, title costs, inspections, etc.

Calculating Profit and Loss

When a property is sold and the cost is subtracted, if there is money ahead; then a profit was made. If you are money behind; you lost money!

Profit

- The Sale Price – Total Cost = Profit
- If there is a net gain!

Loss

- The Sale Price – Total Cost = Loss
- If there is a net loss!

Calculating Profit and Loss

Profit and loss are part of Real Estate. Whether a residence or investment, profit and/or losses have tax ramifications. Investors base many of their buying decisions on profit and loss (and of course, income and taxes). To calculate percentage of profit, take profit and divide by the total cost and you will have the percentage of profit.

% of Profit Formula

- Profit ÷ Total cost = Percentage of Profit

% of Loss Formula

- Loss ÷ Total cost = Percentage of Loss

Profit/Loss Example 1

Here's an example of a problem where you are asked to calculate a percentage of profit: Mighty Ralph bought a property for $98,000. Mighty Ralph sold it for $135,000.

What is Mighty Ralph's percentage of profit?

Profit/Loss Solution 1

If the property cost $98,000 and sold for $135,000, there is a $37,000 profit. $135,000 minus $98,000 is $37,000. To calculate the percentage of profit, divide the $37,000 by the $98,000 cost to equal .378 or 38% of Profit.

- Amount made on sale ÷ Total cost = Percent Profit
- $135,000 price – $98,000 cost = $37,000 profit
- $37,000 profit ÷ $98,000 cost = .377 or 38% profit

Profit/Loss Example 2

A developer purchases 3 lots with 115 ft. frontage each for a total of $150,000. He divides these lots into 5 lots of 69 front feet each and sells them for $500 per front foot. What is the developers' percentage of profit?

Profit/Loss Solution 2

- 3 x 115 ft. = 345 total frontages
- 345 feet of frontage x $500 = $172,500 Sale Price
- $172,500 - $150,000 = $22,500 Profit
- Profit ÷ Cost = % of Profit
- $22,500 ÷ $150,000 = 0.15 or 15%

STEPS TO CLOSING

II) Preliminary steps to a closing

    A) Earnest money deposited

    B) Additional deposit, if required

    C) Loan application

    D) Contingencies

    E) Appraisal

    F) Loan approval

    G) Title insurance

    H) Termite inspection

    I) Required repairs ordered

    J) Survey ordered

    K) Buyer hazard insurance

        1) Hazard insurance policy to closing agent

        2) Flood insurance

    L) Buyer/seller contact for closing appointment

    M) Pre-closing inspection

N) Closing documents reviewed by parties prior to closing

O) Buyer informed of funds needed to close

P) Earnest money transferred to closing agent

Preliminary Steps to Closing

Once you finally have a deal, you have specific steps that must be accomplished to take you from contract to closing. Follow the timelines of these steps carefully as the failure to meet timelines is one of the main things that real estate agents find themselves sued over by their clients when things go wrong.

1. Earnest money deposit
2. Additional deposit if required
3. Loan application
4. Contingencies
5. Appraisal
6. Loan approval
7. Title Insurance
8. Inspections
9. Required repairs
10. Survey
11. Hazard insurance
12. Pre-closing inspection (walk-through)
13. Review closing documents
14. Buyer informed of funds needed to close
15. Earnest money transferred to closing agent

Earnest money deposit - good faith deposit or binder deposit

Additional deposit if required

Loan application

Contingencies

Appraisal

Loan approval

Title Insurance

Inspections

Required repairs

Survey

Hazard insurance

Pre-closing inspection (walk-through)

Review closing documents

Buyer informed of funds needed to close

Earnest money transferred to closing agent

http://www.realtor.com/advice/finance/understanding-the-earnest-money-deposit-2/

Let's take a closer look at each one:

Earnest money deposit, otherwise known as good faith deposit or a binder deposit, is given by the buyer upon submitting an offer. It shows the seller that the buyer has good intention to fulfill purchase agreement.

Sometimes a seller will require an additional earnest money deposit if the seller feels that the buyer has not deposited enough to show real interest in property or to justify taking property off market.

A Loan Application is the first step in applying for a loan. Information is included on the application that helps a loan officer determine if a buyer may qualify for a loan.

Any contingencies in the contract must be tracked and completed to ensure contract fulfillment. This is where the timelines can get tricky. You must pay attention to details such as business days versus calendar days

An appraisal must be ordered by the lender to justify selling price (value) and this value is used to justify a loan on the property at a particular value. Some buyers have their deals subject to appraisals even without a loan involved.

A loan approval is the process where the value of the property and the buyer's ability to satisfy loan debt obligation are finished and the loan can be approved.

Title insurance insures a clear title for the buyer, free from encumbrances i.e. liens, taxes, HOA fees, etc.

An inspection is one way that a buyer protects himself on the purchase of a property. A home inspector inspects the total home structure, major appliances, plumbing, electrical, roof and property near structures. If there are problems with the home found through inspections, depending upon the details of the contract – the seller and buyer will negotiate repairs, or the buyer may be able to cancel the deal.

Required repairs can be included in the purchase contract or because of post inspection negotiations. And sometimes they are flagged and required by the buyer's lender. This is more common with VA and FHA loans than conventional loans. The goal for the lender is make sure the property is suitable for lender collateral.

A survey may be performed to verify property lines and setbacks.

Lenders require proof of hazard insurance before they will fund a loan for a property.

A pre-closing walk-thru is a normal part of closing procedures. A buyer has the right for a final inspection to make sure that things are good for closing. Don't skip this step, it protects all parties involved –even the sales associate.

Closing documents such as loan estimate and closing disclosure let the buyer see close estimates of final loan expenses, title expenses and other costs associated with closing. THIS IS A REVIEW TO VERIFY AMOUNTS.

Funds needed to close are funds that the buyer needs to bring to closing to complete the purchase.

Earnest money or good faith deposit held by a brokerage other than the title company needs to be transferred to the closing agent or title company to be held in escrow until closing.

PRORATIONS

III) Prorated Expenses

    A) Prepaid rent

    B) County and/or city property taxes

    C) Mortgage interest on assumed mortgages

    D) Prorating considerations

        1) Period over which item is prorated

        2) Period allocated to buyer and period allocated to seller

        3) Prorating methods: 360 vs. 365

Prorated Expenses on Closing Documents

Once you finally have a deal, you have specific steps that must be accomplished to take you from contract to closing. Follow the timelines of these steps detailed carefully as the failure to meet timelines is one of the main things that real estate agents find themselves sued over by their clients when things go wrong.

When a buyer and seller go to closing, they are each given a copy of the closing disclosure which shows a financial summary of the deal. Items are credited (+) or debited (-) to each party according to who is liable to or owed monies from the other party. These calculations are based on the day of closing. A credit means that the person who gets the credit is receiving money. A debit means that the person who gets the debit is being charged money.

Closing Disclosure

- Financial summary of the deal

Proration

- Charges and credits divided between parties according to who owes whom

Amounts are calculated based on day of closing

- Credit = one party receives money
- Debit = one party is charged money

http://thismatter.com/money/real-estate/real-estate-closing.htm

What needs to be prorated?

Items that are paid in advance or arrears are prorated between buyer and seller according to date of closing. For investment property that has a tenant, the rent that the seller collected at the first of the month will need to be prorated.

Meaning a credit will be given to the buyer and a debit to the seller for the amount of the rent owed to the buyer who will be taking over the rental property.

- Prepaid Rent
- County and/or city taxes
- Mortgage interest on assumed mortgages
- Home Owner Association Fees

What needs to be prorated?

County and state taxes are paid behind, or in arrears. That means that a tax bill will come that the seller owes after he has passed property onto the buyer. So, the buyer will end up having to pay the tax bill. To make this equitable, the seller must pay his portion of the tax bill at closing. It will be entered as a credit to the buyer and debit to the seller.

- Prepaid Rent

- County and/or city taxes

- Mortgage interest on assumed mortgages

- Home Owner Association Fees

http://www.realtor.com/advice/finance/understanding-the-earnest-money-deposit-2/

What needs to be prorated?

Items that are paid in advance or arears are prorated between buyer and seller according to date of closing. For investment property that has tenant, the rent that the seller collected at the first of the month will need to be prorated. This means a credit will be given to the buyer and a debit to the seller for the amount of the rent owed to the buyer who will be taking over the rental property.

A seller collects rent in advance, so the seller will need to pay the buyer. Any rents already paid are split according to who owns property during period paid or owed – usually split with some of the rent being retained by the seller for the days already passed and rest credited to the buyer. County and city taxes must be prorated, as well as mortgage interest on assumed mortgages and home owner association fees.

- Prepaid Rent

- County and/or city taxes

- Mortgage interest on assumed mortgages

- Home Owner Association Fees

What needs to be prorated?

Mortgage interest is also paid in arrears. That means that if a buyer assumes a mortgage as part of the deal, interest that the seller owes for the number of days he owned the property that month will be given as a credit to the buyer. It will be entered as a debit to the seller.

- Prepaid Rent

- County and/or city taxes

- Mortgage interest on assumed mortgages

- Home Owner Association Fees

What needs to be prorated?

Home owner association fees are paid ahead, meaning that the seller has paid a billing period that the buyer will now owe the seller for at closing. This will be entered as a credit to the seller and a debit to the buyer.

What needs to be prorated?

Know that items that are paid in arrears are entered as a credit to the buyer and a debit to the seller. Items paid ahead are entered as a credit to the seller and a debit to the buyer.

Items paid in arrears-

Entered as a credit to the buyer and a debit to the seller

Items paid ahead-

Entered as a credit to the seller and a debit to the buyer

Proration Methods

When asked to calculate prorations for the end of course exam and the state licensing exam, pay attention to whether you are being directed to use the statutory method or actual calendar days.

The statutory method is basically a shortcut because it assumes that there are 30 days in every month and 360 days in a year, which of course there are not. Thus, this method isn't 100% accurate – and is therefore not used when prorations are calculated for a real closing. If you are directed to use this method, consider it a time saver. More than likely, though, you will be asked to use the actual day method. This means you will have to be able to recall how many days there are in every month.

When calculating using actual days for an entire year, use 365 days.

If you are not told which method to use, always use the actual number of days. Keep in mind, though, that even with the actual day method for the real estate exam; 28 days would be used for February (not 29).

When calculating prorations use either:

- Statutory Method
    - 30-day-month / 360 Days a year
- Actual Number of Days
    - Actual days of the month / 365 Days a year

http://autopia.com.au/novated-leases-the-autopian-special-edition/what-is-the-statutory-method

Proration methods

To prorate using actual number of days may mean using 365 for a full year or it may mean knowing exactly how many days are in the months involved in the calculation. Most people learned the days of the week without any extra effort while in elementary school. However, many other people who struggle to remember utilize a nursery rhyme to recall how many days are in which month.

Thirty Days hath September poem:

**Thirty days hath September,
April, June and November;
February has twenty eight alone
All the rest have thirty-one
Except in Leap Year, that's the time
When February's Days are twenty-nine**

Jan Mar May Jul Aug Oct Dec

Feb Apr Jun

Sep Nov

Yet, others that still struggle to recall which month has how many days find it necessary to resort to the knuckle method. This is a trick that involves counting the months on your knuckles and the grooves between the knuckles. Form two fists and butt your fits together. January is tagged as your far left knuckle. February drops to the right space between the knuckle. March is on the second knuckle. April the space in between the second and third knuckle. May is back on the third knuckle. June drops down and July is on the fourth knuckle. You skip the thumb knuckles, so August is actually on the first left knuckle on the right hand. September drops down etc. And every month that landed on a knuckle has 31 days. Every month that landed on a space between knuckles is 30 days (or 28 for February).

Know that for the real estate test, using the actual number of days ALWAYS use 28 days for February.

http://www.rhymes.org.uk/thirty_days_hath_september.htm

Prorate Rental Income

The best way to explain how to prorate is to demonstrate how it is calculated. In this example a condo unit is being used for rental income. The closing is scheduled for April 15th. The closing day will be the buyer's day meaning the buyer gets to keep the rental income for that day – April 15th. How would a $1,500 rent payment for the month of April, already collected by the seller, be prorated?

- A condo rental unit will close on April 15 and the closing day belongs to the buyer.
- The seller has collected the rent of $1,500 at the beginning of the month.
- What is the proration?
- How will it be applied on the closing statement?

Solution – Prorate Rental Income

Rent has been paid for the month. Seller will not own property for full month, therefore part of the rent is due to the seller, because he will own the property for a portion of the month. With the 15th day due the buyer, the 1st through the 14th is the seller's income.

The seller owes the buyer from the 15th (including the 15th) thru the 30th. There are 30 days in April. $1,500 rent ÷ 30 days in April = $50 per day for rent. $50 x 16 days = $800 due to buyer for time he will own property (a Credit) and this comes from the seller who has already collected so a $800 debit to seller.

- The buyer is due rents from closing date to end of month.
- From the 15th of April to the 30th is 16 days of rent due buyer
- $1,500 ÷ 30 = $50 per day × 16 days = $800.
- Debit seller $800, Credit buyer $800.

http://thismatter.com/money/real-estate/real-estate-closing.htm

Prorate Property Tax

Here's an example of how to prorate property tax. $1,580 in property taxes for the year. Closing day of May 15 with closing day charged to buyer (leaving 14 days charged to seller in May). Use the 365 method.

- The property taxes are $1,580 for the year.
- The day of closing is May 15 and is charged to the buyer.
- Calculate using the 365-day method.
- Who will receive a credit and who will have a debit?

http://thismatter.com/money/real-estate/real-estate-closing.htm

Solution – Prorate Property Tax

- First, know that taxes are paid in arrears. This means that there will be a debit to the seller and a credit to buyer. Calculate how many days the seller will have owned the property and owes for taxes.
- This covers the time period January 1 to May 14. Remember that the buyer owes for the day of closing, the 15th. There are 31 days in January plus 28 days in February plus 31 days in March plus 30 days in April plus the 14 days in May, which equals 134 days.
- Now calculate tax due per day. $1580 ÷ 365days = $4.3287671 per day. Multiply tax per day by number of days that the seller owned the property and still owes tax. $4.3287671 x 134days = $580.05.
- On the closing disclosure, there will be a debit to the seller of $580.05 and a credit to the buyer of $580.05.

- First you must calculate how many days the seller owes the buyer at closing:
  - January 1 to May 14 = 134 days
  - 31 (Jan) + 28 (Feb) + 31 (Mar) + 30 (Apr) + 14 (May)= 134 days
- Then you must calculate how much is owed for each day and multiply the # of seller days owed

- o $1580 ÷ 365 = $4.3287671 per day × 134 days = $580.05
- o Debit seller $580.05, Credit buyer $580.05

http://www.dummies.com/how-to/content/how-to-calculate-proration-for-the-real-estate-lic.html

Prorate Interest on Assumed Loan

A buyer purchases a property scheduled to close on June 10, the 10th going to buyer. The seller owes the buyer for the first 9 days of June since the interest on the mortgage is paid for the previous month and he will not be making the payments in July to cover that. Interest on an assumable mortgage is paid in arrears (pay interest for June in July), so seller owes to buyer for first 9 days of June.

- A buyer is purchasing a property scheduled to close June 10. Closing day to Buyer. The next mortgage payment due July 1.

- There is an assumable loan with a balance of $150,000 @ 5%

- Calculate the proration and how is this is charged on closing statement

http://thismatter.com/money/real-estate/real-estate-closing.htm

Solution - Interest Proration

Know that mortgage interest is paid in arrears. The interest for June won't be paid until July. The interest for the nine days in June that the seller has possession will not be paid until the buyer has possession and making payments. The seller owes 9 days interest to the buyer.

To calculate the daily interest rate, you must first calculate the annual interest by multiplying the interest rate by the balance of the mortgage. You then divide by 365 days to get a daily interest rate of $20.547945. Multiply his daily figure by the 9 days and you have $184.93 (rounded) as the amount owed by the seller for accrued interest. This is paid as a debit to the seller for $184.93 and a credit to the buyer for $184.93.

The interest due for June won't be paid until July, so the seller owes the buyer for the first 9 days of June.

The rate of interest is calculated:

- $150,000 x .05 = $7,500 ÷ 365 days = $20.547945 per day
- $20.547945 x 9 days = $184.93
- Debit the seller $184.93
- Credit the Buyer $184.93

TRANSFER TAXES

IV)   State Transfer Taxes

   A) State documentary stamp tax on deeds

   B) State intangible tax on mortgages

   C) State documentary stamp tax on notes

State Transfer Taxes

In the state of Florida, there are transfer taxes that must be paid by either the buyer or the seller when a property exchanges hands.

Doc stamps on the deed are based on sales price and paid by the seller at $.70 per $100 of sale price. Doc stamps on the mortgages (promissory notes both new and assumed mortgages) are paid by the buyer as $.35 per $100 increments of the total mortgages.

An intangible tax is paid by the buyer on NEW mortgages (not assumed mortgages) and are paid on the value of the new mortgage at $.002 of every dollar.

Deed

- State doc stamp on Deed is $.70 per $100 of sale price.

Mortgages (notes)

- State doc stamp on note(s) is $.35 per $100 of note.

NEW Mortgages (not assumed)

- State intangible tax NEW note is $.002 per $1 of note.

http://dor.myflorida.com/dor/taxes/doc_stamp.html

Let's look at this a different way. The only thing charged to the seller is the doc stamp on the deed. The buyer pays the doc stamp on the note and the intangible tax. The doc stamp on the deed is based on the sale price. The doc stamp on the promissory note is based on the total of the new and assumed mortgages.

The intangible tax is based on the new mortgage only. The doc stamp on the deed is paid on every $100 of value so the purchase price is divided by 100 and then rounded up before multiplying by the .7 tax rate.

The doc stamp on the note is also paid on every 100 increment, so the total mortgages are divided by 100 then rounded up before multiplying by the .35 tax rate. The intangible tax is paid on every dollar of the new mortgage. So, simply take the new mortgage amount and multiply by the .002 tax rate. Memorize this process and memorize these tax rates.

http://dor.myflorida.com/dor/taxes/doc_stamp.html

Rules for Calculating Doc Stamps

On Deed	On Note	Intangible Tax
Charged to Seller	Charged to Buyer	Charged to Buyer
Based on Sale Price	Based on total of New and Assumed mortgages	Based on New mortgage ONLY
Take Sale Price ÷100 Round Up	Take Total of Mortgages ÷100 Round Up	Calculate on EVERY $
× .70	× .35	× .002

Doc Stamps on Deed Example

Seller only pays for doc stamps on the deed. So, the purchase price of $180,000 is what the seller pays doc stamps on.

Doc stamps on the deed are: purchase price ÷ 100 x $.70 = Doc stamps on deed.

- A condo is sold by Bold Realty for $180,550.

- What does the seller pay for documentary stamps?

Solution – Doc stamps on deed

- $180,550 ÷ $100 = 1805.5
- Round up to $1806 Taxable value
- 1806 x $.70 Tax rate

= $1,264.20 Doc stamps on deed.

http://dor.myflorida.com/Forms_library/current/gt800014.pdf

Example of doc stamps on Notes (not intangible)

Doc stamps on the notes (not intangible tax) are on both new and assumed notes(mortgages). There are $153,420 in mortgages.

- A purchaser is assuming a loan for $53,420. And the buyer also takes out a new mortgage for $100,000.

- What are the doc stamps on the mortgages (promissory notes)?

Solution – Doc Stamps on Notes (not intangible tax)

Take the total of all mortgages, new and assumed: $100,000 + $53,420 = $153,420 Total notes. Divide the $153,420 by 100 to equal $1534.20.

Round Up to $1535. Do not round down! Then, multiply the $1535 by .35 to equal $537.25, which is the tax due on the promissory notes.

$100,000 + $53,420 = $153,420 Total notes

$153,420 ÷ 100 = $1534.20

Round Up to $1535

$1535 x .35 = $537.25.

Intangible Tax Example

Intangible tax is due on NEW notes only. New mortgages are taxed at $.002 per dollar of new money.

- A condo is purchased by assuming an existing loan of $53,420 and acquiring a new mortgage for $100,000.

- What is the Intangible Tax due?

Intangible Tax solution

Remember, that you do not pay intangible tax on assumed mortgages. Intangible tax is due on all NEW mortgages only. The rate is $.002 per every dollar of new note. So, simply take the $100,000 new mortgage x .002 = $200 intangible tax due.

- New mortgages x $.002 = Intangible tax due
- $100,000 x $.002 = $200 Intangible tax

OTHER CHARGES

V) Other Charges

    A) Preparation of document

    B) Recording fees

    C) Broker's commission

    D) Title insurance

Preparation of Documents

When preparing for a closing, be aware of how other charges are also handled.

Closing involves the preparation of documents. The person who usually must sign the document pays for it. The deed for example must be signed by the seller and is charged to the seller unless otherwise negotiated. It will be entered as a debit to the seller with no entry on the buyer's side.

This is called a single-entry item rather than as a double entry used with prorations. The mortgage and note are signed by the buyer and are normally paid for by the buyer. It will be entered as a debit to the buyer with no entry for the seller.

The person who usually must sign the document pays for it.

Deed

- Normally paid for by the seller
- Entered as a debit to the seller (NOT entered on the buyer's side)

Mortgage and Note

- Normally paid for by the buyer
- Entered as a debit to the buyer (NOT entered on the seller's side)

Htt p://thismatter.com/money/real-estate/real-estate-closing.htm

Recording Fees

Constructive notice is given when something is recorded. The person who benefits from the document being recorded normally pays to have it recorded. The deed is a good example of this which is paid for by the buyer.

Who benefits from the constructive notice that recording provides?

This is the person who normally pays for the recording.

- o Recorded Deed
  - ▪ Normally paid for by the buyer

- Entered as a debit to the buyer (NOT entered on the seller's side)

http://thismatter.com/money/real-estate/real-estate-closing.htm

Brokers' Commission

The broker commission is usually paid by the seller or whoever employed the broker, unless otherwise negotiated beforehand on the contract. It is entered as a debit to the party being charged.

- Broker commission is usually paid by the seller or whoever employed the broker, unless otherwise negotiated beforehand on the contract.
- Entered as a debit to the party being charged

Title Insurance

There are two types of Title Insurance. The owner's policy is a negotiable item and will be paid by either the seller or buyer depending upon the terms of the purchase contract.

The lender's policy is a buyer's fee as it is something required by the buyer's lender. However, it can be paid by the seller if negotiated in the contract.

- Owner's Insurance
  - o This is a negotiable item as to who pays
- Lender's Insurance
  - o This is mandatory by lenders and is considered a buyer's fee
- Can be paid by the seller if negotiated

http://thismatter.com/money/real-estate/real-estate-closing.htm

RULES OF THUMB

VI) Rules of Thumb

   A) General rule of thumb

      1) Items credited to seller

      2) Items debited to seller

      3) Items credited to buyer

      4) Items debited to buyer

General Rule of Thumb

Memorize these basic rules regarding the closing disclosure.

On the closing disclosure, most items are entered on both the buyer and seller sides. This is called a double entry system. There are some exceptions where the item is only put on either the buyer or seller side as appropriate. These exceptions include the buyer's deposit – credit to the buyer; existing mortgage being paid off – debit to the seller; new mortgage obtained from a financial institution – credit to the buyer; and some other expenses already discussed under "other charges" -- document preparation; recording fees; broker's commission; and title insurance. These items are only going to go to either the buyer or the seller as a credit or debit. Not to both.

Most items are entered on both the buyer and seller sides.

- Called a double entry system

Exceptions (only appear for one party)

- Buyer's deposit – credit to the buyer
- Existing mortgage being paid off – debit to the seller
- New mortgage obtained from a financial institution – credit to the buyer
- Expenses (see other charges)
  - Document preparation
  - Recording fees
  - Broker's commission
  - Title insurance

Items Credited to Seller

The seller receives the purchase price and a 'rebate' on items that were prepaid such as home owner association fees. This is CREDITED to the seller at closing.

- Total purchase price

- Prepaid items

- Home Owner Association Fees

  http://www.realestateproarticles.com/Art/38394/263/Real-Estate-Closing-Costs-Who-Pays-What.html

Items Debited to Seller

Items that the seller usually signs and pays for are charged to the seller including the broker commission, mortgage payoff, buyer's second held by the seller, deed prep, seller attorney fees, doc stamps on deed, owners title insurance, prorated taxes, interest rents and any security deposits held.

- Broker's commission
- Mortgage(s) paid off or held by seller
- Deed preparation
- Seller's attorney fees
- State documentary stamps on the deed
- Owner's Title insurance
- Prorated taxes, interest, advance rent
- Security deposit

http://www.realestateproarticles.com/Art/38394/263/Real-Estate-Closing-Costs-Who-Pays-What.html

Items Credited to Buyer

Credited to buyer: any earnest money (down payment), new or assumed mortgages, prorated taxes, advance rents and security deposits held by the seller.

- Mortgages; new or assumed
- Earnest money deposit
- Prorated property taxes, unpaid interest and paid rents
- Security deposits held by seller

Items Debited to Buyer

Buyer is charged as a debit the purchase price, doc stamps on all mortgages, mortgage note prep, owner's title, recording of dee and mortgage and any attorney fees incurred by the buyer.

- Purchase price
- State documentary stamps on all notes
- Mortgage note prep
- Title insurance (owner's policy)
- Recording Deed
- Recording Mortgage
- Attorney's fees(buyer)

http://www.realestateproarticles.com/Art/38394/263/Real-Estate-Closing-Costs-Who-Pays-What.html

VII) Uniform Settlement Statement

A) Buyer's Transaction Entries

B) Seller's Transaction Entries

C) Settlement Charges for both Buyer and Seller

D) Real Estate settlement example

VII) Uniform Settlement Statement

The Consumer Financial Protection Bureau provides a sample closing summary to teach consumers how to understand their closing statement.

The link to this summary can be found at http://www.consumerfinance.gov/owning-a-home/closing-disclosure/

It is also provided as attached material in this section. This summary is used in the following discussion to present a real estate settlement example.

VII) Uniform Settlement Statement

Michael Jones and Mary Stone currently residing at 123 Anywhere Street, Anytown, ST 12345 are purchasing a property from Steve Cole and Amy Doe of 321 Somewhere Drive, Anytown, ST 12345.

The purchase price is $180,000. Michael and Mary put $10,000 down as earnest money and took out a loan for $162,000 at 3.875%. Their estimated PITI monthly payment, plus mortgage insurance is $1,50.26.

Steve and Amy, the sellers, agreed to pay $2,500 toward the buyer's closing costs. Plus, they paid for a home inspection and a home warranty. At closing, Steve and Amy had their own closing costs to pay which included $11,400 in real estate fees. They also had to pay off their mortgage of $100,000. They had a credit coming for advance home owner association payment, but still owed their part of the year's real estate taxes.

Uniform Settlement Statement

VII) Uniform Settlement Statement

Page 1 of the Closing Disclosure highlights the buyer's loan terms. It is presented in the same format as on the required loan estimate in order for the buyer to make a fair comparison to the terms promised from the lender.

Michael and Mary are getting a loan for $162,000 at 3.875% with a principal and interest payment of $761.78. There is a prepayment penalty.

Loan Terms		Can this amount increase after closing?
Loan Amount	$162,000	NO
Interest Rate	3.875%	NO
Monthly Principal & Interest See Projected Payments below for your Estimated Total Monthly Payment	$761.78	NO
		Does the loan have these features?
Prepayment Penalty		YES • As high as $3,240 if you pay off the loan during the first 2 years
Balloon Payment		NO

Uniform Settlement Statement

VII) Uniform Settlement Statement

Page 1 continues by breaking down the buyer payment.

Projected Payments		
Payment Calculation	Years 1-7	Years 8-30
Principal & Interest	$761.78	$761.78
Mortgage Insurance	+ 82.35	+ —
Estimated Escrow *Amount can increase over time*	+ 206.13	+ 206.13
Estimated Total Monthly Payment	$1,050.26	$967.91

		This estimate includes	In escrow?
Estimated Taxes, Insurance & Assessments *Amount can increase over time* *See page 4 for details*	$356.13 a month	☒ Property Taxes	YES
		☒ Homeowner's Insurance	YES
		☒ Other: Homeowner's Association Dues	NO
		See Escrow Account on page 4 for details. You must pay for other property costs separately.	

Uniform Settlement Statement

VII) Uniform Settlement Statement

Page 1 summarizes the amount of closing costs charged to the buyer and the amount the buyer needs to bring to closing as cash. These numbers are explained on 2 and 3.

Costs at Closing		
Closing Costs	$9,712.10	Includes $4,694.05 in Loan Costs + $5,018.05 in Other Costs – $0 in Lender Credits. *See page 2 for details.*
Cash to Close	$14,147.26	Includes Closing Costs. *See Calculating Cash to Close on page 3 for details.*

Uniform Settlement Statement

VII) Uniform Settlement Statement

Buyer's Transaction Entries

Page 2 begins by breaking down the buyer's transaction entries which includes loan costs.

Closing Cost Details

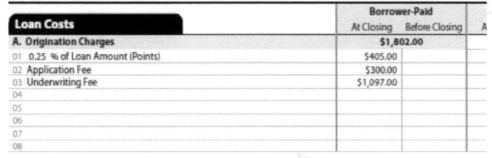

Loan Costs	Borrower-Paid		A
	At Closing	Before Closing	
A. Origination Charges	**$1,802.00**		
01 0.25 % of Loan Amount (Points)	$405.00		
02 Application Fee	$300.00		
03 Underwriting Fee	$1,097.00		
04			
05			
06			
07			
08			

Uniform Settlement Statement

VII) Uniform Settlement Statement

Buyer's Transaction Entries

Page 2 begins by breaking down the buyer's transaction entries .... And then loan service fees are added that the buyer was charged but had no control over such as a credit report fee.

B. Services Borrower Did Not Shop For		$236.55		
01 Appraisal Fee	to John Smith Appraisers Inc.			
02 Credit Report Fee	to Information Inc.		$29.80	
03 Flood Determination Fee	to Info Co.	$20.00		
04 Flood Monitoring Fee	to Info Co.	$31.75		
05 Tax Monitoring Fee	to Info Co.	$75.00		
06 Tax Status Research Fee	to Info Co.	$80.00		
07				
08				
09				

Uniform Settlement Statement

VII) Uniform Settlement Statement

Buyer's Transaction Entries

Page 2 begins by breaking down the buyer's transaction entries .... And things the buyer was able to "shop" for by choosing the provider but were required as a loan cost such as a survey company.

10				
C. Services Borrower Did Shop For			$2,655.50	
01 Pest Inspection Fee	to Pests Co.	$120.50		
02 Survey Fee	to Surveys Co.	$85.00		
03 Title – Insurance Binder	to Epsilon Title Co.	$650.00		
04 Title – Lender's Title Insurance	to Epsilon Title Co.	$500.00		
05 Title – Settlement Agent Fee	to Epsilon Title Co.	$500.00		
06 Title – Title Search	to Epsilon Title Co.	$800.00		
07				

Uniform Settlement Statement

VII) Uniform Settlement Statement

Buyer's Transaction Entries

Until about half way down Page 2, the buyer's transaction entries -the buyer loan fees are totaled.

A. Origination Charges	$1,802.00	
B. Services Borrower Did Not Shop For	$236.55	
C. Services Borrower Did Shop For	$2,655.50	
D. TOTAL LOAN COSTS (Borrower-Paid)	$4,694.05	
Loan Costs Subtotals (A + B + C)	$4,664.25	$29.80

Uniform Settlement Statement

VII) Uniform Settlement Statement

Buyer's Transaction Entries

Page 2 continues by breaking down the buyer's transaction entries …. Other costs to the buyer is then totaled such as insurance money put into escrow

Other Costs		
E. Taxes and Other Government Fees	**$85.00**	
01 Recording Fees Deed: $40.00 Mortgage: $45.00	$85.00	
02 Transfer Tax to Any State		
F. Prepaids	**$2,120.80**	
01 Homeowner's Insurance Premium (12 mo.) to Insurance Co.	$1,209.96	
02 Mortgage Insurance Premium (mo.)		
03 Prepaid Interest ($17.44 per day from 4/15/13 to 5/1/13)	$279.04	
04 Property Taxes (6 mo.) to Any County USA	$631.80	
05		
G. Initial Escrow Payment at Closing	**$412.25**	
01 Homeowner's Insurance $100.83 per month for 2 mo.	$201.66	
02 Mortgage Insurance per month for mo.		
03 Property Taxes $105.30 per month for 2 mo.	$210.60	
04		
05		
06		
07		
08 Aggregate Adjustment	− 0.01	

Uniform Settlement Statement

VII) Uniform Settlement Statement

Buyer's Transaction Entries

Page 2 continues by breaking down the buyer's transaction entries …. Other costs are added until finally the Total Closing Costs (Borrower-Paid) match Page 1

G. Initial Escrow Payment at Closing	$412.25	
H. Other	**$2,400.00**	
01 HOA Capital Contribution to HOA Acre Inc.	$500.00	
02 HOA Processing Fee to HOA Acre Inc.	$150.00	
03 Home Inspection Fee to Engineers Inc.	$750.00	
04 Home Warranty Fee to XYZ Warranty Inc.		
05 Real Estate Commission to Alpha Real Estate Broker		
06 Real Estate Commission to Omega Real Estate Broker		
07 Title – Owner's Title Insurance (optional) to Epsilon Title Co.	$1,000.00	
08		
I. TOTAL OTHER COSTS (Borrower-Paid)	**$5,018.05**	
Other Costs Subtotals (E + F + G + H)	$5,018.05	
J. TOTAL CLOSING COSTS (Borrower-Paid)	**$9,712.10**	
Closing Costs Subtotals (D + I)	$9,682.30	$29.80
Lender Credits		

Uniform Settlement Statement

VII) Uniform Settlement Statement

Seller's Transaction Entries

Also on Page 2, to the far right; any expenses charged to the seller are added such as the real estate commission, seller paid inspection and home warranty.

Closing Cost Details

Loan Costs		Borrower-Paid		Seller-Paid		Paid by Others
		At Closing	Before Closing	At Closing	Before Closing	

Other Costs			Borrower-Paid		Seller-Paid		Paid by Others
E. Taxes and Other Government Fees			**$85.00**				
01 Recording Fees	Deed: $40.00	Mortgage: $45.00	$85.00				
02 Transfer Tax	to Any State				$950.00		
H. Other			**$2,400.00**				
01 HOA Capital Contribution	to HOA Acre Inc.		$500.00				
02 HOA Processing Fee	to HOA Acre Inc.		$150.00				
03 Home Inspection Fee	to Engineers Inc.		$750.00			$750.00	
04 Home Warranty Fee	to XYZ Warranty Inc.				$450.00		
05 Real Estate Commission	to Alpha Real Estate Broker				$5,700.00		
06 Real Estate Commission	to Omega Real Estate Broker				$5,700.00		
07 Title – Owner's Title Insurance (optional)	to Epsilon Title Co.		$1,000.00				
08							
I. TOTAL OTHER COSTS (Borrower-Paid)			**$5,018.05**				
Other Costs Subtotals (E + F + G + H)			$5,018.05				
J. TOTAL CLOSING COSTS (Borrower-Paid)			**$9,712.10**				
Closing Costs Subtotals (D + I)			$9,682.30	$29.80	$12,800.00	$750.00	$405.00

Uniform Settlement Statement

VII) Uniform Settlement Statement

Settlement Charges for both Buyer and Seller

Page 3 details the items prorated between the buyer and seller plus other items that are only attributed to either the buyer or seller.

The purchase price is a debit to the buyer and a credit to the seller.

The total closing costs still to be paid by the buyer at closing from page 2 is added as a debit to the buyer. (It is not entered on the seller's side.)

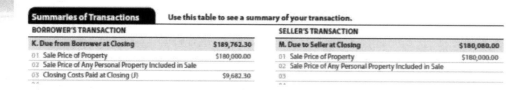

Summaries of Transactions	Use this table to see a summary of your transaction.				
BORROWER'S TRANSACTION			**SELLER'S TRANSACTION**		
K. Due from Borrower at Closing		**$189,762.30**	**M. Due to Seller at Closing**		**$180,080.00**
01 Sale Price of Property		$180,000.00	01 Sale Price of Property		$180,000.00
02 Sale Price of Any Personal Property Included in Sale			02 Sale Price of Any Personal Property Included in Sale		
03 Closing Costs Paid at Closing (J)		$9,682.30	03		

Uniform Settlement Statement

VII) Uniform Settlement Statement

Settlement Charges for both Buyer and Seller

Page 3 details the items prorated between the buyer and seller plus other items that are only attributed to either the buyer or seller... Anything paid in advance by the seller is shown here, such as home owner association dues, and is added as a debit to the buyer and a credit to the seller.

07

Adjustments for Items Paid by Seller in Advance			
08	City/Town Taxes	to	
09	County Taxes	to	
10	Assessments	to	
11	HOA Dues	4/15/13 to 4/30/13	$80.00
12			

08

Adjustments for Items Paid by Seller in Advance			
09	City/Town Taxes	to	
10	County Taxes	to	
11	Assessments	to	
12	HOA Dues	4/15/13 to 4/30/13	$80.00
13			

Uniform Settlement Statement

VII) Uniform Settlement Statement

Settlement Charges for both Buyer and Seller

Page 3 details the items prorated between the buyer and seller plus other items that are only attributed to either the buyer or seller... Anything paid in advance by the buyer or on behalf of the buyer is added here on the left and this includes the earnest money deposit and the buyer's new loan which is shown as a debit to the buyer (and not put on the seller side). Anything still due from the seller is added on the right such as closing costs from Page 2, a mortgage that the seller had on the property, and closing costs the seller agreed to pay to help out the buyer. All debits to the seller.

15

L. Paid Already by or on Behalf of Borrower at Closing	$175,615.04
01 Deposit	$10,000.00
02 Loan Amount	$162,000.00
03 Existing Loan(s) Assumed or Taken Subject to	
04	
05 Seller Credit	$2,500.00
Other Credits	
06 Rebate from Epsilon Title Co.	$750.00
07	
Adjustments	
08	

16

N. Due from Seller at Closing	$115,665.04
01 Excess Deposit	
02 Closing Costs Paid at Closing (J)	$12,800.00
03 Existing Loan(s) Assumed or Taken Subject to	
04 Payoff of First Mortgage Loan	$100,000.00
05 Payoff of Second Mortgage Loan	
06	
07	
08 Seller Credit	$2,500.00
09	
10	

Uniform Settlement Statement

VII) Uniform Settlement Statement

Settlement Charges for both Buyer and Seller

Page 3 details the items prorated between the buyer and seller plus other items that are only attributed to either the buyer or seller... Property taxes and assessment are paid in arrears, so they are added to the buyer side as a credit and the seller side as a debit – prorated.

Adjustments for Items Unpaid by Seller

12	City/Town Taxes 1/1/13 to 4/14/13		$365.04
13	County Taxes	to	
14	Assessments	to	
15			

Adjustments for Items Unpaid by Seller

14	City/Town Taxes 1/1/13 to 4/14/13		$365.04
15	County Taxes	to	
16	Assessments	to	
17			

Uniform Settlement Statement

VII) Uniform Settlement Statement

Settlement Charges for both Buyer and Seller

Page 3 details the items prorated between the buyer and seller plus other items that are only attributed to either the buyer or seller... Until the finally totals are calculated at the bottom of page 3 adding and subtracting the columns.

Summaries of Transactions — Use this table to see a summary of your transaction.

BORROWER'S TRANSACTION		SELLER'S TRANSACTION	
K. Due from Borrower at Closing	$189,762.30	M. Due to Seller at Closing	$180,080.00
L. Paid Already by or on Behalf of Borrower at Closing	$175,615.04	N. Due from Seller at Closing	$115,665.04

CALCULATION		CALCULATION	
Total Due from Borrower at Closing (K)	$189,762.30	Total Due to Seller at Closing (M)	$180,080.00
Total Paid Already by or on Behalf of Borrower at Closing (L)	– $175,615.04	Total Due from Seller at Closing (N)	– $115,665.04
Cash to Close ☒ From ☐ To Borrower	**$14,147.26**	**Cash** ☐ From ☒ To Seller	**$64,414.96**

This Disclosure Summary can be located through The Consumer Financial Protection Bureau.

http://www.consumerfinance.gov/owning-a-home/closing-disclosure/

Closing Disclosure

This form is a statement of final loan terms and closing costs. Compare this document with your Loan Estimate.

Closing Information

Date Issued	4/15/2013
Closing Date	4/15/2013
Disbursement Date	4/15/2013
Settlement Agent	Epsilon Title Co.
File #	12-3456
Property	456 Somewhere Ave
	Anytown, ST 12345
Sale Price	$180,000

Transaction Information

Borrower	Michael Jones and Mary Stone
	123 Anywhere Street
	Anytown, ST 12345
Seller	Steve Cole and Amy Doe
	321 Somewhere Drive
	Anytown, ST 12345
Lender	Ficus Bank

Loan Information

Loan Term	30 years
Purpose	Purchase
Product	Fixed Rate
Loan Type	☒ Conventional ☐ FHA ☐ VA ☐ _____
Loan ID #	123456789
MIC #	000654321

Loan Terms

		Can this amount increase after closing?
Loan Amount	$162,000	NO
Interest Rate	3.875%	NO
Monthly Principal & Interest See Projected Payments below for your Estimated Total Monthly Payment	$761.78	NO
		Does the loan have these features?
Prepayment Penalty		YES • As high as $3,240 if you pay off the loan during the first 2 years
Balloon Payment		NO

Projected Payments

Payment Calculation	Years 1-7	Years 8-30
Principal & Interest	$761.78	$761.78
Mortgage Insurance	+ 82.35	+ —
Estimated Escrow Amount can increase over time	+ 206.13	+ 206.13
Estimated Total Monthly Payment	$1,050.26	$967.91

Estimated Taxes, Insurance & Assessments Amount can increase over time See page 4 for details	$356.13 a month	This estimate includes ☒ Property Taxes ☒ Homeowner's Insurance ☒ Other: Homeowner's Association Dues See Escrow Account on page 4 for details. You must pay for other property costs separately.	In escrow? YES YES NO

Costs at Closing

Closing Costs	$9,712.10	Includes $4,694.05 in Loan Costs + $5,018.05 in Other Costs – $0 in Lender Credits. See page 2 for details.
Cash to Close	$14,147.26	Includes Closing Costs. See Calculating Cash to Close on page 3 for details.

CLOSING DISCLOSURE

PAGE 1 OF 5 • LOAN ID # 123456789

Closing Cost Details

Loan Costs		Borrower-Paid		Seller-Paid		Paid by Others
		At Closing	Before Closing	At Closing	Before Closing	
A. Origination Charges		**$1,802.00**				
01 0.25 % of Loan Amount (Points)		$405.00				
02 Application Fee		$300.00				
03 Underwriting Fee		$1,097.00				
04						
05						
06						
07						
08						
B. Services Borrower Did Not Shop For		**$236.55**				
01 Appraisal Fee	to John Smith Appraisers Inc.					$405.00
02 Credit Report Fee	to Information Inc.		$29.80			
03 Flood Determination Fee	to Info Co.	$20.00				
04 Flood Monitoring Fee	to Info Co.	$31.75				
05 Tax Monitoring Fee	to Info Co.	$75.00				
06 Tax Status Research Fee	to Info Co.	$80.00				
07						
08						
09						
10						
C. Services Borrower Did Shop For		**$2,655.50**				
01 Pest Inspection Fee	to Pests Co.	$120.50				
02 Survey Fee	to Surveys Co.	$85.00				
03 Title – Insurance Binder	to Epsilon Title Co.	$650.00				
04 Title – Lender's Title Insurance	to Epsilon Title Co.	$500.00				
05 Title – Settlement Agent Fee	to Epsilon Title Co.	$500.00				
05 Title – Title Search	to Epsilon Title Co.	$800.00				
07						
08						
D. TOTAL LOAN COSTS (Borrower-Paid)		**$4,694.05**				
Loan Costs Subtotals (A + B + C)		$4,664.25	$29.80			

Other Costs		Borrower-Paid		Seller-Paid		Paid by Others
		At Closing	Before Closing	At Closing	Before Closing	
E. Taxes and Other Government Fees		**$85.00**				
01 Recording Fees	Deed: $40.00 Mortgage: $45.00	$85.00				
02 Transfer Tax	to Any State			$950.00		
F. Prepaids		**$2,120.80**				
01 Homeowner's Insurance Premium (12 mo.) to Insurance Co.		$1,209.96				
02 Mortgage Insurance Premium (mo.)						
03 Prepaid Interest ($17.44 per day from 4/15/13 to 5/1/13)		$279.04				
04 Property Taxes (6 mo.) to Any County USA		$631.80				
05						
G. Initial Escrow Payment at Closing		**$412.25**				
01 Homeowner's Insurance $100.83 per month for 2 mo.		$201.66				
02 Mortgage Insurance per month for mo.						
03 Property Taxes $105.30 per month for 2 mo.		$210.60				
04						
05						
06						
07						
08 Aggregate Adjustment		−0.01				
H. Other		**$2,400.00**				
01 HOA Capital Contribution	to HOA Acre Inc.	$500.00				
02 HOA Processing Fee	to HOA Acre Inc.	$150.00				
03 Home Inspection Fee	to Engineers Inc.	$750.00			$750.00	
04 Home Warranty Fee	to XYZ Warranty Inc.			$450.00		
05 Real Estate Commission	to Alpha Real Estate Broker			$5,700.00		
06 Real Estate Commission	to Omega Real Estate Broker			$5,700.00		
07 Title – Owner's Title Insurance (optional) to Epsilon Title Co.		$1,000.00				
08						
I. TOTAL OTHER COSTS (Borrower-Paid)		**$5,018.05**				
Other Costs Subtotals (E + F + G + H)		$5,018.05				

		Borrower-Paid		Seller-Paid		Paid by Others
J. TOTAL CLOSING COSTS (Borrower-Paid)		**$9,712.10**				
Closing Costs Subtotals (D + I)		$9,682.30	$29.80	$12,800.00	$750.00	$405.00
Lender Credits						

Calculating Cash to Close

Use this table to see what has changed from your Loan Estimate.

	Loan Estimate	Final	Did this change?
Total Closing Costs (J)	$8,054.00	$9,712.10	YES - See Total Loan Costs (D) and Total Other Costs (I)
Closing Costs Paid Before Closing	$0	- $29.00	YES - You paid these Closing Costs before closing
Closing Costs Financed (Paid from your Loan Amount)	$0	$0	NO
Down Payment/Funds from Borrower	$18,000.00	$18,000.00	NO
Deposit	- $10,000.00	- $10,000.00	NO
Funds for Borrower	$0	$0	NO
Seller Credits	$0	- $2,500.00	YES - See Seller Credits in Section L
Adjustments and Other Credits	$0	- $1,035.04	YES - See details in Sections K and L
Cash to Close	**$16,054.00**	**$14,147.26**	

Summaries of Transactions

Use this table to see a summary of your transaction.

BORROWER'S TRANSACTION

K. Due from Borrower at Closing		$189,762.30
01 Sale Price of Property		$180,000.00
02 Sale Price of Any Personal Property Included in Sale		
03 Closing Costs Paid at Closing (J)		$9,682.30
04		
Adjustments		
05		
06		
07		
Adjustments for Items Paid by Seller in Advance		
08 City/Town Taxes	to	
09 County Taxes	to	
10 Assessments	to	
11 HOA Dues	4/15/13 to 4/30/13	$80.00
12		
13		
14		
15		

L. Paid Already by or on Behalf of Borrower at Closing		$175,615.04
01 Deposit		$10,000.00
02 Loan Amount		$162,000.00
03 Existing Loan(s) Assumed or Taken Subject to		
04		
05 Seller Credit		$2,500.00
Other Credits		
06 Rebate from Epsilon Title Co.		$750.00
07		
Adjustments		
08		
09		
10		
11		
Adjustments for Items Unpaid by Seller		
12 City/Town Taxes 1/1/13 to 4/14/13		$365.04
13 County Taxes	to	
14 Assessments	to	
15		
16		
17		

CALCULATION

Total Due from Borrower at Closing (K)	$189,762.30
Total Paid Already by or on Behalf of Borrower at Closing (L)	- $175,615.04
Cash to Close ☒ From ☐ To Borrower	**$14,147.26**

SELLER'S TRANSACTION

M. Due to Seller at Closing		$180,000.00
01 Sale Price of Property		$180,000.00
02 Sale Price of Any Personal Property Included in Sale		
03		
04		
05		
06		
07		
08		
Adjustments for Items Paid by Seller in Advance		
09 City/Town Taxes	to	
10 County Taxes	to	
11 Assessments	to	
12 HOA Dues	4/15/13 to 4/30/13	$80.00
13		
14		
15		
16		

N. Due from Seller at Closing		$115,665.04
01 Excess Deposit		
02 Closing Costs Paid at Closing (J)		$12,800.00
03 Existing Loan(s) Assumed or Taken Subject to		
04 Payoff of First Mortgage Loan		$100,000.00
05 Payoff of Second Mortgage Loan		
06		
07		
08 Seller Credit		$2,500.00
09		
10		
11		
12		
13		
Adjustments for Items Unpaid by Seller		
14 City/Town Taxes 1/1/13 to 4/14/13		$365.04
15 County Taxes	to	
16 Assessments	to	
17		
18		
19		

CALCULATION

Total Due to Seller at Closing (M)	$180,000.00
Total Due from Seller at Closing (N)	- $115,665.04
Cash ☐ From ☒ To Seller	**$64,414.96**

CLOSING DISCLOSURE

Additional Information About This Loan

Loan Disclosures

Assumption

If you sell or transfer this property to another person, your lender

☐ will allow, under certain conditions, this person to assume this loan on the original terms.

☒ will not allow assumption of this loan on the original terms.

Demand Feature

Your loan

☐ has a demand feature, which permits your lender to require early repayment of the loan. You should review your note for details.

☒ does not have a demand feature.

Late Payment

If your payment is more than 15 days late, your lender will charge a late fee of 5% of the monthly principal and interest payment.

Negative Amortization (Increase in Loan Amount)

Under your loan terms, you

☐ are scheduled to make monthly payments that do not pay all of the interest due that month. As a result, your loan amount will increase (negatively amortize), and your loan amount will likely become larger than your original loan amount. Increases in your loan amount lower the equity you have in this property.

☐ may have monthly payments that do not pay all of the interest due that month. If you do, your loan amount will increase (negatively amortize), and, as a result, your loan amount may become larger than your original loan amount. Increases in your loan amount lower the equity you have in this property.

☒ do not have a negative amortization feature.

Partial Payments

Your lender

☒ may accept payments that are less than the full amount due (partial payments) and apply them to your loan.

☐ may hold them in a separate account until you pay the rest of the payment, and then apply the full payment to your loan.

☐ does not accept any partial payments.

If this loan is sold, your new lender may have a different policy.

Security Interest

You are granting a security interest in
456 Somewhere Ave., Anytown, ST 12345

You may lose this property if you do not make your payments or satisfy other obligations for this loan.

Escrow Account

For now, your loan

☒ will have an escrow account (also called an "impound" or "trust" account) to pay the property costs listed below. Without an escrow account, you would pay them directly, possibly in one or two large payments a year. Your lender may be liable for penalties and interest for failing to make a payment.

Escrow		
Escrowed Property Costs over Year 1	$2,473.56	Estimated total amount over year 1 for your escrowed property costs: Homeowner's Insurance Property Taxes
Non-Escrowed Property Costs over Year 1	$1,800.00	Estimated total amount over year 1 for your non-escrowed property costs: Homeowner's Association Dues You may have other property costs.
Initial Escrow Payment	$412.25	A cushion for the escrow account you pay at closing. See Section G on page 2.
Monthly Escrow Payment	$206.13	The amount included in your total monthly payment.

☐ will not have an escrow account because ☐ you declined it ☐ your lender does not offer one. You must directly pay your property costs, such as taxes and homeowner's insurance. Contact your lender to ask if your loan can have an escrow account.

No Escrow		
Estimated Property Costs over Year 1		Estimated total amount over year 1. You must pay these costs directly, possibly in one or two large payments a year.
Escrow Waiver Fee		

In the future,

Your property costs may change and, as a result, your escrow payment may change. You may be able to cancel your escrow account, but if you do, you must pay your property costs directly. If you fail to pay your property taxes, your state or local government may (1) impose fines and penalties or (2) place a tax lien on this property. If you fail to pay any of your property costs, your lender may (1) add the amounts to your loan balance, (2) add an escrow account to your loan, or (3) require you to pay for property insurance that the lender buys on your behalf, which likely would cost more and provide fewer benefits than what you could buy on your own.

Loan Calculations

Total of Payments. Total you will have paid after you make all payments of principal, interest, mortgage insurance, and loan costs, as scheduled.	$285,803.36
Finance Charge. The dollar amount the loan will cost you.	$118,830.27
Amount Financed. The loan amount available after paying your upfront finance charge.	$162,000.00
Annual Percentage Rate (APR). Your costs over the loan term expressed as a rate. This is not your interest rate.	4.174%
Total Interest Percentage (TIP). The total amount of interest that you will pay over the loan term as a percentage of your loan amount.	69.46%

Questions? If you have questions about the loan terms or costs on this form, use the contact information below. To get more information or make a complaint, contact the Consumer Financial Protection Bureau at **www.consumerfinance.gov/mortgage-closing**

Other Disclosures

Appraisal
If the property was appraised for your loan, your lender is required to give you a copy at no additional cost at least 3 days before closing. If you have not yet received it, please contact your lender at the information listed below.

Contract Details
See your note and security instrument for information about
- what happens if you fail to make your payments,
- what is a default on the loan,
- situations in which your lender can require early repayment of the loan, and
- the rules for making payments before they are due.

Liability after Foreclosure
If your lender forecloses on this property and the foreclosure does not cover the amount of unpaid balance on this loan,

☑ state law may protect you from liability for the unpaid balance. If you refinance or take on any additional debt on this property, you may lose this protection and have to pay any debt remaining even after foreclosure. You may want to consult a lawyer for more information.

☐ state law does not protect you from liability for the unpaid balance.

Refinance
Refinancing this loan will depend on your future financial situation, the property value, and market conditions. You may not be able to refinance this loan.

Tax Deductions
If you borrow more than this property is worth, the interest on the loan amount above this property's fair market value is not deductible from your federal income taxes. You should consult a tax advisor for more information.

Contact Information

	Lender	Mortgage Broker	Real Estate Broker (B)	Real Estate Broker (S)	Settlement Agent
Name	Ficus Bank		Omega Real Estate Broker Inc.	Alpha Real Estate Broker Co.	Epsilon Title Co.
Address	4321 Random Blvd. Somecity, ST 12340		789 Local Lane Sometown, ST 12345	987 Suburb Ct. Someplace, ST 12340	123 Commerce Pl. Somecity, ST 12344
NMLS ID					
ST License ID			Z765416	Z65456	Z61616
Contact	Joe Smith		Samuel Green	Joseph Cain	Sarah Arnold
Contact NMLS ID	12345				
Contact ST License ID			P16414	P16160	PT1234
Email	joesmith@ ficusbank.com		sam@omegare.biz	joe@alphare.biz	sarah@ epsilontitle.com
Phone	123-456-7890		123-555-1717	321-555-7171	987-555-4321

Confirm Receipt

By signing, you are only confirming that you have received this form. You do not have to accept this loan because you have signed or received this form.

_____   _____   _____   _____
Applicant Signature   Date   Co-Applicant Signature   Date

15 THE REAL ESTATE MARKET AND ANALYSIS

Learning Objectives:
• Describe the physical characteristics of real estate
• Describe the economic characteristics of real estate
• Identify the factors that influence demand
• Identify the factors that influence supply
• Distinguish among different ways of interpreting market conditions
• Demonstrate understanding of the different market indicators

Key Terms:

buyer's market	seller's market	vacancy rate
demand	situs	
household	supply	

PHYSICAL CHARACTERISTICS OF REAL ESTATE

I) Physical Characteristics of Real Estate

    A) Immobility and importance of location in determining value

        1) The value of real estate is heavily influenced by changes in the surrounding area

        2) Highest and best use is fundamentally determined by alternate types of potential users bidding for a site in accordance with the locational and environmental value of the site in each use

        3) If the value of a site in its current highest and best use declines relative to competing uses, highest and best use may change and land use transition will begin

    B) Indestructibility (durability) of land and fixed location

1) Real estate investment tends to be long term

2) Land does not depreciate

3) Property insurance insures improvements only, not land

C) Non-standardized; non-homogeneous

1) No two parcels are exactly alike

D) Governmental controls the influence of the market through zoning, building codes, taxes, etc.

Physical Characteristics of Real Estate

Real estate economics is the application of economic techniques to understand the real estate market.

It strives to **analyze** the market by describing, explaining, and predicting patterns of prices, supply, and demand.

The real estate market plays a vital role in Florida's growth, and figuring out what lies ahead is a key question for policymakers, residents and real estate licensees.

Florida licensees must closely monitor market trends and forecasts that impact the state's real estate industry to help clients make well-timed buying and selling decisions.

After the downturn in the market with housing hitting a low point around January 2012, the real estate market has been recovering as of the start of 2016.

Yet, mortgage rates and home prices must balance wages and global economic conditions to continue feeding an upward housing trend.

http://finance.yahoo.com/news/florida-realtors-2016-real-estate-183500885.html

This bar graph demonstrates the swing that can result with market changes.

Florida Average Home Sales Price   http://www.zillow.com/fl/home-values/

The dates depicted on the graph are between January 2006 through January 2016 and shows the average sales prices of homes in Florida at the designated dates.

The real estate market, as do all markets, relies on buyers and sellers which creates an interaction between supply and demand.

There are both physical and economic characteristics of real estate that affect the value of real estate and market indicators that can be used to gauge the market trends.

http://www.zillow.com/fl/home-values/

Real Estate has four physical characteristics that affect the value of land.

The first physical characteristic is the fact that real estate is **immobile.** Simply put, it doesn't move. And location is important in determining value.

A second real estate characteristic is that it is **indestructible**.

A third is that it **is non-homogeneous** meaning it is unique.

And the fourth characteristic is that the use of land is **restricted by governmental controls through zoning, building codes,** taxes, etc.

Physical Characteristics Include:

- Immobility and importance of location (in determining value)
- Indestructibility (durable) of land and fixed location
- Non-standardized; non-homogeneous – unique
- Governmental controls through zoning, building codes, taxes, etc.

Immobility of Real Estate (and the importance of location in determining value)

Land is not moveable.

Let's take a closer look at the immobility of real estate. The location of the property is a huge factor in determining value. Immobility of real estate simply means that land cannot be moved to a more suitable location. What you have is what you have.

Many times, working in real estate you will hear a client tell you that a home is perfect – if only it was located somewhere else! Location, location, location… is the defining physical characteristic in real estate!

And yes, technically a house can and occasionally does get moved. It is the land itself that is immobile.

- Land is not moveable

- Influenced by changes in the surrounding area

- Highest and best use if fundamentally determined by alternate types of potential users bidding for a site in accordance with the locational and environmental value of the site in each use.

- If the value of a site in its current highest and best use declines relative to competing uses, highest and best use may change and land use transition will begin.

http://www.realestatemanitoba.com/phase2/unit1/session2_land_character.htm

Because land is immobile, it is heavily influenced by changes in the surrounding area.

An individual may buy their home when they are young and plan to keep the property for years.

That individual may take great care in their maintenance and improvements of the property.

In the end however, the value of the property may be more impacted by the condition of the surrounding properties more than the condition of the individual property.

Highest and best use if fundamentally determined by alternate types of potential users bidding for a site in accordance with the locational and environmental value of the site in each use.

What this means is that if the highest and best use of a land is empty pasture, then the value of that property would be significantly different than a parcel of the exact same size that is located on the busiest intersection in the middle of town.

The highest and best use of the second property might be a fast food restaurant or a gas station.

In the end, the values of the properties will be dramatically affected by the highest and best use that seems the most appropriate for the property.

If the value of a site in its current highest and best use declines relative to competing uses, highest and best use may change and land use transition will begin

Remembering that real estate is immobile, the fact is that land can suffer when the current and best use suddenly shifts.

What once was a profitable endeavor may shift and become unprofitable and vice versa.

A good example of this would be main street in any given town in America. At one-time main street probably was the road that had the most traffic.

As a result, the highest and best uses for a property located on main street may have been a thriving retail business.

As highways were built diverting traffic away from main streets, these businesses became less profitable and no longer fit as the most profitable use for the property.

Indestructibility (Durability) of Land and Fixed Location

- Durability

- Real estate investments tend to be long term

- Land does not depreciate

- Property insurance insures improvements only, not land

Durability

The fact that land is indestructible is another physical characteristic of real estate.

Land is a long-term asset.

It does not get used up, adding to its' allure for investors.

Think about it. What happens if you set off as bomb on the land? If there is a building it may be destroyed, but the land itself will remain. It remains into infinity. It may change in makeup, but it remains. Land is indeed indestructible.

There are very few exceptions to this concept that land is indestructible. The fact is though that land can be lost as mountain tops are removed for coal mining, mudslides wash away entire areas, and land is lost along the coastlines.

https://books.google.com/books?id=4qu_dK7XBI8C&pg=PA11&lpg=PA11&dq=indestructibility+of+real+e state&source=bl&ots=15rV5ulDw6&sig=wbgEzOuAPtFg2BrdGu0J9o9X7-U&hl=en&sa=X&ved=0ahUKEwiF1v7ZlLzKAhUlx4MKHf-CBIA4ChDoAQgxMAI#v=onepage&q=indestructibility%20of%20real%20estate&f=false

Most people that invest in real estate do so as a long-term investment.

The majority purchase for personal use, with the hope that it gains in value adding to the worth of their assets.

For many, their home is their most expensive asset and investment. Others purchase property specifically for the investment opportunities.

Some properties are flipped quickly for a short-term gain.

Most hold property for significant terms. Long term investors purchase a property in an area where the long-term appreciation rate appears favorable and rent the property to tenants, acting as landlord and taking care of all the maintenance that the property requires, while profiting from the monthly rent checks while waiting for the property value to rise enough to sell it for profit.

http://www.yaerd.org/long-term-investment.html

Land Does Not Depreciate

Land is durable and is not calculated into depreciation formulas.

Land is not depreciated because land is assumed to have an unlimited useful life. Other long-lived assets such as land improvements, buildings, furnishings, equipment, etc. have limited useful lives. Therefore, the costs of those assets must be allocated to those limited accounting periods.

Yet, land itself is said to last into infinity.

The whole idea of depreciation is to calculate how long something will last. But long after the remnants of a building remains the land itself will be there.

http://www.yaerd.org/long-term-investment.html

Property insurance insures improvements only, not land.

Because land is said to be indestructible, when insurance is taken out on property, it does not cover the land itself.

Insurance is designed to replace and compensate for lost structures, such as homes and buildings. However, the land itself is not calculated into the insured allowance.

Imagine a tornado, a hurricane, a fire…any calamity that could totally wipe away all signs that a home or a building ever existed cannot wipe away the land itself.

http://www.yaerd.org/long-term-investment.html

Non-standardized: Real Estate is Non-homogeneous

The fact that real estate is unique is the third characteristic of real estate.

- **No two parcels are alike**

- **Real estate is said to be Unique**

- **Value is determined by what users will pay driven by the unique qualities of the real estate**

- **Non-homogeneous – not the same**

No Two Parcels are Alike

Real property has value, which may be viewed as similar to other properties. But make no mistake, there are always differences in the physical characteristics of land.

Real Estate is Said to be Unique

Even if there are a row of homes built using the exact same model. Each home takes on changes based on exactly where the lot is positioned. Real property is said to be unique.

The value of land is influenced by the surrounding area.
The value is determined by what users will pay.

And what they will pay is often dictated by what they view as unique and special about the property.

Real estate is non-homogeneous meaning no two properties are exactly the same.

Government controls influence the market through zoning, building codes, and taxes.

The final physical characteristic of real estate that affects value is the fact that government controls influence the market through zoning, building codes, and taxes.

Zoning literally affects how a property can be used. Placing limitations on how a property can be used directly impacts the value, pricing and demand of property.

- If a seller is trying to monetize property by placing a cell tower on it, for example, and finds that zoning restricts it – that seller might view the zoning as having a negative impact on the value of his property. His neighbor may view the zoning as having protected the value of his property by preventing the cell tower from having been placed in a position that would have destroyed his view of the beach.

These extreme examples demonstrate how zoning, building codes and even taxes can affect the value of property.

Government controls influence the market through zoning, building codes, and taxes.

- Limitations on how a property can be used

- Standards for building size, placement and safety

- Tax assessment affect purchase decisions

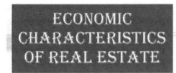

ECONOMIC CHARACTERISTICS OF REAL ESTATE

II) Economic Characteristics of Real Estate

A) Relationship between supply, demand and price

B) Slow to respond to change in supply and demand

C) Demand factors:

1) Price of real estate

2) Population and household composition

3) Income of consumers

4) Availability of mortgage credit

5) Consumer tastes or preferences

D) Supply factors:

1) Availability of skilled labor

2) Availability of construction loans and financing

3) Availability of land

4) Availability of materials

E) Interpreting market conditions

    1) Price levels

    2) Vacancy rates

    3) Sales volume

    4) Area preference—situs

    5) Market adjustment

        (a) Buyer's market

        (b) Seller's market

Four Economic Characteristics of Real Estate

Now, let's look at the economic characteristics of real estate which describes the value of real estate.

Economic characteristic of real estate includes the relationship between supply, demand, and price. Furthermore, real estate is slow to respond to change in supply and demand. Demand is driven by consumer preference and availability driving supply.

- **Relationship between supply, demand, and price**
- **The fact that the market is slow to respond to change in supply and demand**
- **Demand driven by consumer preference**
- **Supply driven by availability**

Relationship between supply, demand and price.

There is a relationship between supply, demand and price. The more real estate that is available, the less demand there is for each individual parcel. Prices in turn go down.

Scarcity of real estate, the lack of real estate, creates higher demand and drives prices upward.

Remember that demand requires buyers and renters that have the ability to pay.

An economic depression can see a high need for housing but still experience a low demand as there are less consumers with the means to pay for the housing.

Relationship between supply, demand and price.

- o Supply
  - How much real estate is available at any one time
  - Affects price by limiting the options or giving too many

- o Demand
  - Willing and able buyers and renters looking for property in a given area
  - Affects pricing by having too many bidding on same property, or too few
- o Price
  - Direct result of the balance between supply and demand
  - Inverse relationship

Slow to Respond

Real estate is generally slow to respond to changes in supply and demand. The fact is that there is not a direct correlation between changes in supply and demand.

Just because there is suddenly more real estate available doesn't mean that you are going to see more demand for the real estate. In fact, it can take years for a real estate market to rebound from an unbalanced level of supply and demand.

The saying "if you build, they will come" can take great patience for economic rewards when it comes to developing following a downward trend in the market.

- **Real estate typically responds slowly to changes in supply and demand**

- **Can take years to recover once unbalanced.**

Demand Factors

Changes in price have an opposite, or inverse, relationship with demand. The higher the price, the less demand. The better or lower the price, the more demand. Age group numbers can influence demand, i.e. 55+ communities. It doesn't take huge changes in interest rates to spur demand.

Tastes and preferences or SITUS make a difference in where homeowners are interested in buying. So what are the variables that influence demand?

They are the price of real estate, the population numbers and household composition, the income of consumers, the availability of mortgage credit, and consumer tastes and preferences.

- **Price of real estate**

- **Population numbers and household composition**

- **Income of consumers**

- **Availability of mortgage credit**

- **Consumer tastes and preferences**

Price of Real Estate

Demand for Real Estate is inverse to its' price. As the price comes down demand rises. As the price rises the demand goes down.

- Inverse relationship between price and demand

Population and Household Composition

Population growth or a declining population affect supply and demand. A declining population has a declining demand and vice versa.

- A declining population has a declining demand

- Multi-generational families typically lived in larger homes.

- A growing population has a larger demand

Availability of Mortgage Credit

Mortgage credit is a fact of life for most Americans. When the mortgage credit market tightens up, less are able to qualify for a mortgage, reducing demand for houses.

- Affects consumer buying power

Consumer Tastes and Preferences

When building tastes change, there is a corresponding change in what buyers are looking for (i.e. what style home, how many bedrooms, size of garage, tile or laminate, granite or Corian). If builders hit it just right, demand spikes.

- Situs

- Home styles

- Home amenities

- Home upgrades

Buyer Preferences Drive Market Conditions

A final economic characteristic of real estate is the fact that buyer preferences drive market conditions and price levels of homes. Personal preference is called situs. This can affect individual perception of value.

These individual preferences can change over time.

When homes are designed to please fads rather than solid architectural standards, properties can quickly become victim to loss of value from functional obsolescence.

- The definition of Situs involves buyer's personal preferences for:

  - Location

  - Accessibility

- Features

Relationship between supply, demand and price.

It's important to have a good understanding of the variables that affect supply and demand. It's important to have a clear understanding of the factors that affect supply verses the factors that affect demand.

The more people there are that are looking to buy, the more chance of someone willing to pay a little more for the same thing particularly since the supply will begin to shrink. Demand drive prices upward putting pressure on pricing as the supply decreases and vice versa.

- Demand drives prices,
    - the more demand there is the more upward pressure there is on pricing as the supply decreases.
    - The less demand there is the less pressure there is on pricing as the supply increases.

Supply Factors

Let's start by taking a closer look at supply. Many variables do influence supply, such as skilled labor to build and clear land, the availability of money to finance growth, how much land is available in the proposed area, and finally whether building materials are readily available.

- Availability of Skilled labor
- Availability of Construction loans and financing
- Availability of Land
- Availability of Materials

Skilled Labor

The supply of housing depends on skilled labor, especially new housing, without which there would be little supply. An abundance of skilled labor could inversely lower costs to build and increase supply.

- Construction depends on skilled labor to complete projects large and small.

Availability of Construction Loans and Financing

Construction financing is the glue that keeps real estate development on course. Developers rely on financing to proceed from stage to stage of their project.

- Developers usually rely on construction financing to supply their projects with needed capital. No financing, little supply.

Availability of Land

The availability of land is a part of the supply side. Availability can be based on type of land, zoning, stability, water table, EPA regulations and other factors.

Availability of Materials

Materials to build can be in good supply or be is short supply. Material availability play a part in availability of new homes. Economics of purchasing, logistics, economy, shipping….all play a part in material availability.

Interpreting Market Conditions

So, how is the market doing? Is it healthy? Is it a buyers' market or a sellers' market? There are several variables that can be analyzed to interpret market conditions. The number of new building permits is a good indicator of the market heading up or down.

More permits usually indicate a strong economy and an upward swing. Rental vacancy rates climbing usually indicate a jump to buying and a prelude to lower rental fees. The number of homes sold usually points to areas of most activity and least activity. This can point to areas that meet buyer preferences (situs); of declining buyer preference.

- Price levels of home sales

- Vacancy rates

- Sales volume—number of homes sold

- Area Preference—Situs

- Market Adjustment—Buyer's versus Seller's Market

Market Adjustment - Buyer's Market

Market conditions dictate demand in the community for real estate. The fluctuation in supply and demand creates either a buyer's market or a seller's market. So, what is a buyer's market? If there is a greater supply of property than buyers to buy, you have a buyer's market. The result is that you can buy real estate for a better price.

Supply exceeds demand

Buyers get better prices and terms

Market Adjustment - Seller's Market

A seller's market exists when there are more buyers (demand) than available real estate for sale. Sellers can hold out for the best price and often buyers will bid up the price of a house in order not to lose it.

Demand exceeds Supply

Sellers able to sell for higher prices

MARKET INDICATORS

III) Market Indicators

    A) Vacancy rates

    B) Price/sales information

    C) Building permits

Market Indicators

A good way to summarize what is going on with a market is to look at the market indicators of vacancy rates, price/sales information, and building permits.

As the rental vacancy rate falls, rental rates tend to spike upward. Eventually, the demand for housing levels then fall as the renters start moving out of an increasingly pricey rental market. This tends to increase the vacancy rate and bring rental rates back down and the cycle begins again, though rental rates tend not to fall to the level they were before.

Vacancy Rates

- # of units vacant, compared to total units available

Occupancy Rates

- # of units filled compared to total units available

Price of Homes Sold

From MLS data, a real estate licensee can garner many different types of data pertaining to sales, i.e. number of homes sold, average prices of homes sold, areas that homes have sold, prices of sold homes. All valuable tools in determining activity and trends of buyers and sellers. If the price levels of new homes are higher, it is a good economic sign.

When sellers struggle to sell their homes at prices that their neighbors had previously sold for this can be an indicator of a downward market. If the values drop low enough, sellers can have trouble selling their homes at a high enough price to clear the debt on their home or to accomplish selling goals such as securing new housing.

Sales Volume

- # of homes sold

Number of building permits

A strong indicator of the market is the number of building permits that are pulled for new housing and new housing developments.

There's no doubt that consumer confidence is increased when they see builders building. The general thought process is that builders are in tune to market conditions. If they are building, then the market is good.

The reality, though, is that builders can be slow to pick up the clues that a market is slowing. As real estate markets slow, builders can end up holding unsold property.

Vacancy Rates

Since vacancy and occupancy rates are a good indicator of the real estate market and also a good indicator that a prospective real estate property is a good investment--real estate professionals need to know how to calculate vacancy and occupancy rates.

These rates are usually expressed as a percentage.

The formula for vacancy rate is the number of vacant units ÷ by the number of total units to= vacancy decimal. Convert to % by moving decimal 2 spaces to the right.

- Calculating Vacancy Rates as a %
  - To calculate the vacancy rate, divide the number of unoccupied units by the total number of units in the building
    - 18 unoccupied(vacant) units ÷150 total units= .12 or 12%
    - The vacancy rate is 12%

Occupancy Rates

It's the same process for calculating occupancy rates, except instead of starting with the number of unoccupied units, you start with the number of units that are occupied. Then, divide by the number of total units to equal the vacancy decimal which you convert to a percentage. The same building will have a vacancy rate and an occupancy rate that when added together will equal 100%.

- Calculating Occupancy Rates as a %
  - To calculate the occupancy rate, divide the number of occupied units by the total number of units in the building
    - 18 unoccupied(vacant) units ÷150 total units= .12 or 12%
    - The vacancy rate is 12%
    - 132
    - The same building has a 12% vacancy rate and 88% occupancy rate

16 REAL ESTATE APPRAISALS

Learning Objectives:

- Describe federal and state regulations pertaining to appraising
- Identify the appraiser's fiduciary relationship
- Identify the economic and physical characteristics of real estate that affect market value
- Explain what the Uniform Standards of Professional Appraisal Practice (USPAP) is and how it affects the appraisal process of real property
- Distinguish among the various types of value
- Define market value and describe its underlying assumptions
- Distinguish among value, price and cost
- Describe the four characteristics of value
- Distinguish among the principles of value
- Differentiate among the three approaches to estimating the value of real property
- Estimate value of subject property using Comparable Sales Approach
- Estimate value of subject property using Cost Approach
- Estimate value of subject property using Income Approach
- Reconcile three approaches to establish final value estimate
- Calculate value using gross multiplier analysis
- Explain how to prepare a Comparative Market Analysis (CMA), comparing and contrasting with sales comparison approach

Key Terms:

appraisal	economic life	over-improvement
assemblage	federally related transaction	plottage
automated valuation models	gross income multiplier (GIM)	principle of substitution
comparative market analysis (CMA)	gross rent multiplier (GRM)	progression
	highest and best use	reconciliation
cost-depreciation approach	income approach	regression
curable	incurable	replacement cost
depreciation	market value	reproduction cost

sales comparison approach	Uniform Standards of	valuation
situs	Professional Appraisal	
subject property	Practice (USPAP)	

FIRREA

Regulation of Appraising – FIRREA

A) Appraisal Foundation

B) Appraisal Qualifications Board

C) Appraisal Standards Board

D) Appraisal Subcommittee

E) State licensed and certified appraisers

      1) Requirements for federally related transactions

      2) Certified appraisal reports

F) Appraisal service of real estate

      1) Part I, Chapter 475

      2) Appraisal reports must conform to USPAP

      3) Comparative Market Analysis (CMA)

      4) Broker Price Opinion (BPO) II

Financial Institutions Reform, Recovery, and Enforcement Act

Working as a real estate licensee, it is important to understand the basics of appraisals. A property appraisal report is requested to obtain an opinion of value.

According to Florida Statutes 475, you can perform an appraisal if you follow certain guidelines. More often than not, though, you will be using other methods to determine value to help guide your buyers and sellers. Regardless of the value methods that you use, it is imperative that you can understand the appraisal process and be able to interpret appraisal reports.

Financial Institutions Reform, Recovery, and Enforcement Act (FIRREA) is a provision under Title XI that mandates states to license and certify appraisers. The goal was to bring accountability and oversight to the appraisal industry.

- (FIRREA)
- Title XI
- Mandates states to license and certify appraiser

https://www.fdic.gov/.../2000-430s

Appraisal Foundation

Authorized by the U.S. Congress in 1989 as the source of professional appraisal standards and qualifications, The Appraisal Foundation and its independent boards work hard to promote stability in the marketplace and maintain the public trust. The professional standards, qualifications, and guidance developed by The Appraisal Foundation advance professionalism in various appraisal disciplines including real estate, business valuation, and personal property. Under the Appraisal Foundation you have the Appraisal Qualifications Board, the Appraisal Standards Board, and the Appraisal Subcommittee.

Source of promotion of professional standards

Appraiser Qualification

Under the Appraisal Foundation

Appraisal Qualifications Board

Appraisal Standards Board

Appraisal Subcommittee

https://www.appraisalfoundation.org/iMIS/TAF/Default.aspx?hkey=87515edb-20e4-40fc-936f-9fe6c3a9532e&WebsiteKey=e12b6085-ff54-45c1-853e-b838ca4b9895

Appraisal Qualifications Board (AQB)

The Appraisal Qualification Board (AQB) of the Appraisal Foundation establishes the minimum education, experience, and examination requirements for real property appraisers to obtain state certification.

Part of the Appraisal Foundation

Sets the standards for appraisers for state certification

Minimum education

Experience

Examination

http://www.appraiser.ne.gov/aqb/pdf/June%202010%20QA.pdf

The Appraisal Standards Board (ASB) develops, interprets and amends the Uniform Standards of Professional Appraisal Practice (USPAP). The ASB is composed of seven appraisers who are appointed by the Board of Trustees of The Appraisal Foundation.

Appraisal Standards Board (ASB):

Develops USPAP

Appraisal standards for federally related transactions

https://en.wikipedia.org/wiki/Appraisal_Standards_Board

Appraisal Subcommittee

The Appraisal Subcommittee's (ASC) mission is to ensure that real estate appraisers, who perform appraisals in real estate transactions that could expose the United States government to financial loss, are sufficiently trained and tested to assure competency and independent judgment according to uniform high professional standards and ethics. Maintains database of state-certified and licensed appraisers eligible for federally related transaction appraisals.

Protects the government from loss due to upholding USPAP standards and professional standards for federally related transactions

Maintains database of state-certified and licensed appraisers eligible for federally related transaction appraisals.

http://www.appraisalfoundation.org/TAF/About_Us/Appraiser_Regulatory_System_/Appraisal_Subcommittee_/T AF/ASC.aspx?hkey=352e1b6b-480b-492d-9d25-0c7dcd63b113

State Licensed and Certified Appraisers

To be a state certified appraiser, you must meet training and education requirements established by the Appraisal Qualifications Boards and the appraisals must follow the guidelines established by the Appraisal Standards Board—meaning it must follow USPAP.

Anytime an appraisal is conducted for a federally related transaction, it must be conducted by a state certified appraiser.

Meet Appraisal Standards Board for experience, training, and education

Follow USPAP standards set by the Appraisal Standards Board

Required for federally related transactions

2 Categories of State Certified Appraisers

There are two types of state appraisers. Those qualified to perform residential properties with four or less units called certified residential appraisers.

And certified general appraisers who can conduct an appraisal on any property. Appraisals are written according to USPAP standards in a Certified Appraisal Report.

Certified residential appraiser (1-4 units)

Certified general appraiser (any property)

Certified appraisal reports

https://www.fdic.gov/.../2000-430

Federally Related Transaction Defined

I keep mentioning the phrase federally related transaction. So, what exactly is it? A federally related transaction is one that involves a federal financial regulatory agency in either the primary or secondary mortgage market. This may involve the sale, lease, purchase, investment or exchange in real property (real estate). It also may apply when refinancing property or when the property is being used as collateral for a loan. These appraisals must be in writing and follow USPAP guidelines. Examples of loans involving a federally related transaction are Fannie Mae, Freddie Mac, FHA, and VA loans.

- Involves federal financial regulatory agency in primary or secondary mortgage market
- Requires services of a state certified appraiser
- Must be written and conform to USPAP
- Applies to real estate related loans
  - Sale, lease, exchange, financing, etc.
  - Also includes appraisals for Fannie Mae, Freddie Mac, FHA, and VA

http://definitions.uslegal.com/f/federally-related-transaction/

Uniform Standards of Professional Appraisal Practice – Defined

Know that USPAP stands for the Uniform Standards of Professional Appraisal Practice. It is what the name implies. It is a standard of professional practice that an appraiser must follow when conducting an appraisal. USPAP is revised periodically, usually annually, and almost never radically. It includes sections covering rules, such as an ethics rule, a departure rule, and a competency rule. It includes standards covering in detail different functions an appraiser might perform. It also includes statements which are used to clarify or supplement the USPAP Standards. Furthermore, it includes Advisory Opinions, such as "When does USPAP apply in valuation services?" and "Clarification of the client in a federally related transaction," which describe real-life problems and how they would be governed under the Rules and Standards of USPAP.

- (USPAP)
- Set of guidelines for appraisal services
- Standards of professional practice
- Ethics
- Competency

http://www.appraisers.org/About/professional-standards-ethics

F.S. 475 and Appraisal Services

According to Florida Statutes 475, real estate licensees may perform appraisal for compensation if the appraisal follows USPAP standards, are not being performed for a federally related transaction, and the licensee is not referring to him or herself as an actual certified appraiser.

- Licensees may perform appraisals for compensation if:
  - o Appraisals must abide by USPAP
  - o Cannot perform appraisals for federally related transactions
  - o Cannot refer to themselves as certified appraiser
  - o Must be a flat fee – not a percentage of the value
  - o Steps of a Real Estate Appraisal

Steps of a Real Estate Appraisal

Preparing to Visit the Property:

- First and foremost, the appraiser will gather information about the subject property that is available through public records, such as tax records.

- Market information is gathered regarding active, pending, and closed sales for the area – including properties that failed to sell.

While at the Property:

- Information already gathered about property is verified – property measurements are taken.

- Pictures of the property and the area are taken.

- Notations are made about condition and upgrades within the home.

Putting Together the Report:

- Choose comparable properties

- Utilize available surveys such as plat maps to include in the pull and upload location map.

- Notations are made about whether in a flood area.

- Verify that the legal description is correct.

- Conditions of the purchase agreement between the buyer and seller is noted, such as whether the seller is paying for any of the buyer's closing costs.

- **The Appraisal Report**

- All the information gathered prior to going to the property and while visiting the property is finally pulled together in written format that meets USPAP standards.

http://theappraisaliq.com/for-consumers/appraisal-steps-determining-market-value-of-property/

Tools to Determine Value

Per Florida Statutes, licensees have three methods for determining value with one being appraisals. More commonly than performing appraisals, though, real estate licensees determine value through either a Comparative Market Analysis (CMA) or a Broker's Price Opinion (BPO).

Appraisal

Comparative Market Analysis (CMA)

Broker's Price Opinion (BPO)

http://www.realtor.org/appraisal/responsible-valuation-policy

Comparative Market Analysis (CMA)

Comparative Market Analysis (CMA) is an assessment of value that a real estate licensee generally gives when helping a seller determine an appropriate list price. Buyers also request CMA's to assist them in deciding how much to offer on a property. An appraisers license is NOT required to conduct a CMA. CMA's may be conducted for a fee and do NOT have to comply with USPAP standards.

- Can be performed by real estate licensee
- Do not have to comply with USPAP
- Are not referred to as appraisals
- Can be done for fee.

http://www.realtor.org/appraisal/responsible-valuation-policy

Broker's Price Opinion (BPO)

A broker's price opinion is an opinion of value for real estate property. Per Florida Statutes, real estate sales associates and real estate broker associates can prepare BPO's so long as it is under the supervision of the broker. When performing a BPO, the licensee must make sure that it is not referred to or represented as being an actual appraisal. The licensee can collect a fee for conducting the BPO. It is common for relocation companies to request a BPO for an employee's home they are relocating. It is also common for lenders of distressed properties to request BPO's as they prepare to make decisions about the property.

- Can be performed by real estate licensee
- Do not have to comply with USPAP
- Are not referred to as appraisals
- Can be done for a fee
- Under the direct supervision of a broker

http://www.realtor.org/appraisal/responsible-valuation-policy

CONCEPT OF VALUE

II) Concept of Value

    A) Concepts of market cost/price/value

B) Many types of value apply to real estate

    1) Assess value for property tax purposes

    2) Insurance value

    3) Value in use

    4) Liquidation value

    5) Investment value

    6) Salvage value

C) Market value

    1) Definition of market value

    2) Assumptions associated with market value

D) Characteristics of value

    1) Demand

    2) Utility

    3) Scarcity

    4) Transferability

Regardless of whether you are utilizing the services of a licensed appraiser, or having a real estate licensee conduct an appraisal, a CMA, or a BPO, the goal is to determine value. The concept of value is driven by the real estate market and is differentiated between cost, price and value

Cost

Cost is how much money is required to produce the item. It includes the land, cost to acquire existing units, labor and materials. In the case of real estate, it means how much it costs to acquire the real estate with the house or building intact – or the cost of the land, plus the cost of materials to erect a building, plus labor.

- How much money is required to produce the item
- Includes the land, cost to acquire existing units, labor and materials

Price

Price is the amount actually paid for an item. This price can be above or below the actual cost of the item. Sometimes in real estate, the seller of a property is not happy to learn that when they add up how much they have invested in a property, that the total cost is not matched or surpassed by a potential sale price.

- Amount paid for an item

- Can be above or below cost

Value

Value is how much something is worth to the average buyer and seller at any given time. Value changes over time. This is often a guessing game for investors in property and even regular sellers who try to determine the best time to sell – to get the most out of their property as possible.

- How much something is worth to the average buyer and seller at the time value is being determined
- Value changes over time.

www.realtor.org/appraisal/responsible-valuation-policy

Types of Value

There are 7 types of value for you to be familiar with: assess value for property tax purposes, insurance value, value in use, liquidation value, investment value, salvage value, and market value.

- Assessed value
- Insurance value
- Value in use
- Liquidation value
- Investment value
- Salvage value
- Market value

www.investopedia.com

Assessed value

The assessed value is the value determined for collecting property taxes.

- The value determined for the purposes of collecting property taxes

www.investopedia.com/terms/a/assessedvalue.as

Insurance Value

When you place insurance on a property, a value is calculated to determine the replacement cost of the property. This is the insurance value.

- When you place insurance on a property, a value is calculated to determine the replacement cost of the property.

Value in Use

Property is not always used as it is intended or as the highest and best use. Value in use is the estimation of value based on how a property is being utilized. It is based on the results and history of a property. This is the value in use.

- Property is not always used as it is intended or as the highest and best use. Value in use is the estimation of value based on how a property is being utilized. It is based on the results and history of a property.

  http://www.appraisers.org/docs/default-source/college-of-fellows-articles/defining-value-in-use.pdf

Liquidation Value

When money is needed quickly, a property can be sold at a value less than it would be within a normal timeframe. This is liquidation value.

- When money is needed quickly, a property can be sold at a value less than it would be within a normal time frame.

  http://www.investopedia.com/terms/l/liquidation-value.asp

Salvage Value

Salvage value is when property is sold piece by piece rather than as a whole unit. With real estate, it would mean taking the building apart and selling off the architectural elements until the land is finally sold. This called salvage value.

- Sold piece by piece rather than as a whole unit

  http://www.investopedia.com/terms/l/liquidation-value.asp

Investment Value

Compared to someone looking to purchase for his or her own use, investors temper the value that a property must consider how much money will need to be invested in order to obtain a desirable return on the investment.

- Investors temper the value that a property must consider how much money will need to be invested in order to obtain a desirable return on the investment.

Market Value

Market value is the highest price a willing buyer would pay and a willing seller would accept. It assumes that both the buyer and the seller are fully informed and equally motivated. It also assumes that the property has been marketed for sale for a reasonable period. Finally, it assumes that the property was not sold under duress, such as with a bank foreclosure or auction. The market value may be different from the price a property can be sold for at a given time (market price).

The highest price a willing buyer would pay and a willing seller would accept.

- It assumes that both the buyer and the seller are fully informed
- Both the buyer and sellers are equally motivated
- The property has been marketed for sale for a reasonable period.
- Was not sold in duress or at auction
- The market value may be different from the price a property can be sold for at a given time (market price).

http://legal-dictionary.thefreedictionary.com/Market+Value

Characteristics of Value

Goods and services, including real estate, have value if four characteristics apply: demand, utility, scarcity, and transferability.

- Demand
- Utility
- Scarcity
- Transferability

Demand

Demand is one of the four characteristics of value. Demand means that there is a demand and an ability to acquire something. It's not uncommon for a real estate licensee to have potential buyers express interest in a property. But the property is only in demand if it is appealing to people who actually have the means to buy it.

- Demand
  - o The desire and ability to acquire something

http://www.investopedia.com/articles/realestate/12/real-estate-valuation.asp?layout=infini&v=1A

Utility

- Utility is one of the four characteristics of value. Utility means that the item provides a useful service or fills a need.
  - o The item provides a useful service or fills a need
  - o The value in use to an owner, which includes the value of amenities attaching to the property.

Read more: http://www.investorwords.com/14953/utility_value.html#ixzz3xdK1BIjq

Scarcity

Scarcity is one of the four characteristics of value. Scarcity means the availability of goods and services. Note that the word used here is scarcity. Not supply. Yet, it is related to supply.

When there isn't enough supply to meet the demand for the item (the real estate), it is scarce. In real estate, scarcity can lead to a seller's market with price increases as more buyers are competing for the same property.

- The item provides a useful service or fills a need
- A lack of supply of some commodity or item; in real estate terms, the scarcity of available properties (supply) tends to lead to an increase in prices if the number of buyers is high (demand)

Read more: http://www.investorwords.com/4402/scarcity.html#ixzz3xdKcAW4y

Transferability
- The more mobile an investment the more valuable
- Freely able to transfer title adds to value

http://mortgage.fastclass.com/courses/MBPUS120824/PDFs/MLPP4e_Ch11_PP.pdf

PRINCIPLES OF VALUE

III) Principles of Value

A) Substitution

B) Highest and best use

1) As if vacant

2) As improved

C) Increasing and decreasing returns

1) Over-improvement

D) Conformity

E) Other valuation terminology

1) Assemblage

2) Plottage

3) Progression

4) Regression

Certain rules apply when determining value. These rules are known as principles of value.

- Substitution
- Highest and best use
- Increasing and decreasing returns
- Conformity

Concept of Substitution

The Concept of Substitution means that a prudent buyer or investor will pay no more for a property than the cost of acquiring, through purchase or construction, an equally desirable alternative property. In clearer language, let's put it this way.

Why would a buyer pay $50,000 more for a property than a neighboring property that is almost identical? Or why would a buyer pay more for an existing property than one that they can build cheaper?

Considering that every property is unique, it is tempting for a seller to view their own property as being so special that it warrants the higher price. Occasionally a buyer will come along that agrees. But generally speaking, the rule of substitution applies and the sale of similar properties sets the upper limit of value.

- An informed and educated buyer will pay no more for a property than the cost of another property – whether through purchasing an existing home or building a similar new home.
- Sets upper limit of value

Principle of Substitution

Principle of Substitution states that no prudent person would pay one million dollars when there is another one readily available that has the same use, design and income for five hundred thousand dollars; the lowest price one is preferred.

http://realestatestudyguides.com/RealEstateStudyGuide/Appraisal_-_Real_Estate_Exam_Content.html

Highest and Best Use

- The most probable use of a property that is legally permissible
- Physically possible
- Financially feasible
- Results in maximum profitability

http://www.propex.com/C_g_hbu0.htm

Highest and Best Use as Vacant

If vacant property:

- Is in an area "zoned" for commercial use, the maximum productivity of the land as though vacant will likely be based on commercial use.

- If, however, the competitive level of demand is greater, for say, residential or multi-family use, then the highest and best use of the property as improved would be for residential use.

  http://www.propex.com/C_g_hbu0.htm

Highest and Best Use as Improved Property

- If the value of the property "as improved" is greater than the value of the site as "if vacant":
  - The highest and best use is usually the "improved" property.
  - Once the value of the vacant land exceeds the value of the improved property (including demolition costs), highest and best use will usually dictate that improvements be demolished.

  http://www.propex.com/C_g_hbu0.htm

Increasing and Decreasing Returns

As a real estate licensee, it is important to understand the principle of value of increasing and decreasing returns. Improvements to land and structures increases value only to the property's maximum value.

Beyond that point, additional improvements no longer affect a property's value. If money spent on improvements produces an increase in income or value, the law of increasing returns applies. At the point where additional improvements do not increase income or value, the law of diminishing returns applies.

A home owner that continues to improve a property past the maximum value is risking over-improvement of the property.

- Improvements to land and structures increases value only to the property's maximum value.
  - If money spent on improvements produces an increase in income or value, the law of increasing returns applies.
- Beyond that point, additional improvements no longer affect a property's value.
  - At the point where additional improvements do not increase income or value, the law of diminishing returns applies.

Over-improvement

- Continuing to improve a property past the maximum value
- Unable to recoup the expense upon the sale of the property

  http://www.propex.com/C_g_hbu0.htm

Conformity

The principle of value of conformity means that value is accomplished when a property is in symmetry with other properties. Think about a homeowner that builds a very unusual looking home. The home is of proper square footage. It follows building rules. It may even be charming. But the fact that it is of an odd design could substantially hurt the actual value due to the principle of conformity.

- An appraisal principle that holds that use conformity is desirable in creating and maintaining higher values

And that maximum value is realized when a reasonable degree of homogeneity of improvements or similarity of properties is present in an area Principle of Conformity.

The Principle of Conformity states that conformity to land use objectives contributes the most to economic stability in a residential community. Therefore, homes are built in the same style as the other properties in that same area, because the values will go up.

http://www.realestatewiki.com/wiki_content/Principle_Of_Conformity_cat40834034_cid20430087.htm

<u>Additional Appraisal Terms to Know</u>

Assemblage - combining of two or more adjoining properties into one

Plottage - added value that results from assemblage

Progression - the value of an inferior property is enhanced by association with superior properties

Regression –the value of a superior property is adversely affected by association with inferior properties

http://www.answers.com/Q/Is_there_a_difference_between_plottage_and_assemblage

Situs – people's preferences for a certain area

The economic attributes of a location, including the relationship between the property and surrounding properties. Situs is the aspect of location that contributes to a property's market value.
http://www.investorwords.com/13858/situs.html

IV) Introduction to the Three Approaches to Value

    A) Sales comparison approach

        1) Theory of method

        2) Steps in the approach

            (a) Making adjustments

            (b) Adjusted sale price

        3) Types of property best suited for this approach

    B) Cost-depreciation approach

        1) Theory of method

        2) Steps in the approach

(a) Reproduction vs. replacement cost

    (1) Cost estimating manuals

(b) Three types of depreciation

(c) Calculating accrued depreciation using age-life method

3) Applications of approach

C) Income approach

1) Theory of method

2) Steps in the approach

    (a) Potential gross income

    (b) Effective gross income

    (c) Net operating income

        (1) Fixed variable, reserve for replacements

    (d) Cap rates

3) Applications of approach

4) Gross rent multiplier (GRM)

    (a) Steps in the multiplier analysis

    (b) Does not act as a substitute for the income approach to valuation

Appraisals Utilize

An appraisal attempts to reconcile three approaches to value. These approaches include the sales comparison approach, the cost depreciation approach and the income approach.

- Sales comparison approach
- Cost depreciation approach
- Income approach

http://www.coestervms.com/3-approaches-to-value

Which Approach to Use?

Not all approaches apply equally to all properties. The sales comparison approach is the strongest way to estimate value for vacant lots and single-family homes. What are comparable properties selling for in the area?

The cost-depreciation approach is used to appraise new homes. It is also used to verify the values obtained through the sales and income approach. Remember the concept of substitution means that it doesn't make sense to pay more for a property that could be built cheaper.

This approach also works well for special-purpose properties that may have trouble finding similar properties to compare to for a sale.

The income approach is a good way to estimate value when the property produces income such as an apartment complex.

Sales comparison

- Vacant lots and single-family dwellings

Cost-depreciation

- New construction
- Verify values found through other approaches
- Special-purpose properties

Income approach

- Income-producing properties

Sales Comparison Approach Method:

Sales of similar properties are a good way to estimate value for a subject property. The subject property is the property that is being appraised. Then, pick comparable properties. Properties are chosen that have sold in a recent timeline and within the same market area.

Properties that are as similar as possible are chosen. Adjustments are made to account for differences in square footage, the number of rooms, existence of garages, pools, etc.

- Based on comparable sales values
  - Similar to subject property
  - Property being appraised
- Recent timeline of sales
- Same market area dictated by type and distance

  http://www2.econ.iastate.edu/classes/econ364/duffy/documents/salescomparisonsfromntbk.pdf

Adjustments

Adjustments are also made based on appeal of location such as whether one property is waterfront and one is not. If properties are chosen that were sold since the market changed in pricing levels, then an adjustment is also made for the market difference.

- Adjustments are made
  - Transactional differences
    - Market has increased or decreased in selling value

- Property differences
  - o Location – waterfront, golf course, etc.
  - o Square footage
  - o Pool, garage, bedrooms, etc.

http://www.readyratios.com/reference/appraisal/sales_comparison_approach_to_value.html

So, how do you make the adjustments? First of all, since you don't yet know the value of the subject property; all adjustments are made to the comparable property's value. If the comparable property is better than the subject property, then you subtract value from the comparable property.

If the comparable property is inferior to the subject property, then you add to the comparable property value. How much you add or subtract depends upon the value attributed to the difference.

- Rules for making adjustments
  - o If the Comparable property is BETTER
    - SUBTRACT value from the comparable property
  - o If the Comparable property is INFERIOR
    - ADD value to the comparable property

Let's look at an adjustment that needs to be made because the comparable property has an extra bedroom. If that home sold for $140,000 and the extra bedroom is worth $5,000, then you would simply subtract $5,000 from the comparable sale price of $140,000 giving you a $135,000 comparable value.

Adjusted Sale Price Example

If a comparable condominium sold for $140,000 and that comparable unit has an extra bedroom that appraiser determines is worth $5,000. What will the adjusted value of the sale price be?

Condominium Sale Price	$140,000
Extra Bedroom	- 5,000
Adjusted sale price	**$135,000**

Adjusting For Time Difference

The process is the same if you are making an adjustment for a time difference. Let's say that the market isn't as strong as what it was nine months ago. The comparable that is used would need to be adjusted down by the 3% change in the market. So $300,000 times .03 equals $9,000. Subtract the $9,000 from the sale price to give you $291,000 as the comparable adjusted sale price.

- Average of Adjusted Sale Prices
  - o An appraiser has found three homes and adjusted their values based on the differences to the subject property.

- ○ He then averages the three values to determine the estimated value of the subject property.
    - $291,000
    - $315,000
    - + $325,000
    - $931,000 ÷ 3 = $310,333 Adjusted Sale Price (rounded)

Weighted Reconciliation

An appraiser may choose three comps that the appraiser believes do not equally represent the subject property. If this happens, he or she can use a process of applying weighted reconciliation to each home rather than taking a mathematical average (as we did in the previous example).

If he believes the home that sold for $291,000 best represents the property and believes it should be weighted as having 50% of the value, he or she would multiply the $291,000 by 50%. Doing the same with the attributed weighted value of the other two comps, the three sums are then totaled together to give the adjusted sale price of the subject property.

- Weighted Reconciliation
    - ○ Attributing different percentage weight based on most like
        - ▪ Based on Adjusted Comparable Sales Price
        - ▪ Apply a % to each comparable
        - ▪ Total for subject property estimated value
            - $291,000 x 50% = $145,500
            - $315,000 x 30% = $ 94,500
            - $325,000 x 20% = $ 65,000
            - $145,500+$94,500+$65,000= **$305,000 Adjusted Sale Price**

Cost-Depreciation Approach Method:

The cost-depreciation approach method is an alternative method of estimating value. It is a good basis for just about anything being appraised. Appraisers like to use the cost-depreciation approach to double check a value found with one of the other methods.

It also may be the only way to value a new home in a newly developed area. Plus, there are those properties that simply defy being able to find a comp – such as a home that was built in 1848 and is in a secluded area. This process involves calculating the reproduction cost of the structure.

Subtracting calculated depreciation from the estimated reproduction cost. Adding in the value of the land. The resulting value is the estimated subject property value.

- Calculate the Reproduction Cost of Structure
- Subtract Accrued Depreciation from the Reproduction Cost
- Add the Estimated Value of Land
- The Resulting Value is the Estimated Subject Property Value

To apply the cost-depreciation approach method, you must break it down into steps. It starts by estimating the reproduction cost of the building or house. First of all, you must understand that there is a difference between the definition of the reproduction cost verses replacement cost.

To remember the difference, think in terms of duplicating an antique with a reproduction. Reproduction cost is as close to an exact duplicate as possible of the original structure. Whereas replacement cost is building a suitable replacement that will meet the same needs at the same quality but will not be exactly the same.

- Estimate Reproduction Cost
  - Reproduction cost
    - "Reproduction" = exact duplicate (as close as possible)
- Replacement Cost
  - Replace with acceptable structure

Reproduction Cost

An appraiser is trying to reproduce the building or house as closely as possible to the original. To make this process easier to calculate, he or she may rely on cost estimating manuals.

These industry accepted manuals will tell an appraiser how much a standard home livable square footage will cost to replace. Or the garage will cost. Or the lanai, etc.

Otherwise, the appraiser would be stuck estimating all the materials that would be necessary bit by bit to reproduce the home.

- Estimate Reproduction Cost
  - Cost Estimating Manuals
    - Comparative livable square footage
    - Comparative garage square footage
    - Comparative lanai square footage

Here's an example of the Cost-Depreciation Approach Method. If the subject property has 1,650 square feet of square footage under heat and air (livable area), plus has a 400 square feet of garage area and a 150 square feet of lanai area, calculate the reproduction cost using the following cost estimating manual figures.

Cost Estimating Manual Figures: Livable Square Foot Cost Estimate $92 Sq. Ft / Garage Square Foot Cost Estimate $45 Sq. Ft / Lanai Square Foot Cost Estimate $32 Sq. Ft. Take $92 x 1,650 = $151,800. $45 x 400 = $18,000. $32 x 150= $4,800. Total the three sums together and you have a total estimated reproduction cost of $174,600.

Solution

Cost Estimating Manual Figures

Livable Square Foot Cost Estimate $92 Sq. Ft

Garage Square Foot Cost Estimate $45 Sq. Ft

Lanai Square Foot Cost Estimate $32 Sq. Ft

- $92 x 1,650 = $151,800

- $45 x 400 = $18,000
- $32 x 150 = $4,800
  - **$174,600   Total Estimated Reproduction Cost New**

Estimate Accrued Depreciation

Once you know what the replacement cost of the structure is, you must calculate and subtract for accrued depreciation. Depreciation is the loss of value for any reason.

Accrued depreciation is the loss of value based on regular use over time. There are three types of depreciation.

- Depreciation is the loss of value for any reason
- Accrued Depreciation is the loss of value based on regular use over time

Types of Depreciation

There are three types of depreciation: Physical Deterioration, Functional Obsolescence and External Obsolescence.

- 3 Types of Depreciation
  - Physical Deterioration
  - Functional Obsolescence
  - External Obsolescence

http://www.workingre.com/estimating-physical-deterioration-2/

Physical Depreciation

Physical deterioration is caused by several factors; ordinary wear and tear from regular use over time, excessive wear and tear from excessive use over time, or physical damage either from use, weather, accidents etc. with the proper maintenance.

- Ordinary wear and tear
  - Regular use
- Excessive wear and tear
  - Excessive use
- Physical Damage
  - Lack of Maintenance

Functional Obsolescence

Functional Obsolescence is a type of depreciation that results in a loss of value. Buyer preferences change over time making the designs of some homes no longer desirable. Examples of functional obsolescence would be a 1 car garage.

Actually, even 2 car garages are becoming less desirable in some areas. A 1 bath home is seen to suffer from functional obsolescence. Buyers also prefer open floor plans today. Thus, choppy floor plans are another example.

- Buyer preferences change over time
  - Design No longer seen as desirable
- Examples
  - 1 car garage (2 car in some areas)
  - 1 bath homes
  - Choppy floor plan

External Obsolescence

External Obsolescence is probably the most frustrating for home owners.

This is a loss of value or depreciation that is suffered due to something literally outside of their control. Let's say that a house has a beautiful view of a lake. But then someone builds a structure that blocks the view of the lake and instead gives them something unsightly to look at. This would alter the value.

A more extreme version would be a noisy freeway that comes close to the boundaries of the property. Suddenly, the home would lose value. This type of depreciation is said to be incurable. There is nothing the owner can do to change or improve it.

- External Obsolescence
  - Outside the control of the owner
  - Incurable
    - Freeway
    - Factory
    - View changes

Age-Life Method

To use the Cost-Depreciation Approach Method, the appraiser first had to calculate the estimated reproduction cost. The age-life method is a popular method to calculate the depreciation that then needs to be subtracted from the estimated reproduction cost. The Age-Life Method requires the appraiser to attribute a total time period that he would expect a similar structure to last.

This is called the economic life estimate. He or she then attributes an effective age to the structure. This means they decide how old the building or house appears to be. This is an opinion and is not based on the actual age of the home.

Think about it this way. If a single person buys a home, pays for a professional crew to keep it maintained and is rarely home to use the property –this home would look substantially younger than a home of equal age that was lived in by a large family that had very little money for upkeep.

Estimate Accrued Depreciation

- Age-Life Method Utilizes
  - Estimated Reproduction Cost
  - Economic Life Estimate

- Appraiser opinion of how long the structure should last under normal use
  - Effective Age Estimate
    - Appraisers opinion of estimated age used up based on condition
    - Does not use actual age of the property!

Age-Life Method Formulas

There are two formulas that you can choose from to calculate the age-life method of depreciation. The first formula is less steps. Simply take the effective age and divide by the total economic age to equal the accrued depreciation.

Although shorter, I prefer the second formula only because the first formula requires that I memorize the formula, whereas the second formula just makes sense to me. I can solve the problem without relying on a formula I memorized. This might not be the case for you, though.

Estimate Accrued Depreciation

2 Age-Life Method Formulas

- Standard Formula
  - Effective age ÷ Total economic life × Reproduction cost new = Accrued depreciation
- Alternative method
  - Reproduction cost new ÷ Total economic life = Annual depreciation
  - Annual depreciation × Effective age = Accrued depreciation

With the second formula, you are simply taking the total reproduction cost and dividing it by the total economic age. This gives you your annual depreciation, meaning how much the building will depreciate each year from year one to the end of the economic life.

You then multiply the 1 year of depreciation by the number of years the appraiser believes have already been used up based on the effective age. This is your total accrued depreciation.

2 Age-Life Method Formulas

- Standard Formula
  - Effective age ÷ Total economic life × Reproduction cost new = Accrued depreciation
- Alternative method
  - Reproduction cost new ÷ Total economic life = Annual depreciation
  - Annual depreciation × Effective age = Accrued depreciation

Estimate Accrued Depreciation - Age-Life Method Practice:

Let's try an example of calculating accrued depreciation using the age-life method. A 4-year old villa was estimated to have a reproduction cost of $180,000. Ignore the fact that the villa is 4 years old. That's extra information that we do not use to solve the problem. The villa has an effective age of 2 years and an economic life of 60 years. To calculate the accrued depreciation, take 2 and divide by 60 and multiply the answer by the reproductive cost of $180,000.

$6,000 is the accrued depreciation.

Or you could have started with the $180,000 and divided by 60 to give you $3,000 of annual depreciation which you then multiply by the 2 years of effective age.

- o   A 4-year old villa was estimated to have a reproduction cost of $180,000.
- o   It has an effective age of 2 years.
- o   It has an economic life of 60 years.

What is the accrued depreciation?

$2 \div 60 = .0333 \times \$180,000 = \$6,000$ Accrued depreciation

Alternative method

$\$180,000 \div 60 = \$3,000$ Annual depreciation

$\$3,000 \times 2 = \$6,000$ Accrued depreciation

Now remember there are several steps to the cost-depreciation approach method. You've learned how to calculate reproduction cost of the structure. You've learned how to calculate accrued depreciation.

To use this approach, you subtract the accrued depreciation from the reproduction cost. You then add in the value of the land. The resulting value is the estimated subject property value.

So, Replacement Cost – Depreciation + Land Value = Estimated Value

- o   Calculate the Reproduction Cost of Structure
- o   Subtract Accrued Depreciation from the Reproduction Cost
- o   Add the Estimated Value of Land
- o   The Resulting Value is the Estimated Subject Property Value

Income Approach Method:

The income approach method is the third way appraisers use to calculate value. This is used when the property produces income such as with rental units.

- o   Basis value on future income generated from the property
- o   Used for income-producing property

http://www.appraisers.org/Disciplines/Personal-Property/pp-appraiser-esources/approaches-to-value

To work with the income approach to value, you need to understand some basic definitions; potential gross income, effective gross income, net operating income, operating expenses, variable expenses, fixed expenses, capitalization rate, gross rent multiplier, and gross income multiplier.

- o   Potential gross income
- o   Effective gross income
- o   Net operating income
- o   Operating expenses
- o   Variable expenses

- o Fixed expenses
- o Reserves for replacements
- o Capitalization rate
- o Gross rent multiplier (GRM)
- o Gross income multiplier (GIM)

Potential Gross Income (PGI)

Potential gross income is the estimated income if the unit is 100% full with no vacancies. It assumes that everyone pays as they are supposed to. Associate the "P" with potential as "Pie in the sky." Because it's not realistic. But it is the starting point for working with the income approach method.

PGI

- o Annual income if fully rented (no vacancies)
- o No collection loss
- o "Pie in the sky"

http://irrsandiego.com/the-difference-between-gross-income-and-effective-gross-income/

Effective Gross Income

The effective gross income does consider the fact that there are vacancies and losses. These are subtracted from the potential gross income. If there is any additional income for the property other than rent, it is added here.

EGI

- o Starts with Potential Gross Income
- o Less vacancy and collection losses
- o Add non-rental income

Potential Gross Income (PGI) – losses + other income = EGI

Net Operating Income

Your net operating income then is your effective gross income minus your operating expenses.

NOI

- o Effective Gross Income
- o Less operating expenses

Effective Gross Income (EGI) – operating expenses = NOI

Operating Expenses

If your net operating income is your effective gross income minus your operating expenses, then you need to know that operating expenses include fixed expenses, variable expenses, and reserves for replacements of building components. Fixed expenses are things that do not change based on occupancy. You must pay it regardless such as property taxes and hazard insurance.

Variable expenses are things that will change depending upon how the unit is being used and how full it is. It includes maintenance, utilities, supplies, etc. Notice that maintenance under variable expenses is different than reserves for replacement, which allows for a methodical outlay of savings toward things like roofing, air conditioners, etc.

- o Fixed expenses
- o Level predictable expenses regardless of occupancy
- o Property taxes & hazard insurance
- o Variable expenses
- o Changes with the occupancy level
- o Maintenance, utilities, supplies, etc.
- o Reserve for replacements
- o Savings for replacement of building components

It's very important that you know that depreciation, costs of the mortgage and income taxes are not included in operating expenses.

Operating Expenses

- o Not included in operating expenses
  - ▪ Depreciation
  - ▪ Costs of mortgage
  - ▪ Income taxes

Capitalization Rate

Your net operating income is important when using the income approach method, because knowing how to calculate it means you can now calculate your capitalization rate. By definition, capitalization rate is the relationship between the net income and the present value of the property. Basically, it's a way for investors to gauge whether a property is going to provide a rate of return on their investment that will make the property appealing enough to invest in.

The basic formula is that you net operating income divided by your capitalization rate equals the value of the property. This means that the net operating income divided by the value of the property is equal to the capitalization rate. Or that the value of the property times the capitalization rate equals your net operating income.

- o Capitalization Rate
  - ▪ Relationship between the net income
  - ▪ And the present value

I (NOI) ÷ R (Capitalization Rate) = V (Value/Sales Price)

I (NOI) ÷ V (Value) = R (Capitalization Rate)

V (Value) x R (Capitalization Rate) = I (NOI)

Let's say an appraiser wants to use the income approach to calculate value on a property that has a net operating income of $52,000.

The appraiser happens to have access to the net operating income of comparable properties. He also has access to their sale prices.

He can take each of their NOI and divide by the sales price which is the formula to determine the capitalization rate that each property produced.

Then, totaling the capitalizations rates of the comps and divide by 3 to get the average capitalization rate, the appraiser can then use this average to divide into the subject's property net operating income to calculate the estimated value of the subject property.

Solution

Capitalization Rate: Subject property has Net Operating Income of $52,000

- o Comparable 1 NOI of $55,000 sold at $550,000
- o Comparable 2 NOI of $40,000 sold at $375,000
- o Comparable 3 NOI of $60,000 sold at $425,000

Use: I (NOI) ÷ V (Value) = R (Capitalization Rate)

$55,000 ÷ $550,000 = 0.1

$40,000 ÷ $375,000 = 0.11   .1+.11+.14=.35 ÷ 3 = .12 Average Capitation Rate

$60,000 ÷ $425,000 =0.14

Use: I (NOI) ÷ R (Capitalization Rate) = V (Value/Sales Price)

$52,000 ÷ .12 = $433,333 Estimated Value

What is the Net Operating Income for a property with a value of $8,500,000 with a capitalization rate of 9%?

Use: V (Value) x R (Capitalization Rate) = I (NOI)

$8,500,000 x 0.09 = $765,000 Net Operating Income

In the previous example, you had to calculate net operating income when you knew the value and the capitalization rate.

Make sure that you can also determine the capitalization rate when you are given the value and the net operating income.

Solution

Take the net operating income of $765,000 and divide by the value $8,500,000 to equal .09 or 9% Capitalization

Rate.

Gross Rent Multiplier (GRM)

An alternative method to calculate value for the income approach is a method called the gross rent multiplier (GRM). This method works well with smaller rental units.

It determines value by measuring sale price against the rent produced each month.

It can also be used even if you do not know exactly how much rent is being collected by the subject property.

By knowing the average rent that is received in an area, this figure can be applied to the subject property to determine is estimated value.

- Gross rent multiplier (GRM)
    - o Ratio between a property's gross monthly rent (no other income)
    - o And its selling price
    - o Expressed as a ratio
- Calculate a Market Area GRM
    - o Taking sale price of comparable properties
    - o Dividing by gross monthly rent
    - o Then calculating average market-area GRM

Gross Rent Multiplier (GRM) Example:

Let's say that a subject property rents for $2,500 a month and the investor wants to know how much the estimated market value of the property should be based on the GRM Method. Knowing that comparable sales with their known monthly rents, calculate the area average GRM and apply to the subject property. First divide each of three sales prices by their monthly rent collected. This gives three GRMs. Total the three together and divide by 3 to give you the average GRM.

Solution

Knowing that comparable sales with their known monthly rent, calculate the area average GRM and apply to the subject property

$$\$250,000 \div \$2,225 = 112.36$$

$$\$210,000 \div \$2,000 = 105.00$$

$$\$180,000 \div \$1,800 = 100.00$$

$$112.36 + 105 + 100 = 317.36 \div 3 = 105.79 \text{ Average GRM}$$

$$\$2,500 \times 105.79 = \underline{\$264,475 \text{ Estimated Market Value}}$$

Gross Income Multiplier (GIM) Example:
    - o Annual Rents plus other Annual Income

Sometimes what you are working with are annual instead of monthly figures. The method to use in this case is the Gross income multiplier (GIM). One of the key differences between GRM and GIM, is the gross income multiplier uses all income, not just rent. The same approach to calculations still apply. However, you substitute the total annual income for the monthly income. So, if a subject property rents for $30,000 a year plus has additional income of $50,000. The investor wants to know how much the estimated market value of the property based on an average market are GIM of 8.81. You would add the $30,000 and the $50,000 for a total annual income of $80,000 which you multiply 8.81 for $704,800 in Estimated Market Value.

Solution

$$\$30,000 + \$50,000 = \$80,000 \times 8.81 = \$704,800 \text{ Estimated Market Value}$$

Averaging the 3 Approaches to Value

It is the appraiser's goal to use two or all three approaches to estimate value. By combining values into an average value of the three, they confirm value. Sometimes though, the appraiser may view one method to be more relevant than another.

So, just as when the appraiser applies a weighted percentage to individual properties with the sales approach, the appraiser can apply a weighted percentage to each resulting value from the various methods.

The appraiser multiplies the percentage by the value and then totals up the sums.

- Sales comparison approach
- Cost depreciation approach
- Income approach

Reconciling with Weighted Values for best Estimate

- Assigns a weight of relevance % to each value

As you can see in this example, these two approaches will result in different figures. Sometimes, as in this example, the difference will be small. But sometimes it can be a lot more significant. It is up to the appraiser to determine which approach is the most relevant for the subject property that is being appraised.

Sales Approach Value	$250,000
Cost-Depreciation Value	$275,000
Income Approach Value	$150,000

$675,000 ÷ 3 = $225,000 Estimated Value

Reconciling with Weighted Values for best Estimate

Sales Approach Value	$250,000 x	.60	= $150,000
Cost-Depreciation Value	$275,000 x	.20	= $ 55,000
Income Approach Value	$150,000 x	.20	= $ 30,000

$235,000 Estimated Value

PREPARING A CMA

V) Preparing a Comparative Market Analysis (CMA)

    A) Gathering appropriate data

        1) MLS

        2) Property appraiser's office

        3) Clerk of Courts

    B) Selecting similar comparables

        1) Recently sold

        2) Currently on the market

        3) Recently expired listings

    C) Common elements of comparison

    D) Adjusting for differences

    E) Computer generated CMAs

    F) Automated Valuation Models (AVM)

Comparative Market Analysis (CMA)

As a real estate licensee, you will prepare many comparative market analyses. So, let's learn some basics about the process.

A Comparative Market Analysis (CMA) is an Estimate of Value used by sellers to determine the best asking price. It's used by buyers to determine an appropriate offer to make on a property. CMAs are not appraisal reports, but they do use some of the same processes. A CMA determines value based on recently sold properties, properties currently on the market, and properties expired unsold.

- Estimate of Value
- Used by sellers to determine asking price
- Used by buyers to determine appropriate offer price
- Not appraisal reports but uses some of the same processes
- Value determined based on
- Recently sold properties

- Properties currently on the market
- Properties expired unsold

Gathering Appropriate Data

When gathering sales data, the best place for a sales associate to start is with the Multiple Listing Service. Remember that the MLS is an exchange of data among members that share information about current listings, listings that have sold, and listings that didn't sell.

The MLS is a valuable resource. Only licensees that have joined their local real estate board office (along with the NAR) and their local MLS have access to this data through the streamlined resources that membership gives. However, today, agreements between the MLS and third party vendors, such as Trulia and Zillow, means that this information is also readily available through other search methods.

- Multiple Listing Service (MLS)
- Property Appraisers Office
- Clerk of the Courts

http://www.realtor.com/advice/sell/how-much-is-your-home-really-worth/

Gathering Appropriate Data

Another resource when gathering sales data is the property appraiser's office. You can access a link directly from the MLS or through an online search.

The property appraiser's office will have access to sales data of houses that sold without being listed in the MLS – usually sold as a For Sale By Owner.

If you happen to know that a property has sold but it hasn't yet been recorded in the property appraiser's office online records, you can access the information directly by visiting the clerk of the courts for actual recorded sales figures.

- Multiple Listing Service (MLS)
- Property Appraisers Office
- Clerk of the Courts

Selecting Similar Properties

Your goal when determining a sales value for your subject property is to pick comparable properties that are as similar as possible to your subject property.

But just as an appraiser may have to adjust values for differences, you may end up doing so as well.

One of the most valuable comparisons you will look to are properties that have sold in the same area as your subject property and within a recent timeline.

Sold properties represent success and are the best measure to determine approximate value.

- **Recently sold properties**

However, the fact is that it is the properties that are currently on the market that your seller's home will be competing with. Therefore, currently listed properties do have some baring on value. Be careful with this, even if you happen to gain a buyer for a property that is priced well above the market average, it will probably only close if the buyer is paying cash.

Lenders require appraisals that justify sales prices through sold data.

- **Properties currently on the market**

And make sure you examine which properties haven't sold.

This can be a real clue as to not setting you and your seller up for failure. Remember that when it comes to analyzing the value of one property as compared to another it can be a bit more of an art than an exact mathematical science.

Just as the appraiser makes an opinion of when one comparable holds more weight over another, you may have to make a judgment as to when sales data do and do not apply.

- **Properties expired unsold**

Common Elements for Comparison

So, what are you looking for when you choose a property as a comparable? You are looking for property of similar style.

Compare single family homes to single family homes not to condominiums. Choose properties in a similar location with similar views.

Choose properties of similar size with similar features. If your property has a pool attempt to find comps that also have a pool. Keep in mind the condition of your subject property and how it compares to the comps.

- Style
- Location
- Square Footage
- # of Bedrooms and Baths
- Garage
- Pool
- Condition

Adjusting for Differences

As hard as you may try to find similar properties, you may end up having to make adjustments to the comps.

Follow the same process that was explained in the sales comparison approach. Make additions and subtractions to the comparable properties for the differences.

- CBS
  - o If the comparable property is BETTER

- ▪ SUBTRACT value from the COMPARABLE property
- CIA
  - ○ If the comparable property is INFERIOR
    - ▪ ADD value to the COMPARABLE property

Computer Generated CMAs

To ease the process of estimating value, a member of the multiple listing service can take advantage of computer generated CMAs as part of the software tools offered.

The results are as good as the time and effort the licensee puts into selecting valid comps to be utilized by the programs.

And you can still make additions and subtractions to the comps to make the results even more effective.

- MLS Generated CMA
  - ○ You pick the properties
  - ○ Can still make add and subtracts

Automated Valuation Models (AVM)

Many lenders utilize AVMs or Automated Valuation Models, which is a computer program that will provide a quick synopsis of value.

This is cheaper for the lender than utilizing an actual appraiser and is deemed appropriate for loans where they need just a cursory affirmation of value.

For example, it might be used with a homeowner who has good credit, good equity in the home, and is choosing to refinance the remaining balance.

The AVM will produce a value based on statistical data without ever visiting the home or examining pictures or even specifics about the property.

- Data analysis
- Lender Software
- Quick value synopsis

17 REAL ESTATE INVESTMENTS AND BUSINESS OPPORTUNITY BROKERAGE

Learning Objectives:

• Distinguish among the different types of real estate investments

• Identify the advantages and disadvantages of investing in real estate

• Distinguish among the various types of risk

• Explain the importance of investment analysis

• Describe the similarities and differences between real estate brokerage and business brokerage

• Describe the types of expertise required in business brokerage

• Distinguish among the methods of appraising businesses

• Describe the steps in the sale of a business

Key Terms:

Appreciation	Equity	Liquidity
Asset	Going concern value	Personal property
Basis	Goodwill	Risk
Capital gain (loss)	Leverage	Tax shelter
Cash flow	Liquidation analysis	

INVESTMENT REAL ESTATE TERMINOLOGY

I)   Investment Real Estate Terminology

  A) Cash flow

  B) Leverage

  C) Capital gain (loss)

  D) Basis E Appreciation

  F) Equity

  G) Liquidity

  H) Risk

  I) Tax shelter

Investment Real Estate Terminology

As a real estate professional, potential investors will look to you for professional guidance in determining whether a piece of property meets their investment goals.

With residential property, you will find investors that are looking to either rent the property or fix-and-flip.

On the selling side of a fix-and-flip, especially in the retail market, there's already room calculated in the selling price by the investor for your commission. Their objective is in getting the property sold as quickly as possible so that they can fund the next. These investors will want a market knowledgeable real estate agent with great marketing reach.

One of the exciting aspects about being adept at working with investors is that these individuals will usually keep coming back to you to purchase or sell more properties. However, just as the potential rewards have increased to you, so has the potential for liability. You will be working with aggressive investors on both ends of the deal; locating and buying properties as well as the listing and sale of the improved property.

To prepare yourself to work in this specialty, start by understanding basic investment terminology.

http://realestate.about.com/od/realestateinvestment/fl/Working-with-Real-Estate-Investors.htm

Cash Flow

The whole point of investing in real estate is to generate income. Your cash flow is defined as the remaining income after you deduct expenses and debt repayment from the income generated from the investment. The resulting cash flow can either be positive – meaning you are making money, or negative– meaning you are losing money.

There is a saying among investors that "cash flow is king." Experienced real estate investors generally buy properties that are cash-flow positive — based on conservative estimates, not perfect world estimates — and skip potentially negative cash flow properties.

To calculate cash flow, take total annual income and subtract all the operating costs, the payments for the debt (mortgage), property taxes and insurance, etc. and any cost to maintain or improve the property. The remaining amount is your annual cash flow. (Note this is NOT the same formula that is used to calculate net operating income.)

http://www.foxbusiness.com/features/2013/07/01/real-estate-investing-why-cash-flow-is-king.html

Total amount of money remaining after all expenses have been paid including **operating expenses, property taxes and insurance, mortgage debt payment and improvements.**

- Can be Positive or Negative

- Income minus expenses and debt repayment

- The resulting remaining income

http://www.investopedia.com/terms/c/cashflow.asp

Calculating Cash Flow Story Problem

Xavier purchased property with total rental income of $30,000. He paid a property management company $4,500 to handle the rental clients. He paid $8,000 total for property insurance and taxes; $5,000 in miscellaneous repairs and expenses; and paid $10,080 for principal and interest payments. What was his year-end cash flow?

Solution

- Income - Expenses (including operating expenses, property taxes and insurance, mortgage debt payment and improvements)
- $30,000 – ($4,500 + $8,000+ $5,000 + $10,080)
- = $2,420 Year-End Cash Flow

http://www.investopedia.com/terms/c/cashflow.asp

Leverage

An investor is said to be leveraging their investments when, instead of using all their own money to purchase a property, they borrow all or part of the funds to make the investment.

In fact, per the rule of investment strategies, the investor increases the rate of return by using borrowed funds. Therefore, financing investments with borrowed money makes them more profitable --when things go as planned – making the debt attractive.

At the same time, though, financing investments with borrowed money also increases the risk involved. Basically, a company that carries little debt relative to its operation stands less chance of going bankrupt than a company with a lot of debt. As such, highly leveraged deals are at greater risk of going bad. The lenders, then, typically demand a high interest rate loan to fund the deals.

http://www.vox.com/cards/bank-capital/if-more-leverage-can-increase-profits-why-dont-companies-borrow

When investors borrow all or part of the funds to make the investment.

- Using borrowed funds

- Finance an investment

The amount in which a purchase is paid for in borrowed money. The greater the **leverage**, the greater the possible gain or potential loss.

http://dictionary.reference.com/browse/leverage

Leverage Story Problem

Xavier purchased a property for $245,000. He took out a loan for $100,000. And the seller gave him a purchase money mortgage of $22,500. Xavier leveraged how much money to purchase the property?

Solution

- Leverage is the use of someone else's money to purchase property. This would include all sources.
- $100,000 + $22,500 = $122,500 leveraged.

http://dictionary.reference.com/browse/leverage

Basis

Your basis is the cost of the property.

This is the original purchase price, plus the fees to buy. However, the basis is then adjusted by taking into consideration that there have been costs to improve the property – capital improvements.

These costs are added to the basis. Then, by subtracting depreciation already taken on tax statements, you have your adjusted basis or your "cost of the property."

No one wants to pay the same tax twice, but that's exactly what happens when they don't correctly figure the cost basis of real estate investment. (This includes investment as a primary residence – a person's home.)

This is a concern when reinvesting the capital gains rather than taking the earnings in cash. These transactions increase the basis, or tax value, of investments.

The basis amount is crucial in determining any capital gains tax bill you owe when you sell your holdings. It also could add to any capital gains tax loss you want to use.

http://www.bankrate.com/finance/money-guides/figuring-investment-cost-basis.aspx#ixzz3xzzRGyH4

Basis = This is the original purchase price plus the fees to buy.

- The original cost to buy the property

- The purchase price

- Less Fees to purchase

The Adjusted Basis is calculated by adding the cost of capital improvements made to the property and subtracting reported depreciation to the IRS on tax statements.

http://www.investinganswers.com/financial-dictionary/tax-center/cost-basis-1037

Calculating Basis Story Problem

Xavier negotiated a purchase of a property at $245,000. He paid 3.5 % in closing costs. All other fees were paid at closing by the seller. What is the amount of his BASIS?

Solution

- *Original purchase price plus the fees to buy = BASIS*
- $245,000 x .035 = $8,575 is the amount of closing costs Xavier paid to purchase. Add $8,575 to the $245,000 to the purchase price to equal his BASIS of $253,575.
- Even if Xavier took out a loan to cover the $245,000, the entire purchase price is still used to calculate basis!

Calculating Basis Story Problem 2

Xavier negotiated a purchase of a property at $245,000. He paid 3.5 % in closing costs. All other fees were paid at closing by the seller. During the five years that he owned the property, he made capital improvements of $50,000. Xavier had already claimed $42,908 in depreciation on his taxes regarding the property. What is the amount of his ADJUSTED BASIS?

Solution

Original purchase price + the fees to buy + capital improvement cost – depreciation already reported to the IRS = ADJUSTED BASIS

$245,000 x .035 = $8,575 is the amount of closing costs Xavier paid to purchase. Add $8,575 to the $245,000 to the purchase price to equal his BASIS of $253,575. Take $253,575 Basis and + the Capital improvements $50,000 = $303,575

Take $303,575 and subtract $42,908 already reported to the IRS ADJUSTED BASES of $260,667.

Capital Gain (loss)

When an investment property is sold, the investor must report either a capital gain or a loss on the income statements for tax purposes.

This is the amount the property is sold for minus the selling expenses such as real estate commissions minus the adjusted basis. If this is a positive amount, then it is a profit. If it is a negative amount, then it is a loss.

No one wants to lose money on an investment. Unfortunately, even in the best planned situations, it does happen. When it does, the capital losses may be claimed on the tax return. All property owners should keep clear, accurate and complete records to claim these losses.

Keep in mind, real estate licensees are not to advise investors on tax issues and should always direct clients to consult with tax professionals.

http://www.geeksonfinance.com/how_5968536_calculate-capital-losses.html

Capital Gain (loss) is the amount the property is sold for minus the selling expenses such as real estate commissions and minus the adjusted basis. If this is a positive amount, then it is a profit. If it is a negative amount, then it is a loss.

- Amount a property is sold for minus selling expenses

- Less adjusted basis of the property

- Can be a gain or a loss

- Tax Term

http://www.investinganswers.com/financial-dictionary/investing/capital-gain-1026

Calculating Capital Gain (Loss) Story Problem

Xavier sold an investment property after holding it for five years. He sold it for $310,000 and paid $24,600 in selling expenses. His Adjusted Basis for the property is $260,667. What is the amount of his Capital Gain or Loss?

Solution

- This is the amount the property is sold for minus the selling expenses such as real estate commissions and minus the adjusted basis. If this is a positive amount, then it is a profit. If it is a negative amount, then it is a loss.

- Sale Price - Selling Expenses – Adjust Basis = Capital Gain (Loss)

- $310,000 - $24,600 - $260,667 = $24,733 Capital Gain

Appreciation

Appreciation is the gain in value that is achieved because the economy is getting better and things are worth more.

Appreciation matters because it can impact the decision for whether it's better to buy a home or continue renting or to sell and move to a different home. Even small changes in appreciation can have a large impact on long-term value.

The increase in the value of a home can be greater than what is paid out in taxes, insurance, maintenance and interest. It is this increased value that older home owners cash in through a reverse mortgage while still maintaining possession of a home.

Appreciation applies to the original purchase and any improvements made to the home.

http://michaelbluejay.com/house/appreciation.html

Appreciation is the gain in value of a property.

- Increase in property value

  - Property Improvements

  - Improvement in the economy

    - (versus improvement that result in increased value)

http://www.businessdictionary.com/definition/appreciation.html

Appreciation Story Problem

Xavier bought a property that appraised for $245,000. When he sold it, it appraised for $310,000. How much had the property appreciated?

Solution

Current Property Value – Original Property Value = Appreciation

$310,000 - $245,000 = $65,000 in Appreciation

(Take $65,000 ÷ $245,000 = 27% Appreciation)

http://www.businessdictionary.com/definition/appreciation.html

Equity

The equity that you have in a property is how much the property is worth minus what is owed on the property.

One of the main benefits of property ownership is the ability to build equity over time. It's also possible to have negative equity. In other words, you owe more than your home is worth.

Equity is an asset. When a property owner builds equity, the net value of the asset is increased. One way to do this is by paying off your mortgage.

http://banking.about.com/od/mortgages/a/Build-Equity.htm

The equity that you have in a property is how much the property is worth, minus what is owed on the property.

- Market Value

- Less Debt (loans/mortgages)

www.investorwords.com/5605/home_**equity**.htm

Equity Calculation Story Problem

Xavier purchased a property that appraised for $245,000. He put 50% down when he bought the property. He sold it five years later at an appraised value of $310,000. His balance on the mortgage when he sold the property was $111,500.

How much was Xavier's equity when he bought the property?

How much was Xavier's equity when he sold the property?

Solution

- Value – Debt = Equity
- $245,000 – ($245,000 x .5) = $122,500 Equity when he purchased.
- $310,000 - $111,500 = $198,500 Equity when he sold it.

Liquidity

When someone invests in a property, one of the things the investor will analyze is how hard the property will be to resell. The ability to sell a property quickly is known as liquidity.

The term liquidity refers to how fast something can be turned into cash – literally cold, hard cash.

When seeking liquidity, there are several options. At one extreme, an investor could hide the cash in a safe. Or they could place the money in a savings or checking account. Money market accounts or certificates of deposit are another option. Investments in United States Treasury bills are a liquid option due to the short duration. However, most investors wish to see greater gain on their cash, so they seek other investment opportunities.

A rule that many investors follow is to keep enough liquid assets that they need to cover expenses for at least several months—investing the rest. Each investor must personally calculate how much liquid cash is needed for their own circumstances.

http://beginnersinvest.about.com/cs/banking/a/091102a.htm

The term liquidity refers to how fast something can be turned into cash – literally cold, hard cash.

- Noncash investments

- Ability to convert to cash quickly

- The opposite **of Illiquidity-** unable to convert to cash quickly

http://www.businessdictionary.com/definition/liquidity.html

Risk

When someone invests in a property, they should face the fact that they potentially risk losing all or part of their investment.

A key concept to understand is the tradeoff between risk and return on an investment.

If a person places cash in a fireproof safe that is huge and bolted in place and then hidden in an unobvious location, it's as close to 100% secure as it can be. But what return will be gained on it? The money will not increase – creating even more cash. The tradeoff, then, is that 100% safe means 0% return on the money.

On the other hand, probably the riskiest option is for someone to play the lottery. With a major lottery, the individual faces more than a 99.999% chance of losing the money invested, but if the person actually wins, the jackpot provides an extremely large return on the "investment."

http://www.fool.com/teens/teens03.htm

Risk is the probability that an actual return on an investment will be lower than the investor's expectations.

- The chance to lose funds invested

- All or Partial

http://www.investorwords.com/8620/investment_risk.html

Tax Shelter

Often investors choose to invest in real estate as a means to avoid paying taxes on money earned from other endeavors. Remember that taxes are not a real estate agent's licensed expertise so always refer clients to real estate tax specialist and income tax specialist for guidance in these areas.

A tax shelter is a legal technique used by tax payers to avoid paying tax (or lowering the amount of tax paid) by reducing taxable income. The lower the taxable income, the lower the taxes that are required to be paid. This technique should not be confused with evading taxes, which is not legal.

Retirement accounts is one example of a type of tax shelter. Legal tax shelters generally create income as does the example of the retirement account.

Investment in real estate is another example of a possible tax shelter that an investor may choose.

http://money.howstuffworks.com/personal-finance/personal-income-taxes/tax-shelters1.htm

Tax Shelter is an investment that shields items of income or gain from payment of income taxes

- Shields from paying taxes

- Advantage of owning real estate

http://www.investorwords.com/4918/tax_shelter.html

Types of investments

A) Residential

B) Commercial

C) Industrial

D) Agricultural

E) Business opportunities

Investors have five types of investments they could make regarding real estate. These areas include residential properties, commercial properties, industrial properties, agricultural properties, and business opportunities.

A real estate license is required to assist others in the sale or purchase of these properties – for a fee.

- **Residential**- Used as homes for individuals or families
- **Commercial** – Used as retail or office buildings
- **Industrial** – Used for manufacturing
- **Agricultural** – Used for farming
- **Business Opportunities** – The sale of the business itself.

Residential

An investor can choose to purchase property with the intention of renting the property for residential use. Single family homes, condominiums, villas, and townhouses can be a good investment when the rents surpass the expenses of the property.

Investment in residential real estate includes single family and multifamily housing. Single family houses may be a detached single-family home, a condominium, a villa, or a townhouse. Multi-family units include a duplex, a multiplex and even large apartment buildings.

- Single-family
    - Single-family homes
    - Condominiums
    - Villas
    - Townhouses
- Multifamily rentals
    - Duplex
    - Multiplex
    - Apartment Buildings

        http://beginnersinvest.about.com/od/realestate/a/Types-Of-Real-Estate-Investments.htm

Investors who invest in residential real estate, may find it as a great compliment to an investment portfolio.

The investor may choose to take out a mortgage, creating more of a hedge against inflation for the investor. The investor may also benefit from increasing rents and property value appreciation. While taxes and repairs could go up in price, mortgage payments can be predictable with a fixed rate amortized mortgage. Even when investors purchase the property without loans, they can still benefit from inflation.

Some investors prefer to invest in single family homes to maximize rental amounts over individual units of multi-unit buildings. Many investors also find it easier to start with single family homes as multi-unit properties generally require a larger outlay of cash.

Other investors prefer multi-family housing investments over single family investments as the cost per unit is usually less. Plus, investing in properties scattered over a geographical area can increase operating expenses as the management process is more involved as compared to a multifamily rental property --with all the units on one site.

Investors will also offset losses from vacant units in a multi-unit property with the income from filled units. For this reason, investors often view these types of properties as posing less risk.

http://www.wealthdaily.com/articles/should-you-invest-in-residential-real-estate/4912

Commercial

Many investors are attracted to investing in commercial properties. This includes both retail and office properties.

One of the attractive features of commercial over residential is that commercial property normally holds long term leases with their tenants. Investors view these leases to mitigate the risk involved with investing in real estate.

- Retail
    - Shopping centers
    - Shopping malls
- Office properties
    - http://beginnersinvest.about.com/od/realestate/a/Types-Of-Real-Estate-Investments.htm

Commercial properties typically offer more financial reward than residential properties, but there also can be more risks.

Tenants of commercial properties may be a mix of large corporate clients and small privately owned companies. Investors find that regardless of the size of the company, tenants of commercial properties tend to take good care of the property as this directly correlates with their rapport with their public image which protects their livelihood. This aligns with the property owner's desire to maintain and improve the quality of the property.

Yet, if one of these tenants goes out of business, it can take a big bite out of the property investment income.

Investors also may find it easy to evaluate the property prices of commercial property requesting the current owner's income statements. An appropriate offer price can be made based on these statements. Many investors prefer the simplicity of the number analysis versus having to negotiate with residential property owners, which often involves more emotions from the seller than with commercial property.

http://www.nolo.com/legal-encyclopedia/pros-cons-investing-commercial-real-estate.html

Industrial

Investors can choose to invest in industrial properties. These properties house manufacturing, assembly and distribution activities.

It may or may not involve the business operations as well.

- Manufacturing

- Assembly

- Distribution

http://beginnersinvest.about.com/od/realestate/a/Types-Of-Real-Estate-Investments.htm

Research reveals that investing in industrial property comprise 15-25% of the total market of investment real estate.

Warehouse property investments have been shown to bring the highest rate of return for all property investment opportunities. Based on reports from the NCREIF - National Council on Real Estate Investments Fiduciaries-investing in industrial properties overall outperforms most other property type investments on an income basis coming in only second to investing in apartment buildings.

Investment in industrial properties has been less volatile than investment in most other property types per NPI data. A stable income component translates into reduced volatility and lower investment risk.

Occupancy levels over the long-term have rarely dipped below 90% for any significant time period. In contrast, office occupancy levels have dipped to 80% or less in most major markets.

http://www.kra-net.com/news/news_a01.htm

Agricultural

Agricultural property which consists of large tracts of farmland is appealing to investors both for current income and also for future development. Leasing the property out to farming businesses in the short run can produce immediate income.

- Large tracts of farmland

- Current Agricultural income

- Future Development

http://beginnersinvest.about.com/od/realestate/a/Types-Of-Real-Estate-Investments.htm

Farmland has very low correlation to financial markets. This means that, traditionally, agricultural farmland investments are largely unaffected by external events such as actions taken by the Federal Reserve Bank. It is also less affected by political turmoil, global conflict, debt defaults, banking crisis, and equity market swings.

Rapidly growing global middle-class and dietary needs are expected to drive up food demand by 70-100% by 2050*.

Investors prefer to invest in large tracts of land to subdivide in the future. Keep in mind, though, that the development of property is restricted by zoning laws which can impede the process of transitioning agricultural land to other uses.

It is important that your investor be educated on current and possible future land use restrictions when making their investment decisions. Also, the investor will be looking to the real estate licensee for assistance with these issues.

http://ifarmshares.com/?page_id=102

Business Opportunities

Legal definitions vary; in its simplest terms, a business opportunity is a packaged business investment that allows the buyer to begin a business. The Federal Trade Commission and 25 states regulate the concept.

A business opportunity, in the simplest terms, is a packaged business investment that allows the buyer to begin a business. (Technically, all franchises are business opportunities, but not all business opportunities are franchises.) Unlike a franchise, however, the business opportunity seller typically exercises no control over the buyer's business operations. In fact, in most business opportunity programs, there's no continuing relationship between the seller and the buyer after the sale is made.

Although business opportunities offer less support than franchises, this could be an advantage for you if you thrive on freedom. Typically, you won't be obligated to follow the strict specifications and detailed program that franchisees must follow. With most business opportunities, you would simply buy a set of equipment or materials, and then you can operate the business any way and under any name you want. There are no ongoing royalties in most cases, and no trademark rights are sold.

Business opportunities are difficult to define because the term means different things to different people. In California, for example, small businesses for sale--whether a liquor store, delicatessen, dry-cleaning operation and so on--are all termed business opportunities, and individuals handling their purchase and sale must hold real estate licenses.

Making matters more complicated, 23 states have passed laws defining business opportunities and regulating their sales. Often these statutes are drafted so comprehensively that they include franchises as well. Although not every state with a business opportunity law defines the term in the same manner, most of them use the following general criteria:

   •A business opportunity involves the sale or lease of any product, service, equipment and so on that will enable the purchaser-licensee to begin a business.

http://www.entrepreneur.com/encyclopedia/business-opportunity

Advantages of Real Estate Investments

A) Rate of return

B) Tax advantages

C) Hedge against inflation

D) Leverage

E) Equity build up

Investing in real estate holds multiple advantages as well as disadvantages over different types of investment opportunities. Investors weigh out the pros and cons to decide which type of market makes the most sense for them to invest their money.

Many others strive for a well-balanced portfolio with varied investments including real estate.

Advantages

Investing in real estate can be appealing over other types of investments because of several advantages including rate of return, tax advantages, hedge against inflation, leverage, and equity buildup.

- **Rate of return**

- **Tax advantages**

- **Hedge against inflation**

- **Leverage**

- **Equity buildup**

http://www.entrepreneur.com/article/250677

Rate of Return

- The amount of income generated in a year by capital invested, expressed as a percentage of the total sum invested.

When choosing whether to invest in real estate verses other types of investments such as stocks, bonds, or precious metals, investors are often attracted to real estate for the rate of return on the money invested that these investments tend to bring.

The rate of return can vary depending upon the nature of the real estate being invested. Single family homes tend to bring the lowest return on investment.

Real estate investment trusts are like mutual funds, but instead of holding shares of stock, they hold commercial real estate properties. Investing in REITs can be a good way to get access to a balanced real estate portfolio without having to spend hundreds of millions or billions of dollars to get it. An index of REITs issued by the National Council of Real Estate Investment Fiduciaries shows that REITs provided an annualized return of 10.91 percent over the 20-year period ending on December 31, 2011.

http://homeguides.sfgate.com/average-rate-return-real-estate-investments-72195.html

NCREIF also tracks the performance of high-quality commercial real estate assets like those owned by pension funds. Their property index includes properties across the country spanning multiple sectors like offices, retail centers, hotels, apartment buildings, and industrial complexes. Over the period from 1978 to 2012, their index achieved an annualized return of 9.19 percent.

Many private investors use income capitalization rates -- more commonly known as cap rates -- to analyze their returns. To calculate a cap rate, you divide a property's net operating income by its purchase price. While the cap rate is not the most exact or detailed valuation metric, it is extremely popular and gives a good general sense of how a property is doing. Cap rate targets differ from property type to property type and based on locale.

http://homeguides.sfgate.com/average-rate-return-real-estate-investments-72195.html

Tax Advantages

- Many investors choose investing in real estate as a way to divert taxes from money earned from other avenues. This is known as a legal tax shelter.

One of the many advantages about being a real estate investor is the many federal income tax advantages that are available. Utilizing real estate investing lets investors keep more of what they make. Tax advantages include a tax deduction for depreciation. Depreciation includes the building structures, plus the capital improvements. Taxes, insurance, and utility expenses are deductible. Repairs are deductible. Commission paid for real estate sales, purchase, and management services are deductible. Office and home office space is deductible. Along with basic office supply expenses. Basic business expenses are also deductible along with mileage related to the real estate business.

Be sure to refer your clients to tax advisors for advice on these matters.

https://www.biggerpockets.com/renewsblog/2013/04/15/income-tax-benefits-real-estate-investors/

Hedge Against Inflation

- The goal of investing is to see a gain in income. Real estate tends to increase in value faster than inflation. Investing in real estate is seen as a hedge against inflation. This is one of the advantages of investing in real estate over other types of investments.

Historically, investing in real estate has been one of the best investments to counteract high rates of inflation. Inflation is a slow, silent killer.

The actual value money at the time that is borrowed is much higher than its value when the loan is repaid. The loan amount stays the same making the investor the beneficiary of having secured the terms before inflation drove up the interest rates and the now higher value of the property. However, this may be negated if a fixed rate has not been utilized for a loan.

For the investor in rental property who has locked in his cost of the loan on the property throughout the 15 to 30-year term, rental rates can be frequently adjusted to increase income.

http://www.creonline.com/blog/investing-in-real-estate-an-exceptional-hedge-against-inflation/#ixzz3y2Vam6vF

Leverage

- Use of borrowed funds

- Increases rate of return

As already explained, an investor is said to be leveraging their investments when instead of using all their own money, they borrow funds to make the investment. In fact, they can increase their rate of return by using borrowed funds.

Because the property itself can act as collateral, real estate is one of the few investment opportunities that truly affords itself to an investor taking advantage of leverage.

http://www.entrepreneur.com/article/250677

Leverage Calculation Story Problem

To understand how this works, let's examine the rate of return achieved if an investor puts up $400,000 to purchase a property that is bringing in a Net Operating Income of $35,000 a year.

The capitalization rate, or rate of return on the investment is 9%.

- $35,000 \div $400,000 = 9% Rate of Return all cash investment

Whereas if the investor limits their cash outlay to only 30% or $120,000 with an annual debt service payment of $19,300, then the return on their investment increases to 13%!

- $35,000 - $19,300 = $15,700

- $15,700 \div $120,000 = 13% Capitalization Rate

Keep in mind that the increase in return on investment is because the outlay of money monthly for the loan debt (principal and interest) is not used in the calculation.

Equity Buildup

- An investor enjoys a gain in equity when he pays down the debt on the property and when the property increases in value due to appreciation.

- Increase through

  - Paying down the debt

  - Increase in value through appreciation

Every payment that is paid on a mortgage involves some level of principal payment. While homeowners pay their own mortgage, investors utilize the rental income itself to pay back the mortgage. So, the investor is using someone else's money for equity buildup.

Many investors forgo cash flow to increase the payment toward the equity building up equity at a quicker pace. While others will allow the equity to build up more slowly and diverting left over cash flow to other business or personal uses.

http://www.entrepreneur.com/article/250677

Disadvantages of Investing in Real Estate

    A) Illiquidity

    B) Market is local in nature

    C) Need for expert help

    D) Management

    E) Risk

Disadvantages

Just as there are many advantages to investing in real estate, there are also many disadvantages. Each investor must personally weigh out the disadvantages to determine whether an investment fits that person's investment criteria.

Disadvantages include:

- Illiquidity
- Market is local in nature
- Need for expert help
- Need for management
- Risk

http://www.investopedia.com/university/real_estate/real_estate4.asp

Illiquidity

- It can be difficult to quickly turn funds invested in real estate back into cash

When deciding where to invest their money, investors consider how easy it will be to sell the investment and turn their money back into liquid assets. Being able to do this quickly is known as liquidity. Real estate has a reputation for having poor liquidity as it can often take a while to sell property – at least to sell it while obtaining a decent sales price. For this reason, illiquidity is one of the disadvantages of investing in real estate.

http://www.investopedia.com/university/real_estate/real_estate4.asp

Market is Local in Nature

- The fact that the buyers of real estate tend to pull from the local geographic area around a property makes investing in real estate to be viewed as a disadvantage.

Don't be confused by the fact that many buyers do come from international areas. Overall, across the country, most real estate sales are between local buyers and sellers.

This is in contrast with most other investment opportunities which is now traded on a global scale.

The fact that real estate is local in nature is considered one of the disadvantages of investing in real estate.

http://www.investopedia.com/university/real_estate/real_estate4.asp

Need for Expert Help

- The exchange of real estate is a complicated process that generally requires the involvement of experts in the field including real estate licensees. This is viewed as a disadvantage of real estate.

  - Real Estate Professionals

  - Title attorneys or companies

  - Accountants and Tax professionals

Even when an investor chooses to take on many of these tasks for him or herself, the investor finds that the property and the tasks take ongoing active attention.

http://www.investopedia.com/university/real_estate/real_estate4.asp

Management

- Managers

- Rent Collection

- Property Maintenance

- Property Improvements

Investing in options other than real estate options can mean making the purchase and then forgetting about it until it is time to cash out the investment.

This is not true with real estate. Real estate requires ongoing attention including the management of the property, the collection of rent, property maintenance, and property improvements. This is seen as a disadvantage compared to other types of investments.

http://www.investopedia.com/university/real_estate/real_estate4.asp

Risk

- As already stated, when someone invests in a property, they must face the fact that they potentially risk losing all or part of their investment.

This is something that must be considered with all types of investments.

Because there are many factors that can affect the success of a real estate investment, this is viewed as a disadvantage of investing in real estate.

http://www.investopedia.com/university/real_estate/real_estate4.asp

ASSESSMENT OF RISK

Assessment of Risk

    A) Risks associated with general business conditions

        1) Business risk

        2) Financial risk

        3) Purchasing-power risk

        4) Interest-rate risk

    B) Risks that affect return

        1) Liquidity risk

        2) Safety risk

            (a) Market risk

            (b) Risk of default

General Business Condition Risks

An investor should weigh out the advantages verses the disadvantages when deciding whether to invest in real estate and when choosing an investment property.

Part of what makes an investment risky are the risks associated with the general business conditions. These include business risk, financial risk, purchasing power risk, and interest-rate risk.

- Business risk

- Financial risk

- Purchasing-power risk

- Interest-rate risk

Business Risk

Business risk is the possibility that a business can fail. Income and expenses are projected, but unforeseen circumstances can result in a shortfall in business income.

If these losses are substantial enough, it can result in the business failing and the investment being lost. This is known as business risk.

- Projected Income and Expenses verses

- Actual Income and Expense

  - Net Operating Income less than expected

  - Can cause the business to fail (default)

https://en.wikipedia.org/wiki/Business_risks

Purchasing-power Risk

An investment is made in real estate with the assumption that the profits from the real estate investment will outpace inflation. This is not always the case.

When expenses go up faster than rents can be increased, for example, the investor can see decline in the value of their investment funds.

This is known as purchasing-power risk.

- Inflation increases faster than the return on investment

- Inflation risk, as the name implies, is the risk that gradual inflation will erode the value of the dollar and reduce the value of long-term investments.

http://www.investopedia.com/ask/answers/101315/why-are-mutual-funds-subject-market-risk.asp

Interest-rate Risk

Increase in interest rate charged on an investment.

The appeal of a variable rate mortgage is lost when suddenly the rate that is being charged by a lender outpaces the rents that are being charged to tenants. This is known as interest-rate risk.

- Interest rates are increased on loans made for the investment

    http://www.investopedia.com/ask/answers/101315/why-are-mutual-funds-subject-market-risk.asp

Risks That Affect Return

Investors must decide how much risk they are willing to take in order to achieve their desired rate of return.

Generally, the higher the risk taken, the higher the expected return. For example, money kept in the bank has no risk (to insured levels). The return on bank accounts, though, tend to only keep up with the inflation rate. This is a low risk, low rate of return.

- Balance risk of liquidating the investment and with how safe it is lower the risk, the lower the return

    - Higher the risk, the higher the return

        http://www.narach.com/investment/risk_and_return.htm

Liquidating the Investment

When things start to go wrong, an investor is going to want to be able to sell quickly.

He must assess the risk and make predictions about how easy it will be to sell a property should he need to do so in a hurry. He will be measuring the liquidation risk against the desired rate of return.

Each individual investor must decide for themselves how much risk they are willing to take.

- Need for a quick sale

How safe is the investment? We've already learned that a type of business risk is the possibility that interest rates on a loan for an investment property can increase.

This is known as interest-rate risk.

This process decreases market value, which is known as market risk. Combined with the risk of default, the overall safety risk must be measured compared to the ability to liquidate quickly and the desired rate of return.

Safety Risk

- How safe is it?
    - Market Risk
    - Risk of default

http://www.investopedia.com/terms/m/marketrisk.asp

Nature of Business Brokerage

   A) Similarities to real estate brokerage

      1) Almost always a sale of real property or an assignment of a long-term lease is involved

      2) Must be licensed pursuant to Chapter 475, F.S., Part I

   B) Differences from real estate brokerage

      1) Usually involve transactions containing assets other than real estate

         (a) Personal property

         (b) Goodwill

      2) The value of the business may be less than, equal to, or greater than the value of the real estate. That is, the "going concern" value may be different than the real estate value

      3) Markets for business enterprises are typically wider in geographic scope than markets for individual parcels of real estate

   C) Expertise required in business brokerage

      1) Corporate finance

      2) Business accounting

      3) Valuation of businesses

         (a) Comparable sales analysis

         (b)Cost approach

         (c)Incomes analysis

         (d)Liquidation analysis

   D) Steps in the sale of a business

Business Brokerage vs. Real Estate

The selling of a business falls under your activities as a licensed real estate agent.

Because business normally involve real estate, either through the sale of the property along with the business or with the buyer taking on a long-term lease for where the property is located, Florida Statutes have deemed the sale of businesses as a real estate license activity.

There are both similarities and differences between business brokerages and real estate.

- Similarities

- Differences

Similarities

Selling both real estate and business brokerages involves the sale of real property or the assignment of a lease of real property.

Because it involves property, per Florida Statutes 475, a real estate license is required to assist in the sale of a business.

Both business brokerages and real estate involves the:

- **Sale of real property**

- **Or assignment of lease**

- **Requires real estate license**

Florida Statute 475.01

Differences

Differences in selling a business as compared to regular real estate includes that most real estate involves the sale of personal property as well as the real estate.

Personal property for a restaurant, for example, could include the perishable food inventory and tables and chairs used in the dining room.

The reputation of a business is often a huge part of the value and sale of a business. This is known as **goodwill** and is involved with the sale of a business compared to regular real estate.

- **Assets other than real estate is the first difference**

  - **Personal property**

  - **Goodwill**

The value of the business may be less than, equal to, or greater than the value of the real estate. That is, the "Going Concern" value may be different than the real estate value.

Because reputation affects the value of a business, the going concern value of a business can be more or less than the value of the property.

- **Going-concern is a second difference in real estate verses business sales.**

Think about the process of valuing a business with many personal assets that would need to be inventoried and assigned a value in order to negotiate and write up a deal for a sale of that business.

The value of the business could be directly tied to its non-real estate inventory. Apply this concept to an award-winning horse farm. If the farm was known for the line of descendants that came from the horses on the farm, then the value of the horse farm would be directly tied to the horses – the personal inventory of the farm rather than the real estate.

What if a virus threatened the stock of horses on the horse farm before a sale was completed?

Or what if the reputation of the horse farm was hurt because rumors spread that illegal hormones where unfairly altering the blood line of the animals? Suddenly the "Going Concern Value" could plummet.

Markets for business enterprises are typically wider in geographic scope than markets for individual parcels of real estate.

For real estate, it is said to draw from a local market. Yet, the opposite is true for the sale of businesses. Buyers tend to pull from a much larger area – even from a global range.

Perhaps it is easier for a buyer to take the plunge of moving across the country, or world, when income from a business is involved.

- **Market wider in geographic scope is the third difference between business brokerages and real estate.**

Florida Statutes 475.01

Nature of Business Brokerages
Business Brokerage vs. Real Estate
Summary:

Similarities

- Involves sale or assignment of long-term lease of real estate
- A real estate license is required per Florida Statutes to sell real either

Differences

- Involves the sale of personal property and goodwill
- The "Going Concern" Value may differ from the real estate value
- Market wider in geographic

Expertise Required in Business Brokerage

If a real estate licensee wishes to specialize in business opportunity sales, it is important to become adept in the areas of corporate finance, business accounting, and valuation of businesses.

- Corporate finance

- Business accounting

- Valuation of businesses

http://www.valuadder.com/valuationguide/business-valuation-three-approaches.html

Corporate Finance

To work with investors, it is important to have knowledge of corporate finance.

Classes can be taken to learn about issues such as corporate sources of funding, the capital structure of corporations, the actions managers take to increase the value to shareholders, corporate stocks, and budgeting.

- Corporate sources of funding

- Capital Structure

- Corporate stocks

  - Preferred and common

- Management to increase value

- Budgeting

http://people.stern.nyu.edu/adamodar/New_Home_Page/background/cfin.htm

Business Accounting

Business accounting consists of three basic activities: identifying, recording and communicating the economic status of a company.

Accountants use bookkeeping techniques to systematically record and report the financial status of a company. Financial statements communicate accounting information.

As a real estate professional selling businesses, it is important to have a basic understanding of these financial statements and how to evaluate cash flow. Remember to stay within the range of your expertise and refer your clients to business accounting experts as needed.

- Income analysis statements

- Cash flow analysis

http://www.ehow.com/info_8120801_business-accounting.html

Valuation of Businesses

Estimating the value of a business is very similar to estimating the value of regular real estate. As with regular real estate you can use the comparable sales approach, the cost approach, and the income approach to evaluate the value.

Another method when a business is involved is the liquidation analysis.

- Comparable sales analysis

- Cost approach

- Income analysis

- Liquidation analysis

http://www.valuadder.com/glossary/business-valuation-methods.html

The basic place to start in determining value is the comparable sales analysis approach.

As with regular real estate, you are looking for similar businesses that have sold. Comparing the attributes of the business, you then determine a close estimation of value of the subject business.

- Comparable sales analysis

  - Sale of comparable businesses

  - Similarities and differences

http://www.valuadder.com/examples/valuing-a-business-based-on-market-comps.html

Cost Approach

For a business that involves real estate, it would be appropriate to determine value by calculating the cost approach. This is the same process as with regular real estate.

Determine the replacement cost. Deduct for depreciation. Add the land value. For a business, remember to add for other assets plus the value of goodwill.

- Reproduction cost

- Replacement cost

The cost approach is based on the principle of substitution, and postulates that a prudent buyer would pay no more for an asset than the cost to replace the service capacity of that asset.

http://www.appraisaleconomics.com/range-of-services/business-valuation/

Income Analysis

Unless an investor is simply looking to invest for appreciation, the income analysis may be one of the most important methods for placing value on a business.

Remember that the income approach looks at projected income and compares it to other businesses that have sold.

There are several methods that accomplish this.

http://www.appraisaleconomics.com/range-of-services/business-valuation/

Liquidation Analysis

Liquidation analysis is a process unique to business valuations verses regular real estate.

Because a business usually involves a great deal of personal property, the value of selling off the assets including the real estate and shareholder stocks is added to the cash on hand to lessen the debt obligations.

- Used for business going out of business

http://www.investopedia.com/terms/l/liquidation-value.asp

Steps in the Sale of a Business

Selling a business is like selling regular real estate. It starts with identifying all the real estate and personal property that is included in the sale. Valuation methods are applied to determine the asking price. The business is marketed to bring a potential buyer. The potential buyer signs a non-disclosure agreement and evaluates financial records of the business. A contract for the sale is entered into. The closing takes place to transfer the property.

1. Identify real estate and personal property (assets) being sold

    - A complete inventory list detailing exactly what is being included with the sale of the business is a necessary test when listing a business for sale

2. Determine the valuation of the business – includes goodwill

    - A combination of the cost approach and income approach are the usual valuation methods used to determine the asking price

3. Market the business to potential buyers

    - Businesses can be included in the Multiple Listing Service. There are also specialty MLS services designed for businesses as well as business brokerage groups that allow for listing and marketing business for a national and global customer reach

4. Buyer signs non-disclosure agreement – keep info. private

    - Before allowing a prospective buyer to take a close look at the private financial information for a business, the buyer will be asked to sign a non-disclosure agreement. This is the buyer's agreement to keep this information, sometimes including the very fact that the business is for sale, confidential

5. Purchase contract negotiated

    - This is very similar to the negotiation process for regular real estate, however lawyers are usually utilized for the drawing up of the agreement

6. Closing to transfer property

    - Before closing can occur, inspection and financing tasks will need to be completed

18 TAXES AFFECTING REAL ESTATE

Learning Objectives:

• Distinguish among immune, exempt and partially exempt property

• Describe the various personal exemptions available to qualified owners of homestead property

• Compute the property tax on a specific parcel, given the current tax rate, assessed value, eligible exemptions and transfer of assessment limitation difference (save our homes portability) if applicable

• List the steps involved in the tax appeal procedure

• Describe the purpose of Florida's Green Belt Law

• Calculate the cost of a special assessment, given the conditions and amounts involved

• Describe the tax advantages of home ownership

• Explain how to determine taxable income of investment real estate

• Distinguish between installment sales and like-kind exchange

Key Terms:

ad valorem	debt service	mill
assessment limitation (save our homes benefit)	exempt properties	special assessment
	installment sale	tax rate
assessed value	immune properties	taxable income
capital gains	just value	taxable value
community development districts	like-kind exchange	

REAL PROPERTY TAXATION

I)   Real Property Taxation

A) Local importance

1) Primary source of revenue

B) Determining "just value"

1) General procedure

(a) Provisions under Amendment I

2) Protest procedure

(a) Property owner contacts property appraiser within legislated time frame

(b) File an appeal with the Value Adjustment Board

(c) Litigation in the courts

(1) Certiorari proceeding

C) Exemptions from property taxes

1) Immune property

2) Exempt or partially exempt property

3) Homestead exemption

(a) Assessment limitation (save our homes benefit, portability)

(b) Surviving spouse exemption

(c) Disability exemption

(d) Blind person's exemption

(e) Cumulative homestead tax exemption

(f) Military service-connected total and permanent disability tax exemption

(g) Tax exemption for certain totally and permanently disabled persons

4) Greenbelt law exemption

(a) Nature

(b) Purpose

(c) Provisions

D) Calculating taxable value

E) Calculating property taxes

F) Special Assessments

    1) Purpose of special assessments

    2) Limitations on use

    3) Computation of assessment rate

    4) Special assessment liens

G) Nonpayment of real property taxes

H) Purchasing tax certificates

Local Importance

Property taxes are used to generate revenue for our government. However, considering that we have governmental powers at the Federal, State, and Local levels, this could get cumbersome to property owners if all levels of government had the power to tax property.

Fortunately for property owners, the Federal government is NOT allowed to impose property taxes per the Constitution of the United States.

Our U.S. Constitution, which created a form of government known as federalism, divided powers between a single national federal government and the individual states. Certain powers were designated as being under the exclusive domain of the federal government while other powers were passed onto the state level. Property taxation is one of the powers that was passed to the state. However, the Constitution also imposes limitations on the laws that states may enact and enforce with the foresight of protecting citizens from over taxation.

https://www.bgdlegal.com/blog/tax-and-finance/constitutional-limitations-on-state-and-local-taxation/

In the state of Florida, though, the state has declined to impose property taxes at the state level and instead has passed the authority for taxation down to the local level of government which includes taxation powers to each **city, county, public school board and special assessment tax district**s.

At the state level, Florida relies on sales and use tax, intangible tax and corporate income taxes to fund the state government. There is no personal income tax in Florida compared to most states which is a draw for people moving to Florida.

Property taxes hold local importance as it provides the funds for the operating budgets of our cities, counties and school districts. In fact, property taxes are the primary source of funding for local government budgets.

http://www.taxpolicycenter.org/briefing-book/state-local/revenues/local_revenue.cfm

Primary Source of Revenue

Property taxes fund a large percentage of the cost paid to teachers, police officers, fire fighters, government staff, administrative staff, etc.

Florida has more than 640 local "governments" that impose a property tax to fund operations. These include the cities, counties, school boards, and special districts. Roughly, 50 percent of Florida's public education funding and 30 percent of its local government revenues come from property taxes.

Each year, in the autumn, locally elected officials in each jurisdiction set a proposed tax rate for the upcoming fiscal year which usually begins on October 1.

The budgets are prepared for each year based on projected total funding costs required to cover operating expenses for the coming year.

http://dor.myflorida.com/dor/property/taxpayers/

Determining "Just Value"

General Procedure

All department budgets are submitted and "totaled" to make the final city or county budget. The budget is used then to determine how much revenue should be required to collect through property taxes which translates into the amount of tax charged to property owners: The total revenue needed is divided between property owners as a **property tax.**

To keep property taxes from being unwieldy, the Florida Department of Revenue reviews the property tax rolls of each county along with the property appraiser's annual budget. This ensures that the tax base established by the property appraiser is equitable, uniform, and in compliance with Florida law.

The Florida Department of Revenue also ensures that local government millage rates do not exceed state-mandated caps. In addition, the Department confirms that local governments properly and timely send notices and advertise public hearings to adopt millage rates and annual budgets.

F. S. 166.211 Ad valorem taxes

http://www.investopedia.com/terms/a/advaloremtax.asp

General Procedure

Property taxes are used to fund local government. The state has oversight to make sure that each property owner is not being unduly taxed by monitoring the budgets and tax rates imposed. How is it decided how much each property owner will have to pay toward property taxes?

To determine the property taxes of an individual property owner, first the property itself must be assigned a value. Then, a tax rate is multiplied by the value to determine the tax amount owed by a property owner.

Florida courts mandate that this value be determined through a fair process that reflects market value. This value is called the **Just Value**.

F.S. 166.211 Ad valorem taxes.

http://www.investopedia.com/terms/a/advaloremtax.asp

Property tax is called an **ad valorem tax** because it is said to be based on a determined "fair value" of the property- not an arbitrary value. (And it is not for a one-time purpose taxation such as a special assessment).

Taxes are assessed and levied for a full calendar year and then collected in **arrears** or for the year past. So, when the tax bill is issued, it is for the previous year or rather for the calendar year that is ending.

Per Florida Statutes 166.211

Ad valorem taxes.—(1) Pursuant to s. 9, Art. VII of the State Constitution, a municipality is hereby authorized, in a manner not inconsistent with general law, to levy ad valorem taxes on real and tangible personal property within the municipality in an amount not to exceed 10 mills.

- **Ad valorem, according to value**

  - Tax is Levied for full calendar year

  - Paid in arrears – for past year

Just Value – defined as market value

166.211 Ad valorem taxes. http://www.investopedia.com/terms/a/advaloremtax.asp

General Procedure

It is the property tax appraiser who determines the assessed value of a property. The appraiser applies value to the property based on:

- The best use of the property, the property location, the property size, the replacement value of the property, and the condition and income generated from the property.

- If the property was sold during the period being assessed, then the sale price will also be taken into consideration.

By looking at the combined property values within a taxable area and the budget needs of the government, a **millage rate** is calculated to multiply by each property value to determine each individual owner taxes owed. This process is designed to cover the expenses carried by the property taxes while fairly dividing them among the property owners.

Florida Statute 195.087

The resulting tax rate is presented in "**mills**" (unit of money) and per Florida Statutes; county, city, and school taxes cannot each exceed 10 mills.

As a real estate licensee, you will be expected to have knowledge of how to apply millage rate to assessed values to determine total property taxes.

That starts by understanding what a mill is and how to work with it as a math problem. **F.S.195.087**

Real Property Taxation

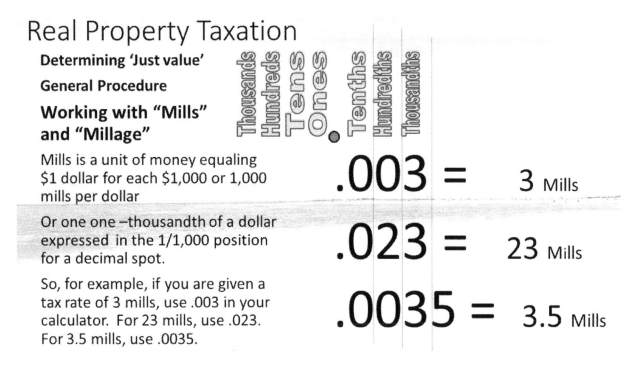

Determining 'Just value'

General Procedure

Working with "Mills" and "Millage"

Mills is a unit of money equaling $1 dollar for each $1,000 or 1,000 mills per dollar

Or one one –thousandth of a dollar expressed in the 1/1,000 position for a decimal spot.

So, for example, if you are given a tax rate of 3 mills, use .003 in your calculator. For 23 mills, use .023. For 3.5 mills, use .0035.

.003 = 3 Mills

.023 = 23 Mills

.0035 = 3.5 Mills

Working with "Mills" and "Millage" Story Problem

Investor Gary bought a property that was assessed to have a just value of $450,000.

The county tax is 8 mills, the city tax is 9 mills, and the school tax is 5 mills.

How much would Gary owe in property taxes?

Investor Gary bought a property that was assessed to have a just value of $450,000. The county tax is 8 mills, the city tax is 9 mills, and the school tax is 5 mills. How much would Gary owe in property taxes?

To solve this problem, you total all three tax rates together, convert the total into a decimal and multiply by the assessed value:

- 8 mills + 9 mills + 5 mills = 22 mills

- Converting 22 mills to decimals is .022 mills

- .022 x $450,000 = $9,900 Property Tax Due

All property assessments and proposed tax rates for the year are to be sent to each property owner by August. This notice is called a TRIM notice.

- TRIM stands for "Truth In Millage"

This notice contains the property's value on January 1, the millage rates proposed by each local government, and an estimate of the amount of property taxes owed based on the proposed millage rates.

The date, time, and location of each local government's budget hearing is also provided on the notice. This gives property owners the opportunity to attend the hearings and comment or object to the millage rates before approval.

The actual tax bill is sent out usually in late October or early November with full payment due for the taxes from the property owner by the following March 31.

Discounts of up to four percent are given for early payments.

The Florida Department of Revenue provides training and certification to tax collectors and their staff to promote fair, uniform, and cost-effective tax collection procedures.

http://dor.myflorida.com/dor/property/taxpayers/

F.S.195.087

Provisions Under Amendment I

In the interest of limiting property tax, On January 29, 2008, citizens of Florida passed an Amendment relating to property tax with four parts.

Part 1. Provides for an increased applicable tax exemption to homesteaded property.

Part 2. Created a Portability provision.

Part 3. Provided for personal property tax exemptions. (Not discussed here.)

Part 4. Placed an Assessment Cap on Non-homestead Property

The benefits of these additional provisions will be discussed in more detail as Homestead exemptions and Save Our Home is examined.

http://www.pcpao.org/Amend1_Instruct.html

Protest Procedure

Not everyone is happy with the tax notice that they receive and find fault with the property's assessed value determined by the property assessor. In addition to attending public meetings to protest tax rates, property owners can also take steps to protest the assessed value of their property.

There are 3 steps that can be taken in protest:

The property owner must act swiftly, as the steps must be implemented within applicable timelines.

The first step involves an informal meeting with the property appraiser to discuss your objections to the appraisal. The second, is to file an appeal with the Value Adjustment Board. The third step is to proceed to the courts for litigation.

1. Meet with Property appraiser
2. File an Appeal with the Value Adjustment Board
3. Litigate in Court

Informal Meeting with Property Appraiser

If a property owner disagrees with the **TRIM** notice, the property owner contacts the property appraiser within the legislated time frame to request a meeting.

By having an informal meeting, the issue may be settled without going to a hearing or going to court. Property owners should take any documentation available that may support a change in the assessment or eligibility for an exemption or property classification.

During the meeting, the property appraiser will present facts that support his or her assessment for the value of the property.

Having an informal conference with the property appraiser **does not extend the deadline** to file a petition with the value adjustment board, which must be done within 25 days of the TRIM notice being mailed.

http://dor.myflorida.com/dor/property/taxpayers/

F.S.194.011-.015

File an Appeal with the Value Adjustment Board

Property owners who want to appeal their property value may do so with the value adjustment board (VAB) by filing a petition (DR-486 form) with the clerk of the court within **25 days** of the Notice of Proposed Property Taxes.

Although a property owner has petitioned the VAB, it is important to pay the tax bill before it becomes delinquent which is usually on April 1.

The members of the **VAB** will decide to either uphold the property tax appraiser's opinion of value or make an adjustment on behalf of the property owner.

- The Value Adjustment Board is made up of two members of the governing body of the county as elected from the membership of the board of that governing body. One member is the elected chairperson. One member is also a member of the school board --as elected from the membership of the school board. Plus, there are two citizen members of the two citizen members; one is appointed by the governing body of the county and must own homestead property within the county. The other must have been appointed by the school board and must own a business occupying commercial space located within the school district.

Litigate in Court

Property owners may also file a lawsuit in circuit court to challenge the property appraiser's assessment or denial of a change from the VAB.

The property owner is not required to go through the steps of the informal meeting with the property appraiser or file a petition with the value adjustment board in order to file a lawsuit.

It is also important for property owners to be aware that even when going through those steps, in order to file a lawsuit in court, it must be filed within 60 days of the date of a VAB decision or the property appraiser's certification of the tax roll, whichever is later.

- The court proceeding is called a **Certiorari Proceeding** as the purpose is for a judicial review of a decision made by an administrative agency—in this case, the VAB. The court could either rule to uphold the decision of the assessed value or force that an adjustment be made.

http://dor.myflorida.com/dor/property/taxpayers/

Exemptions from Property Taxes

Not all property is taxed equally. To be exempt means to be free of an obligation.

Some property owners are free or "exempt" of the obligation to pay property tax either on all of their property value or part of their property value.

Exemptions to property are divided into 3 categories.

1. Immune property- 100% Exempt

2. Exempt property – 100% Exempt

3. Partially exempt – Exempt on part of the property value but still pays some tax.

It is important for property owners to understand the exemptions that may apply to their situation as the exemptions will not be applied unless specifically requested by the property owner. Property owners also look to real estate licensees for guidance in these matters. F.S.196.192, f.s196.199, f.s.195.011

Immune Property

The purpose of property taxes is to support the cost of government. Property taxes, for example, are used to fund a police department. That means that not only are the police officers being paid through the collection of property but also the cost of the building itself.

The police building is in fact government owned. It wouldn't make sense to levy a tax against the police building as doing so would be levying a tax against an entity to support itself. In the end, if a tax was levied, the cost of the tax would drive up property tax for other properties in the community in order to pay the tax on behalf of the police department! Basically, this is a form of double taxation!

To avoid this circular tax trap, government buildings are "immune" to taxation and no tax is assessed.

- Schools

- Municipal buildings

- Police headquarters

- Fire Stations are all examples of immune property.

Florida Statute 196.199

Exempt Property

Some reports claim that as much as one quarter or one-half of a typical U.S. city may be made up of tax-exempt property. Included in this figure are the non-government owned properties such as churches, church schools and other nonprofit organizations.

Exempt property is property that has been assessed, but the property is relieved of paying taxes through their applied tax exemptions.

The tax exempt status of entities such as churches is not without controversy.

Proponents of the exemption argue that that it keeps the government out of church finances and thus upholds the separation of church and state. Furthermore, they point to the crucial social services provided through these organizations.

Opponents argue that giving churches special tax exemptions violates the separation of church and state, and that tax exemptions are a privilege, not a constitutional right.

- Churches

- Church Schools

- Nonprofit Organizations are all examples of exempt property.

http://churchesandtaxes.procon.org/

Partially Exempt Properties

The government has allowed for special circumstances to decrease the tax liability and possible hardship that the tax liability can impose on individual property owners.

Partially exempt property owners are still obligated to pay taxes, however the property tax value that has been assessed is reduced by the exemptions which then reduces the property taxes that are charged by multiplying the rate to the reduced value rather than the full assessed amount.

- Homestead Exemptions

- Greenbelt Law Exemptions are all examples of Partial Property Exemptions.

Homestead Exemption

When a property owner makes a property his or her permanent residence, the property owner may be eligible to receive a homestead exemption up to $50,000.

- The first $25,000 applies to all property taxes, including school district taxes.

- The additional exemption of up to another $25,000 applies to the assessed value between $50,000 and $75,000 and only to non-school taxes. This additional exemption was voted into place through the 2008 Amendment Part I.

A resident of Florida who holds title to a property, resides permanently in the property as of January 1, and makes an application to the county property appraisers office on or before March 1, may establish the residence as a homestead and take advantage of these exemptions.

F.S.196

Exemptions from property taxes

Homestead Exemption

Property Value	County/City	School
$25,000	Exempt	Exempt
$25,000	Taxable	Taxable
$25,000	Exempt	Taxable

* Over $75,000 Value is Taxable

The first $25,000 in value is exempt for County, City and School taxes.

The second $25,000 in value (up to a total of $50,000 in assessed value) is taxable. At this point you have $25,000 in taxable value and $25,000 in exempt value.

The third $25,000 is exempt for both county and city taxes but NOT school taxes. At this point you have $50,000 in exemptions for county and city and only $25,000 in exemptions for school taxes with a total county and city taxable value of $25,000 and a total school taxable value of $50,000 at a total assessed value of $75,000.

Homestead Exemption Example

A homeowner has a property assessed at $49,000. The owner has homesteaded the property. What is the taxable value of the property?

The assessed value in this example is $49,000. The first $25,000 is exempt from taxation. $49,000 value minus the $25,000 exemption leaves a taxable value of $24,000. (The additional homestead exemption does NOT come into play until assessed value is $50,000 or more.)

$49,000	Assessed value
- 25,000	Original exemption (County/City/School)
$24,000	Taxable value

Assessment Limitations - Save Our Homes (SOH)

Controlling property taxes through partial exemptions is only part of the solution. Another method utilized is controlling how much a property owner's assessed value can go up from year to year.

- This limitation in assessments keeps property tax from rising out of control for homestead property per the Save Our Homes amendment as part of the Florida Constitution.

Per Statute 193.155

- **Any change resulting from reassessment shall not exceed the lower of the following: (a) Three percent of the assessed value of the property for the prior year; or (b) The percentage change in the Consumer Price Index …Exemptions from Property Taxes.**

Assessment Limitations - Save Our Homes (SOH)

What this means is that if a property assessed for $100,000 one year (and it is homesteaded which is a requirement for the Save Our Homes provision to kick in); then the next year's property assessed value cannot exceed $103,000.

- Limits increase:

    - To qualify must be legally a permanent resident of Florida

        - Only one homestead can be claimed

        - Hold title to the property as of Jan. 1

        - First year

            - Must be filed with the property appraiser before March 1

    - Currently limits increase in tax to 3% /year or the CPI (Consumer Price Index), whichever is LESS

    - Homestead owner can transfer up to $500,000 to a new homestead.

F.S.196

Why is the Save Our Homes Amendment so important?

Imagine that 50 years ago, Harriet inherited the family cottage from her grandparent. The property had been and still was in the family as it had been for generations.

Harriet didn't have a lot of money. She worked hard, earning a small but manageable income and every day she came home to her tiny home which sat right on the beautiful Gulf of Mexico. For years, life was pretty quiet for Harriet. But over the last couple of decades, her little home had become surrounded by grand mansions.

Without the Save Our Homes Amendment, things wouldn't end so well for Harriet. This is because with every mansion that was built around Harriet, the more her property tax assessed value would have been driven up. Scenarios like this is quite common across the country, with taxes rising to a point that a home owner can no longer to afford to live in their own home.

Fortunately, in Florida, with the Save Our Homes Amendment this is no longer such a risk. Take Harriet for example. Even if property values rose in a given year by 7%, her assessed value would only rise as high as the Consumer Price Index or 3%- whichever was lower.

Real Property Taxation

Assessment Limitations –

Save Our Homes (SOH)

		Value Based On Neighborhood Increase	Assessed Value Based on 3% Cap SOH
Year 1, Harriet's Property Assessed at	$150,000		
Year 2, Values in Harriet's neighborhood increased by 8%;		$162,000	$154,500
Year 3, ...6.5%		$172,530	$159,135
Year 4, ...12%		$193,234	$163,909
Year 5, ...9%		$210,625	$168,826
Year 6, ...11%		$233,794	$173,891
Year 7, ...14%		$266,525	$179,108
Year 8, ...10.5%		$294,510	$184,481

Difference in property value in the 8th year: $294,510 - $184,481=$110,029

If the total tax rate is 26.5 mills times $110,029= $2,915 SAVED! In property taxes!

Assessment Limitations – Portability

Part 2 of the Amendment I created a Portability provision.

- Homestead property owners can transfer their Save Our Homes (SOH) benefit (up to $500,000) to a new homestead within two years of giving up their previous homestead.

- If the just value of the new homestead is more than the previous home's just value, the entire cap value can be transferred.

- If the new homestead has a lower just value, the percentage of the accumulated benefit may be transferred to the new homestead.

Part 2 of the Amendment I created a Portability provision.

What this means is that Homeowners may transfer their SOH benefit (savings of assessed value) to a new homestead anywhere in Florida within two years of leaving their former homestead **if the new homestead is established by January 1**.

For example, if you moved during 2015, the exemption remains on your home until December 31, 2015. You have until January 1, 2017 to qualify for a new exemption and port the benefit to a new homestead. This provision applies to all taxes, including school taxes.

For property owners who have the homestead exemption and the Save Our Homes cap, and who do not give up their homestead, the exemption and cap status remain unchanged.

http://www.pcpao.org/Amend1_Instruct.html

Assessment Limitations – Portability

"Moving Up" Story Problem

Harriet decided to move out of her little cottage on the Gulf. She bought a property with a market (just) value of $340,000. Because her property had been homesteaded, she can bring the value of her assessment caps with her to apply to the new home. The market value of her old home at the time of sale was $294,510. Her assessed value was only $184,481. (This is before her standard homestead exemptions were deducted.)

Solution

- To determine the taxable value of the new home, take the assessed value of the new home and subtract the SOH Benefit (amount of assessed value not taxed) and subtract applicable homestead exemptions.
- $294,510 - $184,481=$110,029
- $340,000-$110,029=$229,971
- $229,971 - $50,000 (Homestead Exemptions) = $179,971 Taxable Value of New Home for City and County.
- $229,971 - $25,000 Taxable Value of New Home for School taxes.

Assessment Limitations – Portability

"Down Sizing" Story Problem

Let's say Harriet decided to downsize (rather than moving up) so when she sold her little cottage on the Gulf, she bought a property with a market (just) value of $175,000. Because her property had been homesteaded, she can bring the value of her assessment caps with her to apply to the new home. The market value of her old home at the time of sale was $294,510. Her assessed value was only $184,481. Determine the taxable value of the new home.

Solution

- Take the market value (just value) of the new home and divide by the market value of the old home. Take the resulting percentage and multiply by the assessed value of the old home.
- $175,000÷294,510=0.5942073x$184,481=$109,620 Assessed Value of New Home
- $109,620 - $50,000 (Homestead Exemptions) = $59,620 Taxable Value of New Home
- For County and City ($84,620 School)

Assessment Limitations

Warning for working with home buyers:

Keep in mind that when a buyer purchases a property, the taxes paid by the seller may not accurately reflect the taxes that the new owner will pay due to the Save Our Home provisions.

If a buyer with a tight budget doesn't understand that their own taxes could be significantly higher, the buyer will look toward the real estate licensee as having not fully informed them prior to the purchase. Included on the state approved purchase agreement is a warning to buyers regarding taxes. Be sure to read the disclosure to the buyers and explain that licensees can in no way guarantee assessed values or tax rates of purchased property.

Real Property Taxation

Exemptions From Property Taxes
Homestead Exemption
Additional Exemptions for homesteaded property F.S.196

To further ease taxable values for individuals with special circumstances, there are additional exemptions available for homesteaded property owners.

- **$500 Additional Exemptions:**
  - Surviving spouse- widowers and widowers
  - Non-veterans who are totally and permanently disabled
  - Legally blind

- **Quadriplegics are totally exempt** – 100% (No property tax paid)

  F.S.196

Real Property Taxation

Exemptions From Property Taxes
Homestead Exemption
Additional Exemptions F.S.196

Disabled Veteran Exemption –
- If at least 10% disabled by military service connected incident
  - Entitled to an **additional $5,000 exemption** from homestead property
  - Not limited to homesteaded property!
  - Includes surviving spouse if married for 5 years upon date of death
  - Once age 65, additional discounts are available connected to % of disability on homesteaded property
- Totally & permanently disabled veterans (includes confinement to a wheel chair)
  - 100% exempt
  - Must be homesteaded property
  - Includes surviving spouse
- Surviving spouses of veterans who died while on active duty
  - 100% Exempt

F.S 196

See addendums for more information regarding these additional exemptions.

Greenbelt Law Exemption

The Greenbelt Law Exemption is a partial exemption that protects agricultural land from being taxed by higher values based on highest and best use.

Development of nearby lands can drive up values of agricultural lands that can drive farmers out of the market.

To help protect this from happening, the greenbelt exemption allows appraisers to assess lands on a basis that can favor the agricultural nature of the land.

Agricultural land:

- Assessment based on use

- Not based on highest and best use

- Protect farmers

- Requires annual classification

F.S. 193.461

Exemptions from Property Taxes

Greenbelt Law Exemption

F.S.193.461 (3)(a) Lands may not be classified as agricultural lands unless a return is filed on or before March 1 of each year. Before classifying such lands as agricultural lands, the property appraiser may require the taxpayer or the taxpayer's representative to furnish the property appraiser such information as may reasonably be required to establish that such lands were used for a bona fide agricultural purpose. Failure to make timely application by March 1 constitutes a waiver for 1 year of the privilege granted in this section for agricultural assessment.

To be classified as agricultural, the property owner does not have to live on the property and does not have to be the person who works the land.

The property owner can lease the land to someone else who conducts the agricultural activities.

In that case, the property owner is responsible for ensuring that the land is used for agriculture.

A property owner who gives false information to obtain or to renew an agricultural classification for the tax savings could be charged with perjury.

http://www.ehow.com/list_6750199_florida-greenbelt-laws.html

Assessment Limitations –Assessment Cap for Non-Homestead Property

Put into place as Part 4 of Amendment I, non-homestead property have a 10% assessment cap (similar to Save Our Homes). This provision took effect for the 2009 tax roll. This provision does not apply to school taxes.

No application is required to receive the benefit of the 10% cap. It will automatically be applied. The Cap is removed when a property changes ownership or changes use.

The 10% cap will sunset (expire) after 10 years, when it will be presented to the voters for re-approval.

http://www.pcpao.org/Amend1_Instruct.html

Calculating Taxable Value

Cumulative Homestead Tax Exemption

To calculate taxable value, start with the property assessor's determination of just value.

Check for whether the property is homesteaded and reduce the assessed value by applicable homestead exemptions. Keep in mind that the exemptions for the county and city taxable values are different from the school exemptions that are allowed.

Check for additional homestead exemptions such as widow/ers, the blind, the disabled, spouses of deceased warriors, etc.…and subtract these exemptions. This is the taxable value.

- Value of real property begins with an assessment by the property appraiser.

- Assessed Value – Exemptions = Taxable Value

http://dor.myflorida.com/dor/property/taxpayers/

Calculating Property Taxes

The taxable value of property in the total taxable area (county/city/school) multiplied by the tax rate, which is expressed in mills.

- A MILL is 1/1,000 of a dollar (1/10 of a cent). Therefore, there are 1,000 mills in a dollar. 15 mills equal a tax rate of .015. There is a top level or CAP on school board, city and county taxes, limited to 10 mills EACH.

  Taxable Value × Tax Rate = Annual Property Taxes Due

http://dor.myflorida.com/dor/property/taxpayers/

Calculating Property Taxes Practice (1)

A widower owns a homestead that is assessed for $180,000. The city tax rate is 6.6 mills; the county rate is 7.3 mills; and the school board rate is 8.4 mills. What will the owner owe in property taxes?

- This example has various rates and amounts to incorporate and add to find a final answer. Remember… School board tax exemption applies to first $25,000 of assessed value only.

Calculating Property Taxes Practice (1)

A widower owns a homestead that is assessed for $180,000. The city tax rate is 6.6 mills; the county rate is 7.3 mills; and the school board rate is 8.4 mills. What will the owner owe in property taxes?

City & County Taxes		School Board Taxes
$180,000	6.6 mills	$180,000
- 25,000	+7.3 mills	-25,000
- 25,000	13.9 mills	- 500
- 500		$154,500
$129,500		X .0084
X .0139		$1297.80
$1800.05		

$1800.05 + 1297.80 = $3097.85

Calculating Property Taxes Practice (2)

A widower owns a homestead that is assessed for $180,000. The city tax rate is 6.6 mills; the county rate is 7.3 mills; and the school board rate is 8.4 mills. What does the owner save in property taxes due to exemptions?

- This is asking for your tax savings using the exemptions available. Remember, school board exemption only applies to the first $25,000 of value. The county and city tax exemptions in this example apply to $50,000 exemption.

Calculating Property Taxes Practice (2)

A widower owns a homestead that is assessed for $180,000. The city tax rate is 6.6 mills; the county rate is 7.3 mills; and the school board rate is 8.4 mills. What does the owner save in property taxes due to exemptions?

City & County	School Board
$25,000	$25,000
+25,000	+ 500
+ 500	$25,500 Exemptions
$50,500 Exemptions	x .0084
x .0139	$214.20
$701.95	

$701.95 + $214.20 = $916.15

Calculating Property Taxes Practice (3)

In 2015, a homestead property was assessed for $200,000. During 2015, the CPI rose 1.5%. What is the maximum the assessed value for 2016?

Solution

- Remember the cap or maximum increase for a homesteaded property is 3% or the CPI- whichever is LESS. Therefore, go with 1.5% because it is LESS than the max of 3%.

- $200,000 x 1.5% = $3,000

- $200,000 + $3,000 = $203,000

- Maximum assessed value for 2016 is $203,000.

Calculating Property Taxes Practice (4)

If a homestead property is assessed at $65,000. What is the taxable value for city taxes only?

Remember that this property has the base exemption of $25,000, plus PART of the 2nd $25,000 exemption (The part over $50,000, but less than $75,000).

Solution

- $65,000 Assessed value
- - 25,000 Base exemption
- - 15,000 Additional exemption on part of assessed value above $50,000.
- **$25,000   Taxable Value**

Calculating Property Taxes Practice (5)

If a homestead property is assessed at $65,000. What is the total tax exemption that applies for city taxes only?

This is the same problem as before, only now it is asking what the total tax exemption is rather than the taxable value.

$65,000	Assessed value		
25,000	Base exemption		
+ 15,000	Additional exemption	**$40,000**	**Total Exemptions for city taxes**

Calculating Property Taxes Practice (6)

If a homestead property is assessed at $65,000. What are the taxes due for city taxes if the city tax rate is 9 mills?

Solution

- Remember that millage is one one-thousandths expressed in a decimal in the third spot to the right of the decimal (for single digit millage)

$65,000   Assessed value

- 25,000   Base exemption

- 15,000   Additional exemption on part of assessed value above $50,000.

      ($65,000 - $40,000 = $25,000 Taxable Value) Only for city, county – not school board.

$25,000   Taxable value

  x .009

$ 225   **City Property Taxes**

Calculating Property Taxes Practice (7)

If a homestead property is assessed at $65,000. What is the taxable value for school taxes if the school tax rate is 12 mills? What are the total school taxes?

Solution

- Remember that millage is one one-thousandths expressed in a decimal in the second spot to the right of the decimal (for double digit millage)

$65,000   Assessed value

- 25,000   Base exemption

- 0   Additional exemption on part of assessed value above $50,000 does not apply for school taxes! ($65,000 - $25,000 = $40,000)

$40,000   **Taxable value**

  x .012

$ 480   **School Property Taxes**

Special Assessments

Purpose of Special Assessments

Taxes that can be imposed on property are not limited to ad valorem taxes. Special assessments are taxes placed on property owners for a one-time purpose. Anything that isn't covered in the budget and directly affects the property owner can be charged as a special assessment.

The most commonly known special assessments are charged when drinking water lines are installed, sewer lines are installed or when streets or sidewalks are updated. However, special assessments are sometimes levied for police, fire, street lights, parking, etc.

Basically, anything that is a public improvement, which is also seen to directly benefit a property owner, can result in a special tax assessment.

These are not ad valorem taxes and are not applied based on property assessments. Instead, the cost levied against an owner is normally calculated on a front-foot basis or per hookup basis.

- For public improvement that benefits the property owner

- Street paving, sidewalks, sewers, etc.

- These are NOT ad valorem taxes

F.S.190

Limitation of Use

To impose a special assessment on a property owner, it is imperative that the governing body take care not to over extend their reach. For an assessment to be imposed, it must specifically improve the value of the property.

When property owners do not feel that the assessment is just, they can take the matter to court. There are many cases that have ended up in the upper level court system with judge's ruling the local governing body that imposed the tax, did so unjustly in that the project did not add value to the property owner charged with the assessment.

Assessments can be issued as a one-time tax or to be paid by the property owner over a period of time. Unpaid special assessments are a point to be negotiated on the sale and purchase agreement. The buyer and seller come to an agreement as to whether the assessment will be paid in full at or before closing or whether the buyer will be taking on the remaining assessment post-closing.

Computation of Assessment Rate

Real estate licensees need to understand how special assessments are calculated and charged to property owners.

As stated, these assessments are not put in place based on the value of the property or "assessed" taxable value.

Instead, calculations are conducted by the governing body imposing the assessment by dividing the total cost of the project by the property owners who have benefited from the expenditure based on the linear frontage (property line butting against the improvement).

Often the governing body imposing the assessment participates by sharing in the expense – covering the share through other revenue sources.

F.S. 190

Here are the steps to solve a math problem involving a special assessment:

The city is paving an unpaved street. The property has 150 feet facing the street. The paving cost is $45 a linear foot, and the city will pay 30% of the total cost. What will be the special assessment for this property?

Solution

- To work through this problem, the 150 ft. frontage is multiplied by cost of $45 per foot to = $6,750 total cost per foot benefiting this property.
- The city pays 30% so multiply $6,750 x .70 (owners share) which brings the total to $4725. BUT - Since a neighbor lives across the street (always assume this!), the cost of the road will be split between the two owners (one living on each side), so $4725 ÷ 2 = $2,362.50 which is the amount billed to each property owner – and the answer to the problem.

Special Assessments

Computation of Assessment Rate Practice (1)

Sunnyside Town is paving a deteriorated street. Property owner Taya owns a property with 200 feet of frontage facing the street being paved. Sunnyside Town has agreed to pay 25% of the cost with the property owners paying the rest through a special assessment. The cost for each linear foot is $30. How much will Taya have to pay?

Solution:

200 x $30 = $6,000

$6,000 x .75 (100% - 25%) = $4,500

$4,500 ÷ 2 = $2,250 charged to Taya

Special Assessment Liens

Property owners are not always happy or able to pay a special assessment that is being imposed on the owner. All such projects are always announced and voted on in public forums before being implemented.

Still, personal situations can make it difficult for a property owner to comply with paying the assessment.

Unpaid assessments become a lien on the property.

Just as with regular property tax, if the property owner fails to pay the property special assessment the government will act to collect on the debt. This collection process can put the property as risk.

http://dor.myflorida.com/dor/property/taxpayers/

Florida Statutes.197

Non-Payment of Real Property Taxes

Purchasing Tax Certificates

A property tax lien is a superior lien, meaning it is above all other liens on the property. The ad valorem tax, if unpaid, takes first positions. Any special assessment liens would be right behind the ad valorem tax lien.

If a property tax bill is not paid by the following March 31, the tax collector sells a **Tax Certificate** on that property in order to collect the unpaid taxes.

A tax deed may be sold if the property owner has not paid all back taxes, interest, and fees within two years. The tax certificate is issued by bid on property certificate. Auction of property can be called for by certificate holder between 2 and 7 years. If no one bids on property, the holder of the certificate is issued a tax deed. If someone bids on property and wins, it will be sold to highest bidder, who will then pay the certificate holder the amount of certificate plus interest.

- Tax certificate- issued for non-payment for interest to be bid upon
- Bid interest rate
  - 18% maximum rate
- Property owner owes taxes plus accrued interest
- Redemption of certificate- owner must pay certificate plus accrued interest

http://dor.myflorida.com/dor/property/taxpayers/

Tax Deed

Anyone can bid at the auction for tax certificate sale. The certificate holder will then be paid what he invested, plus interest. If there are no bidders, the certificate holder is issued a tax deed- ownership of the property with all liens cleared- except government liens.

- If a certificate holder puts the property up for auction, and no one bids on the property, the certificate holder is issued a Tax Deed.

F.S.197

FEDERAL INCOME TAXES

II) Federal Income Taxes

    A) Sale of real property

        1) Amount realized

        2) Capital gain (loss)

    B) Principal residence

        1) Tax advantages

      (a) Mortgage interest deduction on principal residence and second home

      (b) Deduction of property taxes on principal residence and second home

      (c) IRA withdrawal for first time home buyers

      (d) Exclusion of gain from sale of principal residence

C) Investment real estate

  1) Types of income and cash flows

      (a) Potential gross income

      (b) Effective gross income

      (c) Net operating income

      (d) Before tax cash flow (cash throw-off)

      (e) After tax cash flow

  2) Determining taxable income

      (a) Reserve for replacements

      (b) Interest

      (c) Depreciation

  3) Tax from operations

      (a) Capital gain (loss)

         (1) Short-term gain

         (2) Long-term gain

  4) Installment sales (contract for deed)

  5) Like-kind exchange

Sale of Real Property

Owning property and businesses has an impact on federal income taxes. Some of these are tax incentives to encourage home ownership. Real property is a capital asset. It is described by the Federal Government to be any property held by the taxpayer. Therefore, it is subject to CAPITAL gain or loss rules.

Capital Gain is profit from the sale of real property. Taxable gain is determined by calculating the amount realized or "gained" from a sale. This is the sale price minus expenses of the sale. The adjusted basis (the owner's original cost plus expense of the purchase and capital improvements) is then subtracted from the amount realized from the sale. If this calculation results in a positive figure, it is considered a capital gain. If it a negative number, then it is a capital loss.

Taxable gain is determined by:

- **Amount realized from sale**
    - Sale price less expenses of sale
- Adjusted basis
    - Owner's original cost, plus expenses of purchase and capital improvements
- Capital gain
    - Amount realized less Adjusted basis

www.irs.gov/.../**Real-Estate-Tax**

Sale of Real Property Practice (1)

A homeowner sold his house for $225,000 and paid $13,500 for broker's commission, doc stamps on the deed, and owner's title insurance. The owner's original cost was $180,000 with $7,750 in purchase expenses. The owner made capital improvements of $18,000. What were the owner's amount realized from the sale, adjusted basis and capital gains?

Three questions in one. Figure out one part of the question at a time and then solve.

$225,000 - $13,500 = $211,500 amount realized from the sale

$180,000 + $7,750 + $18,000 = $205,750 adjusted basis

$211,500 - $205,750 = $5,750 capital gains

Principal Residence

Tax Advantages

Property owners can claim a mortgage interest deduction on their taxes for their principal residence and also for a second home.

Home ownership is encouraged by current tax laws.

Itemized deductions, not the standard deduction, is generally required to take advantage of these tax benefits.

This is one of the tax advantages of home property ownership.

Taxpayers paying mortgage interest should fill out Schedule A to see if their itemized deductions exceed their standard deduction. If so, taxpayers will save more money on their taxes by itemizing.

Taxpayers who itemize their deductions will need to file the Form 1040 long form.

In order to claim mortgage interest as a deduction, the property owner must be legally liable for the loan. Both the home owner and the lender must intend that the loan be repaid creating a true debtor-creditor relationship between the home owner and the lender.

Deduction of Property Taxes on Principal Residence and Second Home

When property taxes are paid through an escrow account attached to a mortgage loan, the property owner can deduct only the amount paid out of the escrow account for property taxes.

Many monthly house payments include an amount placed in escrow (put in the care of a third party) for real estate taxes. You may not be able to deduct the total you pay into the escrow account. You can deduct only the real estate taxes that the lender paid from escrow to the taxing authority.

The real estate tax bill will show this amount.

IRA Withdrawal for First Time Home Buyers

Individual retirement accounts offer tax benefits such as tax deductible contributions and tax deferred investment gains, but they are also governed by strict rules that limit access to funds.

Federal tax income laws (IRS) imposes a tax penalty on IRA withdrawals made before the age of 59 1/2.

However, a first-time homebuyer can withdraw up to $10,000 from an IRA without paying the early withdrawal penalty to use as a down payment on a home.

Exclusion of Gain from Sale of Principal Residence

Owners who sell a primary residence may be excluded from having to pay any tax on capital gain.

When an individual sells a primary residence, they do not have to pay capital gain on any gain up to $250,000. A married couple is excluded from capital gain for up to $500,000 (must be married filing jointly).

To qualify for this exclusion, the home owner had to reside in the property as a primary residence for two out of the previous five years prior to the sale.

The capital gain exclusion can be claimed repeatedly – after two years between sale.

www.irs.gov/.../**Real-Estate-Tax**

Principal Residence

Tax Advantages

Other Tax Considerations

It is also important to know:

- Interest on **home equity loans** are deductible for the year the interest is paid for loans up to $100,000.

- **Discount points** are prepaid interest on the mortgage loan and can be taken as a tax deduction.

- Refinance points are deducted over the life of the loan

(Always direct clients to tax professionals as tax advice is outside of the scope of a real estate license.)

www.bankrate.com

Purchase of Real Property from Foreign Nationals

The sale of real estate in Florida (as well as throughout the U.S.) that was owned by a seller who is a foreign investor may be subject to U.S. income tax.

In 1980, Congress passed the Foreign Investment in Real Estate Property Tax Act (FIRPTA) because it thought foreign investors were receiving more favorable tax treatment on some of their U.S. real estate investments than U.S. residents.

Due to PIRPTA, 10 to 15 percent of the purchase price may be withheld by the purchaser on a sale by a foreign seller unless certain requirements are fulfilled. If the buyer completes a sale without the required withholding being collected from the seller, then the buyer will have the tax liability shifted to him or her.

Consult a closing agent and/or tax attorney for assistance with the issue.

- **Aim to prevent foreign sellers from avoiding paying taxes**

- **IRS requires buyers to hold 10% of gross sale price**

- **Buyer must report the purchase and pay the IRS the amount withheld**

Investment Real Estate

Federal laws also encourage investment in real estate.

Three types of income – Active, Passive and Portfolio- are all part of the real estate investment scene. Investment in real estate should be done with the advice of a tax consultant.

Maximized return on investment is the goal. Income vs. expenses should be carefully analyzed to determine quality of investment.

Types of Income and Cash Flow

- Active-Wages, commissions, tips

- Passive-rents

- Portfolio-stocks, bonds

www.irs.gov/.../**Real-Estate-Tax**

Potential Gross Income(PGI)

Potential Gross Income includes all projected income without allowing for loss, vacancy or uncollected monies.

All Income with no vacancy/losses deducted.

Potential Gross Income. The maximum rental income possible from a property without vacancy or credit losses.

Potential Gross Income is the basic calculation to determine Effective Gross Income (EGI).

> http://financial-dictionary.thefreedictionary.com/potential+gross+income

Effective Gross Income - EGI

Effective Gross Income is all possible income(PGI) minus vacancy and collection loss to get true gross income or EFFECTIVE Gross Income.

- The amount of income produced by a piece of property,

- Plus, miscellaneous income,

- Less vacancy costs and collection losses.

Effective gross income is a metric commonly used to evaluate the value of a piece of investment property.
http://www.investopedia.com/terms/e/effective-gross-income-egi.asp

Net Operating Income (NOI) Definition

Once effective gross income(EGI) has been determined, operating expenses can be deducted to find Net Operating Income(NOI).

- **Net operating income** (NOI) reflects:

  - **Income** after **operating** expenses are deducted, but before **income** taxes and interest are deducted

Net Operating Income will be used in determining taxable income.

> www.investopedia.com/terms/n/noi.asp

Before Tax Cash Flow

The money left after debt service has been subtracted from the net operating income and before income tax is paid; also called cash throw off or cash flow after debt service

> www.investorwords.com/15294/cash_flow_before_tax.html

After Tax Cash Flow

After tax cash flow is the actual spendable income from and investment; Gross income minus all operating and fixed expenses. This is what you are left with after everything is deducted from gross income including taxes.

- The net spendable income from an investment, determined by:

- deducting all operating and fixed expenses from the gross income.
- when expenses exceed income, a negative cash flow results

http://www.realestateinvestmentsoftwareblog.com/real-estate-cash-flow-types/

Determining Taxable Income

Taxable income is the amount of income that remains after all applicable deductions and adjustments to income are applied.

Three types of expenses that should be taken into consideration when determining taxable income: operating, financing and depreciation expenses.

Operating Expenses

- Replacement expenses but not reserves

Financing expenses

- Mortgage interest

Depreciation

- Deduction of cost of improvements

Operating Expenses

Operating expenses are in three types- fixed expenses, variable expenses, and reserves for replacement. These are expenses that are accrued through day to day business activities. Reserves are a fund to replace those items that wear out quicker than structures.

Variable expenses are things like utility bills, supplies, garbage, management fees etc.

Reserve for Replacement would be equipment for laundry facilities, air conditioning compressors, roof, etc.

Net Operating Income (NOI) - annual mortgage payments = Cash Flow

- Fixed Expenses (i.e. property taxes, insurance)
- Variable Expenses (i.e. utilities, supplies, mgmt.)
- Reserves for replacements (i.e. roof, washers)   www.irs.gov/.../**Real-Estate-Tax**

Financing Expenses

There are also financing related expenses. Types of expenses related to financing expenses includes:

- Mortgage Interest – the cost of leveraged money
- Leasing interest - costs related to leases

- Late penalties- fees charged

- Debt Service- amount of money needed to meet the payments on the loan

Different expenses are treated differently as far as calculating taxable income versus calculating cash flow and monetary demands to keep the business afloat.

Depreciation

Depreciation involves deducting improvements to real property over a period of time. The land itself is not depreciable.

For federal tax purposes, depreciation is allowed only for investment and business property, not personal residences.

At this time the IRS uses a 27.5-year useful asset life for residential rental property and 39 years for non-residential income-producing property.

- Taken on Investment property

- Does not include land (real property)

- Meaning you subtract the value of the land, divide the replacement cost by the IRS allowed useful life. This gives the per year depreciation

www.irs.gov/.../**Real-Estate-Tax**

Depreciation is the write-off over time of acquisitions. Land is not Depreciable. Residential rental property can be depreciated over 27.5 years. Non-residential income-producing property can be depreciated over 39 years.

Depreciable basis

- Land is not depreciated

- Acquisition + acquisition costs minus the value of the land = amount that may be depreciated

Straight-line Depreciation

- 27.5 years residential rental property

- 39 years nonresidential income-producing property

https://www.irs.gov/publications/p527/ch02.html#en_US_2014_publink1000219050

Investment Real State

Depreciation Practice (1)

A residential rental property was purchased for $500,000. $70,000 is the value of the land. What is the amount of the yearly depreciation?

To answer this type of problem, you have to recall that 27.5 years is used to depreciate the structure for residential investment property.   (39 for commercial)

- Meaning you subtract the value of the land, divide the replacement cost by the IRS allowed useful life. This gives the per year depreciation

- $500,000 - $70,000 = $430,000 ÷ 27.5 = $15,636.36 allowable depreciation per year

www.irs.gov/.../**Real-Estate-Tax**

Capital Gains (loss)

Short-term Gain

It is also important to know that the amount of capital gains that is charged on an investment deal upon the sale varies dependent upon how long the property was held.

Capital gains held for one year or less are **short term gains** and are taxed as ordinary income. For 2015, ordinary tax rates range from 10% to 39.6%.

- Short term capital gains do not benefit from any special tax rate – they are taxed at the same rate as your ordinary income.

Long – term Capital Gain

If an investor can manage to hold real estate assets for longer than a year, they can benefit from a reduced tax rate on the capital gains (profits).

For 2015, the long-term capital gains tax rate was between 0 to 20 percent depending upon the normal income tax rate charged.

It is not the real estate licensee's role to council investors on taxes, however, it is within the scope of professional guidance to point out that tax ramifications may change depending upon how long property is held and that a tax professional should be consulted.

- If you hold the asset for more than one year before you dispose of it,

  - your capital *gain* or loss is long-*term*

https://www.irs.gov/taxtopics/tc409.html

Sale of Capital Assets

Capital gain or loss are used to offset taxes. Principal residence excluded, tax benefits can offset taxes on other capital gains. Another example of real estate investment friendly taxation.

Sale of capital assets

- Sold for more than its basis is a capital gain

- Sold for less than its basis is a capital loss

Capital losses can be used to offset capital gains for tax purposes

- Loss on the sale of a principal residence is NOT a capital loss

Capital gains are taxed at the applicable capital gains tax rate
https://www.irs.gov/publications/p544/ch02.html

Installment Sale (Contract for Deed)

The real estate capital gain taxes are designed for investment. Real estate is one of the drivers of our economy. Yet, investors find ways to defer these taxes.

One way to defer capital gains tax is for the investor to sell the property through an installment sale – a contract for deed or land contract, because payments on the sale are NOT taken as one lump sum. Federal income taxes are paid only on the amount received in each year being taxed.

- Installment sale method- taking payments on the sale, thereby deferring taxation until year that payment is received.

Like-Kind Exchange

Like-kind exchange is another way for investors to avoid paying real estate tax.

A like-kind exchange- usually a 1031 exchange, is when the investor sells one property to purchase another – "exchanging" it.

When this process is done per the rules Section 1031 of the Internal Revenue Code, real estate can be sold and bought without paying capital gains tax. These types of transactions have a strict process including a timeline for the sale and purchases and how the money is held. Therefore, closing professionals and attorneys should be consulted by the investor.

- **1031 exchange taxes are deferred on equal amount until sold.**

https://www.irs.gov/publications/p537/ar02.html

Addendum - http://dor.myflorida.com/dor/property/brochures/pt113.pdf

PROPERTY TAX EXEMPTION FOR HOMESTEAD PROPERTY
Property Tax Oversight

When someone owns property and makes it his or her permanent residence or the permanent residence of his or her dependent, the property owner may be eligible to receive a homestead exemption up to $50,000. The first $25,000 applies to all property taxes, including school district taxes. The additional exemption up to $25,000 applies to the assessed value between $50,000 and $75,000 and only to non-school taxes [Section 196.031, Florida Statutes].

Homestead Property Tax Exemption

The application for homestead exemption (Form DR-501) and other exemption forms are on our forms page and on most property appraisers' websites. Click here for county property appraiser contact and website information.

If you are filing for the first time, be prepared to answer these questions:

- Whose name or names were on the title on January 1?
- What is your social security number and your spouse's social security number?
- Were you or your dependent living in the dwelling on January 1?
- Do you claim residency in another county or state?

Your property appraiser may ask for any of the following items to prove your residency:

- Proof of previous residency outside Florida and date ended
- Florida driver license or identification card number
- Evidence of giving up driver license from another state
- Florida vehicle license plate number
- Florida voter registration number (if US citizen)
- Declaration of domicile and residency date
- Name of current employer
- Address listed on your last IRS return
- Dependent children's school location(s)
- Bank statement and checking account mailing address
- Proof of payment of utilities at homestead address

Examples

Assessed Value $45,000
The first $25,000 of value is exempt from all property tax and the remaining $20,000 of value is taxable.

Assessed Value $65,000
The first $25,000 of value is exempt from all property tax, the next $25,000 of value is taxable, and the remaining $15,000 of value is exempt from non-school taxes.

Assessed Value $85,000
The first $25,000 of value is exempt from all property tax, the next $25,000 of value is taxable, the third $25,000 of value is exempt from non-school taxes, and the remaining $10,000 of value is taxable.

If you are moving from a previous Florida homestead to a new homestead in Florida, you may be able to transfer, or "port," all or part of your homestead assessment difference. See Save Our Homes Assessment Limitation and Portability Transfer.

You should complete all required forms and applications for the exemption and file them with your county property appraiser. If the property appraiser denies your application, you may file a petition with the county's value adjustment board. For more information, see Petitions to the Value Adjustment Board.

The Department of Revenue's website has more information about property tax benefits for homestead properties.

http://dor.myflorida.com/dor/property/taxpayers/

PT-113, R. 06/15

Page 1 of 1

Addendum - http://dor.myflorida.com/dor/property/brochures/pt109.pdf

PROPERTY TAX BENEFITS FOR ACTIVE DUTY MILITARY AND VETERANS
Certain property tax benefits are available to members of the Armed Forces.

Property Tax Oversight

Filing and Keeping Your Homestead Exemption

When a person serving in the Armed Forces owns and uses property as a homestead, the servicemember may rent the homestead property without abandoning the claim to the homestead exemption (section 196.061, Florida Statutes).

A servicemember's next of kin or any other person who has written authorization may file a homestead exemption claim on behalf of a servicemember who cannot file in person because of a service obligation (section 196.071, Florida Statutes).

Property Tax Exemptions and Discounts

Eligibility for property tax exemptions depends on satisfying certain requirements. Information is available from the property appraiser's office in the county where the veteran or surviving spouse owns a homestead or other property.

- An ex-servicemember who was honorably discharged, is a resident of Florida, and who is disabled to a degree of 10% or more because of misfortune or while serving during wartime may be entitled to a $5,000 property tax exemption. This exemption is not limited to homestead property. Under certain circumstances, the veteran's surviving spouse may be entitled to carry over the exemption. See Form DR-501. (section 196.24, Florida Statutes)

- Veterans who are Florida residents and were honorably discharged with a service-related total and permanent disability may be eligible for a total exemption from taxes on property they own and use as their homesteads. A similar exemption is available to disabled veterans confined to wheelchairs. Under certain circumstances, the veteran's surviving spouse may be entitled to carry over the exemption. See Form DR-501. (sections 196.081 and 196.091, Florida Statues)

- If they meet certain requirements, veterans 65 or older who are partially or totally permanently disabled may receive a discount from tax on property that they own and use as homesteads. The discount is a percentage equal to the percentage of the veteran's permanent, service-connected disability as determined by the United States Department of Veteran's Affairs. See Form DR-501. (section 196.082, Florida Statutes)

Eligible veterans who want to apply for these exemptions may apply before they receive the necessary documentation from the United States government or the United States Department of Veterans Affairs or its predecessor. After the property appraiser receives the documentation, the exemption will be effective as of the date of the original application. Please see the How to Apply for a Refund brochure for information about refunds.

- A member or former member of any branch of the United States military or military reserves, the United States Coast Guard or its reserves, or the Florida National Guard may receive an exemption if he or she was deployed during the previous calendar year outside the continental United States, Alaska, and Hawaii in support of a designated operation (the Florida Legislature designates operations for this exemption). The percent of the taxable value that is exempt for the current year corresponds to the percent of time during the previous year when the service member was deployed on a designated operation. See Form DR-501M. (section 196.173, Florida Statutes)

You should file all required forms and applications for these exemptions with your county property appraiser. If the property appraiser denies your application, you may file a petition with the county's value adjustment board. For more information, see Petitions to the Value Adjustment Board.

The Department of Revenue's website has more information about property tax benefits for active duty military and veterans and contact information for county officials.

http://dor.myflorida.com/dor/property/taxpayers/

PT-109, R. 06/15

Page 1 of 1

Addendum - http://dor.myflorida.com/dor/property/brochures/pt110.pdf

PROPERTY TAX BENEFITS FOR
PERSONS 65 OR OLDER
Property Tax Oversight

Certain property tax benefits are available to persons 65 or older in Florida. Eligibility for property tax exemptions depends on certain requirements. Information is available from the property appraiser's office in the county where the applicant owns a homestead or other property.

Available Benefits

A board of county commissioners or the governing authority of any municipality may adopt an ordinance to allow an additional homestead exemption of up to $50,000. A person may be eligible for this exemption if he or she meets the following requirements:

- Owns real estate and makes it his or her permanent residence
- Is age 65 or older
- Household income does not exceed the income limitation." (see Form DR-501 and Form DR-501SC) (section 196.075(2), Florida Statutes)

A board of county commissioners or the governing authority of any municipality may adopt an ordinance to allow an additional homestead exemption equal to the assessed value of the property. A person may be eligible for this exemption if he or she meets the following requirements:

- Owns real estate with a just value less than $250,000
- Has made it his or her permanent residence for at least 25 years
- Is age 65 or older
- Does not have a household income that exceeds the income limitation" (see Form DR-501 and Form DR-501SC) (section 196.075(2), Florida Statutes)

- If they meet certain requirements, veterans 65 or older who are partially or totally permanently disabled may receive a discount from tax on property that they own and use as homesteads. The discount is a percentage equal to the percentage of the veteran's permanent, service-connected disability as determined by the United States Department of Veterans Affairs. See Form DR-501. (section 196.082, Florida Statutes)

How to Apply

You should complete and file all required forms and applications for these exemptions with your county property appraiser. If the property appraiser denies your application, you may file a petition with the county's value adjustment board. For more information, see Petitions to the Value Adjustment Board.

*You should check with your property appraiser to find out if an additional homestead exemption is available. The $20,000 income limitation has adjusted annually since 2001 by the percentage change in the average cost of living index, which is the average of the monthly consumer price index figures for the stated 12-month period issued by the United States Department of Labor. For more information, including this year's income limitation, see Florida Property Tax Valuation and Income Limitation Rates (section 196.075(3), Florida Statutes).

The Department of Revenue's website has more information about property tax benefits for persons 65 or older and contact information for county officials.

http://dor.myflorida.com/dor/property/taxpayers/

PT-110, R. 06/15

Page 1 of 1

19 PLANNING, ZONING, AND ENVIRONMENTAL HAZARDS

Learning Objectives:

• Describe the composition and authority of the local planning agency

• Explain the purpose of land-use controls and the role of zoning ordinances

• Identify the provisions of Florida's comprehensive plan and the Growth Management Act

• Distinguish among the five general zoning classifications

• Distinguish among zoning ordinances, building codes and health ordinances

• Explain the purpose of a variance, special exception and a nonconforming use

• Calculate the number of lots available for development, given the total number of acres contained in a parcel, the percentage of land reserved for streets and other facilities and the minimum number of square feet per lot

• Describe the characteristics of a planned unit development

• Understand the basic provisions of the national flood insurance program

• Describe the impact Comprehensive Environmental Response Compensation and Liability Act (CERCLA)

• Explain the various environmental hazards associated with real estate

Key Terms:

asbestos	certificate of occupancy	planned unit development
buffer zone	concurrency	special exception
building code	environmental impact statement	special flood hazard area
building inspection	health ordinance	variance
building permit	nonconforming use	zoning ordinance

PLANNING AND ZONING

I)   Planning and Zoning

   A) City planning

      1) Historical

         (a) Philosophy of laissez faire

         (b) Industrialization and urbanization

         (c) Protecting residential property

Planning and Zoning

As a real estate professional, it is important to understand planning and zoning and how it affects your buyers and sellers.

Imagine …

What would happen to property values if …

- you could build any type of house,

- any type of business or factory,

- anywhere you wanted to

- without any regards to rules.

This story demonstrates what was really happening prior to planning and zoning laws being put into place.

So, to better understand the purpose of land-use controls, let's take a look back in history to see how these rules came into existence.

City Planning

A Historical Perspective - Philosophy of Laissez Faire

Prior to zoning ordinances, the philosophy of Laissez Fair ruled.

- It is a policy that allows businesses, trades, and individuals to operate with very little interference from the government

- It opposes governmental interference beyond the minimum necessary for the maintenance of peace and property rights

The bottom line is that if it was good for the individual property owner-- it happened, regardless of how it affected anyone else.

http://www.merriam-webstr.com/dictionary/laissez–faire

Philosophy of Laissez Faire

As a result of laissez fair, development was happening in a haphazard way. This wasn't such a problem when our country was dominated by farms with miles and miles between them.

The industrial revolution changed all of that.

Urbanization is the process by which cities grow or by which societies become more urban.

Suddenly people were living in tight spaces. Consequently, the needs of the "one" was bumping against the needs of the other. City streets were covered in horse manure. Diseases were spread through common water sources. Furthermore, the quality of housing was becoming questionable.

http://dictionary.reference.com/browse/urbanization?s=t

Industrialization and Urbanization

- Industrialization and urbanization is the process by which cities grow or by which societies become more urban.

http://dictionary.reference.com/browse/urbanization?s=t

The desire to solve urbanization problems created opposing views.

Architects focused on making the city beautiful, while public health officials were connecting the dots between sanitation and health. And social workers were advocating about safer housing. As important as each of their goals were, these forces were not working in unity.

http://www.citylab.com/work/2012/08/brief-history-birth-urban-planning/2365/

Protecting Residential Property

The need for City Planning was born.

- City Planning Defined - the planning and control of the construction, growth, and development of a city or town.

- Also called town planning.

Goal: *To protect residential property*

http://www.oxforddictionaries.com/us/definition/american_english/city-planning?q=city+planning

So, the need for land use controls began to come to city official's attention.

Yet, realizing that the need existed was a long way from understanding how to begin to implement controlled growth.

Fortunately, great minds of the times began to tackle the issue.

America's first urban planning conference was held in New York in 1898. Also, in 1898 Harvard created the country's first Urban Planning School. Classes in City Planning soon followed.

Though the priorities of the social workers and the public health officials continued to resonate, urban planning became grounded in architecture as you couldn't separate design from the main fabric of planned growth.

Although the good of the whole over the good of the one was part of the force that propelled City Planning, it wasn't completely a moral design by today's standards and laws as early planning ordinances helped to foster racial segregation.

Yet, at its core, early city planning efforts did set the stage by what government officials strive for today through land-use controls.

urbanstudies.co.za

What happens when developments grow farther and farther away from the center of a city?

They still need publicly maintained streets, power, and water and sewage management.

If developments are allowed to expand without regard to the impact of the overall infrastructure it can become a huge tax burden of the general public.

The issue of controlled growth within the city becomes a broader issue of how to:

- control growth as the city began to rapidly expand to outside of its boundaries

- constantly widening the area where services were needed.

To accomplish these objectives, specific goals of planning were put into place.

Planning and Zoning

2) Goals of planning include, for example:

> (a) Savings of tax money by preventing sprawl
>
> (b) Adequate provision of services
>
> (c) Providing for road right-of-way and set backs
>
> (d) Protection against costly drainage, flooding or environmental problems
>
> (e) Reduction in political and equity problems in siting landfills, prisons, etc.

City Planning

Goals of planning include, for example

- Savings of tax money by preventing sprawl

One of the goals of city planning is to save tax money by preventing uncontrolled urban sprawl.

- "Urban sprawl" means a development pattern characterized by low density, automobile-dependent development with either a single use or multiple uses that are not functionally related, requiring the extension of public facilities and services in an inefficient manner, and failing to provide a clear separation between urban and rural uses.

Florida Statutes 163.3178 (51)

Goals of planning include, for example

- Adequate provision of services

It's the overall goal of city planners to be able to provide for the safety and welfare of their citizens.

This includes competently being able to provide adequate provision of services including power, water, sanitation, police, ambulances, schools, etc.

Goals of planning include, for example

- Providing for road right-of-way
- Controlling Set backs

Providing adequate services means being able to access property when needed.

This lead to creating rules about exactly where and how a building can be placed on a property.

It controls things like allowing road right-of-way for public vehicles and how far a building must set back from the property lines.

Goals of planning include, for example

- Protection against costly drainage, flooding or environmental problems

When you change the make-up of property, you affect things like drainage.

The act of putting in a parking lot, for example, can create runoff and flooding onto a neighboring property.

So, it has become the goal of city planning to monitor and control improvements to protect against costly drainage, flooding or environmental problems.

Goals of planning include, for example

- Reduction in political and equity problems in siting landfills, prisons, etc.

The placement within the community for city operations such as landfills and even prisons can become a controversial issue as property owners wish to protect the value of their own investments.

One of the goals of city planning is for the reduction in political and equity problems in siting landfills, prisons, etc.

https://www.planning.org/aboutplanning/whatisplanning.htm

Goals of planning include, for example

5 Overall Goals

Today, city planners strive to accomplish all 5 of these goals:

- Savings of tax money by preventing sprawl
- Adequate provision of services
- Providing for road right-of-way and Controlling Set backs
- Protection against costly drainage, flooding or environmental problems
- Reduction in political and equity problems in siting landfills, prisons, etc.

https://www.planning.org/aboutplanning/whatisplanning.htm

II) Local planning agency

   A) Composition

   B) Authority

      1) Subdivision plat approval

2) Site plan approval

3) Sign control

C) Support staff

Composition

So, who oversees of city planning?

- Per Florida Statutes 163.3171 The governing body of each local government, individually or in combination as provided in s. 163.3171, shall appoint a "local planning agency" or commission to guide and make recommendations to city elected officials.

- The state mandates that the commission be made up of individuals that is fairly representative of citizens in the area.

Know that the planning commission members are appointed (not elected), must have a representative of the school district, and that meetings must be held as public hearings and with public notice.

- The Planning Commission was established to act as the Local Planning Agency under Section 163.3174, Florida Statutes.

- The composition of the council must be fairly representative of all the governing bodies in the county or planning area.

    - Appointed

    - Representative of School District – Voting or Nonvoting

    - Involvement of Community College Board

    - Public Hearings with Public Notice

Florida Statutes 163.3174

Mymanatee.org

The Planning Commission is:

- Responsible for the preparation of the comprehensive plan or plan amendment and shall make recommendations to the governing body regarding the adoption or amendment of such plan.

- Monitor and oversee the effectiveness and status of the comprehensive plan

- Review proposed land development regulations, land development codes, or amendments thereto, and make recommendations to the governing body as to the consistency of the proposal with the adopted comprehensive plan

Florida Statutes 163.3174

Authority
To accomplish their planning goals, the planning commission has been given actual and immediate authority over 3 specific area:

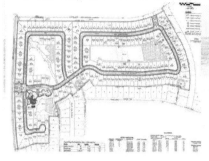

- ## The Planning Commission has authority over
  - ### Plat Map Approval
  - ### Site Approval
  - ### Sign Control

Florida Statutes 163.3174

Subdivision Plat Mat Defined

- A subdivision plat is a map detailing sections of land that has been subdivided into lots showing the location and boundaries of individual parcels with the streets, alleys, etc.

http://legal-dictionary.thefreedictionary.com/Plat

Florida Statute 336.05

Subdivision Plat Mat Approval

- The commission has the authority to approve or reject plat maps
- Per FS 336.05 The commissioners are authorized to refuse to approve for recording in accordance with chapter 177 any map or plat of a subdivision when recording of such plat would result in duplication of names of streets or roads or when such plat, in the opinion of the commissioners, will not provide adequate and safe access or drainage. FS 336.05

http://legal-dictionary.thefreedictionary.com/Plat

Site Plan Defined

Similar to a plat map, a site plan involves larger projects with a broader community impact.

It depicts property lines, outline of existing and proposed buildings and structures, distance between buildings, distance between buildings and property lines (setbacks), parking lots, indicating parking spaces, driveways, surrounding streets, landscaped areas, easements, ground sign location, and utilities.

- **Site Plan Approval**
  - The commission has the authority to approve or reject site plans.

https://en.wikipedia.org/wiki/Site_plan

- **Sign Control**
  - The commission has the authority to approve or reject

Signs erected around a community affect more than aesthetics – it can become a safety issue due to the blocking of one's view such as when they are attempting to pull out into traffic.

The local planning agency has the power to approve or reject sign usage. When planning to erect a sign, it is a good practice to check with the planning commission for rules regulating size and placement.

Support Staff

- Ministerial
- Expert Knowledge
  - Engineering and Environment Issues

Although the commission is an appointed, volunteer, unpaid position, the commission does have the authority to hire support staff and to provide salaries and compensation for their work. They require help ranging from clerical duties to staff members that can provide complex analyses on proposed developments—people they rely upon for decision making.

http://www.fl-counties.com/docs/pdfs/pages-from-florida-county-government-guide---growth-

management.pdf?sfvrsn=2

III) Florida's comprehensive plan

A) Chapter 163, F.S. Growth Policy; County and Municipal Planning; Land Development Regulation

1) Department of Community Affairs (DCA)

B) Plan must contain certain elements to be coordinated with plans of surrounding areas

1) Future land use

2) Traffic circulation

3) Water, sanitary and storm sewers, and solid waste

4) Conservation of natural resources

5) Recreation

6) Housing

7) Coastal zone protection, where relevant

8) Intergovernmental coordination

9) Utilities

(a) Plan must be implemented by adopting sufficient land use control ordinances and capital improvement programs (concurrency requirements)

(b) Optional elements may include: historical, scenic preservation, economic and public buildings

(c) Concurrency allows new development only after a minimum level of public infrastructure is in place around the development site

Florida's Comprehensive Plan

- **The Florida's Community Planning Act** gave authority and responsibility for establishing and implementing the roles, processes, and powers of comprehensive planning to **local governments** because local governments have regulatory authority over the use of land.

- The state's role is to protect the state's resources.

- While the governing body over city planning is implemented locally through the planning commission, Florida saw the need for a **State Comprehensive Plan.**

- The State of Florida has one of the most comprehensive and progressive land use planning programs in the country.

  http://www.fl-counties.com/docs/pdfs/pages-from-florida-county-government-guide---growth-management.pdf?sfvrsn=2

Chapter 163, F.S. Growth Policy; County and Municipal Planning; Land Development Regulation

- Commonly referred to as the "Growth Management Act" and is a broad collection of laws, rules, regulations, and policies affecting all planning and development activities of the state and local governments."

  - This 1985 Act was based upon the successes and failures of previous years' planning efforts experienced by the state and local governments since the adoption of the original planning legislation.

  - One of the major revisions was the requirement that **all local government plans and plan amendments be adopted by ordinance** and that all plans and **amendments must be reviewed and approved by the state.**

  http://www.fl-counties.com/docs/pdfs/pages-from-florida-county-government-guide---growth-management.pdf?sfvrsn=2

Department of Community Affairs (DCA)

- The Florida Department of Community Affairs approves and issues permits for counties to change their growth plan based on availability of public resources such as water, roads, schools, and drainage canals.

- In 2011, there was a massive rewrite of Florida's growth management laws putting enforcement in the hands of the Florida Department of Economic Opportunity.

- The overall goal of the DEO is the development, and support for communities and economic incentives for businesses that create new jobs.

Florida's Comprehensive Plan must contain certain elements to be coordinated with plans of surrounding areas.

- Future land use
- Traffic circulation
- Water, sanitary and storm sewers, and solid waste
- Conservation of natural resources
- Recreation
- Housing
- Coastal zone protection, where relevant
- Intergovernmental coordination

Plan must contain certain elements to be coordinated with plans of surrounding areas.

Utilities -

- Plan must be implemented by adopting sufficient land use control ordinances and capital improvement programs (concurrency requirements).

- Optional elements may include: historical, scenic preservation, economic and public buildings

- **Concurrency** allows for new development only after a minimum level of public infrastructure is in place around the development site.

- Following the rule of Concurrency means that new development can be approved only after a minimum level of public infrastructure is in place around the development site.

- Consistent with public health and safety:

  - Sanitary sewer, solid waste, drainage, adequate water supplies, and potable water facilities shall be in place and available to serve new development no later than the issuance by the local government of a certificate of occupancy or its functional equivalent.

Florida Statutes 163.3180

Born out of the need to control growth, Florida now has in place mechanisms to control growth – helping to foster growth not stifle it—through its state and local authorities.

As real estate professionals, you can rely on clear procedures to protect your client's investments and as a resource for understanding how a property can and cannot be developed.

IV) Zoning, land use restrictions and building codes

    A) Zoning ordinance and classifications

        1) Residential—control of density

            (a) Lot size

            (b) Set backs

            (c) Lot coverage

        2) Commercial—control of intensity of use

            (a) Parking requirements

            (b) Height and size limitations

        3) Industrial—control of emission and effluents

            (a) Control of by-products such as noise, odor, smoke congestion and chemicals

        4) Agricultural

        5) Special use

    B) Building codes

        1) Building permits

        2) Building inspections

        3) R-Value

        4) Certificate of occupancy

    C) Health ordinances

Zoning, Land Use Restrictions and Building Codes

Now it's time to learn about zoning, land use restrictions and building codes.

Zoning ordinances are laws which place restrictions on the way land within its jurisdiction can be used.

Through community planning and development, zoning laws help local governmental agencies preserve property values and ensure communities are functional and safe places.

Zoning laws are what keeps the factory from being built across the street from a mansion.

Among other regulations, zoning requires that properties of certain types be operated within certain areas known as "zones." These zones include:

- Residential

- Commercial

- Industrial

- Agricultural

- Special Use

http://real-estate-law.freeadvice.com/real-estate-law/zoning/zoning_legalese.htm#ixzz3vfSAq8es

Zoning Ordinance and Classifications

Residential-control of Density

- Lot size

- Set backs

- Lot coverage

In residential zones, efforts are made to control "density" – meaning an effort is made to control how many homes can be built within a certain area. According to the Florida Statutes 163.3164

Residential-control of density

- "Density" is an objective measurement of the number of people or residential units allowed per unit of land, such as residents or employees per acre. In regulating residential property rules are put into place as to how big a lot size must be within a certain area, the setback requirements from the edge of the property for buildings, and how much of the lot can be "covered" or built upon.

Florida Statutes 163.3164

Commercial-control of Intensity of Use

- Parking requirements

- Heights and size limitations

In commercial zones, efforts are made to control the intensity of use meaning an effort is made to control public use and access numbers.

Florida Statutes 163.3164

Industrial-control of Emissions and Effluents

- Control of by-products
  - Noise
  - Odor
  - Smoke Congestion
  - Chemicals

Wherever you have the production of a product you potentially have the negative result of emitting noise, odor, smoke and chemical pollution or effluents which are liquid waste or sewage discharged into a river or the sea: zoning attempts to confine industrial businesses to areas approved exclusively for industrial zoning and also places control requirements on emissions and effluents.

http://www.oxforddictionaries.com/us/

Agricultural

- Seeks to preserve farmland

Seeks to preserve the **agricultural** base. It reflects a community-wide policy that farmland is a valuable resource that should be preserved to ensure the continued production of **agricultural** commodities. Agricultural zoning maintains the vitality of the agricultural sector by retaining a critical mass of agricultural land. The segregation of land uses minimizes the number of non-farming landowners impacted by farming activities and reduces the conflicts that arise between farming and non-farming neighbors.

https://pennstatelaw.psu.edu/_file/aglaw/Agricultural_Zoning.pdf

Special Use

A special use permit must be obtained by a landowner who wishes to develop a tract of land whose purpose is included in the special uses ordinances for that zone. The zoning permit allows the owner to develop that land for his own intended use, even if it does not fall within the "by-right" guidelines for that particular zone. Examples of special uses under your local zoning guidelines may include schools, funeral homes, hospitals, cemeteries, and other types of land uses which do not fit exactly into the description of residential or commercial uses.

http://real-estate-law.freeadvice.com/real-estate-law/zoning/special_use_permits.htm#ixzz3vfgXcnfV

Buffer Zone

- An area of land designed to separate different zoned areas, such as industry from housing
- Usually involves green space such as trees or a park
- A builder may include a buffer zone in his development to transition from property types.

http://www.realestatewords.com/buffer-zone

Building Codes

Where zoning ordinances restrict the way land can be used, building codes set minimum standards for how buildings are built.

While zoning and building codes are closely related, they both serve different functions.

In a nutshell, zoning codes regulate how a given section of land can be used and what type of businesses can utilize the land and its structures. On the other hand, building codes regulate the details of the structures themselves.

SETTING minimum standards for safety, health, and general welfare including sanitation, water supply, light, ventilation, means of egress, fire prevention and control, and energy conservation.

Building codes are in place to ensure the safety and wellbeing of tenants, residents and other individuals who occupy buildings and structures. The Great Chicago Fire of 1871 and other examples of structural failures were catalysts for the introduction of stronger codes around the alteration, construction, repair and even the demolition procedures of buildings in the U.S.

- Regulate the details of the structures themselves

- Minimum standards for

    - safety, health, and general welfare

        - including sanitation, water supply, light, ventilation, means of egress, fire prevention and control, and energy conservation.

http://quickbooks.intuit.com/r/compliance-licensing/whats-difference-zoning-building-codes/

https://en.wikipedia.org/wiki/Building_code

Florida Building Commission

The state of Florida has set standards within the Florida Building Codes that is maintained by the Florida Building Commission. Information about the statewide building codes can be found on the floridabuilding.org website which is part of the Department of Business and Professional Regulation.

https://www.floridabuilding.org/bc/bc_default.aspx

Building Permits

- Building Department

Prior to construction or renovation, you must first get a zoning permit before obtaining a building permit through your local planning agency.

Building and other related permits are usually issued by the city where the property is located. This is normally done by the city Building Department. If the property is in an unincorporated area, check with the county to find out what office you should file your application.

http://quickbooks.intuit.com/r/compliance-licensing/whats-difference-zoning-building-codes/

Building Inspections

- Certificate of Occupancy

Building inspections will be conducted at various phases of construction to ensure compliance with building codes.

A certificate of occupancy will be given once the inspector determines that all standards for occupancy has been met.

https://en.wikipedia.org/wiki/Certificate_of_occupancy

Florida's Energy Code

- Federal initiative for all residential and commercial buildings to be energy efficient

Florida's Energy Code was enacted as part of a federal initiative for all residential and commercial buildings (new and old) to be energy efficient.

The Energy Code must be incorporated into the design and construction of all new residential and commercial buildings. Major repairs, additions and equipment replacements in existing residential and commercial buildings must also conform to the Energy Code.

http://www.gordonrees.com/publications/2012/don-t-be-left-out-in-the-cold-florida-s-new-energy-code

http://floridainsulationcontractors.com/high-r-value-chart-florida.html

R-Value

- *The higher the R-value, the greater the insulating effectiveness.*

This includes requirement for the minimum R-Value of insulation depending upon the area of construction being insulated. Insulation is rated in terms of thermal resistance, called R-value, which indicates the resistance to heat flow.

The higher the R-value, the greater the insulating effectiveness. The R-value of thermal insulation depends on the type of material, its thickness, and its density. In calculating the R-value of a multi-layered installation, the R-values of the individual layers are added.

http://www.gordonrees.com/publications/2012/don-t-be-left-out-in-the-cold-florida-s-new-energy-code

http://floridainsulationcontractors.com/high-r-value-chart-florida.html

Health Ordinances

- Sanitary Standards
- Health Departments
  - Minimize the transfer of disease

- Food & drink management

- Waste management

In addition to controls over land use through zoning and building safety through building codes, the safety of the public is also advanced through health ordinances.

The goal is to minimize the transfer of disease through sanitation standards in food management and waste management. All localities have a health department with inspectors that oversee compliance with standards.

http://www.floridahealth.gov/

APPEALS AND EXCEPTIONS

V) Appeals and Exceptions

    A) Zoning Board of Adjustment

        1) Variance

        2) Special exception

        3) Legally nonconforming use

    B) Developments of Regional Impact

        1) Planned unit development

        2) Environmental impact statement

Zoning Board of Adjustment

Not everyone is always happy with how government officials have ruled regarding land use restrictions. So, there are steps you can take to be heard and have your compliance with zoning ordinances being reconsidered.

The adjustment board is an administrative agency for hearing and deciding zoning appeals. It is created for adjusting differences that may from time to time arise between government officials charged with duties under the zoning ordinance and property owners.

It is also referred as board of adjustment or board of zoning appeals. A person going in front of the zoning board of adjustment is seeking either a variance, a special exception, or a legally nonconforming use of the property.

If the owner is unsuccessful in obtaining the change, there may be a possibility to appeal the action, either within the administrative structure of the governmental body or in a court of law.

- Administrative agency to hear and decide zoning appeals

- Seeks variance, special exception, or legally nonconforming use

- If turned down, litigation in court

http://definitions.uslegal.com/a/adjustment-board/

http://realestate.findlaw.com/land-use-laws/zoning-changes-variances-and-more.html#sthash.m2tPA5ZC.dpuf

Variance

A variance is a request to stray from zoning ordinances. It does not result in a change in the zoning law. Instead, it is a specific waiver of requirements of the zoning ordinance for the one owner who sought the variance.

Typically, variances are granted when the property owner can demonstrate that existing zoning regulations present a practical difficulty in making use of the property known as a land hardship. The hardship cannot be self-created…meaning the person caused their own problem.

Additionally, the applicant must show that the variance will be consistent with the intent of the ordinance both securing public safety and achieving substantial equal justice for all citizens.

- Land hardship (not self-created)

http://realestate.findlaw.com/land-use-laws/zoning-changes-variances-and-more.html#sthash.m2tPA5ZC.dpuf

http://canons.sog.unc.edu/?p=7705

Appeals and Exceptions

Zoning Board of Adjustment
Variance
Imagine a lot that narrows dramatically toward the front yard and where the side yard setbacks prohibit the property owner from building an addition.

http://canons.sog.unc.edu/?p=7705

Variance

Not being able to build on a lot such as that by having to follow the setback ordinance would create a hardship for the property owner.

This is an example of a situation where a variance might be granted.

However, if every lot on an entire suffered from the same issue of narrowing at the front, a variance probably wouldn't be considered appropriate – as this would instead be viewed as a problem with the ordinance itself and might justify an actual ordinance amendment instead.

Special Exception

A special exception seeks permission to do something that the zoning ordinance permits only under certain special circumstances.

The permission or special exception is granted by the zoning hearing board in accordance with the standards contained in the zoning ordinance, provided generally that the specific application of the use would not prove injurious to the public interest.

Note that it's not really a "special exception" at all as exceptions have already been written into zoning for possible allowances. The zoning dictates when the special exception can be given.

- Property owner seeks a special exception when their desired use of a property is in direct conflict

- Permitted only under certain circumstances as written into the zoning ordinances

http://www.ccpa.net/DocumentCenter/Home/View/7902

Legally Nonconforming Use

A legally non-conforming use is a use existing on the land that was lawful when the ordinance prohibiting that use was adopted.

You can lose your status if you discontinue your use of the property in manner that no longer is in conflict. You cannot stop and then restart your use of the property just because it used to be used that way.

If a non-conforming use property is destroyed to the point where more than 50% of its value is lost, it may not be rebuilt in the same manner.

- Use of land existed prior to ordnance

- "Grandfathered" usage

- Lost if property is more than 50% destroyed

http://real-estate-law.freeadvice.com/real-estate-law/zoning/non_conforming_use.htm

Development of Regional Impact (DRI)

Florida Statutes 380.06 defines a "development of regional impact," as meaning any development which, because of its character, magnitude, or location, would have a substantial effect upon the health, safety, or welfare of citizens of more than one county.

- Local government to be consistent with state plans and go through approval for large scale projects

- Projects that are so large they affect more than one county

The DRI designated areas that the state would have oversight over such as the Florida Keys, the Big Cyprus Preserve, Apalachicola Bay, and the Green Swamp.

In consideration are:

1) The extent to which the development would create or alleviate environmental problems such as air or water pollution or noise.

2) The amount of pedestrian or vehicular traffic likely to be generated.

3) The number of persons likely to be residents, employees, or otherwise present.

4) The size of the site to be occupied.

5) The likelihood that additional or subsidiary development will be generated.

6) The extent to which the development would create an additional demand for, or additional use of, energy, including the energy requirements of subsidiary developments.

7) The unique qualities of particular areas of the state.

Florida Statutes 380.06

Planned Unit Development (PUD)

Planned unit developments, or PUDs, are homeowner communities that are operated by an association and designed to offer amenities and features not found in traditional subdivisions.

PUDs usually have association dues to cover amenities, maintenance and other usage fees.

They can include single-family homes, condos or town homes or a mixture of both. In some PUDs, the development increases its scope to include retail and other commercial spaces within the development.

- Homeowner communities tightly developed

- Offers special amenities and features

- Variety of single family, condos and townhomes

- Includes retail and commercial spaces

The purpose of the Planned Unit Development is to create more desirable environments through diversified land development.

It is intended to achieve economics in land development, maintenance, street systems, and utility networks while providing building groupings for privacy, usable attractive open spaces, safe circulation, and to protect the general well-being of the inhabitants.

It normally involves Zero Lot Line Development and Clustered Development and is to allow for a combination of condominiums, town homes, office and retail space. Cluster development encourages the preservation of environmentally sensitive areas, open space and agricultural lands.

http://www.delta-co.gov/documents/municipal%20code/chapter16.05.pdf

http://homeguides.sfgate.com/pros-cons-planned-unit-development-2995.html

Statutes 380.06

Purpose of PUD

- Provide a desirable environment

- Economics in land development and maintenance

- Usable attractive green spaces

- Clustered development preserving agricultural land

http://www.delta-co.gov/documents/municipal%20code/chapter16.05.pdf

EIS per U.S. Environmental Law

U.S. Environmental Law requires that an Environmental Impact Statement be prepared describing the positive and negative environmental effects of a proposed action.

It lists one or more alternative actions that may be chosen instead of the action described in the EIS. This study must be provided as a development project may have a sweeping environmental impact. The study must take into consideration the impact not just on the environment, but how waste management will be conducted, how the air quality will be affected, as well as traffic, employment, etc.

The purpose of the Environmental Impact Statement is to look beyond the short term and to instead focus on the long-term consequences of development.

- Study of long term effects of development

- Waste management

- Air Quality

- Traffic

- Employment

https://en.wikipedia.org/wiki/Environmental_impact_statement

FLOOD ZONES

VI) Flood zones

    A) National Flood Insurance Program (NFIP)

        1) Can qualify for Federal Flood insurance program

2) "Special Flood Hazard Areas" are delineated according to NFIP criteria

3) Development within SFHAs must be restricted in a manner so as not to obstruct the natural flow of flood waters

B) Residential structures in the SFHA must have the first floor above the "Base Flood Elevation"

C) Non-residential structures must meet the residential requirement, or be water-tight below the Base Flood Elevation

D) Over 40% of purchasers of National Flood Insurance are in Florida

Flood Zones

National Flood Insurance Program (NFIP)

The National Flood Insurance Program aims to reduce the impact of flooding on private and public structures.

It does so by providing affordable insurance to property owners and by encouraging communities to adopt and enforce floodplain management regulations.

These efforts help mitigate the effects of flooding on new and improved structures.

Overall, the program reduces the socio-economic impact of disasters by promoting the purchase and retention of general risk insurance, but also of flood insurance, specifically.

https://www.fema.gov/national-flood-insurance-program

National Flood Insurance Program (NFIP)

- Reduce the impact of flooding on private and public structures
- Affordable insurance
- Adoption of floodplain management regulation
- Mitigates the effects of flooding
- Promotes the purchase and retention of insurance

https://www.fema.gov/national-flood-insurance-program

Qualifying for National Flood Insurance

You must live in a community that participates in the National Flood Insurance Program (NFIP) to qualify for National Flood Insurance.

The community adopts ordinances to meet or exceed FEMA requirements to reduce risk of flooding.

Participation in the NFIP is based on an agreement between local communities and the Federal government that states if a community will adopt and enforce a flood plain management ordinance to reduce future flood risks to new construction in Special Flood Hazard Areas, the Federal Government will make flood insurance available within the community as financial protection against flood losses.

- You must live in a community that participates in the National Flood Insurance Program (NFIP) to qualify for National Flood Insurance

- Community adopts ordinances to meet or exceed FEMA requirements to reduce risk of flooding

https://www.floodsmart.gov/floodsmart/pages/faqs/am-i-eligible-for-flood-insurance.jsp

http://livethesarasotalifestyle.com/sarasota/owning-a-home-in-florida/flood-insurance/

SFHA - FEMA Flood Hazard Maps

The FEMA Flood Map Service Center (MSC) is the official public source for flood hazard information produced in support of the National Flood Insurance Program (NFIP).

It is the official map of a community on which FEMA has delineated both the special hazard areas and the risk premium zones applicable to the community. Special Flood Hazard Area is identified by FEMA in Flood Hazard Boundary Maps.

A Special Flood Hazard Area (SFHA) or high risk area is defined as any land that would be inundated by having a 1-percent chance of occurring in any given year. This is also referred to as the base flood.

- Delineated according to NFIP criteria
- Flood Insurance Rate Maps (FIRM)
- Special Flood Hazard Areas

In Special Flood Hazard Areas development is restricted to not obstruct the natural flow of flood waters.

- Residential structures in the SFHA must have the first floor above the "Base Flood Elevation"

- Non-residential structures must meet the residential requirements or be water-tight below the Base Flood Elevation

- 40% of purchasers of National Flood Insurance are in Florida

http://livethesarasotalifestyle.com/sarasota/owning-a-home-in-florida/flood-insurance/

https://www.fema.gov/flood-insurance-rate-map-firm

Definition of Base Flood Elevation

- The computed elevation to which floodwater is anticipated to rise during the base flood. Base Flood Elevations (BFEs) are shown on Flood Insurance Rate Maps (FIRMs) and on the flood profiles.

- The BFE is the regulatory requirement for the elevation or flood proofing of structures. The relationship between the BFE and a structure's elevation determines the flood insurance premium.

https://www.fema.gov/base-flood-elevation

ENVIRONMENTAL HAZARDS

VII) Indoor and outdoor environmental hazards

    A) Water supply

        1) Well (adequacy, quality)

        2) Public (quality)

    B) Septic tank

    C) Asbestos

    D) Radon E Toxic waste in soil

    E) Underground storage tanks

    F) Lead paint

    G) Mold

    H) Chemical contamination

    I) Structural damage

        1) Wood-destroying organisms

            (a)Termites

            (b)Carpenter ants

            (c)Decay

Indoor and Outdoor Environmental Hazards

Water Supply

Water is a precious finite resource. Over 50% of the United States population depends on groundwater for drinking water. Groundwater is also one of our most important sources of water for irrigation.

There are many things that can contaminate our water supply. Contamination can potentially come from underground storage tanks, septic systems, storm drains and herbicides.

Drinking contaminated groundwater can have serious health effects. Diseases such as hepatitis and dysentery may be caused by contamination from septic tank waste. Poisoning may be caused by toxins that have leached into well water supplies, even cancer has been attributed to contaminated water.

To ensure that the public water supply is safe to drink, strict water quality standards established by the U.S. Environmental Protection Agency limit the amount of various impurities in drinking water by setting "maximum contaminant levels." Public water suppliers are required to routinely test their water.

http://www.groundwater.org/get-informed/groundwater/contamination.html

http://www.publichealth.lacounty.gov/eh/TEA/ToxicEpi/water.htm

Well (adequacy, quality)

- Finite Resource
- Potential Contamination
    - Underground storage tanks
    - Septic systems
    - Storm drains
    - Herbicides

Public

- Public water suppliers are required to routinely test their water

http://www.groundwater.org/get-informed/groundwater/contamination.html

http://www.publichealth.lacounty.gov/eh/TEA/ToxicEpi/water.htm

Septic Tank

Failing septic systems can be hazardous to your health. The major reason for safe disposal of sewage is to prevent the spread of disease.

Inadequately treated sewage from failing septic systems poses a significant threat to drinking water and human health because diseases and infections may be transferred to people and animals directly and immediately. Dysentery, hepatitis, typhoid fever, and acute gastrointestinal illness are some of the more serious examples.

Inadequately treated sewage from failing septic systems is the most frequently reported cause of groundwater contamination.

- Failing systems

- Ground water contamination

- Diseases

http://www.mass.gov/eea/agencies/massdep/water/wastewater/failing-septic-systems-can-be-hazardous-to-your-health.htm

Asbestos

According to OSHA, asbestos is a naturally occurring mineral fiber. It was used in numerous building materials and vehicle products for its strength and ability to resist heat and corrosion before its dangerous health effects were discovered. Individual asbestos fibers cannot be seen by the naked eye, which puts workers at an increased risk. The Occupational Safety and Health Administration (OSHA) has regulations to protect workers from the hazards of asbestos.

Asbestos fibers are released into the air during activities that disturb asbestos-containing materials. The asbestos fibers can then be inhaled unknowingly and trapped in the lungs. If swallowed, they can become embedded into the digestive tract as well. Asbestos is a known human carcinogen and can cause chronic lung disease as well as lung and other cancers.

Rather than removing existing asbestos, it is best to encapsulate it. Attempting to remove asbestos from a building is more harmful than simply covering it up. When asbestos has been disturbed, small particles of the toxin drift into the air. As a result, an air space can quickly become contaminated. Therefore, the best solution is to manage asbestos by containing it using asbestos encapsulation techniques.

- Naturally occurring mineral fiber

- Used in building materials until 1978

- Chronic lung disease and cancer

- Encapsulate rather than remove

https://www.osha.gov/Publications/OSHA3507.html

http://www.wisegeek.com/what-is-asbestos-encapsulation.htm

Radon

Radon is a natural occurring odorless gas from decaying uranium in the soil. It causes lung cancer.

Some parts of the country have a higher incidence of radon than others. However, new, more efficient "tightly sealed homes" can increase the likelihood of radon becoming trapped inside the home exposing residents to harm.

Because of this, F.S. 404 Mandates Radon Disclosure Warning Prior to a buyer signing a Purchase Agreement for Real Estate. However, there is no requirement for the buyer to test for radon.

Natural Occurring odorless gas from decaying uranium in the soil.

Causes Lung Cancer

- F.S. 404 Mandates Radon Disclosure Warning
  - Prior to signing a Purchase Agreement for Real Estate
  - Does NOT require radon Testing

http://www.floridahealth.gov/environmental-health/radon/mandatory-testing.html

Toxic Waste in Soil

- Toxic waste in the soil also known as **Soil contamination** or **soil pollution** is often caused by the presence of human-made chemicals.

- Typical sources are industrial activity, agricultural chemicals, or improper disposal of waste. Petroleum, solvents, pesticides, lead, and other heavy metals are some examples of contaminants.

- The concern over soil contamination stems primarily from health risks, from direct contact with the contaminated soil, vapors from the contaminants, and from secondary contamination of water supplies within and underlying the soil.

- Soil Contamination or Soil Pollution

- Human-made chemicals

- Industrial activity

- Agricultural chemicals

- Improper Disposal of Waste

https://en.wikipedia.org/wiki/Soil_contamination

Underground Storage Tanks (UST)

Petroleum underground storage tanks, or USTs, have been used throughout the U.S. at gas stations. Many of the aging tanks have leaked, allowing petroleum to contaminate the soil and groundwater.

They end up entering as vapor into buildings and become what is dubbed as brownfields or Superfund sites.

Many USTs installed before 1980 consisted of bare steel pipes, which corrode over time. Faulty installation and inadequate handling may also cause leaks.

Today, UST's are regulated in the United States to prevent release of petroleum and contamination of groundwater, soil and air.

- Old metal UST have leaked petroleum

- Contaminated soil and groundwater

- Today USTs are heavily regulated

https://en.wikipedia.org/wiki/Underground_storage_tank

Lead Paint

If your home was built before 1978, there is a good chance it has lead-based paint.

In 1978, the federal government banned consumer uses of lead-containing. Lead from paint, including lead-contaminated dust, is one of the most common causes of lead poisoning. 87% of homes built before 1940 have lead-based paint; 69% between 1940 and 1969 and 24% between 1960 and 1977.

Lead paint is still present in millions of homes, sometimes under layers of newer paint. If the paint is in good shape, the lead paint is usually not a problem. Deteriorating lead-based paint (peeling, chipping, chalking, cracking, damaged, or damp) is a hazard and needs immediate attention. Keep all paint in excellent shape and clean up dust frequently

- Lead Poisoning

    - Causes learning disabilities

- Houses Built Prior to 1978

  - Disclosure Required before sale or lease

http://www.epa.gov/lead/protect-your-family#sl-home

Residential Lead Based Paint Hazard Reduction Act
- Requires Disclosure
- From Home Owners of Known Lead Hazards Prior to a sale or lease of a home

http://www.epa.gov/lead/protect-your-family#sl-home

Mold

Mold is another potential environmental hazard. Molds can grow on cloth, carpets, leather, wood, sheet rock, insulation when moist conditions exist.

People can become exposed to molds by direct contact on surfaces or through the air. Mold growth is supported by indoor spaces that are wet and contain organic materials that mold can use as a food source.

Mold spores or fragments that become airborne can expose people indoors through inhalation or skin contact. Molds can have an impact on human health.

Health effects generally fall into four categories. These four categories are allergy, infection, irritation (mucous membrane and sensory), and toxicity.

- Poses potential health risk
- Spreads as tiny spores
- DBPR regulates mold assessors and mediators

http://www.mold-survivor.com/harrietammann.html

Chemical Contamination

The U.S. Congress has enacted laws and regulatory procedures aimed at abatement of environmental hazards. The Superfund Act was enacted in 1980 (and amended in 1986) to provide more than $10 billion for the detection and cleanup of sites where hazardous waste is a problem.

The revenue for Superfund is raised through taxes on petrochemical companies and other manufacturers. The EPA, other federal agencies, and individual states can draw the necessary funds to allow them to react in hazardous waste emergency situations and to conduct long-term, permanent cleanups of hazardous waste sites.

Environmental site assessments are classified as either Phase I or Phase II. Phase I assessments identifies and documents possible liabilities from potential or existing contamination. If a problem is discovered under Phase I, a

Phase II assessment will entail chemical analysis of the existing hazardous substances. Environmental site assessments are a necessity when purchasing real estate, such as commercial properties or other properties where the public will have access.

ESAs help estimate potential hazards and accompanying liabilities for site owners or potential purchasers. Consult an attorney to determine federal and state environmental laws control in your situation.

- Commercial Real Estate Screening
    o Phase I
- Environmental Due Diligence
- Superfund Act

http://library.hsh.com/articles/homeowners-repeat-buyers/environmental-hazards-in-the-home/

http://www.realestatelawyers.com/resources/real-estate/commercial-real-estate/phase-i-ii-environmental-site-assessments

Structural Damage

Termite prevention and structural damage cost approximately $1 Billion annually according to the Department of Agriculture and Consumer Service.

It is common for potential buyers of a property to have a pest inspection conducted prior to completing a purchase of a home. Many lenders will require it.

The practice of pest control in Florida is regulated under the Structural Pest Control Act, Chapter 482, Florida Statutes (F.S.). This law is administered and enforced by the Department of Agriculture and Consumer Services.

The inspector must evaluate accessible areas of the property where infestation could occur, including the attic and crawlspace, for signs of live insects, dead insects or insect parts, and signs of infestation such as shelter tubes running through wood or other material, exit holes and insect staining. In addition, the inspector checks for visible damage to wood and other structural materials.

Wood Destroying Organisms

- Termites

- Carpenter ants

- Decay

Florida Statute 482

http://homeguides.sfgate.com/requirements-termite-inspection-real-estate-6730.html

CERCLA

EPA's Superfund program is responsible for cleaning up some of the nation's most contaminated land and responding to environmental emergencies, oil spills and natural disasters.

To protect public health and the environment, the Superfund program focuses on making a visible and lasting difference in communities, ensuring that people can live and work in healthy, vibrant places.

This law was enacted because of the presence of toxic waste dumps such as the one at Love Canal, New York. CERCLA provided liability for those responsible for illegal waste dumping as well as a trust fund to clean up sites when the responsible parties could not be found or determined. Liability is strict, joint and several and retroactive.

Comprehensive Environmental Response, Compensation, and Liability Act

- o   Environmental Protection Agency
    - ▪   Administers and enforces
- o   Identifies Responsible Parties
    - ▪   Strict, Joint and Several, Retroactive liability

http://www.epa.gov/superfund

Strict Liability under CERCLA means:

Owner is responsible to the injured party without excuse or exception

Joint and Several Liability under CERCLA means:

Each individual owner is personally responsible for all the damage liability

Retroactive Liability under CERCLA means:

Prior owners of contaminated property can be held liable and responsible

- •   Just because you sold the property doesn't mean that you're off the hook!

http://lawdigitalcommons.bc.edu/cgi/viewcontent.cgi?article=1436&context=ealr

Superfund National Priorities List

To minimize your liability as a real estate agent, it is important to refer your clients to the Superfund National Priorities List.

This is a list of sites that the government tracks wherever there has been contamination.

TOXMAP is a geographic information system provided by the United States National Library of Medicine (NLM) that uses maps of the United States to help users visually explore data from the EPA Superfund Basic Research Program and the Toxics Release Inventory.

- Contaminated Sites

- Sites with high likelihood of contamination

- Toxmap

http://www.epa.gov/superfund/superfund-national-priorities-list-npl

At times a developer may want to divide property while having to satisfy zoning requirements as far as required square foot per acres.

Following is an example of how to work this type of problem.

- A farmer has 112 acres of land. He wants to preserve 75% of the land for himself and sell the rest as separate lots. If zoning requires the lots to be at least 32,670 square feet, how many lots can he sell?

  Solution

  - Calculate the actual land to be developed by taking the starting acres of 112 and multiply x .25 land available for lots= 28 acres

  - 28 acres x 43,560 sq. ft. per acre= 1,219,680 total sq. ft. available

  - 1,219,680 sq. ft. /32,670 sq. ft. per lot= 37.33 round to 37

  - *Note that with this type of problem you ALWAYS round down. Otherwise you would be developing 1 lot that is too small per requirements.*

TOPIC INDEX

SOURCES AND RESOURCES

Each chapter topics, leaning objectives, key terms, and content of this book follows the Florida Real Estate Commission's curriculum for the Sales Associate Pre-Licensing Course I. When appropriate, the wording from the state syllabus was used exactly to aid the real estate student to prepare for the state licensing exam. In general, the syllabus' words and passages are in bold or are presented in an outline form within the text.

The syllabus can be found at:
http://www.myfloridalicense.com/dbpr/re/documents/FREC080514CourseISyllabusFinal_c_000.pdf

Florida State Statutes and Administrative Code along with Federal Law is quoted throughout the book.

Florida Statutes and Administrative Code can be found at:
http://www.myfloridalicense.com/dbpr/re/statutes.html

Many online sources were consulted in the writing of this book. References to these sources are scattered throughout the book following and to the right of relevant passages. All sources cited were done so by the authors in January 2016. These sources are identified by the web address of the content page.

Visit Azure Tide All Florida School of Real Estate at www.FLREclass.com to find additional source material to expand your real estate knowledge and licensing goals.

<u>Azure Tide All Florida School of Real Estate - Real Estate Mastery Series</u>

Volume 1:   Florida Real Estate Law and Practice Explained

Volume 2:   Florida Real Estate Law and Practice Simplified

Volume 3:   Florida Real Estate Law Primer

Volume 4:   Florida Real Estate Math Primer

Volume 5:   Florida Real Estate Math Formula Reference Guide

Volume 6:   Florida Real Estate Vocabulary Primer

Volume 7:   Florida Real Estate Sales Exam Practice

ABOUT THE AUTHORS

Pamela Kemper is a veteran licensed Florida Real Estate Broker and Real Estate Instructor. She is the Broker of Azure Tide Realty and owns and teaches real estate courses at her school: Azure Tide Realty All Florida School of Real Estate. She also previously practiced Real Estate in Indiana and Michigan. Plus, Pamela holds a Bachelor of Arts Degree from Manchester College.

Heather Raney began practicing real estate in Indiana in 2006 and gained her Indiana real estate broker's license in 2008. Currently, she is licensed as a Florida real estate sales associate with Azure Tide Realty. She is also the student liaison for Azure Tide All Florida School of Real Estate. Plus, she has a law degree from Thomas Cooley Law School.

Jeff Kemper is a practicing Florida real estate licensee with Azure Tide Realty. He is a graduate of Azure Tide All Florida School of Real Estate and Florida State University.

70457529R00327

Made in the USA
Middletown, DE
13 April 2018